THE MOVIES IN OUR MIDST

■ ■ ■ ■

THE UNIVERSITY OF CHICAGO PRESS   CHICAGO AND LONDON

Edited by
GERALD
MAST

THE
MOVIES
IN OUR
MIDST

Documents in the
Cultural History of
Film in America

GERALD MAST is professor of English at the University of Chicago. He is the author of *A Short History of the Movies* and *The Comic Mind: Comedy and the Movies*, both published by the University of Chicago Press.

The University of Chicago Press, Chicago 60637
The University of Chicago Press, Ltd., London

© 1982 by The University of Chicago
All rights reserved. Published 1982
Printed in the United States of America
89 88 87 86 85 84 83 82   5 4 3 2 1

Library of Congress Cataloging in Publication Data
Main entry under title:

The movies in our midst.

   Bibliography: p.
   1. Moving-pictures—United States—History—
Sources.   I. Mast, Gerald, 1940–
PN1993.5.U6M69   1982   791.43'0973   81–16223
ISBN 0–226–50979–6   AACR2
ISBN 0–226–50981–8 (pbk.)

Reproduction of the excerpts, song lyrics, and photographs included in this volume was made possible in part by the kind permission of these publishers, representatives, or authors:

Jane Addams: "The House of Dreams," from *The Spirit of Youth and the City Streets*. Copyright 1909 by The Macmillan Company; renewed 1937. Reprinted by permission of John A. Brittain.

Mortimer J. Adler: "Art and Prudence." Reprinted with permission from the book *Art and Prudence*, by Mortimer J. Adler, copyright © 1937/1964. Published by David McKay Co., Inc.

James Agee: "So Proudly We Fail," 30 October 1943. Copyright 1943 The Nation Associates. Reprinted by permission of *The Nation*.

Maurice L. Ahern: "Hollywood Horizons," *Commonweal*, 21 May 1930. Reprinted by permission of Commonweal Publishing Co., Inc.

Robert Brustein: "The New Hollywood: Myth and Anti-Myth." © 1959 by the Regents of the University of California. Reprinted from *Film Quarterly* 12 (Spring, 1959): 23–31, by permisison of the Regents

William P. Clancy: "The Catholic as Philistine," *Commonweal*, 16 March 1951. Reprinted by permission of Commonweal Publishing Co., Inc.

John Cogley: From *Report on Blacklisting,* Fund for the Republic, 1956. Reprinted by permission of Arno Press, New York, New York.

Michael Conant: "The Paramount Case and Its Legal Background," from *Anti-Trust in the Motion Picture Industry*, University of California Press, 1961. Reprinted by permission of the publisher.

Bosley Crowther: "The Movies," from *While You Were Gone*, ed. Jack Goodman, Simon & Schuster, 1946. Reprinted with the permission of Florence M. Crowther.

Contents

PO essays

3

FEATURE FILMS AND HOLLYWOOD (1914–1927) 101

4

THE TALKIES (1924–1930)   239

5

THE THIRTIES (1931–1940)   315

6

THE WAR ABROAD, A WAR AT HOME (1941–1952) 441

7

HOLLYWOOD IN THE TELEVISION AGE (1953–1977)   643

Introduction

There are many ways to write a history of film. This collection suggests an attempt by film history to "write itself." The documents in this collection span the years 1882 to 1977, almost the entire time that there has been a motion picture or anything resembling one. The individual pieces provide a history of the phenomenon in several senses. First, they chronicle the important events and discoveries in each of those periods. Second, they represent the attitudes of both professional writers and the general public toward those events and discoveries. And third, the evolution of those attitudes in the writings mirrors evolving American attitudes toward not just the movies but the most general and important social issues in the culture as a whole. To compare the censorship activity of the National Board of Censorship in 1909 with the rating activity of the Motion Picture Code and Rating Administration in 1969 is to trace a history of not only film censorship but also the general American attitude toward what is and is not permissible to be seen and done in public and in art.

There are also many kinds of histories that can be written. One might make a broad distinction between "aesthetic" histories of film and "social" or "cultural" histories of film. For the aesthetic history, the important historical documents are the films themselves. Just as the history of the novel might be considered the evolution of all the novels that have been written, and the history of drama the evolution of all the plays, the history of film might be considered the sum and progression of all the films ever produced—a kind of history that inevitably uses key films as examples of both film development in general and the highest kind of achievement of which the film art was capable in each particular period. There are already several of these aesthetic histories with which most readers are familiar; this volume will not be another.

The social history considers films not as works of art but as social and cultural manifestations. Although the movies are the new art of the twentieth century, although some future historians may find it to have been *the* art of the twentieth century, although any number of significant works of movie art have been made, the movies have also been an immensely powerful social and cultural force in our century. They have produced social changes—in ways of dress, patterns of speech, methods of courting. And they have mirrored social changes—in fashion, sexual mores, political principles. The reason for producing a social history of film at this time is that few Americans—even movie buffs—are as familiar with film as a cultural and social phenomenon as they are with movies as works of art. And the reason for producing the social history in this way— as a series of writings which are, in effect, social documents themselves —is that even fewer Americans have been exposed to such documents.

Although every American who has seen some movies knows there was once something called a "Hollywood Code," probably fewer than 5 percent of those people—perhaps even fewer than 5 percent of those who have studied movies—have ever read that Code. Nor do any but some similarly small percentage realize that the famous Code was merely one document among many less famous ones in the more than twenty-year history of producing such codes; nor do any but some such small percentage realize that the Code may well have been written specifically not to be enforced, and that only concerted social and economic pressure forced the film industry into implementing the Code it had written. So, too, most Americans know that there was some sort of congressional investigation of Hollywood in the "McCarthy era," that there was some sort of blacklist, and even, perhaps, that ten people went to jail as a result of those hearings. But probably fewer than 5 percent of those who are aware of these vagaries have ever read any transcripts of those hearings or realize that there were two separate sets of hearings, with very different tones, emphases, and results.

One task this anthology accomplishes, therefore, is to make such primary documents accessible to the public. The reason for our ignorance about such important social documents is that they have been buried in volumes that are difficult to find or peruse. There are over four thousand pages of testimony in the congressional hearings into Communist infiltration of the motion picture industry. Crucial Supreme Court decisions are tucked away in the *Federal Reporter* or *United States Reports,* where only the professional lawyer or law student can readily find them. Many of the articles—particularly those reflecting the attitudes of a contemporary observer toward the social issues of a certain era—were originally published in popular journals long since defunct, of which only the largest libraries own a complete set. Although many cinema books from the earliest periods which were previously out of print have been reprinted in the last decade (this reprinting is itself a cultural sign of contemporary attitudes toward the cinema), collecting the relevant chapters and information together in a single volume such as this saves the reader an enormous amount of time and energy, as well as points the way toward more specific research. Many of these books are still out of print, housed in the rare book rooms of a very few libraries in the country. *The Sins of Hollywood,* to take one example, published in 1922, can be found in only two libraries in the United States and has been seen by almost no one in six decades.

The documents in this anthology are of three kinds. The first might be termed primary documents—Supreme Court decisions and opinions, congressional hearings, official statements by the Motion Picture Producers and Distributors of America, personal statements by inventors about their aims and discoveries, and so forth. Another kind of document might be termed secondary in that it represents a public contemporary response to a specific movie phenomenon—a description of the National Board of Censorship going about its business, written by a reporter who attended several sessions in 1909; the initial press reactions to *The Birth of a Nation* and *The Jazz Singer;* the descriptions of nickelodeon audiences by those who attended these theaters or owned them; defenses of or attacks against institution of the Code in the 1930s or a pamphlet representing the collective position of the "Hollywood Ten" in the 1940s. A final kind of document in the collection is a bit further removed from its immediate period in that it presents the opinions and attitudes of a later generation, looking back on both the events and the documents of an earlier era. Among such documents might be the reminiscences of movie stars about events in which they took part or the probing of scholars into the historical "myths" that have been passed down to us from the past. I have retained the spelling, punctuation, and typographical conventions that obtained in each article as originally published rather than making them conform to current usage and rather than making differing spellings of proper names conform from article to article.

The documents speak to six important social issues, which can be defined as the central problems in the cultural history of American film. First, technology and invention. Without certain kinds of machines there could be no motion pictures, and the mechanical marvels for "recording life" have seized the American imagination in certain periods as powerfully as their products, the films themselves. The three eras in which invention played its most important cultural (and aesthetic) role were the first era of movies (pre-1900), with the initial exhibitions of the original apparatus; the years 1927–30, during which the introduction of synchronized sound revolutionized the industry; and the two years 1952–53, which simultaneously introduced 3-D, Cinerama, and CinemaScope, altering the shape of the film format as much as the coming of synchronized sound altered the patterns of film exhibition. Although by the mid-1960s color filming had made black-and-white theatrical features almost as obsolete as silent or small-screen ones, color's domination was the result of a very gradual takeover, beginning as early as the mid-1920s, rather than of a sudden and violent technological revolution.

Second, economics and industry. It takes money to make movies, which then make money in return. The documents reflect the varying ways of financing the making and selling of films: the system for manufacturing the product, the system for getting it to market, the ways that the theaters which collected the receipts then fed part of that money back into the system so more films could be made and sold. From the initial system of selling films outright to the owners of vaudeville houses or "electric theaters," the film industry evolved a system of renting films to exhibitors, who split their ticket revenues with those who supplied the films. The system moved toward "vertical integration" in the teens and twenties— the organization of a single corporation that would make films, distribute them, and show them in its own theaters—building toward the solid "studio system" of the mid-twenties and the thirties, a system that was really not built on the studios at all but on the interdependent parts of a corporation that controlled everything you could do with a film, from getting the idea for one to projecting it for the customers. The attack on the system by the courts from 1938 to 1948 was accompanied by the loss of vast numbers of its audience to television. Among the economic results were the independent production patterns of the 1950s and 1960s, the conversion of the Hollywood studios from producing companies to distributors and financial backers in the 1960s and 1970s, and the "hype" superhits of the 1970s.

Third (and closely related to economic issues), the industry's relationship to national political issues and governmental regulating bodies. Various congressional committees have attempted to investigate, regulate, or deregulate the commerce of the motion picture industry or the content of the motion picture product over the course of the century. Although early congressional investigations concentrated on restrictive commercial practices—such as block-booking and blind-selling in the 1920s and 1930s—the most dramatic political decade for motion pictures was the 1940s, when governmental committees shifted their concern from finance to ideology. Since the second round of hearings by the House Un-American Activities Committee in 1952, specific governmental concern with motion picture content has steadily lessened, perhaps reflecting an increasingly libertarian attitude in American culture as a whole, perhaps reflecting the waning influence of motion pictures on the American people and the resultant growing indifference of their legislators to movies.

Fourth (and very closely related), the role of specific motion picture content as a barometer of the social and moral climate of American life in general. Attitudes toward both the film industry and the content of films produced by that industry indicate more general attitudes within the culture as a whole. The populist comedies of Frank Capra in the 1930s may have reflected the nation's concern to keep itself together by falling back on the traditional, "homespun" American virtues in the face of a Depression at home and the fascists abroad. The socially rebellious films of the 1960s and the sexually indulgent films of the 1970s may also have revealed some general social attitudes toward personal expression in those decades. But if the motion picture's relation to the culture as a whole shows any evolution over the century, the movies may well have shifted from being a major cultural influence in the first part of the century to a mere cultural mirror in its later part.

Fifth, the specific issue of censorship. Although generally related to both governmental regulation and overall cultural attitudes, film censorship in America has been a practice instituted and regulated by the film industry itself, primarily for economic reasons. Because the movies have sold sex and violence from the beginning (what extremely popular and public art ever sold anything else?), and because they were created within and supported by a society that condoned neither the doing nor the display of sex and violence, the motion picture industry has been in the paradoxical position of trying to set limits on how much it would let itself sell. The primary principle for regulation seems to have been "all that the market will bear," and when the market gets angry and will bear no more, curtailing its expenditures at the box office, the film industry repeatedly catches a severe case of moral fever. The pieces in the collection document a steady succession of committees, boards, codes, and associations with varying degrees of power, influence, and authority, beginning in 1908 and continuing to the present. The most significant points in that continuity are probably 1908 (creation of the National Board of Censorship),

1922 (organization of the Motion Picture Producers and Distributors of America), 1933–34 (creation and implementation of the Production Code Administration), and 1968 (official conversion of the Production Code Administration into the Code and Rating Administration). Between these last two points (particularly in the last half of that wide gulf) lay a series of PCA bendings and easings of the 1930s regulations, reflecting a gradual evolution in cultural attitudes about acceptable sexual behavior in American life.

Finally, the social influence of Hollywood—symbol of American glamour, fashion, and beauty—on American life as a whole. The "movie star" seized the American imagination in the teens, and since that time the "movie colony" or "movie capital" or "superstar" has been front-page news, influencing American attitudes, fashion, behavior, speech, and modes of thinking as much by their off-screen existence as their on-screen performances. In a democratic society, these "movie people," privileged royalty though they may be, seem to indicate the extreme limits of acceptable and respectable social behavior that can be approached and explored by the citizenry at large. In 1922, off-screen sex and drug scandals ruined the careers of several movie stars. Fifty years later, certain movie stars suffered no loss of popularity or employment despite publicly known sexual deviations, illegitimate children, and drug consumption.

Although each of these cultural issues—inventions, economics, politics, social implications of film content, censorship, and the "movie colony" —could easily produce enough documents to merit and fill a volume of its own, this collection seems a richer and more useful one for treating them all. The six issues are not equally important in each period, of course, and the relative emphases of each period's documents indicate the more and less important cultural issues of that time.

One extremely interesting and relevant cultural issue for which major documents do not yet exist (in this collection or elsewhere) is a comparison of the cultural impact of movies and of television. Although television has existed in America since 1938 (television's potential threat to movie commerce is noted in a document as early as 1929), and although television has been a powerful (if not dominant) competitor with the movies for the American leisure dollar since 1948, there has been little careful or systematic attention to the relationship or differences between the two as cultural phenomena. The outlines of an answer to the question would probably take two opposite forms. On the one hand, movies and television can be discussed as complementary parts of the same cultural phenomenon: both combine visual images with sounds; both are "media" of entertainment and information; both use similar narrative conventions and patterns for similar narrative material; both attract a very large audience, converting a vast nation into a unified cultural community; and both have produced parallel political or social efforts to censor or control their content (sex and violence), their cultural power (why should unelected businessmen control the attitudes of the American public?), or their commerce (the FCC's concern with the networks' domination of "prime time" parallels congressional concern with block-booking and blind-selling).

On the other hand, movies and television can be discussed as distinct cultural phenomena: the one enjoyed in public, the other in private; the one capable of great technical assaults on eye and ear, the other offering more modest visual and aural pleasures; the one being a special event, the other being ordinary and everyday. Such a cultural comparison between film and television should probably be broken into two primary questions: (1) What are the cultural similarities/differences between movies in the 1920s and 1930s (when their cultural power was at its height) and television since 1950? (2) What are the cultural similarities/differences between movies since 1950 and television since 1950? Perhaps the lack of attention to this issue in the past will be remedied by the cultural documents of the future.

Although this collection is indeed a thick one, the task of keeping it even this "slim" has required two major decisions. The first, of course, was the necessity of selecting those documents that seemed most interesting, most relevant, most significant, and most representative. The writings in this collection represent a very small fraction of those that exist on each topic in each era. The bibliography will aid the reader in digging more deeply into a particular issue or period. To make any selection, of course, is to interfere with the process of history's "writing itself." Making a selection requires an opinion about the essential cultural issues of each period. Even dividing the material into these (or any other) periods represents a personal judgment and opinion. Such qualifications reveal the inevitable tension between trying to produce a self-contained historical narrative and trying to provide an anthology of individual documents. Despite this tension, the collection again seems richer and more useful for attempting to balance the two intentions rather than excluding either one of them.

The second decision was to restrict the documents to the social and cultural history of film in America. This does not mean that the collection excludes references to "foreign films." Films produced outside America have undeniably been a part of the cultural history of film in America—particularly in the 1920s (with the films from Germany and the Soviet Union) and in the 1950s and 1960s (with the invasion of the "art films" from Italy, France, Sweden, Japan, etc.). But to combine a social history

of the foreign film with that of the American film in a single volume would
be impossible. The primary reason (other than sheer bulk) is that the
term "foreign film" is itself symptomatic of American cultural thinking
about movies, which makes a simple separation between "us" and "all of
them." There is obviously no single "them"; each foreign film-producing
nation has its own social history of film—the conditions of its production,
the economic system of its distribution at home and abroad, the audiences
for which it was produced, its relationships to the moral and political
climate of each nation in each period, and so forth. For this volume, we
must be sketchily satisfied with the cultural-social-moral-economic impact
of foreign films on the film viewing and film thinking of Americans.

1

Beginnings
(1882–1900)

The central issue in this first movie era was to solve the problem of getting a motion picture to its potential public. The invention of the necessary recording and reproducing machines cannot be fixed with any certainty. The complicated tangle of claims and counterclaims arises from several causes. First, a series of inventive steps led to the eventual discovery of both the principles and the methods for recording and reproducing the appearance of animate motion. There was no immaculate conception of a motion picture machine. Second, many different inventors in many different countries had undertaken the task of solving the motion picture problem. Third, many of these inventors borrowed from one another and from earlier research, thereby blurring the line between invention and adaptation. And fourth, although many American inventors were working at motion picture machines, one among them managed to attract all the public attention. Thomas Edison—because his name alone was newsworthy, and because he patented everything that he ever dreamed of inventing, and because he knew the value of publicizing his labors—has received more credit for the invention of the motion picture than many of those lesser known men who may well have contributed more directly to the initial discoveries than Edison. The lawsuits which Edison instigated against all motion picture machines other than his own reveal how complicated it truly is to determine who invented what and when.

Among the other social issues of the period were the public's initial reactions to seeing this scientific miracle of recorded life as well as the founding of the first motion picture companies to supply these films to the public.

■ ■ ■ ■

The Attitudes of Animals in Motion (1882), Eadweard Muybridge

Although born in England, Eadweard Muybridge first achieved fame as a photographer in California. It was Muybridge who, between 1872 and 1877, devised the battery of still cameras for Governor Leland Stanford, proving that all four of a horse's hooves leave the ground during the gallop. Muybridge used his multicamera technique for many other kinds of moving subjects, re-creating the original motion by synthesizing and projecting the individual still photographs with a magic lantern. He gave lectures in both Europe and America, exerting great influence on the future development of motion pictures. Among those who heard his lectures were E. J. Marey (perhaps the "father" of French cinema) and Thomas Edison. Muybridge saw motion photographs as a purely scientific tool, allowing human beings to see locomotion as it had never been seen before—especially by artists. The photographs discussed in the essay are not reprinted here.

The attempts to depict the attitudes of animals in motion probably originated with art itself, if, indeed, it was not the origin of art; and upon the walls of the ancient temples of Egypt, we still find pictures of, perhaps, the very earliest attempts to illustrate animal motion. But artists of all ages seem to have followed peculiar grooves in this matter, and to have adopted uniform notions as to the movement of animals. How inaccurate these notions have been, I shall endeavor to demonstrate to you this evening. I will commence, however, by showing you the apparatus by which the photographs were made; you will then better understand the pictures themselves. Here is the apparatus, consisting of an ordinary camera, in front of which is a strong framework, inclosing a couple of panels, each with an opening in the center, sliding, one up and one down. In connection with it is an electromagnet, which, on completion of a circuit of

Originally delivered before the London Society of Arts in 1882, "The Attitudes of Animals in Motion," by Eadweard Muybridge, was printed in America in July of that year by the *Scientific American Supplement*.

electricity, causes a hammer to strike and release a catch which holds the shutters in position; the back shutter is then drawn upward by a strong India-rubber spring, and the front shutter is simultaneously drawn downward. Here is a photograph of three shutters in position, one showing the panels before exposure, one during exposure, and a third after exposure. The next picture shows the arrangement in front of the cameras. Here are a series of strong threads stretched across the track, each of which being pressed forward, causes two metal springs to touch, and thereby completes the electric circuit. These threads are arranged at a distance of 12 in. from each other, and as the horse passes along he thrusts the strings, one after the other, completes an electric circuit, which operates the shutter of the particular camera which he is passing at the moment.

Twenty-four cameras are arranged parallel with the direction of the animal. The next picture shows the entire photographic arrangements. The track is covered with India-rubber, to prevent dust flying from the horse's hoofs; and there are here five cameras arranged in a semicircle, the object of which I will explain presently. The result is this: A horse, in his progress over the track, comes in contact with these threads successively, and is photographed in the position in which he happens to be when he strikes the thread; then he moves 12 inches, and of course assumes another position, and is so photographed, then another 12 inches, and so on; in this way we have several positions assumed by an animal during an entire stride. The time of exposure, I may say, is the one five-thousandth of a second.

Here is a scale I have drawn out, but which it would take me nearly an hour to explain, illustrating the position of a horse's feet during the various strides, the walk, the trot, the gallop, and the pace; if any one feels sufficient interest in the subject to inquire more thoroughly into it by-and-by, it will afford me a great deal of pleasure to explain it.

Now, as I have spoken of the faults of artists, I must show you what those faults are. Here are some pictures of horses walking, from different sources, with some of which you are all no doubt familiar. One is from Egypt, where they seem to have had two modes only of illustrating the motion of an animal, one the walk, the other the gallop. Here is one walking, with all four feet on the ground at once. As a general rule—indeed almost always—they are going from left to right. You will notice that the lateral legs are represented as moving synchronously, both left legs touch the ground at the same time, and both right legs. Here are other examples of Assyrian and Greek art; a Roman of the first century and one of the eighth century, also a Norman horse from the Bayeux tapestry, a German horse, and one by Flaxman, which is the only correct one of the series. I would particularly call your attention to a representation from the column of Theodosius, where you see two mules, in one of which the hind legs are precisely in the same position as those of the mule in the next illustration, while the fore legs are totally different. Now, a mule or a horse always walks in the same way, so that if one is right the other must be wrong.

Here are photographs of a horse in the act of walking. A horse, while walking, is alternately supported on three feet and on two, and the two are alternately diagonals and laterals. Some very eminent authorities have asserted that a horse, while walking, has never more than two feet on the ground at the same time; but he has always two—that is the characteristic of the walk—and invariably three, four times during each stride, two hind legs and a fore leg, alternately with two fore legs and a hind leg. This horse, you observe, is standing on the right laterals. The most common fault of artists in representing the walk is to mistake the laterals for the diagonals; it arises, I am satisfied, from carelessness and lack of observation. Whenever a horse or any other animal has two suspended feet between two supporting legs, those two suspended feet are laterals, never diagonals. You find them in pictures, engravings, and even in sculpture, quite as frequently represented one way as the other; but they are invariably laterals—that is, when they are suspended *between* two supporting legs. When supported on diagonals, suspended feet are outside the supporting legs. Here is a horse walking, photographed simultaneously from five different points of view, according to the arrangement of the cameras I referred to just now. Next, we have a photograph showing the regular series of positions taken by a horse while walking. Of course, in every thousandth part of an inch a horse really gets into a different position, but these are all the positions of a stride which are worth illustrating.

Next we have the amble; and first I show you some specimens of Egyptian, Assyrian, Etruscan, and Modern Italian art. They are none quite correct, but they approach more nearly to the gait which is ordinarily called the amble than any others I have found. I do not know whether this gait is properly understood or appreciated in this country, because horses are not trained to it, but Spanish horses are invariably taught it. It is faster than a walk, but not quite so fast as a trot, and is an easy, sliding motion, alternately on one foot and on two feet. In this, as in the walk, the horse is never entirely off the ground; in all other gaits the weight is off the ground entirely during a portion of the stride, but in these two he is never clear of the ground. He is alternately on one hind foot, then on two laterals, then upon one fore, then on the diagonals, then on a hind foot again. The succession is very curious; first on one foot, then on two; the two feet being alternately diagonals and laterals.

When these photographs were first made, some experts had doubts as to their accuracy. We have here a little instrument called the zoöpraxi-scope, with which we can throw the various positions in rapid succession on the same spot on the screen, and thus produce apparently the real motion, and you will readily understand that if any of the positions were incorrect, it would upset the experiment altogether.

Next we come to the trot, and as before, I first show you some samples of ancient and modern art. There is Marcus Aurelius on horseback, but that is not a real trot, because in a trot the motion of the diagonals is more synchronous than is here represented. The best example of a trot I have been able to discover of mediæval times is from a stained glass window in the Cathedral of Chartres. There are two from the Louvre, representing Louis XIV and Louis XV; none of them are quite correct, but none have such glaring faults as one by a very celebrated artist, Rosa Bonheur. She is, perhaps, one of the greatest artists of modern times; grand in coloring, splendid in drawing, a great observer of nature, but, unfortunately, she did not pay sufficiently strict attention to the positions of animals in motion. This is a very celebrated picture, and the horse is supposed to be trotting pretty fast. Now, one fore leg is extended back-wards, really beyond the center of gravity of the horse. It would be utterly impossible for him to bring it forward in time, at the rate he is going, to support his body, and he would be obliged to fall down—he could not help it.

Here are a series of photographs of a horse trotting at about ten miles an hour, showing all the various positions at the different periods of the stride. Now, to me it appears almost incomprehensible, but until these experiments were made, it was a question with some very experienced horse drivers whether a horse was entirely clear of the ground during a trot. Some imagined that he always had one foot on the ground, though I cannot see how it was possible for them to come to that conclusion. Even at a moderate rate, in trotting, the weight of the body is entirely unsupported by the feet, though they may drag along the ground at a certain portion of the stride, no matter how slow the pace. This being about ten miles an hour, the horse is entirely clear. Here, again, is a horse trotting at the rate of a mile in 2 min. 20 sec. One thing I would call attention to is this, that when a horse's foot strikes the ground, the leg is always straight; it is never in a bent position. Though you find some eminent artists illustrate a horse striking the ground with his leg bent, it simply is not possible. Another thing is, that he always strikes the ground with his heel first, never with his toe. Here is another horse per-forming a moderately fast trot, about 8 miles an hour, and making a stride of 6 ft. 6 in. Here is another trotting very fast—1 mile in 2 min.

18 sec.; the fastest time ever accomplished being a mile in 2 min. 10 sec. There is also a peculiarity observable with regard to the position of the pastern. When striking the ground it is vertical, but it immediately sinks so as to become almost horizontal. Now, we will try the trot with the zoöpraxiscope, and you will find the motion is perfectly produced. . . .

We now come to the fastest of all gaits—the gallop. Here is the Egyptian representation which, with very slight variations, is the way in which Egyptian horses galloping are always represented; the hind feet are down, and the fore feet in the air. The Assyrian is not much better, but the Greeks evidently understood the motion of a horse better than a great many of the moderns; and this is very nearly the position in which a horse would be, having just landed after a flight through the air. He has struck the ground with his hind feet, one hind foot being behind the other. Here is another from the column of Theodosius; here is a Norman example from the Bayeux tapestry; and here is one by some Italian artist of the fourth century, in which we find a position of the gallop exactly reproduced. Here is one by Albert Dürer; this is the conventional gallop; and, with all due deference to the artists who have palmed it off on the public as being a representation of a galloping horse, I must say it is really absurd, because it is utterly impossible for a horse to get into that position. Here are some ancient pictures, one from the ruins of Angar Wat, in Cochin China; a Japanese, which is tolerably correct; and a very curious one, copied from a painting on the rocks on the banks of the Yenisi by the Tartars. This shows how artists of different ages and different countries have all agreed in representing nearly the same conventional position of the gallop. . . .

Here are some photographs of the dog. In fact, some people might mistake that for a horse, because the position is somewhat like the conventional horse gallop. The motion of the dog is very peculiar. Here he has alighted on one foot, changed it to the next fore foot, and then he leaves the ground with the fore feet. In the next you find him entirely in the air, his feet all doubled up under him; he then comes down on his hind feet. Then he brings the next hind foot down, and leaves the ground again, so that he is in the air twice during a single stride—once with his body curled up, and the other when perfectly extended. I do not think that fact has ever been commented on by a writer on natural history. Here is a photograph of two dogs running a race; they were photographed together; one was a faster dog than the other, and you see how he gradually overtook his competitor. . . .

■ ■ ■ ■

EDISON'S KINETOGRAPH (1891), George Parsons Lathrop

Long before anyone had seen a motion picture, Edison leaked reports about his experiments to the public. This article appeared in *Harper's Weekly* in 1891—perhaps the earliest published report on motion pictures intended for the American public in general.

The name given to Thomas A. Edison's latest invention, the kinetograph, describes briefly the purpose and achievement of that remarkable mechanism. This purpose, it should be said, has nothing directly to do with what scientific men call "kinetic force," *i.e.*, the *force* of a moving body. The aim is simply to produce a perfect and true visual image of men, animals, or other objects as they appear when in actual motion. For some time before the new invention was announced, Mr. Edison thought of calling it, and in fact frequently did call it, the kinetoscope, which would mean "a vision of movement," or "movement sight," but he has finally christened it the kinetograph, a name compounded from two Greek words, meaning movement and writing. The sense, therefore, in which the kinetograph is to be understood is that of a "movement record."

It performs the same service in recording and then reproducing *motion* which the phonograph performs in recording and reproducing *sound*. There, in a nutshell, is the whole object and accomplishment of the kinetograph.

But, as any one may see, moving forms cannot be registered and retained, and then brought before our eyes again, by means precisely similar to those used for sounds. The phonograph does its work by engraving upon wax the almost invisible lines caused by vibrations of the voice or by noise or music, and from these lines the same vibrations may again be set going and heard again. But the function of the kinetograph is to set down and permanently record exact images of men walking, trees waving in the wind, birds flying, machinery in active operation—in fine, to secure pictures of any or everything that is going (*i.e.*, in motion), and then to show us a complete representation of those objects *with* their movement, just the same as though we were looking at the reality. In order to reach this result it must, of course, make photographs—a number of photographs, which, when seen in rapid succession, impress themselves upon the eye in such a blending that we get from them a single clear image of the moving man or brute, bird or machine. The kinetograph, then, is a new application of the art of photography united to peculiar ingenious

"Edison's Kinetograph," by George Parsons Lathrop, was published 13 June 1891 in *Harper's Weekly*.

mechanism, and with a new system of combining many separate photographs in one total effect, which reproduces with absolute fidelity and naturalness the *movement* as well as the form of the original object.

At first glance this may not seem an entirely novel achievement. But it is so, nevertheless, as may easily, I think, be made apparent. It is true that Muybridge and the French investigator Marie made great advances in quick photography, and were able to obtain pictures of men and animals during the transition from one attitude to another. The "horse in motion" is now fully domesticated in our minds. We are familiar with the fact that horses, and even our human fellow-creatures, take the most extraordinary positions when walking, running, leaping, or in other forms of exercise—positions which we cannot perceive with the eye, and only the keen lens and responsive plate of the camera can note down as they exist in fact. But hitherto it has been impossible to blend the separate pictures of these different postures in a single complete, active image. Muybridge succeeded in presenting them to the eye one after another fast enough to give some representation of the way in which they go to make up that general effect which we get in simply looking at a moving horse. But in his experiments the movement was jerky, unpleasant, and not natural. Locomotives also have been photographed while running at high speed, but the result on the negative and in the print was naturally that the engine looked as though it were standing still—a result inevitable with any single instantaneous photograph or series of photographs, unless the series can be passed through our field of vision so rapidly that our eyesight can bunch them together in one harmonious whole. This Mr. Edison has now made it possible and practicable to do. "All that I have done," he says, "is to perfect what had been attempted before, but did not succeed. It's just that one step that I have taken." Yes, that is all. But in science and invention the clever old maxim does not hold true that "it is the first step which costs." Not the first, but the last—the conclusive and triumphant step—is the one that costs and that counts. In this case it has cost Mr. Edison three or four years of study and patient trial (in the midst of his other more engrossing occupations), together with the outlay of much mechanical ingenuity. But it also counts to his great credit, for he has achieved what no man, so far as we know, ever did before. Even though this be but a single step of progress, it surely is a large, important, and even astounding one.

The camera-obscura gives us by reflection and concentration of light rays a perfect reproduction in little of any out-door or street scene upon which it is brought to bear, and this is amusing for the moment. But the effect is transitory; no lasting record is obtained. There is another toy, based on a very simple principle of optics, which roughly illustrates the plan adopted by Edison of mingling visual impressions on the retina so

that we take them all in together instead of separately. This is the gyro-
scope, wherein several small figures or painted slips are so quickly re-
volved that they seem to come together when looked at through an aperture in the surrounding pasteboard; the same sort of thing is done by toy
windmills with parts of a figure depicted on the separate arms. In these
cases, however, the figures, or portions of them, must be painted, printed,
or lithographed on the card-board, and they are at the best only conventional effigies. One striking difference in Edison's machine is that it photographs from life itself, and then reproduces the movement and appearance
of life with such truth of action that if colors could only be given at the
same time, the illusion that one was looking at something really alive
would be absolute. But this is not all. The mere presentation of figures
in action—the "reproduction," as it is called, the creating of the illusion—
is only a part of the invention, and the smaller part. The "recording"—
i.e., the taking of the photographs—is by far the most difficult element
of the kinetograph's duty; that which taxed the inventor's thought most
severely. What mainly concerns us at present, though, is to describe the
reproducing apparatus.

   The kinetograph reproducer now in use at Edison's laboratory (Llew-
ellyn Park, Orange, New Jersey) is regarded only as the basis for still
further development. Photographs are taken first from a living person in
active motion—dancing, gesticulating, bowing, taking off his hat, grimac-
ing, or flinging his arms about. This is done with a camera regulated by
electricity, having a mechanism and other details of preparation specially
devised for the purpose. At the time of the present writing it is impossible
to give any illustration of the recording apparatus.

   But it may be said here that photographic impressions are received
through it upon a thin gelatine band which takes 46 impressions in a
second. The band or strip runs along with prodigious rapidity behind the
lens. Taking 46 pictures in a second, it would take in one minute 2760,
and in one hour 165,600 of them. With the pictures an inch wide, and
spaces of an inch between, it must travel 7⅔ feet in every second. But
since the strip is at rest during nine-tenths of the second, the passing of
these 7⅔ feet is really all done in *one-tenth* of a second. That is, the strip,
when it does move, goes at the rate of about 50 miles an hour. It receives
a perfect photograph of the moving figure in a small fraction of a second.
The shutter closes and opens like a flash, and the gelatine band receives
on another spot another perfect picture. So it goes on. A point of the
utmost importance is this; *only one forty-sixth of a second* can be allowed
for the whole process of taking a photograph *and for also moving the
band along a certain distance,* so that it will be ready for the next impression. It is essential to expose the band to the light for the longest possible
part of this fraction of the second. To give it such exposure as to obtain

a distinct image, yet carry it forward quickly enough to receive another and another, up to the number of forty-six, was perhaps the greatest difficulty which the inventor had to overcome. He solved it, though, and now gets on the gelatine strip with ease the required number of negative images, each one of them being half an inch in diameter. . . .

The continuous strip containing these photo-impressions is, it will be understood, merely a negative. It can be used in the reproducer, and a good telling effect can be got from it. But the intention is always to print from the negative a positive strip. The positive, then, on being put into the "reproducing" box or cabinet, is deftly borne along very fast under a small aperture, in which there is a disk of slightly magnifying glass. A miniature incandescent lamp placed below the translucent filmy band illuminates the figures on it, making them very vivid. And so as they fly past while we are gazing through the disk, they mingle on the retina of the eye, and we see the little man wave his arm without hitch or pause as naturally and flexibly as though he were made of nerve and muscle. . . .

I have spoken of gazing into the glass disk in order to see this illusive figure in action. But that is only a provisional arrangement. The usual and most effective manner of using the kinetograph will be to project the figures from this lens, greatly enlarged, upon a screen, where they may be shown, if need be, as of life size. The explanations just given will make it easier to apprehend the obstacles which Edison had to grapple with in working out the "recorder" part of the process, which is the very nucleus and essence of the invention. . . .

To say that the kinetograph can be nothing more than a marvellous toy would be hasty. It suggests great possibilities, and meanwhile it is as plain as day that the resources which it opens in the way simply of amusement are very large. Mr. Edison's minute inch and half-inch photographs reproduce in action every little muscular movement of the face, can show people laughing, smiling, crying, and so may be used to exhibit the gestures and changing facial expressions of orators, humorists, and actors. By means of them, too, we shall be able to repeat in life-like shadow-play all sorts of dances, the rhythmic whirl of ballrooms, scenes from the theatre, or exciting debates in Congress. Military processions, camp scenes, street scenes (with their accompanying noise and stir), horse-races, prize-fights, athletic games, famous base-ball players batting or catching, colleges crews swinging with a racing stroke in their boat, and the contortions of acrobats, will all be material for the kineto-phonograph. And even the kinetograph alone, by presenting some of these things in dumb-show, without voices, holds in itself a great fund of entertainment. As the speed at which the photographs are run may be greatly increased, so that the figures, if desired, will move three times as fast as the actual persons could, a variety of comic and grotesque exaggerations might be produced by this means. It seems to me just as evident that the kineto-graph may become very useful for instruction in sundry directions. Why not apply it to acting, for the preservation and study of high examples of that art? Mr. Edison expects even that it will some day reproduce the majestic tumult of Niagara. It can picture a locomotive with rods and wheels in full swing of motion, or other machinery and operatives at work. What object-lessons might it not bring to us from foreign lands of literally moving sights or accidents, and the animated presence of far-off peoples! Children could have kinetographic menageries, full of authentic speci-mens taken from life, and moving as in life instead of by crude imitation. We seem to be nearing a time when every man may realize the old philosophical idea of a microcosm—a little world of one's own—by un-rolling in his room a tape which will fill it with all the forms and motions of the habitable globe. By supplying illustrations of this kind for school-books and travels, and by preserving for future ages vitalized pictures of each passing generation or of historic events, the kinetograph may yet play a part of incalculable importance in human life.

■ ■ ■ ■

EDISON'S INVENTION OF THE KINETO-PHONOGRAPH (1894), W. K. L. and Antonia Dickson

Edison's claim to be the inventor of motion pictures is sustained not only by popular pieces hailing "Edison's Kinetoscope" but by William Kennedy Laurie Dickson, the man who worked for him on the project. Although many later scholars, such as Gordon Hendricks, view Dickson himself as the most important pioneer of cinema invention in America, this piece (as do his later writings) reveals Dickson's deference to his boss. Perhaps Dickson felt the power and magnetism of the Edison personality; perhaps he (and his sister) hoped to gain some advantage by claiming little for himself. Whatever the reason, later claims for Dickson's importance get no support from Dickson himself. This piece appeared with an introduction in Edison's own handwriting.

The synchronous attachment of photography with the phonograph was early contemplated by Mr. Edison, in order to record and give back the impressions to the eye as well as to the ear.

"Edison's Invention of the Kineto-Phonograph," by W. K. L. and Antonia Dickson, appeared in the June 1894 issue of the *Century*.

In the year 1887, the idea occurred to me that it was possible to devise an instrument which should do for the eye what the phonograph does for the ear, and that by a combination of the two, all motion and sound could be recorded and reproduced simultaneously. This idea, the germ of which came from the little toy called the Zoetrope, and the work of Muybridge, Marié, and others has now been accomplished, so that every change of facial expression can be recorded and reproduced life size. The Kinetoscope is only a small model illustrating the present stage of progress but with each succeeding month new possibilities are brought into view. I believe that in coming years by my own work and that of Dickson, Muybridge Marié and others who will doubtless enter the field, that grand opera can be given at the Metropolitan Opera House at New York without any material change from the original, and with artists and musicians long since dead. The following article which gives an able and reliable account of the invention has my entire endorsation. The authors are peculiarly well qualified for their task from a literary standpoint and the exceptional opportunities which Mr Dickson has had in the fruition of the work.

Thomas A. Edison

The comprehensive term for this invention is the kineto-phonograph. The dual "taking-machine" is the phono-kinetograph, and the reproducing-machine the phono-kinetoscope, in contradistinction to the kinetograph and the kinetoscope, which relate respectively to the taking and reproduction of movable but *soundless* objects.

The initial experiments took the form of miscroscopic pin-point photographs, placed on a cylindrical shell, corresponding in size to the ordinary phonograph cylinder. These two cylinders were then placed side by side on a shaft, and the sound record was taken as near as possible synchronously with the photographic image impressed on the sensitive surface of the shell. The photographic portion of the undertaking was seriously hampered by the defects of the materials at hand, which, however excellent in themselves, offered no substance sufficiently sensitive. How to secure clear-cut outlines, or indeed any outlines at all, together with phenomenal speed, was the problem which puzzled the experimenters. The Daguerre, albumen, and kindred processes met the first requirements, but failed when subjected to the test of speed. These methods were therefore regretfully abandoned, a certain precipitate of knowledge being retained, and a bold leap was made to the Maddox gelatine bromide of silver emulsion, with which the cylinders were coated. This process gave rise to a new and serious difficulty. The bromide of silver haloids, held in suspension with the emulsion, showed themselves in an exaggerated coarseness when it became a question of enlarging the pin-point photographs to the dignity of one eighth of an inch, projecting them upon a screen, or viewing them through a binocular microscope. Each accession of size augmented the difficulty, and it was resolved to abandon that line of experiment, and to revolutionize the whole nature of the proceedings by discarding these small photographs, and substituting a series of very much larger impressions. . . .

The next step was the adoption of a highly sensitized strip of celluloid half an inch wide; but this proving unsatisfactory, owing to inadequate size, one-inch pictures were substituted on a band one and a half inches wide, the additional width being required for the perforations on the outer edge. These perforations occur at close and regular intervals, in order to enable the teeth of a locking-device to hold the film steady for nine tenths of the one forty-sixth part of a second, when a shutter opens rapidly and admits a beam of light, causing an image or phase in the movement of the subject. The film is then jerked forward in the remaining one tenth of the one forty-sixth part of a second, and held at rest while the shutter has again made its round, admitting another circle of light, and so on until forty-six impressions are taken a second, or 2760 a minute. This speed yields 165,600 pictures in an hour, an amount amply sufficient for an evening's entertainment, when unreeled before the eye. By connecting the two ends of the strip, and thus forming a continuous band, the pictures can be indefinitely multiplied. In this connection it is interesting to note that were the spasmodic motions added up by themselves, exclusive of arrests, on the same principle that a train record is computed independent of stoppages, the incredible speed of twenty-six miles an hour would be shown.

The advantage of this system over a continuous band, and of a slotted shutter forging widely ahead of the film, would be this, that in that case only the fractional degree of light comprised in the 1/2720 part of a second is allowed to penetrate to the film at a complete sacrifice of all detail, whereas, in the present system of stopping and starting, each picture gets one hundredth part of a second's exposure, with a lens but slightly stopped down—time amply sufficient, as any photographer knows, for the attainment of excellent detail even in an ordinarily good light. It must be understood that only one camera is used for taking these strips, and not a battery of cameras, as in Mr. Muybridge's photographs of "The Horse in Motion."[1]

The process of "taking" is variously performed: by artificial light in the photographic department, or by daylight under the improved conditions of the new theater, of which we shall speak. The actors, when more than one in number, are kept as close together as possible, and exposed either to the glare of the sun, to the blinding light of four parabolic magnesium lamps, or to the light of twenty arc-lamps, provided with highly actinic carbons, supplied with powerful reflectors equal to about 50,000 candle-power. This radiance is concentrated upon the performers while the kinetograph and phonograph are hard at work storing up records and impressions for future reproduction.

A popular and inexpensive adaptation of kinetoscopic methods is in the form of the well-known nickel-in-the-slot, a machine consisting of a cabinet containing an electrical motor and batteries for operating the mechanism which acts as the impelling power to the film. The film is in the shape of an endless band fifty feet in length, which is passed through the field of a magnifying-glass perpendicularly placed. The photographic impressions pass before the eye at the rate of forty-six per second, through the medium of a rotating, slotted disk, the slot exposing a picture at each revolution, and separating the fractional gradations of pose. Projected against a screen, or viewed through a magnifying-glass, the pictures are eminently lifelike, for the reason that the enlargement

---

1. See the *Century* for July, 1882. [Ed. Note: And see pp. 3–7 above. Dickson's citation of the *Century* is incorrect.]

need not be more than ten times the original size. On exhibition evenings the projecting-room, which is situated in the upper story of the photographic department, is hung with black, in order to prevent any reflection from the circle of light emanating from the screen at the other end, the projector being placed behind a curtain, also of black, and provided with a single peep-hole for the accommodation of the lens. The effect of these somber draperies, and the weird accompanying monotone of the electric motor attached to the projector, are horribly impressive, and one's sense of the supernatural is heightened when a figure suddenly springs into his path, acting and talking with a vigor which leaves him totally unprepared for its mysterious vanishing. Projected stereoscopically, the results are even more realistic, as those acquainted with that class of phenomena may imagine, and a pleasing rotundity is apparent, which, in ordinary photographic displays, is conspicuous by its absence.

Nothing more vivid or more natural could be imagined than these breathing, audible forms, with their tricks of familiar gesture and speech. The inconceivable swiftness of the photographic successions, and the exquisite synchronism of the phonographic attachment, have removed the last trace of automatic action, and the illusion is complete. The organ-grinder's monkey jumps upon his shoulder to the accompaniment of a strain from "Norma." The rich strains of a tenor or soprano are heard, set in their appropriate dramatic action; the blacksmith is seen swinging his ponderous hammer, exactly as in life, and the clang of the anvil keeps pace with his symmetrical movements; along with the rhythmical measures of the dancer go her soft-sounding footfalls; the wrestlers and fencers ply their intricate game, guarding, parrying, attacking, thrusting, and throwing, while the quick flash of the eye, the tension of the mouth, the dilated nostrils, and the strong, deep breathing give evidence of the potentialities within.

The photographic rooms, with their singular completeness of appointment, have been the birthplace and nursery of this invention; and the more important processes connected with the preparation and development of the film, together with other mechanical and scientific devices, are still carried on in this department. The exigencies of natural lighting incident to the better "taking" of the subjects, and the lack of a suitable theatrical stage, however, necessitated the construction of a special building, which stands in the center of that cluster of auxiliary houses which forms the suburbs of the laboratory, and which is of so peculiar an appearance as to challenge the attention of the most superficial observer. It obeys no architectural rules, embraces no conventional materials, and follows no accepted scheme of color. Its shape is an irregular oblong, rising abruptly in the center, at which point a movable roof is attached, which is easily raised or lowered at the will of a single manipulator. Its color is a grim and forbidding black, enlivened by the dull luster of many hundred metallic points; its material is paper, covered with pitch and profusely studded with tin nails. With its flapping sail-like roof and ebon hue, it has a weird and semi-nautical appearance, and the uncanny effect is not lessened when, at an imperceptible signal, the great building swings slowly around upon a graphited center, presenting any given angle to the rays of the sun, and rendering the operators independent of diurnal variations. The movable principle of this building is identical with that of our river swinging-bridges, the ends being suspended by iron rods from raised center-posts. This building is known as the Kinetographic Theater, otherwise the "Black Maria." Entering, we are confronted by a system of lights and shades so sharply differentiated as to pain the eye, accustomed to the uniform radiance of the outer air. Later we find that the contrasts are effected by the total exclusion of light from the lower end of the hall, heightened by draperies of impenetrable black, against which stands out in sharp relief the central stage, on which are placed the kinetographic subjects, bathed in the full power of the solar rays pouring down from the movable roof. This distribution of light and shade is productive of the happiest effects in the films, as the different figures are thrown into the broadest relief against the black background, and a distinctness of outline is achieved that would be impossible under ordinary conditions.

At the other end of the hall is a cell, indicated by an ordinary door and an extraordinary window, glazed in panes of a lurid hue, which gives the finishing touch to the Rembrandtesque character of the picture. The compartment is devoted to the purpose of changing the film from the dark box to the kinetographic camera, being provided with a special track, running from the mysterious recesses at the back of the stage to its own special precincts, where fresh films are substituted for the ones already employed. The processes of development, etc., are performed in the main photographic building.

The *dramatis personæ* of this stage are recruited from every characteristic section of social, artistic, and industrial life, and from many a phase of animal existence. One day chronicled the engagement of a troupe of trained bears and their Hungarian leaders. The bears were divided between surly discontent and comfortable desire to follow the bent of their own inclinations. It was only after much persuasion that they could be induced to subserve the interests of science. One furry monster waddled up a telegraph-pole, to the soliloquy of his own indignant growls; another settled himself comfortably in a deep arm-chair, with the air of a postgraduate in social science; a third rose solemnly on

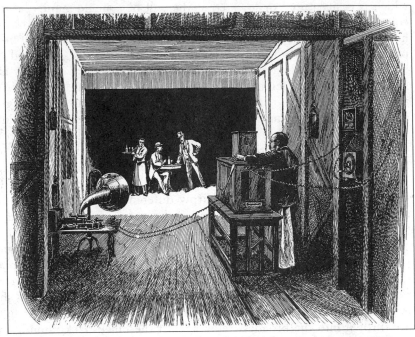

Interior of the Kinetographic Theater, Edison's laboratory, Orange, N.J., showing phonograph and kinetograph.
Drawn by E. J. Meeker.

Exterior of Edison's Kinetographic Theater, Orange, N.J.
Drawn by E. J. Meeker.

his hind legs and described the measures of some dance, to the weird strains of his keeper's music. Another licked his master's swarthy face, another accepted his keeper's challenge, and engaged with him in a wrestling-match, struggling, hugging, and rolling on the ground.

Of human subjects we have a superfluity, although the utmost discrimination is essential in the selection of themes. The records embrace pugilistic encounters, trapeze and cane exercises, dancing, wrestling, fencing, singing, the playing of instruments, speech-making, the motions involved in the different crafts, horse-shoeing, equestrianism, gardening, and many others. . . .

Hitherto we have limited ourselves to the delineation of detached subjects, but we shall now touch very briefly upon one of our most ambitious schemes, of which these scattered impersonations are but the heralds. Preparations have long been on foot to extend the number of the actors and to increase the stage facilities, with a view to the presentation of an entire play, set in its appropriate frame.

This line of thought may be indefinitely pursued, with application to any given phase of outdoor or indoor life which it is desired to reproduce. Our methods point to ultimate success, and every day adds to the security and the celerity of the undertaking. No scene, however animated and extensive, but will eventually be within reproductive power. Martial evolutions, naval exercises, processions, and countless kindred exhibitions will be recorded for the leisurely gratification of those who are debarred from attendance, or who desire to recall them. The invalid, the isolated country recluse, and the harassed business man can indulge in needed recreation, without undue expenditure, without fear of weather, and without the sacrifice of health or important engagements. Not only our own resources but those of the entire world will be at our command. The advantages to students and historians will be immeasurable. Instead of dry and misleading accounts, tinged with the exaggerations of the chroniclers' minds, our archives will be enriched by the vitalized pictures of great national scenes, instinct with all the glowing personalities which characterized them.

■ ■ ■ ■

IN THE HOUSE OF THE WIZARD (1926), Terry Ramsaye

Terry Ramsaye, publisher of the *Motion Picture Herald* and a frequent contributor to *Photoplay* magazine, wrote the first authoritative history of the moving pictures. Chapters of the book were serialized in *Photoplay* between 1920 and 1925, and the full, 700-page-plus book, *A Million and One Nights*, appeared in 1926. One of Ramsaye's emphases was on the earliest era of cinema invention, and it is Ramsaye to whom we owe the myth of Thomas Edison as the sorcerer-wizard-god who spun the motion picture and the American motion picture industry with his own head and hands. Ramsaye's biases are obviously pro-industry and pro-American, attitudes which led him to dismiss the contributions of those two Englishmen who worked in America—Muybridge and Dickson. Although his history is obviously biased, and although Ramsaye is extremely slippery with the data for his claims (not a single specific citation appears in the book), his work remains the liveliest, most authoritative, and most influential study of the earliest years of cinema history. The chapter reprinted below reveals Ramsaye's adoration of the Edison mysteries and his role in the dissemination of the Edison mystique.

We are come now down the path of many years until we stand at the threshold of the House of the Wizard. It is a place deep with awesome mystery and legends of Magic. It is said that strange deeds are done here at strange hours. Here weird lights burn and men toil like gnomes in their cave of the night while God-fearing people are asleep.

Within this place is a wonder trove. Here are, they say, rows upon rows of canisters, bottles, jars and flasks containing curious liquids and powers, crystals, metals, drugs and all manner of substances from the far places of the earth. The black ones might even conceal skulls and reptiles. There are padlocks and chains about, and dark places where the honest light of day never shines. Here are humming, whirring, screaming machines, some of them running endlessly and spitting sparks the color of Fiddlers' Green, which is seven miles south of Perdition.

It is a place of dark Sorceries. Here abides a man who hath a familiar spirit about Things, a worker in the Black Art, which, being rare, is called Common Sense. He who is the master of this place is possessed of twain Devils, one Thought and the other Energy. It is a little Island of Intelligence, located for the while in the city which is called Newark in the state which is called New Jersey.

It is 1886, Anno Domini. May the saints preserve us! We enter.

This is the laboratory of Thomas Alva Edison. He is already known as the Wizard of Menlo Park, who has given to the world the dynamo, the incandescent lamp, the telephone transmitter and the phonograph.

The people call him Wizard because they love magic and mystery, hoping against hope that here is a royal road to All Desire. They believe

"In the House of the Wizard" is from *A Million and One Nights*, by Terry Ramsaye (Simon & Schuster, 1926).

that Principles and the truth about Things and Machines are invented.

All great inventions are greeted as objects of virgin birth, discoveries sprung of inspiration. The popular impression is that the inventor takes smart devices out of his mind as a prestidigitator lifts the long eared rabbit out of the tall silk hat. Hard work, persistence and patience, the bravery of him who walks in the dark alone, the tedious facts of evolution, conscious and unconscious, all these are distasteful and painful to contemplate for the Many. Therefore the fact of effort is ignored, and the fiction of wizardry and miracle is substituted.

Edison was working in this year of 1886 in his laboratory at Newark, busily completing improvements and perfections of the phonograph while waiting the completion of his new establishments at West Orange.

The phonograph had been worked out rather to his liking in the late months of that year. While he had been tinkering along on it, the notion came to Edison that he would like to give it eyes as well as ears. He dallied with the idea of a machine which recorded and transmitted not only the sound but the sight. He felt that it was a somewhat whimsical notion, but that, if it were done, it would be the completion of the phonograph. Eyes have always meant more than ears to Edison—and to every one else since the first sun-up of primeval day. He was, we see, in agreement with the Chinese in their adage, "One hundred tellings are not so good as one seeing."

If Edison appraised this notion at all he thought it trivial. His work was the work of big things, machines and methods that dealt with power, dynamos, batteries, lights that men might see to work, ore crushers, cement mills, giant rolls, and the like. His play was of the little things like the phonograph. This picture machine-phonograph was something to be done when another playtime came.

With the phonograph out of his way for the while, Edison's mind turned again toward a problem that had been long bedeviling him—the magnetic separation of various ores. Smelters were wasteful. He wanted a better way.

It was time to add to his staff of assistants, too. He was inclined to bring in a young fresh mind. He looked about. Over in his electrical plant in New York was a bright English youth, William Kennedy Laurie Dickson. Dickson was young enough and fresh enough, too.

Dickson's job with Edison was a dream come true. While in his teens at home in England Dickson had become fascinated with the published stories of the wonders achieved by "The Wizard of Menlo Park" in New Jersey in that far U. S. A. Dickson took to Edison with all of the fervor with which other youngsters of his age worshipped the dime novel glories of "Deadwood Dick" and "Frank Merriwell."

Young Dickson wrote a letter of application to Edison, offering his small assistance in the business of wizarding the wonders of the laboratory. Edison gave him a grave and solemn reply, stating that he was not contemplating any additions to his staff and advising the young man to stay at home in England.

Whereupon Dickson did precisely the proper thing. He sailed for America, bringing along Edison's letter and various of his own papers to show that he was a research worker, too. He presented himself, and Edison's letter opposing his coming, at the Edison plant.

Edison looked the boy over with a twinkle in his eyes.

"Well, since you have come, you'd better get to work," Edison decided, pointing to the interior of his shop.

This was in 1881. Two years later Dickson, rising in Edison's esteem, was put in charge of an electrical testing department in the plant which was located in the old Roach shipbuilding establishment in Goercke street in downtown New York. It is of incidental interest that in his electrical work for Edison this young Dickson walked along the borderland of the unknown realm of the radio. Dickson made the galvanometer tests for Edison relating to what Sir William Preece later called "the Edison effect" incidental to the operation of the incandescent electric light. . . .

Now in 1886 Dickson was mature and twenty-four. He was absorbedly busy in his work of putting the electric light and telephone wires of New York City underground. An order from Mayor Grant was sweeping the forests of poles from the avenues to save Manhattan from being buried in the wires of its communication.

When Edison called Dickson to join him in his private research laboratory, the young Englishman attained the supreme wish of his ambitions.

Edison gave his new assistant two major assignments, researches aimed at magnetic separation of ores, and, as occasion permitted, an endeavor to construct a combination apparatus for seeing and hearing. This latter was, Dickson says, "to combine Mr. Edison's phonograph with a practical zoetropic moving figure device."

Edison was in some degree familiar with what had been done in the direction of the motion picture. He had available the scientific reviews, and he read them. He watched the Germans especially, and a remarkable zoetrope device invented by Ottomar Anschütz came to his attention. Anschütz, like the rest, used photographic plates on a wheel. But he cleverly illuminated each successive phase of motion with a flash of light from a Geissler tube. The Geissler tube was chosen as a light source because of the rapidity with which its glow is produced and quenched. It gave enough light for direct vision, but not enough for projection on a large screen. This machine, heavy and complicated, saw some slight commercial amusement service in Berlin, Paris and London under the charming name of the Tachyscope.

Edison talked his own ideas over with Dickson while the ore process work went on. Late the next year, 1887, Edison set Dickson to work with experiments aimed at putting eyes into the phonograph.

Edison's thought of the phonograph and the motion picture were inseparable. He thought of the picture as the completion that would give the phonograph a new significance. We shall find the phonograph idea in control through all of Edison's motion picture efforts as an inventor. . . .

It is with no surprise that we find that Edison first set Dickson at the effort to make pictures on what was practically a phonograph cylinder. A little drum was coated with photographic emulsion and was put to recording motion under a tiny camera just as the phonographic cylinder coated with wax records sound under a diaphragm controlled needle.

Dickson had hardly more than got under way with this when it was discovered that while the phonograph record must needs run continuously the picture drum had to be stopped intermittently to permit the recording and perhaps the seeing of the pictures.

This might have been foreseen if enough attention had been given the work that had already been done on the persistence of vision and the illusions of motion. But it was characteristic of the Edison plant to accept little of the work of others lest it be contaminated with errors.

Edison decided that it would be necessary to make about forty pictures a second in order to get a perfect motion record. Trial and commercial practice have proven since that sixteen a second are sufficient, but Edison still views that as a commercial degradation of the picture.

In time Edison and Dickson contrived to get a cylinder picture-recording camera that did start and stop forty-eight times a second. The little pictures on the cylinders were hardly as large as the end of a dance program lead pencil. They were photographed in spirals around the cylinder, just like the spiral sound wave records of the phonograph.

Edison was being controlled with extraordinary persistence by that phonograph idea. From a little scratch in the wax cylinder he could fill the ear with sound. From an almost equally tiny record he was determined to fill the eye with pictures viewed through a microscope over the little cylinder.

Together Edison and Dickson got this cylinder motion picture machine to work well enough to know that it did not offer an important probability of success.

The labor got tedious and trying. The workshop vapored of high tension. This playtime job was getting serious.

Edison, who had made machines that crushed five ton boulders into dust like clods in the hands of a gardener, was all but stumped by a silly little device for making pictures that would dance.

For hours he would sit in abstraction, scratch pad in hand, puzzling over the picture. He sketched out one notion after another, discarding as rapidly as the thoughts grew, tossing the crumpled drawings away. There was a lot of tugging at his left eyebrow in that peculiar nervous mannerism of the inventor's moods of concentration.

Presently a better notion would come, a swift moment of rough drawing, and then Dickson would get instruction to "try this."

And the rough sketches would be formally pasted into the Edison experiment record books on the motion picture, and the work started.

Edison stuck to his task with grim tenacity.

He was making very little progress. He drew, without stint, upon the reservoirs of his energy, which, though apparently unlimited, seemed prodigal even to those who knew his appetite for work.

The cylinder machine would make pictures, but they were exceedingly poor pictures. Again and again, after each defeat, the attack was renewed with unabated ardor.

The first acting for the motion pictures took place before that absurd little phonograph that was trying to be a camera.

And the first actor was Fred Ott, a mechanic and member of the staff, chosen because he was the jester of the works. There were two Otts on the staff, John F. and Fred. . . . Fred Ott was the merry one. He laughed the loudest at Edison's funny stories and had some of his own.

Ott, first of all film stars, has officially told his own story of how he behaved before the camera on those historic occasions. The authenticity of this is guaranteed, under the oath of Ott, sworn as a witness in the case of Thomas A. Edison vs. The American Mutoscope and Biograph Company, in equity No. 8289, before the day of picture press agents.

"I had a white cloth wound around me and then a little belt to tie it in around the waist so as not to make it too baggy—look like a balloon —and then tied around the head; and then I made a monkey of myself."

So the motion picture was born in slapstick comedy, staged in that solemn laboratory. Many a little cylinder full of the gyrations of the monkey-shining Mr. Ott was recorded. Those were "the follies of 1888."

Edison was meanwhile puzzling considerably over photographic matters. Some place in Germany some one was making microscopic pictures of people and buildings, mounting them in tiny tubes with a speck of a lens to magnify them. They became popular toys. And the little pictures, no bigger than a pin head, were perfect. But never could the researchers find just how they were made.

At last the cylinder motion picture was abandoned. There must be a bigger picture, which meant other methods, Edison decided.

Edison did not concern himself with glass plates as the other experimenters had. It is Edison's great characteristic to have what seems to many an instinctive knowledge and discernment concerning materials. He did not have to go up against the limitations of heavy fragile plates in order to recognize them.

The next step was the great one. From John Carbutt, a maker of photographic materials, Dickson obtained some heavy celluloid sheets coated with a photographic emulsion. Carbutt was trying to supplant breakable glass with tough celluloid for general photographic purposes. Only very short bands or strips of this material were obtainable. A new picture device was made with a stop motion and shutter to open the lens and expose the band step by step eight or ten times a second. The stop motion was primitive indeed, just an escapement like that on the balance wheel of a watch, working on notches along the upper edge of the celluloid strip.

By this time the plant at West Orange had been completed and over there Room Five of Edison's private laboratory building was dedicated to the motion picture, and kept locked by night and by day. Workmen came and went on call to do their little parts with various machines. Only Edison and Dickson had access at will. It was the beginning of a profound secrecy about the motion picture which continued for many and many years after there were no secrets to be kept.

Fred Ott and a fellow worker, C. H. Kayser, were the members of the general laboratory staff most often called in for mechanical assistance in the building of the successive experimental machines. The stand of an old Singer sewing machine became the pedestal upon which the tentative mechanisms got their try-outs.

The notches on the top of the celluloid band gave way to a line of perforated holes, and the stop motion device became a Geneva cross and spur wheel which engaged the film by jerks, one jerk per revolution of the wheel. Longer bands were sought by cementing strips cut from the Carbutt celluloid plates together end to end.

Then when Dickson found that the bands did not run very steadily he added another row of perforations at the bottom. This was exceedingly close to the motion picture film of to-day. But the celluloid was heavy, and it was in awkwardly short lengths.

One enduring thing, the present world's standard of size in motion picture photography, was established in these experiments on the slabs of Carbutt celluloid. Every motion picture made today is photographed precisely to the same scale as those monkey-shining pictures of Fred Ott. The motion picture was measured before it was really born.

Edison's subsequent experiments, his perfected machines and those of the competitors and successors who came after, all in due time, adopted the same standard.

Several motion picture experts and inventors have published elaborate accounts of how they set the world's standard gauge for the films. Presumably they are unaware that pictures of that gauge have been in existence for about thirty-nine years. It was all decided in Room Five, even down to the four little perforations which stand at each side of each tiny frame of the motion picture.

A better vehicle for the pictures had to be found. Experiments were made with strips made of thin coatings of collodion, the same sort of stuff called liquid court-plaster, with which one paints a wounded finger. The collodion strips were rough in texture and fragile, but they were good enough to demonstrate the principle.

Now we have come to the late summer of the year of 1889.

Down from Rochester, New York, came word to Edison that George Eastman, the kodak maker, had achieved a thin, flexible film base for photographic emulsions. Eastman was trying to solve the problem of "roller photography." Glass plates were impractical for a popular instrument. Eastman wanted a machine without cumbersome plate holders and fragile glass. He was trying to get photography for the amateur down to a mere press-the-button operation. He had achieved a half-way satisfactory result with rolls of paper coated with a detachable emulsion. But the kodaks had to be sent back to the Rochester plant to be unloaded and to have the pictures processed. This was too complicated. A new material was to be the answer. . . .

Having heard of the new Eastman film Edison dispatched Dickson to Rochester for information and a sample. The first Edison purchase memorandum remitting for a prior delivery of the first motion picture film in the world is still in the files of the Eastman Kodak Company at Rochester, under date of September 2, 1889.

Edison now examined the Eastman film in Room Five.

"That's it—we've got it—now work like hell."

With that material in hand, Edison knew that the solution of the picture puzzle was but a matter of details. There were no important difficulties ahead now. Edison began to think more about the phonograph and other things then. He felt relieved.

Edison interests abroad needed the stimulus of some personal attention and there was time for even a bit of a joy ride. So it came that, after leaving a mass of instructions in Room Five, he said good-bye to West

Orange. When the palatial *La Burgoyne* sailed from New York on the third of August, 1889, Edison stood at the rail waving good-bye toward the dock, clutching a miniature phonograph, delivered at the last moment, under his arm.

That was the year of the Paris Exposition. Edison had a hundred-thousand-dollar exhibit of his works there, centered about the marvels of his incandescent electric light. Edison took a look at the Eiffel Tower, sundry titled persons and some art galleries of note now that the subject of pictures was interesting him.

Europe did not excite Edison very much. In a letter home he shrewdly observed that the much-lauded old masters of the galleries seemed to depend for their value on the rarity of them and the long purses of collectors. To his eyes the old art was dead. And well it might be!

If in all the world there was a man with a right to smile at the labors of Leonardo, Rubens, Hals, Rembrandt, Goya and all those re-creators in paint, that man was Thomas Alva Edison, with his secret of Room Five. He was destined to be at once their heir and their successor—the picture maker to a new and faster age.

Edison had put a blazing electric light into Athanasius Kircher's *Magia Catoptrica* of two hundred and fifty years before, and now he was about to put the essence of life into its shadows on the wall.

Dickson was back home in the House of the Wizard, following instructions to "work like hell." Word came from him that he had something to show his chief.

■ ■ ■ ■

WILLIAM KENNEDY LAURIE DICKSON: MOVIE PIONEER (circa 1935), Merritt Crawford

The later film historian to attack the Ramsaye position most fully and most carefully was Gordon Hendricks. In *The Edison Motion Picture Myth*, Hendricks presents specific data—records of patent applications and correspondence with the patent office, notations in the laboratory log, documents in the Edison archive—that refute the Edison claim. But some contemporaries of Terry Ramsaye also disagreed with the inordinate attention he paid to Edison. One such was Merritt Crawford, a voluminous collector of documents and data on the cinema's inventors and inventions. The collection was clearly intended as a basis for his own history of the cinema—which never appeared. Crawford's attention to the work of Dickson, Eugene Lauste, Jean Acmé LeRoy, and Thomas Armat led to a friendly feud with Ramsaye, which Crawford carried out mostly in private correspondence or letters to the editor. Because Crawford never enjoyed Ramsaye's outlet to the public, his work is so little known today that even many film historians have never heard of him. This piece on Dickson was written in about 1935 but has never before been published.

William Kennedy Laurie Dickson, whose sonorous, fourply moniker receives considerable prominence in the pages of the movie's early history, enjoys the distinction, if it may be called that, of having put the late Thomas A. Edison in the motion picture business. Dickson is the man whose experiments enabled Mr. Edison to invent his famous kinetographic camera and his kinetoscope, or "peepbox," in which the movie first was incubated and then commercialized. Thereby, he helped somewhat to found what has often been called an industry, although it is more frequently referred to as a "game."

Nowadays, Dickson's name is by way of becoming a legend. He was, in a sense, the *alter ego* of the great Edison as far as concerns the development of the processes which made possible the commercial beginnings of the movie. Unbiased historians of the film give Dickson at least equal credit with Edison for the successful outcome of the experiments which took place in Mr. Edison's West Orange, N.J. laboratory between 1888 and 1893. It may be said, however, that they are still in the minority. Most chroniclers of the film's history, hitherto, for many excellent reasons of their own, have tended to be Edison protagonists. The vast reputation, the magnetic and mysterious personality of the great man, added to his even vaster accomplishments, have made it simpler and easier to accept at face value all the claims made for him, rather than to inquire into the facts.

One result of this has been that Dickson's reputation has been handled rather shabbily by most movie chroniclers. His particular place in that select firmament which has been especially assigned to the galaxy of genius and inventive talent, that, combined, have made possible the modern motion picture and its sonant successor, the talkie, has been viewed, when it has been surveyed at all, through the big end of the telescope. In the effulgence of the mightily press-agented reputation of Mr. Edison, Dickson's reputation, like many others, has been made to appear as pallid and unimportant as a rushlight at high noon.

A generation ago Dickson's name was frequently in the headlines during the bitter patent litigation which accompanied Edison's efforts to monopolize the motion picture business. He was a star witness in the

---

"William Kennedy Laurie Dickson: Movie Pioneer" (circa 1935) is in the Merritt Crawford archive of the Museum of Modern Art.

legal battle, which began in 1898 between Edison and the Biograph company, and ten years later, when these two companies had joined forces and with others formed the Motion Picture Patents Company, his testimony figured prominently in the lethal struggle between the "Trust" and the so-called independent producers.

In those days he was considerable of a thorn in the side of his former chief, though it may be said, retrospectively, that his testimony helped rather than hurt Mr. Edison's cause. At all events the revelations regarding his early relations with the "Wizard of Menlo Park," which many of Mr. Edison's opponents anticipated, never materialized. Nowadays, Dickson is almost forgotten. A canvass of a dozen modern cinema audiences, taken at random, probably would not disclose a corporal's guard who could tell a single important fact about him, if, indeed, they had ever heard his name. And these, in all likelihood, would be oldtimers.

Dickson broke with Edison early in 1895 and went off to help Herman Casler, who still lives at Canastota, N.Y., found the American Mutoscope and Biograph Company. With Casler, a mechanical genius, he helped to devise the famous Biograph camera, which gave Mr. Edison a headache during many years. It has been related that the reasons for the differences between Dickson and Edison, ending an association which had been of the closest for a dozen years, was that Edison discovered that Dickson was interested in a concern which had been a customer for their kinetoscope films, but which threatened to become a competitor. This was the Lambda company, an organization composed of a certain Major Woodville Latham and his two sons, Otway and Grey, who were then conducting experiments in a loft at No. 35 Frankfort Street, Manhattan, down under the Brooklyn Bridge. Incidentally, they had obtained the services of a former Edison mechanic, one Eugene Augustin Lauste, a Frenchman. Lauste, who is still living and now has his home at No. 12 Howard Street, Bloomfield, New Jersey, devised for the Lathams the Eidoloscope, the first commercial projection machine and the first to give public exhibitions on the screen of the newly introduced movie, which previously could be seen by but one person at a time.

As a matter of historical interest, it may be mentioned, that this first public showing of a movie on the screen to an audience took place in May, 1895 at No. 153 Broadway, Manhattan. The pictures shown were views of the Griffo-Barnet prizefight, which had taken place at Madison Square Garden a short time before, as specially posed by the obliging principals a few days later on the Garden roof. These pictures were also shown during the balance of that summer in a tent on Surf Avenue, Coney Island, as some old New Yorkers may remember even at this late day. As an after note, it may also be recalled, that the projected pictures of Mr.

Edison, which were first exhibited at Koster & Bial's Music Hall in West Thirty fourth Street in the block now occupied by Macy's department store, did not make their debut until the following year.

Lauste, while working for the Lathams in the Frankfort street loft, also invented the so-called "Latham Loop," an essential feature of every projector down to the present time and one which figured importantly in the patent litigation of those early years. The old Frenchman has since gained fame as the pioneer inventor of the sound-on-film processes, which form the basis for the modern talkie. At present, although in semi-retirement on account of age, he is a member of the consulting staff of the Bell Telephone Laboratory.

Lauste and Dickson had been friends at the Edison plant and the fact that Dickson had obtained him his position with the Lathams may have furnished the original basis for Edison's pique at his chief of staff. Dickson's high spirited temperament and possible resentment at, perhaps, unjust criticism would explain the rest. At all events Dickson and Edison came to a parting of the ways and, once parted, the stubborn and proud character of both men prevented them from ever coming together again. Whatever Edison may have thought, it is clear that Dickson never became associated with the Lathams. It is probable that he never considered such an association in view of his position with Edison, his ample salary and participation in the profits of the kinetoscope. At all events it is of record that he promptly declined overtures which they made to him to join them after his departure from the Edison organization.

Dickson waited around a while after his break with Edison, perhaps in the hope that his old chief would see his mistake and extend the olive branch. When he didn't do so, Dickson eventually joined Herman Casler, as already has been related, in the formation of the American Mutoscope and Biograph Company.

Whatever their differences may have been, Dickson's loyalty to Edison has never wavered. It hasn't even flickered. There is little doubt but that Edison while he lived did his former lieutenant much injustice in failing to deny some of the innuendoes in which partisan film writers have indulged at Dickson's expense, which equally the Wizard refused to confirm. It has made no difference to Dickson, who has generously insisted throughout the years on giving Edison full credit for the experimental work they did together and in which Dickson had at least an equal share.

It is now over twenty years since Dickson has been in America. The last time was some time before the war. He is now nearing his middle seventies and is spending his good gray years amid the gentle airs of Saint Saviour, in old (not New) Jersey, in the Channel Islands. Formerly he spent much of his time in his garden and in long walks amid the picturesque scenery of the island. Until last year Dickson enjoyed excellent health and his tall, spare figure was a frequent sight to the islanders on his daily peregrinations. Nowadays he seldom leaves the house. Even the movies and the newer talkies, which only recently appeared in Saint Saviour, do not attract him. They evoke too many poignant memories. A serious illness last winter, the first in many years, keeps him under the doctor's care. But his mind is just as keen and inquiring, his black eyes just as observant, as they were back in the year 1888 when Mr. Edison first set him to the task of probing the mysteries of animated photography.

Dickson is by no means rich. He counts himself fortunate that he has sufficient to live on in his age. He readily admits, perhaps with a trace of regret, that his exceedingly modest income is not derived from profits from the motion picture business. Such things as profits, he avers, are left for those who come after the inventors and pioneers. . . .

■ ■ ■ ■

Edison v. American Mutoscope Company (1902), Circuit Court of Appeals, Second Circuit

Merritt Crawford mentions Edison's patent suits, and the following court record of one appeal is both important and typical of the whole series of litigations. After Edison's claims had been sustained by lower courts—perhaps on the power of his name—they were usually reversed by higher ones. And for good reason. The legal transcript makes the details of cinema invention a matter of public record—and the record reveals how little Edison actually invented.

This is an appeal from a decree sustaining the validity, and adjudging the infringement by the defendant, of letters patent No. 589,168 for a kineto-graphic camera granted to Thomas A. Edison August 31, 1897. The patent contains six claims; the first, second, third, and fifth being the only ones in controversy. The assignments of error challenge the validity of the claims, and contest the infringement of the fifth claim.

The purpose of the patented invention is to produce pictures, "representing objects in motion throughout an extended period of time, which may be utilized to exhibit the scene including such moving objects in a perfect and natural manner by means of a suitable exhibiting apparatus,"

Edison v. American Mutoscope Company, argued before the Circuit Court of the United States for the Southern District of New York, was decided on 10 March 1902.

such as that described in Edison's patent No. 493,426, granted March 14, 1893. The specification states that the inventor "has found it possible to accomplish this end by means of photography." It further states that the photographic apparatus comprises means, such as a single camera, for intermittently projecting, at such rapid rate as to result in persistence of vision, images of successive positions of the object or objects in motion as observed from a fixed and single point of view, a sensitized tapelike film, and means for so moving the film as to cause the successive images to be received thereon separately and in single-line sequence. It further states that the movements of the tapelike film may be continuous or intermittent, but the latter is preferable, and that it is further preferable that the periods of rest of the film should be longer than the periods of movement. It further states that, by taking the photographs at a rate sufficiently high as to result in persistence of vision, the developed photographs will, when brought successively into view by an exhibiting apparatus, reproduce the movements faithfully and naturally. The patentee says:

> I have been able to take with a single camera and a tape film as many as forty-six photographs per second, each having a size measured lengthwise of the tape of one inch, and I have also been able to hold the tape at rest for nine-tenths of the time; but I do not wish to limit the scope of my invention to this high rate of speed, nor to this great disproportion between the periods of rest and the periods of motion, since with some subjects a speed as low as thirty pictures per second, or even lower, is sufficient, and, while it is desirable to make the periods of rest as much longer than the periods of motion as possible, any excess of the periods of rest over the periods of motion is advantageous. . . .

The claims alleged to be infringed are as follows:

> (1) An apparatus for effecting by photography a representation, suitable for reproduction, of a scene including a moving object or objects, comprising a means for intermittently projecting, at such rapid rate as to result in persistence of vision, images of successive positions of the object or objects in motion, as observed from a fixed and single point of view, a sensitized, tapelike film, and a means for so moving the film as to cause the successive images to be received thereon separately and in a single-line sequence.
>
> (2) An apparatus for taking photographs suitable for the exhibition of objects in motion, having in combination a single camera, and means for passing a sensitized tape film at a high rate of speed across the lens of the camera, and for exposing successive portions of the film in rapid succession, substantially as set forth.

(3) An apparatus for taking photographs suitable for the exhibition of objects in motion, having in combination a single camera, and means for passing a sensitized tape film across the lens of the camera at a high rate of speed, and with an intermittent motion, and for exposing successive portions of the film during the periods of rest, substantially as set forth.

(5) An unbroken transparent or translucent tapelike photographic film, having thereon equidistant photographs of successive positions of an object in motion, all taken from the same point of view, such photographs being arranged in a continuous, straight-line sequence, unlimited in number, save by the length of the film, substantially as described.

According to the views of the expert for the complainant, the first claim covers every apparatus comprising—First, any means whatever capable of intermittently projecting, at such rapid rate as to result in persistence of vision, images of successive positions of the object or objects in motion, as observed from a fixed and single point of view; second, a sensitized, tapelike film; and, third, any means or mechanism or device for so moving the film, either continuously or intermittently, or both continuously and intermittently, as to cause the successive images to be received thereon separately and in a single-line sequence. According to his view, the scope of the second claim is identical with that of the first, except that it is limited to a single camera, with a single lens, as the means for projecting the images onto the sensitized surface, and the third claim differs from the second only in that it is restricted to the intermittent movement of the film, and to the exposure of the film during the periods of rest. We think this interpretation of the claims is the reasonable one, and the question of their validity is to be determined by giving to them this scope.

The photographic reproduction of moving objects, the production from the negatives of a series of pictures representing the successive stages of motion, and the presentation of them by an exhibiting apparatus to the eye of the spectator in such rapid sequence as to blend them together, and give the effect of a single picture in which the objects are moving, had been accomplished long before Mr. Edison entered the field. The patent in suit pertains merely to that branch of the art which consists of the production of suitable negatives. The introduction of instantaneous photography, by facilitating the taking of the negatives with the necessary rapidity to secure what is termed "persistence of vision," led to the devising of cameras for using sensitized plates and bringing them successively into the field of the lens, and later for using a continuously moving sensitized band or strip of paper to receive the successive exposures.

The invention of the patent in suit was made by Mr. Edison in the summer of 1889. We shall consider only those references to the prior art which show the nearest approximation to it, and are the most valuable of those which have been introduced for the purpose of negativing the novelty of its claims.

The French patent to Du Cos, of 1864, describes a camera apparatus consisting of a battery of lenses placed together in parallel rows, and focused upon a sensitive plate; the lenses being caused to act in rapid succession, by means of a suitable shutter, to depict the successive stages of movement of the object to be photographed. . . .

The expert for the complainant, Prof. Morton, concedes that the Du Cos camera would be capable of taking a series of photographs on a strip of sensitized paper, such as subsequently came into commercial use, at the rate of eight or ten a second, supposing them to be two or three inches square; but he insists that the dry paper then known was not suffciently sensitized to permit this to be done.

Prior to January, 1888, a sensitive film better adapted for instantaneous impression was in commercial use with photographers, and in that month a patent was obtained in this country by Le Prince for a method of, and apparatus for, producing animated pictures. The apparatus included a camera for producing the negatives upon an endless strip of sensitive film, "or any quick-acting paper, such as Eastman's paper film." The camera apparatus was a series of lenses arranged in two or more rows, and two or more strips of film. Each strip of film is unwound from a supply spool, and drawn across the field of its row of lenses by a take-up spool. The lenses are provided with shutters which open and allow them to operate upon the film at the proper time. . . .

Le Prince subsequently, and in 1888, obtained an English patent for the same apparatus, a complete specification of which was published December 8, 1888. This patent contains a suggestion that only a single lens may be employed, as follows:

> When provided with only one lens, as it sometimes may be, it is so constructed that the sensitive film is intermittently operated at the rear of said lens, which is provided with a properly timed intermittently operated shutter.

The mechanism adapted to co-operate with a single-lens camera is not described.

The camera apparatus of M. Marey, described in the Scientific American of June, 1882, and used by him, mounted in a photographic gun, to produce a series of instantaneous photographs, showing the successive phases of motion of birds and animals, describes a single-lens camera, and clock mechanism which actuates the several parts. The apparatus is shown in detail by woodcuts. M. Marey conceived the idea of equipping a gun with the apparatus from the astronomical revolver invented by Mr. Janssen for observing the last passage of Venus. . . .

He states that he has photographed with his apparatus horses, asses, dogs, and men on foot and on velocipedes, but he has not followed such experiments up, as they entered into the programme that Mr. Muybridge had carried out with so much success. He proposes especially to study by photography the mechanism of flight in different animals. . . .

It is apparent from the references considered that while Mr. Edison was not the first to devise a camera apparatus for taking negatives of objects in motion, and at a rate sufficiently high to result in persistence of vision, the prior art does not disclose the specific type of apparatus which is described in his patent. His apparatus is capable of using a single sensitized and flexible film of great length with a single-lens camera, and of producing an indefinite number of negatives on such a film with a rapidity theretofore unknown. The Du Cos apparatus requires the use of a large number of lenses in succession, and both the lens and the sensitized surface are in continuous motion while the picture is being taken; whereas in the apparatus of the patent but a single lens is employed, which is always at rest, and the film is also at rest at the time when the negative is being taken. Nor is it provided with means for passing the sensitized surface across the camera lenses at the very high rate of speed, which is a feature, though not an essential feature, of the patented apparatus.

The Le Prince apparatus employs two or more rows of lenses, and two or more strips of film, which move alternately and successively, the lenses of each operating upon its appropriate strip, and the shutters of the lenses opening successively as the strips are brought to rest; and, although its devices permit the exposures for the production of successive pictures to be made in rapid succession, they require a slow movement of the film. Pictures taken in such apparatus are not taken from the "same point of view" as they are when taken from a single stationary lens. This would result in producing, when such pictures are subsequently combined for persistence of vision in their exhibition, a greater or less indefiniteness of outline and conformation as to movement. Again, the pictures are not taken in a regular succession, as on a single strip, but a short series are taken on one strip, then a short succeeding series on another strip, and so on, with the result that to use these pictures for exhibition in any convenient way would require them to be cut up and rearranged, or apparatus would have to be employed for so moving and feeding them as to obtain the proper arrangement of their positives for the purposes of exhibition, which is indicated in the Le Prince patent. Those taken by the apparatus of the patent in suit can be reproduced by a precisely corresponding positive. The suggestion that one lens may be employed, implying, of course, the use of a single film, is quite enigmatical, and would seem to be impracticable, without altering the principle of his apparatus. The problem of dispensing with the other lenses would involve changing the mechanism so as to secure a rapid movement of the film. We are not satisfied that the apparatus is inoperative, but incline to the opinion that the alleged defects are merely in details of construction, which would be readily obviated by the skilled mechanic. The presumption arising from the grant of the United States patent must prevail in the absence of proof to overthrow it.

The Marey apparatus employs the same general combination of parts specified in the first and third claims of the patent, except the tape film, to produce the negatives; but it is not adapted to produce them upon the film of the patent, and it would require modifications to enable it to do so; but whether such as would involve invention, or merely mechanical skill, is a debatable question. It enables negatives of an animate object, showing the various phases of motion, to be produced by projecting images of the moving object, as observed from a fixed and single point of view, or from a fixed and successive point of view, upon the successively advanced portions of the sensitized surface, and in sequence thereon, and at such a rapid rate of succession that the movements can be naturally reproduced to the eye by bringing the developed photographs successively into view. It is capable of taking 12 pictures per second, each image requiring an exposure of 1/720th part of a second. Although his revolver was designed to get successive pictures for an analysis of the movements of objects, and not for the purpose of taking negatives for reproduction and use in an exhibiting apparatus, it seems manifest that it could have been adapted by changes in the parts, obvious to the skilled mechanic, to produce negatives suitable for reproduction and use in such an apparatus. . . .

The important question is whether the invention was in such sense a primary one as to authorize the claims based upon it. The general statements in the specification imply that Mr. Edison was the creator of the art to which the patent relates, and the descriptive parts are carefully framed to lay the foundation for generic claims which are not to be limited by importing into them any of the operative devices, except those which are indispensable to effect the functional results enumerated. It will be observed that neither the means for moving the film across the lens of the camera, nor for exposing successive portions of it to the operation of the lens, nor for giving it a continuous or intermittent motion, nor for doing these things at a high rate of speed, are specified in the claims otherwise than functionally. Any combination of means that will do these things at a high enough rate of speed to secure the result of persistence of vision, and which includes a stationary single lens and tape-like film, is covered by the claims.

It is obvious that Mr. Edison was not a pioneer, in the large sense of the term, or in the more limited sense in which he would have been if he had also invented the film. He was not the inventor of the film. He was not the first inventor of apparatus capable of producing suitable negatives, taken from practically a single point of view, in single-line sequence, upon a film like his, and embodying the same general means for rotating drums and shutters for bringing the sensitized surface across the lens, and exposing successive portions of it in rapid succession. Du Cos anticipated him in this, notwithstanding he did not use the film. Neither was he the first inventor of apparatus capable of producing suitable negatives, and embodying means for passing a sensitized surface across a single-lens camera at a high rate of speed, and with an intermittent motion, and for exposing successive portions of the surfaces during the periods of rest. His claim for such an apparatus was rejected by the patent office, and he acquiesced in its rejection. He was anticipated in this by Marey, and Marey also anticipated him in photographing successive positions of the object in motion from the same point of view.

The predecessors of Edison invented apparatus, during a period of transition from plates to flexible paper film, and from paper film to celluloid film, which was capable of producing negatives suitable for reproduction in exhibiting machines. No new principle was to be discovered, or essentially new form of machine invented, in order to make the improved photographic material available for that purpose. The early inventors had felt the need of such material, but, in the absence of its supply, had either contented themselves with such measure of practical success as was possible, or had allowed their plans to remain upon paper as indications of the forms of mechanical and optical apparatus which might be used when suitable photographic surfaces became available. They had not perfected the details of apparatus especially adapted for the employment of the film of the patent, and to do this required but a moderate amount of mechanical ingenuity. Undoubtedly Mr. Edison, by utilizing this film and perfecting the first apparatus for using it, met all the conditions necessary for commercial success. This, however, did not entitle him, under the patent laws, to a monopoly of all camera apparatus capable of utilizing the film. Nor did it entitle him to a monopoly of all apparatus employing a single camera.

We conclude that the functional limitations which are inserted in the claims do not restrict the patent to the scope of Mr. Edison's real invention. We cannot undertake to point out the differences between the scope of the real invention and the claims. The real invention, if it involved invention as distinguished from improvement, probably consists of details of organization, by which the capacity of the reels and the moving devices are augmented and adapted to carry the film of the patent rapidly and properly. It suffices to say that the modifications required to conform old apparatus to the use of the tape film, and which would define the real invention, cannot be imported into the first and third claims without violence to their terms; and the second claim is broader than the third.

The fifth claim of the patent is obviously an attempt by the patentee to obtain a monopoly of the product of the apparatus described in the patent, so that in the event it should turn out that his apparatus was not patentable, or the product could be made by apparatus not infringing his, he could nevertheless enjoy the exclusive right of making it. A claim for an article of manufacture is not invalid merely because the article is the product of a machine, whether the machine is patented or unpatented; but it is invalid unless the article is new in a patentable sense, —that is, unless its original conception or production involved invention, as distinguished from ordinary mechanical skill. If it is new only in the sense that it embodies and represents superior workmanship, or is an improvement upon an old article in degree and excellence, within all authorities the claim is invalid. . . .

By the terms of the claim the length of the film is not defined, nor is the number of photographs which it is to represent defined. It is to be an unbroken transparent or translucent, tapelike photographic film; it is to have thereon equidistant photographs of successive positions of an object in motion; these photographs are to be arranged in a continuous, straight-line sequence; and the number of them is not limited, save by the length of the film. The film was not new, and if the other characteristics of the product are not new, or are new only in the sense that they add to the article merely a superiority of finish or a greater accuracy of detail, the claim is destitute of patentable novelty. . . .

We conclude that the court below erred in sustaining the validity of the claims in controversy, and that the decree should be reversed, with costs, and with instructions to the court below to dismiss the bill.

2

Nickelodeon
(1900–1913)

The motion picture entered its second era in America when it moved out of the vaudeville houses—where it was featured as a single "turn" on the vaudeville bill—and into the little storefront theaters that featured it exclusively. The statistics alone reveal how swiftly and how dramatically the new entertainment at the nickelodeons, or "nickelets," captured the attention and allegiance of vast numbers of the American public. In 1907 attendance at the nickel theaters was estimated to have been as high as ten million admissions each day. Only three years earlier no such entertainment institution had even existed.

The nickelodeons attracted their audiences for many reasons. First, the entertainment was very cheap. A nickel or dime bought over an hour's worth of amusement. Second, the entire family could enjoy the activity together. The varied kinds of short films that made up the nickelodeon program appealed to different tastes and age-groups. Third, the nickelodeon allowed a largely poor and working-class audience to escape into more pleasant surroundings. The motion picture not only provided "escape" in the psychological sense; it simply created a pleasanter, more comfortable social environment than did the typical, cramped tenement home. And fourth, the motion picture allowed a largely immigrant audience to enjoy narrative entertainment in a "language" they knew how to read.

Along with attracting so many ardent admirers, the motion picture necessarily attracted its first ardent enemies as well. The Nickelodeon Era marked the beginning of social legislation and agitation against the motion picture. Many Americans—particularly those who were rich, powerful, or educated enough not to want or need this kind of entertainment—worried about what so many of their fellow citizens might be learning or enjoying inside the nickelodeon. Laws were passed to regulate the operation and licensing of theaters; many cities and states established censorship boards to control the content of the films; the motion picture industry itself established its first self-regulating body of "voluntary" content control. Educators wondered what the motion picture would do to children's minds; social workers wondered what experiencing this world of fantasy would do to the attitudes of the eventual adult citizens of a real society; police commissioners wondered more about the crimes committed inside the theaters than those depicted on the screens.

But most Americans, remaining faithful to their entertainment at the nickelodeon, began to wonder more about the movies themselves— how they were made, where they were made, and, especially, who were the people that made them.

■ ■ ■ ■

The Nickelodeon (1907)
The Nickel Madness (1907), Barton W. Currie
The Nickelodeon (1908), Lucy France Pierce

These three pieces reflect representative views of the new entertainment phenomenon. The first appeared in the 4 May 1907 issue of the *Moving Picture World and View Photographer* (later to be known simply as *Moving Picture World*) in that trade journal's first year of publication. The fact that the motion picture industry required a trade journal of its own was itself indicative of its new commercial power. The Currie article appeared in the *Harper's Weekly* of 24 August 1907, and the Pierce article appeared in the *World Today* of October 1908.

The Nickelodeon

There is a new thing under the sun—at least new within a short period of time—and entirely new in the sense that the public is waking up to what it means.

It is the 5-cent theater.

The nickel place of amusement made its appearance with no greater blare of trumpets than the noise of its phonograph horn and the throaty persuasions of its barker. It came unobtrusively, in the still of night. It is multiplying faster than guinea pigs, and within a few months has attained to that importance where we may no longer snub it as one of the catch-pennies of the street.

One day a Pittsburg man hit on the 5-cent theater idea. He equipped a building at a cost of $40,000, bought a phonograph with a big horn, hired a leather-lunged barker and threw his doors open.

The theater was such an unqualified go in Pittsburg that the men who started in competition with the originator of the scheme decided that a new popular chord had been struck in the amusement line. They

"The Nickelodeon" appeared in the 4 May 1907 issue of the *Moving Picture World and View Photographer*.

hiked to Chicago and opened a theater near State and Van Buren streets. The theater prospered from the moment the barker first opened his mobile face to extol the wonders of the show "upon the inside." That was the beginning in Chicago.

Of course, they were opened in other cities, until now it is estimated there are from 2,500 to 3,000 5-cent theaters in the United States.

One of its chief attractions is the knowledge that if you are stung it is for "only a nickel, five pennies, a half a dime," as the barker says, and that if you don't like the show they can inflict only fifteen minutes of it on you.

Here are the ingredients of a 5-cent theater:

One storeroom, seating from 200 to 500 persons.

One phonograph with extra large horn.

One young woman cashier.

One electric sign.

One cinematograph, with operator.

One canvas on which to throw the pictures.

One piano.

One barker.

One manager.

As many chairs as the store will hold.

A few brains and a little tact. Mix pepper and salt to taste.

After that all you have to do is to open the doors, start the phonograph and carry the money to the bank. The public does the rest.

It makes little difference what time of day you go to a 5-cent theater. The doors are opened as early in the forenoon as there is an chance of gathering in a few nickels, the downtown theaters opening earlier than those in the outlying districts to accommodate the visitors. Each "performance" lasts fifteen minutes. At the end of each a sign is thrown from the cinematograph on the canvas announcing that those who came late may stay for the next "performance."

Often they stay for several. After they find out that nobody cares and that they can stay all day and far into the night and bring their lunch if they want to, they leave, disappointed because nobody tried to get the best of them.

They are great places for the foot-sore shopper, who is not used to cement sidewalks, to rest; and it took the aforesaid foot-sore shoppers about one minute to find this out. It is much more comfortable than to take street-car rides to rest, and they don't have to pay the return nickel.

The name of the play is flashed on the canvas, so that it may be identified if ever seen again. Understand that the young men who sing the "illustrated songs" are the only live performers in these theaters. The rest is moving pictures; and that is the startling part of the great favor with which these theaters have been received by the public.

The plays that are put on at the 5-cent theaters are for the most part manufactured abroad. Paris is a great producing center. London has numerous factories that grind them out. They are bought by the foot.

This system of buying drama and comedy by the foot has its distinct advantages. If the piece grows dull at any point the manager can take a pair of shears and cut out a few yards or rods, thereby enlivening the whole performance.

The worst charge that has been made against the 5-cent theaters is that some of them put on pieces of the blood-and-thunder type, depicting murders, hold-ups, train robberies and other crimes. This charge has led the managers of the new style theaters into a hot discussion with the up-lifters of the public morals.

Few people realize the important part these theaters are beginning to play in city life. They have been looked upon largely as places of trivial amusement, not calling for any serious consideration. They seem, how-ever, to be something that may become one of the greatest forces for good or for evil in the city.

On the other hand, in the congested districts the 5-cent theaters are proving a source of much innocent entertainment. The mothers do not have to "dress" to attend them, and they take the children and spend many restful hours in them at very small expense.

The possibilities of them in an educational way are unlimited. The tuberculosis society already has seen this and has under way a plan for having the cinematograph theaters show pictures which will instruct the public, of and precautions to be taken against consumption. A great many educational lines might be developed among the people in this way.

THE NICKEL MADNESS

THE AMAZING SPREAD OF A NEW KIND OF AMUSEMENT ENTERPRISE WHICH IS MAKING FORTUNES FOR ITS PROJECTORS

The very fact that we derive pleasure from certain amusements, wrote Lecky, creates a kind of humiliation. Anthony Comstock and Police-Commissioner Bingham have spoken eloquently on the moral aspect of the five-cent theatre, drawing far more strenuous conclusions than that of the great historian. But both the general and the purity commissioner

"The Nickel Madness," by Barton W. Currie, was published in *Harper's Weekly* on 24 August 1907.

generalized too freely from particulars. They saw only the harsher aspects of the nickel madness, whereas it has many innocent and harmless phases.

Crusades have been organized against these low-priced moving-picture theatres, and many conservators of the public morals have denounced them as vicious and demoralizing. Yet have they flourished amazingly, and carpenters are busy hammering them up in every big and little community in the country.

The first "nickelodeon," or "nickelet," or whatever it was originally called was merely an experiment, and the first experiment was made a little more than a year ago. There was nothing singularly novel in the idea, only the individualizing of the moving-picture machine. Before it had served merely as a "turn" in vaudeville. For a very modest sum the outfit could be housed in a narrow store or in a shack in the rear yard of a tenement, provided there was an available hallway and the space for a "front." These shacks and shops are packed with as many chairs as they will hold and the populace welcomed, or rather hailed, by a huge megaphone-horn and lurid placards. The price of admission and entertainment for from fifteen to twenty minutes is a coin of the smallest denomination in circulation west of the Rockies.

In some vaudeville houses you may watch a diversity of performances four hours for so humble a price as ten cents, provided you are willing to sit among the rafters. Yet the roof bleachers were never so popular or profitable as the tiny show-places that have fostered the nickel madness.

Before the dog-days set in, licenses were being granted in Manhattan Borough alone at the rate of one a day for these little hurry-up-and-be-amused booths. They are categorized as *"common shows,"* thanks to the Board of Aldermen. A special ordinance was passed to rate them under this heading. Thereby they were enabled to obtain a license for $25 for the first year, and $12.50 for the second year. The City Fathers did this before Anthony Comstock and others rose up and proclaimed against them. A full theatrical license costs $500.

An eloquent plea was made for these humble resorts by many "friends of the peepul." They offered harmless diversion for the poor. They were edifying, educational, and amusing. They were broadening. They revealed the universe to the unsophisticated. The variety of the skipping, dancing, flashing, and marching pictures was without limit. For five cents you were admitted to the realms of the prize ring; you might witness the celebration of a Pontifical mass in St. Peter's; Kaiser Wilhelm would prance before you, reviewing his Uhlans. Yes, and even more surprising, you were offered a modern conception of Washington crossing the Delaware "acted out by a trained group of actors." Under the persuasive force of such arguments, was it strange that the Aldermen befriended the nickelodeon man and gave impetus to the craze?

Three hundred licenses were issued within the past year in the Borough of Manhattan alone for *common shows*. Two hundred of these were for nickelets. They are becoming vastly popular in Brooklyn. They are springing up in the shady places of Queens, and down on Staten Island you will find them in the most unexpected bosky dells, or rising in little rakish shacks on the mosquito flats.

Already statisticians have been estimating how many men, women, and children in the metropolis are being thrilled daily by them. A conservative figure puts it at 200,000, though if I were to accept the total of the show-men the estimate would be nearer half a million. But like all statisticians, who reckon human beings with the same unemotional placidity with which they total beans and potatoes, the statistician I have quoted left out the babies. In a visit to a dozen of these moving-picture hutches I counted an average of ten babies to each theatre-et. Of course they were in their mothers' or the nurse-girls' arms. But they were there and you heard them. They did not disturb the show, as there were no counter-sounds, and many of them seemed profoundly absorbed in the moving pictures.

As a matter of fact, some mothers—and all nurse-girls—will tell you that the cinematograph has a peculiarly hypnotic or narcotic effect upon an infant predisposed to disturb the welkin. You will visit few of these places in Harlem where the doorways are not encumbered with go-carts and perambulators. Likewise they are prodigiously popular with the rising generation in frock and knickerbocker. For this reason they have been condemned by the morality crusaders.

The chief argument against them was that they corrupted the young. Children of any size who could transport a nickel to the cashier's booth were welcomed. Furthermore, undesirables of many kinds haunted them. Pickpockets found them splendidly convenient, for the lights were always cut off when the picture-machine was focussed on the canvas. There is no doubt about the fact that many rogues and miscreants obtained licenses and set up these little show-places merely as snares and traps. There were many who thought they had sufficient pull to defy decency in the choice of their slides. Proprietors were said to work hand in glove with lawbreakers. Some were accused of wanton designs to corrupt young girls. Police-Commissioner Bingham denounced the nickel madness as pernicious, demoralizing, and a direct menace to the young.

But the Commissioner's denunciation was rather too sweeping. His detectives managed to suppress indecencies and immoralities. As for their being a harbor for pickpockets, is it not possible that even they visit these humble places for amusement? Let any person who desires—metaphorically speaking, of course—put himself in the shoes of a pickpocket and visit one of these five-cent theatres. He has a choice of a dozen neighborhoods, and the character of the places varies little, nor does the class of patrons change, except here and there as to nationality. Having entered one of these get-thrills-quick theatres and imagined he is a pickpocket, let him look about him at the workingmen, at the tired, drudging mothers of bawling infants, at the little children of the streets, newsboys, bootblacks and smudgy urchins. When he has taken all this in, will not his (assumed) professional impulse be flavored with disgust? Why, there isn't an ounce of plunder in sight. The pickpocket who enters one of these humble booths for sordid motives must be pretty far down in his calling—a wretch without ambition.

But if you happen to be an outlaw you may learn many moral lessons from these brief moving-picture performances, for most of the slides offer you a quick flash of melodrama in which the villain and criminal are always getting the worst of it. Pursuits of malefactors are by far the most popular of all nickel deliriums. You may see snatch-purses, burglars, and an infinite variety of criminals hunted by the police and the mob in almost any nickelet you have the curiosity to visit. The scenes of these thrilling chases occur in every quarter of the globe, from Cape Town to Medicine Hat.

The speed with which pursuer and pursued run is marvellous. Never are you cheated by a mere sprint or straightaway flight of a few blocks. The men who "fake" these moving pictures seem impelled by a moral obligation to give their patrons their full nickel's worth. I have seen a dozen of these kinetoscope fugitives run at least forty miles before they collided with a fat woman carrying an umbrella, who promptly sat on them and held them for the puffing constabulary.

It is in such climaxes as these that the nickel delirium rises to its full height. Young and old follow the spectacular course of the fleeing culprit breathlessly. They have seen him strike a pretty young woman and tear her chain-purse from her hand. Of course it is in broad daylight and in full view of the populace. Then in about one-eighth of a second he is off like the wind, the mob is at his heels. In a quarter of a second a half-dozen policemen have joined in the precipitate rush. Is it any wonder that the lovers of melodrama are delighted? And is it not possible that the pickpockets in the audience are laughing in their sleeves and getting a prodigious amount of fun out of it?

The hunted man travels the first hundred yards in less than six seconds, so he must be an unusually well-trained athlete. A stout uniformed officer covers the distance in eight seconds. Reckon the handicap he would have to give Wefers and other famous sprinters. But it is in going over fences and stone walls, swimming rivers and climbing mountains, that you mount the heights of realism. You are taken over every sort of jump and obstacle, led out into tangled underbrush, through a dense forest, up the face of a jagged cliff—evidently traversing an entire county— whirled through a maze of wild scenery, and then brought back to the city. Again you are rushed through the same streets, accompanying the same tireless pack of pursuers, until finally looms the stout woman with the umbrella.

A clerk in a Harlem cigar-store who is an intense patron of the nickelodeon told me that he had witnessed thief chases in almost every large city in the world, not to mention a vast number of suburban towns, mining-camps, and prairie villages.

"I enjoy these shows," he said, "for they continually introduce me to new places and new people. If I ever go to Berlin or Paris I will know what the places look like. I have seen runaways in the Boys de Boulong and a kidnapping in the Unter der Linden. I know what a fight in an alley in Stamboul looks like; have seen a paper-mill in full operation, from the cutting of the timber to the stamping of the pulp; have seen gold mined by hydraulic sprays in Alaska, and diamonds dug in South Africa. I know a lot of the pictures are fakes, but what of that? It costs only five cents."

The popularity of these cheap amusement-places with the new population of New York is not to be wondered at. The newly arrived immigrant from Transylvania can get as much enjoyment out of them as the native. The imagination is appealed to directly and without any circumlocution. The child whose intelligence has just awakened and the doddering old man seem to be on an equal footing of enjoyment in the stuffy little box-like theatres. The passer-by with an idle quarter of an hour on his hands has an opportunity to kill the time swiftly, if he is not above mingling with the *hoi polloi.* Likewise the student of sociology may get a few points that he could not obtain in a day's journey through the thronged streets of the East Side.

Of course the proprietors of the nickelets and nickelodeons make as much capital out of suggestiveness as possible, but it rarely goes beyond a hint or a lure. For instance, you will come to a little hole in the wall before which there is an ornate sign bearing the legend:

FRESH FROM PARIS
Very Naughty

Should this catch the eye of a Comstock he would immediately enter the place to gather evidence. But he would never apply for a warrant. He would find a "very naughty" boy playing pranks on a Paris street—annoying blind men, tripping up gendarmes, and amusing himself by every antic the ingenuity of the Paris street gamin can conceive.

This fraud on the prurient, as it might be called, is very common, and it has led a great many people, who derive their impressions from a glance at externals, to conclude that these resorts are really a menace to morals. You will hear and see much worse in some high-priced theatres than in these moving-picture show-places.

In some of the crowded quarters of the city the nickelet is cropping up almost as thickly as the saloons, and if the nickel delirium continues to maintain its hold there will be, in a few years, more of these cheap amusement-places than saloons. Even now some of the saloon-keepers are complaining that they injure their trade. On one street in Harlem there are as many as five to a block, each one capable of showing to one thousand people an hour. That is, they have a seating capacity for about two hundred and fifty, and give four shows an hour. Others are so tiny that only fifty can be jammed into the narrow area. They run from early morning until midnight, and their megaphones are barking their lure before the milkman has made his rounds.

You hear in some neighborhoods of nickelodeon theatre-parties. A party will set out on what might be called a moving-picture debauch, making the round of all the tawdry little show-places in the region between the hours of eight and eleven o'clock at night, at a total cost of, say, thirty cents each. They will tell you afterwards that they were not bored for an instant. Everything they saw had plenty of action in it. Melodrama is served hot and at a pace the Bowery theatres can never follow. In one place I visited, a band of pirates were whirled through a maze of hair-raising adventures that could not have occurred in a Third Avenue home of melodrama in less than two hours. Within the span of fifteen minutes the buccaneers scuttled a merchantman, made its crew walk the plank, captured a fair-haired maiden, bound her with what appeared to be two-inch Manila rope, and cast her into the hold.

The ruthless pirate captain put his captive on a bread-and-water diet, loaded her with chains, and paced up and down before her with arms folded, à la Bonaparte. The hapless young woman cowered in a corner and shook her clankless fetters. Meanwhile from the poop-deck other pirates scanned the offing. A sail dashed over the horizon and bore down on the buccaneers under full wing, making about ninety knots, though there was scarcely a ripple on the sea. In a few seconds the two vessels were hurling broadsides at each other. The *Jolly Roger* was shot away. Then the jolly sea-wolfs were shot away. It was a French man-of-war to the rescue, and French men-of-war's men boarded the outlaw craft.

There were cutlass duels all over the deck, from "figgerhead" to taffrail, until the freebooters were booted overboard to a man. Then the *fiancé* of the fair captive leaped down into the hold and cut off her chains with a jack-knife.

Is it any wonder, when you can see all this for five cents and in fifteen minutes, that the country is being swept by a nickel delirium? An agent for a moving-picture concern informed the writer that the craze for these cheap show-places was sweeping the country from coast to coast. The makers of the pictures employ great troops of actors and take them all over the world to perform. The sets of pictures have to be changed every other day. Men with vivid imaginations are employed to think up new acts. Their minds must be as fertile as the mental soil of a dime-novelist.

The French seem to be the masters in this new field. The writers of *feuilletons* have evidently branched into the business, for the continued-story moving-picture has come into existence. You get the same characters again and again, battling on the edges of precipitous cliffs, struggling in a lighthouse tower, sleuthing criminals in Parisian suburbs, tracking kid-napped children through dense forests, and pouncing upon would-be assassins with the dagger poised. Also you are introduced to the grotesque and the *comique*. Thousands of dwellers along the Bowery are learning to roar at French buffoonery, and the gendarme is growing as familiar to them as "the copper on the beat."

And after all it is an innocent amusement and a rather wholesome delirium.

The Nickelodeon

"What is it?"

"The academy of the workingman, his pulpit, his newspaper, his club."

"Where is it located?"

"On every thoroughfare in every large city."

"Why was it established?"

"To afford an inductive method of instructive entertainment for five cents."

"How is it governed and regulated?"

"By me," said the Chief of Police.

"Is the nickelodeon a municipal institution?" finally questioned the investigator, as an officer of the law posted the weekly instruction of the Chief of Police in the entrance.

Lucy France Pierce's "The Nickelodeon" ran in the October 1908 *World Today*.

"It isn't, but it is good enough to be," replied Jane Addams. "It is one of those peculiar mushroom growths in the amusement of a great city that sprang up suddenly, somehow, no one knows why, and it had to grow because the good in it was too big and splendid at rock bottom to allow the little evil to control and destroy it."

A fascinating ribbon of incandescent light wriggles around and around the word "Motion" strung out before the gaudy blue and yellow Moorish entrance, flaming with posters, which leads into the place itself. On the edge of the sidewalk the persuasive notes of the barker rise fitfully above the roar of the elevated trains. His eloquence in many cases stamps him as a person who might have been a United States senator, only he considered the show world less corrupt than politics. One can't miss him. He never permits it. An army of men and women and children, a million strong, march and countermarch past him nightly, past that flaming yellow entrance, as they spring out of the dark to plunge headlong into the dark again. How many thousands know no other light! They pause and look, startled, pleased, drawn by the brilliancy. The eloquence of the barker, the purring of a string band hold them. The conscious thought of relaxation, of recreation, is upon them. The subconscious desire of being a unit in the passing show seizes them. "It is only five cents!" coaxes the barker. 'See the moving-picture show, see the wonders of Port Said tonight, and a shrieking comedy from real life, all for five cents. Step in this way and learn to laugh!" And the thousands venture.

Three years ago the nickelodeon was unknown. Cheaply made moving pictures on indifferent topics were utilized to fill up the bills of vaudeville theaters. As the machines became perfected, and every phase of life was drawn upon to enhance the novelty of motography—notice the new word—it was found expedient to create a place devoted solely to the bringing of this practical and inexhaustible form of entertainment to the people. . . .

There is no town of any size in the United States which does not contain at least one nickelodeon. It has become a kind of recreative school for the whole family. On Sunday with its religious subjects it takes the place of the sermon. On week days with its current events of the city, of the world, it takes the place of the newspaper. The clerk, the mechanic, the student, each with his "lady friend," the mother with her brood, young schoolchildren in droves, spend the day and a greater part of the evening loitering in these places. They command a vaster patronage than any school or church. The nickelodeon is more varied than any other type of amusement. It presents its lessons more graphically, more stupendously, reproducing in heroic action life itself without the limitations of art. It is evident that so far-reaching and commanding an institution among the masses may work irreparable evil or boundless good.

Municipal ordinances in New York and Chicago covering the exhibition of what is termed immoral pictures, and a strict police censorship, ever vigilant, are reducing the baneful influences to the minimum. All representation of criminal acts, violent scenes, or questionable social incidents calculated to arouse harmful emotions, is prohibited. Careful inspection is made of every picture which is thrown on the screen. A heavy fine is imposed for every infringement of the law. Its moral tone is thus carefully supervised. . . .

Few nickelodeons, no matter how gaudy or alluring on the outside, can be described as more than puritanically simple within. They are little more than academic halls, given over to a direct and vital appeal to the eye from the screen alone. Sometimes they are fitted up to look like the interior of a railway car and the workingman may take a quick, imaginative journey into a strange land. Sometimes it is a submarine boat, and he looks out (through the screen) to behold the giants of the deep hobnobbing with curiously humanlike mermen. And sometimes it is a thick jungle overhung with tangled growths, and by the aid of the phonograph he hears the very scream of almost real monkeys disporting themselves in what looks like a farther glimpse of a tropical wilderness. But usually it is only a plain, neat hall, scrupulously clean, with the usual uniformed group of ushers as in an ordinary theater, and a "ticket-chopper" at the door. . . .

The past year has developed a remarkable phase of mechanical amusement, housed in the nickelodeon, which may in time revolutionize the whole amusement world. The action of entire dramas of recognized artistic worth is now being projected to the screen, not in movement alone to satisfy the eye, but with the sound of the voices of living actors speaking the lines. This is accomplished in two ways: first by stationing a group of actual actors behind the screen, and second, by means of the phonograph synchronized with the kinetoscope or projecting machine. In the former case companies of actors are trained to follow the movement of the figures in the motographs, reciting the lines of the action as the play progresses on the screen, but always concealed from sight. In the second place science alone gives the whole show and its cost is then reduced to the minimum.

The operator in the kinetoscope cabinet, stationed at the farther end of the theater from the screen, turns the crank of his projecting machine, which simultaneously opens up the phonograph, and the play begins. The whole drama thus comes from the machine. Ibsen and Shakespeare need no longer reasonably turn in their graves over the unintelligible

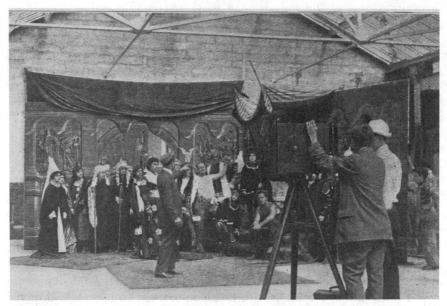

PREPARING "RICHARD III" FOR FIVE-CENT PATRONS
A scene from Shakespeare's well known play is being motographed in
the glass studio

THE INDOOR STAGE
The stage manager directing the scene painters and stage carpenters in
setting the throne-room scene in "Richard III"

mouthings of lesser players. The real machine is safer, and in many instances no more automatic. Here again the possibilities are without limit.
Famous old pieces, such as "East Lynne," "Camille," "Monte Cristo" and
"The Rivals" have been "canned," to use a commercial vulgarism, and
great spectacular melodramas such as "Quo Vadis" and the Passion Play
of Oberammergau have been put on the market by great film-makers. It
brings to the common people, the world over, the greatest plays of
modern times with little less of the reality of a first performance, and
yet for only the trifling price of five cents.

The nickelodeon is still a novelty to a large portion of the public.
Motography itself is still in its infancy. The talking machine is yet to be
exactly synchronized with the projecting machine in order to avoid ridiculous lapses between speech and action at the screen. Yet the future is rich
with promise. To create complete poise and exact concerted action is the
mechanical problem of the hour. Considerable curiosity is being manifested in the possibilities of a device which claims to produce speech at
the screen as if emanating from the throats of the figures in the picture. It
is operated by electricity on the plan of the telephone. A switchboard
erected on the stage behind the screen will receive impressions from a steel
ribbon in the projecting cabinet, and turn them into sound.

When some such invention has been exactly synchronized with the
picture machine, it will materially change the working scheme of the
world's theater. The first performance of a new play given in Paris or
London will echo around the world in ten thousand simultaneous performances, giving not only the actual movement of the original actors,
but the sound of their voices. The *modus operandi* is simple. Henri Bernstein will write a tragedy for Sarah Bernhardt. The actress will rehearse
her company to the point of perfection. A dress rehearsal will be given
before the moto-camera and a giant talking machine loaded with blank
disks. When the play is over a complete record has been obtained of
both speech and action. Then any one may hang up a sheet anywhere,
press the button, and the play is reenacted exactly as the original—and
for five cents! . . .

While it is announced by a famous French firm of moving-picture makers that their output last year reached the seven million dollar mark, it
has been roughly estimated that the profits to American manufacturers
of films and projecting machines amounted last year to $75,000,000. The
middlemen, or rental agents, buy annually from the manufacturer
$4,000,000 worth of films, from which they derive a rental from the ex-
hibitor in the nickelodeon of $8,000,000. It requires an army of ninety
thousand or more persons to conduct the rental agencies and the theaters
proper. It is estimated that four times that number are employed in the

manufacturing corps. In the season just past $65,000,000 were spent in paid admissions to the nickelodeon in the United States alone.

Competition has lately become very keen between French and American manufacturers. The American is better able to cope with native demands because he understands the taste of his own countrymen. However, it has been found that while French pictures are often immoral from a social standpoint, American ones have often been found to encourage violent crimes and daring deeds of robbery and brigandage. Such pictures invariably fail to pass the censorship of the police. . . .

■ ■ ■ ■

THE DRAMA OF THE PEOPLE (1910)
THE MOVING PICTURE AND THE NATIONAL CHARACTER (1910)

While some articles merely chronicled the statistical spread of nickelmania, others attempted to relate the new entertainment to both traditional art and morals. The first piece, prepared by the editors of the *Independent,* compares the popular, democratic motion picture with the elitist and traditional live drama; the second, prepared by the editors of the *American Review of Reviews,* assesses the impact of the motion picture on American moral values.

THE DRAMA OF THE PEOPLE

The cinematograph is doing for the drama what the printing press did for literature, bringing another form of art into the daily life of the people. Plays are now within the reach, literally, of the poorest, as are good books and good pictures. The secret of cheapness in art as in other things is mechanical multiplication. So long as a play required for each presentation the active co-operation of a considerable number of more or less talented persons it could never be cheap, and in its better forms it was necessarily accessible to a comparatively small part of the population. But once on a celluloid film a spectacle can be reproduced indefinitely, the good as cheaply as the poor, and superiority is no longer handicapped. The same effect is shown in the field of literature. Among the dollar and a half books published every year there is a large proportion of trash or worse, but the volumes sold for fifty cents or less comprise the world's best literature.

"The Drama of the People" appeared in the 29 September 1910 *Independent.*

The moving picture shows are in general superior, both artistically and morally, to the vaudeville and melodrama that they have driven out of business. It is a mistake to suppose that their amazing popularity is due altogether to their low price of admission. On the contrary the cinematograph has some advantages, not only over the cheap shows which it at first rivaled, but over any previous form of dramatic art. The most conspicuous of the advantages is spaciousness, distance. The stage is at the best but a narrow platform. The characters must dodge out of the wings or pop out of a door at the back. They have their exits and their entrances, but all both necessarily sudden, more "dramatic" than lifelike.

But the moving picture show has a third dimension. The characters have a gradual approach and recession. The railroad train rushes out toward the spectator; the horseman rides off thru the woods or across the plain until he disappears in the distance. The scene of action is all outdoors. Rejoicing in this release from the limitations of the old drama, the moving picture plays at first were mostly routs. They gave the spectator a run for his money, a chase of comic or tragic character. . . .

The moving picture has it in its power by alternating scenes to show us what is going on simultaneously in two different places, inside and outside a house, for example, or in adjoining rooms. He can vary at will the distance of the stage, giving us a closer view at critical moments. When we would see more clearly what emotions the features of the heroine express or what is in the locket she takes from her bosom we have no need to pick up opera glasses. The artist has foreseen our desire and suddenly the detail is enlarged for us until it fills the canvas.

On the ordinary stage there is no good way of showing what is being written or read, however essential this may be to the plot. The actor has to read aloud his letter as he writes it as tho he was not sure of its grammar. This device is no longer necessary. The incriminating note, the long lost will, the visiting card, the portrait, and the newspaper paragraph are shown to us directly and we do not have to hear of them at second hand. We see instantly what the hero sees when he puts the spyglass to his eye, and what the housemaid is looking at thru the keyhole. Ghosts, visions and transformation scenes are accomplished in a manner truly magical, without the aid of the old stage contrivances, the steam curtain, the trap and the *deus ex machina*. Flying is as easy as walking. Acrobatic feats are unlimited. All miracles are possible, even that most marvelous of miracles, the reversal of the course of life. . . .

The disadvantages of the cinematograph in comparison with the ordinary drama cannot well be discussed at present because we do not know which of them are inherent and which remediable. The flickering and jerky action, now often so disagreeable, can be obviated by more rapid exposures and better adjustment of apparatus. The cinematograph drama is still pantomime as was all drama everywhere in its primitive form. But the phonograph is losing its metallic twang and may soon be satisfactorily synchronized with the running film. The problem of photography in natural color may be regarded as solved altho it cannot in its present stage stand the quick exposure and great enlargement necessary for moving pictures. If once the cinematograph drama can be made vocal and given lifelike color, the only thing further required for a perfect illusion of reality is a real perspective. It can be done by giving our two eyes different pictures and this is not impossible. It has been accomplished for small stationary pictures by means of red and blue spectacles and other contrivances. How it can be managed we do not know. If we did we would not be engaged in writing editorials for a living. But we expect to see some time a stereoscopic colored speaking moving picture drama and it will be well worth seeing. It will be a new form of fine art not unworthy to rank with the elder arts.

THE MOVING PICTURE AND THE NATIONAL CHARACTER

Moving pictures are the main American amusement of to-day. You must appreciate this first of all. Study this table:

CITIES	POPULATION	M. P. THEATERS	SEATING CAPACITY
New York	4,338,322	450 (est.)	150,000
Chicago	2,000,000	310 "	93,000
Philadelphia	1,491,082	160 "	57,000
St. Louis	824,000	142 "	50,410
Cleveland	600,000	75 "	22,500
Baltimore	600,000	83 "	24,900
San Francisco	400,000	68 "	32,400
Cincinnati	350,000	75 "	22,500
New Orleans	325,000	28 "	5,600

In New York City, the moving-picture center of the world, there are 250 "shows" against only 76 regular theaters. Some of the latter include moving pictures on their bills.

The chief combination of manufacturers produces 20,000 feet a week of new films—of which eighty copies apiece must be made. Mr. Edison's royalty, begun only recently, amounts from this source to an income of $8000 a week. The middlemen or "exchanges" pay manufacturers $9,000,000 for films, which the former rent at about $18,000,000 a year

"The Moving Picture and the National Character" appeared in the September 1910 *American Review of Reviews.*

to the actual exhibitors or showmen. They in turn collected nickels and dimes in 1909, at their 10,000 ticket-windows, amounting to $57,500,000. And these audiences numbered more than two and a quarter million souls *per day*—three times the audiences of all the regular theaters in America put together!

When an enterprise as vast as this gets into the field of morals, something serious is bound to happen one way or the other. So far, it is happening both ways. For instance, we quote from a last month's newspaper:

> Charles Judson witnessed a "suicide" scene last night in a moving picture show at Newark. Then he went home and copied the plan of the picture heroine. His body was found in his gas-filled room this morning.
>
> The suicide was nineteen years old. The picture that he saw last night showed a young woman going through all the preliminaries to suicide by gas, finally reclining on her bed and awaiting death calmly.
>
> What was thrown on the screen Judson copied to the last detail, even to the stuffing of the cracks of the windows and doors.

In the files of any newspaper office can be found story after story like the above. Only a few weeks ago the newspapers told of a tragedy in Philadelphia. A clerk, unreasonably jealous of his wife, went with her to a moving-picture melodrama. It showed a home disrupted by a friend's attentions to the wife. The suggestion of fancied wrongs fanned the clerk to a murderous rage. The next morning this clerk shot his wife dead in the presence of their seven-year-old son. The police had no trouble in learning the immediate incitement.

With young, formative, and impressionable minds the results are, of course, worse. Indeed, the motion-picture show is as widely suggestive to this class as the cheap sensational novel used to be. Recent records show that three Brooklyn lads committed burglary to get the price of admission to unlimited "Wild West" pictures. To obtain free tickets from the criminals who run shows in sections of large cities, many boys and girls have been led into all sorts of vice. Two Pittsburg youths tried to "hold up" a street car after viewing a train robbery enacted on a moving-picture screen.

Only a few weeks ago, the President of Police in Berlin forbade children under fourteen to attend moving pictures at night under any circumstances. Before that, the efforts of the S. P. C. C. of New York City had resulted in a similar law against the admission of any children under sixteen unaccompanied by an adult. The International Police Association adopted William A. Pinkerton's resolution at its last meeting for the suppression of moving pictures calculated to increase crime. The agitation in July against the moving pictures of the prizefight at Reno, Nevada, became nation wide.

THE CONSTRUCTIVE SIDE

Is there any reason why so compelling a force cannot be thrown entirely to the aid of education and inspiration?

No reason at all appears to an observer of the uplift and public service already credited to the best film manufacturers. To popularize the Navy, a few motion pictures were made, by order of the Government, for exhibition in recruiting offices. Then one of the "Edison" film company's operators suggested that mere views and naval drills were all right, but that adventures, romances, and spirited action would be better. Whereupon Paymaster George P. Dyer became an active playwright, with motion pictures as his material. His first production was "Up the Ladder with Tom Bowline," a country lad's rise in the service and the heroism that wins him a beautiful bride. "The Sea Hounds" was another romance dealing with torpedo boats. The Government cheerfully furnished as "stage properties" the battleship *Texas,* at Charleston; the *Reina Mercedes* at Newport; the entire torpedo fleet of eleven craft at Newport; a half-dozen torpedo boats at Charleston, and a squadron at Magdalena Bay. The method has proved a convincing recruiting method. . . .

William H. Maxwell, the New York City Superintendent of Schools, demonstrated this year, before the Board of Education and a number of visiting educators and clergymen, a history lesson in motion pictures— scenes from the life of George Washington, including a highly realistic crossing of the Delaware, a triumph of "make-believe" more impressive to the school child's imagination than any book could possibly be. The scenes were directed by the late Prof. Charles Sprague Smith, head of the People's Institute, a pioneer in the movement for wholesome pictures. Another film-history just completed is the life of John Paul Jones. During months past actors and stage managers have been at work dramatizing historical paintings of the sea-fighter's life with high accuracy. The battle between the *Serapis* and *Bon Homme Richard* is unquestionably convincing, although it actually took place in the Bronx Borough of New York City on a miniature scale, in a tank. . . .

THE NATIONAL BOARD OF CENSORSHIP

The big practical step toward eliminating pictures that are dangerous, and encouraging wholesome ones, was the formation, by the People's Institute of New York, of the National Board of Censorship. This is composed of public-spirited men and women, persons of high professional standing, representatives of the municipal government, and of social organizations, along with those of the main combination of manufacturers. Many of the so-called "independents," however, voluntarily submit their films also for the National Board's "O K"—which, as a certificate of good standing and respectability, has business value.

Four times a week the censors meet, passing each time upon fifty-odd series of films. Slips of paper are handed around, and criticisms and suggestions are written on them by the censors. These command the manufacturers' attention, although, in many cases, the rearrangement of plot and picture means an immediate money loss. . . .

WHAT EVERY COMMUNITY CAN DO

Enough examples have been given of moving pictures that are very bad and very good to show how simply the problem could be solved by organized supervision. Any religious or public-spirited organization can obtain from the National Board of Censors of New York City lists of pictures that have been approved, so that improper ones may rigidly be boycotted. Such an arrangement in every section of the country would clear the situation immensely. On the circulating library plan, catalogues could be examined, and the desirable films marked. Thus it would readily become apparent to both manufacturer and exhibitor what the better element of the public admired, and what it condemned.

The exclusion of improper books from public libraries and circulating libraries is pretty closely attended to. Yet no group of libraries in the world have ever possessed the influence over susceptible children, and over all minds in the formative and impressionable stage, that the motion picture exerts to-day. It is probably the greatest single force in shaping the American character.

■ ■ ■ ■

CHEAP THEATERS (1911), Chicago Vice Commission

In its general study of crime and vice in the city of Chicago, the Chicago Vice Commission devoted this brief section to the nickelodeon's contribution to that evil.

The five and ten cent theaters which have sprung up all over the city are conducted in an orderly manner. The entertainment consisting of moving pictures is generally clean. The vaudeville acts and singing are very often

"Cheap Theaters" is from *The Social Evil in Chicago,* published in 1911 by the Chicago Vice Commission.

coarse and inclined to be vulgar but not immoral. The great danger seems to be that which always besets children congregated without proper supervision. We believe that the pictures are a menace to the eyes, which will be shown later in life. The use of glass screens with lighted interior of theater would undoubtedly do much to remove moral dangers and eye strain.

The police are to be commended for their strict censorship over all films exhibited in Chicago. No film may be shown without the signature of the General Superintendent of Police.

It is estimated that there are over 310 of these places of amusement in Chicago. Investigations by individuals interested in the welfare of children have pointed out many instances where children have been influenced for evil by the *conditions surrounding* some of these shows. Vicious men and boys mix with the crowd in front of the theaters and take liberties with very young girls.

The men and boys outside the theaters speak to the young girls and invite them to go to the show.

In one very respectable residential district three very serious things have happened in connection with these theaters.

A man by the name of (X1230), a proprietor of one of these nickel theaters, assaulted fourteen young girls.

Another man, seventy-six years of age, was in the habit of enticing young girls to go to the show.

At another theater the stage manager committed a serious offense with several little boys.

All these things happened in the afternoon.

Many liberties are taken with young girls within the theater during the performance when the place is in total or semi-darkness. Boys and men slyly embrace the girls near them and offer certain indignities.

The following extracts from conferences with widely known workers on the influence of the nickel theater in child protection are worthy of note:

"I think the nickel theaters have an immoral tendency. While I believe some are instructive, the general tendency is toward immorality. I know a good many of my young girls have told me their first wrong came when they attended nickel theaters. The people who conduct them may be morally all right and the shows instructive to the class of people who go there ofttimes, but they are not what they should be. That applies also to dance halls and is one of the great sources of their downfall.

"I think the nickel theater is a recruiting station for vice. In the first place from the type of pictures often shown there; in the second place from the association. Often young people are without supervision, and it is an easy matter for a wrong character to get acquainted with a girl.

Evil minded men can very easily make an acquaintance there, when it wouldn't be possible under other circumstances.

"Nickel theaters exert an evil influence. Parents and in some cases delinquent children testify that they started in these places. They have a tendency to keep the children out away from home at night very late.". . .

■ ■ ■ ■

CENSORING THE FIVE-CENT DRAMA (1910), Charles V. Tevis

The result of such attacks on the moral responsibility of the motion picture was the industry's creation of the National Board of Censorship (its name was later changed to the less imposing title of the National Board of Review). Given so many conflicting censorship laws, boards, and standards in so many different localities, the film industry (represented at the time by the monopolistic "Trust—the Motion Picture Patents Company and the General Film Company) decided to protect its commercial product and profits by censoring films before their release. Its hope was to satisfy a great number of these local boards at one time with one series of decisions based on a single set of standards, thereby eliminating the need to make costly changes and deletions for each city or state. This self-regulation of film content begins a history of such practices by the American film industry that has continued to the present. The principles and procedures of this first board compare interestingly with the problems of the Production Code Administration and the Code and Rating Administration of later periods (see pages 321–33 and 693–715). Indeed, the evolving standards of these censorship boards reflect the evolving moral and social standards of American society as a whole.

A SESSION IN THE "JUDGMENT CHAMBER"
OF A MOTION-PICTURE FACTORY, WHERE
"THE COURT OF LAST REPORT" CONDEMNS
OR COMPLIMENTS UNTRIED FILMS

It seemed to be a quite informal reception, at first. On one side of the room several ladies were gaily chatting about the weather with several gentlemen, and on the other side several gentlemen were pointing out the merits of a number of art-prints to several ladies. The writer's initial impulse was to glance out of the window to see if the sun were still shin-

"Censoring the Five-Cent Drama," by Charles V. Tevis, appeared in the World Today of October 1910.

ing. Then a pile of blank slips on a long table in the center of the room caught his eye. They had a cold, businesslike appearance.

All at once the lights went out. Somebody came softly into the room and screened the windows. The buzz of conversation gave way to a b-r-r-ring sound, and, upon a white background, which had been dropped from the ceiling at the end of the room, there appeared a round blotch of light which slowly evolved into the announcement that "The Judgment of the Mighty Deep" was about to be depicted.

The man on the left muttered something about "another sea picture," and one of the ladies exclaimed, "Oh, look at the surf!" The end of the room had become a reef, a ragged, desolate, forbidding reef, on which wild storm-waves were venting their fury. The try-out of a new idea, a new story, which was to be told in pictures to hundreds of thousands of people, was in process. And in anything but a grim, condemning mood sat the official censor committee.

It did not take long for the story to be told. The pretty fisher maiden made her choice between two lovers in record-breaking time, and it took about as long for the discarded one to plot dire vengeance and scuttle his rival's boat.

According to melodramatic ethics, the hero was a laggard, so, of course, the heroine took the boat to sea. And, again of course, the villain discovered the result of his work too late and endeavored to make amends, only to accomplish nothing and, perforce, return to the blind father of the girl and confess his evil doing. Thereupon the father did some quick work in the midst of which the life of the villain was choked out. Then the old man groped his way out of the little cabin onto the shore in search of his daughter.

"How in the world will he find her?" some one asked in a loud whisper.

Certainly he did. In a riot of surf on the rocky reef he stumbled across her. How he bore her back to the hut was not shown. The moving-picture audience must be credited with some imagination. There the hero and heroine were reunited and the object-lesson of villainy made plain.

"That's a good picture," one of the audience remarked, as the secretary of the committee passed around the slips for a vote. "But why do not heroes sometimes deserve the reward they get?" Then he voted "approved" on one of the blanks like the following:

Title—Judgment of the Mighty Deep.

Maker—E.

Approved. Disapproved. Question. Educational.

Signature—*John Smith.*

"These votes," explained one of the committee, "all are collected and counted by the secretary, who then issues a bulletin announcing the result. Sometimes an argument is necessary. Some may believe that the film should be changed; some that it is altogether bad; some that it is worthy. This film is not passed until there is a consensus of opinion one way or another. If the vote is unanimous either for or against, no further action is taken. Our conclusions are then published in a bulletin and circulated over the country among the managers of moving-picture houses. If they want authorized films they order those we have O. K.'d. Otherwise they take chances—not only with their local authorities but with the manufacturers from whom they rent their stock in trade."

"But what of these manufacturers—do they not lose a lot of money in making films which may not get any farther than this judgment chamber?"

"Sometimes—yes," the censor replied. "But that is their lookout. Our committee is their own institution, you know. They want us as a sort of moral certificate of the high character of their product.

"Consider these pictures on the screen now. Henry is trying to deliver a package and Levi is wildly searching for his lost money. There is much character in both of them. Henry's hilarity might be toned down some, but there is nothing really harmful for man or child in the story he tells. As for Levi, I think that is really humorous. The character burlesque is possibly a trifle strong, but one has no difficulty in imagining such a person doing what Levi is. And notice the interesting little love affair on the side, between his daughter and the clerk in the store? That is well worked out and quite effective. If the idea is old—well, that is not our affair, you know. We are only moral critics.

"Here comes one that will serve to illustrate this, I think," he concluded, as a Persian slave-market scene appeared upon the canvas, following the announcement that the story to be told was "Her Life for Her Love."

Far eastern costumes, camels and picturesque tents predominated in the first scene. After one minute's wait, the tents had metamorphosed into a sixteenth-century castle with a modern Queen Anne back porch, and the dress was of almost every period and country in the European calendar.

"Do we condemn on account of historical incongruity or inappropriate and inartistic stage settings? No," explained the censor. "If, when the maiden loses her life for her love, there is any gruesome detail of crime accentuated, we will take notice at once. They can call a present-day bungalow a medieval castle for all we care. Or they can dress all the characters as American Indians. See—now the plot thickens. She is impersonating her lord, and the band of desperadoes ought to be coming along soon. There they are, lurking behind that stone wall. They are starting to follow her."

A bold, bad-looking crowd it was, indeed. One might have belonged to Captain Kidd's crew; another be a member of the Jesse James gang; another a Parisian Apache; another a seventeenth-century knave; and the captain surely had stepped out of the pages of the "Three Musketeers." None in any moving-picture audience in any part of the United States could have for a moment mistaken their identity.

They overtook the disguised maiden in a secluded part of Central Park —no, it was somewhere in the domain of her fascinating lord—and there they fell upon her in relays, and, as one of the committee expressed it, "did her to dreadful death."

Then they arose from the prostrate form, and each wiped his dripping blade upon his mantle, doublet, overcoat or shirt—whatever sort of garment he wore. Horrors! The committee, as one person, sat up stiffly and took a long breath.

"That will have to be changed," declared a member in no uncertain tone of voice.

"The knife-cleaning business especially," suggested another.

"And those horrible grins!" exclaimed one of the ladies. "They seem to think that murdering a girl is the finest kind of sport."

As a rest, probably, a floricultural exhibit was flashed upon the screen. Roses, lilies, chrysanthemums, tulips and violets, all colors and sizes, appeared and disappeared in all sorts of arrangements.

"Such a picture we class under the head of education," explained one of the critics. "It encourages a love for the beautiful in nature, at least. Here is another." He read from the screen, "The Sisal Industry in the Bahamas." "Teaching the public by this method is much more productive of lasting result than by any other."

"What is sisal?" some one interrupted.

"I—er—don't know," the critic honestly acknowledged, then continued: "As I was saying, this type of film we encourage because of its educational value. You may know all about the sisal industry, but I don't, so I'm going to pay attention and learn something."

A series of pictures showing the way salt is harvested from the sea, gathered up, transported, cleaned and refined, followed. Like the sisal film, it received a large O. K.

Would you consider a surgical operation an unfit subject for public exploitation? Everybody in the judgment chamber asked everybody else this question when, during the film "The Brave Deserve the Fair," one hundred dollars' worth of blood was given by the hero to save the life of the heroine.

THE JUDGMENT CHAMBER
Seven members of the Censor Committee inspecting films in the private
exhibition room of one of the large moving-picture companies

THE STAGE MANAGER INSTRUCTING THE PLAYERS

There was a real operating table. A real looking nurse and a bewhiskered doctor handled real knives and other necessary surgical instruments. Apparently, there was nothing faked in the mannner and method of the transfusion of blood from one patient to the other. The spectacle was interesting, undoubtedly. But was it "fit" for the great public?

The secretary smiled when he was asked to announce the vote. There are rules, you know. It is safe to predict, however, that that film will be seen many times in public during the present year.

"Over the Cliff" was a meaty film from the viewpoint of the critics. In the first place, the heartless villain, a wicked-looking French sailor, made the mistake of kidnaping the pretty little girl in a manner quite taboo. When the "coast was clear," he stole up and ruthlessly enveloped her in a large, dirty sack, very plainly choking her cries by means of a throttle hold upon her throat. This was exceedingly careless of him, or the manufacturers. He should have waited until she had wandered behind the scenes, for an intimation of a kidnaping is about all the committee will allow to pass through its hands.

Then he made another mistake. He climbed upon a high cliff in plain view of the audience, and, sneering fiendishly at an inoffensive little cloud in the northwest, flung the sack and its human freight into the sea far below. One could almost hear him say some thrilling French curseword. The exclamations of the ladies in the audience were quite plain, though.

Luckily, the child did not sink for a good five minutes, and the little boy who went to her rescue was able to reach and carry her to safety. To be sure, in the last scene, the guilty man was apprehended and marched away to his punishment, and all that sort of driving-home-a-lesson business. But the scoundrel had scoundreled too well. His acting had been so good that it had hurt the drama—according to several of the moral censors, who neglected to obscure the "disapproved" mark on their slips.

With this picture the morning's session came to an end. The windowcurtains were raised and the white background taken down. Introductions were in order for late comers. Small talk, for the most part, was again the rule.

But work had been accomplished during the morning. There had been nothing even remotely frivolous in the method by which each had observed and judged and voted for or against the eight films shown. Nothing which might in any way influence the public in the wrong direction had escaped attention and notation. There had been no partiality whatever shown. One film had received the same careful consideration as another. To the guarantors of the moving-picture drama of the United States the affixing of their guarantee mark is a serious proposition.

Since March, 1909, this sort of work has been going on five days in a week, every week in the month. Prior to that date effort had been made by the managers of the show-houses in New York to organize such a committee, but internal dissension among the producers hurt whatever success they might have had. Then the manufacturers of films, trust firms and independents, took the matter up and formed a permanent organization.

Chosen members from fully a score of charitable, religious and educational institutions in the metropolis were sent as delegates to the manufacturers to make up a committee which should sit in judgment on their work. The men and women were from the Young Men's Christian Association, the Young Women's Christian Association, the Children's Aid Society, the People's Institute, the Women's Municipal League, the different branches of the city's associated charities, the Society for the Prevention of Cruelty to Animals, the Purity League, the Women's Christian Temperance Union, a number of denominational societies and many other civic and private organizations. There was no remuneration; the services of the members were donated in the interest of public morals. There was even no law to direct the forming and working of such a body. It existed purely on invitation of the manufacturers. Yet, since its inception, not one verdict of the committee has been set aside.

Every Monday and Friday morning members of the censor committee attend the exhibitions in the offices of the trust. The other days of the week are given over to the independents, who entertain the censors in their different places of business. Sometimes there are a dozen members present. Sometimes there are only four or five. The dictum of the four is as binding, however, as that of the dozen.

On an average thirty-five films are inspected every week. Since the working start of the committee, about four-fifths of all the films passed upon have been approved. Some of these have been changed before final approval, but the remaining one-fifth has been deemed so bad that improvement was out of the question. In the early days of the censors about one in every ten French pictures had to be condemned. Now the foreign manufacturers are working so well with the committee that it is seldom that any of their films are returned to them.

Mr. John Collier, the member of the committee representing the People's Institute, who has made several years' study of the matter of moving-picture morals, has expounded some of the unwritten "don'ts" according to the lights of the censors.

"All obscene subjects are strictly taboo. If manufacturers put them out the local boards and police authorities over the country will place the ban on them.

"All crime pictures, showing gruesome details or tending to teach the technique of crime, are voted against. The suggestion is too strong, even where the picture brings out a strong lesson. The minds of the young to-day are too fertile to trust such pictures to. And we believe that the same lessons can be shown as effectively in other ways.

"All suggestive crime, that is, crime like arson or suicide, is taboo. We do not object to a Shakespearean suicide. But we do object to a picture which shows a man or a woman jumping off the Brooklyn Bridge into the East River. That picture would possibly be the cause of several people trying such a leap for themselves.

"Unmitigated sensationalism and malicious mischief we do not believe should be exploited. We are not prudes in this direction, however. We can encourage innocent mischief.

"Nothing that is in any way offensive to any religious sentiment is allowed to pass. Biblical pictures and stories we do not object to, and we do not demand historical accuracy in them. We are not censoring for theological seminaries. And, if they want to make George Washington the discoverer of America, why, as far as we are concerned, they may.

"We discourage pictures dealing with the subject of marital infelicity. But in some cases we do not condemn them. We believe that the problem play is all right, if it is presented in a proper manner.

"Kidnaping pictures we do not like and seldom pass. In New Jersey there is a law against producing them. Also pictures which show wanton cruelty to animals, even hunting scenes, we cut out, except in remote cases where there is a moral pointed that could not be shown in any other way.

"There has been much debate among our members about allowing pictures of prize-fights to be reproduced. The final decision was, in effect, tolerant of such films where there was nothing extremely brutal shown and where the persons who took part in them were of a better grade.

"We also had much debate over several series of bull-fight pictures. The result of this was that we are now 'agin' them.

"As the audiences of the moving-picture shows over the United States are between twenty and twenty-five per cent children, we give special consideration to subjects of interest wholly, or in great part, to the little ones. This phase of our work is most difficult. Herein our responsibility is heavy indeed. We, therefore, do not approve anything which by any chance might be harmful."

The finished film, the one you may see at any moving-picture exhibition, be you in Oshkosh, Wisconsin, or Tallahassee, Florida, really passes through three boards of censor nowadays. Besides the official one, each manufacturer has two and sometimes three of his own. The studio "round table" reviews it first, then the officers of the company, and, after a final revision, the whole staff gives it another inspection. The negative is then sent to the central office, and the real censor committee acts upon it.

It is an expensive business, the making of films only to have them thrown away. Even the altering of a scene or a piece of scene costs a lot of money. Therefore, abiding by the judgment of the censors as they do, the manufacturers have come to take little chance with their studies. They feel reasonably certain that a film will meet with all requirements before they let it go out of their hands. And they wait before making their positives and scheduling the date of release of the subject until it has been fully approved by the committee.

It really does not need the word of the censor committee now to convince the manufacturers that by extra care they are saving themselves money. One film, a very well-known one, made an elaborate dramatization of "Michael Strogoff," Jules Verne's novel of life in Siberia. It was passed without a single question by the committee and duly scheduled and sent out upon the road.

Almost with its first appearance in Chicago objection was made to it by the authorities and it had to be taken off the boards and altered to meet this city's requirements. It was said that the scene where "Strogoff's" eyes were burned out was too gruesome for public display.

In the picture the man impersonating "Strogoff" sat with his back to the audience and when his captors apparently passed a hot iron across his eyes, he blew out a large mouthful of cigarette smoke. The illusion was complete. Members of the censor committee remarked the cleverness with which this scene was accomplished and passed the film unquestioningly. The Chicago police held it up on its first try-out.

A remarkable picture, "The Fly," was forced off the board in Indianapolis by the police for the same reason. They saw in the exposition of a fly's disease-spreading proclivities something fearfully gruesome. The city board of health, however, had the picture restored to the theater program, claiming that its educational value was immeasurable. The censor committee's judgment was thoroughly upheld in this case.

All of this allied supervision, seconding as it does the work of the New York body, means much for the future of the motion-picture business. With the exception of a very few small dealers in the country, every manufacturer of films is subscribing to the decisions of the board of censors. Every firm is turning out from two to five pictures a week, which approximate about 1,000 feet of film each. These films, when approved, are sent out on their rounds of 10,000 motion-picture houses in the country, and most of them also see the inside of 1,411 theaters where moving pictures form a part of the program. A minimum of 2,250,000 people flock to see them daily. In New York city alone there are 450 picture shows, which enjoy a weekly attendance of 1,100,000.

Measured by the past the coming year will see many changes in the style of pictures shown. Branches of trade to handle subjects for hospital and schoolwork have been established. The educational is to be accented strongly. History is to receive the attention previously given to melodrama. Science, art and religion are to be expounded through the medium of the stage picture. The possibilities opened up and proved by the past year's activities of the board of censors are unlimited.

■ ■ ■ ■

The House of Dreams (1909), Jane Addams

Jane Addams, founder of Chicago's Hull House and a close observer of the ills of American urban, working-class life, discusses the effects of motion pictures on urban children in this chapter from *The Spirit of Youth and the City Streets*. Although aware of the forces that lure children to the "house of dreams," she worries about the American adults that will emerge from a youth of escape and fantasy. Her answer to the house of dreams was parks and playgrounds—where children could enjoy the outdoors (rather than sit imprisoned inside the nickelodeon), where they could play together, establishing a social communicality (rather than sit and fantasize alone), and where they could be active participants (rather than be passive receivers).

To the preoccupied adult who is prone to use the city street as a mere passageway from one hurried duty to another, nothing is more touching than his encounter with a group of children and young people who are emerging from a theater with the magic of the play still thick upon them. They look up and down the familiar street scarcely recognizing it and quite unable to determine the direction of home. From a tangle of "make believe" they gravely scrutinize the real world which they are so reluctant to reënter, reminding one of the absorbed gaze of a child who is groping his way back from fairy-land whither the story has completely transported him.

"Going to the show" for thousands of young people in every industrial city is the only possible road to the realms of mystery and romance; the theater is the only place where they can satisfy that craving for a conception of life higher than that which the actual world offers them. In a very

"The House of Dreams" is from Jane Addams's *The Spirit of Youth and the City Streets* (Macmillan, 1909).

real sense the drama and the drama alone performs for them the office of art as is clearly revealed in their blundering demand stated in many forms for "a play unlike life." The theater becomes to them a "veritable house of dreams" infinitely more real than the noisy streets and the crowded factories.

This first simple demand upon the theater for romance is closely allied to one more complex which might be described as a search for solace and distraction in those moments of first awakening from the glamour of a youth's interpretation of life to the sterner realities which are thrust upon his consciousness. These perceptions which inevitably "close around" and imprison the spirit of youth are perhaps never so grim as in the case of the wage-earning child. We can all recall our own moments of revolt against life's actualities, our reluctance to admit that all life was to be as unheroic and uneventful as that which we saw about us, it was too unbearable that "this was all there was" and we tried every possible avenue of escape. As we made an effort to believe, in spite of what we saw, that life was noble and harmonious, as we stubbornly clung to poesy in contradiction to the testimony of our senses, so we see thousands of young people thronging the theaters bent in their turn upon the same quest. The drama provides a transition between the romantic conceptions which they vainly struggle to keep intact and life's cruelties and trivialities which they refuse to admit. A child whose imagination has been cultivated is able to do this for himself through reading and reverie, but for the over-worked city youth of meager education, perhaps nothing but the theater is able to perform this important office.

The theater also has a strange power to forecast life for the youth. Each boy comes from our ancestral past not "in entire forgetfulness," and quite as he unconsciously uses ancient war-cries in his street play, so he longs to reproduce and to see set before him the valors and vengeances of a society embodying a much more primitive state of morality than that in which he finds himself. Mr. Patten has pointed out that the elemental action which the stage presents, the old emotions of love and jealousy, or revenge and daring take the thoughts of the spectator back into deep and well worn channels in which his mind runs with a sense of rest afforded by nothing else. The cheap drama brings cause and effect, will power and action, once more into relation and gives a man the thrilling conviction that he may yet be master of his fate. The youth of course, quite unconscious of this psychology, views the deeds of the hero simply as a forecast of his own future and it is this fascinating view of his own career which draws the boy to "shows" of all sorts. They can scarcely be too improbable for him, portraying, as they do, his belief in his own prowess. A series of slides which has lately been very popular in the five-cent theaters of Chicago, portrayed five masked men breaking into a humble dwelling, killing the father of the family and carrying away the family treasure. The golden-haired son of the house, aged seven, vows eternal vengeance on the spot, and follows one villain after another to his doom. The execution of each is shown in lurid detail, and the last slide of the series depicts the hero, aged ten, kneeling upon his father's grave counting on the fingers of one hand the number of men that he has killed, and thanking God that he has been permitted to be an instrument of vengeance.

In another series of slides, a poor woman is wearily bending over some sewing, a baby is crying in the cradle, and two little boys of nine and ten are asking for food. In despair the mother sends them out into the street to beg, but instead they steal a revolver from a pawn shop and with it kill a Chinese laundryman, robbing him of $200. They rush home with the treasure which is found by the mother in the baby's cradle, whereupon she and her sons fall upon their knees and send up a prayer of thankfulness for this timely and heaven-sent assistance.

Is it not astounding that a city allows thousands of its youth to fill their impressionable minds with these absurdities which certainly will become the foundation for their working moral codes and the data from which they will judge the proprieties of life?

It is as if a child, starved at home, should be forced to go out and search for food, selecting, quite naturally, not that which is nourishing but that which is exciting and appealing to his outward sense, often in his ignorance and foolishness blundering into substances which are filthy and poisonous.

Out of my twenty years' experience at Hull-House I can recall all sorts of pilferings, petty larcenies, and even burglaries, due to that never ceasing effort on the part of boys to procure theater tickets. I can also recall indirect efforts toward the same end which are most pitiful. I remember the remorse of a young girl of fifteen who was brought into the Juvenile Court after a night spent weeping in the cellar of her home because she had stolen a mass of artificial flowers with which to trim a hat. She stated that she had taken the flowers because she was afraid of losing the attention of a young man whom she had heard say that "a girl has to be dressy if she expects to be seen." This young man was the only one who had ever taken her to the theater and if he failed her, she was sure that she would never go again, and she sobbed out incoherently that she "couldn't live at all without it." Apparently the blankness and grayness of life itself had been broken for her only by the portrayal of a different world.

One boy whom I had known from babyhood began to take money

from his mother from the time he was seven years old, and after he was ten she regularly gave him money for the play Saturday evening. However, the Saturday performance, "starting him off like," he always went twice again on Sunday, procuring the money in all sorts of illicit ways. Practically all of his earnings after he was fourteen were spent in this way to satisfy the insatiable desire to know of the great adventures of the wide world which the more fortunate boy takes out in reading Homer and Stevenson. . . .

One Sunday evening last winter an investigation was made of four hundred and sixty six theaters in the city of Chicago, and it was discovered that in the majority of them the leading theme was revenge; the lover following his rival; the outraged husband seeking his wife's paramour; or the wiping out by death of a blot on a hitherto unstained honor. It was estimated that one sixth of the entire population of the city had attended the theaters on that day. At that same moment the churches throughout the city were preaching the gospel of good will. Is not this a striking commentary upon the contradictory influences to which the city youth is constantly subjected?

This discrepancy between the church and the stage is at times apparently recognized by the five-cent theater itself, and a blundering attempt is made to suffuse the songs and moving pictures with piety. Nothing could more absurdly demonstrate this attempt than a song, illustrated by pictures, describing the adventures of a young man who follows a pretty girl through street after street in the hope of "snatching a kiss from her ruby lips." The young man is overjoyed when a sudden wind storm drives the girl to shelter under an archway, and he is about to succeed in his attempt when the good Lord, "ever watchful over innocence," makes the same wind "blow a cloud of dust into the eyes of the rubberneck," and "his foul purpose is foiled." This attempt at piety is also shown in a series of films depicting Bible stories and the Passion Play at Oberammergau, forecasting the time when the moving film will be viewed as a mere mechanical device for the use of the church, the school and the library, as well as for the theater.

At present, however, most improbable tales hold the attention of the youth of the city night after night, and feed his starved imagination as nothing else succeeds in doing. In addition to these fascinations, the five-cent theater is also fast becoming the general social center and club house in many crowded neighborhoods. It is easy of access from the street, the entire family of parents and children can attend for a comparatively small sum of money, and the performance lasts for at least an hour; and, in some of the humbler theaters, the spectators are not disturbed for a second hour.

The room which contains the mimic stage is small and cozy, and less formal than the regular theater, and there is much more gossip and social life as if the foyer and pit were mingled. The very darkness of the room, necessary for an exhibition of the films, is an added attraction to many young people, for whom the space is filled with the glamour of love making.

Hundreds of young people attend these five-cent theaters every evening in the week, including Sunday, and what is seen and heard there becomes the sole topic of conversation, forming the ground pattern of their social life. That mutual understanding which in another social circle is provided by books, travel and all the arts, is here compressed into the topics suggested by the play.

The young people attend the five-cent theaters in groups, with something of the "gang" instinct, boasting of the films and stunts in "our theater." They find a certain advantage in attending one theater regularly, for the *habitués* are often invited to come upon the stage on "amateur nights," which occur at least once a week in all the theaters. This is, of course, a most exciting experience. If the "stunt" does not meet with the approval of the audience, the performer is greeted with jeers and a long hook pulls him off the stage; if, on the other hand, he succeeds in pleasing the audience, he may be paid for his performance and later register with a booking agency, the address of which is supplied by the obliging manager, and thus he fancies that a lucrative and exciting career is opening before him. Almost every night at six o'clock a long line of children may be seen waiting at the entrance of these booking agencies, of which there are fifteen that are well known in Chicago.

Thus, the only art which is constantly placed before the eyes of "the temperamental youth" is a debased form of dramatic art, and a vulgar type of music, for the success of a song in these theaters depends not so much upon its musical rendition as upon the vulgarity of its appeal. In a song which held the stage of a cheap theater in Chicago for weeks, the young singer was helped out by a bit of mirror from which she threw a flash of light into the faces of successive boys whom she selected from the audience as she sang the refrain, "You are my Affinity." Many popular songs relate the vulgar experiences of a city man wandering from amusement park to bathing beach in search of flirtations. It may be that these "stunts" and recitals of city adventure contain the nucleus of coming poesy and romance, as the songs and recitals of the early minstrels sprang directly from the life of the people, but all the more does the effort need help and direction, both in the development of its technique and the material of its themes. . . .

This spring a group of young girls accustomed to the life of a five-cent theater, reluctantly refused an invitation to go to the country for a day's outing because the return on a late train would compel them to miss one evening's performance. They found it impossible to tear themselves away not only from the excitements of the theater itself but from the gaiety of the crowd of young men and girls invariably gathered outside discussing the sensational posters.

A steady English shopkeeper lately complained that unless he provided his four daughters with the money for the five-cent theaters every evening they would steal it from his till, and he feared that they might be driven to procure it in even more illicit ways. Because his entire family life had been thus disrupted he gloomily asserted that "this cheap show had ruined his 'ome and was the curse of America." This father was able to formulate the anxiety of many immigrant parents who are absolutely bewildered by the keen absorption of their children in the cheap theater. This anxiety is not, indeed, without foundation. An eminent alienist of Chicago states that he has had a number of patients among neurotic children whose emotional natures have been so over-wrought by the crude appeal to which they had been so constantly subjected in the theaters, that they have become victims of hallucination and mental disorder. The statement of this physician may be the first note of alarm which will awaken the city to its duty in regard to the theater, so that it shall at least be made safe and sane for the city child whose senses are already so abnormally developed.

This testimony of a physician that the conditions are actually pathological, may at last induce us to bestir ourselves in regard to procuring a more wholesome form of public recreation. Many efforts in social amelioration have been undertaken only after such exposures; in the meantime, while the occasional child is driven distraught, a hundred children permanently injure their eyes watching the moving films, and hundreds more seriously model their conduct upon the standards set before them on this mimic stage.

Three boys, aged nine, eleven and thirteen years, who had recently seen depicted the adventures of frontier life including the holding up of a stage coach and the lassoing of the driver, spent weeks planning to lasso, murder, and rob a neighborhood milkman, who started on his route at four o'clock in the morning. They made their headquarters in a barn and saved enough money to buy a revolver, adopting as their watchword the phrase "Dead Men Tell no Tales." Once spring morning the conspirators, with their faces covered with black cloth, lay "in ambush" for the milkman. Fortunately for him, as the lariat was thrown the horse shied, and, although the shot was appropriately fired, the milkman's life was saved. Such a direct influence of the theater is by no means rare, even among older boys. Thirteen young lads were brought into the Municipal Court in Chicago during the first week that "Raffles, the Amateur Cracksman" was upon the stage, each one with an outfit of burglar's tools in his possession, and each one shamefacedly admitting that the gentlemanly burglar in the play had suggested to him a career of similar adventure.

In so far as the illusions of the theater succeed in giving youth the rest and recreation which comes from following a more primitive code of morality, it has a close relation to the function performed by public games. It is, of course, less valuable because the sense of participation is largely confined to the emotions and the imagination, and does not involve the entire nature. . . .

To fail to provide for the recreation of youth, is not only to deprive all of them of their natural form of expression, but is certain to subject some of them to the overwhelming temptation of illicit and soul-destroying pleasures. To insist that young people shall forecast their rose-colored future only in a house of dreams, is to deprive the real world of that warmth and reassurance which it so sorely needs and to which it is justly entitled; furthermore, we are left outside with a sense of dreariness, in company with that shadow which already lurks only around the corner for most of us—a skepticism of life's value.

■ ■ ■ ■

CAME THE DAWN (1962), Edward Wagenknecht

One of the children who spent his time in the house of dreams was Edward Wagenknecht—who grew up to become a professor of English literature. He recalls the hours he spent there in *The Movies in the Age of Innocence,* a book he describes as that of a scholar on vacation. In this excerpt on the films of Vitagraph and Essanay, Wagenknecht provides valuable information about how it felt to be a member of a nickelodeon audience and what he saw there—the kinds of films, the qualities of the players, and the characteristics of several of the little companies which made the one-reel films.

Vitagraph, a Brooklyn concern in which J. Stuart Blackton, Albert E. Smith, and William T. Rock held the controlling interest, has been

"Came the Dawn" appeared in *The Movies in the Age of Innocence,* by Edward Wagenknecht (University of Oklahoma Press, 1962).

neglected by film historians—Norma Talmadge says the firm burned many of its negatives for lack of storage space—but it loomed very large in the lives of contemporary movie fans, and by 1912–13, its profits were in the neighborhood of $1,250,000 a year. Next to Biograph, Vitagraph had the most impressive stock company, and it anticipated Biograph by several years in publicizing its players. I should say that the first real approach to the star system among the Patents companies was made at Essanay with the Broncho Billy pictures, which were produced and acted by G. M. Anderson, the "A" or "ay" of that concern (George K. Spoor was the "Ess"); not only was the name Broncho Billy generally a part of the name of the picture, but it became the custom to print a circled photograph of Mr. Anderson, with his name under it, in one corner of the poster. Vitagraph approached this, however, with the John Bunny comedies, generally directed by George D. Baker, which often carried such titles as *Bunny's Birthday, Bunny in Disguise,* and *Bunny Dips into Society.* The first great comic of the screen, Bunny (1863–1915) had had rather more success on the stage than most of the early film stars, having played Bottom in Annie Russell's production of *A Midsummer Night's Dream,* and when he first approached Vitagraph they were very doubtful of their ability to use him, simply because they did not think they could pay him what he was worth. He agreed to start at $40 per week; according to Norma Talmadge, he rose to $200, thence to a percentage, being the only Vitagraph player to be so treated. "This is my work," he told an interviewer, after he had established himself in the new medium. "Here every day is a first night. It keeps you alive, stimulates your imagination, and compels a constant thinking out of new ideas."

How good was Bunny? Not much of his work is available for reinspection, but what I have seen leaves me with the impression that he was an artist of considerable gifts. "When Mr. Bunny laughs," observed the London *Spectator,* "people from San Francisco to Stepney Green laugh with him. When Mr. Bunny frowns, every kingdom of the earth is contracted in one brow of woe. When he smells a piece of Gorgonzola cheese there is no doubt whatever that his nose has been seriously offended. His despair is incredible. His grief is unendurable. His wrath is apoplectic. His terror is the terror of a whole army."

His materials were generally quite unliterary. It is true that in 1913, Vitagraph sent him to England to do a *Pickwick Papers* and that in 1914 he made a picture of Ellis Parker Butler's *Pigs Is Pigs.* He sometimes appeared in minor roles in serious pictures; he was, for example, the Jos Sedley in Vitagraph's big production of *Vanity Fair* at the end of 1911. But in the typical comedies which he made his own, he simply devoted himself to high jinks, often in association, for purposes of contrast, with

Flora Finch, "in all her Scrawny, Skinny Majesty," as she was later billed when, after his death, she tried a starring career of her own. Like "Fatty" Arbuckle a little later, Bunny was fond of disguising himself as a woman, and they both did it extremely well; in *Bunny's Dilemma* our hero became a maid to avoid meeting a woman visitor and then found himself greatly attracted to her. There was a great deal of flirting and other extramarital shenanigans in the Bunny films; there was also considerable drinking and smoking (this was also true of the domestic comedies produced by Mr. and Mrs. Sidney Drew with which Vitagraph found another profitable "line" after they had lost Bunny); in this respect they conformed to the Age of Innocence pattern less than one might have expected. In spite of his enormous bulk, however, Bunny had considerable charm as well as great vitality, and those who worked with him generally remembered him affectionately.

The great dramatic stars at Vitagraph were Maurice Costello and Florence Turner. Costello, who may be identified for a later generation as Dolores Costello's father—both Dolores and her sister Helen played with him as children in Vitagraph films—was the first great matinee idol of the screen, and Florence Turner was "The Vitagraph Girl" before anybody knew her name. Costello won the first popularity contest conducted by *The Motion Picture Story Magazine* in 1912 with 430,816 votes. I myself was mad about him in those days; when I recently, somewhat shamefacedly, mentioned my enthusiasm for him to Zena Keefe, who played with him, she replied, a bit reproachfully, I thought, "Well, he *was* very good, you know." So I think he was, not only in the big roles, like Sydney Carton in *A Tale of Two Cities* (1911), which roused Rex Ingram's interest in motion pictures and caused the British press to speak of Costello in the same breath with Martin Harvey, but in hosts of now completely forgotten one-reelers. Obscene as I find the kind of psychological slang now in vogue, I suppose it would not be too far beyond the mark to speak of Costello as a "father image." Already a mature man when success came to him (he had been on the stage in stock), Costello did not go in for "sex appeal." Neither did he try to overwhelm you with his athletic prowess, and I am sure he would have felt nothing but disgust for the "sullen slobber" kind of thing, as it has been called, associated with some later screen idols. He may sometimes have been slightly conscious of his charm, but there was always a relaxed friendliness in his exercise of it.

Florence Turner was, I suppose, a more serious artist, and a more ambitious one, and nobody in my generation could have had any difficulty in understanding the young Norma Talmadge's enthusiasm for her even before she herself had become a Vitagrapher: "I would rather have

touched the hem of her skirt than to have shaken hands with Saint Peter."
Miss Turner's ambition finally proved her undoing, for she left Vitagraph
early in 1913 and went to England, with Lawrence Trimble as her director, to produce independently. Her films were at first very successful,
and Rachael Low, the authoritative historian of the British film, speaks
of them with great enthusiasm, but the war intervened and brought hardship and failure. Miss Turner returned to America, but she never regained her old position on the screen.

From 1907 on at Vitagraph, however, she played everything from
Lucie in *A Tale of Two Cities* and Elaine in *Lancelot and Elaine* down to
broadest farce. She loved "mugging" and never considered it beneath
her; this, no doubt, was one of the reasons why she was so successful
in English music halls. In her serious work she never overacted, however;
unsatisfactory though *The Deerslayer* is as a motion picture, I was much
impressed, when I saw it recently, by the fine restraint with which she
played Hetty. In 1911 she did a solo performance as a discarded harem
favorite whose life ends in murder and suicide in a one-reeler called
Jealousy; this of course antedated Chaplin's solo film *One A.M.* by a
number of years. Miss Turner had enthusiasm and a quick, eager mind
which addressed itself to every aspect of film-making. When I met her
in 1945, only a year before she died, I asked her, "Do you remember a
film called *The Closed Door?*" This was an oppressively moral Vitagraph
of 1910 in which Miss Turner played an unfaithful wife who ran off
with Leo Delaney from her husband (Maurice Costello) and her child
(Adele de Garde). I can still see the radiant smile on her face as she looked
up adoringly at Delaney when they passed down the street together, and
I can see her too, broken and white-haired, as she returned on the eve
of her daughter's wedding to be self-righteously shown the door in one
of Costello's most theatrical gestures. It was of course the *East Lynne*
motif, which was used again and again in early films, but this time it
had not come from *East Lynne* directly. "Do I *remember* it?" Miss
Turner exclaimed in answer to my question. "I *wrote* it. I went to see
Madame X one night, and the next morning I came down to the studio
and said to Mr. Smith, 'I have a *wonderful* idea for a picture!' " She
was a lovely, idealistic, and unselfish woman, and such she remained,
through good fortune and bad, to the end. . . . In 1912, Clara Kimball
Young came along with her first husband James Young, who was director as well as actor; she was a very beautiful girl in those days, and
she made her first appearance as Anne Boleyn in *Cardinal Wolsey*, in
which Tefft Johnson was the Henry VIII, Julia Swayne Gordon the
Catherine of Aragon, and Hal Reid (Wallace Reid's father) the Wolsey.
Many years later I told Mrs. Young I had seen her in her first film;

she was not able to remember it, but she admitted that it had been made in 1912, and she seemed so appalled by the date that I felt very rude for having mentioned it. That same year Ralph Ince brought his sister-in-law to the studio, a fresh, distractingly pretty little slip of a girl named Anita Stewart, and Vitagraph found just the right showcase for her personality in *The Wood Violet*. Another little girl who has already been mentioned, Norma Talmadge, had arrived two years before. She made her first important appearance with Florence Turner in *A Dixie Mother*, and she was the girl who held Carton's hand on the way to the guillotine in *A Tale of Two Cities*. Norma learned film-acting rather slowly, and her ability was not highly regarded at first, but Costello believed in her and championed her. She was not the kind of person to forget such a service; when in 1927 she produced *Camille* she gave Costello one of the best roles of his later years as the elder Duval.

Vitagraph even had the first dog star, Larry Trimble's beautiful collie, "Jean the Vitagraph Dog." Trimble was a wizard with animals; I have heard it said that to know him was to have no difficulty in crediting what has been written about Saint Francis of Assisi and the Wolf of Gubbio; after his picture career was over, he carved another for himself as a trainer of "seeing-eye" dogs. As Miss Turner remarked, Jean did not do tricks; she was simply an actress! She appeared in innumerable Vitagraphs; she even shared with Bunny the distinction of having some of them carry her name—*Jean the Matchmaker, Jean Goes Foraging*, etc. —and when she reproduced herself she was given part of a reel to display her proud family. Vitagraph's idea of a very poetic final fade-out in those days was Jean silhouetted against the sunset on a seaside rock, and Miss Turner told me a delightful anecdote of what happened one day when she, Trimble, Charles Kent, and others were out on location making such a scene. "Do you suppose," Kent asked Trimble, "that you could get that dog to do something you told her *not* to do?" "I don't know," replied Trimble. "I never thought of that. Let's try it." Then he turned to her. "Jean," he said, "go over and sit on that rock, and when I call you, *don't come*." Jean went over and sat on the rock, and Trimble proceeded to wear out his lungs shouting to her. She did not come, and she did not even condescend to turn her head. Then Trimble changed his tone. "Jean," he said, "come here to me, *and this time I mean it*." Jean trotted obediently to his side.

Essanay and Selig were Chicago firms, though both began producing in California also at a very early date. Essanay's great Chicago star was Francis X. Bushman, who with Beverly Bayne later formed one of the screen's legendary teams of "great lovers." Bushman's last big role was as Messala in the 1925 *Ben Hur*, though he has appeared occasionally since then in sound films, still looking very much as he always did—and he might have appeared more frequently if he had not preferred his own self-respect to the kind of kowtowing that is favored in the film industry today. Bushman always did have a mind of his own; it is said that he broke with Essanay when he was asked to "support" Viola Allen when she was brought in from the stage for *The White Sister*. Like Bunny, he came to films because he loved them, becoming a fan while he was still in stock, and describing pictures as "the only practical Esperanto that is understood by the whole world" and a greater influence for good than press or pulpit. They keep men "from the saloon," he declared, "the pool parlor and the cabaret and other forms of amusement that are not agents for health or morals." He also believed that pictures would break down barriers between nations and make us realize "that we are all brothers of God's family." Such were the high hopes we had for the films in the early days. They turned out, alas! no better than the men who controlled them.

Gloria Swanson and Wallace Beery also began their careers at Essanay's Chicago studio, and of course Chaplin went to Essanay for a year after leaving Keystone. But perhaps the name one thinks of first of all in connection with Essanay is that of G. M. Anderson, who was born Max Aronson and became world-famous as Broncho Billy.

Anderson did not confine himself entirely to cowboy films. In 1911 he appeared as a prize fighter in *"Spike" Shannon's Last Fight;* in 1914 he was in a four-reeler, *The Good-for-Nothing,* wherein he impersonated both "a man of a large eastern metropolis and a man of the far and unsettled West"; in 1914–15 he appeared in a whole series of multiple-reel "mystery plays." Anderson is recorded as having established an Essanay studio at Niles, California, as early as the fall of 1908, and it is said that he got his screen name from a Peter B. Kyne story, "Broncho Billy and the Baby." But the earliest Broncho Billy film title recorded seems to be *Broncho Billy's Redemption,* which was released July 30, 1910.

He was a heavy-set, rather stolid actor, with amazing, white-gleaming eyes. He was not exactly a romantic figure, and at the beginning of his career as the first great cowboy hero of the screen, he could not even ride a horse. He himself says that he never became more than a fair rider, and he claimed even less for his marksmanship. Nevertheless his contemporaries loved him, and if I were ever tempted to forget it, I should have to recall the old German lady, mother of many children, who lived downstairs in my aunt's house on Sawyer Avenue. "Ach!" she would say as often as occasion warranted, "ich muss tonight nach der White Palace. Der Broncho Billy ist da. Ach, der ist zu schön!"

When you have to think up a story a week, it does not pay to be fussy about consistency, and Broncho Billy's admirers could never be quite sure which side of the law he was going to be on. In *Broncho Billy Reforms* (1913) he was an outlaw who refused to join his fellows in robbing a store kept by the local schoolteacher, and in *Why Broncho Billy Left Bear County* he not only reformed but got religion. In *Broncho Billy's Scheme* he was a medical man, but in *Broncho Billy's Mother* he was a "booze fighter" who shot up the town. In *"Alkali" Bests Broncho Billy* he was teamed with the diminutive Augustus Carney, who had a series of his own, and whose name had to be changed from "Alkali Ike" to "Universal Ike" when he deserted Essanay for Carl Laemmle. In *Broncho Billy's Conscience* he was even killed, but few of his followers can have entertained any real fears that he would turn out to have been "kilt entoirely." Anderson was probably most popular in the films in which he exemplified the spirit of renunciation, like *Broncho Billy's Christmas Spirit*, where he sacrificed his horse for a destitute family. Frequently he gave up a girl, and then we might see him gazing in upon her happiness with his rival from the wrong side of a lighted window and trudging out into the night with his traps as sadly as Chaplin ever walked down the lonesome road. . . .

The informality of early film-making is hard to realize today. "In those days if there was a fire or a procession or a circus," wrote Hobart Bosworth, "we 'grabbed' it and wrote a story around it afterward." Vitagraph, according to Albert Smith, wrote no contracts until 1916, and seasonal layoffs were so common that they used a form letter to announce them. Biograph worked more systematically and carefully. "On Mondays," writes Mary Pickford, "we would rehearse. Mr. Griffith would call the company round him and assign our parts. Then and there the story would be written or built up. Tuesdays we took interior scenes and Wednesdays we took exteriors." But even Biograph improvised, as one may tell by reference to Miss Pickford's own account of the making of *Wilful Peggy*. Thanhouser used a Siberian locale in one film because a sudden snowstorm had buried the New Rochelle studio; when the snow melted before the picture was finished, they simply inserted a subtitle: "Later—A Warmer Clime." In one early Vitagraph, *The Life of Washington*, William Shea played fifteen parts and died twice in one scene; in *The Servant Girl's Problem* he was a Jew, a Dutchman, and three old maids. When in 1911 somebody asked *Motion Picture's* "Answer Man" how long it took to make a film, he replied that "a week to ten days should cover the ordinary production." But Bosworth said the early Seligs were made in two days, and Gene Gauntier claims to have ground out Kalems at the rate of one a day. Warren Kerrigan, the first player to be engaged by American, testified in 1914 that for three and a half years he played the leads in two pictures a week, or everything that the com̄, produced. When Herbert Brenon and Annette Kellerman were hurt while filming *Neptune's Daughter* in the Bahamas, *The Moving Picture World* conjectured that other members of the company would probably make other pictures while waiting for them to recover. All this made for roughness of course, but it also made for spontaneity, and Gilbert Seldes reports so meticulous a worker as Chaplin eyeing his elaborate equipment during the filming of *Modern Times* and remarking wistfully, "We used to go into the park with a stepladder, a bucket of whitewash, and Mabel Normand, and make a picture." . . .

■ ■ ■ ■

WHEN THE MOVIES WERE YOUNG (1925), Linda Arvidson Griffith

One of the actresses to work in the early films was Linda Arvidson, D. W. Griffith's first wife. Mrs. Griffith, who usually played lesser roles in her husband's Biograph films, kept her marriage to the director a secret from the other members of the company. These excerpts, describing the making of one-reelers under Griffith at Biograph, are from her collection of reminiscences about the early years of movies, published in 1925 after she and Griffith had been divorced.

DIGGING IN

It was an easy matter in those days to get into the studio. No cards of announcement were needed—no office boy insulted you, no humiliation of waiting, as to-day. A ring of the bell and in you'd go, and Bobbie Harron would greet you if he chanced to be near by. Otherwise, any one of the actors would pass you the glad word.

On an ordinary kitchen chair a bit to one side of the camera, Mr. Griffith usually sat when directing. The actors when not working lingered about, either standing or enjoying the few other kitchen chairs. During rehearsals actors sat all over the camera stand—it was at least six feet square—and as the actors were a rather chummy lot, the close and informal intimacy disturbed them not the least.

A "scene" was set back center, just allowing passage room. What

Linda Arvidson Griffith, *When the Movies Were Young* (E. P. Dutton, 1925; Blom, 1969).

little light came through the few windows was soon blocked by dusty old scenery. On the side spaces of the room and on the small gallery above, the carpenters made scenery and the scene painters painted it—scenery, paint pots, and actors were all huddled together in one friendly chaos. We always had to be mindful of our costumes. To the smell of fresh paint and the noise of the carpenters' hammers, we rehearsed our first crude little movies and in due time many an old literary classic.

Rolls of old carpet and bundles of canvas had to be climbed over in wending one's way about. To the right of the camera a stairway led to the basement where there were three small dressing-rooms; and no matter how many actors were working in a picture those three dark little closets had to take care of them all. The developing or "dark" room adjoined the last dressing-room, and all opened into a cavernous cellar where the stage properties were kept. Here at the foot of the stairs and always in every one's way, the large wardrobe baskets would be deposited. And what a scramble for something that would half-way fit us when the costumes arrived!

We ate our lunches in the dingy basement, usually seated on the wardrobe baskets. Squatted there, tailor-fashion, on their strong covers, we made out pretty well. On days when we had numbers of extra people, our lunch boy, little Bobbie Harron, would arrange boards on wooden horses, and spread a white cloth, banquet fashion. Especially effective this, when doing society drama, and there would be grand dames, financiers, and magnates, to grace the festive board.

In a back corner of the studio reposed a small, oak, roll-top desk, which the new director graced in the early morning hours when getting things in shape, and again in the evening when he made out the actors' pay checks. When the welcome words came from the dark room, "All right, everybody; strike!" the actors rushed to the roll-top, and clamored for vouchers—we received our "pay" daily. Then the actor rushed his "make-up" off, dressed, passed to the bookkeeper's window in the outer office, presented his voucher, and Herman Bruenner gave him his money. And then to eat, and put away a dollar towards the week's rent, and to see a movie for ten cents!

A little group of serious actors soon began to report daily for work. As yet no one had a regular salary except the director and camera man. "Principal part" actors received five and "extras" three dollars.

In August this first year Mr. Griffith began turning out two releases a week, usually one long picture, eight to eleven hundred feet, and one short picture, four to five hundred feet. The actors who played the principal parts in these pictures were Eddie Dillon, Harry Salter, Charles Inslee, Frank Gebhardt, Arthur Johnson, Wilfred Lucas, George Nichols,

John Compson, Owen Moore, Mack Sennett, Herbert Pryor, David Miles, Herbert Yost, Tony O'Sullivan, and Daddy Butler. Of the women Marion Leonard, Florence Lawrence, and myself played most of the leading parts, while Mabel Stoughton, Florence Auer, Ruth Hart, Jeanie Macpherson, Flora Finch, Anita Hendry, Dorothy West, Eleanor Kershaw (Mrs. Tom Ince), and Violet Mersereau helped out occasionally. Gladys Egan, Adele DeGarde, and Johnny Tansy played the important child parts.

Though I speak of playing "principal parts," no one had much chance to get puffed up, for an actor having finished three days of importance usually found himself on the fourth day playing "atmosphere," the while he decorated the back drop. But no one minded. They were a good-natured lot of troupers and most of them were sincerely concerned in what they were doing. David had a happy way of working. He invited confidence and asked and took suggestions from any one sufficiently interested to make them. His enthusiasm became quite infectious.

In the beginning Marion Leonard and I alternated playing "leads." She played the worldly woman, the adventuress, and the melodramatic parts, while I did the sympathetic, the wronged wife, the too-trusting maid, waiting, always waiting, for the lover who never came back. But mostly I died.

Our director, already on the lookout for a new type, heard of a clever girl out at the Vitagraph, who rode a horse like a western cowboy and who had had good movie training under Mr. Rainous. He wanted to see her on the screen before an audience. Set up in a store on Amsterdam Avenue and 160th Street was a little motion picture place. It had a rough wooden floor, common kitchen chairs, and the reels unwound to the tin-panny shriek of a pianola. After some watchful waiting, the stand outside the theatre—the sort of thing sandwich men carry—finally announced "The Dispatch Bearer," a Vitagraph with Florence Lawrence. So, living near by, after dinner one night we rushed over to see it.

It was a good picture. Mr. Griffith concluded he would like to work with Mr. Rainous for a while and learn about the movies. For one could easily see that besides having ability Florence Lawrence had had excellent direction.

Well, David stole little Florrie, he did. With Harry Salter as support in his nefarious errand, he called on Miss Lawrence and her mother, and offered the Vitagraph girl twenty-five dollars a week, regular. She had been receiving fifteen at Vitagraph playing leading parts, sewing costumes, and mending scenery canvas. She was quite overcome with Mr. Griffith's spectacular offer, readily accepted, and by way of celebrating her new prosperity, she drew forth from under the bed in the little boarding-house room, her trombone—or was it a violin?—and played several selections. As a child, Miss Lawrence, managed by her mother, and starred as "Baby Flo, the child wonder-whistler" had toured the country, playing even the "tanks."

Immediately she joined the Biograph, Florence Lawrence was given a grand rush. But she never minded work. The movies were as the breath of life to her. When she wasn't working in a picture, she was in some movie theater seeing a picture. After the hardest day, she was never too tired to see the new release and if work ran into the night hours, between scenes she'd wipe off the make-up and slip out to a movie show.

Her pictures became tremendously popular, and soon all over the country Miss Lawrence was known as "The Biograph Girl." . . .

AT THE STUDIO

An especially busy hour 9 A.M. when we were to start on a new picture. What kind of a picture was it to be? The air was full of expectancy. Who would be cast for the leads? How keen we were to work! How we hoped for a good part—then for any kind of a part—then for only a chance to rehearse a part. In their eagerness to get a good part in a movie, the actors behaved like hungry chickens being fed nice, yellow corn, knocking and trampling each other in their mad scramble for the best bits.

This Mr. Griffith did enjoy. He would draw his chair up center, and leisurely, and in a rather teasing way, look the company over. And when you were being looked at you thought, "Ah, it's going to be me." But in a few minutes some one else would be looked at. "No, it was going to be he." A long look at Owen, a long look at Charlie, a long look at Arthur, and then the director would speak: "Arthur, I'll try you first." One by one, in the same way the company would be picked. There would be a few rough rehearsals; some one wouldn't suit; the chief would decide the part was more in Owen's line. Such nervousness until we got all set!

Indeed, we put forth our best efforts. There was too much competition and no one had a cinch on a line of good parts. When we did "The Cricket on the Hearth," Mr. Griffith rehearsed all his women in the part of *Dot*, Marion Leonard, Florence Lawrence, Violet Merserau, and then he was nice to me. Miss Merserau, however, portrayed *May Plummer*—making her movie début. Herbert Pryor played *John Perrybingle,* and Owen Moore, *Edward Plummer.*

Sometimes after rehearsing a story all day our director would chuck it as "no good" and begin on another. He never used a script and he rehearsed in sequence the scenes of every story until each scene dovetailed smoothly, and the acting was O. K. He worked out his story using his actors as chessmen. He knew what he wanted and the camera never began to grind until every little detail satisfied him.

There was some incentive for an actor to do his best. More was asked of us than to be just a "type," and the women couldn't get by with just "pretty looks." We worked hard, but we liked it. With equal grace we all played leads one day and decorated the back drop the next. On a day when there would be no work whatever for you, you'd reluctantly depart. Sometimes Mr. Griffith almost had to drive the non-working actors out of the studio. The place was small and he needed room.

Sometimes when rehearsing a picture he liked a lot, it would be as late as 3 P.M. before a fainting, lunchless lot of actors would hear those welcome words, "All right, everybody, get your lunches and make up." Then Bobbie Harron would circulate the Childs' menu card and the thirty-cent allotment would be checked off. Roast beef or a ham-and-egg sandwich, pie, tea, coffee, or milk usually nourished us. And it was a funny thing, that no matter how rich one was, or how one might have longed for something different, even might have been ill and needed something special, none of us ever dreamed of spending a nickel of his own.

While the actors ate and made up, and the carpenters were getting the set ready, Mr. Griffith, accompanied by three or four or five or six actors not on the working list that afternoon, would depart for a restaurant near by. But no woman was ever invited to these parties. This social arrangement obtained only on days when a new picture was to be got under way. David Griffith was a generous host, but he always got a good return on his investment. For while being strengthened on luscious steak, steins of Pilsener, and fluffy German pancakes all done up in gobs of melted butter, lemon juice, and powdered sugar, ideas would sprout, and comments and suggestions come freely from the Knights of Lüchow's Round Table, and when the party was over they returned to the studio all happy, and the director ready for a big day's work.

But the other actors, now made up and costumed but fed only on sandwiches, were wearing expressions of envy and reproach which made the returning jolly dogs feel a trifle uncomfortable.

"Well, let's get busy around here—wasting a hell of a lot of time— six o'clock already—have to work all night now—now come on, we'll run through it—show me what you can do—Bitzer, where do you want them? Come in and watch this, Doc." Mr. Griffith was back on the job all right.

One such rehearsal usually sufficed. Then Johnny Mahr with his five-foot board would get the focus and mark little chalk crosses on the floor, usually four, two for the foreground and two for the background. Then

Johnny would hammer a nail into each cross and with his ball of twine, tying it from nail to nail, enclose the set. Now a rehearsal for "lines." And when Bitzer would say it was O.K. and Doc beamed his round Irish smile, we would take the picture, and God help the actor who looked at the camera or at the director when he was shouting instructions while the scene was being photographed.

The old ways of doing were being revolutionized day by day with the introduction of the close-up, switchback, light effects, and screen acting that could be recognized as a portrayal of human conduct. Exhibitors soon began clamoring for A. B. pictures, not only for the U. S. A. but for foreign countries as well; and as Mr. Griffith had a commission on every foot of film sold, it was an easy matter for us to judge our ever-increasing popularity.

The Biograph Company readily acknowledged its young director's achievements, and the other companies soon took cognizance of a new and keen competitor. The first metropolitan showings began a rivalry with the other companies. Once in the race, we were there to win— and we did. Biograph pictures came to mean something just a little different from what had been. There was a sure artistic touch to them; the fine shadings were there that mark the line between talent and genius.

David Griffith had found his place; found it long before he knew it. In ways, it was a congenial berth. Mr. Marvin, once he saw how the wind blew, seldom came into the studio. He was willing to let the new producer work things out his own way. An occasional conference there was, necessarily—a friendly chat as to how things were coming along.

Mr. Marvin was tall and dark, quite a handsome man—so approachable. The actors felt quite at ease with him. Had he not been one of us? Had he not directed even Mr. Griffith in a penny-in-the-slot movie? Years later I recalled the incident to Mr. Marvin. He had forgotten it completely, but with a hearty laugh said: "No did I really? Well, God forgive me."

"God forgive us all," I answered. . . .

■ ■ ■ ■

GROWING UP WITH THE MOVIES (1915), Florence Lawrence

A far more important film actress in the Nickelodeon Era was Florence Lawrence, one of the first movie names to become a household word. She was the "Biograph Girl," featured in many of the best Griffith one-reelers, and when she was stolen away by an independent company, IMP (Independent Motion Picture), she became one of the first motion picture players to receive screen credit. Biograph, incensed at the loss of their star, circulated the report that she had been killed by a streetcar in St. Louis. Miss Lawrence made several public appearances to put an end to the rumor. She was not so fortunate in 1915. Badly injured in a studio fire (when she returned to a blazing building to rescue another actress), Miss Lawrence was temporarily paralyzed. She continued as a minor player in motion pictures until her death (a suicide) in 1938. This piece was one of a series of three articles by Miss Lawrence to appear in *Photoplay* (January 1915), then only in its third year of publication. Both the birth of such a magazine and the existence of articles like this are indicative of America's growing fascination with the "photoplay" and "photoplayers."

When I presented myself at the Biograph studio I was exceedingly anxious and nervous. I have always been so in new and strange surroundings. I inquired for Mr. Solter, who had urged me to try my luck with the Biograph, and later, brought me word that Mr. Griffith desired to see me. While waiting for Mr. Solter an exceedingly lanky and tall young man came into the general waiting room. He seemed to know who I was at a glance, and, though he was shabbily dressed and wore a badly battered hat, I grasped the fact that he was an important official of some sort. It was a certain matter-of-factness about him that impressed me. He came towards me saying: "I was just inquiring about you, Miss Lawrence." Then I knew that he was Mr. Griffith. Mr. Solter entered the room at the moment and was a little surprised to find Mr. Griffith talking to me about the work to be done.

"Can you ride horses?" asked Mr. Griffith.

"I would rather ride than eat," I told him, which was the truth. My folks used to say that they never waited meals for me if they knew I was horseback riding. When I am riding before the moving picture camera, I really forget the picture and everything else. And I always act better in such scenes because I am not acting at all. I am just having fun. Of late the pictures I have appeared in have not called for much of this kind of work, but that fact has not dampened my ardor for galloping 'cross country at break-neck speed. Also, I intend working in some pictures soon in which my equestrian abilities will be needed, and then you shall see.

"You worked in Vitagraph's "The Despatch Bearer," didn't you?" Mr. Griffith asked.

"You were very good in that—it was a good picture," he added, after

"Growing Up with the Movies," by Florence Lawrence, appeared in the January 1915 issue of *Photoplay*.

I had answered his question and explained the difficulties under which the picture was produced. Mr. Solter had stepped to one side and was standing near a door that led back into the studio, when Mr. Griffith turned away saying:

"Wait just a few minutes. I'll be right back."

"I think she is the very person I want," I heard him say to Mr. Solter as he passed out of the room. I could not imagine where he had gone, and thought that if he intended giving me work, I was the person to be told and not Mr. Solter. Hardly a minute had passed when he re-entered the room accompanied by a great, big, dignified man who stopped just inside the door, looked me over from head to foot, spoke a few words to Mr. Griffith, and disappeared back into the recesses of the studio. As Mr. Griffith came forward I came near asking who the dressed-up individual was, then thought better of it. At the Vitagraph studio I had learned that it didn't pay to be inquisitive. But Mr. Griffith knew what I was about to ask.

"That was Mr. Kennedy," he explained. "He said he hoped you could ride just as well as you look."

After I had got over my embarrassment we talked of the salary to be paid, the work expected, and a lot of other details.

"You might as well begin right now," he remarked and, though I was just a little afraid of myself, I was eager to do so. One hour later I was dressed like a cow-girl—knee-length skirt, leggings, blouse waist with sleeves rolled above my elbows, pistol holster swung about my waist, a water pouch slung carelessly over my shoulder, and a big sombrero on my head. My hair was loose. The camera was clicking off a scene for "The Girl and the Outlaw." Charles Ainsley was the outlaw and I was the girl.

As the title suggests, it was a story of the wild and woolly west, and produced in the vicinity of peaceful Coytesville, New Jersey, a town which was the scene of most all the sensational western dramas until about three years ago, and this in spite of the fact that it was almost impossible to make a scene that even remotely resembled the west. There was always a telephone pole around close enough to come within range of the camera which was never discovered until after the scene had been photographed. In "The Girl and the Outlaw" one of the scenes was supposed to represent a section of primeval forest on a mountain side. The finished print showed some perfectly lovely and well pruned maple trees on the slopes of the towering mountain. It was only after the film manufacturers realized that California afforded continuous sunshine as well as an infinite variety of background that the fields and hills of New Jersey were discarded for the real thing. While with the Biograph Company

I appeared in no less than a dozen wild west pictures, all of which were made just outside of New York City or in some New York park.

There was certainly need of a good horseback rider for leading woman in "The Girl and the Outlaw," and I was in the saddle in almost all of the exterior scenes. The story, if my memory serves me rightly, concerned a young eastern girl who had gone west and fallen in love with an outlaw. She brought about his reformation by keeping him from holding up the stage coach, or robbing the village bank—I forget which it was. In several of the scenes I had to ride like fury to overtake the outlaw and prevent him from carrying out his plans. I think it was my riding in that picture that made me a permanent fixture around the Biograph studio. But the work was so severe and trying that I was unable to work in the next western picture Mr. Griffith proposed to make. He was rather disappointed, too, but soon "framed-up" a story with many interior scenes. "Betrayed by a Handprint," was its melodramatic title, and in which I portrayed a society belle, who, losing at bridge, stole a beautiful diamond necklace from her hostess only to be found out by a handprint she made in the dust on the dresser while stealing the necklace. From cow-girl to society belle was rather a change, but all in the day's work just a few years back. Nowadays if a director should ask his leading lady to do as much she would certainly have something to say. Edith Storey of the Vitagraph players and Pauline Bush of the Rex-Universal pictures are the only two actresses I know who seem to be as much at home on the back of a cayuse as in a drawing room.

The very next picture in which I appeared was a Mexican drama with soul stirring action. Throughout my year at the Biograph studio I worked along this plan—a western picture, a society drama or comedy, and then a frontier or Indian picture. "The Red Girl" was the title of the first Indian picture produced by Mr. Griffith after I began playing "leads," and of course I was the red girl. Every time I think of that picture I have to smile. My make-up was so realistic that I looked more like a tramp than a fetching daughter of Lo. At the studio I canvassed the opinions of everybody to learn just how to make up for the part. Nobody seemed to know how I ought to look. So I did the best I could and the result was hideous. And the strange part of it all was that Mr. Griffith did not object to my make-up in any way whatsoever. I hope that picture is never reissued, for I don't want anyone ever to see my idea of what an Indian girl should be. No, I won't tell you how I was painted up. Suffice it to say that I was anything but "darling." And think of it—that picture was one of the first Biograph features, being one thousand and fourteen feet in length, and positive prints sold for fourteen cents a foot. It was released for exhibition on the fifteenth day of September, 1908.

One of the greatest bothers we had to contend with during my Biograph days was the assembling of large crowds whenever we had to make an exterior street scene. I say "exterior street scene" to make it plain that we frequently made interior street scenes. I recall several pictures in which I worked in which the street scenes were painted sets and all the camera work was done inside the studio, though the finished picture looked much as if we had found the very location we wanted right in New York City. All the directors were bothered with the crowds which gathered whenever it was discovered that we were going to do outside work, particularly if the scene was to be made in the business section or in a tenement district. And even today the collecting of large crowds, the tying up of traffic occur as a result of the insatiable curiosity of the passers-by and are a source of annoyance to the director. Nowadays it is the custom to "slip" the first policeman who comes upon the scene a five dollar bill and everything is O. K. until another "copper" comes on the scene. Then the wheels of progress must be greased anew. . . .

In the studio we generally have two rehearsals of a scene before it is finally recorded by the camera. The first is called a rehearsal for "mechanics." That is, we just go through the pantomime which the director tells us is necessary for that particular situation. Next, we go through it with "feeling," as the saying is. Then we are ready for the camera. It often happens that a player is called upon to rehearse comedy, drama and tragedy, one after the other. Once Mr. Griffith directed me in a scene for a comedy—"The Road to the Heart," I think it was called—in the morning, in several scenes of a problem melodrama called "What Drink Did," immediately after luncheon, and we completed the day's work by retaking a scene for a near-tragedy—"The Romance of a Jewess." This is one of the most trying experiences that happens to the moving picture player who conscientiously tries to feel his part. . . .

I have seen many players lose their nerve in front of the camera—old-timers, at that, who think nothing of acting before a vast throng of people within a theatre. Others can't keep from looking into the camera while they are performing, which is "bad acting" in the movies, and something we are never supposed to do unless we have a situation that requires us to look directly at an audience. This is frequent in comedy, since there are many scenes which require the player to look straight at his audience and to go through facial contortions to bring the laugh. It is especially so in the lower forms of comedy such as slap-stick, and rough-and-tumble. As a general rule the best actors and actresses of the stage do not make the best moving picture players because of the fact that their stage success is due largely to a magnetism exercised by means of the voice. Quite recently I saw one of the best known actors in the United

States in a five reel motion picture play, and though the audience "stood for it" I am confident that there were many who would vastly have preferred to see their movie matinee idol portraying the role. The actor I speak of would strike a pose in nearly every other scene which seemed to ask, "Now am I not the handsome lover?" or "Don't you think I'm some hero." To me, the picture was disgusting in spite of the fact that the play was a picturization of one of the best novels I have ever read.

I had been with the Biograph Company but a short time when plans were begun for the formation of the Motion Picture Patents Company. Up to this time the method of distributing the positive prints of the picture plays being manufactured was very poor. Also, certain manufacturers had sprung up almost overnight whose business methods were questionable. It was necessary to place the motion picture industry on a better footing and one which would preserve it as well as protect those manufacturers who had paved the way. Negotiations were begun by the interests controlling the Edison studio. At this time the Essanay, Selig, Kalem, Lubin, Biograph, Vitagraph, Pathe, Edison and Melies films were the best to be had. Some of these brands of films were being marketed under licenses issued by the holders of the Edison camera patents. The other big factor was the licenses of the holders of the patents on the Bioscope, or in other words, the Biograph Company. Of course all of the individual manufacturers possessed certain patents, but decisive lawsuits might have proven these to be infringements on either the Edison or the Bioscope patents. Under the name of the Motion Picture Patents Company the nine different manufacturers pooled their patent rights and formed the General Film Company for the owning of film exchanges throughout the country. With the exception of Pathe, this arrangement still stands, and no one questions the statement that the General Film Company is the most thorough and efficient agency of its kind in the world, and in spite of the fact that there are numerous other large agencies, namely, the Universal, the Mutual, the Paramount, the Eclectic and the World.

The formation of the Patents Company with the Biograph Company as one of the chief producers gave added impetus to our work, for the studio output was increased. Prior to that time there had been talk of long legal battles, seizure of cameras, and the like, and no one would have been surprised had the studio been suddenly closed and notices posted. But the motion picture industry began to get its second wind. Many of the mushroom concerns which had not been included in the Patents Company were forced out of business. The elimination of their product made way for more and better pictures. Mr. Griffith was now permitted to spend from $500 to $600 on a single-reel picture, although he had been getting along with allowances of $300 and $400 previously. Better studio sets, better costumes, and better studio conditions were now possible. The feeling of more freedom had as much to do with the result as did the actual change. . . .

When I joined the Biograph Company the players then engaged for regular work were George Gebhardt, Charles Ainsley, Ashley Miller, David Miles, Anita Hendrie, Harry Solter, John Cumpson and Flora Finch. Two or three weeks later Mack Sennett, Arthur Johnson, Herbert Prior, Linda Arvidson and Marion Leonard were added to the company. Arthur Johnson had been playing extra parts for Mr. Griffith before I joined the company. Miss Leonard had been a member of the company prior to my advent among them, but had left to go on the road with a theatrical company. I had always admired Miss Leonard for her remarkable beauty, and when she renewed her connections with "the Biographers" as we came to call ourselves, we became close friends.

Of these pioneers, only John Cumpson has passed over the great divide. It was Mr. Cumpson who helped to make the "Jonesy" pictures so popular, for he was "Jonesy." When we undertook the first picture there was no intention of making a series of comedy productions, but when the exchanges began asking for more and more "Jonesy" pictures, we kept it up until I left the Biograph Company. Mr. Cumpson was the most serious comedian I have ever known. Nothing was ever funny to him, and he never tried to be funny. When all the rest of the company would laugh at something he had said or done he would become indignant, thinking we were making fun of him. . . .

Mr. Cumpson left the Biograph Company to appear in Edison pictures at about the same time I became identified with "Imp" pictures. There he was known as "Bumptious," but the series of comedies put out under that name failed to interest as had the "Jonesy" pictures.

Arthur Johnson and I played opposite each other in a great many Biograph pictures, the first of which I think was "The Planter's Wife." Others were "Confidence," "The Test of Friendship," "A Salvation Army Lass," "The Resurrection," and "The Way of a Man." Mr. Johnson was such a delightful artist that it was always a pleasure to be cast to play opposite him. He is even funnier off the stage than on. When he gets one of those sanctimonious parts, which he just delights in, he keeps the whole company in a roar. He likes to josh the other players and he sometimes says the funniest things.

I enjoyed playing opposite him in "The Resurrection" more than any other part during my Biograph days. . . . In "The Resurrection," Mr. Johnson seemed so earnest and looked so handsome, and I so poor and ragged —I was playing the part of a housemaid in his gorgeous palace—that the play appealed to me greatly. According to the story, he makes love to me, surreptitiously. When we are found out, and I, the maid, must pay the penalty "the woman always pays" Mr. Johnson seemed the most broken-hearted man in the world. Afterwards, as the story continues, we meet again in Siberia, and his penitence seemed so real and earnest as he repeated the words of the Father, "I am the resurrection and the life; he that believeth in me, though he were dead, yet shall he live; and whosoever liveth and believeth in me shall never die," that our souls seemed to rise above our earthly thoughts and surroundings.

During those early days of motography's struggle for existence there was no greater student of the art to be found than was Mack Sennett, now the famous star of Keystone comedies. He was known around the Biograph studio as "the villain in the play." Excepting the western dramas, Mr. Sennett played the role of the villain in nearly every picture in which I appeared. There were one or two exceptions. In "A Salvation Army Lass," he was the leader of the Salvation Army band; a guard in "The Slave," in which some one else played the villain. He was always the bartender, in a saloon scene, too. It seems strange that he never worked in comedy.

Mr. Sennett and Mr. Solter were always planning and arguing with Mr. Griffith. Mr. Sennett wanted to do certain things his way—Mr. Solter had an entirely different view of the matter, and Mr. Griffith, being the director and boss, insisted on having his way. They say that the proof of the pudding is in the eating, and when Mr. Sennett was given his way some few years back, his famous Keystone comedies leave little if any cause for complaint.

About four months before I left the Biograph studio an elfin like little girl, hardly more than a child, with beautiful golden hair, came into our midst. Mary Pickford was her name. From the first, Mary won our hearts with her charming ways. She possesses a pout and a frown all her own, which are irresistible. I am unable to recall all of the pictures in which we worked together, but my scrap book reveals a scene from "The Way of a Man," in which the three chief characters were portrayed by "Little Mary," Arthur Johnson and myself. In this, according to the story, I am blind, and my lover falls in love with my sister, "Little Mary," and I discover this fact when my sight is restored and relinquish my claim upon the man to make my sister happy.

"Little Mary," Gertrude Robinson—she had joined us about the same time as did "Little Mary"—and myself were all jealous over our height. Mary did not like being called little and Gertrude claimed to be taller than Mary and me. In spite of our arguments not a one of us would ever stand the test of measurement. But the truth will out. One day Mary wore a dress that I had worn on a previous occasion, and I noticed that it touched the floor as she walked, while it certainly did not on me, so after starting a happy little argument I remarked on this fact and they all agreed that I was the tallest.

"Well, I knew it all the time," said Mary with a frown and a pout, then smiled, and forgot the matter. Even to this day, and now that all three of us have really grown up, whenever I meet Mary we always start that same old argument.

I am glad of Mary's success, and hope that she will always remain just as unspoiled, as little and sweet and dear as she really is today. . . .

What seemed to annoy us "Biographers" very much and hold us back from achieving greater artistic success was the speed and rapidity with which we had to work before the camera. Mr. Griffith always answered our complaint by stating that the exchanges and exhibitors who bought our pictures wanted action, and insisted that they get plenty of it for their money.

"The exhibitors don't want illustrated song slides," Mr. Griffith once said to us.

So we made our work quick and snappy, crowding as much story in a thousand foot picture as is now portrayed in five thousand feet of film. Several pictures which we produced in three hundred feet have since been reproduced in one thousand feet. There was no chance for slow or "stage" acting. The moment we started to do a bit of acting in the proper tempo we would be startled by the cry of the director:

"Faster! Faster! For God's sake hurry up! We must do the scene in forty feet."

In real life it would have taken four minutes to enact the same scene. The reason for this is explained as follows—the buyers of the films saw their money being wasted if there was a quiet bit of business being portrayed. They didn't want, as Mr. Griffith had said, "illustrated song slides," when they had to pay so much money for the illustrated celluloid.

About this time the Pathe Company imported several one reel length pictures which they called features since the leading actors and actresses of the prominent theatres of Paris appeared in them. These pictures were released under the Film D'Art brand and created quite a stir in motion picture circles and especially among all directors. In naturalness, they were far ahead of anything yet produced in this country, and largely for the reason that the important artists portraying the chief roles were permitted to do things as their training had taught them to do. These artists would never have consented to appear in motion pictures at all if they had had to follow the instructions of the ordinary directors. The purpose of the Film D'Art pictures was to record the work of the best artists of France by means of cinematography as a permanent tribute to that artist's ability. So naturally they were permitted to act before the camera as they thought proper.

Following the appearance of the Film D'Art pictures nearly all of the Biograph players asked Mr. Griffith to be allowed to do slow acting, only to be refused. He told us it was impossible since the buyers would positively not pay for a foot of film that did not have action in it.

But before I severed my connection with the Biograph Company Mr. Griffith did commence the production of pictures employing "the close-up" and slow acting, working along the lines suggested by the French actors and actresses. And simultaneously, the American film manufacturers woke up to the fact that they were on the wrong track in producing pictures showing human beings doing things at about four times the speed of real life.

This, then, is the story of my Biograph days, those days in which I was always known as "The Biograph Girl."

At the Moving Picture Ball

Hip Hooray!
I feel delighted.
Yesterday
I was invited
To a swell affair—
All the movie stars were there.

Oh what fun!
The party lasted till the break of dawn.
Famous Players
Turned to cabareters
How they fooled and carried on!

While dancing at that moving picture ball
(So scenario!)
Great big stars paraded round the hall.
(They were merry, oh!)
Handsome Wallace Reid
Stepped out full of speed,
And Theda Bara
Was a terror—
She vamped a little lady,
So did Alice Brady.

Douglas Fairbanks shimmied on one hand
(Like an acrobat!),
Mary Pickford did a toe-dance grand
And
Charlie Chaplin with his feet
Stepped all over poor Blanche Sweet
Dancing at that moving picture ball.

Lyric by Joseph Santly, music by Howard Johnson, copyright 1918.

3

Feature Films and Hollywood (1914–1927)

The motion picture entered its next era in America when it altered its exhibition pattern from a one-hour program of one-reel films to a two-hour-plus program of a feature film, supported by a few short films. The longer film demanded more of those who made it—the actors, cameramen, directors, writers, producers, publicists, and designers; it also demanded more of those who watched it—more time, more attention, more concentration, more money. The audiences, in turn, demanded more of it—greater narrative complexity, subtler acting, more careful and consistent scenic design, and more comfortable theaters for watching it. With the coming of the feature film, the motion picture moved one step closer to the live drama—both in its duration and in the kind of customer it attempted to satisfy—and one step further from the informal, lower- and working-class atmosphere of the nickelodeon. The one anachronism (as was true of his entire career) was the sensational success of Charles Chaplin, whose short films were more popular than most features and whose tramp character was more rooted in the earthy attitudes of the one-reelers than in the genteel grace of the features.

Perhaps the two most important feature films in America, the two most responsible for establishing the feature film as the American industry's essential product, were

Queen Elizabeth and *The Birth of a Nation*. The former, produced in France by the Film d'Art Company and starring Sarah Bernhardt, was distributed in America by Adolph Zukor. The latter, directed by the master of one-reel Biographs, D. W. Griffith, ran over three hours, was financed independently for a total cost of $125,000, and earned over $2 million within a year. Whatever these films may have revealed about the "art of the film" (and the Griffith film revealed much more than did that of the Film d'Art Company), they revealed an enormous amount about the film audience and its commercial potential. Audiences wanted to see feature films; theater owners saw they could make much more money with feature films than with short films; therefore, feature films would have to be made. As was true of the Nickelodeon Era (and has been true ever since), the demands of exhibitors determined the kinds of films that would be produced.

There were other significant social issues in the teens. In 1915, the Supreme Court handed down a major decision that excluded motion pictures from protection by the First Amendment right to free speech. The decision was to stand for thirty-seven years. The debate over censorship continued as the National Board of Review drew increasingly heated criticism that it was merely the tool of the film industry and would, therefore, merely serve the will of the industry rather than the American people. The movies probably came closest to formal federal censorship in the 1920s. At the same time that several personal scandals in the film colony became highly public news—particularly the deaths of Virginia Rappe (at a Fatty Arbuckle party), Thomas Ince, Wallace Reid, and William Desmond Taylor—the content of films in the "Flapper Era" also became more openly flirtatious and salacious. (Indeed, the industry itself would repudiate the moral looseness of some of these films a decade later when writing and enforcing its Production Code, blaming the moral laxity on the sensual temper of the times—see pages 340–44.) The censorship debate culminated in 1922 with the industry's hiring Will H. Hays to serve as president of the Motion Picture Producers and Distributors of America, becoming, in effect, the movies' "moral czar."

Two prominent members of the film audience, Hugo Munsterberg, the Harvard psychologist, and, even more important, Vachel Lindsay, the noted poet, took the motion picture seriously enough to write the first theoretical investigations of its artistic values and principles. The two works appeared in almost the same year as *The Birth of a Nation*. At the same time, the nation participated in a European war in which the movies played a significant role—both providing the home audience with information about the battle "over there" and building the plots of the new feature films around issues and attitudes that would sustain the public morale and support the principles for which Americans were fighting. By the time Johnny came marching home, the American movie had marched off to Hollywood and established the world capital of a new art.

The first seven years of the 1920s in that capital were devoted to stabilizing previous practices rather than striking off in a new direction, to improving and consolidating those patterns of exhibition, production, and distribution which had been established in the previous decade. This commercial stability created an appropriate climate for one of the richest periods in the art of the motion picture, the "Golden Age" of the silent film, which produced the comedies of Chaplin, Keaton, Lloyd, Langdon, and Lubitsch, the films of Vidor, von Stroheim, von Sternberg, Ford, Cruze, King, Ingram, and De Mille, and the European contributions of Lang, Murnau, Pabst, Stiller, Sjøstrøm, Eisenstein, Pudovkin, Dreyer, Gance, and many others.

Hollywood's attraction upon the fancies of the American public grew even stronger. Young girls especially liked to read about their heroes and heroines; they were also likely to emulate their behavior—their ways of dressing, walking, making themselves up, or flirting—and at least to dream of running off to Hollywood themselves. A group of eastern wits and writers also ran off to Hollywood, either to write scripts for the films or to send cynical chronicles of Hollywood banalities to their eastern magazines for the amusement of their eastern readers.

The period of commercial stability and artistic growth also led to an increasing consciousness of both the potential of the motion picture as an art and its usual failure to realize that potential in America. This consciousness was partially stimulated by the imported films from Europe—especially those from Sweden, Germany, the Soviet Union, and France—which impressed critics with their innovative visual styles, their intellectual complexity, and their social-psychological-moral maturity. The consciousness was also stimulated by the growing seriousness of film critics and film criticism, the fact that writing about films had begun to attract such insightful and thoughtful analysts as Gilbert Seldes, Alexander Bakshy, Francis Hackett, Aldous Huxley, Robert E. Sherwood, Harry Alan Potamkin, and Herman G. Weinberg.

■ ■ ■ ■

A New Epoch in the Movies (1914), Walter Prichard Eaton

Walter Prichard Eaton, the influential drama critic for the *American Magazine,* was one of the first to perceive the growing closeness of the motion picture and the "legitimate" stage. Although he shares the typical prejudice against the artistic integrity of the "movies" (note his use of the word in print is the earliest in this collection) in comparison to the stage, he finds their apparent clumsiness a matter of their youth and inexperience rather than of their essence. Eaton saw the coming of the feature film as beneficial for both the movies and the stage—an early insight that has probably proved true.

The moving pictures are moving in more senses than one. It has been scarcely a decade since they jumped into prominence as a popular form of entertainment. In ten years the land became covered with nickel and dime screen theaters, and the so-called "legitimate" theater began to shake with apprehension. And now, within the last year or two, there has begun a new epoch in the meteoric career of the "movie" dramas, and the situation has changed again. The cause for this, in a word, is the "feature film."

A feature film is a motion picture drama (or even a record of actuality, like the "Rainey Hunt" film) which is so long that it runs an entire evening, and is well enough produced to hold the attention for this period. A feature film, just because it does last the whole evening, must of necessity be carefully done. Because care costs money, the rental of a feature film is always greater than the rental of three, four, or even five ordinary single reel dramas. Consequently, the proprietor of the movie theater must either raise his prices or enlarge his seating capacity in order to exhibit it profitably. Some proprietors have done either one, or both. Still others, however, have been forced out of business. The general result, already apparent and destined to become more apparent in the next year or two, is a distinct decrease in the number of screen theaters, the

"A New Epoch in the Movies," by Walter Prichard Eaton, appeared in the October 1914 *American Magazine.*

smaller and shabbier ones giving way to the larger and more prosperous; and, especially in the large cities, an increase in the price of admission for the more prominent feature films, with an attendant increase of comfort for the audience, better music, and a general rise in dignity.

For instance, in New York last summer "Cabiria," by Gabriele D'Annunzio, shown at the Knickerbocker Theater, cost seventy-five cents and a dollar if you sat down-stairs. The regular theater ushers were in attendance, and the large orchestra was a good one. Between reels the audience went out to the lobby, quite as between the acts of a play. At the Candler Theater seats were fifty and seventy-five cents, and Modest Altshuler, conductor of the Russian Symphony orchestra, led the band. Similar prices were charged for Paul Armstrong's "The Escape," and for the picture called "Neptune's Daughter," featuring Annette Kellermann.

In time, of course, all these films will go to smaller theaters at lower prices, but they are bound to take some of their dignity with them, for they are not planned for the complete unsophistication of the former nickel audiences. They are sustained picture narratives, demanding concentration of the attention, and their producers have made honest, and at times successful, attempts to achieve either genuine dramatic effectiveness or real pictorial charm. Crude as it is, there is a social message, an intellectual point in "The Escape." In "Cabiria," D'Annunzio's opulent imagination has woven a story of the war between Rome and Carthage, so that there is a distinct historical perspective to the narrative, as well as a rare pictorial charm, especially in those scenes which have been photographed on the north African desert, with trains of camels or Numidian horsemen or the Roman legions winding over the ridges of sand against the sunset sky.

In other words, the day of the brief, careless, artless, and too often pointless film seems to be passing. More and more a sustained story, well told and well photographed, is demanded in the screen theaters. The movies are becoming more nearly allied to dramatic and pictorial art. They are gaining in dignity and value, for any change from carelessness and lack of concentration to artistic carefulness and a demand on the concentrated attention of the crowd, is a distinct gain in both qualities.

As a result of this condition (or, perhaps, in part a cause), the film producers are turning more and more to the real stage for material. The Famous Players Film Company and many other concerns have, in the past year, put out feature films which are not only adaptations of spoken plays but which are also played by well-known actors.

For the season of 1913–14, for example, the Famous Players Film Company made the following productions, after the success of Bernhardt in

"Queen Elizabeth" and James K. Hackett in "The Prisoner of Zenda" the year before: Mrs. Fiske in "Tess of the D'Urbervilles;" Mary Pickford in "In the Bishop's Carriage;" Henry E. Dixey in "Chelsea 7750;" Mrs. Langtry in "His Neighbor's Wife;" James O'Neill in "The Count of Monte Cristo;" Mary Pickford in "Caprice," "Hearts Adrift," "A Good Little Devil," and "The Eagle's Mate;" Carlotta Nillson in "Leah Kleschna;" Cecilia Loftus in "A Lady of Quality;" Cyril Scott in "The Day of Days;" John Barrymore in "An American Citizen;" Charlotte Ives in "Clothes;" William Farnum in "The Redemption of David Corson;" Pauline Frederick in "The Eternal City;" Malcolm Williams in "The Brute;" Arnold Daly in "The Port of Missing Men;" Bruce McRae in "The Ring and the Man;" Hazel Dawn in "One of Our Girls," "An Hour Before Dawn," "The Port of Doom," "A Daughter of the Hills," "The Pride of Jennico," and "A Woman's Triumph;" Bertha Kalisch in "Marta of the Lowlands;" Carlyle Blackwell in "The Spitfire;" Jane Grey in "The Little Gray Lady;" Paul McAllister in "The Scales of Justice;" William Courtleigh in "The Better Man;" Herbert Kelcey and Effie Shannon in "Aristocracy."

Next season, among other stars who will act before the camera for this company are Maclyn Arbuckle and Willis Sweatnam in George Ade's "The County Chairman," and Margaret Anglin, probably in "The Taming of the Shrew."

Nor does this begin to exhaust the list of well-known American players who have become temporarily or even permanently movie stars. Ethel Barrymore has succumbed; Dustin Farnum has acted "The Squaw Man" and "The Lightning Conductor;" Edmund Breese, "The Master Mind;" Maude Fealy is now a movie actress; John Bunny is the low comedian par excellence of the canned drama, and is making more money than he ever made on the stage; Gail Kane, Gertrude Coghlan, Josie Sadler, and scores of others, have been recently added to the list.

Moreover, there is hardly a producer of plays in the country now who has not also allied himself with some film producer, or else organized a film company of his own. Jesse Lasky has secured the screen rights to all of Belasco's plays. The Shuberts and William A. Brady have organized a company to put their plays out as canned dramas. In the next few seasons about every play which can be turned into a film story will be shown on the screens. Even Hippodrome productions are to be photographed. It almost looks as if the man or woman who wishes to be a motion picture "author" must now become a regular dramatist first.

Yet this apparent union between the films and the stage is not nearly so close as at first it would seem to be. The reasons are interesting and illuminating.

In the first place, not every actor or actress can be successful on the screen. Some of the very greatest are comparative failures as movie players. And this is not alone because of the different technic required. Of course, if a player belongs to the so-called modern or naturalistic school of acting, and especially if a measure of his charm lies in his vocal skill, his ability to waft an epigram or point a comic sentence or stab home a tragic line, it may very well be that he will find it extremely difficult to express himself effectively solely by pantomime and facial play. It is said that Bernhardt spoiled two reels of film before her "Camille" was fit to exhibit. A player like Mrs. Fiske, for instance, who is one of the greatest actresses on our English speaking stage, has made almost a gospel of "repression," and her art is the art of under-emphasis. No one is so eloquent in moments of total inaction, no one so icily brilliant in passages of staccato repartee. But most of these, her greatest distinctive qualities, go for nothing before the camera, and she must adopt much the same method as any movie heroine unknown to fame. For this reason, those of the "legitimate" actors who were trained in the "old school" of free gesticulation and constant pantomime are very often the most successful in the movies.

But the player's methods have less to do with his success or failure than his physical characteristics. It is well known that some voices reproduce well on the phonograph, while others, perhaps better voices, reproduce badly. Just so certain faces seem made for the camera, while others, apparently no less striking, no less attractive, do not "register" on the film at all, to employ the technical term. When so much of the story has to be expressed by the faces of the players it is of prime importance that every change of expression, every passing thought and emotion, be caught clearly by the camera. If it isn't, that player, however famous on the dramatic stage, is a failure in the movies. And the layman would be surprised if he knew how many players whom he has admired for their skill or their beauty have to be given up as hopeless when the first trial hundred feet of film (which is always taken as a precaution) is developed and run across the screen.

Of all the famous players so far employed by the Famous Players Film Company, by far the most popular with the movie audiences is Mary Pickford, with Hazel Dawn a not very close second. Mary Pickford is only a famous player by courtesy of the press agent. She appeared in "The Good Little Devil," and then went back to the movies, whence she had come. Certainly she wasn't famous enough to make "The Good Little Devil" a success, even under the Belasco banner, nor to cause any suspicion that a second Duse was in our busy midst. But before the camera she is supreme, and as a film drama "The Good Little Devil" is a huge success. Similarly, Hazel Dawn, who has been the star of six film dramas, was hitherto known only as the heroine in "The Pink Lady," a mild musical comedy. Neither woman stands as high on the dramatic stage as Mrs. Fiske's shoe laces, yet both are more successful and popular before the camera.

This is not because they are better known to movie audiences, either, for Hazel Dawn has not been in the movies before. It is because they have, in addition to youth and prettiness (which are always valuable in a photograph), the peculiar power of maintaining a constant play of facial expression which always registers clearly and sharply on the film, and becomes for the audience pantomime easily seen and instantly comprehended. If you take a series of enlarged sections from any film showing Mary Pickford, you can always say exactly what emotion her face is expressing without knowing so much as the name of the story. It is like a series of illustrations for one of those funny old books teachers of "expression" used to affect—Fear, Horror, Disappointment, Anticipation, and the like. This power doesn't make Mary Pickford a great actress, but it makes her a great film player, a great instrument for recording in the superficial language of photographs the thread of a narrative.

Of all the men so far photographed by the Famous Players Film Company it is said that John Barrymore made one of the best subjects, because he, also, "registered" well before the camera. Here again, judging from the records of the dramatic stage, is a most unpredictable result.

But not only is the apparent union between movies and the stage seen to be a very incomplete alliance because of this difference in the technical and physical requirements of the players; it is also an incomplete alliance because of the difference between a good drama and a good motion picture scenario. Some plays, of course, cannot be made into motion pictures at all. Shaw's "Getting Married," for example, or Wilde's "The Importance of Being Earnest," would baffle the most optimistic scenario writer! You cannot photograph an epigram. In general, it may be said that the more a play depends for its appeal upon its intellectual ideas, its poetry of diction, its wit, its whimsy, the less fitted it is for a motion picture. The more it depends for its appeal upon physical action, upon the climaxes of melodrama, or the complications of farce, the better adapted it is for the screen.

But even the farce or melodrama must inevitably emerge a different thing before the camera. Mr. Schulberg, who makes the adaptations of the plays for the Famous Players Company, says that only one third of a play is ever used bodily, one third is adapted, and one third has to be made up out of entirely new cloth. At most, the original author has supplied a title and an idea. The thing which emerges is a new work altogether. It belongs to a different art, represents a different technic, and has a different appeal.

The rush for famous players, then, and for famous dramatic pieces, to show upon the screen, does not really mean that the stage and the screen are wedded, are now one and the same. It only means that the movie public is demanding better and longer stories, and the producers are seeking these stories in the most likely and readiest place, and trying to advertise them by the names of actors and actresses known to the wider public.

To those interested in such problems, a comparison of the technic of a film drama with that of a modern naturalistic play is sure to prove fascinating. Take, for example, D'Annunzio's "Cabiria," of which we have already spoken. What is the first technical consideration this play awakens? I can best answer, perhaps, by quoting part of a letter from Winthrop Ames:

> I went to see "Cabiria" in the movies the other night, and later happened to take up Shakespeare's "Antony and Cleopatra." The similarity of dramatic construction amazed me. Shakespeare had all the characteristic tricks of modern movie writers—the various sets of characters brought successively into action, the alternation of "feature" and plot scenes, the short detached interludes like "close-ups," and even the "throw-backs."
>
> Working independently, the movie men have apparently arrived at a Shakespearean type of scenario construction; and, of course, for the same reason—the ability to shift the scene at will.

"Antony and Cleopatra" is naturally the Shakespearean drama one puts into comparison with "Cabiria," because the scenes are Rome and northern Africa; but the technic of "Cabiria" would compare with equal closeness to almost any drama of the loose Elizabethan period, and so would the technic of any other movie play. A scene shows one set of characters in action. It is interrupted to flash on a scene showing another set, and then the picture jumps back to the first scene, thus indicating to the audience that the two events are happening at the same time. We jump with ease across the Mediterranean, or plunge from daylight into moonlight.

When Shakespeare wanted his stage to represent "a blasted heath" he put words of shivery portent into the witches' mouths. When he wished to evoke Cleopatra's barge upon the Nile, he inserted a lyric passage of glowing description. In either case, there was no trouble with scene shifters. Similarly, the movie producer has only to take his actors out on a blasted heath, or photograph Cleopatra's barge reconstructed upon the real Nile, and insert those photographs into their proper place in his film. Run off on the screen, there is no delay. The scene may be changed a hundred times in a single play.

The movie producers, however, are still a long way from being as proficient in their craft as Shakespeare was in his. Shakespeare, in all his changes of scene, never forgot the dramatic integrity of each individual episode, but about nine tenths of the movie men do. How seldom you see a motion picture in which the number of scenes could not be reduced perhaps by half, and the remainder developed to twice their present length, with great advantage. The individual episodes are not worked out fully; they are not long enough to build up a dramatic situation. The eye and mind are both bewildered by the too sudden and too frequent shifts of scene. There is a terrible sense of rush and hurry and flying about, which is intensified by the twitching film and the generally whang-bang music.

The movies, of course, are young, and even though Augustus Thomas does bear the portentous title of "Director General of Productions for the All Star Feature Corporation," they have not yet developed the artists to give them the ultimate technic and raise them nearer, at least, to the level of an art. Just now they are rather stumbling along instinctively on the technical path that Marlowe and Shakespeare trod over three centuries ago.

And what of the future? What will the effect be upon the stage?

One effect is already apparent. The actors have a new and added source of revenue, and possibly the dramatists have, also. Not all players can get $30,000 for acting a single play in front of a camera, as Bernhardt did when she acted "Queen Elizabeth." But Miss Anglin, and players of her rank, get as high as $5,000 for the single performance, which includes from one to four weeks of rehearsals. The dramatists, also, whose plays are adapted, get an added revenue, sometimes in the form of royalty, sometimes a flat sum divided with the theatrical manager who has previously produced their play on the stage. These revenues have, in some cases, amounted to as much as $8,000 or $10,000. But it is yet an open question whether this is not offset by a depreciation of their property in the stock theaters.

A popular feature film generally rents for $40 a day, while it is new and fresh, and from twenty-five to thirty-five prints are sent out. That means a gross return of from $1,000 to $1,400 per day, or from $7,000 to $9,000 a week. The life of the average feature film is about three months (at a lesser rental during the last month). So it is easy to see that the gross return is very large. Some films, such as Hackett in "The Prisoner of Zenda," or the "Rainey Hunt," have continued popular for more than a year, with fresh prints being produced.

The copyright laws are lax and rather chaotic concerning motion pictures, and the Authors' League of America is working better to protect authors whose books and stories are used for films, since a popular book often makes as good a movie drama as a play. But these conditions will doubtless be corrected, and it may be said that the author and perhaps the dramatist of the immediate future, if he writes the kind of books or plays which have interesting plots, and especially if the scenes can be put into pictorial setting, will have a new source of revenue from the motion pictures.

Our actors used to fear that if they appeared on the screens the public would no longer pay to see them in person. That fear has been dissipated. James K. Hackett took out "The Prisoner of Zenda" after he had acted it for the camera and the film had been widely shown, and he has testified that in all towns where the photo-play had preceded him the attendance upon the real play was noticeably larger. Feature films, then, with "real actors" in them, or made from real plays, are potentially a feeder for the dramatic stage. The step up from short, scatter-brained films to the long photo-play telling a sustained story for two hours or more, is a step forward in the process of educating a wider public for the enjoyment of dramatic art. We can say even more confidently than we said in this place a year ago, that the movies are not a menace to the theater.

But the movies will probably have one permanent effect on the dramatic stage. Just because the camera can be carried so easily far afield, to show mountains and gorges, rivers and caverns, deserts and jungles, which all people love to look upon and which the pasteboard stage of the theater can never hope to depict with a thousandth part of the camera's realism, it is more than likely that the old-fashioned spectacular play will fall more and more into disrepute, and the drama will more and more concentrate upon modern realistic plays with an intellectual drift, or upon poetry and that form of scenery which is not realistic but consciously artificial, calculated to achieve a decorative or suggestive effect. The old-fashioned popular melodrama has already disappeared from the stage, and re-appeared upon the movie screen. After seeing the marvelous siege of a Carthaginian city in "Cabiria," it is easy to believe that the spectacles will go the same way. Not even on the Hippodrome stage could such an effect be achieved. On the other hand, of course, Shaw and Barrie and Galsworthy and a hundred other modern dramatists can no more be adapted into films than gold can be transmuted into tin. The movies are here to stay—and so is the theater. Just now the movies are attracting the more attention. The film business is greatly inflated, as the theatrical business was a few years ago. When it settles down to a normal level we shall find that the movies have made audiences for the theaters, that they have risen to a higher level of artistic worth, and that they fill a useful and by no means to be despised place in the life of the people.

■ ■ ■ ■

ORIGIN AND GROWTH OF THE MOVIES (1927), Adolph Zukor

Adolph Zukor rode to success on the feature film and *Queen Elizabeth*. In 1913 he founded the production company Famous Players in Famous Plays, which would become Paramount Pictures in the next decade. The Zukor lecture reprinted below was one of a series delivered by members of the film industry to students in the business school of Harvard University in 1927. Joseph P. Kennedy, an alumnus of the school and the new president of a recently amalgamated film company—FBO–Keith–Orpheum—put the lecture series together and published the addresses as *The Story of the Films*. Kennedy's film company would become known as RKO after the coming of talking films; Kennedy would become ambassador to the Court of St. James and the father of three famous sons. Zukor's address is interesting for the folksy vagueness of its details and the smoothly genteel way he manages to turn some of his most vicious, cutthroat battles for power and money into mere ripples in the historical stream. Zukor would live long enough to outlive his ruthless reputation (block-booking—see pages 400–403—was one of his commercial innovations) to become the unofficial grand old man of the movies and the honorific chairman of the board of Paramount Pictures until his death at the age of 103 in 1976.

It is indeed a privilege to have the opportunity to address a class in Harvard College. You gentlemen living here and developing your ideals and ambitions here are so close to the institution that I do not believe you can appreciate the opportunities you have. To a man like myself who never had the chance of a college education, this a great opportunity, and if I am a bit nervous it is not because I am not glad to be here. Even if it should

"Origin and Growth of the Movies," by Adolph Zukor, was published in *The Story of the Films*, edited by Joseph P. Kennedy (Shaw, 1927; Ozer, 1971).

be an ordeal to talk to you I do it with pleasure and I hope that it may do some good.

MODEST BEGINNINGS

I may begin by referring to my early experiences in the business. About twenty-two years ago we had "Hale's Touring Car," which was a Pullman car constructed with the rear end open. A picture was thrown some twenty feet from the rear, and one would turn around, as if in an observation car, and watch the scenery. These pictures were taken in Switzerland, Italy, and all parts of the world. That was the first moving picture that attracted my attention seriously. I thought it was very interesting and I knew that it would appeal to most of the people. William A. Brady, a theatrical manager in New York, who had bought the rights for that state, asked me to join him in exploiting this form of entertainment.

We started out by taking a store on Fourteenth Street and put this Pullman car in. We made the front of the store look like a depot and we were able to get films for about six different tours. The first day was a big success. It was very interesting. We also had a lecturer who pointed out the interesting points, such as mountains, rivers, and buildings, and I felt sure we were on the road to success. But it did not last long because there were not enough subjects to make changes. We found that after about two weeks we had to repeat the subjects and, of course, when they were once seen people were no longer interested. Pretty soon we found ourselves with no business.

We approached all of the people who had made pictures in this country—Edison, Biograph, Lubin, and Selig, and the Belasco Company—and tried to get them to supply these travelogues, but they did not think we could dispose of enough to warrant their spending money for the negatives. So we had to shut down.

VOGUE OF THE CHASE PICTURES

In the meantime they had been making a lot of short subjects that ran about 150 to 200 feet in length. By putting together several of these, they made up 1,000 feet of what they called "chase pictures." Many of you will remember that every picture finished with a man who was painting, or washing a window, using a ladder. Somebody passed by and kicked the ladder. Then he ran away, and the man who was painting ran after him and the police chased him, and the dogs and the cats and the children ran after him. That was the climax of every picture; it seemed they could not think of any other.

We were compelled to remove the cars and put seats in our stores and show these chase pictures. That lasted about three years. All the subjects were of much the same type, though occasionally some director hit upon the idea of making a picture with a story to it that had some heart interest. Each time we were lucky enough to have a subject of that kind our business felt it. The response to that kind of picture was surprising. It was really a foretaste and a prophecy of what we have now.

THE MECHANICAL SIDE DOMINANT

At this time the men who made these pictures earned most of their money on the projection machines. The main business of the Edison Company, as well as of Lubin and Selig, was to make these machines. Naturally, they all concentrated on the mechanical end of the business. That was very necessary and very important for this reason: In those days you could buy a projection machine for $75 or $95. People with money or with a substantial business would never think of opening a little store show, but as long as it did not take more than $300 or $400 to open up a theatre, a good many small investors took a chance, and that helped to develop the business. The making of these low-priced projection machines made it possible for a number of store shows to come into existence, without which I believe there would be no moving picture industry today. The great number of these store shows created a market for the moving picture producers and gave them an opportunity to develop.

THE SEARCH FOR PICTURES

The novelty of the chase pictures began to wear out, too, and about 1907 or 1908 we found ourselves where we could not carry on the business profitably. There were plenty of pictures made but they were so much alike that there was no more public interest in them.

In those days when anybody wanted a lease he had to put up a good deposit and take the lease in his own name. I had taken about fourteen leases and found myself where I had to go through bankruptcy to get out of the leases or else continue in business. I chose to continue in business. So I made every effort in this country as well as in Europe to obtain pictures. They were making the best pictures in Europe then, in France and Italy. We did not make very good pictures in this country. As luck would have it, the Pathé Company in Paris made a picture, "The Passion Play," which was in three reels and hand-colored. That was really the first picture of any consequence that I can recall. When I saw that picture I made up my mind to bring it to America.

SUCCESS OF THE PASSION PLAY

We arranged for an organ and a quartet to play and sing appropriate music. I did not dare open in New York. So we tried it first in Newark.

We were on a street adjoining a big department store and opened up Monday morning. A great many of the bargain hunters—I mean the ladies—dropped in early to see and hear the performance. As they walked out, I stood at the door eager and anxious to hear the comments. People with tears in their eyes came over to me and said, "What a beautiful thing this is." I felt instinctively that this was the turning point, that my rent would be paid from now on.

About eleven o'clock, a priest who was in the audience came over and said he thought that showing a picture like that in a theatre was sacrilegious and he would have to report it to the city authorities. I could see that rent staring me in the face again, so I had a talk with him and asked him what objection he had and why he objected. He said he did not object to the picture itself, that everything in it was fine, but that the subject belonged to the church and not the theatre. He did not think the church and the theatre had the same mission. I told him the plight I was in; I told him my circumstances; I told him all about it, and I said, "If you have this place closed you see what will happen to me." He looked at me and sympathized and he thought he would let it go, and so the picture stayed on. We stayed on with that picture for months and did a land office business.

That gave me courage to go into New York and wherever else I had theatres, and we showed that picture with the same success everywhere. Then it occurred to me that if we could take a novel or a play and put it on the screen, the people would be interested. We should get not only the casual passers-by but people leaving their homes, going out in search of amusement. However, I had no experience in making pictures and nothing was farther from my mind. I did approach all the producers then in the business and tried to sell the idea of making big pictures.

At that time the producers numbered ten, and so many store shows had jumped up—thousands throughout the country—that there developed a great demand for the one-reel and two-reel pictures that were being made. They were so busy turning out these pictures that they would not undertake anything else. In fact, they did not believe that people would sit through pictures that ran three, four, or five reels. I tried for a number of years to convince them, but nobody would undertake to make big pictures. . . .

STAGE CELEBRITIES SOUGHT

In 1911 I made up my mind definitely to take big plays and celebrities of the stage and put them on the screen. While I was looking around to get an organization together, word came to me that Sarah Bernhardt was appearing in Paris in a play called "Queen Elizabeth" and that she would be willing to put that play into motion pictures for $35,000. Of course that was an awful lot of money. There was a Mr. Porter at the head of Rex, which was the trade name of a one-reel picture released weekly. They knew I was interested in going into this big picture making. Sarah Bernhardt's agent cabled to Mr. Porter, and he came to me with the proposition and said, "I merely mention it to you, because the price is prohibitive." I asked him what it was, and he said she wanted $35,000. I said, "All right; I will take it," and we cabled $5,000 that very day.

Sarah Bernhardt in "Queen Elizabeth"

That was in November, 1911, and in March, 1912, we released the picture in this country. By the time that picture was finished there had been formed what was called the General Film Company and the Patents Company. They had everything in their control. The Patents Company controlled the patents not only of the camera but of the projection machine, and they made it a condition in leasing a machine that only their pictures could be shown on the screen. So I found myself with "Queen Elizabeth" and no place to go. There was only one thing I could do and that was to take the legitimate theatres. I went to Klaw and Erlanger and got bookings. It was in the spring, and there were not many shows on the road. I booked Daly's in New York and the Powers Theatre in Chicago.

We found that our matinees were fine. I remember in Chicago I stood in the lobby and I was very proud. We had almost a full house at the matinee. The show went off well and everything was lovely. A great many thought Sarah Bernhardt was there in person. I may mention that this was the first time lithographs were made of the pictures. We had used lithographs before, but they had nothing to do with the pictures shown. We also advertised in the newspapers.

Just about that time I interested Mr. Daniel Frohman in the enterprise and told him what I thought could be accomplished. He used his influence with the Patents Company to have this Bernhardt picture licensed, and that opened the doors and I was able to distribute the picture. I believe we had to gross about $60,000 to cover expenses, but we took in enough so that our first experiment was not costly. We did gain the knowledge that made us absolutely certain that pictures of the right type had a great future.

The First American Photoplay

At that time Mr. Frohman had the late James K. Hackett under contract. He was on the road with "The Prisoner of Zenda." I asked Mr. Frohman to see Mr. Hackett, who was then playing in St. Louis, and explain that we wanted him to go into pictures and assure him that it would not hurt his reputation or affect his popularity. Mr. Frohman prevailed on Mr. Hackett to appear in a picture, though it was a very hard job. At that time it was beneath the dignity of a well-known star to appear on the screen. But Mr. Hackett was a good business man as well as a good actor. He realized that this was an art that was going to amount to something and thought he might as well have the honor of being its first American star.

The first long picture made in this country was "The Prisoner of Zenda," with Mr. Hackett as star. We had all sorts of handicaps to overcome but finally, after a great deal of trouble, the picture was made. Of course, everybody who heard about it in the theatrical world thought I was crazy. Nobody believed that people would sit through a picture for hours as they would a play. There were all sorts of reasons why the thing would not succeed. However, when we finished the picture and had a showing at the Lyceum Theatre to invited guests and critics, the thing was pronounced a great success. The characters were recognized and called by name. People said, "See who is playing Black Michael! Look at so and so! Isn't that so and so?" The effect was tremendous. I was sure then that personalities plus a good story were all that we needed in pictures.

Two Monte Cristos

Following that we made a picture of "The Count of Monte Cristo," with James O'Neill. By this time the Patents Company had almost come to the realization that perhaps I was right, and yet they did not feel like changing their method or their line of business. But when they heard that I was going to make this picture, "The Count of Monte Cristo," with O'Neill, they made another on the same subject in a hurry. By the time my picture was finished they had theirs in circulation, and, although it was so inferior to the one we made that it would not be in the same class at all, nevertheless the damage was done. I could not release mine because they would not license it as long as they had their own, and we had to put "The Count of Monte Cristo" on the shelf. That was our first financial setback.

The Rise of Mary Pickford

Just about this time Belasco had a little girl in a play called "The Good Little Devil." She played a blind girl's part and her name was Mary Pickford. I knew Mary Pickford had had picture experience, because she had been with Biograph a couple of years before and knew the camera. We had already discovered in making these pictures that the makeup and action required were entirely different from those of the regular stage.

The regular actors did not have screen experience and they did not seem to want to learn. We tried people who were well advanced on the stage, but the director could not make them do things to suit the camera.

I felt, if we could get people who had experience on the stage and also had some camera experience, the results would be much better. It appeared to me that Mary Pickford would be a good choice, so I made Mr. Belasco a proposition to produce "The Good Little Devil" on the screen. While the play was going on we would take the picture during the day. As soon as she came into the studio we recognized her ability, and I induced her to stay in the motion pictures permanently. Her salary with Belasco was $175 a week. I offered her $500. Of course, that was a great deal of money and she could not resist it. So she joined the Famous Players. About the same time we contracted for several other stars of Broadway, such as Mrs. Fiske, John Barrymore, and many others, and prepared to do about six pictures that year.

Difficulties in Distribution

As that plan worked along I found that we could not release the pictures through the General Film Company. We had to work out some other method of distribution. The only method we could think of at that time was to sell our pictures through state rights, meaning that to take care of a section like this we would organize the Famous Players' Company of New England; in Michigan we would have the Famous Players' Company of Michigan; and so on. We divided the country into fifteen units, and each unit would buy and distribute the pictures in a certain territory. One unit had no connection financially or otherwise with the others.

When we got to that point we realized that a distributor could not maintain an office and do business on six or eight pictures a year because the overhead would not permit it. So we decided to make thirty pictures a year. We felt that that number of pictures would give an office about two and one-half pictures a month, and on that they could maintain an organization and run their business. So we made thirty pictures a year.

These state rights buyers to all appearances operated successfully, but they had no uniform policy. One man who owned a picture in New England would handle it on one policy and somebody who owned the rights in the west or in Pennsylvania would operate it on a different policy. For example, we insisted that our pictures should not be exhibited for less than ten cents. A good many of the exhibitors had been charging an admission price of five cents. In many places editorials were written, attacking the ten-cent charge. I remember distinctly in Colorado there appeared an editorial stating that there was no picture made that was worth ten cents.

We soon discovered that the state rights men in the different sections booked their pictures "hit or miss," that some were successful and others were not, and we found ourselves making no progress. We kept on making pictures and we tried to make better pictures, but as far as distribution was concerned the business was chaotic.

A New Distributing System

At this stage we called our state rights buyers to New York in the spring of the year, when we had our convention preparing for the next fall, and told them that we were not making headway and could not continue on the same basis. Out of that meeting developed an organization which we now call the Paramount. A number of the state rights men got together and organized the Paramount Pictures Corporation. This distributing organization made a contract with Famous Players and also with the Lasky Company, which came into existence that same year, and with another company, I think the Morosco Company out in Los Angeles. These three organizations agreed to deliver to Paramount eighty-four pictures a year. The Paramount hoped to pick up twenty more pictures in the open market because a great many other companies had started out making big pictures. They felt that a hundred and four pictures, which meant two a week, would be the necessary supply to maintain the organization.

The Ratio for Production and Distribution

It may interest you to know that the arrangement provided for thirty-five per cent to the distributor and sixty-five per cent to the producer. That is about the ratio today. When we analyzed the cost of handling the product during the year in which they distributed our pictures, we found it had cost about twenty-five per cent to distribute and we figured they should have ten per cent net profit. We also figured that as the volume of business became greater the cost of handling would be reduced, and in this way the profit for the distributor would be proportionately increased. That is the way we established the ratio of thirty-five to sixty-five.

A Union of Producers to Improve Quality

When the Paramount organization took over these productions, they began to advertise the product nationally. Then we found that each producer tried to make pictures according to his own ideas without any reference to the other producers. The Famous Players had already established a policy of showing famous players in famous plays. We took well known stories and well known artists and used them in our pictures. The others had not developed that part of the business. When it came to national distribution their product did not meet with the response that ours did. The result was that the exhibitor would protest to the distributor and the distributor would complain to the producers. The pictures were uneven in quality and in drawing power. We found ourselves, therefore, in this position; that although distribution throughout the country was unified, the interest between the producer and the distributor was not one. The machinery as it was set up could not continue successfully and build up the industry.

So in order to get the product of a more uniform standard we felt that the producers ought to get together. Thus the Famous Players, the Lasky, and the Morosco companies put their business into one and the Famous Players-Lasky Corporation was organized. Then the Paramount Distributing Company was taken over about six months or a year afterward. That was the first time the producing and distributing departments were put under one management with one policy for the whole.

TROUBLE WITH THE EXHIBITORS

From that point on we continued until we had nearly all the well known stars within our organization. Then the fear developed in the minds of a good many exhibitors throughout the country that our control of the best material in the business was not a good thing for them, wherefore the First National Exhibitors Circuit was organized. Primarily it was organized to buy, outside of the pictures we controlled, any good pictures that might come into the country. Subsequently they decided they would go into producing themselves. We saw that coming. We often had meetings with them and pointed out that if the exhibitor was going to create product for himself and endanger the producer's outlet, particularly the first-run outlet, we could not hope to succeed in our business.

We were prepared to make any kind of an agreement with the exhibitors that would assure them that they would not have to pay more than they should for the product. But irrespective of whether our suggestion was practicable or not, there were ambitious people in their organization who were determined to go into the producing business for themselves because they felt that was the only way they could protect their theatres.

We had a very interesting conference in Los Angeles at which were represented practically all of the producers then in the business, like Metro, Fox, Famous Players, and others. There we met the exhibitors and pointed out to them that if they went into producing, we would have to go into the theatres to protect our product, especially in the key cities.

At that time the finances of any one group were limited because we could not get credit from the banks. Financing ourselves was out of the question because the industry had not advanced far enough to enable us to do it. Confronted with this problem, I did not fear so much the fact that the exhibitors were going to make their own pictures. The danger lay in another direction. Most of the popular stars were in our camp, and the first thing the opposition would do would be to make overtures to them. Some of their contracts would be expiring within a few months or a year, and the exhibitors' organization, we felt sure, would make all sorts of inducements to get the stars to join them.

I told them if they did that, somehow or other I would protect my business by building or buying theatres. They laughed at me. They did not think I was serious. They went ahead and made an offer to Griffith, Mary Pickford, and two or three others, and very soon they had the whole business in an upheaval. All the stars were going with them, because they pointed out that they could do more for the stars. All I could do, they said, was to take their pictures and book with the exhibitors and, if the latter did not want to exhibit the films, I would be helpless.

The Stars Organize Independently

While these negotiations were going on, the United Artists organization was formed, and the stars, instead of going with the First National, went into business for themselves and I was relieved of embarrassment on that score.

The Producers Need Theatres

Still, the exhibitors' organization was a threat. So I came back to New York with the idea that one thing we must have was a house on Broadway. The Broadway house we had played in, the Strand, had joined the First National. That meant that I was out as far as the Strand was concerned. There were two other theatres on Broadway, the Rivoli and the Rialto. They were both the same type of house—first run.

I sent for the owners of these two theatres and told them we were out of the Strand and would like to make arrangements to book our pictures in their theatres. They hesitated because they were thinking of the high prices they had to pay for our pictures. I think we charged them $1,000 a week. We are getting $15,000 a week now. Finally they made a proposition to sell the theatres, which was just what I wanted. I said, "I will if the price is right." The man with whom I was talking took out a pencil and figured how much preferred stock they had outstanding and how much common stock and said, "We will sell the common stock at $55 a share." I do not know to this day how many shares he had, but I grabbed him by the hand and said, "All right; I will take them."

The next day the announcement was made that the Famous Players had bought the Rivoli and the Rialto. The stars and everybody in our world realized that the Famous Players had a plan and a policy and that we were going to protect our business by having representation in the key cities. So we started out on Broadway, which was a great turn in our affairs. We now had two first-run motion picture houses which guaranteed us an outlet on Broadway for our product in the event that we could not at any time secure bookings in any other theatres. . . .

■ ■ ■ ■

THE BIRTH OF A NATION (1915)

This review of *The Birth of a Nation* appeared in the *New York Times* on 4 March, 1915.

FILM VERSION OF DIXON'S "THE CLANSMAN"
PRESENTED AT THE LIBERTY

"The Birth of a Nation," an elaborate new motion picture taken on an ambitious scale, was presented for the first time last evening at the Liberty Theatre. With the addition of much preliminary historical matter, it is a film version of some of the melodramatic and inflammatory material contained in "The Clansman," by Thomas Dixon.

A great deal might be said concerning the spirit revealed in Mr. Dixon's review of the unhappy chapter of Reconstruction and concerning the sorry service rendered by its plucking at old wounds. But of the film as a film, it may be reported simply that it is an impressive new illustration of the scope of the motion picture camera.

An extraordinarily large number of people enter into this historical pageant, and some of the scenes are most effective. The civil war battle pictures, taken in panorama, represent enormous effort and achieve a striking degree of success. One interesting scene stages a reproduction of the auditorium of Ford's Theatre in Washington, and shows on the screen the murder of Lincoln. In terms of purely pictorial value the best work is done in those stretches of the film that follow the night riding of the men of the Ku-Klux Klan, who look like a company of avenging spectral crusaders sweeping along the moonlit roads.

The "Birth of a Nation," which was prepared for the screen under the direction of D. W. Griffith, takes a full evening for its unfolding and marks the advent of the two dollar movie. That is the price set for the more advantageous seats in the rear of the Liberty's auditorium.

"The Birth of a Nation," a review of the film, appeared in the 4 March 1915 *New York Times*.

It was at this same theatre that the stage version of "The Clansman" had a brief run a little more than nine years ago, as Mr. Dixon himself recalled in his curtain speech last evening in the interval between the two acts. Mr. Dixon also observed that he would have allowed none but the son of a Confederate soldier to direct the film version of "The Clansman."

■ ■ ■ ■

FIGHTING A VICIOUS FILM: PROTEST AGAINST "THE BIRTH OF A NATION" (1915), Boston Branch, National Association for the Advancement of Colored People
THE RISE AND FALL OF FREE SPEECH IN AMERICA (1916), D. W. Griffith

Although *The Birth of a Nation* produced public and critical respect for its visual and narrative power, it also aroused violently hostile reactions to its racist reading of American history. Leading the fight against the film was the Boston branch of the NAACP, which published a forty-seven-page pamphlet attacking the film's insulting portrayal of the Negro, supported by the endorsements of leading American public figures. Ironically, *The Birth of a Nation* may owe its position as the most influential film in American film history (if not in the world's film history) as much to the public controversy it generated as to its artistic powers. There had been feature films in America for at least two years prior to the release of *The Birth of a Nation* (clearly indicated by the Eaton article on pages 104–12 above); that the Griffith film irrevocably set the exhibition pattern for the future might well be as attributable to its social power (which contributed to its commercial success) as to its art.

D. W. Griffith wrote and privately published his own pamphlet, responding to the charges of his detractors on the constitutional grounds of the right to free speech. Whatever his opponents thought of the film's ideas, Griffith rejected their attempts to censor and suppress it. The next turn in Griffith's campaign would be his film *Intolerance*, which implied many of the same positions as his pamphlet (indeed, the film's opening titles quoted freely from Griffith's prose argument). It is quite possible that the Griffith pamphlet was written as much for the purpose of plugging his new film (the commercial power of controversy and "hype" had perhaps been discovered by 1915) as for the purpose of defending free speech. This suspicion that the movie producers who wanted to "speak freely" were not completely disinterested would influence a crucial Supreme Court ruling about films (see article following the two below).

FIGHTING A VICIOUS FILM

In its advertisement we are told that *The Birth of a Nation* is founded on Thomas Dixon's novel *The Clansman;* that it is a war play "that worked the audience up into a frenzy"; that "it will make you hate."

In an interview with a Boston editor, Thomas Dixon said, "that one purpose of his play was to create a feeling of abhorrence in white people, especially white women, against colored men"; "that he wished to have all Negroes removed from the United States and that he hopes to help in the accomplishment of that purpose by *The Birth of a Nation.*"

In furthering these purposes the producers of the film do not hesitate to resort to the meanest vilification of the Negro race, to pervert history and to use the most subtle form of untruth—a half truth.

Well knowing that such a play would meet strong opposition in Boston, large sums of money were spent in the employment of Pinkerton detectives and policemen to intimidate citizens, and the managers of the theatre refused to sell tickets to colored people. To soften opposition, the impression was given that the president of the United States had endorsed the play and that George Foster Peabody and other distinguished people favored it. One method of working up support was to pass cards among the auditors asking them to endorse the play. These cards were circulated, signed and collected at the end of the first act and before the second act in which appear the foul and loathsome misrepresentations of colored people and the glorification of the hideous and murderous band of the Ku Klux Klan.

The indignation against the play grew in intensity. The colored people in greater Boston rose in mass against it. It was opposed by many distinguished citizens including Governor Walsh, Lieutenant-Governor Cushing, Mr. Moorfield Storey, Hon. Albert E. Pillsbury, Hon. Samuel W. McCall, Rev. Samuel M. Crothers, D.D., Dr. Alexander Mann of Trinity Church, a majority of both branches of the legislature and many religious and civic organizations. A series of public meetings, remarkable for the spirit of unity and brotherhood and a very pronounced desire to save every group of our varied citizenship from insult and indignity, resulted in securing a new Censor Law for the City of Boston. . . .

Disregarding this law, plainly intended to stop the play, two of the censors refused to revoke its license. . . .

The failure of the censors to stop *The Birth of a Nation* would have been a very grievous disappointment if the agitation against it had not

Fighting a Vicious Film: Protest against "The Birth of a Nation" was written and published by the Boston Branch of the NAACP in 1915.

brought good of a very deep and satisfactory kind. To learn that on a question of decency and self-respect they could get together and in a dignified, law-abiding manner resent, as one man, the insult offered to their race by this play was a wonderfully heartening result to the twenty thousand colored people of greater Boston. . . . With a view to giving some idea of the scope of the agitation and the spirit in which it was conducted a few of the many letters, resolutions and speeches produced by the opposition to the play in April are put in permanent form with the further purpose of aiding other communities in opposing this and all such productions. . . .

ANALYSIS BY FRANCIS HACKETT

If history bore no relation to life, this motion picture drama could well be reviewed and applauded as a spectacle. As a spectacle it is stupendous. It lasts three hours, represents a staggering investment of time and money, reproduces entire battle scenes and complex historic events; amazes even when it wearies by its attempt to encompass the Civil War. But since history does bear on social behavior, *The Birth of a Nation* cannot be reviewed simply as a spectacle. It is more than a spectacle. It is an interpretation, the Rev. Thomas Dixon's interpretation, of the relations of the North and South and their bearing on the Negro. . . .

In *The Birth of a Nation* Mr. Dixon protests sanctimoniously that his drama "is not meant to reflect in any way on any race or people of today." And then he proceeds to give to the Negro a kind of malignity that is really a revelation of his own malignity.

Passing over the initial gibe at the Negro's smell, we early come to a negrophile senator whose mistress is a mulatto. As conceived by Mr. Dixon and as acted in the film, this mulatto is not only a minister to the senator's lust but a woman of inordinate passion, pride and savagery. Gloating as she does over the promise of "Negro equality," she is soon partnered by a male mulatto of similar brute characteristics. Having established this triple alliance between the "uncrowned king," his diabolic colored mistress and his diabolic colored ally, Mr. Dixon shows the revolting processes by which the white South is crushed "under the heel of the black South." "Sowing the wind," he calls it. On the one hand we have "the poor bruised heart" of the white South, on the other "the new citizens inflamed by the growing sense of power." We see Negroes shoving white men off the sidewalk, Negroes quitting work to dance, Negroes beating a crippled old white patriarch, Negroes slinging up "faithful colored servants" and flogging them till they drop, Negro courtesans guzzling champagne with the would-be head of the Black Empire,

Negroes "drunk with wine and power," Negroes mocking their white master in chains, Negroes "crazy with joy" and terrorizing all the whites in South Carolina. We see the blacks flaunting placards demanding "equal marriage." We see the black leader demanding a "forced marriage" with an imprisoned and gagged white girl. And we see continually in the background the white Southerner in "agony of soul over the degradation and ruin of his people."

Encouraged by the black leader, we see Gus the renegade hover about another young white girl's home. To hoochy-coochy music we see the long pursuit of the innocent white girl by this lust-maddened Negro, and we see her fling herself to death from a precipice, carrying her honor through "the opal gates of death."

Having painted this insanely apprehensive picture of an unbridled, bestial, horrible race, relieved only by a few touches of low comedy, "the grim reaping begins." We see the operations of the Ku Klux Klan, "the organization that saved the South from the anarchy of black rule." We see Federals and Confederates uniting in a Holy War "in defence of their Aryan birthright," whatever that is. We see the Negroes driven back, beaten, killed. The drama winds up with a suggestion of "Lincoln's solution"—back to Liberia—and then, if you please, with a film representing Jesus Christ in "the halls of brotherly love."

My objection to this drama is based partly on the tendency of the pictures but mainly on the animus of the printed lines I have quoted. The effect of these lines, reinforced by adroit quotations from Woodrow Wilson and repeated assurances of impartiality and goodwill, is to arouse in the audience a strong sense of the evil possibilities of the Negro and the extreme propriety and godliness of the Ku Klux Klan. So strong is this impression that the audience invariably applauds the refusal of the white hero to shake hands with a Negro, and under the circumstances it cannot be blamed. Mr. Dixon has identified the Negro with cruelty, superstition, insolence and lust. . . .

Whatever happened during Reconstruction, this film is aggressively vicious and defamatory. It is spiritual assassination. It degrades the censors that passed it and the white race that endures it.

PURPOSE OF THE FILM

I, Rolfe Cobleigh, of Newton, in the County of Middlesex and Commonwealth of Massachusetts, being duly sworn depose and say, that:

I am associate editor of *The Congregationalist* and *Christian World*, published at 14 Beacon St., Boston, where our offices are located.

My attention was attracted to the moving picture play entitled, *The Birth of a Nation,* by editorials which appeared in the *New York World,* the *New York Evening Post*, the *New York Globe* and other newspapers condemning the production when it was first shown in New York. Several of my friends, who saw the show in New York, soon reported to me their disapproval on the grounds that it incited race prejudice against the Negro race, that it glorified lynching and falsified history. Influenced by this evidence I wrote a letter to Mr. D. W. Griffith, who was advertised as the producer of the film, and protested against the exhibition of such a series of moving pictures as these were represented to be. I received in reply a letter from Mr. Thomas Dixon, whose interest in *The Birth of a Nation* was indicated by the paper upon which he wrote, the letter-head being printed with the words: "Thomas Dixon's Theatrical Enterprises," under which was *The Birth of a Nation*, with D. W. Griffith, following the titles of five other plays written by Mr. Dixon. He said in the letter referring to "our picture": "The only objection to it so far is a Negro Society which advises its members to arm themselves to fight the whites." He also wrote that Rev. Charles H. Parkhurst, D.D., was "making a report on this work," and that if I would "await Dr. Parkhurst's report" he would send it to me. This letter was dated March 27.

Under date of April 3, I wrote in reply: "I shall await Dr. Parkhurst's report, which you say you will send to me, with interest." I asked for the name of "a Negro society which advises its members to arm themselves to fight the whites."

Mr. Dixon wrote again under date of April 5, enclosing Dr. Parkhurst's report of which he said: "As this letter has been forwarded to Mayor Curley by Dr. Parkhurst I will appreciate it if you will publish it in *The Congregationalist*, with any comment you may make. Also Dr. Gregory's letter except one clause." Both the Parkhurst and Gregory letters were in approval of *The Birth of a Nation*. Mr. Dixon referred to his opponents as a "Negro Intermarriage Society," a term used in Mr. Gregory's letter to Mayor Curley and he gave the name of the organization as the National Association for the Advancement of Colored People, and suggested that it might produce a play to answer him, and that, "The silly legal opposition they are giving will make me a millionaire if they keep it up." I did not reply to this letter.

On the morning of April 9, 1915, Thomas Dixon called at my office and I had a long talk with him about *The Birth of a Nation*. He tried to convince me that it deserved my approval. He referred especially to the favorable reports of Dr. Parkhurst and Mr. Gregory. Mr. Dixon asked what I thought of Dr. Parkhurst's approval of the play. I replied that the evidence which had come to me was so strongly against the play that I was not influenced by Dr. Parkhurst, but that I would try to judge the play impartially when I saw it. He talked at length with reference to the artistic and dramatic merits of the play and of its value for the teaching of history, and ridiculed those who disapproved it. In reply to my questions with reference to the treatment of the Negro race in the play, he said that the subject was a debate, that he presented one side and that those who disagreed were at liberty to present the other side.

Mr. Dixon admitted that some of the scenes as originally presented in New York were too strongly suggestive of immorality and that he told Mr. Griffith they went too far.

I asked Mr. Dixon what his real purpose was in having *The Birth of a Nation* produced, what he hoped to accomplish by it. He began to read from the copy of Thomas B. Gregory's letter to Mayor Curley six things that Mr. Gregory said the play did in its effect on an audience. I interrupted to say, "Yes, but what is your chief purpose, what do you really want to accomplish through the influence of this play?" He replied in substance that he wanted to teach the people of the United States, especially the children, that the true history of the Reconstruction period was as it was represented in *The Birth of a Nation*. He said that in the play he presented the historical fact that Thaddeus Stevens became dictator of the United States government immediately after the death of President Lincoln, and that he appeared in the play under the name of Stoneman. Mr. Dixon said that one purpose in the play was to suggest Stevens' immorality in his relationship to his colored mistress for many years. He said the alleged sensual character of this woman, who in the play is called "Lydia Brown, Stoneman's mulatto housekeeper," was emphasized. Mr. Dixon described bad conditions in the South during the Reconstruction period, alleging that the Negroes gained control politically incited chiefly by Thaddeus Stevens, that the white Southerners were insulted, assaulted, robbed and disfranchised and that white girls and women were in constant danger of assault by colored men. He emphasized the alleged dominant passion of colored men to have sexual relations with white women and said that one purpose in his play was to create a feeling of abhorrence in white people, especially white women against colored men. Mr. Dixon said that his desire was to prevent the mixing of white and Negro blood by intermarriage. I asked him what he had to say about the mixing of the blood outside marriage and if it was not true that white men had forced their sexual relations upon colored girls and women all through the period of slavery, thus begetting children of mixed blood outside marriage, and if it was not true, as I am creditably informed, that such conditions prevail to a wide extent even among white men who occupy high social and political positions in the South today.

Mr. Dixon hesitated and finally answered that there was less of such conditions than there had been. Mr. Dixon said that the Ku Klux Klan was formed to protect the white women from Negro men, to restore order and to reclaim political control for the white people of the South. He said that the Ku Klux Klan was not only engaged in restoring law and order, but was of a religious nature, as represented in the play, having religious ceremonies and using the symbol of the cross. He said that the best white men of the South were in it, that Mr. Dixon's father was a Baptist minister in North Carolina and left his church to join the Ku Klux Klan, and that he remained with the organization until it was disbanded.

I asked Mr. Dixon what solution of the race problem he presented in *The Birth of a Nation* and he replied that his solution was Lincoln's plan. He said this was the colonization of the Negroes in Africa or South America, which he said President Lincoln favored during the last of the Civil War. Mr. Dixon said that he wished to have that plan carried out, that he wished to have all Negroes removed from the United States and that he hoped to help in the accomplishment of that purpose by *The Birth of a Nation*.

I suggested the difficulty of getting ten million people out of the country, and asked if he seriously advocated such a scheme. He replied with great earnestness that he did, that it was possible to create public sentiment such that a beginning could be made in the near future, that a large faction of the Negroes themselves would cooperate in the enterprise and that within a century we could get rid of all Negroes.

Mr. Dixon informed me that the first presentation of *The Birth of a Nation* in Boston would be given that evening for censorship before the mayor and other city officials and newspaper critics and gave me two tickets for that exhibition. He said that in anticipation of a hostile demonstration he and his associates would have thirteen Pinkertons scattered through the audience at the first performance and that as many or more Pinkertons would be employed in the Tremont Theatre at the exhibitions that would follow in Boston, with orders to rush anyone into the street instantly who started any disturbance. He said that he had feared there would be trouble in New York and that many Pinkertons were employed when the show was presented in New York, but that up to the time I saw Mr. Dixon there had been no disturbance in the Liberty Theatre, where the play was presented in New York. Mr. Dixon said that he owned a one-fourth interest in *The Birth of a Nation* Company.

I asked Mr. Dixon to what cities the show would be taken next and he replied that all plans had been held up until they knew the result of the protests in Boston. He said he regarded Boston as the critical point for their enterprise, that it was more likely to object to such a play than any other city and that he and his associates believe that if they could get by in Boston they would be able to go anywhere else in the country with the show without trouble.

As he went away he asked me to let him know what I thought of the play after I had seen it and expressed the hope that I would approve it.

I saw *The Birth of a Nation* that evening, April 9, and saw it again three weeks later, after omissions had been made to comply with the decision of Judge Dowd. I have expressed my disapproval of *The Birth of a Nation,* following each view of it on the grounds of falsifying history, in a riot of emotions glorifying crime, especially lynching, immorality, inviting prejudice against the Negro race, falsely representing the character of colored Americans and teaching the undemocratic, unchristian and unlawful doctrine that all colored people should be removed from the United States. I especially disapprove the play because Mr. Dixon frankly explained to me that his purpose in the play was to promote a propaganda with the desire to accomplish the results that I have stated.

Rolfe Cobleigh

Personally appeared Rolfe Cobleigh and made oath to the truth of the foregoing affidavit by him subscribed before me in Boston, Massachusetts, this 26th day of May, A.D. 1915.

George R. Brackett,
NOTARY PUBLIC

DUTY OF THE WHITE SOUTH

. . . An author like Mr. Dixon and the producer, Mr. Griffith, ought to realize that if the Negro was as bad as they paint him in the film he was what the South made him; he was the shadow of her own substance; and pride of race, if there were any in the white South, ought to suppress this exposition of their own shame. . . .

William Stanley Braithwate

PORTRAYS NEGROES AS BEASTS

I, Oswald Garrison Villard, testify that I have witnessed the performance of *The Birth of a Nation* at the Liberty Theatre in New York, and that I unhesitatingly testify that I consider said production improper, immoral, and unjust to the colored people of the country. I further testify that if the matter of race were eliminated, the play would, in my judgment, as to the objectionable scenes at least, be unfit for public production, since there is a suggestiveness about it of the kind which physicians and alienists know too often incites to crime with certain types of minds. The attack upon the Negro in this play is entirely unnecessary; it is not directly related to the story, nor is it proportional to the space given to the big things with which the play deals. In my judgment it is a deliberate attempt to humiliate ten million American citizens, and to portray them as nothing but beasts. In my judgment the play should not be tolerated in any American city.

Oswald Garrison Villard

GROSS LIBEL

This pictorial recrudescence of the rebellion is a gross libel upon the Union cause, upon its public leaders, Lincoln only excepted, upon every soldier, living or dead, who fought for it, and upon the whole people who supported it. Slavery and rebellion were right, the South was outraged by emancipation, the attempt to secure the Negro in his freedom was a crime for which wholesale murder was the proper remedy, the Negro was unfit for freedom and is unfit for civil rights, the Yankees were vandals, the rebels the true chivalry, and the Ku Klux Klan the heroes of the whole drama. This is the moral of the tale, conveyed with skillful innuendo and most consummate art. It gambles on the public ignorance of our own history, and as a vast majority of people are more impressed by what they see than by what they read or hear, it is liable to win by permanently lodging a radically false conception in the public mind.

A. E. Pillsbury

NOT ENDORSED BY THE PRESIDENT

. . . Referring to your recent favor containing copies of statements in which it was claimed that President Wilson had given his endorsement and approval of the photoplay which was presented before the president some time ago called *The Birth of a Nation,* I beg to say that I called at the White House, and the president's secretary the Honorable J. P. Tumulty made a most emphatic denial of the above statement that the president had endorsed the play. I have today received from Mr. Tumulty the following letter:

THE WHITE HOUSE
Washington, April 28, 1915

My dear Mr. Thatcher:—

Replying to your letter and enclosures, I beg to say that it is true that *The Birth of a Nation* was produced before the president and his family at the White House, but the president was entirely unaware of the character of the play before it was presented and has at no time expressed his approbation of it. Its exhibition at the White House was a courtesy extended to an old acquaintance.

Sincerely yours,
(Signed) *J. P. Tumulty,*
SECRETARY TO THE PRESIDENT

THREE MILES OF FILTH

It is three miles of filth. We believe this film teaches a propaganda for the purpose of so stirring up the people of the East and the West and the North that they would consent to allowing the Southern programme of disfranchisement, segregation and lynching of the Negro and finally to the repeal of the fourteenth and fifteenth Amendments to the Constitution.

Hon. W. H. Lewis

THE RISE AND FALL OF FREE SPEECH IN AMERICA

WHY CENSOR THE MOTION PICTURE—THE LABORING MAN'S UNIVERSITY?

Fortunes are spent every year in our country in teaching the truths of history, that we may learn from the mistakes of the past a better way for the present and future.

The truths of history today are restricted to the limited few attending our colleges and universities; the motion picture can carry these truths to the entire world, without cost, while at the same time bringing diversion to the masses.

As tolerance would thus be compelled to give way before knowledge and as the deadly monotony of the cheerless existence of millions would be brightened by this new art, two of the chief causes making war possible would be removed. The motion picture is war's greatest antidote.

INTOLERANCE: THE ROOT OF ALL CENSORSHIP

Ours is a government of free speech and a free press.

Intelligent opposition to censorship in the beginning would have nipped the evil in the bud.

But the malignant pygmy has matured into a Caliban.

Muzzle the "Movies" and defeat the educational purpose of this graphic art.

Censorship demands of the picture makers a sugar-coated and false version of life's truths.

The moving picture is simply the pictorial press.

The pictorial press claims the same constitutional freedom as the printed press.

Freedom of speech and publication is guaranteed in the Constitution of the United States, and in the constitution of practically all the states.

The 1916 pamphlet *The Rise and Fall of Free Speech in America* was written and published by D. W. Griffith.

A publicity photograph of a reflective D. W. Griffith, contemporaneous with his pamphlet in defense of free speech

Unjustifiable speech or publication may be punished, but cannot be forbidden in advance. Mayor Gaynor, that great jurist who stood out from the ordinary gallery-playing, hypocritical type of politician as a white rose stands out from a field of sewer-fed weeds, said in vetoing a moving picture censorship ordinance in the city of New York:

> Ours is a government of free speech and a free press. That is the cornerstone of free government. The phrase "The Press," includes all methods of expression by writing or pictures. . . . If this (moving picture) ordinance be legal, then a similar ordinance in respect to the newspapers and the theaters generally would be legal.

Today the censorship of moving pictures, throughout the entire country, is seriously hampering the growth of the art. Had intelligent opposition to censorship been employed when it first made itself manifest it could easily have been overcome. But the pigmy child of that day has grown to be, not merely a man, but a giant, and I tell you who read this, whether you will or no, he is a giant whose forces of evil are so strong that he threatens that priceless heritage of our nation—freedom of expression.

The right of free speech has cost centuries upon centuries of untold sufferings and agonies; it has cost rivers of blood; it has taken as its toll uncounted fields littered with the carcasses of human beings—all this that there might come to live and survive that wonderful thing, the power of free speech. In our country it has taken some of the best blood of our forefathers. The Revolution itself was a fight in this direction—for the God-given, beautiful idea of free speech.

Afterwards the first assault on the right of free speech, guaranteed by the Constitution, occurred in 1798, when Congress passed the Sedition Law, *which made it a crime for any newspaper or other printed publication to criticize the government.*

Partisan *prosecution of editors and publishers took place at the instance of the party in power,* and popular indignation was aroused against this abridgement of liberty to such an extent that Thomas Jefferson, the candidate of the opposition party for president, was triumphantly elected. And after that nothing more was heard of the Sedition Law, which expired by limitation in 1801.

The integrity of free speech and publication was *not again attacked* seriously in this country until the arrival of the *motion picture*, when this new art was seized by the powers of intolerance as an excuse for an assault on our liberties.

The motion picture is a medium of expression as clean and decent as any mankind has ever discovered. A people that would allow the suppression of this form of speech would unquestionably submit to the suppression of that which we all consider so highly, the printing press.

And yet we find all through the country, among all classes of people, the idea that the motion picture should be censored.

Now, the same reasons which make a censorship of the printed press unconstitutional and intolerable to Americans, make a censorship of the pictorial press unconstitutional and intolerable.

The theory of the constitutional guarantee, in brief, is this: Every American citizen has a constitutional right to publish anything he pleases, either by speech, or in writing, or in print, or in pictures, subject to his personal liability *after publication* to the penalties of violating any law, such as the law forbidding obscenity, libel, and other matter legally unfit for publication.

But the distinction between this theory and a censorship is that a censorship passes upon and forbids printing a picture *before publication*, and so directly controverts the most valuable of all our liberties under the Constitution, which our fathers established for our guidance and our protection.

If the pictorial press can be subjected to censorship by a mere act of Congress, then so can the printed press. And, of course, there would be an end, at once, to the freedom of *writing and printing*.

The constitutional and rightful manner in which to keep the moving pictures within proper bounds is simply to make and to enforce laws which will severely punish those persons who exhibit improper pictures.

As a matter of fact, there are laws now on the statute books which are ample to punish all who deserve punishment. It is simply a question of enforcement. So that the creation of Federal censorship is absolutely unnecessary.

It is said the motion picture tells its story more vividly than any other art. In other words, we are to be blamed for efficiency, for completeness. Is this justice? Is this common sense? We do not think so.

We have no wish to offend with indecencies or obscenities, but we do demand, as a right, the liberty to show the dark side of wrong that we may illuminate the bright side of virtue—the same liberty that is conceded to the art of the written word—that art to which we owe the Bible and the works of Shakespeare.

■ ■ ■ ■

MUTUAL FILM CORP. V. INDUSTRIAL COMMISSION OF OHIO (1915), United States Supreme Court

One of the states where *The Birth of a Nation* encountered severe difficulties was Ohio, whose strong censorship board refused to permit its exhibition. Early in 1915 the Mutual Film Corporation, distributor of the film, lost a crucial appeal to the Supreme Court of the United States in its suit against the Ohio censorship board. The Court, in a landmark decision, maintained that motion pictures were not "speech" and were therefore not entitled to speak freely. The decision, quoted by a member of the United States Senate in 1941 (see pages 476–81), stood until the famous "*Miracle* Case" of 1951 (see pages 615–19). Behind the Mutual suit was not so much their abstract desire to speak freely but the pragmatic desire to protect their interstate commerce (for a film was such a commerce) from expensive alterations as it traveled from state to state. In deciding against the Mutual Film Corporation, the Court also seemed to view the motion picture people as having a greater interest in money than in freedom of expression.

Appeal from the District Court of the United States for the Northern District of Ohio to review a decree refusing to restrain the enforcement of a state statute for the censorship of motion picture films. Affirmed. . . .

Statement by Mr. Justice McKenna:

Appeal from an order denying appellant, herein designated complainant, an interlocutory injunction sought to restrain the enforcement of an act of the general assembly of Ohio, passed April 16, 1913 (103 Ohio Laws, 399), creating under the authority and superintendence of the Industrial Commission of the state a board of censors of motion picture films. The motion was presented to three judges upon the bill, supporting affidavits, and some oral testimony.

The bill is quite voluminous. It makes the following attacks upon the Ohio statute: (1) The statute is in violation of §§ 5, 16, and 19 of article 1 of the Constitution of the state in that deprives complainant of a remedy by due process of law by placing it in the power of the board of censors to determine from standards fixed by itself what films conform to the statute, and thereby deprives complainant of a judicial determination of a violation of the law. (2) The statute is in violation of articles 1 and 14 of the Amendments to the Constitution of the United States, and of § 11 of article 1 of the Constitution of Ohio, in that it restrains com-

Mutual Film Corp. v. Industrial Commission of Ohio was argued before the United States Supreme Court 6 and 7 January 1915 and decided 23 February 1915.

plainant and other persons from freely writing and publishing their sentiments. (3) It attempts to give the board of censors legislative power, which is vested only in the general assembly of the state, subject to a referendum vote of the people, in that it gives to the board the power to determine the application of the statute without fixing any standard by which the board shall be guided in its determination, and places it in the power of the board, acting with similar boards in other states, to reject, upon any whim or caprice, any film which may be presented, and power to determine the legal status of the foreign board or boards, in conjunction with which it is empowered to act.

The business of the complainant and the description, use, object, and effect of motion pictures and other films contained in the bill, stated narratively, are as follows: Complainant is engaged in the business of purchasing, selling, and leasing films, the films being produced in other states than Ohio, and in European and other foreign countries. The film consists of a series of instantaneous photographs or positive prints of action upon the stage or in the open. By being projected upon a screen with great rapidity there appears to the eye an illusion of motion. They depict dramatizations of standard novels, exhibiting many subjects of scientific interest, the properties of matter, the growth of the various forms of animal and plant life, and explorations and travels; also events of historical and current interest,—the same events which are described in words and by photographs in newspapers, weekly periodicals, magazines, and other publications, of which photographs are promptly secured a few days after the events which they depict happen; thus regularly furnishing and publishing news through the medium of motion pictures under the name of "Mutual Weekly." Nothing is depicted of a harmful or immoral character.

The complainant is selling and has sold during the past year for exhibition in Ohio an average of fifty-six positive prints of films per week to film exchanges doing business in that state, the average value thereof being the sum of $100, aggregating $6,000 per week, or $300,000 per annum.

In addition to selling films in Ohio, complainant has a film exchange in Detroit, Michigan, from which it rents or leases large quantities to exhibitors in the latter state and in Ohio. The business of that exchange and those in Ohio is to purchase films from complainant and other manufacturers of films and rent them to exhibitors for short periods at stated weekly rentals. The amount of rentals depends upon the number of reels rented, the frequency of the changes of subject, and the age or novelty of the reels rented. The frequency of exhibition is described. It is the custom of the business, observed by all manufacturers, that a subject shall be released or published in all theaters on the same day, which is known as release day, and the age or novelty of the film depends upon the proximity of the day of exhibition to such release day. Films so shown have never been shown in public, and the public to whom they appeal is therefore unlimited. Such public becomes more and more limited by each additional exhibition of the reel.

The amount of business in renting or leasing from the Detroit exchange for exhibition in Ohio aggregates the sum of $1,000 per week.

Complainant has on hand at its Detroit exchange at least 2,500 reels of film which it intends to and will exhibit in Ohio, and which it will be impossible to exhibit unless the same shall have been approved by the board of censors. Other exchanges have films, duplicate prints of a large part of complainant's films, for the purpose of selling and leasing to parties residing in Ohio, and the statute of the state will require their examination and the payment of a fee therefor. The amounts of complainant's purchases are stated, and that complainant will be compelled to bear the expense of having them censored because its customers will not purchase or hire uncensored films.

The business of selling and leasing films from its offices outside of the state of Ohio to purchasers and exhibitors within the state is interstate commerce, which will be seriously burdened by the exaction of the fee for censorship, which is not properly an inspection tax, and the proceeds of which will be largely in excess of the cost of enforcing the statute, and will in no event be paid to the Treasury of the United States.

The board has demanded of complainant that it submit its films to censorship, and threatens, unless complainant complies with the demand, to arrest any and all persons who seek to place on exhibition any film not so censored or approved by the censor congress on and after November 4, 1913, the date to which the act was extended. It is physically impossible to comply with such demand and physically impossible for the board to censor the films with such rapidity as to enable complainant to proceed with its business, and the delay consequent upon such examination would cause great and irreparable injury to such business, and would involve a multiplicity of suits. . . .

Messrs. William B. Sanders and Walter N. Seligsberg argued the cause, and, with Mr. Harold T. Clark, filed a brief for appellant:

Appellant is entitled to invoke the protection of the constitutional guaranty of freedom of publication as fully as any person with whom it does business could do. . . .

Motion pictures are publications. . . .

Motion pictures constitute part of "the press of Ohio within the comprehensive meaning of that word. . . .

The Ohio motion picture censorship law is in direct contravention of the guaranty of freedom of publication contained in § 11 of article 1 of the Constitution of Ohio. . . .

The question is not whether or not the framers of our state and Federal Constitution had in mind this particular method of publication by motion pictures at the time when the Constitution was adopted. Obviously they did not, but this fact does not in any way remove this form of publication from the protection of the constitutional guaranty if it is within the spirit thereof. . . .

Neither the legislative nor the judicial branches of the government can, through censorship or injunction or by any other means, constitutionally impose a previous restraint upon publications, whether these publications be made through the medium of speech, writing, acting on the stage, motion pictures or through any other mode of expression now known or which may hereafter be discovered or invented. . . .

However far-reaching the police power vested in the legislature of Ohio may be, it is always subject to the limitation that the legislature may not pass an act which is in direct conflict with any provision of the Constitution of the United States or of the state of Ohio. . . .

The Ohio censorship law violates the provisions of art. 2, § 1, of the Constitution of Ohio, in that it attempts to delegate legislative power. . . .

A constitutional guaranty need not embody a specific prohibition in order to be entitled to protection against violation by legislative act. . . .

Even as to theaters, the legislature of Ohio could not demand the surrender of rights guaranteed by the Constitution as a condition precedent to the issuing of a license. The conducting of a theater or other place of amusement is a perfectly lawful business, and can only be subjected to such regulations as may other legitimate businesses. . . .

Under the law of Ohio, just as elsewhere, a corporation has the right to avail itself of these constitutional guaranties. . . .

Mr. Justice McKenna delivered the opinion of the court:

Complainant directs its argument to three propositions: (1) The statute in controversy imposes an unlawful burden on interstate commerce; (2) it violates the freedom of speech and publication guaranteed by § 11, article 1, of the Constitution of the state of Ohio;[1] and (3) it attempts to delegate legislative power to censors and to other boards to determine whether the statute offends in the particulars designated.

---

1. "Section 11. Every citizen may freely speak, write, and publish his sentiments on all subjects, being responsible for the abuse of the right; and no law shall be passed to restrain or abridge the liberty of speech, or of the press. In all criminal prosecutions for libel the truth may be given in evidence to the jury, and if it shall appear to the jury that the matter charged as libelous is true, and was published with good motives and for justifiable ends, the party shall be acquitted."

It is necessary to consider only §§ 3, 4, and 5. Section 3 makes it the duty of the board to examine and censor motion picture films to be publicly exhibited and displayed in the state of Ohio. The films are required to be exhibited to the board before they are delivered to the exhibitor for exhibition, for which a fee is charged.

Section 4. "Only such films as are, in the judgment and discretion of the board of censors, of a moral, educational, or amusing and harmless character shall be passed and approved by such board." The films are required to be stamped or designated in a proper manner.

Section 5. The board may work in conjunction with censor boards of other states as a censor congress, and the action of such congress in approving or rejecting films shall be considered as the action of the state board, and all films passed, approved, stamped, and numbered by such congress, when the fees therefor are paid, shall be considered approved by the board.

By § 7 a penalty is imposed for each exhibition of films without the approval of the board, and by § 8 any person dissatisfied with the order of the board is given the same rights and remedies for hearing and reviewing, amendment or vacation of the order "as is provided in the case of persons dissatisfied with the orders of the Industrial Commission."

The censorship, therefore, is only of films intended for exhibition in Ohio, and we can immediately put to one side the contention that it imposes a burden on interstate commerce. It is true that, according to the allegations of the bill, some of the films of complainant are shipped from Detroit, Michigan, but they are distributed to exhibitors, purchasers renters, and lessors in Ohio, for exhibition in Ohio, and this determines the application of the statute. In other words, it is only films which are "to be publicly exhibited and displayed in the state of Ohio" which are required to be examined and censored. . . .

It is true that the statute requires them to be submitted to the board before they are delivered to the exhibitor, but we have seen that the films are shipped to "exchanges" and by them rented to exhibitors, and the "exchanges" are described as "nothing more or less than circulating libraries or clearing houses." And one film "serves in many theaters from day to day until it is worn out."

The next contention is that the statute violates the freedom of speech and publication guranteed by the Ohio Constitution. In its discussion counsel have gone into a very elaborate description of moving picture exhibitions and their many useful purposes as graphic expressions of opinion and sentiments, as exponents of policies, as teachers of science and history, as useful, interesting, amusing, educational, and moral. And a list of the "campaigns," as counsel call them, which may be carried on, is given. We may concede the praise. It is not questioned by the Ohio statute, and under its comprehensive description, "campaigns" of an infinite variety may be conducted. Films of a "moral, educational, or amusing and harmless character shall be passed and approved," are the words of the statute. No exhibition, therefore, or "campaign" of complainant will be prevented if its pictures have those qualities. Therefore, however missionary of opinion films are or may become, however educational or entertaining, there is no impediment to their value or effect in the Ohio statute. But they may be used for evil, and against that possibility the statute was enacted. Their power of amusement, and, it may be, education, the audiences they assemble, not of women alone nor of men alone, but together, not of adults only, but of children, make them the more insidious in corruption by a pretense of worthy purpose or if they should degenerate from worthy purpose. Indeed, we may go beyond that possibility. They take their attraction from the general interest, eager and wholesome it may be, in their subjects, but a prurient interest may be excited and appealed to. Besides, there are some things which should not have pictorial representation in public places and to all audiences. And not only the state of Ohio, but other states, have considered it to be in the interest of the public morals and welfare to supervise moving picture exhibitions. We would have to shut our eyes to the facts of the world to regard the precaution unreasonable or the legislation to effect it a mere wanton interference with personal liberty.

We do not understand that a possibility of an evil employment of films is denied, but a freedom from the censorship of the law and a precedent right of exhibition are asserted, subsequent responsibility only, it is contended, being incurred for abuse. In other words, as we have seen, the Constitution of Ohio is invoked, and an exhibition of films is assimilated to the freedom of speech, writing, and publication assured by that instrument, and for the abuse of which only is there responsibility, and, it is insisted, that as no law may be passed "to restrain the liberty of speech or of the press," no law may be passed to subject moving pictures to censorship before their exhibition.

We need not pause to dilate upon the freedom of opinion and its expression, and whether by speech, writing, or printing. They are too certain to need discussion—of such conceded value as to need no supporting praise. Nor can there be any doubt of their breadth, nor that their underlying safeguard is, to use the words of another, "that opinion is free, and that conduct alone is amenable to the law."

Are moving pictures within the principle, as it is contended they are? They, indeed, may be mediums of thought, but so are many things. So is the theater, the circus, and all other shows and spectacles, and their performances may be thus brought by the like reasoning under the same immunity from repression or supervision as the public press,—made the same agencies of civil liberty.

Counsel have not shrunk from this extension of their contention, and cite a case in this court where the title of drama was accorded to pantomime; and such and other spectacles are said by counsel to be publications of ideas, satisfying the definition of the dictionaries,—that is, and we quote counsel, a means of making or announcing publicly something that otherwise might have remained private or unknown,—and this being peculiarly the purpose and effect of moving pictures, they come directly, it is contended, under the protection of the Ohio constitution.

The first impulse of the mind is to reject the contention. We immediately feel that the argument is wrong or strained which extends the guaranties of free opinion and speech to the multitudinous shows which are advertised on the billboards of our cities and towns, and which regards them as emblems of public safety, to use the words of Lord Camden, quoted by counsel, and which seeks to bring motion pictures and other spectacles into practical and legal similitude to a free press and liberty of opinion.

The judicial sense supporting the common sense of the country is against the contention. As pointed out by the district court, the police power is familiarly exercised in granting or withholding licenses for theatrical performances as a means of their regulation. . . .

It seems not to have occurred to anybody in the cited cases that freedom of opinion was repressed in the exertion of the power which was illustrated. The rights of property were only considered as involved. It cannot be put out of view that the exhibition of moving pictures is a business, pure and simple, originated and conducted for profit, like other spectacles, not to be regarded, nor intended to be regarded by the Ohio Constitution, we think, as part of the press of the country, or as organs of public opinion. They are mere representations of events, of ideas and sentiments published and known; vivid, useful, and entertaining, no doubt, but, as we have said, capable of evil, having power for it, the greater because of their attractiveness and manner of exhibition. It was this capability and power, and it may be in experience of them that induced the state of Ohio, in addition to prescribing penalties for immoral exhibitions, as it does in its Criminal Code, to require censorship before exhibition, as it does by the act under review. We cannot regard this as beyond the power of government.

It does not militate against the strength of these considerations that motion pictures may be used to amuse and instruct in other places than theaters,—in churches, for instance, and in Sunday schools and public schools. Nor are we called upon to say on this record whether such exceptions would be within the provisions of the statute, nor to anticipate that it will be so declared by the state courts, or so enforced by the state officers.

The next contention of complainant is that the Ohio statute is a delegation of legislative power, and void for that if not for the other reasons charged against it, which we have discussed. While administration and legislation are quite distinct powers, the line which separates exactly their exercise is not easy to define in words. It is best recognized in illustrations. Undoubtedly the legislature must declare the policy of the law and fix the legal principles which are to control in given cases; but an administrative body may be invested with the power to ascertain the facts and conditions to which the policy and principles apply. If this could not be done there would be infinite confusion in the laws, and in an effort to detail and to particularize, they would miss sufficiency both in provision and execution.

The objection to the statute is that it furnishes no standard of what is educational, moral, amusing, or harmless, and hence leaves decision to arbitrary judgment, whim, and caprice; or, aside from those extremes, leaving it to the different views which might be entertained of the effect of the pictures, permitting the "personal equation" to enter, resulting "in unjust discrimination against some propagandist film," while others might be approved without question. But the statute by its provisions guards against such variant judgments, and its terms, like other general terms, get precision from the sense and experience of men, and become certain and useful guides in reasoning and conduct. The exact specification of the instances of their application would be as impossible as the attempt would be futile. Upon such sense and experience, therefore, the law properly relies. . . . If this were not so, the many administrative agencies created by the state and national governments would be denuded of their utility, and government in some of its most important exercises become impossible. . . .

We may close this topic with a quotation of the very apt comment of the district court upon the statute. After remarking that the language of the statute "might have been extended by description and illustrative words," but doubting that it would have been the more restrictive might be more easily thwarted, the court said: "In view of the range of subjects which complainants claim to have already compassed, not to speak of the natural development that will ensue, it would be next to impossible to devise language that would be at once comprehensive and automatic."

In conclusion we may observe that the Ohio statute gives a review by the courts of the state of the decision of the board of censors.

Decree affirmed.

■ ■ ■ ■

CENSORSHIP AND THE NATIONAL BOARD (1915), John Collier

While state and local boards continued their work, the National Board of Censorship continued the industry's scrutiny of its own product. John Collier, cofounder and first president of the National Board, published this article describing and defending the practices of his panel.

The National Board of Censorship was founded in March, 1909, as an undertaking local to New York, through the initiative of The People's Institute assisted by the genius of Charles Sprague Smith. . . . The board was first locally organized at the request of the motion-picture exhibitors, who undertook to shut out from exhibition any film not approved. The work became national through the request of the manufacturers of films. The original governing committee of the board was composed of representatives from seven civic agencies. There are now thirty-two members on the general or governing committee. This committee is self-perpetuating and adds to its own membership; it creates the censoring committees which now use the regular voluntary services of 120 men and women.

The general committee has final control of policy, finance and administration, and is a court of last review in appeals from the censoring committees. No system of national representation has yet been devised, and such representation is probably impracticable; but a bulletin goes from the board's offices each week to about 450 collaborators in all parts of America, and a voluminous correspondence is maintained with agencies of all sorts which are concerned with the improvement of films. Many of the Board's correspondents are legally required to inspect the motion programs shown in their cities, and others operate as voluntary committees or advisory boards attached to the license departments.

To this day, not merely has the board no legal powers, but it has no contractual relations with the producers, distributers or showmen of films. The board has power only through the positive and continuing wish of those interested in the film business; yet no member of the board is obligated to the film business or is permitted to have even an indirect interest in the commercial phases of the motion-picture art.

The situation of the national board is so unusual as to be almost picturesque. Intense competition reigns among film-makers, film distributors and film showmen, yet the national board censors for them all. Trade arrangements come and pass, combinations are formed and broken up,

"Censorship and the National Board," by John Collier, appeared in the 2 October 1915 issue of *Survey*.

but the national board cooperates right through. Only if all, or nearly all makers of films submit their product and obey the board's findings, can the board's efforts be of value to any one of them. Only through manifest fair play can the board hold hungry rivals in this concensus of submissiveness. In spite of all its internecine struggles, the film art rises or falls as one, and the national board is an expression of this fact in the moral field.

While from the above standpoint the national board is really a trade institution, from another standpoint it is a public institution. The board must substantially satisfy the public, else its usefulness to the film business is gone and its power vanishes. Yet the board and its members have no possible fiscal interest in keeping the work alive. The board succeeds or fails by the economic test—that is, the test of value rendered alike and inextricably to the public and to the art.

Even the board's executive expenses are and always have been paid by voluntary subscription, rather unequally distributed among the manufacturers of films, the very interests whose product it censors—whose product, to the value of a half-million dollars a year, it prohibits from the market. But no one who censors films, arbitrates policy or chooses the committees or administrative staff of the board, receives even his expenses from the trade interests or from the board.

The board's procedure in judging films is described in testimony by the present writer, at that time secretary of the national board, before the assistant attorney-general of the United States, February 24, 1914:

Q. "Will you tell us something about the actual work of passing upon motion pictures and criticizing them, how it is done, and where?

A. "The censoring is done by this large sub-committee on censoring, of about one hundred and forty members. This committee is broken up into smaller committees, which are at work in New York every day except Sunday. . . . Two or three committees are at work on the same day. . . . Every foot of every film is looked at by the censoring committee, sample copies being submitted to it. If there is a disagreement in the censoring committee, or if the secretary disagrees, or if the manufacturer is aggrieved, the film is then appealed to the general committee which passes on it with final power. As soon as the board censors the film, it is listed, or is condemned, or passed, or passed with eliminations, and a bulletin is sent each week to over three hundred cities, containing statements of all the approved, condemned, or changed films."

At the time of its establishment, the board looked to many people impossible, utopian; only the personnel of its governing committees preserved it from suspicion and ridicule. It is still viewed with suspicion and incredulity by many, in spite of large visible results which have been achieved under its hand and of its influence, daily felt in every motion-picture showhouse in America. The more insistent attacks upon the board are directed against its virtues; but its principal opponents—the advocates of legal pre-censorship—are unanimously silent concerning its one great practical weakness and limitation. For their own compulsory censorships, existing and proposed, are afflicted with the same limitation. The national board advertises its limitations and makes no false promises. The legal boards and their advocates make promises which they must know to be impossible of fulfilment; when confronted with the national board's handicap and their own, they "hasten by with averted gaze."

It accords with the superficially-paradoxical nature of the whole origin and position of the national board, that the condition which permanently handicaps it is the very one which, as suggested at the beginning of this article, necessitates its existence.

This is the handicap: Although the national board inspects with final power all but a handful of the films shown in America, it is powerless to direct where any given film shall or shall not be shown. Nay, more; it knows that virtually every film will be seen everywhere, by every possible kind of audience, by people of every possible grade of culture and of all ages from four years to seventy.

Most states and most cities are, when viewed from the standpoint of the censorship problem, practically as heterogeneous as is the entire country. No censorship, whether voluntary or legal, under existing fundamental laws and trade conditions, can direct the use or restrict the audience of any film after it is once approved.

By this fact, any censor of motion-pictures is compelled to choose between one of two policies: He may fix his mind on one element among the very composite audience, or pay attention to some one use among the many and complex uses of films, and he may censor with reference to that one human element or that one use, ignoring the rest. Or again, he may try to bear in mind the whole audience and the many vital uses of the film, remembering that each film is for all the audience and that most films have complex uses; and cautiously proceeding, he may try to accomplish something or other under these conditions. The censor who worked consistently by the first method, focusing his mind on, for example, the juvenile and pathological elements in the audience, or on the narrowly moralistic uses of the film, would promptly be driven from office by an outraged public. The censor who tried to work consistently by the second method would find his judgment entirely sophisticated, his action paralyzed; and he would resign in sheer discouragement.

In real life, the legal censors have generally rushed to battle on the first policy, only to find themselves bathed in gore from slaughtered films and reprobated by nearly the whole public which has created their office. They have then retreated toward the second policy, accepting more or less the guidance of the national board but wakening to an occasional erratic severity through the pressure of one or another element of tax-payers, office-holders or interests. The national board has from the beginning planted itself theoretically on the second policy, but in an empirical way has been more or less inconsistent. No judicial body is immune, fortunately and unfortunately, from the infection of public opinion, and public opinion is only approximately rational.

At this point should be mentioned the comparative results of the national board and the various legally compulsory censorships. . . . The Chicago board, like many of the legal boards, views films simultaneously with the national board, so that many of the verdicts of all the boards duplicate one another. But the Chicago board takes the viewpoint of the child more exclusively than does the national board, and in considering films, is in the habit of judging each scene out of reference to the general plot. And . . . the Chicago board is more sensitive—more prudish—than the national board in sundry matters.

Other boards, like those of Ohio and Pennsylvania, publish meagre reports or no reports, rendering impossible a detailed comparison with the national board. But as their methods (not to mention ideals) diverge excessively from those of the national board, a divergence of results may be taken for granted. A report by the Portland Board of Censorship for the five months ending July 31, last, may be compared with the statistics of the national board published elsewhere in this article. During that period, 2,003 pictures, or 3,538 reels, were viewed by the Portland board. Of this number twelve pictures were condemned and 148 eliminations were made. A fair proportion of these condemnations represented verdicts going beyond those of the national board. The secretary of the Portland board adds that many of the films censored were old pictures made before censorship began.

Viewing the national board internally: Many of its members are predominantly concerned with the child and have blind spots for other social problems. Others are swayed more or less unconsciously by their own rebellion against the aesthetic, not moral, standards of the millions. There are members with religious bias, members deeply schooled in submissive morality, members with a strong property loyalty, members with sympathies for the industrial revolution, members with hatred for caricature or libel directed against downtrodden elements of the nation.

Details of the board's theories and formulae in judging films would require a long article. The latest printed copy of its standards (which can be had free of charge from the board) fills twenty-three pages and is still far from exhaustive. These formal standards are designed primarily for the guidance of film-makers and incidentally for the enlightenment of the public, and within broad limits they are binding on the action of the board itself. The accompanying excerpts from the "Standards" are given merely to suggest its contents.

These examples, and practically all the rules of the published "Standards," are wisely general and serve well their proper aim—namely, to suggest the temper of the board and its probable action and reasons for action in any given case.

Certain recent developments are less reassuring, indicating a tendency in the board to over-specialize its rules, always in a prohibitive direction, in a fashion that may ultimately limit the board's own freedom of action and even of debate and may discourage the creative producer of films. The board sincerely aims to keep itself free and to encourage responsible freedom in the film-makers. Dramatic art is an organ of life, and life is unforeseeable, tameless and profound. Let the board of censorship not become, as William James said that academic philosophy had become, "too buttoned-up and white-chockered and clean-shaven a thing to speak for the vast slow-breathing unconscious Kosmos with its dread abysses and its unknown tides. The freedom *we* want to see there, is not the freedom with a string tied to its leg and warranted not to fly away."

TYPICAL STANDARDS OF THE NATIONAL BOARD

SECTION 36. "Nor has the board felt that it should insist that the struggle be robbed of elements of treachery or trickery, or dictate who shall win or what the weapons shall be . . . though it will not tolerate the rough handling of women and children except where the life depicted is undoubtedly pioneer."

SECTION 39. "As a general rule it is preferable to have retribution come through the hands of authorized officers of the law, rather than through revenge or other unlawful or extra-legal means."

SECTION 41. "An adequate motive for committting a crime is always necessary to warrant picturing it. . . . It is desirable that the criminal be punished in some way, but the board does not always insist on this. . . . The results of the crime should be in the long run disastrous to the criminal so that the impression is that crime will inevitably find one out. The result (punishment) should always take a reasonable proportion of the film."

SECTION 42. "The producer should remember that he is not writing a detailed exposition of a crime, but is telling a dramatic story which most often does not need such detail."

Consistency is the original sin of intellect, and it is also practically expedient. The writer has always been more afraid of the national board's consistency than of its inconsistency; though it is plain that the board is here merely struggling in a net of perplexity which tangles all of human life. A committee on standards has recently been formed. This committee does not censor, but analyzes cases which are referred to it after action by the board. It tries to generalize from such cases and prepares resolutions which, when adopted by the board, become more or less binding on the future. The following recommendation from the standards committee is at this writing pending before the board. It is just the kind of rule that one has to formulate if he insists on abstracting general and future-limiting laws from the solutions and compromises arrived at in facing concrete problems of art or morals; but to the lover of dramatic art or to the pragmatist in philosophy it would appear that the standards committee is more audacious than were Moses and Confucius:

"The National Board of Censorship will condemn the presentation of complex and intricate themes presenting the details of the life of the so-called 'wanton heroine' and her companion when these are shown as attractive and successful. It will not allow the extended display of personal allurements, the exposure of alleged physical charms and passionate, protracted embraces. It will also disapprove the showing of men turning lightly from woman to woman, or women turning lightly from man to man in intimate sexual relationships. It prohibits the spectacle of the details of actual physical fights engaged in between women and disapproves of all such contests in which a woman is roughly handled. It disapproves also of the condoning by pure women, in motion pictures, of flagrant moral lapses in men, presented in detail and at length."

A recent example of *inconsistency* on the part of the national board is of interest, especially because the inconsistency was due to an attempt at consistency. The board refused to prohibit the film "The Birth of a Nation," which in the view of many persons was an insult to a defenceless race, calculated to intensify race hatred and even to cause violence. This action of the board, taken after prolonged and conscientious discussion, was based on a necessary ruling by which the national board refuses to stand guard on behalf of the pride or interests of any special faction, section or race, but aims to censor for the whole people of all the country. This ruling acted as a stay against action which might otherwise have been taken, based on the alleged libelous character of "The Birth of a Nation" and its possible tendency to provoke lynchings and riots.

Shortly thereafter, the national board condemned a film which depicted outrages by German soldiers, alleged to have been committed in 1870 in the Franco-Prussian war. The owner of the film attempted to overrule the board's verdict in New York. The license commissioner concurred with the board and announced that he would revoke the license of theaters showing this film. The dispute was carried to the courts, and an injunction was secured against the license commissioner, permitting the film to be exhibited. Said the court, in effect, "We cannot take

THREE CENSORSHIP PROBLEMS
Murder: Rape: Vice

Above: A typical crime-episode from
The Diamond from the Sky showing
murder and robbery. The National
Board considered it justified through
its relation to a significant plot.

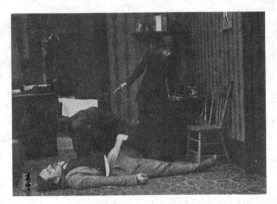

To the Left: A scene from The Outcast
based on a well-known story of
Thomas Nelson Page. The heroine, defending herself against assault, has
killed the man. A scenario well within
the National Board's standards.

Below: The extreme of sensuousness
permitted by the National Board of
Censorship. Episode from The Toast
of Death, an East Indian melodrama,
which was approved because of its
tragic-moral ending.

PASSED. The National Board of Censorship bars gruesome brutality in most contexts, but approved this scene as essential in a plot dealing with the relation of defective mentality to juvenile crime. The boy who is here shown torturing a cat is later restored by medical treatment to normality.

PROHIBITED. The kind of vulgarity which the National Board does not pass. A dancing party is being held upstairs; a woman falls through the ceiling.

cognizance of national prejudices; this court does not recognize hyphenated Americanism." This injunction was contested and the case is still being appealed.

In this second case, the national board had acted on a ruling adopted at the outbreak of the Great War, that films likely to cause unneutral acts, or riots between (for example) Franco-Americans and German-Americans, should not be permitted. This ruling sufficed to neutralize and to override the ruling which had been applied in refusing to condemn "The Birth of a Nation." . . .

Is it possible to state briefly the controlling positive ideal of the board in censoring films? The board has in fact an implicit ideal. There is a tradition which its members share in common; and which reveals itself in the fact that a new member can nearly always be readily identified. The most steadfast part of this tradition is mentioned nowhere in the printed standards of the board; it is nothing more nor less than a recognition that the board is *collaborating* in an improvement of motion-pictures which is desired by all, and by none so much as by the heads of the great film studios. The board is not at work to force an improvement or to hand down its own greater wisdom, for the board has no such wisdom and makes no pretense to having it. The national board is a clearing house and a means by which many factors—business factors, esthetic factors, moral factors and personal factors—represented by divers individuals, groups and corporations, are enabled to do team-work for the educational, moral and to some extent the artistic development of the film art. This does not mean that the national board is merely an advisory agent. It has great powers, greater with each year, and it sometimes uses them with cruel effect. But these powers are neither legal, contractual nor mandatory in any sense whatever; the board is voluntarily exercising a *trust* which is voluntarily reposed with it.

To execute wisely, moderately and fearlessly this trust; to aspire toward no vested power, contractual or legal; to make no false claims; to do its unpretentious best under the limitations, described in this article, which are beyond its power to modify; this is the implicit but perfectly conscious ideal of the more than 150 men and women who, without pay or recognition, examine and debate that ceaseless stream of film-drama flowing six days in the week, fifty-two weeks in the year. And thus working, the national board has written itself pretty deeply into the history of motion-pictures during six years. Mistakes by the hundreds or thousands, which have been made and will continue to be made, are compensated for by this steadfast, earnest ideal of the board; and its own position, alike with the film-art and the public, grows ever stronger. . . .

ONE YEAR'S WORK [1914] OF THE NATIONAL BOARD OF CENSORSHIP

Total number of reels inspected, including those inspected more than once   9,496

Total number of subjects first inspected   5,770

Number of reels condemned in toto in the form presented by the manufacturer   167

Number of subjects condemned in toto in the form presented by the manufacturer   79

Number of subjects condemned in toto even after pictures had been re-made by the manufacturer   27

(In other words, about two-thirds even of condemned films were, through being reconstructed, made acceptable to the National Board).

Number of subjects in which changes were made by the National Board   522

Total cost to manufacturers of negative, sample copies and sales copies kept off the American market $513,853.20

Number of meetings of the original Censoring Committee for 1914, divided into sub-committees of 4 to 12 members   1,011

Number of meetings of the General Committee for 1914   45

The proportion of all films viewed by the National Board two years ago   95%

Proportion viewed one year ago   97%

Proportion now viewed   99%

(The one percent not at present viewed includes some melo-dramas and dubious crime films and some films of local interest publicly shown over limited areas. A few obscene films are always being secretly passed around for private exhibition before festive gatherings of men.)

■ ■ ■ ■

PLUTARCH LIGHTS OF HISTORY, NO. 5: CHARLES CHAPLIN (1916), FPA

CHARLIE CHAPLIN'S ART (1917), Harvey O'Higgins

Charles Chaplin appeared in his first Keystone Comedy in January 1914, and by the end of that year he had become a national craze among the audiences at the nickelodeons. Yet these two articles, published in 1916 and 1917, respectively, were among the very first in the major national magazines to take any notice of this phenomenon. The first piece, published in *Harper's Weekly,* indicates the reasons for ignoring the clown's arrival. The sneering author refuses to believe that any motion picture comedian—not to mention any motion picture—is worth taking seriously. The second piece, published in the *New Republic,* is more observant of Chaplin's magic and more sensitive to his aims. The *New Republic* was, of course, a new magazine at the time, and its birth was almost simultaneous with Chaplin's appearance in motion pictures.

PLUTARCH LIGHTS OF HISTORY, NO. 5: CHARLES CHAPLIN

Pericles is said to have received, in the Golden Age, 2 drachmæ per word for a speech he made at a dinner of the Athens Chamber of Commerce; and Cæsar's scale of remuneration, when he was war-correspondent to the Rome *Tribune,* was 15 sestertia a column, albeit his book publishers hoodwinked him, Herodotus has it, forasmuch as they sell millions of his Commentaries every year, and neither Cæsar nor his estate ever received a denarius for it. But this, continueth Herodotus, may be because Cæsar thrice refused the crown, and his publishers deemed that he hated royalty, therefore paid him none; but this, I think, is naught but a joke of the old historian's, and not, I fear, a very merry one. As to disproportionate emoluments, there is the absurd sum ($1.50) with which I am rewarded for these chonicles, that price being enough to purchase, at the moment of going to press, near 5 gallons of petroleum, which I use in 5 hours; and I can write a chonicle of this length in less time than two hours, on a clear day.

But of great rewards, the greatest in all history is that of Charles Chaplin, the cinematograph actor, who receiveth $10,000 a week for making grimaces, sitting in custard pies, hurling pancakes into human countenances, walking with strange anticks, and doing all manner of grotesque steps, which are enough, say those who have seen him, to make a cat laugh. Of his drollness I am not fit to judge, never having seen him, nor indeed any motion pictures soever, which is a great distinction in itself.

As to the justice of the great guerdon he getteth for this clowning, I am not one to say he doth not merit it. For there be men of greater skill and ability than are mine, who do not earn ten dollars for a week's work. Money is but a relative term, says Plato, and I envy no man his earnings. For I can not wear two suits of clothing at once; nor smoke synchronously

"Plutarch Lights of History, No. 5: Charles Chaplin," by FPA, was published in the *Harper's Weekly* of 25 March 1916.

more than one cigar. And I crave no greath wealth, forasmuch as I need no dimes to spend upon the motion pictures.

Charlie Chaplin's Art

There died last winter, in New York, a notable artist who was comparatively unknown because he had the ill-luck to miss his right artistic medium. He was a circus clown—"Slivers" of the delectable "baseball game." He should have been "Frank Oakley of the movies." He was condemned to pantomime because of a voice that was inadequate to public utterance, but he was a comedian of surprising imagination, a serious observer, a real student of comic effects, and inherently pathetic even at his funniest.

Charles Chaplin has come into the kingdom that poor Slivers missed. He wears, as Slivers did, a grotesque costume. He has the same gift for clowning—an ability to translate any natural gesture into caricature without the slightest apparent exaggeration—a gift that seems inherent in his body as grace is so often in the body of beauty. Slivers used to say: "Put a real clown in the middle of a three-ring circus, with nothin' to work with but a shoe-lace, an' he'll make the whole tent laugh." Slivers did it by virtue of a penetrating imagination. He would see the shoe-lace as anything from an angle-worm to a string of spaghetti, and see it and relate himself to it so convincingly that he made you see it as he did. Chaplin performs the same miracle with a walking-stick. He will see it—outrageously—as a tooth-pick, but he will use it exactly as you see tooth-picks used at a lunch counter, looking at you with an air of sad repletion, with a glazed eye from which all intelligence has withdrawn, inwardly, to brood over the internal satisfaction of digestive process— absurdly, but with unimpeachable realism. Or, he is a clerk in a pawn-shop, and a man brings in an alarm clock to pledge it. Chaplin has to decide how much it is worth. He sees it first as a patient to be examined diagnostically. He taps it, percusses it, puts his ear to its chest, listens to its heart-beat with a stethoscope, and, while he listens, fixes a thoughtful medical eye on space, looking inscrutably wise and professionally self-confident. He begins to operate on it—with a can-opener. And immediately the round tin clock becomes a round tin can whose contents are under suspicion. He cuts around the circular top of the can, bends back the flap of tin with a kitchen thumb gingerly, scrutinizes the con-

Harvey O'Higgins's "Charlie Chaplin's Art" was carried in the 3 February 1917 *New Republic*.

tents gingerly, and then, gingerly approaching his nose to it, sniffs with the melancholy expression of an experienced housekeeper who believes the worst of the packing-houses. The imagination is accurate. The acting is restrained and naturalistic. The result is a scream.

And do not believe that such acting is a matter of crude and simple means. It is as subtle in its naturalism as the shades of intonation in a really tragic speech. In one of Chaplin's films, another actor, disguised as Chaplin, walked into the picture and was received by the audience with a preliminary titter of welcome. He went through a number of typical Chaplin antics with a drinking fountain that squirted water in his face. There was half-hearted laughter. He was not funny. He moved through a succession of comic "stunts" unsuccessfully before it dawned on me that this was not Chaplin at all. When Chaplin followed in, and repeated the exact passages that had failed, the laughter was enormous. It was the difference between a man acting a comic scene and a man living it, and the difference was apparent in a thousand niceties of carriage and gesture and expression of face. In this hairbreadth of difference lies the triumph of Chaplin's art. Expressed in salary, it is the difference between a few dollars a day and a half-million a year. In reputation, it is the difference between the obscurity of the still unknown comedians who competed with Chaplin in the early films and the success of the most famous clown in the world—for Chaplin is as preëminent a favorite in Paris, for instance, as he is here. It is the difference between a genuine artist and an artificial one.

That difference goes very deep. Slivers used to say: "It's imitatin' life— that's what does it. You can't get it by muggin'—" making faces—"it has to be real to you. Why, in that baseball game—"And he would describe how he had built up his elaborate caricature of a catcher from innumerable observations, holding his glove between his knees instead of dropping it on the ground—when he paused to put on his chest-pad because So-and-So always did it that way, and snatching off his mask with just *this* gesture because it was the way he had seen another catcher do *that*. And he would say: "You know, it's hard work—that turn. You have to keep in your mind where all the players are, on the field and on the bases, all the time. It keeps you watchin'." He was as serious about it as a Russian realist. And, as a result, you would see the baseball fans at the circus wiping the tears of helpless laughter from one eye at a time so as not to lose sight of him for an instant.

The curious thing is that none of the clowns who worked with Slivers in the circus learned the lesson from him. They imitated his "make-up." They stole his "business." But they never reached his secret. And on the films, to-day, as on the stage, you will find all the would-be comedians "mugging" diligently, trying to "put over comedy" with consciously comic gesture and intonation, saying to the audience tacitly, "I'm funny—laugh at me," and concluding that the audience is "a bunch of bone-heads" because they do not laugh. The author gives the stage comedians amusing lines, and Chaplin has no lines. Elaborately humorous plots are invented for the spoken drama, and Chaplin's plots are so simple that the popular legend credits him with improvising them as he goes along. He is on a stage where the slapstick, the "knockabout," the guttapercha hammer and the "roughhouse" are accepted as the necessary ingredients of comedy, and these things fight against the finer qualities of his art, yet he overcomes them. In his burlesque of Carmen he commits suicide with a collapsible dagger, and the moment of his death is as tragic as any of Bernhardt's. His work has become more and more delicate and finished as the medium of its reproduction has improved to admit of delicate and finished work. There is no doubt, as Mrs. Fiske has said, that he is a great artist. And he is a great lesson and encouragement to anyone who loves an art or practises it, for he is an example of how the best can be the most successful, and of how a real talent can triumph over the most appalling limitations put upon its expression, and of how the popular eye can recognize such a talent without the aid of the pundits of culture and even in spite of their anathemas.

■ ■ ■ ■

THE INTIMATE PHOTOPLAY (1916), Vachel Lindsay

The motion picture has spurred as much abstract, theoretical speculation in this century as any other art ever did in the past. The reason is that the cinema has challenged many of the assumptions that have dominated traditional aesthetic thinking about the older arts: the cinema is produced by a machine; its products can be infinitely duplicated; it is produced for mass consumption; it seems to contain "nature itself"; it operates "automatically," almost by itself; its production is dependent on large sums of money; it is produced by a community of artisans rather than by a single artist; it seems totally "impure" in its ability to select and synthesize the methods and materials of almost every other art; and so forth.

In America this kind of theoretical speculation began extremely early—and at a very distinguished level. Vachel Lindsay, the American poet noted for his verbal symphonies such as "The Congo" and "General William Booth Enters Heaven," loudly proclaimed (he could never do anything softly) that the motion picture was a "great high art" in *The Art of the Moving Picture*. Lindsay was extremely sensitive to Griffith's work, recognizing him as a superior artist long before anyone else did (perhaps even before Griffith himself came to think so). Lindsay's prescience with Chaplin was less acute; he found the tramp vulgar. (But then humor was never Lindsay's long suit as a poet.) Interestingly, in this era of the feature film, Lindsay preferred the compactness of the shorter films, finding many of the long films several reels too long. Perhaps the poet preferred the shorter works, which felt more like poems. Or perhaps Lindsay was right; many of the early features were too long, growing longer without growing more complex.

Let us take for our platform this sentence: THE MOTION PICTURE ART IS A GREAT HIGH ART, NOT A PROCESS OF COMMERCIAL MANUFACTURE. The people I hope to convince of this are (1) The great art museums of America, including the people who support them in any way, the people who give the current exhibitions there or attend them, the art school students in the corridors below coming on in the same field; (2) the departments of English, of the history of the drama, of the practice of the drama, and the history and practice of "art" in that amazingly long list of our colleges and universities—to be found, for instance, in the World Almanac; (3) the critical and literary world generally. Somewhere in this enormous field, piled with endowments mountain high, it should be possible to establish the theory and practice of the photoplay as a fine art. Readers who do not care for the history of any art, readers who have neither curiosity nor aspiration in regard to any of the ten or eleven muses who now dance around Apollo, such shabby readers had best lay the book down now. Shabby readers do not like great issues. My poor little sermon is concerned with a great issue, the clearing of the way for a critical standard, whereby the ultimate photoplay may be judged. I cannot teach office-boys ways to make "quick money" in the "movies." That seems to be the delicately implied purpose of the mass of books on the photoplay subject. They are, indeed, a sickening array. Freeburg's book is one of the noble exceptions. And I have paid tribute elsewhere to John Emerson and Anita Loos. They have written a crusading book, and many crusading articles.

After five years of exceedingly lonely art study, in which I had always specialized in music exhibits, prowling around like a lost dog, I began to intensify my museum study, and at the same time shout about what I was discovering. From nineteen hundred and five on I did orate my opinions

"The Intimate Photoplay," from *The Art of the Moving Picture* by Vachel Lindsay, was published in 1916 by Liveright. The book was revised in 1922.

to a group of advanced students. We assembled weekly for several winters
in the Metropolitan Museum, New York, for the discussion of the
masterpieces in historic order, from Egypt to America. From that standpoint, the work least often found, hardest to make, least popular in the
street, may be in the end the one most treasured in a world-museum as
a counsellor and stimulus of mankind. Throughout this book I try to
bring to bear the same simple standards of form, composition, mood and
motive that we used in finding the fundamental exhibits; the standards
which are taken for granted in art histories and schools, radical or conservative, anywhere. . . .

Just as the Action Picture has its photographic basis or fundamental
metaphor in the long chase down the highway, so the Intimate Film has
its photographic basis in the fact that any photoplay interior has a very
small ground plan, and the cosiest of enclosing walls. Many a worth-
while scene is acted out in a space no bigger than that which is occupied
by an office boy's stool and hat. If there is a table in this room, it is often
so near it is half out of the picture or perhaps it is against the front line of
the triangular ground-plan. Only the top of the table is seen, and nothing
close up to us is pictured below that. We in the audience are privileged
characters. Generally attending the show in bunches of two or three, we
are members of the household on the screen. Sometimes we are sitting
on the near side of the family board. Or we are gossiping whispering
neighbors, of the shoemaker, we will say, with our noses pressed against
the pane of a metaphoric window.

Take for contrast the old-fashioned stage production showing the room
and work table of a shoemaker. As it were the whole side of the house
has been removed. The shop is as big as a banquet hall. There is something
essentially false in what we see, no matter how the stage manager fills in
with old boxes, broken chairs, and the like. But the photoplay interior
is the size such as a work-room should be. And there the awl and pegs
and bits of leather, speaking the silent language of picture writing, can
be clearly shown. They are sometimes . . . the principal actors.

Though the Intimate-and-friendly Photoplay may be carried out of
doors to the row of loafers in front of the country store, or the gossiping
streets of the village, it takes its origin and theory from the snugness of
the interior.

The restless reader replies that he has seen photoplays that showed
ball-rooms that were grandiose, not the least cosy. These are to be classed
as out-of-door scenery so far as theory goes, and are to be discussed
under the head of Splendor Pictures. Masses of human beings pour by
like waves, the personalities of none made plain. The only definite people
are the hero and heroine in the foreground, and maybe one other. Though

these three be in ball-costume, the little triangle they occupy next to the camera is in sort an interior, while the impersonal guests behind them conform to the pageant principles of out-of-doors, and the dancers are to the main actor as is the wind-shaken forest to the charcoal-burner, or the bending grain to the reaper.

The Intimate Motion Picture is the world's new medium for studying, not the great passions, such as black hate, transcendent love, devouring ambition, but rather the half relaxed or gently restrained moods of human creatures. It gives also our idiosyncrasies. It is gossip *in extremis*. It is apt to chronicle our petty little skirmishes, rather than our feuds. In it Colin Clout and his comrades return.

The Intimate Photoplay should not crowd its characters. It should not choke itself trying to dramatize the whole big bloody plot of Lorna Doone, or any other novel with a dozen leading people. Yet some gentle episode from the John Ridd farm, some half-chapter when Lorna and the Doones are almost forgotten, would be fitting. Let the duck-yard be parading its best, and Annie among the milk-pails, her work for the evening well nigh done. The Vicar of Wakefield has his place in this form. The Intimate-and-friendly Motion Picture might very well give humorous moments in the lives of the great, King Alfred burning the cakes, and other legendary incidents of him. Plato's writings give us glimpses of Socrates, in between the long dialogues. And there are intimate scraps in Plutarch.

Prospective author-producer, do you remember Landor's Imaginary Conversations, and Lang's Letters to Dead Authors? Can you not attain to that informal understanding in pictorial delineations of such people?

The photoplay has been unjust to itself in comedies. The late John Bunny's important place in my memory comes from the first picture in which I saw him. It is a story of high life below stairs. The hero is the butler at a governor's reception. John Bunny's work as this man is a delightful piece of acting. The servants are growing tipsier downstairs, but the more afraid of the chief functionary every time he appears, frozen into sobriety by his glance. At the last moment this god of the basement catches them at their worst and gives them a condescending but forgiving smile. The lid comes off completely. He himself has been imbibing. His surviving dignity in waiting on the governor's guests is worthy of the stage of Goldsmith and Sheridan. This film should be reissued in time as a Bunny memorial.

So far as my experience has gone, the best of the comedians is Sidney Drew. He could shine in the atmosphere of Pride and Prejudice or Cranford. But the best things I have seen of his are far from such. I beg the pardon of Miss Jane Austen and Mrs. Gaskell while I mention Who's

Who in Hogg's Hollow, and A Regiment of Two. Over these I rejoiced like a yokel with a pocketful of butterscotch and peanuts. The opportunities to laugh on a higher plane than this, to laugh like Olympians, are seldom given us in this world.

The most succeful motion picture drama of the intimate type ever placed before mine eyes was Enoch Arden, produced by Cabanne.

Lillian Gish takes the part of Annie, Alfred Paget impersonates Enoch Arden, and Wallace Reid takes the part of Philip Ray. The play is in four reels of twenty minutes each. It should have been made into three reels by shortening every scene just a bit. Otherwise it is satisfying, and I and my friends have watched it through many times as it has returned to Springfield.

The mood of the original poem is approximated. The story is told with fireside friendliness. The pale Lillian Gish surrounded by happy children gives us many a genre painting on the theme of domesticity. It is a photographic rendering in many ways as fastidious as Tennyson's versification. The scenes on the desert island are some of them commonplace. The shipwreck and the like remind one of other photoplays, but the rest of the production has a mood of its own. Seen several months ago it fills my eye-imagination and eye-memory more than that particular piece of Tennyson's fills word-imagination and word-memory. Perhaps this is because it is pleasing to me as a theorist. It is a sound example of the type of film to which this chapter is devoted. If you cannot get your local manager to bring Enoch Arden, reread that poem of Tennyson's and translate it in your own mind's eye into a gallery of six hundred delicately toned photographs hung in logical order, most of them cosy interior scenes, some of the faces five feet from chin to forehead in the more personal episodes, yet exquisitely fair. Fill in the out-of-door scenes and general gatherings with the appointments of an idyllic English fisher-village, and you will get an approximate conception of what we mean by the Intimate-and-friendly Motion Picture, or the Intimate Picture, as I generally call it, for convenience.

It is a quality, not a defect, of all photoplays that human beings tend to become dolls and mechanisms, and dolls and mechanisms tend to become human. But the haughty, who scorn the moving pictures, cannot rid themselves of the feeling that they are being seduced into going into some sort of a Punch-and-Judy show. And they think that of course one should not take seriously anything so cheap in price and so appealing to the cross-roads taste. But it is very well to begin in the Punch-and-Judy-show state of mind, and reconcile ourselves to it, and then like good democrats await discoveries. Punch and Judy is the simplest form of marionette performance, and the marionette has a place in every street in history just as the dolls' house has its corner in every palace and cottage. The French in particular have had their great periods of puppet shows; and the Italian tradition survived in America's Little Italy, in New York for many a day; and I will mention in passing that one of Pavlowa's unforgettable dance dramas is The Fairy Doll. Prospective author-producer, why not spend a deal of energy on the photoplay successors of the puppet-plays?

We have the queen of the marionettes already, without the play.

One description of the Intimate-and-friendly Comedy would be the Mary Pickford kind of a story. None has as yet appeared. But we know the Mary Pickford mood. When it is gentlest, most roguish, most exalted, it is a prophecy of what this type should be, not only in the actress, but in the scenario and setting.

Mary Pickford can be a doll, a village belle, or a church angel. Her powers as a doll are hinted at in the title of the production: Such a Little Queen. I remember her when she was a village belle in that film that came out before producers or actors were known by name. It was sugar-sweet. It was called: What the Daisy Said. If these productions had conformed to their titles sincerely, with the highest photoplay art we would have had two more examples for this chapter.

Why do the people love Mary? Not on account of the Daniel Frohman style of handling her appearances. He presents her to us in what are almost the old-fashioned stage terms: the productions energetic and full of painstaking detail but dominated by a dream that is a theatrical hybrid. It is neither good moving picture nor good stage play. Yet Mary could be cast as a cloudy Olympian or a church angel if her managers wanted her to be such. She herself was transfigured in the Dawn of Tomorrow, but the film-version of that play was merely a well mounted melodrama.

Why do the people love Mary? Because of a certain aspect of her face in her highest mood. Botticelli painted her portrait many centuries ago when by some necromancy she appeared to him in this phase of herself. There is in the Chicago Art Institute at the top of the stairs on the north wall a noble copy of a fresco by that painter, the copy by Mrs. MacMonnies. It is very near the Winged Victory of Samothrace. In the picture the muses sit enthroned. The loveliest of them all is a startling replica of Mary.

The people are hungry for this fine and spiritual thing that Botticelli painted in the faces of his muses and heavenly creatures. Because the mob catch the very glimpse of it in Mary's face, they follow her night after night in the films. They are never quite satisfied with the plays, because the managers are not artists enough to know they should sometimes put her into sacred pictures and not have her always the village hoyden, in plays not even hoydenish. But perhaps in this argument I have but betrayed myself as Mary's infatuated partisan.

So let there be recorded here the name of another actress who is always in the intimate-and-friendly mood and adapted to close-up interiors, Marguerite Clark. She is endowed by nature to act, in the same film, the eight-year-old village pet, the irrepressible sixteen-year-old, and finally the shining bride of twenty. But no production in which she acts that has happened to come under my eye has done justice to these possibilities. The transitions from one of these stages to the other are not marked by the producer with sufficient delicate graduation, emphasis, and contrast. Her plots have been but sugared nonsense, or swashbuckling ups and downs. She shines in a bevy of girls. She has sometimes been given the bevy. . . .

■ ■ ■ ■

Movies in the World War (1939), Lewis Jacobs

Perhaps the best summary of the contribution of movies to American life during the First World War is a chapter of Lewis Jacobs's classic study, *The Rise of the American Film*. Although the relationship between film content and government policy was not as fully and as officially articulated during the First World War as it was in the Second (see pages 453–76), the earlier war provided extremely valuable lessons on the use of film for both instruction and uplift which would become important some twenty-five years later. Professor Jacobs was one of the first Americans to make a vocation of film scholarship; he continues to research, to write, and to teach on the university level today.

The critical war period proved motion pictures to be one of the most powerful social agencies of modern times, especially when mobilized officially as a propaganda tool. Films of these years present a vivid and lively picture of American opinion changing from tolerance to intolerance, from progressivism to reaction, from pacifism to militarism. Not only did they reflect the rising war spirit, but they were used to intensify it, to "sell" the public on participation in the world conflict.

The outbreak of war in Europe in 1914 startled and shocked a peace-minded America. The growth of pacifistic sentiment in the United States in the preceding years had been phenomenal in speed and vigor. In 1906 Andrew Carnegie had given ten million dollars for the establishment of

"Movies in the World War," from Lewis Jacobs's *The Rise of the American Film* (Teachers College Press, 1968), was originally published in 1939.

the New York Peace Society; in 1911 wealthy Edwin Ginn had endowed the World Peace Foundation; in 1912 the American Peace Society— the first of its kind in the world—had been revitalized. The ideal of pacifism had been carried into religious quarters by the Church Peace League. Business circles had been similarly influenced by the National Association of Cosmopolitan Clubs—the organization that was later to sail for Europe in Henry Ford's historic Peace Ship.

Despite this ascendancy of pacifism in America, pro-war sentiment began growing rapidly soon after the outbreak of war in Europe. Until now united in a firm anti-war stand, the nation found itself suddenly divided by conflicting opinions. Partisan and opposition groups hurled accusations at one another, and pacifist ideology split into a hundred inconsistent variations. In President Woodrow Wilson the American people saw a staunch advocate of peace, and most of them for a time rallied around his neutrality policy. But during the next two years that policy was undermined. Regarded with mounting disfavor, it was finally abandoned for outright pro-war demonstrations. The transition from peaceful idealism to the violent war passion in two short years culminated, in 1917, with the entrance of the United States into the World War on the side of the Allies. Nowhere is that transition revealed more patently than in the newly found language of movies.

At the beginning of the conflict in 1914 the American movie industry was poorly prepared to act as a war-news agency for the nation. Within two months' time, however, hundreds of appropriate political and military films were ready for public showing. At first, to meet the emergency, old newsreels of military maneuvers and parades, views of Berlin, Paris, and St. Petersburg; and pictures of the Kaiser, King Albert, Franz Josef, Woodrow Wilson, Theodore Roosevelt, Taft, Poincaré, and Nicholas of Russia, were shown at random. All the nations involved in the war had equal attention on the screen and were applauded in accordance with the President's neutrality proclamation, which urged people to maintain a non-partisan attitude. Germans were represented, on the whole, without undue animosity. The United States even imported German films that presented the German side of the war: *The Cruise of the M, The Log of U-35, Behind the German Lines. The German Side of the War,* in particular, attracted audiences of thousands. All these films were shown in American theatres as late as 1916. The tendency to sympathize with England and the other Allies, however, was apparent in the titles of otherwise objective newsreel compilations: *The Battling British, The Kaiser Challenges, The Great War in Europe, Germania, England's Menace.* The general public's attitude toward the European struggle was summed up best, perhaps, in the title of the picture *War Is Hell.*

Neutrality and pacifistic sentiment were further indicated in most of the war dramas which movie producers began to turn out as rapidly as possible. The war drama *Neutrality* pointed the lesson that in a neutral country one should be neutral. The story showed how a Frenchman and German now in the United States remained friends, despite the antagonism of their now fighting fatherlands. It did not attempt to paint the German character as villainous, rather it attempted to ease the mounting friction among the various nationalities represented in the United States.

Strong preachments against war, consistent with the public's attitude, emphasized again and again, in the spectacular style of the day, war's futility, destructiveness, and tragedy. *Civilization, or He Who Returned,* one of the outstanding pictures of the day, directed by Thomas Ince, preached peace in the lofty terms characteristic of Wilsonian idealism. In this picture the spirit of Christ returns to earth in the body of a great soldier who, insulted and persecuted while trying to restore the world to peace, fiinally triumphs. The film attempted a profound interpretation of the grim disaster—the bereavements, disunions, tragedies— caused by war. It was said to have helped to re-elect Wilson on his platform, "He kept us out of war."

War Brides, a distinguished film directed by Herbert Brenon, was another anti-war production which purported to show the unwillingness of the German people at large to participate in war, although the reference to Germany was veiled. The story was both strikingly conceived and strikingly executed.[1] Joan (Alla Nazimova), a vigorous young woman, begins to question the sufferings of her fellow workers in a factory town, "underpaid and overworked." Arousing them to strike, she leads them to victory and thus gains the confidence and leadership of the town. She falls in love with a farmer and marries him.

Then war is declared. Her husband goes to the front and, with his three younger brothers, is killed. The king of the country soon decrees that men shall marry all the available single girls and produce more offspring. (The girls who marry under the decree are the "war brides.") Now pregnant, Joan foresees the fate of her child in future wars, and decides to try to win over the women and stop the present war. As her campaign becomes more effective, Joan is arrested, but since she is the expectant mother of a soldier she cannot be executed. She escapes from prison and organizes the women to demonstrate before the king on his return from the front to his palace. Robed in black, contrary to the law, the women greet him with anti-war chants. The king tells Joan that there will always be war. Thereupon Joan, with the shout "No more children

1. It is described fully in *Photoplay,* 1916.

for war!" shoots herself. The women take up her body, hold it aloft as a symbol, and with renewed courage determine to carry on their campaign.

Exceedingly well received when shown, *War Brides* was suppressed upon our entrance into the World War on the grounds that "the philosophy of this picture is so easily misunderstood by unthinking people that it has been found necessary to withdraw it from circulation for the duration of the war."

Unlike *Civilization* and *War Brides,* the pacifistic film *Intolerance*, conceived and made at a time when the national viewpoint was predominantly peace-minded, appeared at the flood of the tide of preparedness and pro-war films. Because it was perhaps the strongest outcry against the forces that lead to war, the very forces that were then being used to whip the nation into the war spirit, the film was nationally condemned and religiously boycotted. Being out of step with changed public opinion, *Intolerance* was so great a failure financially that it led to the wrecking of Griffith's (its director-producer's) career. If *Intolerance* had been released six months earlier, it would no doubt have been passionately acclaimed.

Pro-war agitation rapidly mounted despite government disapproval. Preparedness, regarded dubiously by the populace, was soon being earnestly urged by many groups. Its outstanding advocate in the movie industry was J. Stuart Blackton, always a pronounced nationalist. An old hand at patriotic propaganda, he now made some of the first flaming pro-war films: *The Battle Cry of Peace, Wake up America!, Womanhood, The Glory of the Nation.*

Of *The Battle Cry of Peace* Blackton himself said:[2]

> It was propaganda for the United States to enter the war. It was made deliberately for that purpose. It was against the administration because at that time Mr. Wilson was arguing for neutrality and peace, and talking about being too proud to fight. But nevertheless *The Battle Cry of Peace* went out as a call to arms. It had collaterally associated with it Theodore Roosevelt. I lived next door to him at Oyster Bay, New York . . . he and I were very good friends. We worked out a very splendid idea. We had the Army, Navy, Church and State, represented in that picture. . . . Roosevelt said, "When you have the Army, Navy, Church and State, you don't want anything else." Mr. Roosevelt would not get into the picture.

The film, based on Hudson Maxim's *Defenseless America,* emphasized an armament program for America as the only means of maintaining peace. Its treatment set the style for all future anti-German propaganda

2. In a lecture at the University of Southern California, February 20, 1929.

dramas. "Huns" were portrayed as leering, mustached, lustful scoundrels whose only instincts were those of rape and plunder. So incendiary was the film that Henry Ford wrathfully denounced it in full-page newspaper advertisements, pointing out that Maxim's munitions-corporation stock was on the market and that the film was merely a ruse to promote his and other war merchants' profit. But fewer people read the advertisements than saw the film. Preparedness, moreover, had become deeply instilled by this time in the national mind. In October 1916 a reader sent in the following comment to *Film Pictorial:* "Every American including Henry Ford should see *The Battle Cry of Peace.* . . . We would better be up and doing, or it will be too late. . . ."

Preparedness and pro-war sentiment, supported by Blackton, began to supersede the pacifistic and neutral attitude for which Wilson stood. Nationalist zeal was stimulated by picture slides issued by the New York Mayor's Committee in National Defense. The committee's chairman, Jesse Lasky, one of the leading producers in the movie industry, declared: "If you are an American, you should be proud to say so." More and more movie producers settled down to serving the new cause of militarism and nationalism.

Pro-war and preparedness propaganda was now subtly and astutely injected into satires, comedies, dramas, romances. *In-Again, Out-Again* jibed at the pacifist-minded sweetheart of a preparedness hero, and finally exposed the leading "pacifist" as a manufacturer of explosives. A baby-food factory was shown canning shrapnel, a wheat shreddery loading high explosives, a pill foundry making mines. In *A Man Without a Country* a pacifist was persuaded to become a recruit. *Motherhood* was eloquently summarized by a reviewer of the day as "a smug, diabetic preachment of American insular security. . . . All I can say is that it will be a mournful sugar plum for pacifists in hiding."

Battling for one's country, espionage, and other war activities were glorified and romanticized in *The Wall Between, Shell 42, The Flying Torpedo, On Dangerous Ground,* and *The Fall of the Nation.* How evident the strategy of the movie propagandists was, is apparent in the lengthy protest that appeared in *Motion Picture Magazine* in February 1916:

> Strangely enough, these pictures have not presented to our view the actual proof of the toll of war. They have not shown us the millions of widows and the millions of orphans that are the results of this conflict. They have not proved to us the hopelessness, the despair, the hunger and suffering that have been inevitable consequences of the War. And—having failed to present these consequences . . .—these pictures have not been logical arguments in favor of

Peace. They have been military—they have been martial in the extreme. . . .

Public opinion, however, was being quickly heated to a fighting temper. Anglophiles multiplied; sympathy for the Allies became the fashion. Leaders in the movement for international peace, heretofore respected as humanitarians, were regarded with increasing distrust and contempt by the man in the street. Popular emotions began to be rallied for America's participation in the War. With such noble phrases as a "war to end all wars" and "make the world safe for democracy," President Wilson finally asked Congress to take sides against Germany. The Carnegie Peace Foundation led the way for other peace organizations by announcing in the words of Charles and Mary Beard,[3] that "it could serve the ideal of its founders best by lending all its strength to the prosecution of the armed conflict to a triumphant conclusion."

When the United States declared war officially on Friday, April 5, 1917, the transition from mere anti-pacifism to out-and-out pro-war passion was already complete. As soon as war was declared, pacifists, socialists, Germans, and unionists became suspects. Refusal to salute the flag became cause enough for imprisonment and persecution. Mrs. Carrie Chapman Catt, the feminist leader, condemned Representative Jeanette Rankin's lone vote against war as an unpatriotic stand not to be countenanced by the women of the nation. Spy scares filled the news hourly. War posters, parades, war tunes, flag waving, and singing of the national anthem on all occasions sold super-patriotism to the people and kept their excitement at fever heat. The moving pictures were immediately conscripted along with other social agencies.

Peace pictures were placed under a government ban; all anti-war films became so much junk. Movie companies zealously produced pictures in key with the emotional necessities of a warring nation and, like newspapers and other organs of propaganda, distorted, omitted, or deliberately misrepresented facts for the sake of immediate ends.

The Committee on Public Information, a federal organization with George Creel as chairman, created a Division of Films to sell the war to America. Two days after the war declaration, posters, slides, and slogans filled the screens. Four patriotic dramas were produced by the Division in quick succession: *Pershing's Crusaders*, *America's Answer*, *Under Four Flags*, *The Official War Review*. The Exhibitors' Branch of the National Association of the Motion Picture Industry, organized in peace time by William A. Brady, was appointed by President Wilson to organize the private producers as a fighting arm of the government. In New

3. *The Rise of American Civilization*, p. 537.

York City a newly organized bureau of motion pictures produced two feature pictures for recruiting purposes, showing mobilization and the life and problems of the army and navy. Fourteen sets of slides were released at once to be used daily until pictures were ready.

Motion picture theatres became centers for patriotic rallies. The populace was urged to attend; the war tax on admission prices was explained as a chance for every citizen to do his bit. The movie, a quick and vital means of communication between the government and the people, became the traveling salesman for war and war discipline. It imparted the latest "news," taught citizens how to help shamed "slackers" and encouraged recruiting, and glorified fighting for one's country, loyalty to an ideal, heroism, and sacrifices for a great and noble cause.

The financing of the war was aided by films promoting the sale of Liberty Bonds throughout the nation. A "trailer" distributed to nearly all theatres showed President Wilson dictating his Buy-Liberty-Bonds message to the American people. Adolph Zukor lent a helping hand by distributing 70,000 slides and 500,000 feet of film which appealed for public support of the bond issue. *Sic 'Em Sam* typified the general appeal of the movies to the fighting instincts of audiences.

In teaching war discipline and war organization to citizens the motion picture was remarkably effective. Slides, shorts, and "picturettes," featuring popular favorites such as Marguerite Clark, Mabel Normand, and Elsie Ferguson, pleaded on behalf of the U.S. Food Administration for "economy for democracy." The Red Cross also found movies a lucrative means of arousing support. Hundreds of Red Cross "trailers," including *The Spirit of the Red Cross,* by James Montgomery Flagg, were displayed everywhere.

Screen players, "symbols" of American manhood and womanhood, stepped down from their pedestals to lead in the mobilization of patriotic activity. They co-operated in Red Cross drives, exhorted audiences to be loyal, become "minute men," soldiers, or nurses, and appeared on the screen to urge people to buy government bonds. Fan magazines on page after page displayed photographs of the public's favorites in uniform, buying Liberty Bonds, knitting for "the boys Over There," and training as Red Cross nurses. "Fatty" Arbuckle, in the peculiar position of having to apologize for his fatness in view of the food-conservation drive, was shown holding out his trousers to indicate how much weight he was losing in doing his bit. At a tremendous patriotic rally of motion picture people, Cecil B. DeMille was master of ceremonies, and Dustin Farnum, in uniform, passed the hat. William S. Hart, Douglas Fairbanks, and Mary Pickford were a few among many movie notables who made speeches and cross-country tours in support of Liberty Loan drives.

Having seen their sons go overseas to battle and die, movie-goers in time began to feel hostile toward prominent screen actors who stayed safe at home. Some bad public feeling was excited when J. Warren Kerrigan, answering demands that he enlist, declared that the world needed his art now more than ever. People reacted cynically; criticisms were hurled at him. Movie producers rushed to close the breach, explaining that many of the stars who appeared extremely youthful on the screen were, in reality, closer to thirty-five than to twenty-five years of age, and therefore had sound reasons for not enlisting. They assured the public that when the government was in need of them, these men would wholeheartedly do their duty. At the same time the producers pointed out that movies generally were valuable for entertainment in the camps, and that movie actresses were the sweethearts and inspirations of countless soldiers.

D. W. Griffith and Herbert Brenon were both invited to make authentic movies of the war at the front. *Intolerance* having brought down international condemnation on his head, Griffith reversed his pacifistic stand and accepted the invitation. Fan magazines now pictured him in full uniform in the trenches. The film he made abroad, *Hearts of the World,* showed German militarism as a frightful threat to civilization and demanded that it be wiped from the face of the earth.

Very little of the war "news" was authentic. Exhibitors did not hesitate to prepare war bulletins which they assumed approximated the situation abroad: these bulletins always represented the Allies as winning, and thus kept up the public morale. Nationalism was inspired by glowing tributes to the American heritage, as in *The Settlement of America, Independence, World Recognition, American Achievement.* Flag waving and super-patriotism marked such films as *My Own United States, The Great Love,* and *Patria.* The last, a serial made by William Randolph Hearst, glorified not only American womanhood in the person of Irene Castle, but the Du Pont family, munitions makers. The government ordered its anti-Japanese sentiment to be deleted, since Japan was now an ally of England.

Sympathy for the Allies was intensified by films about England and France. *The Victoria Cross, Whom the Gods Destroy, An Enemy of the King,* and *Heroism of a Spy* romantically praised the Englishman and his history. *Joan the Woman* spectacularly pointed out that it was the inherited duty of Anglo-Saxons to aid France and thus expiate their part in the killing of France's savior, Joan of Arc, centuries before. *Hearts of the World, Somewhere in France, Daughter of France, The Belgian,* and *For France* (which *Wids,* the trade paper, said "shows too many men being killed to please American families today") idealized France and

kept the flame of kinship burning. French-produced films, such as the famous Sarah Bernhardt plea, *Mothers of France,* supported American pro-French propaganda.

While England, France, and even Russia were depicted as heroic and godly nations, Germany was painted utterly black, without a saving grace. Atrocity films that rivaled newspaper headlines in sensationalism stigmatized the whole German nation as a mass of "Kaisers." No longer was it necessary, as it had been until the declaration of war, to veil the identity of the Opposing Power. "The ruthless monarch" was now revealed as the Kaiser, "the military nation" as Germany. In the fashion established by Blackton, the "Huns" were characterized as brutal, barbaric, shameless. Nothing was too savage and uncivilized for "these primitive beasts."

A Daughter of France, War and Woman, A Maid of France, and *The Little American* were only a few of the many films in which raping, pillaging, village-burning by the Germans were featured. In *The Little American,* Mary Pickford, America's symbol of sweetness and innocence, is saved at the eleventh hour from a fate worse than death at the hands of barbaric Huns. A French spy arrested by the Germans, she demands an explanation of their savage action in raping a fellow-prisoner. The Prussian colonel, with a sneer under his waxed mustache, tells her that "My men must have relaxation."

Photoplay, reviewing *For France,* declared:[4]

> There is, of course, pillaging of the farmhouse and the terrorization of people by the Hun horde—and such applause as burst forth spontaneously when the leading Hun offenders were shot! . . . *For France* means for our own homes and fire-sides.

The Kaiser became the symbol of hatefulness for the whole nation. No epithet was too vile for him. Pictures were titled *The Kaiser, Beast of Berlin; To Hell with the Kaiser; The Prussian Cur.* Charlie Chaplin in *Shoulder Arms* heaped ridicule upon this arch villain of the world. Particularly notable for its picture of the German ruler was *The Kaiser, Beast of Berlin,* advertising as "giving an insight into the man guiding the most horrible outrages." Rupert Julian, hated villain of the screen, portrayed the Kaiser as the "enemy of world progress," weak, insane, arrogant, and colossally conceited. He was nationally greeted with spontaneous and hearty hissing. Americans were thus conditioned to pour all their aroused spleen into one stream. In their minds the Kaiser was mercilessly burned at the stake, and the heat and light concealed, at least for a time, other possible objects of hate behind the blaze.

4. January 1918.

Other films were designed to provoke Americans to seek vengeance. *Till I Come Back to You* urged the punishment of Germany for the Belgian "atrocities." *Lest We Forget* showed the heroine defying Prussianism and preaching vengeance. Germany had to be chastised also for her designs on America, as was made clear in *Inside the Lines, The Spy, Daughter of Destiny,* and *Joan of Plattsburg.*

Perhaps the most powerful vehicles of hatred were the allegedly authentic newsreels of German cruelty. One of the most sensational of these films was *My Four Years in Germany,* based on Ambassador James Gerard's book. Supposed to be the camera record of a tour through German prison camps and courts, it pointed out that Germans now in America had the same reason for fighting their fatherland that the rest of the world had: namely, to stamp out Prussian cruelty.

The German Curse in Russia, advertised as the 'inside facts" on the revolution in Russia, aroused Americans further by showing that German "lies," if given the chance to breed here, might do to America what they had done to Russia: "The world believes Russia sold out her Allies knowingly, but my camera will show that it was the German propaganda of lies that undermined this great country. . . ."

Another film dealing with the Kaiser's evil plots against America was *The Evil Eye,* compiled by William J. Flynn, Chief of the U. S. Secret Service, which showed the defensive secret warfare being waged by the government at home.

Anti-German sentiment was pitched so high that soon everything and everyone with a tincture of the Germanic were despised. So strong was this passion that Gustav von Seyffertitz, a leading player of the screen, was forced to change his professional name. According to the publicity, he had "a perfect right" to his new name, C. Butler Clonebaught, as "it belonged to his mother." But other complications created by the anti-German fashion were not so easily coped with. The greatest task was that of convincing millions of people of German extraction, now living peacefully in America, that Germany was no longer the home of friends. German-Americans had to be "educated" to hate their German relatives, to despise German culture, to be passionately loyal to their new country. *The Immigrant,* a government-made picture, taught the Americanized German-born that they owed first allegiance to the United States and must salute the Stars and Stripes.

To inspire and stimulate patriotism, films varied from plain recruiting advertisements, as in *The Spirit of '17, Vive la France, Over There, A Call to Arms,* and *Draft 258,* to dramas shaming the slacker, as in *The Man Who Was Afraid, The Slacker* (in a potpourri of American history containing tableaux of Paul Revere, Lee's surrender, Abraham Lincoln, and Nathan Hale), *The Unbeliever,* and *A Man Without a Country.*

The recruiting of women in a moral sense was just as vital as enlisting men in the army or navy. Such films as *Sweetheart of the Doomed, Missing, An Alien Enemy, Womanhood, Daughter of Destiny,* and *Betsy Ross* praised woman's heroism, bravery, loyalty, and sacrifice. Women and young girls were taught to smile and sing at home while their loved ones carried out their duty at the front. In DeMille's spectacle *Joan the Woman,* Geraldine Farrar inspired feminine militarist sentiment as Joan of Arc. This film, with its panorama of war scenes and dream effects, ritual-like in their presentation, aroused patriotism through its appeal to the richest emotional sources: love and religion.

Another film, *The Whispering Chorus,* employed the Enoch Arden theme to exploit "the religious teaching of loyalty to principle and duty as well as to flag and country." *We Can't Have Everything,* dealing with "the restless spirit of the times," advocated self-denial and self-sacrifice as ways to win the war. Like other films, this one urged women in particular to give freely, to sacrifice heroically, not to mind the tragedy of losing a son, to be brave "Gold Star mothers."

The common stay-at-home man was proved to be extremely important to the nation. *Berlin Via America* showed an unknown citizen heroically risking his life by posing as a traitor in order to make a triumphant raid on Berlin possible. *The Gown of Destiny* revealed how the poor man could be as valuable to his country as the rich man who, in exemplary fashion, celebrated his wedding anniversary by giving three ambulances to France. Mr. and Mrs. Sidney Drew in *The Patriot* comically showed how Henry and his wife decided to out-Hoover Hoover in conserving food. *For Freedom of the World,* an eighty-five minute film on doing one's bit, covered about every possible angle of patriotism. A mother gives up her son; a father leaves his child; a husband bids farewell to his wife; a slacker is converted. Enlistment, trench life, Red Cross work, and Over the Top are all exploited as themes, and an aphasia victim is cured upon seeing the American flag. In such films no avenue of appeal to human emotions was neglected.

One of the noblest reasons for America's prosecution of the war was that this was not only "a war to end all wars," but "a sacrifice for the democratization of the world." Again and again pictures showed that in the trenches all classes were leveled; the rich man's son and the poor man's son fought shoulder to shoulder. *Safe for Democracy, The Pride of New York,* and *The Battle Cry of Liberty* predicted that a wonderful sociological melioration would result from the war, that the benefits of the people's struggles and sacrifices were to be shared by everyone regardless of class and wealth, that all together were now bettering the world.

The American flag was waved on the slightest provocation. So often was it waved without apparent reason, except perhaps to lend dignity to worthless photoplays, that movie-goers in time criticized needless displays of the flag as in bad taste and insulting to the flag itself. Although such criticism was open and vigorous, the flag waving continued.

Battle scenes of every description abounded in films. Movie-goers were insatiably interested in them, perhaps because every individual, through his soldier relatives or friends, was personnally concerned. Bloody, frightful engagements in the trenches and in No Man's Land were exhibited by the thousands, and apparently the more the public saw of such films, the more they wanted to see them. Pictures were terrifying in their depiction of mysterious gases destroying cities and helpless human beings. Airplanes, machine guns, submarines, and other modern war instruments were represented with more regard for effect than for truth.

War pictures conventionally ended with the soldier boy safe behind the firing line in France. When one picture, *The Slacker,* did not follow the usual pattern, *Photoplay* (its critical faculties not altogether impaired by propaganda) commented:[5]

> Mr. Cabanne [the director] had the self-restraint to send the soldier boy off to war and end the picture there instead of Inceing and Blacktoning through a reel of smoke and horror to an amorous half nelson. . . .

The movies became a sort of military textbook in which those at home could follow their sons' and brothers' experiences in the training camps. To reinforce the psychological effects of such popular songs as "Keep the Home Fires Burning," "Over There," "Smile a While," "A Baby's Prayer at Twilight," "My Buddy Lies over the Ocean," the screen showed loyal kisses, courageous good-bys and "home stuff," hospital pictures, German prisoners being brought in, and the ambulance boys at work.

In the Allied countries, no less than in the United States, pictures proved of incalculable help to the governments. Not only did they bolster public morale, but they proved valuable emotional safety valves. *Photoplay* editorialized,[6]

> The reports of Mr. Hoover and his aides and successors in Belgium tell us that no matter how destitute a district, or how utterly dependent on funds from America, a portion of every family's pittance was put aside for the beloved cinema, and the oppressed Belgians went out of their troubles by going through the screen to other lands.

At the front movies were also a salve and inspiration for the fighting soldiers. Ninety feet under shell-torn Verdun crude theatres were re-

5. November 1917.
6. July 1918.

ported to have been constructed for the army. Projector operators, exchange men, and necessary mechanical equipment for first-class moving-picture presentations were provided by both army and navy.

Army cantonments—cities with an average of 40,000 population—had theatres of their own built. It was advertised that one of the many advantages soldiers enjoyed was their exemption from paying any war tax. To relieve them of the five- or ten-cent admission price, "smileage" was invented. This was a system whereby railway mileage books, sent as gifts to soldiers, were accepted as tickets of admissions.

Ernest A. Dench in *Motion Pictures*[7] reported,

> As is perhaps natural, comedy is the thing, for the soldier wants his thoughts to be taken away from the serious work ahead of him. . . . If a soldier has survived a big battle he will say, "I was in the picture show at Ypres."

One of the greatest favorites was Charlie Chaplin. Young English subalterns with a sense of humor cultivated his characteristic mustache, and cut-outs of Charlie were set up as mascots. Even the movie companies were represented appreciatively. Dugouts were named after movie trademarks, as Keystone Kottage and Vitagraph Village.

Movies proved enormously helpful in hospitals, also. Nicknamed "The Soul Doctor," they relieved the monotony of hospital existence and helped the wounded to forget their misery. Often the pictures were projected on the ceilings so that prostrate sufferers could watch them.

American films thus carried the banner of "victory for democracy" into all the corners of the Allied countries, and helped to relieve the stress of the times whenever shown. The motion picture industry was not unaware of its powerful role in the war. Louella O. Parsons summarized that role:[8]

> If German vandalism could reach overseas, the Kaiser would order every moving picture studio crushed to dust and every theatre blown to atoms. There has been no more effective ammunition aimed at the Prussian empire than these pictures of German atrocities. . . . The followers of the cinema have seen with their own eyes how German militarism is waged against civilization. They have seen the rape of Belgium, the devastation of France and the evil designs against America. . . . And while these films have been raising the temperature of the Allies' patriotism to a blood heat, Germany has been gnashing its teeth.

7. October 1916.
8. *Photoplay*, September 1918.

Astonishingly effective for so young a medium, the movie was among the most valuable war-time assets the United States government had at its disposal. Conversely, when the armistice was signed, the motion picture was enlisted in the promotion of international understanding and goodwill.

But the movies were themselves all but transformed by World War influences, industrially, socially, artistically. The entire European continent having been drawn into the conflict, American motion pictures had the world to themselves. Hollywood became securely established as the international production center for movies. Having become recognized as a leading agency for propaganda and as a remarkable social therapeutic and palliative, the motion picture was viewed with new and deeper respect. On the other hand, given a message to deliver to the public, movie makers learned how to deliver it eloquently and entertainingly.

By the close of 1918 the industry had grown self-assured and was consciously directing itself as big business putting on the screens what the populace sought in life. When the war ended, producers feared that the motion picture's great era was done, but a greater era was actually about to begin.

■ ■ ■ ■

The Sins of Hollywood (1922)

The Sins of Hollywood was a small pamphlet, published anonymously in 1922, just after the Rappe-Arbuckle murder case hit the headlines. Subtitled, "An Exposé of Movie Vice," the book presents a series of the most salacious and scandalous Hollywood clichés (without naming any actual names), including detailed descriptions of drinking, dope smoking and taking, sex orgies, strip-poker parties, kept men and women, sodomy, and so forth. These are the first two chapters of (as the title page announces) "A Group of Actual Happenings Reported and Written by a Hollywood Newspaper Man."

The Reasons for the "Sins of Hollywood"

To the public:
The sins of Hollywood are facts—NOT FICTION!
    The stories in this volume are true stories—the people are real people—

The Sins of Hollywood (Hollywood Publishing Co., 1922).

Most of those involved in the events reported herein are today occupying high places in motion pictures—popular idols—applauded, lauded and showered with gold by millions of men, women and children—ESPECIALLY THE WOMEN AND CHILDREN!

To the boys and girls of the land these mock heroes and heroines have been pictured and painted, for box office purposes, as the living symbols of all the virtues—

An avalanche of propaganda by screen and press has imbued them with every ennobling trait.

Privately they have lived, and are still living, lives of wild debauchery.

In more than one case licentiousness and incest have been the only rungs in the ladders on which they have climbed to fame and fortune!

Unfaithful and cruelly indifferent to the worship of the youth of the land, they have led or are leading such lives as may, any day, precipitate yet another nation-wide scandal and again shatter the ideals, the dreams, the castles, the faith of our boys and girls!

It is for these reasons that the SINS OF HOLLYWOOD are given to the public—

That a great medium of national expression may be purified—taken from the hands of those who have misused it—that the childish faith of our boys and girls may again be made sacred!

Fully eighty per cent of those engaged in motion pictures are high-grade citizens—self-respecting and respected.

In foolish fear of injuring the industry, Hollywood has permitted less than one per cent of its population to stain its name.

The facts reported in these stories have long been an open book to the organized producers—No need to tell them—they knew!

They knew of the horde of creatures of easy morals who hovered about the industry and set the standard of price—decided what good, clean women would have to pay—have to give—in order to succeed—

They knew of the macqueraux—of the scum that constituted the camp followers of their great stars. They knew of the wantonness of their leading women—

They knew about the yachting parties—the wild orgies at road houses and private homes—

They knew about Vernon and its wild life—Tia Juana and its mad, drunken revels—

They knew about the "kept" women—and the "kept" men—

They knew about the prominent people among them who were living in illicit relationship—

There was a time at one studio when every star, male and female, was carrying on an open liason—The producer could not help knowing it.

Eight months before the crash that culminated in the Arbuckle cataclysm they knew the kind of parties Roscoe was giving—and some of them were glad to participate in them—

They knew conditions—knew about the "hop" and the "dope"—but they took the stand that it was "none of our business"—

Their business was piling up advance deposits from theater owners and manipulating the motion picture stock market.

They frowned on all attempts to speak the truth—

Any publication that attempted to reveal the real conditions—to cleanse the festering sores—was quickly pounced upon as an "enemy of the industry"—A subsidized trade press helped in this work!

Any attempt to bring about reform was called "hurting the industry."

It was the lapses and laxities of the producer that precipitated the censorship agitation—that led a nauseated nation, determined to cleanse the Augean stables of the screen, into the dangerous notion of censorship—almost fatally imperilling two sacred principles of democracy—freedom of speech and freedom of the press!

They have made "box office" capital of everything—Nothing has been too vile to exploit—

They created the male vamp—

Nothing was sacred—nothing was personal—if it had publicity possibilities—

In the Daniels case they exploited the courts and made them a laughing stock—

At this moment Taylor's tragic death is being exploited in connection with his last production—

* * *

If the screen is to be "cleaned-up," the sores must be cut open—the pus and corruption removed—This always hurts! But it is the only known way!

THE AUTHOR
Hollywood, April 1, 1922

DOPE!

During the throbbing, feverish years of the World War all roads led to France or—Hollywood.

The conglomerate, nondescript mass of beings of every hue and type that swept over the battlefields was no more complex in its composition, no more a mixture of oil and water, than were the high and the low, the vile, the vain and the vicious that made up the mob which swarmed into Hollywood to dip its fingers into the pot of gold that was being poured from the movie crucible.

No mining camp ever equalled it. No mad, lurid, wild and woolly border town ever attracted so many men and women of so high a station in life or so vilely sunk as did Hollywood.

None of the country's historic bonanza towns ever beheld one half the real money that Moviedom bathed in.

The Hollywood of those days will go down in history as the Rainbow Age of the mountebank and the mummer.

The circus, the Uncle Tom show, the medicine show, the carnivals, the physical culture fakes, the pony shows, the wild west outfits, the concert halls, the dives, the honk-a-tonks—and in many cases—the bawdy houses—all contributed their quota to the studios of Hollywood.

With them came men and women who had achieved world wide fame —actors, authors, dramatists, composers, dancers, whose names are indelibly written in the list of the world's great artists.

When the shower of gold fell this latter group held its wits—in the main. Here and there one dropped into the mire of licentiousness and incest. But this was rare.

The great actor of the spoken drama rarely got very far in the movies. He refused to fit into the scheme as laid out by those who held the purse strings.

It was the upstarts, the poor uncouth, ill-bred "roughnecks," many of whom are to-day famous stars, and who never knew there was so much money in the world, who made the Sins of Hollywood the glaring, red sins they are to-day.

After the first few weeks of plenty, of full feeding, the days of penury and vagabondage faded into the dim vistas of the past. Then came indulgence in the common, ordinary vices of the average being. And still the money lasted and even increased. Then the appetites became jaded and each tried to outdissipate the other.

Strip poker parties of both sexes, wild drinking debauches and lewdness, motor cars in designs and colors that screamed and shrieked—dogs and cats as aids to stimulate the imagination. The odors of the Tenderloin and the lobster palaces. Poor, futile mimicry!

Then one day a certain well-known and muchly adored heart-breaking star of the so-called "manly" type taught them something new. And this is how it came about:

This star—who shall be called Walter[1]—had tried out something. In his mad endeavor to provide for himself a thrill not written down in the Movie Vicealogue, Walter sought out several habitues of the underworld of Los Angeles and visited with them, consorted with them for the purpose, he explained, of obtaining "local color."

1. Ed. Note: "Walter" is probably Wallace Reid.

Once they induced him to try "a shot of hop." It was great, he told some of his friends and "Yes men." They agreed that if he said it was great, it was indeed great.

Yes, Walter smoked an opium pipe and went back for more. He then tried "snuffing" a bit of cocaine. That too gave him the desired kick. He "took a few shots in the arm." Ah, that was still better. He was getting on.

But why have his pleasures all alone? Walter was a good sort. He wanted his friends to taste of the sweets of life as he found them. Here's what he would do—he would give a "dope party."

Obviously he could not hold this party at his own home. His wife—she, too, a star—would object. She didn't even know that Walter had been trying out various kinds of dope.

But that was easy. Walter merely leased a cabin in Laurel Canyon and invited a few select friends to come and enjoy something new. Many attended: Margaret and Mae, Vincent and Jay, Frank and Louise, Mary and Jack and Juanita—all good fellows and friends of Walter.

Oh, yes, there was a Chinaman there with his layout—pipes and little pellets of opium.

But first they must try "a shot in the arm." My! How they enjoyed that "shot in the arm." It thrilled the blase actor folk as they had not been thrilled since Clara Kimball Young auctioned off her teddy bears, removing them right before all the crowd.

"Sniffing cocaine" through a little tube, one end of which hung inside a vial of "snow," was another pastime which all hugely enjoyed. It exalted and made other beings of them. It was thoroughly a worth-while party, his guests told Walter, and he was pleased—very pleased, indeed, if he had succeeded in bringing a few thrills into their uneventful lives—lives, too, made up of many thrills, but little else.

But the crowning event was when the Chinaman entered and gave each of them a pipe and a pellet of opium.

Walter had fitted up cosy lounges for them to lie in. Soft, clinging curtains hung about them, pink-shaded lamps shed a soft glow, and the Chinaman worked fast and soft-footedly.

Luckily the night was long—it was Saturday. None of them had to appear for work on Sunday. So all the rest of the night and far into the next day did they loll there upon the soft cushions and dream—and—well, there are things that cannot be printed even for truth's sake.

One by one they staggered homeward, vowing to return—any time—and partake of handsome Walter's hospitality.

And they did. For that was but the beginning. Today the Chinaman has increased his output of pipes and pellets. He has two assistants and he holds himself in readiness to answer a summons at a moment's notice to appear at somebody's home and help to make the night short and the dreams long.

Today the dope peddlar is a common sight around the streets of Hollywood. And once, not so long ago, the Federal officers called upon Handsome Walter and talked things over with him. They wanted to know if he was the go-between—the man who acted as middleman for the actors and the peddlars of drugs. Somehow he got out of it. At least, he is still in pictures and out of jail.

But the dope users are increasing; dope peddlars prevail.

There is a handsome home, closed temporarily, on a certain fashionable street in Los Angeles, where if you could enter you would find the finest equipped dope outfit in America.

Here come the players—mostly stars and near stars—to revel in Poppyland; here are held high revels—or such was the case only a few months ago—and here are the wildest of wild parties staged.

Not so long ago Dottie Pitchfork fought a duel with a former Follies girl with fist and vases; though it is claimed that hair pulling constituted and really ended the argument.

But they are interesting parties for all that. They must be interesting, for there have been as many as a hundred guests at these "affairs," not all of them dope fiends, but many of them are.

Most of them are easy to pick out. Their nervousness betrays them. The twitching of their mouths, the "snuffles," the listless air of many of them.

A rather new and somewhat unusual dope lately employed is that of bromidia, a drug which taken in teaspoonsful drives the user to continuous sleepiness, swelling of the limbs and a lassitude that brings great surcease.

There are but a few of these, however, more of them preferring cocaine, a "shot in the arm," and an occasional drag at the pipe.

Take for instance a certain young actor, son of one of the country's foremost exponents of the spoken drama. His face is yellow as saffron. He is a pipe smoker. Twice his father has had him committed to sanitariums. When his father's company comes to Los Angeles now the son secretes himself and after his father's departure writes and tells him how sorry he was to be away on location during his stay in the city.

Then there is the case of the blonde with the Scandinavian name. Last year it cost her a thousand dollars a month for her dope supply. She uses cocaine and heroin, goes to sleep on the set, slips over to her dressing room, takes a few "sniffs" and returns full of ginger, only to fade away in a short time again.

A once noted song writer, now a movie scribbler, spends the greater part of his income for drugs.

An actor who has had a long and successful career with two of the big companies is one of the list.

A well known director is another.

A young woman star, whose name has been very much in the public print of late, is still another.

The list is interminable—almost inexhaustable.

These indulgences are not always confined to the privacy of the home, either. In certain more or less public resorts one may upon occasion find well known movie people partaking of ether cocktails or other concoctions—perfume dripped on sugar, for instance. Anything and everything in the nature of what the jazz mad world knows as a "kick."

Walter, they say, still persists in giving an occasional party, though his wife has long since learned of his condition. But Walter has stamina. He is still the handsome young devil he always was. He gets away with it.

And even whiskey still has a thrill for him. He dearly loves to go out— to some other town, of course—and fight a couple of policemen, tear out sections of the hotel lobby and throw dishes at the head waiter.

But there are two young girls who regret that they ever attended one of Walter's parties. They were new at the game, but they wanted to be "good fellows." They "hit the pipe," they "took a shot in the arm," they snuffed cocaine, just as the others did.

One has returned to her home in Illinois—back to her parents—where they say that the drugs have so eaten into her system that she is dying of tuberculosis.

The other, driven to desperation because of the insistent demand of her nerves calling for the drugs, is now an ordinary street walker. Her place of "business" is a shabby rooming house in the underworld district of Los Angeles; her "beat" is Main and Los Angeles streets. Occasionally when she can lure a sailor or a stranger to her room she gets from him whatever money she can and then, as soon as she can rid herself of her companion, she rushes frantically down to "John" and buys another "shot." It is all she lives for, that "shot." And she prays nights that she will not live very long.

There are other cases, of course. For it is the young and inexperienced who suffer most. It is they who are driven to despair, and there are many in Hollywood today.

The Federal officers are trying to stamp out the plague, but somehow the dope users manage to obtain enough to keep them happy. It has made wrecks of several once good men. One of them, in his efforts to break off the habit, has gone into the wilderness. He is trying to make a little farm pay him a livelihood, and his estimable wife is helping him. She has had a hard fight, but they say she is winning over the drug.

But Walter, handsome, debonair, smiling Walter, goes serenely on, having a handsome salary, feeling, no doubt, that he is a benefactor to his friends.

Didn't he give them a new thrill?

■ ■ ■ ■

STATE CENSORSHIP OF MOTION PICTURES (1923), J. R. Rutland

This introduction to the issues of motion picture censorship, followed by an outline of those issues, was published in a 1923 pamphlet compiled by J. R. Rutland, *State Censorship of Motion Pictures,* as one number in the Reference Shelf series. That series was devoted to providing "briefs, bibliographies, debates, reprints of selected articles and study outlines on timely topics"; the Reference Shelf was especially useful for debating societies since it set forth the abstract arguments both for and against a particular position as well as gathered the necessary evidence to support either side. The Rutland pamphlet is an extremely revealing summary of contemporary attitudes toward the movies and toward censorship.

INTRODUCTION

The motion picture industry has grown in a decade from a very insignificant business to what producers claim is the fourth largest industry in America. Starting as a one-reel comedy of fights, fallings, and a chase or two, the film has challenged competition with the drama and the novel in the field of fiction, with the newspaper and the magazine in the field of news and art, and with books and lectures in school work. No town is complete without its picture houses; cities have scores of them for all classes and at all prices, some of them in palatial homes; almost every village community in the land either has its own exhibitor or is in easy reach of one. In fact, it is estimated that ten million people in the United States alone go to the movies every day and that thousands more see American pictures in all countries of the earth only a little less frequently. By all odds, the motion picture is now the world's largest commercialized form of entertainment.

Its influence is effective and far-reaching. In the days before prohibition, it was heralded as the conqueror of saloons. Some critics feared years ago that the "legitimate" drama could hardly survive the severe

J. R. Rutland, *State Censorship of Motion Pictures,* Reference Shelf series (1923).

competition of the movies. During the war with Germany, our leaders made extensive use of motion pictures not only to urge us to buy bonds, to economize on clothes and food, and to look out for the ubiquitous spy, but also to tell us what to think and to keep us passionately determined to do our bit. Big business has found that moving pictures are short cuts in teaching employees technical manipulation as well as wholesome entertainment in leisure hours. Even churches have found it necessary to adapt pictures to the service of religion. It may be true, as a recent contributor to the magazines has said, that the Hollywood state of mind is entirely too common and that we are in process of changing our national character under the influence of a machine that can tell us the news, give us the exhilaration of travel, show us the ends of the earth, portray all kinds of human conflict, make us laugh and cry at will, and point its own moral in a most effective way.

Social workers, teachers, and parents are calling attention to what seems to them to be a direct connection between the movies and child crime. Psychologists tell us why children and adults of limited intelligence may be tempted to imitation by the glamor of a criminal act in the pictures and lack the self-restraint or the ability to foresee the consequences of crime in real life, with which they might hold themselves in check. Some think that manners are being vitiated by "comics" in which pie-plastering, Falstaffian fighting, pitching unwelcome guests out of windows, dumping heroines into mud puddles, and so forth, descend in deluges upon the impressionable youth and the untutored mind. Others see as much danger to normal adults in the reiteration of criminal themes, the popularity of the domestic triangle situation, the visualization of vamping and attempted seduction, as zealous patriots saw not long ago in German propaganda. Thus, it may be seen, its critics flatter the motion picture by seeing in it a power that uncurbed may disrupt the bonds of society and government and destroy our dearest ideals.

Business men's organizations, women's clubs, chambers of commerce, religious and charitable organizations have made extensive investigations of moving picture conditions and influences and have proposed a variety of remedies for the evils involved. One serious student has recommended a system of state or Federal licensing of producers to curb the publication of vicious pictures. A bill has been introduced in the House of Representatives for the purpose of establishing a national commission of censorship. About thirty states have considered some sort of state censorship and seven have adopted it. On the other hand producers and their friends object to any outside regulation, claiming the right, accorded to newspapers, to publishers of books, and to dramatic producers, of doing their own censoring and of accepting punishment at the hands of the law when they violate it. Many authors, publishers, and others to whom censorship sounds un-American and who fear the possibility of further extension of censorship, agree with picture makers and dealers that public opinion, and not a board of censors, should be their sole judge. That this plan will succeed is shown, producers claim, by the undoubted improvement made in recent months.

Censorship is a vital question. All agree—even the producers and distributors—that some sort of regulation is necessary, that unlimited publication in pictures is unwise. What, then, is the best kind of regulation? Among the many answers to this question—of which probably the most important are Federal censorship by the Bureau of Education, censorship by the National Board of Review, a general system of licensing producers and distributors, state censorship, and the judgment of public opinion voiced by the patrons of the pictures—this volume presents the pros and cons of state censorship. Although it has been planned for debaters, the general reader will find it helpful in the formation of an intelligent opinion on the subject.

BRIEF

RESOLVED: *That state censorship of motion pictures should be adopted in the United States.*

Affirmative

I. The existing methods of censorship and regulation, other than state regulation, are unsatisfactory.
   A. The National Board of Review is insufficient.
      1. It has no legal power to enforce its decisions.
      2. It may be, or can easily become, a tool of the producers.
         a. They contribute to its support.
      3. A New York city board cannot represent satisfactorily all parts of the United States.
   B. Existing laws are inadequate.
      1. Complaint from the public or a lawsuit is necessary to have a film withdrawn from exhibtion.
      2. In some cases, present laws governing immoral entertainments have not been interpreted to cover motion pictures.
      3. Responsibility for the exhibition of a vicious picture is not adequately placed.
      4. Offenders are punished only after bad pictures have been shown and have been seen by thousands of people.
   C. Local or municipal censorship is not satisfactory.
      1. Only larger communities have adopted the plan.

2. The plan cannot easily function in a small community.
    a. The producers would not likely submit expensive films.
    b. Competent censors are not easily available in all small communities.
D. Advisory organizations—like women's clubs, community motion picture bureaus, and like organizations—are helpless when exhibitors and producers find a strong public (?) demand for salacious pictures.
    1. They cannot punish violators of the laws of decency, except as heretofore explained.
    2. Even their children's curfew and special selected program schemes have not been successful.

II. State censorship would improve the present situation.
  A. It would simplify regulation.
    1. It would fix responsibility on a board of censorship.
    2. It would create a uniform standard of judging films for a whole state.
  B. It would be less expensive.
    1. Money spent for municipal censorship could be saved.
    2. State boards of censorship are self-supporting.
  C. It would safeguard society from the insidious influences patent in unregulated exhibition of moving pictures.
    1. It would protect the small child and the adolescent from the shock of witnessing violence.
    2. It would curb that encouragement of crime inherent in the reiteration of criminal themes.
    3. It would prevent the derision of racial or religious groups and officers of the law.
    4. It would protect poorer sections against low, vulgar, or worthless films.
    5. It would elevate the tone of pictures intended for adults by excluding pictures of low moral influence, such as vulgar comedies, over-emphasis on the domestic triangle, and other sex themes.
      a. What happened to "Carmen" is an example.
    6. It would eliminate from films suggestions that might give foreigners false impressions of America.
      a. Many of our films shown abroad have given foreigners false ideas about our manners and morals.
      b. Immigrants get warped ideas of American social standards.
  D. Censorship has already improved conditions.
    1. The "thirteen points" subscribed to by several producers are

a concession to constructive censorship already established in certain states and municipalities.

2. Supporting producers are slow to send out through exchanges pictures that have been condemned by official and unofficial boards.

3. Censors eliminate unfit scenes and reels very frequently.

III. State censorship is in harmony with American ideas and ideals.

  A. It is constitutional.

    1. A liberty may be infringed upon by legislation with the consent of the Supreme Court, when restriction results in a benefit to all the people.

      a. The 18th Amendment prohibiting the manufacture and sale of alcoholic liquors has stood the test.

    2. If state censorship were not constitutional, the laws creating state censorship boards in Ohio, Pennsylvania, Maryland, Virginia, New York, Florida, and Kansas would have been declared unconstitutional.

      a. Courts have sustained these laws.

  B. If picture censorship seems to discriminate against the movies in favor of the press and the drama, the immensely greater immediate influence of the movies makes the problem different and more serious.

    1. The movie has a vastly larger audience than both the press and the drama.

    2. The conditions for "crowd psychology," which causes people in the mass to yield to suggestions that they would instantly reject in the office or at home or elsewhere, are normally present in the movie theater.

    3. James' idea of the "moral holiday" in the lives of respectable people is apparently confirmed by the fact that audiences will applaud movie pictures of the subtly salacious type or of a crime that breaks an otherwise impassable barrier between the hero and the heroine.

    4. The visual appeal is stronger than any other.

  C. State censorship is fair to the producer and distributor.

    1. Censorship prevents violation of the law.

    2. The fourth largest interstate business must be suitably regulated, like other big business.

    3. Community or local censorship, if generally adopted, would work a greater hardship.

      a. The number of varying opinions would be greater.

      b. Expense and delay would be greater.

4. Censors are considerate.
   a. They respect the producer's rights as well as the public's.
     (1) Changes in decisions show willingness to take produc-
       er's point of view.
5. Delay of releases would not be very serious.
   a. Cooperation between state boards would be feasible.
   b. Pictures recommended by reputable agencies could, in some
     cases, be passed tentatively without review.
6. The procedures and distributors must share with the exhibitors
  the responsibility for bad pictures.
   a. Common law governing local amusements, now in force,
     reaches only the local picture show manager.
7. Expense of eliminations would be reduced to a minimum.
   a. Manufacturers would know what the legal standards were.
D. State censorship is fair to the individual and to the local community.
  1. Small communities are unable to cope singly with the giant
    movie business.
    a. Without cooperation, such as state censorship gives, small
      communities have to take what the exchanges send or
      nothing.
  2. Political perversion of news and senseless mangling of edu-
    cational pictures are very rare, and, sometimes, may be justified
    in view of local conditions.
  3. Absurdities and inconsistencies of elimination, denying the
    citizen's right to see all that may be shown, will grow fewer
    year by year.
    a. Producers will meet the new demand of public opinion.
    b. Censors will profit by experience and by cooperation.
  4. No pictures of really great merit will be denied exhibition.
    a. Boards of censors, in the long run, will consist of intelli-
      gent people who will adequately enforce public opinion.
    b. Narrow-minded censors who mangle pictures passed else-
      where will be dismissed.

Negative
I. State censorship, as it is practiced today, is undemocratic.
  A. It is out of harmony with the spirit of the American Constitution.
    1. It provides for punishment before crime has been committed.
    2. It limits freedom of speech and publication necessary in a
      democracy and guaranteed by the Constitution.
      a. It restricts publication to the private opinion of a few po-
        litically appointed individuals.

3. It takes away from communities the right of self-government in matters not affecting other communities.

B. It is class legislation and as such discriminates against moving pictures, as compared with other forms of free speech, the newspaper, the book, the magazine, and the drama.

    1. Other organs of free speech are not called to trial until they have published offensive material.

    2. Other publishers are allowed to defend themselves in open court before a jury of their fellows.

    3. Censorship retards unjustly the natural development of pictures.

        a. It seriously limits the right of experimentation.

        b. It would compel, if adopted by forty-eight states, forty-eight differing conceptions of morality and good taste.

    4. It would delay releases.

        a. Forty-eight state boards would have to pass upon a picture.

II. State censorship is not satisfactory where it has been tried.

A. What one board eliminates another passes.

    1. Whole reels condemned by one state are permitted in another.

    2. No two boards make the same eliminations in the same film.

B. News and educational films are sometimes tampered with.

    1. News reports of Hughes' condemnation of movie censorship were forbidden in Kansas.

    2. Scientific and educational films have been mangled to conform to rules formulated for amusement films.

C. The censor privilege has been perverted for political reasons.

    1. The negro vote in Ohio prevented the showing of "The Birth of a Nation" in that state.

    2. The Ohio and Pennsylvania censorship boards eliminated pictures of the coal strike in 1919—the latter at the request of the governor.

D. Reasons for elimination are often inconsistent and absurd.

    1. "Carmen" was rejected in three states for three different reasons.

    2. Ohio permits no pictures of smoking women.

    3. Pennsylvania prevented the showing of a farcical scene in which a man burns a letter from his wife, because (forsooth) it showed contempt of the marital relation.

E. No universal, absolute standard of morals and good taste can be formulated.

    1. The conception of what is immoral, indecent, or not in good taste varies with the individual, social group, or in accordance with one's experience, education and environment.

     a. Pictures of bathing girls, of dancing in short skirts, etc.,
       would be received differently in different communities.

     b. Although Schnitzler's "Anatol" on the stage or in the
       pictures would excite little adverse comment in Paris or
       Vienna, it would be considered unfit in many an American
       community.

   2. Censorship is helpless in dealing with slapstick comedy, ro-
     mantic tommyrot, scientific misinformation, inartistic plots,
     many distasteful views of life that may be true.

     a. No two people react similarly.

     b. Taste and good judgment are products of slow growth
       and maturing intellect.

F. Pictures in censorship states are not better than those in other
  states.

   1. No state board can meet absolutely all community conditions.

   2. Elimination often mars the author's or the producer's intended
     artistic effect.

G. Censorship creates the wrong attitude of mind for censors and
  producers.

   1. The censor feels compelled to eliminate.

   2. The producer makes up films with obvious faults so that
     there may be something to delete.

H. It is not a satisfactory solution of the child problem.

   1. Pictures for adults must not be censored for children.

     a. It is unfair to adults, for whom pictures are chiefly made.

     b. Parents must protect children from these as they protect
       them from vicious books and periodicals.

   2. It is the parent's business to censor for his children.

     a. Parents, like censors, differ.

      (1) One parent is known to have taken his daughter to see
         "Damaged Goods," a play on a subject usually banned
         from the conversation of young girls.

     b. Pennsylvania prevents the display of a layette or any sug-
       gestion of approaching maternity, whereas many parents
       believe in dispelling the "stork" illusions by talking about
       natural facts in a frank manner.

III. State censorship, if censorship there must be, is not the best method of
  protecting the public from bad pictures.

A. If censorship before publication be essential, national censorship
  is better.

   1. It would be less expensive to the people.

     a. One board could serve for all the states.

     b. It would eliminate opportunities for graft by state boards.

2. It would set the same standards of taste and morals, right or wrong, everywhere.

B. A licensing system would be better.

   1. The responsibility for bad pictures would then be placed, where it ought to be, on the producer and distributor as well as on the exhibitor.

   2. Fear of loss of license to continue business would deter manufacturers from making pictures about which they had any doubts.

C. Local public opinion is the best judge of the fitness of local amusements.

   1. Churches, clubs, parents, and good citizens may enforce local standards of taste and morals.

   2. The local exhibitor can then be held responsible.

D. The National Board of Review is impartial and efficient.

   1. Its nearly two hundred members receive no salaries—not even carfare.

   2. Its work is supported by taxes on films reviewed, by sale of its services, and by subscriptions from persons and organizations interested in the production of good pictures.

   3. It serves directly large cities in thirty-eight states through bulletins and other means.

   4. It assists churches and educational organizations in finding suitable pictures.

■ ■ ■ ■

State Censorship of Motion Pictures (1921), National Board of Review

The National Board of Review, representing both the opinion of the movie industry and its own traditional practice of self-regulation, published this 1921 pamphlet that took a strong stand against legal censorship on constitutional grounds.

An Invasion of Constitutional Rights

The Constitution of the United States and those of the several states guarantee freedom of speech and the press. Motion pictures have arisen

State Censorship of Motion Pictures was written and published by the National Board of Review (1921).

since the framing of the Constitution, but they are obviously a means whereby opinion is expressed, and as such are entitled to the same right of liberty as is accorded speech and press.

On this ground many state legislatures have repeatedly killed censorship legislation. In New York City, Mayor Gaynor vetoed an ordinance providing for censorship in 1912, and a second attempt was frustrated in 1919, the official report against it concluding:

> Your committee is opposed to the creation of a censorship *because it regards the remedy suggested as far more inimical to our institutions than the evil sought to be corrected thereby.*

A Defiance of Democratic Principles

Legalized state censorship empowers a small group, usually three persons, politically appointed and of inferior ability, to decide what all the people of the state may see on the screen. *It takes away from local authorities who are elected by the people power to regulate the pictures shown in their own communities.*

Censors Cannot Agree

Only four states have boards of censorship, and these continually contradict one another in their decisions. If every state had censorship, there would be forty-eight independent, conflicting, arbitrary standards to which motion pictures must conform. It is inconceivable that this could make for better pictures.

No Popular Demand for Censorship

There is no popular demand for state censorship. The average American family attend the show once a week and enjoy it. Censorship agitation is artificially stirred up by well-meaning but insufficiently informed reformers, who wish to impose their own standards of taste upon everybody else. It is encouraged by certain political elements who covet the patronage and the power over channels of public information which it would give them.

Unjust Discrimination

Compared with other forms of dramatic entertainment, the motion picture is the least objectionable of all on the score of morals. To single it out for censorship, therefore, is on the face of it indefensibly unjust and stupid.

Censorship No Solution of the Child Problem

The chief reason advanced for state censorship is that ordinary shows are unfit for children to attend.

In the first place, no censorship can banish melodrama from the screen, or expurgate it into a commendable entertainment for children.

In the second place, nobody has any business to try to do this. The motion picture is the chief amusement of the adult public, and any attempt to standardize it as a child's entertainment is as intolerable as it is impossible.

The only solution of the child problem is to provide children with special programs.

Confusion of Taste with Morals

Most clamor for censorship makes no distinction between bad taste and bad morals. It is chiefly concerned with the former, quite oblivious of the fact that standards of taste are irreconcilable. What is good taste to one is bad taste to another.

Public Opinion the Only Effective Censor

Awakened public opinion is the only effectual guaranty of safety and decency. Responsibility for public morals should therefore be put squarely up to the community and its constituted authorities. Any scheme which takes responsibility and authority away from the community and vests them in a distant and small committee is plainly dangerous and vicious, particularly if such a board is clothed with arbitrary authority and is not directly responsible to the people.

The standards of the local theater audience differ from the average standards of a whole state. The legal censors would have us believe that state censorship is based on the state average of opinion. But there is no state average which legal censors may voice in their decisions. The opinions of the people of an entire state are composed of a conglomerate mixture of opinions and standards which no one board can possibly combine so as to give it a real gauge of public opinion. For instance:

The mayor of one of the leading cities of Ohio recently said that the Ohio Board of Censors were allowing in his city pictures which the citizens would not permit, had the power of regulation not been taken from them and vested in the state board.

In another great city of Ohio, a federation of churches and other organizations are at work enforcing higher standards than those endorsed by the state censors. Since the managers have a legal right to exhibit pictures passed by the state board, the federation must depend upon the good-will and cooperation of these men.

If, then, the public and the managers in one of the largest cities of the country voluntarily agree that their standards are different from those of the state board of censors, *what is the use of the board?* Its claim that its decisions represent state sentiment is contrary to fact.

Such a board, then, is clearly a drag upon public opinion and the motion picture producers in any attempt to further the development of the artistic picture. It is an authority to be invoked by the unthinking or the prejudiced or those with special axes to grind who see in the motion picture an enemy to their own particular point of view or their own interests. It is an engine to frustrate the will of the people, to interfere with the only healthy and efficient regulation of public morals....

NATIONAL BOARD AND THE FREEDOM OF THE SCREEN

Fundamental in the theory of the National Board of Review is the recognition of *the screen's right to freedom.*

The conviction that there can be no complete convergence of opinion as to what is precisely moral and what is precisely immoral, or as to where questions of taste and morals overlap, is basic in its conception of motion picture regulations.

The national board believes that public opinion, which is the compound of all tastes and all ideas of morals, is the only competent judge of the screen.

But public opinion cannot regulate if there is no freedom of the screen to allow it to decide for itself what shall and shall not be presented to it....

■ ■ ■ ■

SEX PICTURES (1922), Ellis Paxson Oberholtzer

Ellis Paxson Oberholtzer was the chairman of the Pennsylvania Board of Censors, by reputation the strictest board during the period. In 1922 Oberholtzer published *The Morals of the Movie* (the title page describes its author as Litt.D, Ph.D.), defending the practice of motion picture censorship despite its theoretical and constitutional problems. This chapter from the book is the most explicit (and salacious) in its describing the unacceptable sexual activities and innuendos that have found their way into films.

Sex is the one potently dominant idea in the minds of the men who are gambling in the public taste for nasty photographic stories. The capitalist who is financing the picture-producing company, the executive officers whom he hires to make money for him, and the directors in the studios

"Sex Pictures" is from the book *The Morals of the Movie,* by Ellis Paxson Oberholtzer (Penn, 1922; Ozer, 1971).

expend much of their time and energy in trying to devise that which will show the male and the female in some unusual and new relationship. The public, sated by much looking at film, night after night, must be aroused from the apathy which comes from having long ago seen all that is proper to be shown, and we have been plunged into an abysmal morass of fornication, adultery, pandering and prostitution. The seduction of mill girls and stenographers by their employers, men living with mistresses and women consorting with men without marriage are flashed into the eyes of old and young, willy nilly, in our "movie" houses.

The owner or distributor of such film often comes to me with the statement that it is educational. He is engaged in teaching the people lessons which it will be good for them to learn. For example he wishes to circulate a picture which tells about "white slavery." An innocent country lass arrives in town. She is accosted at the railway station by a procurer. This man is in league with a taxicab driver. They offer the girl counsel, and, by one dishonest device or another, before she quite realizes what she is about, she finds herself in a sumptuously furnished house ready to be inducted into a life of shame.

The changes have been rung upon this theme for years. Sometimes the portly "madame," with the jet-black female servant, who receives the girl, is the "mother," and sometimes the "aunt" of the young man who interested himself so deeply in the welfare of the country lass at the railway station. Sometimes it is a procuress who greets her upon her arrival and ensnares the young victim. Occasionally the girl is saved from the fate which faces her; again she may be submerged in the life to which she has been introduced to break the hearts of her parents and some farmer boy who loves her at home.

The dealer who wishes to persuade me that this is a film suitable for public showing argues with me vigorously and tediously. He asserts that young girls should be instructed as to a matter of this kind and that there is no better medium for popular education than picture film. How can they protect themselves from the pitfalls which are prepared for youth and beauty if these revelations are not made to them in as public a manner as possible? Would I bar them from knowledge which is capable of being of so much indispensable worth?

At times lecturers will accompany pictures of this character with remarks most stupid, most vulgar and most ungrammatical. I have in mind three or four shabby fellows. They hoisted sensational banners outside of the houses in which they were to speak and filled the theatre lobbies with like announcements. In the afternoons, perhaps, "ladies only" would be admitted; at night, only men. At all times boys and girls under sixteen might not enter, so it would be said, although in such cases any who may have the price of admission are seldom excluded. In little towns the advance advertising put the entire population upon the tiptoe of expectancy. Here was an exposé of fearful wickedness which all wished to know more about. I have pursued, prosecuted and driven these men out of our state, but not before they took the opportunity to tell me, of course, that I had no interest in the reformation of the race. Statistics were cited to me about the large numbers of young women who annually are led astray. Here was a sermon which was being taken to the hearths and firesides of the people and it was a hard heart, and an unsympathetic one, which would prevent those who were bearing such a message from delivering it.

I asked one of the fellows why he did not choose another subject for his lectures. He told me that he could not get the people to come and hear him on other topics, a fact so obvious, taken in connection with his appearance, address and general equipment for the service, that the conversation was abandoned at once.

A few years ago the "educators" in the film business invaded another field. It was their "mission" to persuade women to avoid malpractitioners and abortionists. Every reluctant mother should be instructed as to the dangers of "birth control," and she should be made to understand the emptiness of a childless life. Though it might seem, on superficial view, that such a subject could not well be dramatized and incorporated in film several producers, nothing daunted, set themselves to the task. The first of these pictures, unless my memory is at fault, was "Where Are My Children?" which was followed by "The Unborn," "Enlighten Thy Daughter," "The Law of Nature," and others—all dealing in one way or another with the same theme. Considerable sums of money, some talent in direction and in acting, though it is difficult to conceive how women, even if they were generously compensated for the service, would consent to appear in such scenes, were expended in filming these stories.

It is a sorry part of the business that our degeneration is progressive. At first pictures of this kind were considered bold. In particular did women feel and express a resentment that the producers should make such films and that the theatres should exhibit them. But after the first was seen the second shocked no one very much, and the public was ready for some fresh exploitation of the intimacies of life.

The absolute assurance of large profits from the exhibition of such material led the distributors to put forth exceptional efforts to market it with the greatest possible amount of prestige and publicity. They ran off the reels privately before doctors and ministers with the purpose of securing endorsements from at least some of the number who might be drawn to witness the "shows." Engraved invitations were issued. Expensive apartments in fashionable hotels were secured for the exhibitions. The names of bishops and other men, well known in the community, were used by the audacious fellows who held the distribution rights. Because of the variety that there is in human nature, by flattery and sometimes by bribery, endorsements of this kind were obtained. These were printed in the newspapers or set out in large letters in front of the theatres, thus creating an impression which lulled into insensibility many who were on the point of protesting against such a commercialization of sacred things, and enabled those who had set out to speculate upon the curious and prurient in public taste to gather in the money from the crowds which formed long queues at the doors of the theatres.

Now and again we have had pictures to illustrate the processes of human birth. I do not allude to scenes in pictures, which are so numerous as to be common, showing the obstetricians and nurses around the mother in travail upon her bed and of the father pacing outside the door. These scenes are introduced for entertainment. I refer instead to pictures, made originally, perhaps, for limited use to instruct women as to their own care and the care of their children. But they come into other hands. Someone sees value in them for general sale and exhibition and he takes them out on circuit for gain.

A picture of the kind which I have in mind is introduced by observations quite common to propaganda film—therein is contained the apology, as the distributor would have us think, for their manufacture and exhibition:

> Birth is not the commencement of life. Every baby is alive for several months before birth, therefore, it is necessary to consider the welfare of the mother and child.
>
> In the production of this remarkable series of motion pictures, the Eugenic Film Company and its co-workers have been prompted by a realization of the dire effects resulting from ignorance of eugenic and hygienic principles.
>
> These effects are most glaring, especially during the periods of expectancy, confinement and the urgent necessity of fostering baby's health and well being.
>
> "Last year in spite of the great work done by the Department of Health, out of ten babies born here, taking only the first year of life, *one* died in every ten! So that with nearly 40,000 births per year, New York City shows an annual appalling loss of *fourteen thousand* baby lives.
>
> We offer these pictures to the adult public, sincerely anticipating that they will teach the great lesson, which, if heeded, will do much toward the preservation of the all too often sacrificed little lives.
>
> These pictures have been produced under the supervision of the

attending staff of physicians and surgeons of a prominent New York hospital and the methods illustrated herein have the stamp of their approval.

It is, therefore, in deepest appreciation of the opportunities afforded that we convey to you a visualized scientific precept of what Every Woman Should Know.

At least one picture there has been, "The Solitary Sin," which was designed to "educate" us on the question of masturbation.

Venereal disease has lately received a considerable amount of attention and several films have been made to illuminate this subject. Some, like "Damaged Goods," are held to have literary support. Others, such as "Fit to Fight," "The End of the Road," and "Open Your Eyes," were called out by the war. I know not in what spirit they were originated, but I can believe that one or more of them may have been born of some honesty of motive. It is barely possible that they may have had their uses in camps or before selected audiences, gathered together to be instructed under the direction of reverent persons. But others hold a different opinion. . . .

Of this character, too, we are asked to believe, are the "drug pictures," three or four years ago very numerous, though of late their production has nearly ceased. "The Secret Sin," "The Devil's Needle," and a long series of films, having to do with the use of morphine, cocaine, opium and other narcotics, which we have been endeavoring to suppress with the whole power of the law, have swept across the screen. All classes of the population who know nothing of these vices, have been made intimately acquainted with the names of the various drugs and their seductive influence, the manner of applying them by the needle, by smoking them, by sniffing them, et cetera, the devices which may be employed for smuggling them into the country for a forbidden trade, and for procuring them from peddlers and other persons engaged in their distribution.

In general such pictures as I have been describing are called "Enlightenment Films." They have attracted notice in other countries as well as our own, and they, everywhere, meet with protest and condemnation. The allegation about their "mission" is pure "humbug." . . .

Such communications on the subject of eugenics, race suicide, sex disease and the most successful methods of avoiding the pitfalls of large cities can be made, one might suppose, through the home, the church, the school and those social agencies which have been established for ordering our civilization. The theatre manager is another type of citizen. He keeps a place of amusement for his own gain. His lesson is mixed with a seductive love story "to get it across"; he advertises it luridly that he may draw all classes to his doors in a spirit of morbid curiosity. They do not come in a frame of mind for learning. They are wrought up to the point of believing that they are to see hitherto unseen and to hear hitherto untold things, having to do with their procreative organs. The lesson goes astray; if it shall ever be taught them at all it must be conveyed by wiser teachers under more favorable conditions at some later day.

In the case of most of our sex stories in pictures, however, no lesson is intended. I am aware that this plea is sometimes offered and we are asked to give it serious attention. A line at the end and a few scenes, fifty feet in length, after we have dragged our helpless limbs for an hour and a half through the sewers of picturedom, remind us that "the wages of sin is death." We are shown, perhaps, in accordance with a moral code which is very familiar in the "movie" house, that there is retribution for the girl, though seldom enough for him who has tempted and wronged her.

But no such defense as that which is set up unsuccessfully in behalf of the "Enlightenment Films" can now avail in this wider field. That virtue is rewarded and sin is punished before the audience is sent home, or that the whole sorry relation was "only a dream," cannot excuse gross and deliberate offending, and those who have brought these sex pictures to me and my associates have fallen back upon their rights and privileges as purveyors of the drama. They ask us to think that they are artists who must enjoy a free scope for their talents. They must have contrasts, climaxes and situations for the "people's drama," no less than for the play that belongs to the stage.

Let us look at some of their themes. I am bound to think that no one familiar with the history and spirit of the drama would wish to say very much in extenuation of such a perversion of art in the interest of low and nasty commerce. The stories are summarized not unfairly. Their titles are given, though not the names of the manufacturers, so that any who may care to investigate the subject on his own account may have a clue for doing so.

THE SCARLET WOMAN.—The story of a woman whose husband, while robbing a cash box to meet losses he has sustained in stock speculations, has killed another man. To save him from the electric chair she sells her honor to the district attorney. The husband, learning of what she has done, repudiates her and she becomes a prosperous prostitute. At length she marries again. When her second husband learns of the errors of her past life she commits suicide by inhaling gas.

WHAT THE BRIDESMAID KNEW.—A young girl from the country comes to town at the invitation of a friend to serve as the maid of honor at her wedding. The train is late; the girl is not met at the station; she falls into the hands of a "cabby" who is in league with a procuress, and is taken to a house of ill fame. The prospective groom, after a night of debauchery at an ushers' dinner, visits the house for a "last fling," discovers that he is in a room with the girl who is to be the maid of honor at his wedding on the following day, and agrees to aid her to escape from "white slavery," if she will take a pledge to say naught about his misconduct. They together leave the house by a rope made of the sheets on the bed and the next time they face each other it is at the man's wedding.

GOD'S COUNTRY AND THE WOMAN.—A story about a Hudson Bay Company agent in the Canadian Northwest and his wife and daughter. An earlier lover of the wife returns to her. She has a child by him in the absence of her husband. The daughter comes to her mother's defense. She finds a man who is willing to pose as her husband and she takes the responsibility of her mother's new-born infant which is offered to the absentee upon his return as his grandson. Later the man with whom the wife has had adulterous relations abducts and attempts to seduce the daughter.

TWELVE TEN.—The manager of a rich old man's business affairs makes improper advances to his adopted daughter. The manager tries to poison his employer. He is foiled. To gain his sensual ends he alters the old man's will and inserts a provision in it requiring the girl, who is the principal heir, to repair at night to a deserted castle to pray over his corpse. The old man, suspecting his manager of evil designs, takes some drug which is warranted to bring about the appearance of death for a number of hours or days. His supposedly dead form is put in a great bed in the castle. The young woman is terrified but betakes herself to the place for the services required of her. Soon there is a rustling under the covers and the villain, who has somehow put himself in the place of the corpse, comes forth to rape the girl. He is confronted, to his great surprise, by the old man, who, lying in the next room, has recovered from the effects of the drug in time to rescue the girl.

THE AMAZING WOMAN.—The story of a girl from the country who is enticed into the home of a rich man who has promised to advance her in art or music. She lives with him for a time under the hope of marriage, but is disappointed. A discarded mistress, she wanders into the slums of the city where she is touched by the sufferings of crippled boys. That she may establish a hospital for them she adopts an unusual course. She plies a prostitute's vocation at night. The money which she thus gains from rich men she applies during the day to the comfort and relief of the poor. She falls in love at length with a young soldier, who proves to be the son of the man who originally betrayed her. She is forgiven by her lover and marries him. . . .

■ ■ ■ ■

Motion Pictures and Crime (1921), Dr. A. T. Poffenberger

Dr. Poffenberger, of Columbia University, published this article in the
Scientific Monthly in 1921. More concerned with the effect of motion pictures on crime than on morality, the piece reveals a contemporary suspicion about another social effect of watching movies. In his book *Art and
Prudence* (see pages 365–79), Dr. Mortimer J. Adler singles out this
Poffenberger article as a classic example of fallacious scientific reasoning,
its conclusion based on conjecture, supposition, and assumption rather
than on any concrete data. For Adler, the piece was an example of opinion
masquerading as science.

One of the surprising things about the wave of crime which is reported
to be raging throughout the country is the large number of very young
persons found implicated in crimes of all sorts. Much attention has recently been given to the matter in newspaper articles and editorials, and
blame is placed rather frequently upon the motion picture. Various sorts
of censorship have been proposed, most of them drastic in form. The following article taken from a recent issue of the New York *Times* will serve
as an illustration:

> Motion pictures portraying criminals at work have been barred in
> ————. Chief of Police ———— announced today that three weeks
> ago he had given orders to movie censors not to issue permits for any
> screen drama that showed a crime committed, even though the end
> of the picture might show the criminal in a prison cell.
> "It will make no difference whether the criminal shown is a hero
> or a villain," said the chief. "Even the showing of a policeman dis-
> guised as a burglar is taboo."
> The order became public when three youthful robbers, who were
> sentenced to the State Reformatory, said their crimes had been in-
> spired by a "crook" moving picture.

Prohibitions and censorships of any sort are distasteful to the American people, except in cases where the general welfare can be proved to
be at stake. Therefore an inquiry into the accusations that have been made
against the motion picture seems justified at this time when attention is
being centered upon the means of crime prevention. The question is a
psychological one, and concerns the effects of motion picture experience
upon the mind of the young person. The average adult can not interpret

"Motion Pictures and Crime," by Dr. A. T. Poffenberger, appeared in the *Scientific
Monthly* of April 1921.

the reactions of a child in terms of his own reactions, because there are fundamental differences between the two. A knowledge of child psychology is needed to understand what the motion picture means to the child.

As an agent of publicity, with its immense daily audience of young people, it has great possibilities for creating and developing in them a spirit of true Americanism, a respect for law and social order which are recognized as essentials for a democracy. Rightly used, the motion picture is indeed one of the most powerful educational forces of the twentieth century. Its possible influence in the Americanization of our foreign population, through a medium which shall be intelligible to all, regardless of race, is scarcely yet realized. But wrongly used and not carefully guarded, it might easily become a training school for anti-Americanism, immorality and disregard for law—a condition in which each individual is a law unto himself. We have therefore, in a sense, to meet an emergency, to begin in time to make of this truly public school the kind of educational force that it should be—to prevent rather than to prohibit.

In a consideration of the young, we must not fail to include that great class of unfortunates designated as the mentally deficient. They are individuals, who, though physically and chronologically adults, are still children mentally. The problem of the mentally retarded individual is essentially the same as that of the normal person of younger years. The moron, the highest type of the feeble-minded, usually defined as an individual whose mental development has ceased at about the age of eleven years, has most of the mental traits of the child of eleven years. He has, however, the physical strength, instincts and desires of the adult. The moron is seldom confined in an institution, because his defects are not considered by family and friends as great enough for that. As a result, this type of individual is at large, and must be protected from evil suggestions and from too complex an environment. Such persons, when the higher forms of control which they lack are supplied by guardians or are made unnecessary by simplified living conditions, may well become useful and self-supporting members of society. Without this control, they constitute a real danger, since their physical age, which may be from fifteen years up, places them in a position to act upon evil suggestions more readily than the child.

What, then, are the mental characteristics of these two groups, children and mentally deficient adults, which mark them off from normal adults?

One respect in which they differ from the adult is in suggestibility; another is the lack of ability to foresee and to weigh the consequences for self and others of different kinds of behavior; another is the lack of capacity and willingness to exercise self-restraint; and still another is an imagination less controlled and checked by reference to the realities. All these traits taken together make the child and the mentally deficient person especially susceptible to evil influences. That is why one expects the majority of certain kinds of crimes to be committed by persons of retarded mental development. And recent statistical studies of the relation between crime and mental defect confirm the expectation. One needs only to recall the epidemics of suicide and murder by such means as cyanide of potasium, chloride of mercury, carbolic acid and the like; to notice the likenesses in the technique of burglars at different periods of time; to note the cases of false testimony in court and false confessions of crime to realize the great suggestibility of such persons and their lack of foresight. Unlike the normal adult, they are unable to resist the sug- gestions of advertisements, posters, newspapers and magazines, and of their associates. Naturally, these traits may be played upon either for good or evil. One who knows the mechanism of suggestion would expect the prevalence of crime, especially when it is advertised by these agencies of publicity, to breed more crime.

Motion pictures, containing scenes vividly portraying defiance of law and crimes of all degrees, may by an ending which shows the criminal brought to justice and the victory of the right, carry a moral to the in- telligent adult; but that which impresses the mind of the mentally young and colors their imagination is the excitement and bravado accompanying the criminal act, while the moral goes unheeded. Their minds can not logically reach the conclusion to which the chain of circumstances will drive the normal adult. A little questioning of such persons who attend moving pictures and read stories will indicate how different are the factors which impress their minds, from those which impress the intel- ligent adult. This failure to grasp the significance of the story is even more pronounced when it is conveyed only by the posters advertising it. Here it seems to be the rule to portray only the most glaring and exciting portion of the plot with no possibility of right interpretation. A survey of any group of posters advertising motion pictures, with only their direct appeal in mind, will show a surprisingly large portion of them sug- gesting murder, burglary, violence or crime of some sort. The pistol seems to be one of the commonest of the stage properties of the motion picture advertisement. And a very frequent pose is that of the frenzy of rage and the clenched fist ready to strike a blow. Those young people and even adults who are limited to the advertising posters for their entertain- ment may get evil and anti-social suggestions from them. Considering the almost unlimited audiences which the advertising posters command, their careful control would seem a greater necessity even than that of the play itself.

It is just on account of this susceptibility to suggestion that the mentally retarded criminal and the child criminal need a special kind of treatment and special courts to handle their cases. Indeed, much has been done in recent years toward the proper treatment of these two classes of criminals. What needs most emphasis now, however, is prevention, not cure. Proper control of their environment is the one factor which will do much to make of these two classes respectable members of society instead of criminals.

There are many sources of evil suggestions which can not be eliminated, so long as there are immoral and anti-social persons, and to that extent the atmosphere in which children develop and the feebleminded live, must remain far below the ideal. But that is a good reason why those evils which can be eliminated should be. Such organs of publicity as moving pictures, newspapers, magazines, advertising posters and the like, should not be allowed to contribute to the necessary burden of evil suggestion by the character of their productions. The purely commercial spirit should be tempered by a spirit of social welfare and education.

The matters here discussed have not entirely escaped attention hitherto. For instance, there was introduced, some time ago, into the New York State legislature a bill providing for the limitation by newspapers of the publicity which may be given to reports of crime. The width and height of headlines for such material was specified. The nature of these provisions does not especially concern us here, but the fact that the matter is receiving attention is interesting.

These are preventive measures applied from the outside. The remedy should come from within. It can be done, and in fact has been done by newspapers. A survey, recently made of a large number of metropolitan newspapers, shows that they differ strikingly in the way they handle reports of crime. In some cases crimes are not featured in big headlines and favored positions, and only facts that the reading public can profit by knowing are printed. If the motion picture is to become the educational force that it is capable of becoming, the censorship must be an internal one. The old notion is outworn that it is necessary "to give the people what they want." It is the function of an educational medium and an entertaining medium also, to give the public what they should have, in order that they may learn to want it. The function of education is to create as well as to satisfy wants. The future of the motion picture is limited only by the foresight of its leaders.

■ ■ ■ ■

THE MOTION PICTURE INDUSTRY (1923), Will H. Hays

The industry's official response to such charges came from its new official
spokesman, Will H. Hays. This article, published in the *American Review
of Reviews,* is typical of the positive picture Hays attempted to paint for
the general public of the social concern and responsibility of the motion
picture industry.

*About ten months ago the leaders in the motion picture industry, on their
own initiative, inaugurated a new effort for the industry's improvement,
and there has been much inquiry as to just what this new effort may be.
It is merely that these men who make and distribute pictures, recognizing
their duty and responsibility and determined to discharge it, have become
associated to deal with those things in which they are mutually but non-
competitively interested, having as the chief purposes of this organization
two great objectives—and I quote from the formal articles of association,
which have been filed in the office of the Secretary of State at Albany,
New York:*

> *"Establishing and maintaining the highest possible moral and artistic
>   standards in motion-picture production"; and,*
> *"Developing the educational as well as the entertainment value and
>   the general usefulness of the motion picture."*

*This is not a vague gentlemen's agreement; it is the legal statement of
a legal purpose by a legally organized body. It creates no super-court auto-
cratically to pass upon pictures, nor to do many of the other things which
have been suggested. The purposes of the association are exactly those
stated in their articles; and I respectfully suggest that no charter breathing
more important purposes could well be found. It is a large service in which
everyone is interested.*

AWAKENED RESPONSIBILITIES

The motion picture is an institution operating all around us, with which
we are all familiar yet about which we know little. Its potentialities are
recognized by few, and by many they are entirely misunderstood.

The fact is, it is a great *Institution of Service,* just as the Postal Establishment, the Newspaper, the Public School, and the Church are institutions of service.

"The Motion Picture Industry," by Will H. Hays, appeared in the 23 January 1923
American Review of Reviews.

Evil pictures have been produced, yes—but incalculable good has been accomplished. The motion picture has carried the silent call for virtue, honesty, ambition, patriotism, hope, love of country and of home, to audiences speaking twenty different languages but understanding in common the universal language of pictures. There may be fifty different languages spoken in this country; but the picture of a mother is the same in every language. It has brought to narrow lives a knowledge of the wide, wide world; it has clothed the empty existence of far-off hamlets with joy; it has been the benefactor of uncounted millions.

In a little over twenty years, the motion picture has grown from a mere idea until to-day it is the principal amusement of the great majority of all our people and the sole amusement of millions and millions. It is not only one of the greatest industries in the country, but it is an instrument and means of immeasurable education and moral influence; and we must not forget that even as we serve the leisure hours of the people with right diversion so do we rivet the girders of society.

It is our earnest purpose to stimulate the development of the spirit of service among all branches of the industry. The camera-man performs a service when he clicks his camera. The operator in the booth contributes a public service when he handles the projector. The director, author, actor, mechanic, and exhibitor, all serve the public, just as do the producer and distributor. Everyone must know that he is a partner in this industry, without whose wholehearted coöperation we cannot succeed.

The motion-picture theater owner builds a structure in which to show pictures, but he also builds an institution to exert an influence for good. The motion-picture theater is an asset to a community. The public has just begun to realize the influence of motion pictures upon thought, taste, conduct and morals, and the consequent influence upon our national life.

It may be that the makers of motion pictures have not been as alert as they should have been in sensing their responsibility; but it is true that the men who pioneered in this industry have already accomplished marvelous things. It has been like an Arabian Nights story. There is little wonder that these crowded years have been, in some respects, a chaos. The development of this industry is analogous to the development of no other. When keen men saw the commercial possibilities in it, they set out in feverish haste on the world-old quest for gold, just as the Forty-niners did when the word came from Sutter's Hill then sent them around Cape Horn and overland across desert, mountain, and plain, undaunted by peril, hardship, or savage. Picture pioneers set out to dig gold just as men went to get it in Alaska when the Klondike flashed the golden invitation to the spirit of adventure.

Nor do we forget, as a matter of history, that while the pioneer in any business is always a romantic figure, his conduct frequently does not measure up to the best boarding-school standards. Force and trickery and even homicide were common incidents in the opening of yesterday's oil fields, and in the mighty struggle for supremacy of the railroads of the country. It is strongly suspected, too, that commerce was begun in piracy, and we know that organized society itself was born in the little group which lifted its hand against all other groups in the fierce, skin-clad clan which knew no law but violence and no purpose but the defense of its own cave.

It is a far cry from many phases of the development of those industries to the development of this; but there is not an entire absence of analogy. There has been competition of the fiercest kind, of course. There has been no opportunity for adequate reflection. The mere physical and mechanical expansion of the early years has been so rapid and so great that there was neither time nor the proper mood to consider adequately the moral and educational responsibility inherent in this great new thing.

Twenty Years' Growth

But those days are over. At the end of this period of incredibly compressed physical, mechanical, financial, and artistic development, the pioneers have caught their second breath. They find themselves the responsible leaders and custodians of one of the greatest industries in the world, with limitless commercial possibilities and perhaps more income than all the public utilities in the country combined. The business is seeking and is finding a firm anchor, in the same way that banking and manufacturing and other mercantile enterprises have done. Sober business men, with vision clarified, old rivals now seeing their common interest, know better than anyone else that the future of the business, as well as the future of society, demands better and still better pictures. . . .

Primarily an instrument of amusement, new uses are developed almost every day. Surgery is taught by motion pictures; secretion of glands is studied by motion pictures; many old-time remedial measures of medicine are supplanted by motion pictures; milder forms of insanity and mental instability, as well as several forms of nervousness, are being cured by motion pictures. They are, in many hospitals, a part of the treatment of children.

Motion pictures are used to demonstrate machines and inventions to prospective buyers who sit in their office chairs and view the projection of the apparatus on the screen, which they will not go miles to see in actual operation. Every "movie" fan is acquainted with the slow-motion effect that can be obtained in pictures, which enables the eye to see the most minute movements of every intricate mechanism. Instead of spending three days in inspecting properties upon which a bond issue was to be floated, representatives of important bond houses recently spent three hours seeing the properties in motion pictures and then purchased the bonds. A stockbreeder clinched his deal with his prospects through motion pictures. Goods are sold at home and in foreign countries through motion pictures. During the trying times of soldiers in camp and during the lull in battle, motion pictures maintained that all-important factor —the morale.

Chambers of commerce are using motion pictures in place of speakers to promote civic interests, such as zoning, recreation and city management. Legends, stories, and local historical events are perpetuated, and religious, civic, and charitable movements are made successful by motion pictures. The flight of a bullet can now be seen in motion pictures. Voice waves shown by motion pictures are studied by telephone engineers in connection with problems of long-distance telephony. The secrets of nature are revealed to the eye by motion pictures.

The Agricultural Department has more than half a million feet of motion-picture films which are used in the promotion of farming and stock-raising. Other Government establishments use the motion picture to show their activities.

MAGNITUDE OF THE INDUSTRY

Millions and millions of dollars are invested by theater owners in the theaters. There is an investment in real estate, equipment, and property of approximately $500,000,000, without including the investment in allied business which has sprung up to supply the wants of the motion-picture industry. There is probably $50,000,000 paid annually in salaries and wages, $200,000,000 spent annually in production, and possibly $600,-000,000 taken in each year for admissions.

Exportation of American-made pictures continued large during 1921, although under the peak established during the previous year. We exported 140,878,345 linear feet of film in 1921, valued at $6,513,567. In 1913 we had exported only 32,192,018 feet of motion pictures. Canada, Australia, England, Argentina and France lead in the use of our films, Canada using over 18,000,000 feet and Australia nearly as much. These are large figures, and as a business the industry now commands the respect of the commercial world.

There are about 15,000 regularly operated motion-picture houses in the United States, with several more thousands operated only during the winter or summer season or once or twice a week.

From the "Nickelodeon" of a decade ago, where motion pictures were shown in some old storeroom for a nickel admission price, to the three or four million dollar theater devoted exclusively to motion pictures, seating several thousand, with unexcelled orchestration and pipe-organ accompaniment, with stage and lighting effects unsurpassed, is an amazing record of progress. All these developments surrounding motion pictures have been so gradual and steady that we fail usually to appreciate the vast improvement of every phase of the industry.

The motion-picture business has its production, sales, and retail branches just as in other industries, which are represented by the producer, distributor, and exhibitor.

Knowledge of the motion-picture industry, to many people, is limited to their own neighborhood theater. They do not realize how many persons find employment in the industry, nor how much the human element enters into it. In production plants and studios, in distributing organizations located in forty different large cities in the United States and at thirty points abroad, and in 15,000 theaters throughout the United States, there are probably 150,000 men and women employed.

The magnitude of the industry may be grasped from a recital of a few of the estimated larger items of expense of the motion-picture business, omitting the exhibiting branch. From the producing end nearly $5,000,000 annually—and many more millions from the theaters—go into advertising, such as newspapers, magazines, trade papers, handbills, theater programs, etc. Perhaps $2,000,000 more go for glass slides, lobby photographs, mats, window cards and posters; another $2,000,000 are spent for lithographs. Lastly, $3,000,000 are spent for printing and engraving.

Thus the newspaper, magazine, advertiser, printer, engraver, typesetter, photographer, lithographer, artists, bookbinders, ink and paper manufacturers, bill-posters, and their help, are all benefited by these immense sums spent.

Whole cities are built for motion pictures. The item for material and labor in "sets" will reach over $5,000,000 annually. Millions of feet of lumber are used, from pegs to palaces. Thus the lumberman, carpenters, builders, and architects come in for benefits. The clothing trade benefits to nearly $1,000,000 in the wardrobes of the studios. All manner of costumes, modern and medieval, are kept and made. The drapery departments contain rare fabrics, priceless tapestry, and modern textiles. Furniture of every period is made or the originals purchased. Wild and domestic animals and birds are kept, and plant nurseries are maintained; for everything must be true to form in motion pictures. The railroads and hotels receive almost $5,000,000 annually through travel expenses of the industry. Hundreds of thousands of metal cases are used for shipping films, benefiting the metal trade, not to mention the cameras and projecting machines. Cost of transporting films by express and parcel post is enormous, and the insurance runs into large sums. Real estate and rents figure in an important way, both in ground and buildings of the producing plants and in the theaters. The electrical trade, the coal industry, the electric power companies, the telegraph and telephone, the optical trade, and the automobile industry all participate in the benefits. The film industry furnishes not far from one billion feet of films annually to the motion-picture producers, enough to encircle the earth eight times.

Every time one pays an admission to his neighborhood theater, a large portion of it goes to benefit men and women employed in the supplying industries the world over. . . .

GOOD PICTURES, AND CENSORSHIP

It has been said repeatedly that certain objectionable pictures which have been made are the class of pictures which the public wants, and that such productions have been meeting the demands of the public, based on box office receipts. That is not true. The American people want —and must have—nothing but good pictures. One way for the public to help the industry to make good pictures is easy; and that is to support the good pictures. I am not suggesting an alibi for the motion-picture business, for that business is coming through on the highway that leads to better pictures. I am only emphasizing that this is not a one-man job, nor the job of a single group; it is a task for the multitude, and in doing it there is work for all.

The American public, of course, is the real censor for the motion picture, just as it is for the press and the pulpit. The people of this country are against censorship fundamentally—against censorship of press, against censorship of pulpit, and against censorship of pictures. But just as certainly is this country against wrong doing; and the demand for censorship will fail when the reason for the demand is removed. As the motion-picture industry moves toward the consummation of its newer ideals, just in like degree all demands for censorship will recede.

An interesting thing happened in Massachusetts at this last election. In 1921 a bill was passed by the legislature providing for a censorship of motion pictures, and under a Massachusetts statute came before the voters for approval. So, at this election, the people of the Bay State had opportunity to vote directly as to whether or not there should be a political censorship of this method of expression. When the Act was originally passed there had been generous support of the measure and many civic and religious organizations favored its enactment. Last summer, however, some three hundred splendid Massachusetts men and women formed a citizens' committee and made it their own fight. The newspapers took it up and were practically a unit in declaring for the defeat of the measure, with full appreciation of the fact that it is not so much the length of the step as the direction of the step that is important in anything.

It is well known that the vote of any referendum question or constitutional amendment is usually but a small part of the vote cast for the political offices. With this in mind, the result of this Massachusetts referendum is most remarkable. The vote against censorship was 552,345 and the vote for censorship was 210,500: a majority against censorship of 341,845. The largest number of votes cast for any candidate for any office on any ticket was that cast for the successful candidate for Governor, 468,277, which was 84,000 less than the "no" vote on censorship. I rather think this is an unprecedented performance; it certainly shows the deep interest that people have in pictures.

This rejection of censorship was a splendid response to the appeal of the press and the citizens of Massachusetts against undue political aggression. But just as certainly is it a challenge to the motion-picture industry to work out successfully its own program for betterment; and that responsibility is accepted by the industry and will be discharged. . . .

The motion-picture business objects to political censorship for one great reason: because it is un-American. Political censorship drove the Pilgrims to Plymouth Rock; political censorship faced the Minute Men at Concord; political censorship caused the Boston Tea Party; in this new effort to control politically a great method of expression, Massachusetts has taken a characteristically American position. . . .

WHAT OF THE FUTURE?

Continuing this new drive for the best possible pictures, measuring up toward what the standard should be—a standard which many pictures already had achieved—earnestly asking the public's cooperation, and desiring from every possible standpoint, selfish and unselfish, to move in the right direction, they have brought out, and are bringing out, a series of pictures which we are hoping will attract the public's attention, as evidence both of good faith and ability to accomplish, and as an augury for still better things to which every effort shall be directed. The better pictures are here. The maintaining of the highest standard is quite essential as its attainment, and there can be and will be no slipping backward, nor loss of any improvement that may be accomplished. These pictures are being received with appreciation and the *public will not be unmindful either of the impossibility of pleasing every one with every picture or of the necessity for different types of pictures to meet various tastes and interests.*

As is well known, the great center of the industry is in Los Angeles County, California, possibly 75 per cent. of the pictures being made there. It is an interesting fact that the third largest industry in Los Angeles

County is food production, with an expenditure last year of $92,000,000 and with a weekly payroll of $260,000; the second largest industry in the county is petroleum, spending last year $104,000,000, with a weekly payroll of $353,000 (and probably one-fourth of the oil produced in the country last year was produced in Los Angeles County). But the largest industry in Los Angeles County is the motion-picture business, spending last year $140,000,000 and having a weekly payroll of over $500,000. It is the earnest purpose of the Association that everything possible shall be done toward maintaining an industrial community which will be a model not only as regards the activities of the industry itself, but also in its relations with the splendid community of which it is a part. Definite steps are being taken by the Association in Los Angeles toward that end.

I have come to visualize this new thing as my attachment to it becomes deeper. I have come to know it as an unbelievably great, three-fold instrument for good. It can do three great things, and it will do these three things as no other instrument that I know of can do them.

In the first place, it can and will *fill a necessity*—the necessity for entertainment.

In the second place, it can and will *instruct*—which is, indeed, a most precious power.

In the third place, and I am sure that my enthusiasm does not warp my judgment, it will do more than any other existing agency to *unite the peoples of the world*—to bring understanding between men and women, and between nation and nation.

I know there will everywhere be abundant sympathy with all of these things; and those within the industry, on whom the first duty lies, do not minimize their responsibility nor would they shirk it. With the sympathetic and active coöperation of the public, we can accomplish the purposes of this Association. I believe that any job in this life which ought to be done can be done.

The motion-picture industry accepts the challenge in the demand of the American people for a higher quality of art and interest in their entertainment.

The industry accepts the challenge in the demand of the American youth that its pictures shall give the right kind of entertainment and instruction.

We accept the challenge in the righteous demand of the American mother that the entertainment and amusement of that youth shall be worthy of its value as a most potent factor in the country's future.

We accept the challenge in the proper demand of educators and religious leaders that the full instructional and religious value of the motion picture shall be developed and used.

We accept our full responsibility. It is a service, and "service is the supreme commitment of life." It is a service which needs the best from us all, and I have great faith in its fulfillment.

■ ■ ■ ■

THE DON'TS AND BE CAREFULS (1927), Motion Picture Producers and Distributors of America

To support the industry's contention of its social and moral concern, it passed the first of a series of official moral rules, or "codes," in 1921— the Thirteen Points of the National Motion Picture Industry. These codes were to be formulated, passed, and, evenutally, enforced for the next twelve years as a specific commercial antidote against censorship agitation. The second of these series of resolves was stronger and longer than the Thirteen Points—"The Don'ts and Be Carefuls"—passed in October of 1927 on the occasion of a Federal Trade Commission hearing into the practices of the motion picture industry. The final statement of moral resolves, which would replace these "Don'ts and Be Carefuls," was to be the more famous Hollywood Production Code of three years later (see pages 321–33).

Resolved, That those things which are included in the following list shall not appear in pictures produced by the members of this Association, irrespective of the manner in which they are treated:

1. Pointed profanity—by either title or lip—this includes the words "God," "Lord," "Jesus," "Christ" (unless they be used reverently in connection with proper religious ceremonies), "hell," " damn," "Gawd," and every other profane and vulgar expression however it may be spelled;
2. Any licentious or suggestive nudity—in fact or in silhouette; and any lecherous or licentious notice thereof by other characters in the picture;
3. The illegal traffic in drugs;
4. Any inference of sex perversion;
5. White slavery;
6. Miscegenation (sex relationships between the white and black races);
7. Sex hygiene and venereal diseases;

Motion Picture Producers and Distributors of America, "The Don'ts and Be Carefuls," October 1927.

8. Scenes of actual childbirth—in fact or in silhouette;
9. Children's sex organs;
10. Ridicule of the clergy;
11. Willful offense to any nation, race or creed;

And be it further *resolved,* That special care be exercised in the manner in which the following subjects are treated, to the end that vulgarity and suggestiveness may be eliminated and that good taste may be emphasized:

1. The use of the flag;
2. International relations (avoiding picturizing in an unfavorable light another country's religion, history, institutions, prominent people, and citizenry);
3. Arson;
4. The use of firearms;
5. Theft, robbery, safe-cracking, and dynamiting of trains, mines, buildings, etc. (having in mind the effect which a too-detailed description of these may have upon the moron);
6. Brutality and possible gruesomeness;
7. Technique of committing murder by whatever method;
8. Methods of smuggling;
9. Third-degree methods;
10. Actual hangings or electrocutions as legal punishment for crime;
11. Sympathy for criminals;
12. Attitude toward public characters and institutions;
13. Sedition;
14. Apparent cruelty to children and animals;
15. Branding of people or animals;
16. The sale of women, or of a woman selling her virtue;
17. Rape or attempted rape;
18. First-night scenes;
19. Man and woman in bed together;
20. Deliberate seduction of girls;
21. The institution of marriage;
22. Surgical operations;
23. The use of drugs;
24. Titles or scenes having to do with law enforcement or law-enforcing officers;
25. Excessive or lustful kissing, particularly when one character or the other is a "heavy."

■ ■ ■ ■

Don't Go to Hollywood (1924), Ruth Waterbury

One of the social problems of the 1920s—for both Hollywood and the rest of the nation—was the number of young girls who ran off there each year. These runaways were perhaps the predecessors of those runaways and dropouts who disappeared into the hippy colonies of the big cities in the late 1960s. This article in *Photoplay* warns the potential runaway to stay away. *Photoplay* in the 1920s, edited by the literate James Quirk (he is mentioned by H. L. Mencken as one of his Hollywood drinking buddies on page 228), with contributing writers such as Terry Ramsaye and Adela Rogers St. John, was perhaps the most literate and mature "fan magazine" America ever produced.

THE ADVICE OF PHOTOPLAY'S WRITER WHO TRIED BREAKING INTO THE MOVIES

Don't go to Hollywood! Don't go! Don't go, no matter what beauty, talent or youth you have, no matter what inducements are offered you.

I have no words to express it strongly enough. Stay away! I saw things in Hollywood, heard them, learned of them, when I was posing as a girl trying to break into the movies that I want to forget.

Understand, there is no vice, as such, among the extra girls of Hollywood. Their only vice is ambition. But that vice consumes them.

Adela Rogers St. John, in her story of *Greta* in "The Port of Missing Girls" in this issue of PHOTOPLAY, states that stellar success in Hollywood is a ten thousand to one chance. That amazing figure is absolutely true. And a girl's even getting a single day's work is a thirty to one chance, with the cards stacked against her.

For every Betty Bronson, for every Sally O'Neill, talented, beautiful, lucky little kids who get the break and rise to sudden stardom, there are 9,999 girls who never get anywhere—who strive, suffer, and starve, and never get a close-up.

It is not alone that a girl cannot reach fame in Hollywood. She can not reach anything there—not that tenderest dream of women, the love of some good man; not that maintainer of self-respect—a good job. Nothing, unless she is the lucky girl.

This is not the fault of Hollywood, the city.

My call on the Hollywood Chamber of Commerce persuaded me of

"Don't Go to Hollywood," by Ruth Waterbury, was published in the March 1924 issue of *Photoplay*.

Hollywood's merchandising
and packaging of "it":
The "It Girl" Clara Bow;
an alluring Lupe Velez;
an uplifting Vilma Banky;
an inspirational Pola Negri

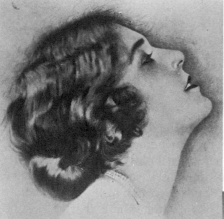

that. To get to see the publicity man of the office, I had to pass five very beautiful girls.

"All trying to break into the movies," he explained. "When Central Casting turns them down on registration, they come to us. We always issue the same advice. Go back home. If a girl has to have help, we have an arrangement with the Chamber of Commerce in other cities that helps us get her back to her own city."

"The city of Hollywood is for the movie people, absolutely. But as its representative, the Chamber of Commerce is bending every effort to keep these unwanted people from coming here. Unemployment produces bad conditions. After all, Hollywood's only a small place, not a manufacturing community or a big trade center. They can't get work in the movies and they can't get work in ordinary lines. The jobs aren't here, that's all, and for those that there are, the supply is ten times too great and pulls down the wage scale. But we get these aspirants back to their homes somehow, if we even have to make them accompany a body."

Then it was explained to me how many a disillusioned girl reaches home by acting as chaperon to a corpse. The dead are not supposed to travel alone. So when a body must be shipped out from Hollywood, the railroad lets the Chamber of Commerce know, and some girl gets a free ticket for performing this gruesome job. Adventure can not possibly end more abjectly than this. Don't go to Hollywood!

There simply is not room for another girl in any line in Hollywood. The girls who go there and stay in face of all the pressure there is on them to make them return to their homes must face utter failure.

I know what I am talking about. I gathered these facts for myself, living as the extra girl lives.

Take, first, the simplest thing, loneliness.

I have no conception how the average girl, fresh from home, stands the loneliness of Hollywood. Its kindliness, its charity is there, but it is extremely difficult to get at either. Friendships are quite impossible. You see, very occasionally, intense attachments between two individuals on sets, but Hollywood is primarily a city of individuals, intent on self, as any city must be where everyone is excessively ambitious. Everyone is afraid of everyone else, as it must always be where the only standard is that whoever can get in movies, can get in, and whoever can't can not. Hectic wealth on the one hand, hectic poverty on the other, unreality and sunshine, silence and watchfulness. There can be little conversation in such an atmosphere. Few can afford to be helpful. The two-faced to-

morrow is always just ahead, tomorrow equally compounded of fear and
hope.

Long before I lost my editor's bet of five hundred dollars that I couldn't
break into the movies, I moved from the Studio Club, for I regarded those
girls, protected from Hollywood, some of them supported by indulgent
parents, the others within reach of charity when it was needed, as no true
picture of the extra girl. I moved, still under an assumed name, to a cheap
little hotel, in search of local color. And it was there that the Hollywood
loneliness got me, as I was facing my first Sunday alone.

There are three movie houses on the main section of Hollywood Boulevard, and those are the only amusements you can reach without a car. One
is the luxurious Egyptian Theater, but its cheapest seats cost more than
a dollar. The other two, offering pictures I had already seen, did not seem
worth fifty cents. I knew no one to telephone. I wanted plain, human
companionship. Finally I went for a walk.

He was standing near the corner of Las Palmas Avenue as I approached it. His face, though young, was marked by the heavy lines
which almost always characterize the actor. His smile insinuated many
things. I tried to ignore him. I bought popcorn from a curbside stand.
I bought magazines in a drug store. I went back to the quietest corner of
the hotel lounge, but I couldn't discourage him. He sat opposite me,
staring, until curiosity conquered me.

"Why do you follow me?" I asked.

He seized the opening quickly. "I know when a girlie's lonesome," he
said. "I've been getting bad breaks lately and if you want to buy me my
dinner, I'll see you get less lonesome."

The white pages of the magazines fluttered to the floor as I fled from
him toward the elevator.

When I came down stairs, two hours later, I stopped to speak to the
room clerk. It was largely because I wanted to hear my own voice.

"Mr. Blank over there could help you break into the movies," said the
clerk, to whom I had deliberately confided my supposed ambition. "He's
an assistant director and lives here in the hotel. I'll introduce you."

Mr. Blank spent an hour impressing me with his importance at an unimportant studio. Then he whispered, "Say, a friend of mine's got a house in
Laurel Canyon. He's away and I've got the key. Let's go up there for the
evening. I can help you a lot and I bet we'll find we're on the same mental
plane."

I knew we wouldn't, so I ate dinner alone. I took another walk. Suddenly in the stillness of a little dark street I heard a scream. I saw two

figures twisting together before a stucco wall, and as I flew forward, with some vague idea of being of help, I recognized the girl. You would have known her, too, for she had been a well known leading woman. Her head was being vigorously slammed against the stucco by a thick throated gent. I stopped aghast but a girl, passing me, grinned unconcernedly. "It's only her husband," she explained. "He's a chauffeur and every time he gets tight he knocks her around trying to spoil her face. He's jealous of her success, I guess. No use to interfere. He's never spoiled her expression yet and she keeps on loving him."

Nor had I reached the limit for that day. I had been put on the trail of a certain assistant director at one of the largest studios. Knowing he had much to do with hiring extras, I rang him up, explaining who I really was and my connection with PHOTOPLAY, and asked him if he could give me some human interest stories.

Central Casting has tried to do away with the power of the assistants, the camera men, the prop boys over extra girls' destinies, but it hasn't succeeded conspicuously. When Central was formed, a rule was made that any girl recommended by any studio official must be placed on their lists. The result is that when a call comes from a studio asking for eighty girls, say, seventy-seven of the names are frequently already on the call. And behind each of those demanded names there is always a story of personal influence. Central protects itself by marking the girl's pay check "requested." Then if such a girl is unsatisfactory to the studio for any reason, the blame can not fall on the agency.

In this case, the assistant knew perfectly well I wasn't some poor kid up against it, looking for a job and willing to pay almost anything to get it. Yet that stupid boob proceeded on the supposition I wanted to mix kisses with my facts and when I refused to give them, he refused to give the facts.

These are the types of men the lonely girl encounters. Not that a girl might not encounter such men in other lines of work, but in Hollywood there are more of them because there are more beautiful girls there, freed from all restraints of home.

That is that side of it. To get the other side I moved to Hollywood's best hotel, which is an excellent one, and registered for the first time under my own name.

I had little more than got to my room when the telephone began ringing. The hotel press agent wanted to give out a little story to the papers. A woman's press club asked me to be their guest at dinner. A man who manages a rising young star asked me to lunch with the little star and himself and maybe I could write something about the dear in PHOTOPLAY. The leading Hollywood restaurant invited me to dine there as its guest.

And those things are Hollywood, too, as much as extras are. I knew perfectly well it was only my association with PHOTOPLAY that made me suddenly so important, but I accepted all invitations as they came. Throughout a hectic week I went everywhere, for lunch with stars, for tea with stars, for dinner with stars and it was all perfectly marvelous. I went to the Writers' Club and to the magnificent beach clubs at Santa Monica. I attended a meeting at the Thalians, a club organized by young Lincoln Stedman to which the movie youngsters who are climbing toward stardom belong. Earnest and ambitious, they held a solemn meeting, talked of their careers and art, and left at ten after a supper of ham sandwiches and cider. A more circumspect group couldn't have been found at the most select prep school.

Everywhere I saw the miracles of the movies, the luxurious homes of Colleen Moore and Tony Moreno, the veritable palace set in formal gardens that Milton Sills recently purchased for his bride, Doris Kenyon, the apartments in Los Angeles that Norma Talmadge owns—wealth and ease purchased by movie success. I saw, too, an old woman come into a casting office and faint from hunger though she is the mother of one of our most successful stars. I went to cabarets near Culver City and to Henry's, the sandwich emporium run by a former Chaplin comedian. You see the crowd there, but never a star. A star who matters today can not afford night life.

There is little bohemianism in the upper ranks of the movies. Their work demands too much. . . .

I went to the opening of "Bardelys the Magnificent" that night. It was the first Hollywood premier I had seen and I was totally unprepared for the brilliance of it. It was the sort of scene that lures girls to Hollywood as inevitably as a candle flame lures the moths of a summer night.

Great sunlight arcs around the theater, great piercing searchlights crossing and recrossing the sky. The scream of motor cars, the rattle of trolleys, the noise of loaded busses. The crowd of fans, roped off at either side, the police holding them back. The "cash customers" coming in one path, the stellar world down another before the camera under the arc lights. Everyone of the movie world was present, out to see and be seen, out to watch John Gilbert, whose story is so typical of Hollywood. There was what Hollywood gave you if you won out, adulation, awe, money, beauty, luxury, jewels, clothes, comfort.

When I returned to my hotel I was still dazed with the exotic magnificence of it all. And there in the lobby was a girl weeping, a girl who had been a star and who has been off the screen for three years.

Now the Hollywood hotels have a habit of what is called "plugging keyholes." So many girls register with them while waiting the lucky break. A hotel bill doesn't have to be paid for a week. Sometimes it can be stalled a month. And in that time luck may turn. If it doesn't the girl can, if she's smart, drop her clothes out the window after dark, walk out and collect them and disappear, leaving the bill. And just this happened until the hotels learned their little trick. Now when a bill stays too long unpaid they plug the keyhole of the room, leaving the girl locked outside and her possessions inside.

The girl in the lobby was locked out of her room.

"I haven't a friend or a dollar left," she sobbed. "Used to have both. I've tried to get work but they don't believe I'm off the hop. I haven't a place to sleep. When I found my door plugged, I got drunk and raised a row on the Boulevard thinking I'd get pinched and locked up. That'd give me a place to sleep anyhow. Instead I just get dragged back here. Make 'em lock me up."

I rushed to the desk for a telegram blank.

"Lost our bet," I wired my editor. "Returning East immediately where jobs are jobs and where the women have wide, homely faces." But he wouldn't let me pay it. He raised my salary instead.

Gee, I'm glad I didn't break into the movies.

■ ■ ■ ■
___

HOLLYWOOD'S EXTRAS (1941), Murray Ross

As the previous article implied, one of the industry's most serious problems was managing its army of extras, who were susceptible to both sexual and financial abuses. Because the movies required the services of this human scenery, the industry itself cleaned up the mess in 1925 by creating the Central Casting Corporation—in effect, the first formal organizing of any members of the Hollywood labor force. This chapter from Murray Ross's *Stars and Strikes* (a history of labor relations in the movie industry published in 1941) describes the founding of Central Casting.

___

Motion pictures must have a human backdrop. Film stars need the support of lesser luminaries to enhance their own brilliance and to lend authenticity to scenes. To supply this background all sorts of people and

"Hollywood's Extras" is from *Stars and Strikes,* by Murray Ross (Columbia University Press 1941).

all types of ability are needed. Eskimos and Fiji Islanders, infants and bearded men, ice skaters and soprano singers—all must be available at a moment's notice. It is difficult to anticipate what the next script may contain or what a new director may demand. To meet all possible contingencies, the reservoir of extra players from which the studios draw their human atmosphere must be vast and of a polyglot character. This creates a tragic situation, since the industry cannot provide these essential people with sufficient employment. There are too many of them to exist comfortably on the annual studio expenditure for extra talent. Their lot is a sad one, and they constitute Hollywood's most serious labor problem.

The problem of "extras" is not new; its roots are a quarter of a century old. Almost from the day of the location of the film industry on the sunny shores of the southern Pacific, the flow of extras became discernible. Show business throughout the country supplied a large share, especially between 1914 and 1918. Many of these recruits became professional extras in stock companies maintained by studios in the early days. A second migration of show people, refugees from the rapidly declining theater and vaudeville, occurred after the World War. In addition, a heterogeneous group of ex-service men and expatriates of many nations drifted into Hollywood. Thousands of movie-struck youngsters flooded the film capital annually during the 1920s. The best-looking girl in a high school graduating class, the best-dressed boy in a small-town competition, the winner of a local bathing-beauty contest, all set out for movieland. Most of them finally became extras. Local residents who had been used during the shooting of spectacles requiring large crowds decided that this experience was sufficient to make them actors and further overcrowded the extra field.

This enormous oversupply of both professionals and amateurs who were determined to "break into the movies" presented a social, moral, and economic hazard. They had no protective organization to look after them and fell prey to all sorts of minor abuses. Unscrupulous individuals concocted numerous schemes by means of which the gullible extras were looted of their last pennies. "Acting" and "make-up" schools which guaranteed studio jobs, "influential" commercial placement agencies, and still less legitimate enterprises mushroomed. The studios themselves aggravated the situation by their haphazard hiring procedure. Since no studio offered regular or steady employment, extras had to "make the rounds" of the studios daily. This procedure burdened them with large traveling expenses and wasted a great deal of their time and energy. They frequently carried complete wardrobes in order to fit into whatever opening occurred.

Persistent complaints to the public authorities drew attention to the plight of the extras. Championing their cause were publications which dramatized their difficulties. Charges of underpayment, of overwork, of maltreatment, and of other forms of exploitation were widely circulated. The California Department of Industrial Relations and the Association of Motion Picture Producers became actively interested in the extra problem in the middle 1920s. Several of the complaints had resulted in well-deserved adverse publicity. The industry had just been very badly shaken by a public scandal—the Arbuckle episode. Eager to avoid further notoriety, it took steps to remedy the glaring abuses to which the extras were subjected.

Hays engaged Mary Van Kleeck of the Russell Sage Foundation to make a study of social and employment conditions in Hollywood, with special emphasis on the situation of the extras. Her survey failed to disclose "evidence of any deliberate intention of exploiting anybody in the industry." On the contrary, it found "many signs of goodwill and kindliness and wholesomeness of attitude in casting directors' offices."

But despite these generally favorable conclusions, the report criticized the industry for neglecting its employment problems. All the companies lacked records of labor turnover, which Miss Van Kleeck regarded as essential for the development of sound industrial relations. Specifically referring to the extra problem, the survey condemned the absence of a definite policy toward this group.

The Russell Sage survey criticized the high fees legally charged by the commercial placement agencies which supplied extras to the studios. It called attention to the fact that the studios paid in non-negotiable vouchers and that the extras assigned part of their unearned wages to the placement agencies. These were both violations of the California labor laws. Miss Van Kleeck recommended the immediate establishment of a free central registration and placement bureau for extras. The California Department of Industrial Relations, which was then making an independent study of the situation, concurred in her recommendation. Miss Van Kleeck divided the extra problem into two phases: (1) the difficulties resulting from the casual nature of the work; and (2) the abuses pertaining to the placement and employment practices. The root of the first problem lay deeply buried in the technical conditions prevalent in the industry and would take a long time to erase through the gradual process of decasualization; the second problem was of a more immediate character and could be substantially rectified by a free central placement agency.

Although somewhat reluctant at the outset to assume the large financial burden, the Association of Motion Picture Producers established the Central Casting Corporation on December 4, 1925, fifteen months after the completion of the Russell Sage survey. The new organization was to be the employment office for all the association's members. The California Bureau of Labor Statistics stated its purposes as follows: (1) the elimination of high fees charged by private employment agencies; (2) the prevention of violations of law arising out of methods of paying the extras; (3) the discouragement of would-be additions to the extra ranks; (4) the development of a residue of efficient extras who would be called upon frequently and who would be able to earn a decent living from their employment as extras.

Immediately upon assuming its arduous task in January, 1926, Central Casting registered all the available extra players. For the actual casting, it developed a unique procedure of placing entirely by telephone. This method was not altogether new to Hollywood, since many extras who were frequently used had become so well known to studio casting directors and to the casting agencies that they were able to solicit work in this manner. Realizing its advantages, Central established an efficient system which enables extras to call in for work at any time. Records indicate that as many as 4,000 inquiries for work have been received by Central in a single hour.

Placement by telephone provides a case study in efficiency. From the casting offices of the studios, requests come over the teletype daily for extras needed during the following day's shooting. The studio casting directors usually supply specific directions as to the type of player and the kind of wardrobe wanted. The order may call for ten couples to dance at a fashionable social function or for fifty mourners to take part in a funeral procession. All studio requests are in at the close of the business day. This is the hour when Central Casting begins its feverish activity. Thousands of calls pour in from the extras, who have been instructed to announce their names and to wait for a reply. As the Central Casting operator repeats the name, a well-trained casting personnel peruses the studio order sheets. These casting directors are familiar with the qualifications of the most frequently used extras. If the player who is on the wire can fill one of the studio requests, the director will take the call and give the necessary directions as to the place of work and the wardrobe required. Extras whose services are not needed are told "Try later." They may continue to call during the evening until they get an assignment for the next day or until they give up in discouragement. If on any day the demand for certain types is greater than the number of inquiring extras, Central obtains additional players by making use of its exhaustive files. The process is now reversed; Central itself telephones to suitable extras. Such a situation, for example, may arise when some studio sends in a call for unusual types or for a large number of Orientals, Negroes, or other "racials." Most of the assignments are made between five and eight P.M., since the casting personnel has learned from experience that it is difficult to locate extras during later hours.

The entire casting procedure is remarkably smooth in its operation. Orders for extras filled by Central are very seldom rejected by studio directors. Before this situation was achieved the casting personnel had been thoroughly trained and was well acquainted with picture requirements. As a result of constant repetition, at least 2,000 names are recorded photographically in the minds of the casting directors. To some extent, selection has reached the conditioned-reflex stage. This familiarity with available players is essential since casting must be done too rapidly to permit reference to files. Central Casting is one of the largest placement agencies in the country. It fills as many as 1,000 jobs a day in this expeditious manner.

Central Casting remedied many of the employment abuses to which the extras had previously been subjected. Since the placement expenses were borne by the producers, the annual savings to these players have averaged $300,000. Commercial placement agencies had deducted seven to ten percent of their daily earnings. Out-of-door interviewing yards in each studio, popularly known as "bull pens," where candidates for extra work assembled daily in all kinds of weather, were abolished. It was no longer necessary for extras to waste time, money, and energy making the rounds from studio to studio. The undesirable practice of payment in non-negotiable vouchers was also eliminated. These vouchers could be cashed only at the employment agency, after the deduction of the placement fee. Extras who were too tired at the end of the day to spend several hours traveling to the agency and waiting in line for the cash had been subjected to another petty abuse: scalpers accosted them at the gates of every studio and offered to cash the vouchers for a small consideration.

State authorities, meanwhile, kept a vigilant eye on developments. By prevailing upon the producers to exercise more rigid control over the entire situation, they had been instrumental in the establishment of Central Casting. In addition, they helped the extras in a number of other ways. As early as 1922, the California Bureau of Labor Statistics investigated fake "movie make-up" schools which promised employment to film aspirants. It revealed that a number of these schools worked in collusion with private employment agencies to defraud prospective extras of their money. The schools were prosecuted and forced to liquidate. A number of motion picture employment agencies forfeited their licenses. Although after 1925 about ninety percent of all extras were placed by Central Casting, some commercial film employment agencies continued to operate. Several of these were disreputable. The studios frequently employed unlicensed "runners" to engage large groups of extras for location work. Like the dishonest agencies, they often exacted exorbitant commissions and tampered with wages. The state labor law enforcement officers rapidly put an end to this cheating of the poorest workers.

Acting under the authority of the state minimum wage law, the Division of Industrial Welfare of the California Department of Industrial Relations promulgated a set of uniform rules for women and minor extras in January, 1926. Since Central Casting was being organized just at that time, these rules standardized the procedure under which the placement agency has operated ever since. They were revised in April, 1931.

Thse state regulations eliminated many evils by establishing maximum hours of work and by laying down the broad principles governing employment conditions. A woman or minor receiving a wage of $15 or less a day or $65 or less a week was defined as an extra. For all those coming under this classification, the working day is limited to eight hours. Overtime with pay is permitted in case of emergency. Under no circumstances may an extra be required to work more than sixteen hours, including mealtime, during any twenty-four hour period. A six-day week was instituted for the few extras who work on a weekly basis. If these players are required to work on the seventh day they must be paid time and one-half for the first eight hours and double time for additional work. Extras must be compensated for all time occupied at the direction of the studio. This includes rehearsal, lengthy interviews, and delayed salary payment. Carfare is allowed for all interviews and for "weather permitting" calls when studios cannot work because of unfavorable weather conditions. In addition to transportation costs, the time necessary for traveling to and from location is paid for at half the standard rate. Meal periods must be provided at reasonable intervals. Extras required to report for costume fittings are entitled to a full day's salary if not given employment in the production for which they are fitted.

In case of "weather permitting" calls, the studio is required to give extras carfare and to discharge them immediately. Otherwise they are entitled to a quarter of a day's pay for each two hours until paid. When work calls are canceled for reasons beyond the studio's control after the extras report, they are entitled to one fourth of the daily check. If any recording or photography is done when extras report for a "weather permitting" or canceled call, they are to be paid the agreed daily wage. Day workers must be paid at the completion of their work in cash or in negotiable checks.

Conditions of employment were greatly improved. Employers are required to inform extras at the time of call if they are to do night work, "wet" work, or work of a rough or dangerous character. If extras are not previously advised of the type of work, the studio is responsible for any injury to health or damage to property. Extras have the option of refusing such work and must be paid for all the time they are kept until they are dismissed. If the personal wardrobe or property of extras is damaged as a result of their work, they are to be compensated for the loss. This was a concession important to the extras, as their wardrobes are, to a large extent, their stock in trade. Companies frequently work into the early hours of the morning. If extras are dismissed after public transportation service has ceased, the studios are required to provide transportation home. Food and hot drinks must be served to women extras working at midnight. The producers are required to provide adequate dressing facilities, safe locker rooms, and sanitary water and toilets. Although the Division of Industrial Welfare was empowered to decree these conditions for women and minor extras only, the studios voluntarily extended them to men. . . .

■ ■ ■ ■

INTERLUDE IN THE SOCRATIC MANNER (1927), H. L. Mencken

H. L. Mencken, the noted American journalist, essayist, linguist, and cynic, wrote this summary of his Hollywood observations for the magazine he edited, the *American Mercury*. As opposed to that other newspaperman who chronicled *The Sins of Hollywood*, Mencken found the legends depicting Hollywood as Sodom and Gomorrah to be—like so much else about Hollywood and America in his view—"bunk."

Having completed your æsthetic researches at Hollywood, what is your view of the film art now?

I made no researches at Hollywood, and was within the corporate bounds of the town, in fact, only on a few occasions, and then for only a few hours. I spent my time in Los Angeles, studying the Christian pathology of that great city. When not so engaged I mainly devoted myself to quiet guzzling with Joe Hergesheimer, Jim Quirk, Johnny Hemphill, Jim Tully, Walter Wanger and other such literati. For the rest, I visited friends in the adjacent deserts, some of them employed in the pictures and some not. They treated me with immense politeness. With murderers as thick

"Interlude in the Socratic Manner" is from *Prejudices: Sixth Series,* by H. L. Mencken (Knopf, 1927).

in the town as evangelists, nothing would have been easier than to have had me killed, but they let me go.

Did any of them introduce you to the wild nightlife of the town?

The wildest night-life I encountered was at Sister Aimée McPherson's tabernacle. I saw no wildness among the movie-folk. They seemed to me, in the main, to be very serious and even gloomy people. And no wonder, for they worked like Pullman porters or magazine editors. When they are engaged in posturing for a film and have finished their day's labor they are far too tired for any recreation requiring stamina. I encountered but two authentic souses in three weeks. One was a cowboy and the other was an author. I heard of a lady getting tight at a party, but I was not present. The news was a sensation in the town. Such are the sorrows of poor mummers: their most banal peccadilloes are magnified into horrors. Regard the unfortunate Chaplin. If he were a lime and cement dealer his latest divorce case would not have got two lines in the newspapers. But, as it was, he was placarded all over the front pages because he had had a banal disagreement with one of his wives. The world hears of such wild, frenzied fellows as Tully, and puts them down as typical of Hollywood. But Tully is not an actor; he eats actors. I saw him devour half a dozen of them on the half-shell in an hour. He wears a No. 30 collar and has a colossal capacity for wine-bibbing; I had to call up my last reserves to keep up with him. But the typical actor is a slim and tender fellow. What would be a mere apéritif for Tully or me would put him under the table, yelling for his pastor.

So you caught no glimpses of immorality?

Immorality? Oh, my God! Hollywood, despite the smell of patchouli and rattle of revolver fire, seemed to me to be one of the most respectable towns in America. Even Baltimore can't beat it. The notion that actors are immoral fellows is a delusion that comes down to us from Puritan days, just as the delusion that rum is a viper will go down to posterity from our days. There is no truth in it. The typical actor, at least in America, is the most upright of men: he always marries the girl. How many actors are bachelors? Not one in a thousand. The divorce rate is high among them simply because the marriage rate is so high. An actor, encountering a worthy girl, leaps from the couch to the altar almost as fast as a Baptist leaps from the altar to the couch. It is his incurable sentimentality that fetches him: if he was not born a romantic he is not an actor. Worse, his profession supports his natural weakness. In plays and movies he always marries the girl in the end, and so it seems to him to be the decent thing to do it in his private life. Actors always copy the doings of the characters they impersonate: no Oscar was needed to point out that nature always imitates art. I heard, of course, a great deal of gossip in Los Angeles, but all save a trivial part of it was excessively romantic. Nearly every great female star, it appeared, was desperately in love, either with her husband or with some pretty and well-heeled fellow, usually not an actor. And every male star was mooning over some coy and lovely miss. I heard more sweet love stories in three weeks than I had heard in New York in the previous thirty years. The whole place stank of orange-blossoms. Is honest love conducive to vice? Then one may argue that it is conducive to delirium tremens to be a Presbyterian elder. One of the largest industries in Hollywood is that of the florists. Next comes that of the traffickers in wedding silver. One beautiful lady star told me that buying such presents cost her $11,000 last year.

But the tales go round. Is there no truth in them at all?

To the best of my knowledge and belief, none. They are believed because the great masses of the plain people, though they admire movie actors, also envy them, and hence hate them. It is the old human story. Why am I hated by theologians? It is because I am an almost unparalleled expert in all branches of theology. Whenever they tackle me, my superior knowledge and talent floor them. In precisely the same way I hate such fellows as the movie Salvini, Jack Gilbert. Gilbert is an amiable and tactful young man, and treats me with the politeness properly due to my years and learning. But I heard in Culver City that no less than two thousand head of women, many of them rich, were mashed on him. Well, I can recall but fifteen or twenty women who have ever showed any sign of being flustered by me, and not one of them, at a forced sale, would have realized $200. Hence I hate Gilbert, and would rejoice unaffectedly to see him taken in some scandal that would stagger humanity. If he is accused of anything less than murdering his wife and eight children I shall be disappointed.

Then why do you speak for Mr. Chaplin?

Simply because he is not a handsome dog, as Gilbert is. The people who hate him do so because he is rich. It is the thought that his trouble will bust him that gives them delight. But I have no desire for money and so his prosperity does not offend me. I always have too much money; it is easy to get in New York, provided one is not a professing Christian. Gilbert, I suppose, is rich too; he wears very natty clothes. But it is not his wealth that bothers me: it is those two thousand head of women.

So, failing researches, you continue ignorant of the film art?

Ignorant? What a question! How could any man remain ignorant of the movies after three weeks in Los Angeles? As well continue ignorant of laparotomy after three weeks in a hospital sun-parlor! No, I am full of information about them, some of it accurate, for I heard them talked day and night, and by people who actually knew something about them. There was but one refuge from that talk, and that was La McPherson's basilica. Moreover, I have hatched some ideas of my own.

As for example?

That the movie folks, in so far as they are sentient at all, are on the hooks of a distressing dilemma. They have built their business upon a foundation of morons, and now they are paying for it. They seem to be unable to make a presentable picture without pouring out tons of money, and when they have made it they must either sell it to immense audiences of halfwits, or go broke. There seems to be very little ingenuity and resourcefulness in them. They are apparently quite unable, despite their melodramatic announcements of salary cuts, to solve the problem of making movies cheaply, and yet intelligently, so that civilized persons may visit the movie-parlors without pain. But soon or late some one will have to solve it. Soon or late the movie will have to split into two halves. There will be movies for the present mob, and there will be movies for the relatively enlightened minority. The former will continue idiotic; the latter, if competent men to make them are unearthed, will show sense and beauty.

Have you caught the scent of any such men?

Not yet. There are some respectable craftsmen in Hollywood. (I judged them by their talk: I have not seen many of their actual pictures.) They tackle the problems of their business in a more or less sensible manner. They have learned a lot from the Germans. But I think it would be stretching a point to say that there are any artists among them—as yet. They are adept, but not inspired. The movies need a first-rate artist—a man of genuine competence and originality. If he is in Hollywood to-day, he is probably boot-legging, running a pants pressing parlor, or grinding a camera crank. The movie magnates seek him in literary directions. They pin their faith to novelists and playwrights. I presume to believe that this is bad medicine. The fact that a man can write a competent novel is absolutely no reason for assuming that he can write a competent film. The two things are as unlike as Pilsner and coca-cola. Even a sound dramatist is not necessarily a competent scenario-writer. What the movies need is a school of authors who will forget all dialogue and description, and try to set forth their ideas in terms of pure motion. It can be done, and it will be done. The German, Dr. Murnau, showed the way in certain scenes of "The Last Laugh." But the American magnates continue to buy bad novels and worse plays, and then put over-worked hacks to the sorry job of translating them into movies. It is like hiring men to translate college yells into riddles. Æschylus himself would have been stumped by such a task.

When do you think the Shakespeare of the movies will appear? And where will he come from?

God knows. He may even be an American, as improbable as it may seem. One thing, only, I am sure of: he will not get much for the masterpieces. He will have to give them away, and the first manager who puts them on will lose money. The movies today are too rich to have any room for genuine artists. They produce a few passable craftsmen, but not artists. Can you imagine a Beethoven making $100,000 a year? If so, then you have a better imagination than Beethoven himself. No, the present movie folk, I fear, will never quite solve the problem, save by some act of God. They are too much under the heel of the East Side gorillas who own them. They think too much about money. They have allowed it to become too important to them, and believe they couldn't get along without it. This is an unfortunate delusion. Money is important to mountebanks, but not to artists. The first really great movie, when it comes at last, will probably cost less than $5000. A true artist is always a romantic. He doesn't ask what the job will pay; he asks if it will be interesting. In this way all the loveliest treasures of the human race have been fashioned—by careless and perhaps somewhat foolish men. The late Johann Sebastian Bach, compared to a movie star with nine automobiles, was simply a damned fool. But I cherish the feeling that a scientific inquiry would also develop other differences between them.

Are you against the star system?

I am neither for it nor against it. A star is simply a performer who pleases the generality of morons better than the average. Certainly I see no reason why such a performer should not be paid a larger salary than the average. The objection to swollen salaries should come from the stars themselves— that is, assuming them to be artists. The system diverts them from their proper business of trying to produce charming and amusing movies, and converts them into bogus society folk. What could be more ridiculous? And pathetic? I go further: it is tragic. As I have said in another place, nothing is more tragic in this world than for otherwise worthy people to meanly admire and imitate mean things. One may have some respect for the movie lady who buys books and sets up as an intellectual, for it is a creditable thing to want to be (or even simply to want to appear) well-informed and intelligent. But I can see nothing worthy in wanting to be mistaken for the president of a bank. Artists should sniff at such dull drudges, not imitate them. The movies will leap ahead the day some star in Hollywood organizes a string quartette and begins to study Mozart.

■ ■ ■ ■

A CHILD OF THE CENTURY (1952), Ben Hecht

Another newspaperman from the East was Ben Hecht, who came to Hollywood to write the screenplays for such films as *Underworld, Scarface, The Front Page* and *Twentieth Century* (he had also written both plays), *Nothing Sacred, Gunga Din, His Girl Friday, Spellbound,* and *Notorious.* Despite his success there, Hecht never abandoned his cynicism about Hollywood, as revealed in this section from his autobiography, *A Child of the Century,* which chronicled his introduction to the movie colony in the twenties.

Hollywood, 1925, was another boom town, and my nerves were alive to its hawker's cry an hour after I had left the train. It reminded me happily of that other Eldorado—Miami. Miami had run up the price of its real estate. Hollywood was doing the same thing for talent, any kind of talent, from geese trainers to writers and actors.

Hungry actors leaped from hall bedrooms to terraced mansions. Writers and newspapermen who had hoboed their way West began hiring butlers and laying down wine cellars. Talent, talent, who had talent for anything—for beating a drum, diving off a roof, writing a joke, walking on his hands? Who could think up a story, any kind of story? Who knew how to write it down? And who had Ego? That was the leading hot cake—Ego or a pair of jiggling boobies under morning-glory eyes. Prosperity chased them all. New stars were being hatched daily, and new world-famous directors and producers were popping daily out of shoe boxes.

I went to work for Paramount Pictures, Inc., over which the Messrs. Zukor, Lasky and Schulberg presided. They occupied the three Vatican suites on the main floor of a long, plaster building that looked like a Bavarian bathhouse. It still stands, empty of almost everything but ghosts.

Most of the important people got drunk after one o'clock, sobered up around three-thirty and got drunk again at nine. Fist fights began around eleven. Seduction had no stated hours. The skimpy offices shook with passion. The mingled sound of plotting and sexual moans came through

Ben Hecht, *A Child of the Century* (Simon & Schuster, 1952).

the transoms. It was a town of braggadocio and youth. Leading ladies still suffered from baby fat (rather than budding wattles as today) and the film heroes had trouble growing mustaches.

Nor was the industry yet captive. There were as many wildcatters around as bankers. And the movies, God bless 'em, were silent. The talkies had not yet come to make headaches for the half-illiterate viziers of the Front Office. In fact, to the best of my recollection, there were no headaches. There were no unions, no censor boards, no empty theater seats. It was Round Three and everybody looked like a champion.

Movies were seldom written. They were yelled into existence in conferences that kept going in saloons, brothels and all-night poker games. Movie sets roared with arguments and organ music. Sometimes little string orchestras played to help stir up the emotions of the great performers—"Träumerei" for Clara Bow and the "Meditation" from Thais for Adolphe Menjou, the screen's most sophisticated lover.

I was given an office at Paramount. A bit of cardboard with my name inked on it was tacked on the door. A soiree started at once in my office and lasted for several days. Men of letters, bearing gin bottles, arrived. Bob Benchley, hallooing with laughter as if he had come on the land of Punch and Judy, was there; and the owlish-eyed satirist Donald Ogden Stewart, beaming as at a convention of March Hares. One night at a flossy party Don appeared on the dance floor in a long overcoat. "That's silly and showing off to dance in an overcoat," said the great lady of the films in his arms. "Please take it off." Don did. He had nothing on underneath. F. Scott Fitzgerald was there, already pensive and inquiring if there were any sense to life, and muttering, at thirty, about the cruelty of growing aged.

Listening to Mankiewicz, Edwin Justus Mayer, Scott Fitzgerald, Ted Shayne and other litterateurs roosting in my office, I learned that the Studio Bosses (circa 1925) still held writers in great contempt and considered them a waste of money. I learned, also, that Manky had gotten me my job by a desperate coup. The studio chieftain, the mighty B. P. Schulberg, smarting from experience with literary imports, had vowed never to hitch another onto the pay roll. Manky had invaded the Front Office, his own two-year contract in his hand. He had announced that if his friend Hecht failed to write a successful movie they could tear up his contract and fire us both.

I was pleased to hear this tale of loyalty and assured Manky The New York Times would be happy to take him back on its staff if things went awry.

On my fourth day, I was summoned and given an assignment. Producer

Bernard Fineman, under Schulberg, presented me with the first "idea" for a movie to smite my ears.

An important industrialist, said he, was shaving one morning. His razor slipped and he cut his chin. He thereupon sent out his butler to buy an alum stick to stop the flow of blood. The butler was slowed up by a traffic jam and the great industrialist, fuming in his onyx bathroom, had to wait fifteen minutes for the alum stick. The movie I was to make up was to show all the things that were affected in the world by this fifteen-minute delay. I recall of the details only that something went wrong with the pearl fisheries. The whole thing ended up with the great industrialist's mistress deserting him, his vast enterprises crashing, and his wife returning to his side to help him build a new life.

I relate this plot because my distaste for it started me as a successful scenario writer. I had seen no more than a dozen movies but I had heard in my four days in Hollywood all that was to be known about the flickers.

"I want to point out to you," said Manky,[1] that in a novel a hero can lay ten girls and marry a virgin for a finish. In a movie this is not allowed. The hero, as well as the heroine, has to be a virgin. The villain can lay anybody he wants, have as much fun as he wants cheating and stealing, getting rich and whipping the servants. But you have to shoot him in the end. When he falls with a bullet in his forehead, it is advisable that he clutch at the Gobelin tapestry on the library wall and bring it down over his head like a symbolic shroud. Also, covered by such a tapestry, the actor does not have to hold his breath while he is being photographed as a dead man."

An idea came to me. The thing to do was to skip the heroes and heroines, to write a movie containing only villains and bawds. I would not have to tell any lies then.

Thus, instead of a movie about an industrialist cutting his chin, I made up a movie about a Chicago gunman and his moll called Feathers McCoy. As a newspaperman I had learned that nice people—the audience—loved criminals, doted on reading about their love problems as well as their sadism. My movie, grounded on this simple truth, was produced with the title of *Underworld*. It was the first gangster movie to bedazzle the movie fans and there were no lies in it—except for a half-dozen sentimental touches introduced by its director, Joe von Sternberg. I still shudder remembering one of them. My head villain, Bull Weed, after robbing a bank, emerged with a suitcase full of money and paused in the crowded

---

1. Ed. Note: Herman J. Mankiewicz, a journalist friend of Hecht's from the East, who wrote the scripts for *Dinner at Eight, Citizen Kane,* and many others.

street to notice a blind beggar and give him a coin—before making his getaway.

It was not von Sternberg who helped me put the script together but another director, Arthur Rossen. Art Rossen was the first of these bonny directorial gentlemen with whom I was for many years to spend happy days locked away in fancy hotel rooms sawing away at plots. Art was one of the best of them, but, with a few nightmarish exceptions, they were all good. They were the new sort of storyteller produced by the movies, and, to this day, they remain the only authentic talent that has come out of Hollywood.

The Paramount Viziers, all four of them including the ex-prize fighter Mr. Zukor, listened to my reading of *Underworld*. It was eighteen pages long and it was full of moody Sandburgian sentences. The viziers were greatly stirred. I was given a ten-thousand-dollar check as a bonus for the week's work, a check which my sponsor Mankiewicz snatched out of my hand as I was bowing my thanks.

"You'll have it back in a week," Manky said. "I just want it for a few days to get me out of a little hole."

My return to New York was held up for several weeks while Manky struggled to raise another ten thousand to pay me back. He gambled valiantly, tossing a coin in the air with Eddie Cantor and calling heads or tails for a thousand dollars. He lost constantly. He tried to get himself secretly insured behind his good wife Sarah's back, planning to hock the policy and thus meet his obligation. This plan collapsed when the insurance company doctor refused to accept him as a risk.

I finally solved the situation by taking Manky into the Front Office and informing the studio bosses of our joint dilemma. I asked that my talented friend be given a five-hundred-dollar-a-week raise. The studio could then deduct this raise from his salary and give it to me. Thus in twenty weeks I would be repaid.

I left the Vatican suite with another full bonus check in my hand; and Manky, with his new raise, became the highest paid writer for Paramount Pictures, Inc.

If I Had a Talking Picture of You

I talk to your photograph each day,
You should hear the lovely things I say.
But I've thought how happy I would be
If your photograph could speak to me.

If I had a talking picture of You-oo,
I would run it every time I felt blue-oo.
I would sit there in the gloom
Of my lonely little room,
And applaud each time you whispered, "I love you!
Love you!"

On the screen the moment you came in view-oo,
We would talk the whole thing over, we two-oo.
I would give ten shows a day,
And a midnight matinee,
If I had a talking picture of you.

Lyrics and music by B. G. DeSylva, Lew Brown, and Ray Henderson;
from the motion picture *Sunny Side Up,* 1929.

4

The Talkies
(1924–1930)

Chronologically, the years of Hollywood's conversion to synchronized-sound films overlap those of its silent films of the twenties. But the final years of the decade are different enough from those that preceded them to produce a period that can be considered an era of its own. As in the Nickelodeon and Feature Film eras, the introduction of a radical change in exhibition patterns produced radical changes in both the film industry and the expectations of the film audience. The technological innovation disrupted the production methods and exhibition attitudes of an industry that had become increasingly stable over the years since 1915. But the audience's demand for the new films was so insistent that by the end of the decade there was almost no silent film production and exhibition in America at all.

As with the earliest era of film history, many of the issues of this first "sound" era relate to matters of invention, innovation, and introduction. Although sound-film processes had been patented and exhibited in America since 1907, such experiments did not attract the public fancy or the public's attention until the mid-1920s. Lee De Forest's Phonofilms were one of the first highly publicized sound-film processes, but the industry's conversion to synchronized-sound films was effected by the Vitaphone of the four Warner brothers.

The issues that arise from the

Warners' introduction of the Vitaphone are both economic and theoretical. Why did they invest in the Vitaphone and market it? (Was it a desperate commercial gamble or a shrewdly conceived commercial strategy?) Why did other film producers and exhibitors resist it? (Was it a blindness to its possibilities or an awareness of the commercial chaos it would cause?) Why did they capitulate to "talkies" so quickly? Why did audiences prefer synchronized-sound films to the old nontalking ones with musical scores? And how did serious critics and theorists view the new talkies? (Were they a deplorable vulgarization of the "art of the film," or did synchronized-sound films present interesting and valid artistic possibilities that had merely been obscured by the cheapness and crudeness of the initial talkies?)

■ ■ ■ ■

Pictures That Talk (1924)

This article on Lee De Forest's Phonofilms in the July 1924 issue of *Photoplay* was one of the first notifications to movie fans that something new might lie in their entertainment future.

DR. LEE DE FOREST HAS AT LAST SUCCEEDED
IN SYNCHRONIZING THE ACTION WITH SOUND

And now the motion pictures really talk. It has been almost twenty years since Thomas A. Edison first tried to accomplish this, but it has remained for Dr. Lee De Forest to bring the "talkies" to their present stage of advancement.

Mr. Edison's first attempt was made by the simple process of playing stock cylinder records on a phonograph and having the actors sing, or pretend to sing, with the record, while the camera photographed the lip movement. By this method synchronization was impossible. Sometimes the singer would be so far ahead or behind the record that the result was laughable.

Edison knew this would never do, so he finally invented the "kinetophone." Again he used the phonograph, but he obtained better results by making the phonograph record at the same time as the motion picture negative. This gave perfect synchronization in the taking of the pictures, but two operators were needed for the projection—one for the film in the booth and the other, back stage, to run the phonograph.

Sometimes the results were good. More often they were not. But, nevertheless, these pictures had quite a vogue and drew great audiences all over the country. Edison was not satisfied, but he never was able to get perfect synchonization, nor was any of a dozen others who tried.

About this time Lee De Forest, then a young electrical engineer in the West, was experimenting with wireless, or radio, as it is now called. Out of this came the "audion," which is now a part of every radio set and which makes broadcasting and receiving possible. Three years ago De

"Pictures That Talk" was published in the July 1924 *Photoplay*.

Forest became interested in motion pictures and began his experiments to make them talk. He realized that synchronization and audibility were essential. After three years he has worked out his "Phonofilm." He has synchonized the picture and the voice by photographing the sound on the same strip of film with the action and at the same time. Instead of the voice being phonographed, it is radioed from the speaker's lips, by sound waves, to the camera. There these sound waves are converted into light waves and photographed on the left side of the film.

All of this is accomplished with any standard motion picture camera, to which has been added an attachment for photographing sound.

The negative thus produced is developed in the usual manner and prints made exactly similar to the prints of any other motion picture.

In projecting the De Forest Phonofilms, an inexpensive attachment is necessary, which fits on any standard projection machine. In this attachment is a tiny incandescent lamp. As the film passes this light, the lines made by the voice become "flickers" or light waves. These light waves are picked up by infinitesimal wires and converted into sound waves again. Other larger wires take the sound waves into the amplifier, from which they are carried from the projection room by ordinary wires back-stage, amplified again, and thrown on the screen in precise synchronization with the action of the scene.

"But what if the print should break?"

That is one of the first questions asked by exhibitors. And the answer is always ready for them.

If the print breaks, it is patched together just like any other motion picture print. The pictures are taken at the rate of twenty to twenty-two per second, so that two, or even three "frames" may be cut out of a film without being noticed in the synchronization.

"My talking pictures have not yet been perfected," says Dr. De Forest. "I never said they were. But I will make this prediction: Within a year from now we will have perfected talking pictures to a point where the voices will be recorded with such clarity that it will be impossible to distinguish between the actual human voice as spoken by a person present and the voice of the same person recorded on the film. We have found out what causes the metallic sound that makes the voice unnatural. It is so simple that I am amazed we did not discover the cause at the start. That will be remedied immediately.

"It is perfectly possible now to record different voices so that they are instantly recognizable to one familiar with them, just as it is possible for you to recognize the voice of a friend over the telephone."

Dr. De Forest's first experiments with recording sounds on film with the Phonofilm were in connection with the reproduction of music. Every-

one knows how absurd it is to see a motion picture of a man playing, for
example, a saxphone. His cheeks puff out and he gets red in the face
with the exertion, and never a sound is heard. De Forest made his saxo-
phone player heard.

Then he experimented on dance numbers. The motion picture producer always steers clear of dancing on the screen as much as possible because it is impossible, even in the best theaters, for the orchestra to play
so that the dancers will be "in step." So Dr. De Forest photographed the
music and the dancer on the same film.

Through the interest of Dr. Riesenfeld, permission was given Dr. De
Forest to experiment with "Covered Wagon" film. Dr. Riesenfeld arranged the musical score for this production, and Dr. De Forest is photographing this music on the negative of the picture. This means, if the
work is successful, that "The Covered Wagon" may be seen in any theater,
no matter how small, with the same musical program that was played
with it for more than a year in New York.

■ ■ ■ ■
_____

The Voice of Vitaphone (1975), Harry Geduld

Although *The Jazz Singer* has received most of the credit for the talkie revolution, the real landmark event was probably the first Vitaphone program of several short films and the sonorized feature, *Don Juan*, which
predated the famous Jolson film by more than a year. In this chapter from
his book *The Birth of the Talkies,* Harry Geduld, a film historian and
American literary scholar, provides an excellent survey of the events and
decisions that produced the first Vitaphone program.
_____

The decisive events leading to the coming of talkies occurred during the
mid-twenties and involved the association of Warner Bros. Pictures, Inc.,
with Western Electric and Bell Telephone Laboratories.

Warner Bros. followed no long-term policy with regard to the development of sound cinema. Indeed, they were to be directed by the unpredictable nature of public response (particularly as far as reception of
The Jazz Singer was concerned) rather than by any astute insight into
the future of the medium. However, in retrospect, we can now discern
three major phases in Warner Bros.' involvement with sound films. The

"The Voice of Vitaphone" appeared in *The Birth of the Talkies,* by Harry Geduld
(Indiana University Press, 1975).

first culminated with the making of *Don Juan* (1926), in which, following the tradition of silent cinema, the sound used was primarily musical accompaniment. The second phase was to produce *The Jazz Singer* (1927), out of which the transitional concept of the part-talkie emerged. The third and final phase was realized with *Lights of New York* (1928), which inaugurated the conventional dialogue film of the sound era.

Some three years before the Warners were to come into the picture, a little-publicized experiment took place. It was eventually to have shattering consequences on film industries all over the world, but at the time not one studio head seems to have bothered about it. In October 1922 at Woolsey Hall in Yale University, Edward B. Craft demonstrated the synchonization of a phonograph record and a projected motion picture. Sound engineers, the only people seriously interested in the experiment, were more concerned with the record itself than with the synchronization, for Craft was giving the first public demonstration of a system for the electrical recording of phonograph disks. It was the outcome of combining electromagnetic reproducers (the work of Crandall, Kranz, and H. D. Arnold, c. 1913–15) with improvements (by J. P. Maxfield and his associates and H. C. Harrison) in wax disk recording and the phonograph.

The recording system was imperfect, but its possibilities aroused the interest and activity of researchers at Bell Telephone Laboratories. Bell Labs and Western Electric Company were both subsidiaries of American Telephone and Telegraph Company; the former was the research branch, the latter the manufacturing and marketing arm. These organizations had obvious, vested interests in technological developments relating to sound.

Mainly through their invention of a mechanical filter that greatly refined the quality of sound recording, Bell engineers managed to improve considerably upon Craft's system. Their apparatus was ready by 1924, and RCA, Victor, and Columbia, the major phonograph recording companies, promptly obtained licenses from Western Electric to use the new system (whose advancement of the art and science of sound recording was to be paralleled only by the much later development of the long-playing high-fidelity microgroove record). This successful and lucrative outcome of their work encouraged Bell engineers to consider further applications of the new sound system. Recalling Craft's attempt to synchronize film and phonograph record, they proceeded to experiment along the same lines. Only after the expenditure of millions of dollars did they become aware of Hollywood's indifference—even downright hostility—to sound pictures. Then it became clear to them that most, if not all, film companies regarded sound pictures as the kiss of death.

It was well known in Hollywood that previous dabblings with such innovations had proved to be technical failures and financial disasters. And even if a new system turned out to be technically perfect, it was generally agreed among studio heads that the transition to sound would be a very costly gamble that could be disastrous to the whole industry. Sound studios would have to be built, and theaters would have to be equipped with the new apparatus. And what would happen to all those millions already invested in silent films? What would be the effect on the industry's lucrative overseas market if talking pictures with American dialogue replaced silent films whose titles could be easily translated? What would become of silent movie stars who were not trained to deliver spoken dialogue, but whose reputation as silent stars had been "created" by expensive promotional campaigns and whose popularity sustained the studios and represented their greatest assets? "What," as *Variety* asked, "would happen to the class theatres with expensive orchestras and stage shows, if any jerk-water movie joint was to be able to give its patrons gorgeous feasts of music via the screen?" Oblivious to these and other questions, Western Electric and Bell sank more and more time and money into experiments they felt sure would interest the film industry as eagerly as the development of electric recording had interested the phonograph record industry.

The energies of the Bell people were concentrated on perfecting a sound-on-disk system. Their ignorance of the needs of the film industry may be gauged from the fact that the apparatus they originally built was designed to synchronize records with films running at 75 feet per minute. As film was normally projected at 90 feet per minute, their system would have required modifications to every projector wired to their apparatus. Fortunately, this little oversight was corrected when, in due course, Warner Bros. came onto the scene. But, as we shall see, other shortcomings were not discovered until their system was already in use for the production of sound movies for commercial exhibition.

As Edward Kellogg noted, "To provide sound for pictures, using the disk-record system, it was necessary to have records which would play continuously for at least the projection time of a 1000-ft. reel (about 11 min.), to plan a synchronous drive, and to use electrical reproduction in order that, with the help of amplifiers, adequate sound output could be had."

After much trial and error, what the Bell people eventually produced was a combination of several important technical developments: First, "an electrical system of recording, employing a high quality microphone and a record-cutting mechanism . . . second . . . an electrical needle reproducer in the grooves of a sound record [where it was sensitized] by electrical vibrations. The electrical currents from this device pass[ed] into an amplifier and then operate[d] a high quality speaker capable of filling the largest motion picture auditorium." Third, a method for making the change from one record to the next without any interrupation in the recorded sound.

Sixteen-inch one-sided disks were used; when played at 33⅓ rpm, the speed at which the sound had been recorded, this size supplied the sound equivalent of a standard thousand-foot reel of film. Interconnected projectors providing imperceptible transitions from reel to reel were already in general use in most cinemas. The corresponding switch from one record to another was managed by the use of a double-amplifying rheostat, "the points on one side of which led to the electrical 'pick-up' of one reproducing instrument, those on the other side leading to the other. These points were numbered, and the switch served both as amplifier control and as switch-over. If record number one was being played on point 5, record number two could be switched to by a single quick turn of the dial to point 5 on the other side. This would open the circuit between number one's pickup and the loudspeaker, and close that between number two's pickup and the same loudspeaker. The amplification would be the same in both cases." The final development in the Bell system was the use of a "link between the reproducer and the audience in a theater. An adaptation of the public address system . . . [made] it possible to pick up electric vibrations from the reproducer, amplify them, and by means of properly located loudspeaking telephones, transform them into sound."

One of the first uses of the new system was the completion, in 1924, of *Hawthorne,* a talking picture about the Western Electric factory in suburban Chicago. E. S. Gregg has described it as "the first industrial sound picture ever to be seen and heard." During the same year, Bell technicians prepared a number of short test films of songs and dance bands to demonstrate their newly developed system to the heads of the most important Hollywood film companies. The Warner brothers were not invited. Their company was too small and insignificant at that time. But Edison, Jesse Lasky, and several executives from MGM were among those who attended the demonstration programs. Their responses, when enthusiastic, stopped short at investing in the system or at expressing any interest in the production of sound movies in Hollywood.

Meanwhile, separate and more aggressive approaches to the film industry were being made by Walter J. Rich, an independent entrepreneur with little direct knowledge of Hollywood. He nevertheless convinced Western Electric that he was the man to promote the new synchronization system and to persuade the Hollywood companies that the sound era had arrived and that they should make haste to join it. Rich's agreement with Western Electric provided that licenses to use the system were to be negotiated with him as well as with Western Electric. (In due course this provision was to involve him in dealings with Warner Bros., whom he had not bothered to contact during his promotional efforts.) By spring 1925, before Warner Bros. came into the picture, Rich had spent $36,000 of his own money in promoting the system without managing to sign up a single company. He thought and talked on the grand scale but achieved little and was never more than incidental to events that led to the coming of sound.

Despite Rich's activities, during 1923–25, events were transpiring that would involve Warner Bros. in the experiments of Bell Laboratories. Since 1903, when they traveled through Pennsylvania and Ohio, exhibiting an overworked print of *The Great Train Robbery,* Sam, Harry, Jack, and Albert Warner had been active in the film industry—first as small-time exhibitors, and later, with increasing success, as distributors and producers. In 1923 they established Warner Bros. Pictures, Inc., a production company whose greatest assets were the popular dog-star Rin-Tin-Tin and the talents of John Barrymore (in that order of importance). When the new corporation began to rack up healthy profits and a rapid increase in production became desirable, more studio space and equipment and an effective, widespread distribution system were needed. These requirements were fulfilled by buying the ailing Vitagraph company, with its acres of well-equipped studios and an established network of foreign film exchanges.

Stepped-up production meant that more publicity would be needed. At that period radio offered the most exciting medium for advertising films, and a film company that was affluent enough owned a radio station or even a radio network. Warner Bros. could not afford to establish a new radio network, but late in 1924 it did buy the equipment of a radio station that had gone bankrupt. It was the best investment the company ever made. As Jack Warner notes: it was "one of those freak rolls of dice—a radio station was almost directly responsible for the fantastic upheaval which took us from a net income of $30,000 for the first eight months of 1927, to a staggering profit of $17,000,000 for a similar period only two years later." However, such a development was inconceivable in 1924. The immediate concern of the Warners was to transport the heap of apparatus to their studio and get it working.

The installation job was given to Western Electric. As a result, Benjamin Levinson, a radio expert and Western Electric's engineer in charge of the work of setting up KFWB (as Warner Bros.' station came to be known), got to meet Sam Warner. The two men became close friends, and Levinson enjoyed explaining to Sam Warner the intricacies and marvels of the apparatus that the studio had just acquired.

Early in 1925, Levinson visited Bell Labs in New York and chanced upon a showing of one of the short test films that had been prepared the year before to demonstrate the new system to the Hollywood executives. According to E. S. Gregg, "He heard the natural sounds of the steps of a pianist going to his instrument; he heard the clicks as the pianist unbuttoned his gloves, the life-like sounds as cane, gloves, hat and coat were tossed aside. He heard for the first time the music of the piano as it came from the screen with startling fidelity. He was greatly impressed." Back in Los Angeles and in the company of Sam Warner, Levinson could not contain his enthusiasm.

"Listen," he said, "I'm bringing you hot news. I just saw in our New York Laboratories the most wonderful thing I ever looked at in my life. A moving picture that talks!"

... "Benny," said Sam with a shake of the head, "haven't you been around the show world long enough now to know that a picture that talks is something to run away from?"

"I know, I know," said Levinson impatiently. "You're thinking about the old ones. 'Cameraphone,' 'Kinetophone,' all those things. But this is different. This is a talking picture that works like radio! Vacuum tubes. Amplifiers. Listen while I explain it to you. . . ."

According to Fitzhugh Green, Levinson made Sam Warner promise to attend a demonstration at Bell Labs, telling him, persuasively, "there's more money in it than there ever was in movies." Green, writing close to the events, nowhere mentions that Jack Warner influenced Sam's decision to attend the demonstration. However, as recently as 1965, Jack Warner claimed in his autobiography that it was on his "enthusiastic urging" that his brother "went to New York and there, with eyes popping like a kid at a French peep show . . . saw a series of shorts in which voices and music came from the screen." It is not clear why Jack Warner should have been so enthusiastic about an invention he had never seen or heard. What is clear is that he wants his readers to believe that he was the most prescient of the Warner brothers. (Later in the same book he states, "I started production on our first sound film, *Don Juan*." [Notice the "I."] Elsewhere brother Jack speaks of "we" [all the Warner brothers], but here he claims credit for being the sole, personal producer of the first sound feature film, a claim that this writer has been unable to substantiate in Warner Bros. promotional material, in trade advertising for the film, or in any of the published and unpublished sources he has consulted. It should be noted, incidentally, that while Jack Warner clearly identifies himself as the producer of *Don Juan,* he somehow omits to mention the name of the man who directed the picture. He does remember Alan Crosland when he gives his account of the making of *The Jazz*

Singer, but this little piece of information is overshadowed by the revelation that it was none other than Jack Warner who had the brilliant idea of offering the lead to Al Jolson.)

With or without the inspiration of his brother, Sam Warner attended a demonstration of sound films at Bell Labs in April 1925, when he was visiting New York to finalize the takeover of Vitagraph. If anything, he was even more impressed than Levinson. The synchronization and the sound quality seemed remarkably natural and clear to him. The idea of producing sound movies began to appeal to his imagination. Back in California he tried to convey his excitement to his brother Harry. But Harry was ice-cold on the subject of talking pictures; he knew all the horror stories about earlier ventures into sound movies. Also, as he was in charge of the company's financial affairs, he knew better than Sam did how heavily it had gone into debt to buy Vitagraph. It would be lunacy to gamble even more borrowed money on an untried novelty. Accordingly, he refused to see the invention or even talk about it.

Undaunted, Sam arranged what was ostensibly a social meeting between his brothers and officials from Bell Labs and Western Electric. Actually, it was a ruse to get Harry Warner to attend a demonstration of sound movies, and it worked. Harry "was very much impressed, but didn't want the Western people to know it. It was when they showed an orchestra that he got his great inspiration of providing film with musical accompaniment." He was to explain subsequently:

> "The thought occurred to me that if we quit the idea of a talking picture and brought about something the motion picture theatre of the present day really needs—music adapted to the picture—we could ultimately develop it to a point at which people would ask us for talking pictures. If I myself would not have gone across the street to see or hearing a talking picture, I surely could not expect the public to do it. But Music! That is another story. . . ."

Later, when he was alone with his brother, Harry admitted that he thought the system had possibilities.

> "But Sam," he added, "I wouldn't be so foolish as to try to make talking pictures. That's what everybody has done, and lost. No, we'll do better than that: we can use this thing for other purposes. We can use it *for musical accompaniment to our pictures!* We can film and record vaudeville and musical acts, and make up programs for houses that can't afford the real thing or can't get big-time acts. Think of what it would mean to a small independent theatre owner to buy his orchestra with his picture! Not to have an organ! Not a musician in the house! Not an actor—and yet his whole show. . . ."

Thus was envisaged what was to be the first of the three major phases of Warner Bros.' development of sound cinema.

Now that Sam and Harry were both seriously interested in the new sound system, Warner Bros. was ready to open negotiations with Western Electric. At this point it was discovered that the company would first have to settle with Walter J. Rich. Rich was promptly approached, and having given up hope of interesting any of the big film companies, he was more than willing to deal with Warner Bros. For a fee of $72,000 he agreed to "go in with [Warners] on a share and share alike basis" and permit them to negotiate freely with Western Electric for permission to use the new sound system.

In June 1925, "Stanley Watkins, who had been head of [J.P.] Maxfield's experimental sound crew at Western Electric, took his men to the Vitagraph studio, in Brooklyn, and set up shop. Inside the big glass stages, they built a box 50 feet square and 30 feet high. This would be their new set, but it had to be sound-proofed. So the crew and Sam Warner, who . . . left the studio only to sleep, hung rugs over the walls of the box stage to insulate the place for sound." Vitagraph studios had not, of course, been designed for the making of sound movies. Despite the efforts of Watkins and his crew, acoustic problems arose from the outset. "Draperies were hung up in the rafters to muffle sound. . . . Ed DuPar . . . was the cameraman on this early project. He achieved as much camera mobility as possible by running four cameras on a take. One master camera ran continuously on a long-shot set-up while the others were used to get cut-in shots. Sometimes he would make ten or twelve changes on the close-up camera in the course of one ten-minute recording. At this period, the sound system was being used at Vitagraph on the basis of Rich's agreement with Western Electric and his recently-formed partnership with Warner Bros. So far Warner Bros. had not signed a contract with Western Electric.

By spring 1926 short test films using the new sound system were being made quite regularly at Vitagraph. Two of the short experimental pictures made at this time were later released for public exhibition. The first was a speech by elderly Dr. Watson, who had collaborated with Alexander Graham Bell in inventing the telephone. The second, rather more ambitious effort was titled *The Volga Boatmen*. It required the construction of a studio set depicting a river bank along which eight sturdy men— two quartets of Russian singers—proceeded laboriously while singing the "Volga Boat Song" and tugging at a rope supposedly attached to an unseen boat. "For this opus they imported loads of salt to simulate snow and braced one hefty member of the [sound] crew off stage so the 'boatmen' could have something to pull on." The inspiration for this masterpiece, reputedly directed by Sam Warner himself, was doubtless the release, early in April 1926, of Cecil B. DeMille's feature film *The Volga Boatman,* starring William Boyd, Robert Edeson, and Victor Varconi. If DeMille heard about the competition he was unlikely to have been disturbed by it. The Warners would have a much longer haul than their boatmen before they could make sound pictures that offered any serious opposition to the ambitious silent features of the major studios.

Before legalizing their arrangements with Western Electric, the Warners decided to keep their venture into sound films separate from the regular, silent film-making activities of their Hollywood studios. Early in April 1926 they established a new company, Vitaphone Corporation (no doubt a deliberate echo of Vitagraph), and named the sound system Vitaphone. On April 20, 1926, the new corporation formally leased the Vitaphone system from Western Electric and also secured rights to sublicense the system to other film companies. In due course, Warner Bros.' control of these sublicensing rights was to antagonize other studios when they in turn sought to make the transition to sound; and more than any other single factor it was to lead to the promotion of rival systems and the eventual triumph of sound-on-film over sound-on-disk.

But at this stage Warner Bros. had the field to itself. It was a questionable advantage when none of the other studios had shown any interest in sound movies, but nevertheless one that had to be exploited in view of the company's heavy and increasing investments in the system. Rich suggested arranging demonstration programs for film exhibitors, who might thereby be induced to sink some of *their* money into Vitaphone. But the Warners knew show business better than Rich did. Realizing that they had something unique, they decided that the best way to exploit it was to use it in a unique way—to present it in a package that no other film company could offer. Instead of demonstrating experimental films to exhibitors, they would use the system to create a spectacular show that everyone would want to see. (The same idea was behind Clément-Maurice's Phono-Cinéma-Théâtre of 1900 and in the exploitation, years later, of such technical developments as Cinerama and 3-D) Thus, from the outset the public would associate Vitaphone with entertainment of the highest order. The inspiration was Harry Warner's. As he subsequently explained, "I said to my partners, 'Let's get the greatest artists and the best orchestra in the country. Let's have confidence in this and put all our muscle behind it. We'll know the result after we have opened the first show. . . .'" He conceived a long, elaborate program, consisting of a number of short films exhibiting the talents of musical virtuosi of the concert stage and opera house, followed by a lavish feature film. In every part of the show the "miracle" of Vitaphone would be evident.

Once the die had been cast and the Warners were firmly committed to promoting Vitaphone on the grand scale, it became imperative for them to raise large amounts of capital. The creation of the whole program for the premiere of Vitaphone would finally involve Warner Bros. in an expenditure of almost $3 million. Within a year after the agreement with Western Electric, the company had so overextended itself that the future of Warner Bros. Pictures, Inc., depended entirely on the success or failure of the gamble with Vitaphone.

For the short films that would make up the first part of the program the Warners planned to present leading artists of the Metropolitan Opera Company of New York. Eventually, upwards of a million dollars was spent in hiring the chosen artists, obtaining their temporary release from contracts with Metropolitan Opera and various record companies, hiring the New York Philharmonic Orchestra, and securing rights to use certain copyrighted music.

It was decided that the program's feature film would be *Don Juan,* the latest vehicle for John Barrymore. Originally intended as a silent movie, the film was already in production in Warner Bros.' Hollywood studios. Its budget had been fixed at half a million dollars, but when the decision was made to include the movie in the Vitaphone program, an additional $200,000 was ploughed into the picture, thus insuring that it would be one of the most expensive films of 1926, and certainly the costliest Warner production up to that time. This additional investment did not include the considerable expense of supplying the sound accompaniment, which utilized a specially commissioned score.

The short films for the premiere program were made in Manhattan. Vitagraph studios proved to be totally unsatisfactory. The production crew was "isolated in Flatbush from everything, except the subway. The Coney Island line of the BMT ran above the surface—right past the studio windows. Every time a train passed, the record needle jumped in anguish. Working conditions in Flatbush went from bad to worse."

Obviously, at this period no sound studio where feature films could be made existed anywhere in the world, and Warner Bros. had no immediate plans to build one. A compromise location had to be found, and the old Manhattan Opera House, which was known to have good acoustics, was chosen. The Vitaphone Corporation took a year's lease on the building, and soon electricians, carpenters, and sound engineers were swarming over the place, installing miles of wiring, and setting up arc lamps, cameras, and recording equipment.

"S. S. A. Watkins was in charge for Western Electric. He had a group of men including H. C. Humphrey, R. C. Sawyer, and George Grove. Sam Warner carried on the Warner Brothers' end. With him he had Ed

DuPar, a cameraman, and Bert Frank, a cutter. On occasion Herman Heller, musical director of the Warner Theatre in New York, came over. Heller was the first 'Talkie' director because all the first numbers were musical."

Now that production had begun, in earnest, on a program intended for the largest possible public audience, a series of difficulties became apparent that had been latent or nonexistent while the test films were being made. As Fitzhugh Green observed: "It was easy to make pictures, easy to make records; but another matter to make them together. Conditions that were ideal for the one were so often not at all ideal for the other." The Manhattan Opera House turned out to be scarcely any improvement over the Vitagraph studios. The most serious problems arose from noise of all kinds, which impaired the quality of the sound recording. Close to the Opera House, part of the New York City subway system was being excavated, and workmen were blasting into the rocky surface of Manhattan while recording sessions were in progress. Aside from the disruptive sounds of explosions, shock waves would knock the stylus out of the groove and ruin a well-nigh perfect disk.

A host of other unexpected noises plagued the recording engineers: interference from static electricity; echoes, resonances and various extraneous sounds (such as coughs, footsteps, passing traffic), most of which were inaudible to listeners in the Opera House but were nevertheless picked up and amplified by the Vitaphone system. The system also proved to be ultrasensitive to the sounds emitted by the studio arc lights: not only the barely audible "sizzle" but also the normally inaudible emission of radio waves and harmonics. In addition, the records themselves produced uncontrollable surface noise, and it was discovered that the Vitaphone apparatus was sensitive to radio broadcasts and was sometimes unexpectedly recording radio programs along with the intended sounds.

But the most serious obstacles were created by the cameras themselves. First, they were hand-cranked, which meant that even the most assiduous and unwearying cameraman could not maintain a speed regular enough to insure perfect synchronization with phonograph recordings. Motor-driven cameras had to be devised to replace the standard hand-cranked apparatus, but the sound of their whirring mechanism was clearly discernible on every recording made at the outset of production in the Manhattan Opera House. Most, if not all these difficulties had to be mastered quickly. Unfortunately, not all the immediate solutions were ideal ones for the art of motion picture making. Thus by housing the camera in a soundproof booth, camera noise was eliminated—but at the cost of the camera's former mobility and flexibility. The booth constructed for this purpose was about seven feet high, four feet deep and three feet wide, mounted on rubber tired swivel wheels, with a door cut in the back for the ingress and egress of the camerman and his machine. There was a square hole in the front of it for the camera to "shoot" through. And in order that no camera noise should come through this hole, felt sound insulating material was fastened, in the shape of an inverted pyramid between its edges and the outer part of the lens; the lens stuck its glassy eye out from the depths of a felt-sided tunnel.

After one occasion when the door of the booth had been left open accidentally and the camera noise ruined the take, it became the practice to lock cameramen into the booth during the recording sessions. But no way was found to avoid frequent disruptions from noises outside the Opera House; this problem was not solved until the construction of sound studios insulated against exterior noise.

The other difficulties were easier to cope with. Radio sounds and some surface noise were prevented by covering every part of the Vitaphone apparatus with a metallic "shield" that was impervious to static and radio waves. Unfortunately, this shield proved ineffective as a barrier to sounds emanating from the arc lamps; the only solution here was for Frank N. Murphy, Warner Bros.' chief electrician, to devise an entirely new lighting system employing incandescent lamps. The system he developed was a major advance in studio lighting, and within a short time in most studios it had entirely replaced the old arc lighting that had been used during the silent era. Echoes and resonances inside the building were reduced or eliminated by hanging heavy drapes or placing scenery flats at suitable locations to break up extensive wall surfaces. With these and other quickly improvised methods, the shooting and recording sessions were able to proceed more or less on schedule.

■ ■ ■ ■

THE VITAPHONE (1926), Mordaunt Hall

This review of the first Vitaphone program appeared in the *New York Times* of 7 August 1926.

THE VITAPHONE, a new invention synchronizing sound with motion picture; DON JUAN, with John Barrymore, Mary Astor, Willard Louis, Estelle Taylor, Warner Oland, Montague Love, Helene Costello, Jane Winton, Myrna Loy, John Roche, June Marlowe, Yvonne Day, Phillipe de Lacy, John George, Helene d'Algy, Josef Swickard, Lionel

Braham, Phyllis Haver, Nigel de Brulier and Hedda Hopper, inspired by the legends of "Don Juan," written for the screen by Bess Meredyth, directed by Alan Crosland; Vitaphone music score. At Warners' Theatre.

A marvelous device known as the vitaphone, which synchronizes sound with motion pictures, stirred a distinguished audience in Warners' Theatre to unusual enthusiasm at its initial presentation last Thursday evening. The natural reproduction of voices, the tonal qualities of musical instruments and the timing of the sound to the movements of the lips of singers and the actions of musicians was almost uncanny. This "living sound" invention, without a musician being present, also furnished the orchestral accompaniment to an ambitious photoplay entitled "Don Juan," in which John Barrymore plays the title role.

The future of this new contrivance is boundless, for inhabitants of small and remote places will have the opportunity of listening to and seeing grand opera as it is given in New York, and through the picturing of the vocalists and small groups of musicians, or instrumental choirs of orchestras, the vitaphone will give its patrons an excellent idea of a singer's acting and an intelligent conception of the efforts of musicians and their instruments. Operatic favorites will be able to be seen and heard, and the genius of singers and musicians who have passed will still live.

The introductory Vitaphone feature which incidentally prefaced the program, was that of Will H. Hays delivering a speech congratulating the Warner Brothers, the Western Electric Company, the Bell Telephone laboratories and Walter J. Rich on this remarkable achievement. There was no muffled utterance nor lisping in the course of the talk; it was the voice of Hays, and had any of his friends closed their eyes to his picture on the screen they would have immediately recognized the voice. Every syllable was audible and clear.

This was followed by a vitaphone of the Philharmonic Orchestra under the direction of Henry Hadley, in which one was not only impressed by the clarity of the tonal colors and softer interludes, but also by the thrilling volume of the full orchestra. During the exhibition of this subject the screen scenes swayed from those of the whole body of musicians to small groups as each instrumental choir took up its work.

ELMAN HEARD IN "HUMORESQUE"

Mischa Elman, the noted violinist, was seen and heard playing Dvorak's "Humoresque," with Josef Bonimo at the piano, and every note that

"The Vitaphone," by Mordaunt Hall, appeared in the 7 August 1926 *New York Times.*

came to one's ears synchronized with the gliding bow and the movements of the musician's fingers. It seemed at times that the sound was so distinct that during a pause had a pin been dropped in the studio it would have been heard.

The "Caro nome" aria from "Rigoletto," rendered by Marion Talley, gave one an excellent idea of the qualities of the singer's voice and also of her acting. As she retreated from the front of the stage her voice became modulated, and then there were times when one heard her as if from a front seat in the Metropolitan Opera.

"An Evening on the Don," delivered by Russian dancers and singers, contained a wealth of charm. Then the seductive twanging of a guitar manipulated by Roy Smeck captured the audience. Every note appeared to come straight from the instrument and one almost forgot that the Vitaphone was responsible for the realistic effect.

There was a decided opulence about the entertainment, for next on the list was Efrem Zimbalist, violinist, accompanied by Harold Bauer. Mr. Zimbalist played variations of Beethoven's "Kreutzer Sonata," and whether it was a note from the piano or the plucking of the violin strings, it was audible throughout the theatre and just as inspiring as if Mr. Zimbalist and Mr. Bauer had themselves been before the audience.

The powerful voice of Giovanni Martinelli then came from the screen, singing in an enthralling fashion "Vesta la giubba" from "Pagliacci," accompanied by the Philharmonic Orchestra. Nothing like it had ever been heard in a motion picture theatre, and the invited gathering burst into applause such as is seldom heard in any place of amusement. The singer's tones appeared to echo in the body of the theatre as they tore from a shadow on the screen—a shadow that appeared earnest and intense in the delivery of Leoncavallo's well-known composition.

The final special Vitaphone feature was of Anna Case, supported by a dance divertissement of the Cansinos, accompanied by the Metropolitan Opera chorus and Herman Heller's orchestra. This was also pleasing and extraordinarily effective in delivering the singer's glib and quickly turning tones.

JOHN BARRYMORE IN "DON JUAN"

And so one came to the picture, "Don Juan," and it can readily be appreciated that only a cleverly produced film could hold its own against the entertainment that had preceded it. Messrs. Warner were sufficiently astute to screen the prologue, or the first chapter of the photoplay, before announcing an intermission. By the time the first stretch of "Don Juan" faded out the spectators were in the mood of a person who does not wish to leave an interesting novel. . . .

■ ■ ■ ■

"DON JUAN" AND THE VITAPHONE (1926), Robert E. Sherwood

One of the most receptive reviewers of the new talkies was Robert E. Sherwood, the film critic (and later editor) of *Life* magazine. This review of the first Vitaphone program appeared in *Life* in 1926.

DON JUAN

Some press matter issued in connection with the showing of DON JUAN assures us that, in the course of this lengthy film, John Barrymore receives or delivers exactly one hundred and ninety-one kisses.

This figure is probably correct, but it seems extremely conservative to me. Certainly, Mr. Barrymore has established a new record for running broad osculation over the twelve-reel route. As the most celebrated lover in history, he literally leaps from lip to lip, with optional stopovers at each point of interest.

Among the actresses who are favored by his lingering caresses are Estelle Taylor, Mary Astor, Jane Winton, Phyllis Haver, June Marlowe, Helene D'Algy, Hedda Hopper and various unidentified but luscious extra girls.

More darned fun. . . .

DON JUAN has been as liberally panned by the United Brotherhood of Movie Critics as has any picture within my memory. Strain my ears as I might after its New York opening, I could hear no kind word for it from any one.

For all that, I confess that I enjoyed it. The backgrounds are awful, and the costumes grotesque in their inaccuracy; Mr. Barrymore himself is almost as bad, at times, as he was in THE SEA BEAST; the story is dragged out and frequently confused. But the fact remains that DON JUAN engaged my humble interest and provided me with considerable entertainment.

Much of this merit is traceable to good direction by Alan Crosland, and to the efforts of a generally good cast. There is one splendid performance by Nigel de Brulier, and some effective work by Willard Louis, Warner Oland, Phillipe de Lacy and Myrna Loy.

As the father of Don Juan, Mr. Barrymore is his old self. When he steps down a generation into the title role, he becomes the movie Barrymore, with a few flashes of brilliance and a great many glints of supreme silliness.

"*Don Juan* and the Vitaphone," by Robert E. Sherwood, appeared in the 26 August 1926 issue of *Life* magazine.

You may take or leave DON JUAN, as you yourself may choose. I hesitate to recommend either course.

THE VITAPHONE

In connection with the "world premiere" (as it is fatuously called) of DON JUAN, there was a demonstration of the Vitaphone, a new device for the synchronization of shadow and sound.

There can be no doubt that the Vitaphone is a real triumph. It is as far ahead of De Forest's Phonofilm as the Phonofilm was ahead of Edison's ill-fated Kinetophone (I think it was called that).

The Vitaphone has reproduced speeches, songs and instrumental numbers by Marion Talley, Will H. Hays, Mischa Elman and others. On the female voices, the choruses and the violin solos it is a trifle unsure of itself, but in a solo by Giovanni Martinelli and a ukulele number by Roy Smeck it proved to be extraordinarily impressive.

DON JUAN was accompanied by the New York Philharmonic Orchestra via the Vitaphone, indicating that it will be possible in the future to dispense with orchestras and organists in movie theatres.

Well, I for one will shed no tears. I'm tired of hearing "Hearts and Flowers" during the views of the United States Cavalry riding to the rescue, and "Horses—Horses—Horses" during the tender love scenes.

■ ■ ■ ■

FUTURE DEVELOPMENTS (1927), Harry M. Warner

Harry Warner appeared as one of the speakers in Joseph Kennedy's series of lectures on the film industry for the Harvard business school (see page 112). Warner's lecture—delivered after the appearance of the first Vitaphone program but before the opening of *The Jazz Singer*—suggested the difficulties of selling the Vitaphone to others in the industry (not to the public) and implied that the company's entire "life's wealth" was invested in the project.

The Vitaphone is, I presume, the thing that you all want to hear about, so I will step outside of formalities and try to give you a little outline of it. As a preliminary and a sort of parallel case, I would like to tell you

"Future Developments," by Harry M. Warner, was published in *The Story of the Films,* edited by Joseph P. Kennedy (Shaw, 1927; Ozer, 1971).

about a picture we had in Newcastle, Pennsylvania, twenty-four years ago. When the theatre was all finished, we found we had no chairs. My brothers and I got together and tried to decide where we were going to get them. One said, "What's the matter with the undertaker?" So we went over and engaged ninety-six chairs from a neighboring undertaker. The consequence was that whenever there was a funeral we had to ask the audience to stand up. Picture that theatre with those ninety-six chairs and then picture the Roxy Theatre today, and you will have an idea of the development of the motion picture industry. When I first saw the vitaphone, I remembered that little theatre with ninety-six chairs.

A New Idea

It may be this thought would never have come to my mind if my brother, who had been fooling around with radio stations, had not wired me one day: "Go to the Western Electric Company and see what I consider the greatest thing in the world." After a while I went and heard it and wired him back, "I think you are right." Had he wired me to go up and hear a talking picture I would never have gone near it, because I had heard and seen talking pictures so much that I would not have walked across the street to look at one. But when I heard a twelve-piece orchestra on that screen at the Bell Telephone Laboratories, I could not believe my own ears. I walked in back of the screen to see if they did not have an orchestra there synchronizing with the picture. They all laughed at me. The whole affair was in a ten by twelve room. There were a lot of bulbs working and things I knew nothing about, but there was not any concealed orchestra.

Music Needed for the Pictures

The thought occurred to me that if we quit the idea of a talking picture and brought about something the motion picture theatre of the present day really needs—music adapted to the picture—we could ultimately develop it to a point at which people would ask us for talking pictures. If I myself would not have gone across the street to see or hear a talking picture, I surely could not expect the public to do it. But Music! That is another story. An organ playing to a picture was the thing that I visualized. I stopped and thought a minute and said: "Here's a theatre that seats four or five thousand people, runs a motion picture, which is the most important part of its business, and neglects the most important part of the picture, which is music. The manager plays his music as an overture and does not play it to the picture." Try this experiment some day. Take a motion picture, a silent one, and run it off. Then take the same picture and run it with an orchestra, and you will see the difference. That vision came to me. So I took it up with the head of the Western Electric Company and arrived at an understanding with him. I will give our arrangement as briefly as I can.

They were to agree to discontinue the use of the name "talking picture" and devote their time entirely to music. Then the question came up, What is the proper method of bringing this instrument before the public? Some members of our firm were for taking a little theatre, making up a few vaudeville numbers and asking the different exhibitors throughout the country to come in and hear it. That would be a long drawn out process and the objection came up that we would be competing with the "short-reel" subject, which does not cost the theatre man much, and he might say, "Why should I throw out the short-reel subject and take on something new which I know so little about?"

THE FIRST DEMONSTRATION

So the battle was on and it lasted several weeks. I finally decided to do the thing on a liberal scale, because if it was worth doing at all it was worth doing well. I said to my partners: "Let's get the greatest artists and the best orchestras in the country. Let's have confidence in this and put all our muscle behind it. We'll know the result after we have opened the first show." I banked on the ability of the Western Electric Company, with the thirty-five hundred people employed in the Bell laboratory, to take care of the proper working of the instrument itself. As long as the telephone company and its subsidiaries were lending their name to an instrument, it was up to them to make sure that it was right, because they had just as much at stake as we had. While we could go broke and they could not, nevertheless the stake was there for both of us.

So we put on a first-class show and opened it to the public. The critics lauded it as a great success. Everybody talked about it but everybody still continued saying that talking pictures were not a success. Still the show went on. Now, the question arose, "The show is open and everything is fine, but who is going to buy our machines?"

OVERCOMING VESTED INTERESTS AND HUMAN INERTIA

Here is the problem that we were confronted with and are confronted with yet. I do not want you to think for a minute that the victory has been won. New ideas do not penetrate the human mind as easily as that. They take more time. We have confidence in our idea and we have put our money in it, but it still furnishes us serious problems.

The main problem is this. The people in the amusement business have developed mammoth enterprises and they have built them along certain lines. Some give just motion pictures and some motion pictures and vaudeville and some vaudeville alone. Now they say: "We have built these institutions, and they are successful. Why should we discard any part of that which is successful to try something new?" After establishing the success of the invention, we found that we had that difficulty in front of us. I read in a magazine only yesterday that the Keith-Albee people have put a clause in their contract forbidding any actor that works for them to appear on the vitaphone. I have gone around to the heads of several companies and tried to persuade them to participate and become a part of our company, but as yet I must admit we have not succeeded.

Selling the Machines

We cannot take defeat so easily, so we set out to prove to them that we are right. Now, if you think right, you cannot do wrong. So we went out and convinced the first man that the vitaphone was a good thing, and he put in a machine. Then we opened more shows on Broadway. I will admit to you that it is not good business for a firm to open three shows on Broadway, but, to convince the theatre people that the vita-phone is all right, we opened number two and number three shows and showed them just what they were doing. We wanted to prove that there was a public that wished to see good pictures with good music, that the vitaphone helped the picture by its orchestration, and, if so, they ought to put it in. Well, we convinced them one at a time, until today—the wire I had Saturday was one hundred and forty convinced theatre people. That is quite a lot, because when we made the contract we agreed only to in-stall one hundred and sixty the first year.

If one hundred and forty theatres will have these machines installed by August first, why, of course, the machine will be able to speak for itself. After that it will not be necessary, I am positive, for us to worry about its success. The theatre man is no different from any other business man. When he sees the man around the corner doing well, he wants the same thing and he wants it on the same terms.

Prospects of Success

Now for the benefits. We must always try to visualize these, because that which is visualized is that which we can do. And visualization of the final result helps us over the discouraging moments. I was very sorry a couple of weeks ago to read the headlines of a New York newspaper, which said that Edison called the talking pictures a failure. You know it is not so comfortable to have your life's wealth invested in a thing which such a great authority as Edison says cannot succeed. I wrote an answer and pointed out that they may have been a failure fifteen years ago but if Edison himself looked at his own bulb of that period and compared it with the bulb of today he would not know it. We have parts in our vita-phone today which even he did not know about fifteen years ago.

Young men like you must never get discouraged when others say that some enterprise in which you are interested will not be a success. You must be satisfied in your own mind, as I was about the vitaphone when I saw that it would bring to the small hamlet and the small theatre the same performance that the big theatre has. There is no reason why an instru-ment of this kind cannot bring into a town of ten thousand with a theatre of eight hundred seats the same show that is being performed in a theatre of five thousand seats in a big city.

But the introduction of a novelty like that takes time, and just how it is going to be done I cannot yet say. There are a great many problems to solve in the distributing end of the vitaphone. You have to deal with the big theatre and you have to deal with the small one. The problems are many and different, but I am sure we will ultimately overcome them all, particularly as we have the assistance of the Western Electric Com-pany, whose name the machine carries.

Other New Developments

There are other new inventions, or new methods, that are required in the picture business. Let me tell you about one. About three years ago I saw them making pictures with a carbon light. A set the size of this room would take possibly forty or fifty electricians to light it. I asked why they could not get a bulb that would do the work. Everybody said it could not be done. Last Saturday we finished our first picture with an incandescent lamp doing the work. Now, that is quite a step forward in the motion picture business. Suppose you had to light up an enormous street scene and you had to have two or three hundred electricians. Instead of that, you can do it with buttons at one desk. I saw some of the reels of the first picture, and the lighting is better than with carbon because it is softer. You cannot get as soft a light with carbon as you can get with the regular bulb. You can divide your light better and when you work with the carbon you have to work with more powerful electricity. There you have an important technical advance in the making of motion pictures. . . .

Suitable Material for the Vitaphone

The big job before us is to provide the proper kind of entertainment through the vitaphone. We are confident people will go to hear the vita-phone but we know the proper kind of entertainment must be supplied, if it is going to be a great success.

This coming year we are to make three pictures in which the vitaphone will play an important part. For instance, in the making of a scene in which a stage forms part of the view and the actors are seen playing, we intend to bring out the actors' singing and the actual performance of each person on the stage. Our first picture embodying that feature will be "The Jazz Singer," with Al Jolson. Then we are going to perform a wedding ceremony. As you see it today, a wedding ceremony performed on the screen takes place in complete silence. Nobody knows what the priest or the preacher or the rabbi has said. We will actually perform a wedding ceremony and try to make it as real as life. In talking to a big man in the business not long ago, who tried to make a deal for some vitaphone machines, I told him exactly what I am telling you. He said, "I did not think you could do that with it; I thought you could just play short numbers." . . .

■ ■ ■ ■

A SOLDIER FALLS (1929), Fitzhugh Green

The most romantic history of the coming of sound was Fitzhugh Green's *The Film Finds Its Tongue,* which characterizes the four brothers Warner as the four Musketeers, gallant gamblers who staked all on a single roll of the dice so that art and science could go forth and forward. This chapter from the book describes the death of one of the "soldiers," Sam Warner, just prior to the premiere of the film that would make the Warners' name and fame.

The *Jazz Singer,* starring Al Jolson, was finished as a Talkie at the Warners' Hollywood studio in the summer of 1927. The last "take" had been made on August 7th. The film was developed that night for the "rushes"; and after those were seen by Alan Crosland, who had directed the picture, by the cutter, by Sam and Jack Warner . . . and talked over . . . they were locked in the big film vaults to await the return of the records from the Victor Talking Machine Company's plant at Oakland, California. The records were made up there; the "waxes," as the original records were called, having been shipped in special boxes so constructed as to allow nothing to touch or mar their perfect surface. These waxes were then, at the Victor plant, covered with graphite and electroplated with copper. The copper conformed to each delicate groove and made a "master" die from which the commercial records were pressed.

"A Soldier Falls" is from Fitzhugh Green's *The Film Finds Its Tongue* (G. P. Putnam's Sons, 1929).

A week later the records were back; and the difficult task of cutting, scoring and duping the picture began, a task of great delicacy. It is easier now, for it has been done many times, and those who make talking pictures have grown skillful at it. Then, it was pioneering, experiment, every step of the way.

It should be remembered that the *Jazz Singer* was as much of an innovation as *Don Juan*. It was the first true Talkie. It had been projected at a time when it seemed mathematically certain that it could not return its costs, due to the small number of places where it could be played. Yet as a silent picture it could not succeed. Harry Warner knew this when he hired Al Jolson.[1] He calculated that success in "wired" houses would force the silent houses to install reproducing apparatus. He was right. For at least 100 houses that failed with it as a silent picture played it again as a Talkie and cleaned up.

The middle of September, and the job was done, the records ready. Special messengers carried it all across the country to New York as though it were most precious jewels.

This now-famous Talkie was to open at the Warner Theatre on October 6, 1927. The theatre was being renovated especially for the great occasion. Huge electric signs were being built to cover the big marquee. Posters flared on billboards all over the city: "COMING—AL JOLSON IN THE JAZZ SINGER" . . .

It was all pretty good. It was so good that there was a feeling on the Warner lot and in the Warner offices, that it might be the turning point of this long heart-breaking fight. The feeling of success was in it. On the tryouts those songs of Jolson's had gone over with a ring that ought to bring down the house. But there had been too many setbacks to be sure.

The four Warner brothers had that feeling of hope; and yet they bore the undercurrent of anxiety that is always present when one's work is to be submitted to the public. It meant so much to them: it meant the future. They had been skating on thin ice for so long, following their dream. The ice seemed thinner than ever now, even though there promised to be solid footing just ahead.

Days went on, drawing closer and closer to that opening night. It didn't seem that anything could happen . . . they were so carefree. But something did happen.

Sam Warner was tired. He had been in the thick of battle ever since the day he saw that first Talkie demonstration. He had been putting

1. Ed. Note: Originally they hired George Jessel, who had starred in the play on Broadway, for the role. Jessell was replaced either because he refused to sing for the same money (Jessel's story) or because the Warners wanted a bigger star.

all his force, all his energy, all his vitality into it; carrying it on his shoulders, lending strength, cheer . . . continually fighting.

The last week in September he was ill, just one day. It didn't seem much; just a cold. He'd been just about to start for New York with Jack and Albert to see the premiere. Now he wasn't well enough to go. Jack went alone, under protest; Albert stayed. Sam continued work, literally dying on his feet.

Two days later Sam went to the hospital. A sinus was infected. Then the poison swept down into his system and all through it. The surgeons operated. Jack, in New York, turned and raced for the coast. Harry dropped everything. The premiere was forgotten in this moment of threat to one of those four warriors. He sat, an anxious man, waiting for telegrams in a train that seemed to crawl when it was going seventy miles an hour.

For twenty-four hours the news was reassuring. Then there was a relapse. Sam, who had been in full vigor a week before, a giant just turned forty, was fighting for his life in the California Lutheran Hospital, Los Angeles. It was pneumonia with complications. They were operating again. They were feeding him oxygen. . . .

In three frantic days Harry Warner crossed the country, hoping against hope. Albert was in Los Angeles, hurrying to the hospital, when Harry got the telegram he had been dreading: Sam was dying—he was not going to get well.

Harry was in Phoenix, Arizona. Time and miles seemed insurmountable barriers. He was trying to get a plane to take him the rest of the way. He failed. He chartered a special train. When he reached Los Angeles at six o'clock on the morning of October 5, 1927, his brother had been dead for three hours.

But the public must be amused, regardless of life or death. The Pagliacci theme is not all confined to the actor. And so, on the 6th of October, the next night after Sam's death, the *Jazz Singer* had its premiere: without Sam—without any of the Warner brothers. None of them could summon up enough feeling to care much about the *Jazz Singer* at that moment.

On Broadway the new Warner signs came to life with the dusk. Striking posters of Jolson, just eyes, mouth, collar, and white gloves in a dead black sheet, but Jolson to the last detail, stood in the theatre's lobby. Crowds pushed by, swarmed, shoved. Taxis drew up carrying the cream of the profession, possessors of choice tickets . . . taxis carrying Broadway to something new. A line swayed about the box office. But there were no more seats.

It was a New York audience, come to see a New Yorker, to hear him sing for them, to judge his song—*which came out of a can!* They had a good time that night. They were wild about the singing. They seemed almost wilder about one other thing: that little impromptu speech of Jolson's, to his mother. *"Come on, Ma. Listen to this . . ."*

When Jolson began to speak, the audience reacted as though to wine. It was an epochal moment. They couldn't get over it—he had spoken . . . to *them*, from that screen! It was a little strange, too; for there had been much Vitaphone speech before, in many of the shorts. But this, coming from a picture that the crowd was interested in, a picture that was swaying their emotions, that they were for the moment *living* with the players, struck deeply home.

Telegrams started west now that were business: *"Jazz Singer a hit. Went over big. Jolson's talking hit the high spot. Work dialogue into them. Give us more like Jazz Singer, with more talk."*

The public knew what it wanted; the theatre men at last knew what the public wanted. The public wanted talking pictures, now. They wanted the characters to start talking and go on talking.

The dam was broken: Dynamite the crevice and let the flood through! It was victory! It meant dollars; it meant fortune, fame, success. . . . But at the moment it didn't mean very much to Harry Warner, and Albert Warner, and Jack Warner. Where would be the victory, how could there be anything in the reward . . . without Sam.

And yet they could not stop now. A great fight still lay ahead. This was only the merest crack. There was the forcing of the issue concerning the equipping of the theatres. After all these months, only a hundred of them were yet equipped to take the Talkie product. There was the making of pictures that must now take advantage of the "break." There was the surpassing of other producers who might now see the merits of Talkies and try to capitalize on Warners' pioneer venture.

The brothers did not want to fight for themselves any more. For Sam's sake, they could not lie down. They must carry on. They must finish the task he had started, must between them do his share. They must see it through to the end, and that end must be a triumphant one.

Harry and Albert were sober and determined when they started back for New York after Sam was buried. Jack, in the studio, squared himself. He was alone, now, in the west. There were those telegrams from the east. He must give them "more talk."

The public knew at last who the Warners were.

■ ■ ■ ■

WARNER BROS. INNOVATES SOUND: A BUSINESS HISTORY (1977), Douglas Gomery

The young film historian Douglas Gomery looks skeptically at the romantic myths of gambling and financial flamboyance that have attached themselves to the history of Warner Bros. and the Vitaphone. In this previously unpublished monograph Gomery surveys the development and expansion of the Vitaphone from a strictly economic point of view, developing the position that the triumph of Vitaphone was a carefully conceived business strategy that revealed itself in a series of cautious, steady, expansionary steps. Although the success of *The Jazz Singer* may have exceeded the Warner expectations (and everyone else's, for that matter), that success could be properly exploited because it had been carefully built.

The transition of the American film industry from silent to sound films is an important historical epoch in any history of film. Yet for no comparable period do so many legends, unproved hypotheses, and unverified facts exist. The framework and data provided by Lewis Jacobs and Benjamin Hampton have remained unchallenged for nearly forty years.[1] To begin a reexamination of this important period, this article will adopt a new approach and will employ previously unexamined primary documents. The approach emphasizes economics: this article assumes that the entrepreneurs of the American film industry converted to sound to increase their profits. The men who controlled the American motion picture industry were in business primarily for one reason: to maximize the long-run profits of their firms. The giant communications firms, such as American Telephone and Telegraph (AT&T), that supplied the film industry with sound equipment were also eager to maximize long-run profits. These assumptions explain *why* all the firms which contributed to the transformation acted as they did, and thus frees the historian to concentrate on the who, what, where, and how of the change.

The economic theory which treats the introduction of any new product or new production process is called the theory of technological innova-

"Warner Bros. Innovates Sound: A Business History" (1977) is adapted from chap. 3 of Douglas Gomery's Ph.D. dissertation, "The Coming of Sound to the American Cinema: The Transformation of an Industry" (University of Wisconsin–Madison, 1975).

1. Benjamin B. Hampton, *History of the American Film Industry* (New York: Covici-Friede, 1931); Lewis Jacobs, *The Rise of the American Film* (New York: Columbia University Press, 1939).

tion. This theory develops three different stages of change: invention, innovation, and diffusion. Even more important than the creation of the necessary inventions is the innovative activity of the entrepreneur who revamps his or her firm's means of production and devises ways to market a new product based on the new technology. An executive will take such actions because he or she determines that the adoption of these untried methods is this firm's best avenue of expansion (i.e., this investment will add the most to the firm's long-run profit for the least cost). Such a change requires many practical judgments. A firm must have the necessary managerial talent to organize and effect the innovation. Its managers must estimate the future costs for the needed capital investment and for changes in production, distribution, and exhibition. On the demand side, they must estimate the effects of new pricing policies and marketing techniques. Finally there is the risk factor. It takes a bold entrepreneur to undertake such speculative activity. Later, other entrepreneurs imitate the innovator and industry-wide diffusion occurs.

This new historical approach can provide fresh insights only if there is adequate primary evidence with which to work. Fortunately for studying the coming of sound, such data exist in congressional investigations of the American Telephone and Telegraph Corporation, the testimony and exhibits in court records, and motion picture trade papers such as *Moving Picture World, Motion Picture News,* and *Variety.* We can now describe and analyze how Warner Bros. handled the issues posed by the theory of technological innovation.

Previous historical research has conclusively established that Warner Bros. innovated synchronized-sound movies. Yet researchers always argue that the cause of this risky behavior was desperation: Warner Bros. was nearing bankruptcy, and its quick conversion to sound was the only means of avoiding going out of business. Although such reasoning paints a very romantic portrait, it is much too simplistic. In fact, Warner Bros. imposed a substantial short-term debt on itself to enable its rapid expansion. In 1924 Warner Bros. was a prosperous, albeit small, production company. Lack of size, of distribution exchanges, and of theaters made it quite difficult for Warner Bros. to acquire financial backing for production. Prior to 1925, Warner Bros. used two methods to raise the necessary capital. One was to seek out a rich individual and trade a percentage of the firm's potential profits for part of the necessary capital. As a consequence, real interest rates effectively ran well in excess of 100 percent. More frequently, Warner Bros. followed the "franchise" technique. First, Warners' divided the United States into twenty-eight "franchise" zones and secured from each "franchise holder," usually a major exhibitor, backing for five to ten films. Then, Warners' guaranteed each "franchise holder" first rights to a fixed percentage of the profits. Here the effective rate of interest usually approached 100 percent.

No wonder that in 1924, Harry Warner, president of Warner Bros. and the eldest brother, sought an alternative method of financing. In December 1924, he met Waddill Catchings, head of the investment division of Wall Street's Goldman, Sachs. Catchings was famous for his willingness to back small firms he thought could grow into giants; in 1924 he was in the process of helping Woolworth's and Sears, Roebuck grow from small, regional businesses into large, national chains. Moreover, by 1924 Catchings had reasoned that the motion picture industry was ripe for expansion. In December 1924, Catchings carefully scrutinized the operations of Warner Bros. Previously, because they doubted that upstart movie moguls could enforce reasonable limits on the cost of films, Catchings and other partners in Goldman, Sachs had not been confident enough to finance a motion picture concern. Warners' rigid accounting procedures, especially the day-to-day audits by production manager Jack Warner, made Warners Bros. far more attractive than the other firms Catchings had investigated.

However, in February 1925, just before Harry Warner and Catchings were to consummate a deal, the Warner Bros. franchise holders rebelled; they had heard rumors of a Warner–Goldman, Sachs alliance. Normally unorganized, they appointed a committee to meet with Harry Warner; they did not want Warner Bros. to terminate what had been an extraordinarily profitable relationship. At this point Harry Warner devised a counterstrategy. He know that Vitagraph, a pioneer motion picture concern with an international network of exchanges, was verging on bankruptcy. Harry approached Vitagraph president Albert E. Smith and offered to relieve the corporation of its current liabilities of $980,000 and to purchase enough shares to acquire majority control. Smith agreed, and on 22 April 1925 Harry advised the franchise holders' committee that Warner Bros. now had twenty-six exchanges in the United States, twenty-four in foreign countries, a new studio in Brooklyn, and another in Hollywood. This bold action broke the Warner dependency on the franchise system. Catchings was impressed and decided to use the resources and power of Goldman, Sachs to orchestrate and support all future financial operations of Warner Bros.

Catchings immediately set out to obtain permanent financing for production. Initially, he established a revolving credit line of $3 million; then he raised $4 million more through a bond issue. Both Catchings and Harry Warner agreed that if Warner Bros. was to grow more profitable, it must also expand its holdings in distribution and exhibition, becoming completely vertically integrated. Thus, in the fall of 1925 Warner Bros. opened two new distribution exchanges in the United States and twenty-nine more in foreign countries. In six months Warners' had created a distribution system equal to those of Famous Players, Loew's (MGM), and First National. At the same time, it purchased ten first-run houses to form the basis of a chain of theaters, including Broadway's Piccadilly theater (renamed the Warners) as the flagship. Harry also leased a half-dozen first-run theaters in key locations, beginning with the Orpheum in Chicago's Loop.

As part of this wave of expansion, Warners' acquired a Los Angeles radio station. Through this deal Sam Warner met Nathan Levinson, a salesman of Western Electric radio equipment. The two became fast friends, and in April 1925 Levinson introduced Sam to the new Western Electric system for recording and reproducing sound motion pictures. Sam was fascinated, and in May 1925 he and Levinson tricked Harry into attending a demonstration. Harry almost did not go, for, as he later recalled, "if [they] had said talking picture, I never would have gone, because [talking pictures] had been made up to that time several times, and each was a failure."[2] A recording of a five-piece jazz band sparked Harry's interest, and within a week he had conceived of a plan to use this new invention. He explained to Catchings, "If it can talk, it can sing."[3] Warner Bros. could record the greatest musical acts and present them in their theaters. This would provide their theaters with the best added attractions, albeit on film, currently available. It was an entrepreneurial vision that would require the large amounts of financing which only an investment banker as skilled as Catchings could provide. At once Harry Warner and Catchings opened negotiations with Western Electric's agent, Walter J. Rich. The three met with executives from Western Electric throughout June 1925. On 25 June 1925 Warner Bros. and Western Electric signed a letter of agreement calling for an experimental program of at least a year's duration. Experiments began in October. Slowly, Sam Warner and his assistants integrated the Western Electric inventions into a workable production system.

During this experimental phase, Warner Bros. did not cease its other expansionary activities. It even began to experience some return on these other investments. Ernst Lubitsch's *Lady Windemere's Fan* established box office records in its debut in January 1926 at the Warners' theater in New York City; *The Sea Beast* with John Barrymore opened the follow-

2. General Talking Pictures Corporation et al. v. American Telephone and Telegraph Company et al., 18 F. Supp. 650, *Record,* p. 1108.

3. Koplar, 19 F. Supp. 173, *Record,* p. 368.

ing month to the same reception. To extract the maximum revenue from these hits and to overcome Warners' lack of first-run theaters, Harry even rented a number of legitimate theaters to "road-show" these and later films at a two dollar admisison price. Even more important were the immediate returns from foreign operations. Despite these improvements, it was not surprising that Warners' yearly financial statement, issued in March 1926, stood in the red. The loss was a large $1.337 million. Yet the company did not face bankruptcy. Its loss was self-imposed, for now Warners' possessed an international distribution network, owned a growing chain of theaters, was producing higher-priced films, and had established the line of credit necessary to continue its climb to the top of the industry.

By December 1925 the experiments were going so well at the Brooklyn studio that Rich proposed to Harry Warner and Catchings that negotiations for a permanent agreement begin immediately. By the end of 1925 all the interested parties had come to substantial agreement. However, as they hammered out the specific details of the contract in January and the early part of February, an important change in the negotiators took place. John E. Otterson became Western Electric's sole representative. Upon assumption of power, he expressed his disappointment that Western Electric was not negotiating with Famous Players, Loew's, or First National. Otterson began to try to rectify Western Electric's mistake. In order to assure Western Electric of a maximum profit, he demanded complete authority over any future developments and immediate control of all prices to be charged exhibitors for equipment. Otterson was unable to secure such power; the backing of Goldman, Sachs gave Warner Bros. the strength to command parity with Western Electric. Thus, on 20 April 1926 Western Electric signed an exclusive agreement with Warners' newly created subsidiary for sound-film production and distribution, the Vitaphone Corporation. Western Electric granted Vitaphone a permanent license and established 8 percent (of Vitaphone's gross revenues) as its royalty fee. An annual minimum, ranging from $40,000 for the first year to $100,000 by 1930, was also fixed. The agreement looked to a gradual sale of apparatus to theaters: the sale of sound-film equipment to 160 theaters in 1927 and to a total of 2,400 theaters by 1931. To satisfy Otterson, Warner and Catchings granted Western Electric a permanent representative on Vitaphone's board of directors and guaranteed that Goldman, Sachs would stand behind all Vitaphone debts for at least five years.

As the trade papers were announcing the first news of the alliance, Vitaphone was organizing its assault on the marketplace. Harry signed a great number of the popular musical artists monopolized by the Victor

Phonograph Company, negotiated contracts with the stars of the Metropolitan Opera, and secured the New York Philharmonic to record orchestral accompaniments for feature films. By June 1926 Vitaphone was ready to begin recording musical shorts and orchestral accompaniments for features to be released during the following season. Because of Otterson's insistence, Vitaphone moved its studio to the vacant Manhattan Opera House on 34th Street in New York City. Sam Warner and his crew rewired the theater, added lights, and even built a deck over the seats in the orchestra section. To keep costs to a minimum, Vitaphone rented part of the building to the Shriners for evening meetings.

Vitaphone's 6 August 1926 premiere reflected the strategy that Harry Warner had been following for more than a year. A "Vitaphone prelude" replaced the overture, vaudeville acts, newsreel, and comedy short usually presented at a first-run theater. There were seven numbers in the prelude. The first presented Will Hays congratulating Warner Bros. and Western Electric for their pioneering efforts. The stage "illusion" was complete; Hays bowed at the end, anticipating applause. Next came the overture from *Tannhauser* played by the New York Philharmonic. Conductor Henry Hadley also bowed. Six "acts" in a colossal "headliner" presentation followed. Five performed serious music. Only Roy Smeck, with his harmonica and banjo act, provided an alternative. Tenor Giovannni Martinelli's aria from *I Pagliacci* was the hit of the evening, his segment receiving a two-minute ovation. Harry Warner's strategy of providing the most popular musical stars had begun very conservatively. No one could object to a new mechanical device that would bring classical music to the masses. Moreover, since the shorts cost an average of only $12,000, they provided a cheap way to experiment with sound while still ensuring a large audience.

After a ten-minute intermission came the feature film, *Don Juan*, accompanied by a Vitaphone recording of the New York Philharmonic Orchestra. Most reviewers failed to comment on this music, since the recording simply replaced the usual pit orchestra. The film *Don Juan* did impress most observers. It was Warners' most expensive feature to date, and promised, with or without sound, to be its most popular. Moreover, few could fail to notice Vitaphone's initial popularity. Scalpers sold $3.30 tickets for $10. The first five public performances established a record gross for the Warners' theater. In the short run, Vitaphone seemed an immediate success; its future remained still very much in doubt.

When the 1926–27 motion picture season opened in September 1926, Warner Bros. was clearly on its way up in the American film industry. Only the Vitaphone operations expanded at a slow rate. This infuriated

John Otterson; repeatedly, Harry Warner tried to reassure Otterson and convince him that Vitaphone should continue at its present rate of growth. Harry argued that for the present he should book sound films only in a selected number of large cities throughout the United States. Each first-run theater need not be the largest, but should be big enough to attract attention, yet cheap enough so Vitaphone could *continuously* present a show before the public for at least one season. Following up on that publicity, Vitaphone should gradually place shows in smaller, surrounding cities. By this time Vitaphone would have increased production so that any theater could have a continuous flow of the Vitaphone product. Simultaneously, Vitaphone would adapt its shorts and later its features to meet maximum audience approval. Thus, in the not too distant future, with Vitaphone's resources for production and distribution of sufficient size, Warners' could reap the maximum rewards from a hit Vitaphone show.

Following this strategy, on 6 September 1926 Warner Bros. opened the *Don Juan* package at the Globe Theater in Atlantic City. The show drew a packed house, an especially good sign since Atlantic City was a popular summer resort. Next Vitaphone rented the McVickers Theatre in Chicago's Loop and opened the *Don Juan* package to overflow crowds. In October Vitaphone repeated this process and opened the *Don Juan* show in more than a half-dozen major American cities.

A second Vitaphone package, with the feature *The Better 'Ole,* premiered at Moss's Colony Theatre in New York on 7 October 1926. This not only gave Vitaphone two "shows" on Broadway, but, more importantly, represented a major shift in programming strategy. The program's shorts all featured vaudeville artists whom (according to *Variety* estimates) only the four largest motion picture theaters could have afforded to present live. The show opened with another overture, "The Spirit of 1812." *Variety* estimated that the New York Philharmonic would cost $6,000 per week. The Four Aristocrats came next and would cost $1,000 per week. Then recordings of four of the most popular vaudeville stars of their day appeared; the aggregate salaries of such stars could total $25,000 per week. The first was George Jessel, who performed a short monologue and sang Irving Berlin's "At Peace with the World and You." Elsie Janis followed with four songs. Mordaunt Hall of the *New York Times* found this Vitaphone recording so convincing that "one forgot all about the Vitaphone in listening to the distinct words of the songs . . . it was just as if Miss Janis were on the stage." This was high praise for a vaudeville artist popular enough to command $3,000 per week. Eugene and Willie Howard followed with a comic sketch. And the "headliner" was Al Jolson, who did three songs, standing before a set of a southern plantation. *Variety* could only see a bright future for an invention that could place this much high-priced vaudeville talent on one stage at one time.

Despite these early triumphs, Vitaphone experienced its share of disappointments during its first season. At Grauman's Egyptian theater in Los Angeles, *Don Juan* with sound lasted only two weeks. (Later the silent version with Grauman's own prologue ran for eleven weeks.) In St. Louis, Vitaphone withdrew *Don Juan* after seven losing weeks and put silent program releases in the Capital for the remainder of its lease. At the McVickers, Vitaphone experienced a 50 percent drop during the usually active Christmas season. Only at Broadway's Colony and Warner theaters did Vitaphone shows generate extraordinary revenues. Overall there was no clear-cut trend. Thus, it surprised no one in the film industry when, in December 1926, Warner Bros. released *Don Juan,* and, a month later, *The Better 'Ole* as individual silent films.

Despite this lukewarm response, Catchings and Harry Warner remained optimistic. Harry continued to sign every available concert, musical, and vaudeville star. He consciously followed the model of the Victor Phonograph Company, wanting to make the Vitaphone trademark as famous in its field as Red Seal was in its own. By February 1927 Vitaphone had fifty vandeville subjects on disc and was recording five new shorts per week. In April 1927 Vitaphone signed its last major vaudeville holdout, Weber and Fields. Still, tenor Giovanni Martinelli and Al Jolson made the most shorts, received the highest fees ($5,000 per recording), and received the most praise from the reviewers of the time. Vitaphone's key problem became how to maintain a balance between opera stars, variety acts, and big-name bands. Like big-time vaudeville, Vitaphone found it should construct thirty-minute-long preludes, with its biggest stars coming last. Moreover, the shorts gradually became unlike "canned" vaudeville, as Sam Warner and his assistants eliminated mandatory bows (by May 1927) and extremely long takes, employing more traditional strategies of camera work and editing.

Simultaneously, Vitaphone began to interest exhibitors in leasing and installing reproducing equipment. Between November 1926 and April 1927, 132 exhibitors signed installation contracts. Of the first 74 theaters wired, the majority were in the East. In the spring of 1927 Harry secured three very important accounts. The first was the Stanley Company of America, owners of more than 300 theaters in the mid-Atlantic states. (Warner Bros. would merge with the Stanley Company in 1928.) Stanley installed Vitaphone equipment in 13 of its theaters. In Minnesota the Finkelstein and Rubin circuit held dominion. It installed Vitaphone in the Capital theater in St. Paul and the State in Minneapolis. The final, key account consisted of only one theater: New York City's Roxy. In March 1927 Samuel Rothafel opened America's largest theater, the Roxy, and featured Vitaphone shorts. Recognition by such a noted theater entrepreneur produced extremely favorable publicity. Most theaters that used Vitaphone kept their regular prices despite the additional cost. Still no trends emerged. Vitaphone failed and succeeded; it had long runs in some theaters and closed within a week in others. Most exhibitors waited, hoping to learn more before deciding.

Warner Bros. continued to improve financially despite the drain from Vitaphone. As of 26 February 1927 Warner Bros. had invested over $3 million in Vitaphone, yet its quarterly losses had declined to less than a third of the previous year's loss. Foreign operations grew extremely profitable. Rentals in Great Britain alone rose by two million for the fiscal year ending 31 August 1927. Waddill Catchings was always able to generate the necessary financing for all of Warners' new investments, including Vitaphone. To finance more costly products, he established a new revolving credit account of $4 million; to facilitate production, he secured a $1 million loan to construct a new Hollywood studio. He negotiated extensions on outstanding loans and refinanced others.

Such extraordinary financial support did not satisfy John Otterson. Still wanting to control all Vitaphone operations directly and then to grant direct licenses to Famous Players, Otterson continued to harass Catchings's and Harry Warner's efforts at every turn. He set the cost of the reproduction equipment at $16,000 to $25,000, not at the promised $3,700 to $7,000. This price crippled Vitaphone's ability to interest independent theater owners of limited means. Harry Warner countered by granting liberal time-payment plans: 25 percent down, the balance due over a period of twelve to twenty-four months. Otterson kept requesting that Vitaphone supply detailed, long-range plans; he pressured Harry Warner to move toward rapid expansion. By the end of 1926 Otterson had totally broken with Warner and Catchings; he detailed his thoughts in a memo:

> the present management of the Vitaphone Corporation is incompetent to properly exploit the Vitaphone, to conduct relationships with the motion picture industry and to execute the contract with the Western Electric Company.[4]

Otterson hoped Western Electric could purchase Vitaphone, and then let Warner Bros. make shorts and scores, while Western Electric directed

4. United States Federal Communications Commission, *Staff Report on Electrical Research Products, Inc., Volume II, Report A* (pursuant to Public Resolution No. 8, 74th Congress, 1937), p. 169.

all the technical and licensing activities. He was convinced that only then would Western Electric be able to gain a monopoly position and, hence, not be "out-manuevered and-distanced by competitors who have started later in the field."[5]

In December 1926 Otterson took the offensive. First, he organized Electrical Research Products, Inc. (ERPI), as a wholly owned subsidiary of Western Electric solely to market sound equipment. From this new base Otterson pressured Famous Players, Loew's, and Fox to take out direct licenses for sound, even though this activity was legally reserved for Vitaphone. The Fox Film Company did contract for such a license on 31 December 1926. Still, Otterson could not pursuade Famous Players or Loew's. Competition from RCA provided one stumbling block, but Otterson's demands proved to be the largest impediment. Neither Famous Players nor Loew's would contract to pay the 8 percent of gross royalities Otterson sought; it was too high a rate. Moreover, legally Vitaphone would have to grant the license to Famous Players or Loew's, and neither giant wished to become the licensee of a subsidiary of a competitor. Thus, in February 1927 Famous Players and Loew's postponed any decision concerning sound for one year. In reaction, Otterson campaigned more intensely to separate Warner Bros. from Vitaphone. He could then reopen negotiations with Famous Players and Loew's. On 14 March 1927 he called on Catchings and demanded termination of the current Vitaphone–Western Electric agreement. The next day Catchings approached Edgar S. Bloom, Otterson's immediate superior. Bloom supported Otterson and said that ERPI's lawyers had prepared an opinion proving that Vitaphone was in default of its contract. Bloom threatened to release this information to the press. Catchings knew this would cripple his delicate operations with key banks. Thus, he concluded that Warner Bros. must give in and negotiate a new contract.

Signed on 18 May 1927, two documents formed the heart of the new Warner Bros.–Western Electric agreement. The first terminated the earlier contract as of 2 April 1927 and transferred to ERPI all of Vitaphone's theater reproducing equipment, its contracts with 136 exhibitors, and its sublicense with Fox-Case. In return, ERPI paid Vitaphone $1,322,306 and agreed not to license any other motion picture producer at a rate less than that which Vitaphone paid. In the second contract ERPI granted Vitaphone a nonexclusive license to employ Western Electric sound-recording equipment and patents at cost plus the usual 8 percent (of gross revenues) royalty fee against an annual minimum of $100,000. In retrospect this new agreement denied Warners' millions in profits. Yet at the

5. Ibid.

time, in the short run, the deal was a good one for both sides. Warners' secured over $1 million in cash, kept strong relations with key banks, and retained its lead in the production and distribution of sound films. On the other hand, Otterson had achieved his goal: he now had total control over all matters concerning future contracts and prices and, thus, could reopen negotiations with Famous Players and Loew's. This new agreement marked the end of the close working alliance of Warner Bros. and Western Electric. Yet it would be nearly a year before Otterson could sign Famous Players and Loew's.

After its settlement with ERPI, Warner Bros. was free to continue expansion. In May 1927 it announced new plans for the 1927–28 season. It would release 26 features and 4 road-show specials—all with Vitaphone accompaniments. In addition, Harry Warner proclaimed that Vitaphone would add talking sequences to some of its feature films. The Vitaphone short had become an accepted part of the motion picture industry's presentations. Throughout the slack summer period, Vitaphone continued to produce shorts at the rate of 5 per week and release them to the growing number of theaters with installations. By October 1927 at least 150 of these shorts had been recorded and released. Two new shows opened: *Old San Francisco* on 22 June 1927 at the New York Warners', and *The First Auto Race* at New York's Colony Theatre on 28 June 1927. The 3 original shows were playing now at popular prices in New York, Chicago, Minneapolis, Dayton, Denver, Philadelphia, Detroit, Buffalo, and Portland, Oregon. Vitaphone opened on Labor Day in theaters in Newark and Milwaukee. And, of course, the Roxy continued to use Vitaphone shorts.

To meet its new schedule of "talkers" and shorts, Warner Bros. instituted an intensive building program. As early as May 1927, it completed the first of four new Hollywood stages completely devoted to the production of Vitaphone shorts and features. In October, when all were finished, Warner Bros. could shift its production of shorts to Hollywood. The new stages were 90 by 150 feet; all walls were felt-lined and specially sealed. Fifteen feet above the floor was a glass-enclosed booth to monitor the recording. The camera was enclosed in a soundproof, movable booth. To maintain absolute quiet, Sam Warner installed incandescent lamps to replace the usual motor-driven arc lights and carbon lamps.

Sam needed talented people to produce the new sound films. Gradually he built his staff: Herman Heller to head the music department, Nathan Levinson to head a sound department, and two full-time writers, Grant Clarke and Murray Roth. Bryan Foy, a former member of vaudeville's

Seven Little Foys and an experienced silent films director, became chief
director and production manager. With his connections in both vaudeville
and motion pictures, Foy was a natural choice. Foy quickly established
a rigid schedule for the production of shorts; Sam then moved to concentrate on features with Vitaphoned segments. The first was *The Jazz
Singer;* finished in August 1927, it cost an estimated $500,000, making
it the most expensive feature in the history of Warner Bros. Sam immediately began production of more feature films with Vitaphone sequences. In all, Warner Bros. looked forward to a prosperous 1927–28
season.

Despite gaining control over all contracts and prices for equipment,
John Otterson continued to harass Vitaphone's efforts. He repeatedly
favored ERPI's only other licensee, Fox. For example, he promised Fox
and Vitaphone one price for certain new equipment and then, at the last
minute, doubled only Vitaphone's rate. Harry Warner and Waddill
Catchings still thought Vitaphone could work with ERPI; then Otterson's
agents began directly to obstruct exhibitors presenting Vitaphone products. Typical was the case of the Smith Amusement Company of Ohio.
One of Vitaphone's first accounts, Smith followed perfectly the marketing
plan Harry Warner had proposed for Vitaphone's films. Its presentation
of Vitaphone shows in Warren and Alliance, Ohio, and Huntington, West
Virginia, gradually created interest throughout the upper Ohio River
Valley. Smith lost $25,000 during the 1926–27 season and counted on
The Jazz Singer to recoup its losses. However, on the day before the
premiere, ERPI pulled its appartus from all three theaters and took Smith
to court. Vitaphone had lost an important account, and the word soon
spread of the power of ERPI. A few exhibitors even began to return
their equipment and went back to silent films.

Catchings and Harry Warner tried to reason with Otterson, but without success. As an alternative, they approached C. M. Bracelen, vice-
president and general counsel of AT&T, ERPI's parent company. Would
Bracelen serve as an informal arbitrator? Upon hearing of this suggestion, Otterson became enraged; he reasoned that the parent company
had no authority in this matter. Otterson soon became even more uncooperative. Vitaphone's contract with ERPI provided for formal arbitration (under New York law) for any unresolved disputes. Catchings knew
formal arbitration might take years to settle, but it was the only way
to impede further abuses by Otterson. So on 30 January 1928 Vitaphone
formally notified ERPI of its contractual defaults. ERPI responded on 8
February, denying all of Vitaphone's contentions. Vitaphone issued further complaints on 30 March; ERPI countercharged with twelve new
violations on 6 April. Formal hearings began in October. In the mean-

while, Otterson reduced his direct harassment of Vitaphone and its exhibitor accounts, freeing Warner Bros. to concentrate on its innovative and expansionary activities.

As the 1927–28 season opened, Vitaphone began to add new forms of sound films to its program. Though *The Jazz Singer* premiered on 6 October 1927 to lukewarm reviews, its four Vitaphoned segments of Jolson's songs proved a success. Vitaphone contracted with Jolson immediately to make three more films for $100,000. (The four Warner brothers did not attend *The Jazz Singer*'s New York premiere because of Sam Warner's death in Los Angeles on 5 October. Jack Warner took over Sam's position as head of Vitaphone production.) Bryan Foy pushed his unit to create four new shorts each week, becoming more bold in programming strategies. On 4 December 1928 Vitaphone released the short *My Wife's Gone Away,* a ten-minute, all-talking comedy based on a vaudeville playlet developed by William Demarest. Critics loved this short; so did audiences. Thus, Foy, under Jack Warner's supervision, began to borrow even more from available vaudeville acts and playlets to create all-talking shorts. During Christmas week of 1927, Vitaphone released a twenty-minute, all-talking drama, *Solomon's Children*. Again revenues were high, and in January 1928 Foy moved to schedule production of two all-talking shorts per week.

Warner Bros. had begun to experiment with alternative types of shorts as a cheap way to maintain the novelty value of Vitaphone entertainment. Moreover, with such shorts it could develop talent, innovate new equipment, and create an audience for feature-length, all-sound films. In the spring of 1928, with the increased popularity of these shorts, Warner Bros. began to change its feature film offerings. On 14 March 1928 it released *Tenderloin*—an ordinary mystery that contained five segments in which the actors spoke all their lines (for twelve of the film's eighty-five minutes). More part-talkies followed that spring.

Harry Warner and Waddill Catchings knew that the investment in sound was a success by April 1928. By then it had become clear that the *The Jazz Singer* show was more than a mild success; it was the most popular entertainment offering of the 1927–28 season. In cities that rarely showed films for more than one week *The Jazz Singer* package set records for length of run: five weeks in Charlotte, North Carolina, Reading, Pennsylvania, Seattle, Washington, and Baltimore, Maryland. It also began to appear on return engagements. *The Jazz Singer* played the Fox Theater in Philadelphia for two return weeks in mid-February, holding its own at Philadelphia's second largest theater. By mid-February, it was in its (record) eighth week in Columbus, Ohio, St. Louis, and Detroit, and its (record) seventh week in Seattle, Portland, Oregon, and Los

Production stills from two short Vitaphone novelties of 1928:

The Kiddies Kabaret and *The Big Paraders*, the last of which featured over two tons of talent, according to its press release

THE BIG PARADERS.

VITAPHONE № 1538
REL. № 840

Angeles. Samuel Rothafel even booked *The Jazz Singer* package for an unprecedented second run in April 1928, where it grossed in excess of $100,000 each week, among the Roxy's best revenues that season. Perhaps more important, all these first-run showings did not demand the usual expenses for a stage show and orchestra. It took Warner Bros. only until the fall of 1928 to convert to the complete production of talkies—both features and shorts. Catchings and Harry Warner had laid the foundation for this rapid growth and, hence, maximum profit with Vitaphone's slow, steady expansion in production and distribution. In 1929 Warner Bros. had the largest profits of any motion picture company and had moved to third in the industry in total assets. Others quickly moved to imitate Warners' behavior, and soon the American film industry's rapid switch to sound was on in full force. Diffuson had begun.

BIBLIOGRAPHIC NOTE

The most important government documents employed in the author's research were the following: (*a*) United States Congress, House, Committee on Patents. *Hearings on H.R. 4523: Pooling of Patents* (74th Congress, 1st Session, 1935. (*b*) United States Federal Communications Commission. *Telephone Investigation Exhibits.* (pursuant to Public Resolution No. 8, 74th Congress, 1936–37).

Data from the following court cases proved most significant: (*a*) Electrical Research Products, Inc., v. Vitaphone Corporation, 171 A. 738 (1934). (*b*) General Talking Pictures Corporation et al. v. American Telephone and Telegraph Company et al., 18 F. Supp. 650 (1937). (*c*) Koplar (Scharaf et al., Interveners) v. Warner Bros. Pictures, Inc., et al., 19 F. Supp. 173 (1937).

■ ■ ■ ■

SILENCE IS GOLDEN (1930), Aldous Huxley
WITH ALL DUE RESPECT TO MR. HUXLEY (1930),
Robert E. Sherwood

A typically cynical response to *The Jazz Singer* was that of Aldous Huxley, who saw the film as taking another step toward the famous "Feelies" of his *Brave New World,* the fit entertainment for Delta-Minus Morons. The noted British essayist and novelist spent much of his life in Hollywood, writing for, about, and against the movies. The essay was originally published as a debate on the talkies ("Do You Like the Talkies?") by *Golden*

Book magazine in 1930. The affirmative rebuttal to Mr. Huxley's nay was by Robert E. Sherwood.

SILENCE IS GOLDEN

I have just been, for the first time, to see and hear a picture talk. "A little late in the day," my up-to-date readers will remark, with a patronizing and contemptuous smile. "This is 1930; there isn't much news in talkies now. But better late than never."

Better late than never? Ah, no! There, my friends, you're wrong. This is one of those cases where it is most decidedly better never than late, better never than early, better never than on the stroke of time. One of the numerous cases, I may add; and the older I grow, the more numerous I find them. There was a time when I should have felt terribly ashamed of not being up to date. I lived in a chronic apprehension lest I might, so to speak, miss the last bus, and so find myself stranded and benighted in a desert of demodedness, while others, more nimble than myself, had already climbed on board, taken their tickets and set out toward those bright but, alas, ever receding goals of Modernity and Sophistication. Now, however, I have grown shameless, I have lost my fears. I can watch unmoved the departure of the last social-cultural bus—the innumerable last buses, which are starting at every instant in all the world's capitals. I make no effort to board them, and when the noise of each departure has died down, "Thank goodness!" is what I say to myself in the solitude. I find nowadays that I simply don't want to be up to date. I have lost all desire to see and do the things, the seeing and doing of which entitle a man to regard himself as superiorly knowing, sophisticated, unprovincial; I have lost all desire to frequent the places and people that a man simply *must* frequent, if he is not to be regarded as a poor creature hopelessly out of the swim. "Be up to date!" is the categorical imperative of those who scramble for the last bus. But it is an imperative whose cogency I refuse to admit. When it is a question of doing something which I regard as a duty, I am as ready as anyone else to put up with discomfort. But being up to date and in the swim has ceased, so far as I am concerned, to be a duty. Why should I have my feelings outraged, why should I submit to being bored and disgusted for the sake of somebody else's categorical imperative? Why? There is no reason. So I simply avoid most of the manifestations of that so-called "life" which my contemporaries seem to be so unaccountably anxious to "see"; I keep out of range of the "art" they

"Silence Is Golden," by Aldous Huxley, and "With All Due Respect to Mr. Huxley," by Robert E. Sherwood, appeared in the April 1930 issue of *Golden Book* magazine.

think is so vitally necessary to "keep up with"; I flee from those "good times" in the "having" of which they are prepared to spend so lavishly of their energy and cash.

Such, then, are the reasons for my very tardy introduction to the talkies. The explanation of my firm resolve never, if I can help it, to be reintroduced will be found in the following simple narrative of what I saw and heard in that fetid hall on the Boulevard des Italiens, where the latest and most frightful creation-saving device for the production of standardized amusement had been installed.

We entered the hall halfway through the performance of a series of music-hall turns—not substantial ones, of course, but the two-dimensional images of turns with artificial voices. There were no travel films, nothing in the Natural History line, none of those fascinating Events of the Week—lady mayoresses launching battleships, Japanese eathquakes, hundred-to-one outsiders winning races, revolutionaries on the march in Nicaragua—which are always the greatest and often the sole attractions in the programs of our cinema. Nothing but disembodied entertainers, gesticulating flatly on the screen and making gramophone-like noises as they did so. Some sort of comedian was performing as we entered. But he soon vanished to give place to somebody's celebrated jazz band—not merely audible in all its loud vulgarity of brassy guffaw and caterwauling sentiment, but also visible in a series of apocalyptic close-ups of the individual performers. A beneficent Providence has dimmed my powers of sight so that at a distance of more than four or five yards I am blissfully unaware of the full horror of the average human countenance. At the cinema, however, there is no escape. Magnified up to Brobdingnagian proportions, the human countenance smiles its six-foot smiles, opens and shuts its thirty-two-inch eyes, registers soulfulness or grief, libido or whimsicality, with every square centimeter of its several roods of pallid mooniness. Nothing short of total blindness can preserve one from the spectacle. The jazz players were forced upon me; I regarded them with a fascinated horror. It was the first time, I suddenly realized, that I had ever clearly *seen* a jazz band. The spectacle was positively terrifying.

The performers belonged to two contrasted races. There were the dark and polished young Hebrews, whose souls were in those mournfully sagging, seasickishly undulating melodies of mother love and nostalgia and yammering amorousness and clotted sensuality which have been the characteristically Jewish contributions to modern popular music. And there were the chubby young Nordics, with Aryan faces transformed by the strange plastic forces of the North American environment into the likeness of very large uncooked muffins or the unveiled posteriors of babes. (The more sympathetic Red Indian type of Nordic-American face was completely absent from this particular assemblage of jazz players.) Gigantically enlarged, these personages appeared one after another on the screen, each singing or playing his instrument and at the same time registering the emotions appropriate to the musical circumstances. The spectacle, I repeat, was really terrifying. For the first time, I felt grateful for the defect of vision which had preserved me from an earlier ac-quaintance with such aspects of modern life. And at the same time I wished that I could become, for the occasion, a little hard of hearing. For if good music has charms to soothe the savage breast, bad music has no less powerful spells for filling the mildest breast with rage, the happiest with horror and disgust. Oh, those mammy songs, those love longings, those loud hilarities; How was it possible that human emotions intrinsi-cally decent could be so ignobly parodied? I felt like a man who, having asked for wine, is offered a brimming bowl of hogwash. And not even fresh hogwash. Rancid hogwash, decaying hogwash. For there was a hor-rible tang of putrefaction in all that music. Those yearnings for "Mammy of Mine" and "My Baby," for "Dixie" and the "Land Where Skies Are Blue" and "Dreams Come True," for "Granny" and "Tennessee and You"—they were all a necrophily. The Mammy after whom the black young Hebrews and the blond young muffin-faces so retchingly yearned was an ancient Gorgonzola cheese; the Baby of their tremulously gargled desire was a leg of mutton after a month in warm storage; Granny had been dead for weeks; and as for Dixie and Tennessee and Dream Land—they were odoriferous with the least artificial of manures.

When, after what seemed hours, the jazz band concluded its dreadful performances, I sighed in thankfulness. But the thankfulness was prema-ture. For the film which followed was hardly less distressing. It was the story of the child of a cantor in a synagogue, afflicted, to his father's justifiable fury, with an itch for jazz. This itch, assisted by the cantor's boot, sends him out into the world, where, in due course and thanks to My Baby, his dreams come tree-ue, and he is employed as a jazz singer on the music-hall stage. Promoted from the provinces to Broadway, the jazz singer takes the opportunity to revisit the home of his childhood. But the cantor will have nothing to do with him, absolutely nothing, in spite of his success, in spite, too, of his moving eloquence. "You yourself al-ways taught me," says the son pathetically, "that the voice of music was the voice of God." *Vox jazzi vox Dei*—the truth is new and beautiful. But stern old Poppa's heart refuses to be melted. Even Mammy of Mine is unable to patch up a reconciliation. The singer is reduced to going out once more into the night—and from the night back to his music hall.

The crisis of the drama arrives when, the cantor being mortally sick and unable to fulfil his functions at the synagogue, Mammy of Mine and the Friends of his Childhood implore the young man to come and sing the atonement service in his father's place. Unhappily, this religious function is booked to take place at the same hour as that other act of worship vulgarly known as the First Night. There ensues a terrific struggle, worthy of the pen of a Racine or a Dryden, between love and honor. Love for Mammy of Mine draws the jazz singer toward the synagogue; but love for My Baby draws the cantor's son toward the theater, where she, as principal Star, is serving the deity no less acceptably with her legs and smile than he with his voice. Honor also calls from either side; for honor demands that he should serve the God of his fathers at the synagogue, but it also demands that he should serve the jazz-voiced god of his adoption at the theater. Some very eloquent captions appears at this point. With the air of a Seventeenth Century hero, the jazz singer protests that he must put his career before even his love. The nature of the dilemma has changed, it will be seen, since Dryden's day. In the old dramas it was love that had to be sacrificed to painful duty. In the modern instance the sacrifice is at the shrine of what William James called "the Bitch Goddess Success." Love is to be abandoned for the stern pursuit of any sort of newspaper notoriety and dollars.

In the end the singer makes the best of both worlds—satisfies Mammy of Mine and even Poor Poppa by singing at the synagogue and, on the following evening, scored a terrific success at the postponed first night of My Baby's revue. The film concludes with a scene in the theater, with Mammy of Mine in the stalls (Poor Poppa is by this time safely under ground), and the son, with My Baby in the background, warbling down at her the most nauseatingly luscious, the most penetratingly vulgar mammy song that it has ever been my lot to hear. My flesh crept as the loud speaker poured out those sodden words, that greasy, sagging melody. I felt ashamed of myself for listening to such things, for even being a member of the species to which such things are addressed. But I derived a little comfort from the reflection that a species which has allowed all its instincts and emotions to degenerate and putrefy in such a way must be pretty near either its violent conclusion or else its radical transformation and reform.

To what length this process of decay has gone was very strikingly demonstrated by the next item on the program, which was the first of that series of music-hall turns of which the dreadful jazz band had been the last. For no sooner had the singer and My Baby and Mammy of Mine disappeared into the limbo of inter-cinematographic darkness than a very large and classically profiled personage, dressed in the uniform of a clown, appeared on the screen, opened his mouth very wide indeed and poured out, in a terrific Italian tenor voice, the famous soliloquy of Pagliacci from Leoncavallo's opera. Rum, tum, ti-tum, tum; Rum-ti-ti, tum, ti-tum, tum—it is the bawling-ground of every Southern virtuoso, and a piece which, at ordinary times, I would go out of my way to avoid hearing. But in comparison with the jazz band's Hebrew melodies and the singer's jovialities and mammy yearnings, Leoncavallo's throaty vulgarity seemed not only refined and sincere, but even beautiful, positively noble. Yes, noble; for after all, the composer, whatever his native second-rateness, had stood in some sort of organic relationship, through a tradition of taste and of feeling, with the men who built Santa Maria del Fiore and the Malatestan temple, who painted the frescoes at Arezzo and Padua, who composed the Mass of Pope Marcellus and wrote the *Divine Comedy* and the *Orlando Furioso*. Whereas the Hebrew melodists and the muffin-faced young Nordics, with their Swanee whistles and their saxophones, the mammy songsters, the vocal yearners for Dixie and My Baby are in no kind of relationship with any of the immemorial decencies of human life, but only with their own inward decay. It is a corruption as novel as the régime under which they and all the rest of us now live—as novel as Protestantism and capitalism; as novel as urbanization and democracy and the apotheosis of the Average Man; as novel as Benjamin Franklinism and the no less repulsive philosophy and ethic of the young Good-Timer; as novel as creation-saving machinery and the thought-saving, time-killing press; as novel as Taylorized work and mechanized amusement. Ours is a spiritual climate in which the immemorial decencies find it hard to flourish. Another generation or so should see them definitely dead. Is there a resurrection?

WITH ALL DUE RESPECT TO MR. HUXLEY

Mr. Aldous Huxley pronounces the talking picture to be "the latest and most frightful creation-saving device for the production of standardized amusement."

I can't very well dispute that statement, nor can I deny that Mr. Huxley's description of his first and last talkie show is excruciatingly realistic. I happened to visit that same "fetid hall on the Boulevard des Italiens," and saw the same "muffin-faced" jazz boys, and heard the same "rancid hogwash" that had so dreadfully offended the senses of the author of *Point Counter Point;* and when I came out of that Paris theater after the performance, I thought bitterly that the talkies were destined to provide Europe with final proof of its pet theory, which is that the United States is the home of a race of loud, vulgar, oversentimental and obscene morons.

So I sha'n't attempt to quarrel with Mr. Huxley's estimate of the awful offering at the Auber Palace, or of the mechanical contrivance that made that offering possible. I shall, however, reiterate my belief that the talking picture is an honest medium through which an artist may express himself intelligibly, eloquently and effectively. If it may be used—and, alas, usually *is* used—for the dissemination of distasteful junk, it may also be used for the dissemination of ideas that are beautiful and important.

When the silent movies were young, I liked them and studied them and even, on occasion, cheered for them—and I suffered social ostracism as a result. I ventured to express publicly the opinion that some of them were "artistic"; and I was told, vehemently, that nothing that came out of a machine could possibly be Art.

Then, after years of effort by Charlie Chaplin, Ernst Lubitsch, Erich von Stroheim, Douglas Fairbanks and a few others, the humble cinema began to assume a certain respectability in the eyes of the intellectually elite. I felt that vindication had come at last. My championship of the movies no longer disqualified me from membership in the better literary clubs. (The admissions committees had to think up other reasons for keeping me out.)

With the arrival of the Vitaphone and Movietone, I had the effrontery to predict that talking pictures would eventually be just as worthy of serious attention as the silent films had been—and I was once more convicted of heresy. I still dwell under a cloud of disapproval, but there are hopeful signs that I will again be vindicated. Even now, many of the more lordly condemners of sound on the screen are unobtrusively eating their words.

For the despised movie producers of Hollywood have made enormous and admirable progress with the new medium in an extremely short space of time. The early atrocities are being forgotten. In a few pictures—such as "Hallelujah," "Seven Days Leave," "Men Without Women," "Disraeli," "Anna Christie"—have been unmistakable intimations of high artistic merit. The talkies have managed to overcome most of their obvious mechanical disadvantages; they have begun to assume a character of their own that is not imitative of the speaking stage; there is no question of doubt that they will improve incalculably.

There will always be plenty of decayed mammy songs, and muffin-faced crooners to interpret them; but there will also be, here and there, manifestations of genius comparable to "The Last Laugh," "Nanook of the North" and the Chaplin comedies. . . .

Perhaps when Johann Gutenberg was experimenting with his wooden blocks, he elected to inscribe on them some stanzas of one of the more bawdy ballads of the time, and this was the first printing. Some of the results of his labor fell into the hands of the local churchmen and one of them, a singularly high-minded and erudite Abbot, protested that Gutenberg's invention "is the latest and most frightful creation-saving device for the production of standardized amusement."

Later, however, the Abbot had a second thought, which was: "If Gutenberg can print bawdy ballads for wholesale distribution, he can also print the Bible." This, accordingly, was done.

I earnestly commend the Abbot's second thought to the attention of Aldous Huxley and other artists who may contribute sage advice, and possibly more tangible benefits, to the young talkies.

■ ■ ■ ■

Notes on the Movies (1928), George Jean Nathan

George Jean Nathan, one of the most respected (and feared) drama critics of his generation, turns his feisty bile on the Vitaphone in this section from his book, *The Art of the Night*. Since Nathan believed that movies and literacy were antithetical, he could see no future in a literate cinema that was able to use words.

The theatre need not be worried over the Vitaphone, the mechanical invention which synchronizes the movies and human speech. If there is any worrying to be done, it is the movies that should do it. For if the Vitaphone or its like is ever adopted generally by the movies, it will not be long before the galleries of the legitimate theatres are again filled with the class of individuals who deserted them some years ago for the films.

The Vitaphone is an interesting device, despite certain crudities that still exist in it, crudities that will doubtless be eliminated as time goes on. It does succeed in dovetailing speech and music with the movements of persons on the screen, and dovetailing them exactly. Its words and its tones are identical in time with the opening of persons' lips and the movement of violin bows. It still betrays an audible mechanism and it still possesses no light and shade; it is deafening. It makes the actor, the singer and the musician alike so many boiler factories. But that is not the point. The point, rather, is that, aside from its commercial value in certain short-reel subjects, such as an opera singer doing her bit or a politician

"Notes on the Movies" is from the book *The Art of the Night,* by George Jean Nathan (Knopf, 1928).

exuding the usual platitudes or a musician making pretty sounds, it will bring to the motion picture exactly the thing that the motion picture should have no use for, to wit, the human voice, and that, further, once it brings it, the motion picture will have a difficult time holding its own even among the jays who now make it the profitable institution it is.

If the Vitaphone gets its deadly hold on the movies, it won't be long before the latter's current millionaires are driven back to their former pants and delicatessen businesses. It is, of course, conceivable that once in a great while, once the machine is perfected, a reputable talking picture may be made by hiring expert legitimate actors to enact a first-rate legitimate drama for the articulate screen. But even that is shadowed o'er with doubt, for moving picture audiences would care no more for, say, "Hamlet" thus done than "Hamlet" audiences would care for Miss Gloria Swanson in one of her present masterpieces. Furthermore, since the actors who appear in the movies, even the very best of them, are panto-mimists rather than dramatic performers, any effort to make them articulate would be not only paradoxical and absurd, but utterly futile. To expect a pantomimist, talented though he be, to be the possessor of a vocal organ capable of expressing all the shadings of dramatic speech is surely expecting a lot. The theatre, so far as I know, has not, in all its history, owned more than one or two pantomimists, pantomimists, that is, by strict profession, who were simultaneously gifted with the requirements of such dramatic speech. One may easily imagine, therefore, what nine hundred and ninety-nine out of every thousand movies would be like once the Vitaphone recorded and duplicated the voices of their performers. The result, one allows one's self to believe, would be like so many phonograph records of a Brahms concerto played by a speak-easy orchestra.

To wish the movies to be articulate is about as sensible as wishing the drama to be silent. The movies are designed for pantomime, nothing more. The titles that they generally employ, despite the criticism of them, are legitimate for the same reason that the program synopses of stage pantomimes are. It is all very well to pretend that pantomine should be made so lucid by gifted performers that any one can tell what it is meant to convey, but for one such pantomime, or movie, there are a hundred that need the assistance of the printed word to make them properly clear. If a drama has a program, why shouldn't a pantomime have a program also?

But—imagine such a pantomime as "L'Enfant Prodigue" with articulate pantomimists, with words accompanying the actions! That is precisely what the mechanical gentlemen who are responsible for the Vitaphone are eager to bring about. It would be not more ridiculous for them to

invent a machine to give a Rodin sculpture, say, the semblance of movement. The movies have succeeded among the peculiar audiences they
cater to for exactly the same reason that the tabloid newspapers have
succeeded among the peculiar audiences they, in turn, cater to. Both have,
for the greater comfort of their illiterate publics, boiled down the number of words to a minimum and substituted readily comprehensible pictures in place of less easily comprehensible speech and type. The moving picture fortunes have been built upon the sagacious business theory
of showing the boobs everything and telling them nothing. As Barnum
catered to the public's eye and got rich, so have the movie magnates catered and got rich. To the producers of fine drama who cater to the public's ear, both Barnum and the movie magnates have willed the poor-
house.

The regular and enthusiastic movie patron is a person upon whom a
strain may be placed only at the risk of losing him. When he is asked
to use his eyes, that is enough. To bid him use his ears as well and
coincidentally his intelligence—or at least that modest share of intelligence that is demanded to assimilate dramatic speech—is to ask the
impossible. He likes the movies as they presently are for the simple reason that they impose not the slightest tax upon his imagination. All that
he has to do is to open his eye, occasionally at least, and allow the screen
balderdash to impress itself easily and casually upon his half-conscious
retina. Words would change this acceptable situation, and enormously.
The spoken word demands attention, not the semi-attention that pantomime demands, but taut attention. There is something commanding,
challenging, about the human voice. And, in addition, there is something that calls for a degree of understanding. If the Vitaphone were to
stick to words of one syllable, the movies might use it to some advantage. That is possible. But the moment it went in for words of two
or, on gala occasions, three, Mr. Adolph Zukor would have to sell his
twelve Rolls-Royces and 82-carat diamond suspender buckles, learn
English, and go back to work.

■ ■ ■ ■
_____

The Cultural Influence of the "Talkies" (1929),
Ralph L. Henry

In addition to the aesthetic controversy, the new talking films generated
social and moral controversies as well. This article reveals the continuing
concern of professional educators with the informal education that chil-

dren were receiving in the movie house. The principles underlying the concern expressed in this sort of article would emerge more fully in the next decade with the provisions in the Hollywood Production Code against certain kinds of ungenteel speech and with the exhaustive demonstrations of the Payne Fund Studies of the amount of influence that films have in shaping the attitudes and values of American youth.

The talkies will make Hollywood the slang center of the United States. . . . A wisecrack recorded in Hollywood will be heard in all corners of the country months before the same quip could travel from town to town across the continent with a road show or a vaudeville troupe.

Wade Werner, prophesying in a newspaper article appearing in the California capital of moviedom on December 8, 1928, broadcasts this comforting news to the world at large. The prospect which his words conjure up should be particularly interesting to the teachers of the children in American schools. What influence are the talking movies to have on the speech habits of those who hear them? What is going to happen to the American-English language and to American culture generally once every small-town movie house is equipped to reproduce night after night the language which the current cult of realism in all things literary will demand of successful screen plays?

The outlook is by no means assuring. Judging by the past there is little to indicate that moving-picture producers will be actuated by any principles of social responsibility which extend beyond tangible results in the box office. The written conversations already necessary for the silent pictures have never been models of good English. Their influence, however, has been small because the emphasis in the movies has always been on action rather than on speech. It has not mattered much what the actors said— though there has been a brave attempt at making the lips of the players seem to say what the screen (an instant later) recorded in the written words. What the actors *did* carried the drama, and the occasional direct conversations, aside from a few borrowings from the vaudeville stage, have probably not had an appreciably bad effect on national habits of speech. Alongside the comic strips, the movies up to the present moment have been relatively harmless. They have not ranked with illiterate or foreign home environment, with street and playground associations, with the vaudeville shows, or with cheap books and magazines as influences

"The Cultural Influence of the 'Talkies,'" by Ralph L. Henry, appeared in the 2 February 1929 *School and Society*.

which make for degeneration of the language and the consequent lowering of the general cultural standard.

In the last years of this third decade of a wonder-working century we are witnessing the end of the first phase of the moving-picture industry. Apparently no one is quite sure what the second phase will be—one writer suggests that the movies are committing suicide.[1] But whatever the second phase is, it will be upon us shortly; it has already arrived in our large cities, and it will reach down to touch the whole population of America, urban and rural, just as the first phase has done. The unique contribution of the "new movies" will clearly be the spoken word synchronized with the dramatization of events on the screen. The speech level of the Hollywood "lot" seems likely to be reproduced millions of times in the ears of millions of people, including practically 100 per cent. of the children of the country from the kindergarten to college.

No one can doubt that this tremendous reiteration of the spoken word under conditions tending greatly to emphasize a certain style of language will have its effect on the speech habits of impressionable young people who have no mind-set or philosophy to resist it. Nor can we hope that the producers will make willingly any altruistic effort to raise the level of the great majority of "talkies" above the vaudeville-show patter of the present moment. There is no particular incentive for the makers of commercial pictures, with or without the talking accompaniment, to do anything more than appeal to the rather low group tastes of the masses of people, reproducing for them their own language with appropriate profane, suggestive and obscene decorations such as have delighted the "groundlings" since Shakespeare's time. We may expect no higher standard in the "out-loud" movies than we have previously had in the pictures themselves. We may look forward to no noticeably higher ideal in the "realistic" talking movies than we have had in recent stage successes which have masqueraded behind the amusingly naïve contention that "This is pure art" the most daringly profane and pornographic literature since the drama of the Restoration Period in England—a span of two centuries and a half.

Mr. Werner says on this point:

Modern stage plays with a high profanity content can not be made into talking pictures without considerable deletion of language likely to excite the scissor muscles of the screen censors. Even original movie dialogue has to be carefully composed to satisfy picturegoers

1. Gilbert Seldes, "The Movies Commit Suicide," *Harper's Magazine*, November, 1928.

accustomed to stage profanity, without offending censors *not yet ready* [the italics are not Mr. Werner's] to allow such profanity on the talking screen.

James Gleason, the author of "Is Zat So?" and other plays, who is writing talking-picture dialogue now, is working out a vocabulary of expletives which sound nearly enough like the cusswords of the up-to-date stage to pacify the spectator who would rebel at substitutions like "My Goodness!" or "Dear Me!" and yet are utterly innocent of profanity in themselves.

Perhaps censorship will save the moral situation, although it is not impossible that the censors who are "not yet ready" for the last word in profane speech will find it as hard to keep profanity out of the "talkies" as other types of censorship have in the fields of the novel and the modern drama. Whatever the event in that direction, he is indeed a sanguine observer of the present-day trend who believes that we shall hear good English from the talking movies. Inherent in the situation is the plain demand of the mass mind for something easy and for something broadly humorous. Slang, profanity, even obscenity have always satisfied that demand and probably always will. It is, of course, altogether true that the language level of any people can not rise higher than its cultural and intellectual level. It is a question—still debatable it is to be hoped— whether in America our average cultural and intellectual plane is above the movie and vaudeville standard of the present moment.

■ ■ ■ ■

TALKIES' PROGRESS (1929), Gilbert Seldes

Gilbert Seldes was an "intellectual" film critic who refused to give up on the talkies. This theoretical discussion, from *Harper's Magazine,* considers the errors of the specific talkies he has seen and suggests the general problems of technique and material that the talkies needed to solve. The early references to both "home movies" and television indicate the length of time Hollywood has had to live with these threats to its entertainment sovereignty.

When I wrote about the talking films in these pages a year ago, the sentimental interest lay entirely with the silent movie. At the end of the

"Talkies' Progress," by Gilbert Seldes, was published in the August 1929 *Harper's Magazine.*

first decade of their existence the movies had threatened the legitimate theater in spite of its glorious record of twenty centuries; at the end of the third decade the movies were being bustled off into obscurity by the novelty of the talkies, brash, loud, and vulgar. When invention, mechanism, and commerce are concerned, the acceleration in the rate of change is high: the talkies, as a successful entertainment, are only two years old and already they are threatened in turn. Within twelve months—eighteen months at the latest—the talkies will have to meet the competition of the talkie-projector in the home—something resembling the popular amateur movie projector, but equipped with synchronized sound. And within another year we shall probably have the simple and comparatively inexpensive mechanisms, now being perfected, which will throw on a small screen set up beside the home radio set a moving picture projected from a central broadcasting station; it is only a matter of time before this televisual entertainment is extended so that it, too, will have speech and sound in perfect synchronization. Thus two separate ways of having the talkie without going to the theater will challenge the talkie which stays in the theater.

To overcome these rival novelties, the talkie will have to be a much better entertainment than it has proved itself in the past two years; and the way to become a better entertainment is to stop the senseless sacrifice of good movie elements in making the talkies. Purists, aesthetes, and a few practical makers of movies assert that the talkies can never be a good movie; my own feeling a year ago, when I said "the movies commit suicide," was that the two forms had to develop separately and that, while the talkie went forward to an assured commercial success, the silent movie would proceed to an unexampled artistic one. I am now not nearly so certain of the talkie's inevitable success and quite willing to believe that an intermediate form can be created. If it cannot the talkie will be the loser.

Not one of the talkies shown by mid-summer, 1929, is worth a minute of any intelligent person's time. In themselves, that is. A number of them are good enough entertainment because they are transpositions to the screen of good stage melodrama or of good musical shows; some are good entertainment only in the accidental moments when they remain movies. But as a self-contained, self-sufficient form they are wholly negligible and are worth consideration only because they are beginning to show signs of knowing what direction they want to take. Up to the present they have lived on borrowed material; and the trouble with living on the energies or emotions of others is that one doesn't live.

The same situation occurred in the movies about twenty years ago. The movie had begun in all ignorance and innocence to find its own way; in the pictures of Western adventure, the serials, and slapstick comedy it made a fortune and almost created an art. Then the major portion of the industry contracted a mesalliance with the theater; actors from the stage condescended to play in the movies, and the hits of the season were transferred to the screen. The result was that for ten years the movie stood still. In spite of the lesson of D. W. Griffith, who threw out the novel and the play on which he was supposed to base his masterpiece, and made "The Birth of a Nation," in terms of pure cinema, the movie clung to the skirts of the stage and called itself "the photoplay" and "the silent drama," as if it were proud of being kept by the respectable old theater. It is as if the art of painting had insisted for years on being known as "flat sculpture," or symphonic orchestras as "operas without singing." "The Birth of a Nation" was not a drama; it was a movie, and its elements were the series of movements, the flow of images, the special tone and the special rhythm which the movie alone could create; it was the product of the camera. Five years after its production the lesson it taught was reinforced by a few other American directors and by the German films which began to come into America; the movie threw off the stage and began again to make its own way, going back to some of the first principles of the Western thriller and to those principles of good movie making which Chaplin, for instance, had never abandoned.

The ten dead years in the development of the silent movie may be repeated in the talkie unless the producers of the new type are capable of discovering their own materials and their own methods. It is hard to say what these materials and methods are; it is easier to say what they are not. For instance, the talkies use the technic of the musical show of ten years ago when they make excuses for introducing a song; they use the technic of vaudeville when they treat speech or song as something extraordinary, like card tricks or swinging by the teeth, and work out the most elaborate pretexts for introducing perfectly simple things. They use the technic of the stage where people are always being urged to "tell me all about it" in order to explain the action. In "Alibi" the director even used the old stage-aside by the expedient of cutting one character out of the picture while the others plotted against him—a trick which infuriated the editor of The Film Spectator, who made it a text for a warning sermon to the talkie-directors, the excellent theme of which was, "Find your own technic."

The most significant instance of failure to find a proper technic appeared in the early days of the talkie when, entranced by the novelty of synchronized speech, the directors trained the camera upon the speaker, usually in a close-up of the throat or gullet. This was unpleasant to look at, but was passable when the subject was a tenor singing a ballad; when the speaker came to take part in an action, the isolation of his vocal cords in the close-up made it impossible for us to observe the effect on his listeners of what he said; the camera had to shift back to the next speaker. It required a year before the directors saw that they could include three or four people in a scene and let them talk in succession without focusing attention exclusively on the speaker. In the last pictures I have seen the directors are awkwardly fumbling for a technic by which they indicate that a person is speaking and then let him disappear from the screen, to make way for the people who are listening.

The whole problem could have been solved at the beginning if the producers of the talkies had troubled to look carefully at their instruments. The voice in the talkies is recorded by one mechanism, the movement by another; by one method the voice goes on a record synchronized with the film; the other method sets the voice on the film itself; but even here the recording mechanism is separate and the studio custom is to use two separate films, one for the voice, one for the action. The microphone is comparatively stationary; the camera is mobile to the highest degree. From this separation of function it should have been clear at the start that, while the voice might go on steadily, the camera could leave it behind, could show not only the listeners, but whatever else was relevant to the action at the moment. The producers immobilized the camera in favor of the microphone; the result was not a new form of entertainment—the true talkie—but a combination of movie and phonograph.

The problem of talkie material can best be approached by observing the material actually used in the successes of the year. "Noah's Ark" was not properly a talkie and owed its success to the spectacular film as we have known it since the time of Griffith's "Intolerance"; "Bulldog Drummond" and "Broadway" are melodramas imported from the stage; "The Coconuts" is a musical show transported to the talkies with only a barely perceptible change of *décor;* "The Singing Fool" is an "original" story (the quotation marks will be forgiven by all who know what constitutes originality in Hollywood), but it lives by the perverse exploitation of the talents of Al Jolson, talents so great that even the perversion cannot conceal them; "The Broadway Melody" is a synthetic talkie made up of bits of movie, bits of vaudeville, bits of musical revue. The last, however, begins definitely to be a talkie, because the mixture is so skilfully compounded that one does not recognize any one element as dominant. It is certainly not a movie with sound effects and dialogue—which is what most of the others are.

Consider some of these outstanding films in detail. "Bulldog Drummond" adds to Sapper's exciting melodrama an exciting motor chase in the rain, also a lovesick yokel who sings a ballad. The former, which fits perfectly and enhances the speed of the melodrama, is pure movie; the latter, which is an interpolation so awkwardly made that it does not even give suspense, is talkie.

The stage version of "Broadway" concentrated the action in the small ante-room of a night club, the club itself was never seen. In the ante-room took place a series of dramas, a little love-duel between a dancer and a dancing girl, a sinister duel between two hijackers, a duel between criminals and the law, and the fundamental drama of the entire piece, the struggle between the earnestness and purity and decency of the two dancers and the foul crime and lasciviousness of their surroundings. To give this drama point, the life of the night club had to be suggested— and was, by a miracle of direction and staging; it was never seen, hardly heard when the doors opened, but you felt it there, pressing against the walls of the ante-room, forcing the dancer to break off in the midst of his love and anguish to go on and dance, disgorging drunkards and de- tectives and waiters, calling for the liquor which in turn calls for two murders. In the talkie version the director added the scene which the play omitted: the night-club was there, elaborate and noisy; and the moment you saw it, it ceased to exert its power, it had lost the mystery of the unknown. Once, *in a silent sequence,* the director shot the cabaret scene from above while scrubwomen cleared away the smashed glasses, the soiled confetti, the torn menus; and this scene became a sour com- mentary on the nervous gaiety of the night before. Otherwise, visualiz- ing the cabaret stopped the imagination. It added to the talkie an element of spectacle and gave excuse for that combination of singing and dancing which the directors think essential, reducing "Broadway" to the Pagliacci- plot, the clown with the breaking heart.

To "The Coconuts" nothing was added. I am obliged to assume that the beach was a real beach and the palm grove had real palms; but they seemed to be stage sets. Like all the other musical talkies, it had one supreme advantage over stage production: there are no encores. In this special case, however, there was a notable disadvantage. Of the four Marx Brothers, Harpo is constitutionally mute on the stage. Carrying this muteness over into films, still excited by their capacity to make noises, was a delicate job not successfully done; the close-ups seemed to be pleading with Harpo to talk, his muteness seemed unreal. With that much lost, the film was remarkable only for the brilliant recording of the speech of Groucho and Chico Marx; the famous delivery of the former, which I should have thought baffling to the mechanism, was almost flawless, and this is all the more remarkable because Groucho speaks at a terrific speed, the speed being part of the fun. Everyone else I have heard from the screen enunciates painfully, to carry out the director's illusion that speech is unnatural to human beings; Groucho and Chico chatter along.

Al Jolson's two successes were both critical points in the history of the talkies; it was "The Jazz Singer" which sent all the producers scurrying for equipment, and the cumulative effect of "The Singing Fool," dispelling all notions of a fluke, persuaded them that the silent movie was done. The second picture was still another version of the obligatory plot, only this time the clown had to live through the departure of his wife and finally the death of his son. So long as Jolson was the Jolson of his stage days, unctuous, energetic, dynamic, possessed, the talkie was held together by his genius; when he was compelled to act, to surrender his genius to the necessities of the talkie, it lapsed into dullness and vulgarity.

Next to the Jolson pictures, the decisive factor in the progress of the talkies was the critical praise and the financial success of "The Broadway Melody." It happens that both were well-deserved; "The Broadway Melody," unimportant as adult entertainment, is the beginning of a real talkie. Edmund Goulding, who wrote the story, and Harry Beaumont, the director, were apparently not oppressed by their own experience in the silent movies. They used the obligatory setting of the 1929-model talkie: back-stage of a musical show; they interpolated a revue number (in color) which had nothing to do with their story; they had one of those theme songs which are rapidly becoming the most insufferable pest of the talkies; they created, in short, a potpourri of all the safe elements. But they justified the high praise given to the production by a sort of simple acceptance of their medium: it is, in the ancient phrase, "not a movie." Nor is it a play. It hangs together, and surpasses all the others, through inner conviction that this is what the talkie ought to be doing. It tells the story of a "sisters act"—two small-time song and dance artists, both pretty bad, and one destined to "get by on her legs," the other, to return from a Ziegfeld dress-rehearsal to the sticks. The ill-fated one loves, and at the beginning is loved by, a composer of popular songs; his love turns to the younger sister. The complication lies in the attempted double sacrifice; the younger sister, to efface herself, tries to accept the proposals of a man about town; and the elder, to leave the field clear, persuades the man she loves that she has been using him only for advancement in her profession. This is a competent plot for a movie or a play, but nothing in it is specifically outside the province of the talkie; and the singing and dancing require the talkie with its opportunities for verbal fun, its comparatively easy handling of singing crowds, its use of the old movie spectacle, and all its other capacities.

Derived material and an undeveloped technic make these talkies unsatisfactory even when the original source is not entirely spoiled; a stock company performance of "Sherlock Holmes" gives about the same satisfaction and the same feeling that something is lacking. How can the talkie go about discovering material which is not only suitable to itself, but more suitable to it than to any other form?

There are two ways. The way of the theorist would be to learn the capacities of the talkie mechanism, to develop the technic and, with each gain in mastery, to try something new. The way of the practical man is to take whatever comes to hand, make it as a talkie and, in the process, master the technic. The instinct of the first producers led them to musical shows and to melodrama; it was sound because in both of these the movements are broad, the lines of development are coarse, the action simple. In the melodramas the fights and the chases revert to the silent movie; in the musical shows all action is stopped for a ballet number or a vocal solo. Most of the talkies promised for the next half year lie in these two fields: talkies built around the songs and dances and camp meetings of negroes, talkies of the sounds of cities, talkies of Tin Pan Alley and the radio, talkies about composers; and melodramas reworked from the stage or straight mystery stories transferred from books.

Until they develop a group of special writers, conversant with the talkie mechanism, knowing its capacities, and intelligent enough to direct experiments, the talkies will naturally borrow, and their growth will depend on the skill with which they reduce their material to their own terms. They would do well to observe the radio-playlet to see how completely material can be worked and handled and made to fit in a difficult medium. The radio playlet, totally insignificant in itself, instantly separates itself from the same playlet broadcast from the theater. Action is reduced to sound as far as possible, and nothing which cannot be adequately described or made immediately audible is admitted. Change of place and time are easily indicated by a phrase; but the directors are not satisfied and find a characteristic noise for the new setting, so that at the end of a scene in a drawing-room, if the characters go to the street, you may hear a parade, or if they go to a store, the cash register will ring. On the other hand, new characters have to be carefully planted, because the person cannot be seen and the new voice may not be recognized. If in a stage play a character indicates awkwardness by dropping a felt hat, in the radio version he will drop a gong or a glass. These are elementary things, but the result is that when you listen to a radio play, you do not

Clarence Brown (*in the white visor*) and Greta Garbo shooting *Anna Christie*, her first talkie, for the blimped camera and the microphone boom

feel that you are missing any significant element, just as in the few good silent movies you do not miss sound, or as in certain paintings or statues you are not aware of the lack of motion, but say with complete justice, "Look at the movement in those bodies."

In its first excitement over the new trick of speech, the talkie forgot that it was still a movie; it chose to exploit the phonographic and to neglect the cinematic. But the cinema is still the greater marvel, it is younger and more mysterious than the talking machine; and as the talkie develops it will choose such material as does not too violently conflict with its cinematic nature. For if the movie part of the talkie stops moving, the talkie becomes merely a phonograph. To avoid that, to keep the movie going while speech is heard, is the actual problem of the talkie. . . .

■ ■ ■ ■

COLOR AND SOUND ON FILM (1930)

Even before the talkie revolution had been fully accomplished another technological revolution seemed about to begin. The Technicolor Corporation had neared the development of a technically perfect system of color filming at almost the same time as the Vitaphone and Movietone reached the public. This article, from *Fortune,* surveyed the economic results of the talkie revolution and examined the economic outlook for color filming. Its prediction—that all films would be made in color when the audience's "psychological adaptation" noticed its absence—would come true some thirty-five years later.

REFLECTIONS ON A REVOLUTION

The talkie revolution having been accomplished (beyond comparison the fastest and most amazing revolution in the whole history of industrial revolutions), the producers say they are glad it happened. Talkies, they say, came just as the popularity of the movies was beginning to wane. Despite the general agreement on this proposition, it remains absolutely unprovable and extremely doubtful. Already—after only two years of talkies and long before they have been perfected—there is another distinct drop in movie attendance. Looking for a reason ("bad times" is inadequate) we find a circumstance which contains one of those strange paradoxes which haunt the showman's career. The talkies, bad though they

"Color and Sound on Film" appeared in the October 1930 issue of *Fortune.*

may be, are *too* good. This is the theory: in the silent days people were kept movie-minded by the few great pictures (Chaplin, Fairbanks, etc.) which appeared every year; but also, and much more importantly, they made a regular habit of going to the movies several times a week; if the picture were fair they got a thrill; if it were poor, they communed peacefully and beneficially with their cud-like souls. Now the talkie brings them a definitely higher form of entertainment; from a good talkie they get a far greater thrill than from any except the very best silents; but before going to it they want to be sure that the talkie is good; otherwise, they are not thrilled but simply disturbed; in short, the talkie has made the public critical.

Nevertheless the talkie has completely nullified the silent screen. This is entirely characteristic of the machine. A new machine (or process) does not merely *add;* it *replaces.* In most lines the replacement is gradual, but in the show business nothing can prevent the replacement from being almost instantaneous. The reasons are obvious. Price, for example, is no object. A public which has tasted talkies cannot be lured to silents by offering the latter at cut-rates. (On the contrary, a conviction that brass pipes or colored porcelains are best for bathrooms does not lead to immediate replumbing.) Now this also results in the fact that in the show business it is quite possible for a relatively unimportant innovation to have consequences almost as serious as a major invention.

An ideal illustration of the weird relation between Science and Showmanship is to be found in the most hotly disputed of current developments: color. The importance of color to drama is as nothing compared with the importance of voice. But, even though it may add little to dramatic interest, it obviously has the possibilities of *replacing* black and white. This replacement threat makes color a deuce in a game wherein all deuces are wild. While the players bet millions pro or con, let us see whether this latest threat can be rationalized from the side lines.

The first surprising detail about color is that it makes Boston a sort of sub-capital of the movie world. It is a better than ten to one bet that every color film you have seen was made in Boston. For the history of colored movies is almost entirely the history of Technicolor, which began in Boston years ago and whose main plant is still there. A new plant in Hollywood went into operation last spring. The hero of Technicolor is Dr. Herbert T. Kalmus.

Forty-nine next month, Dr. Kalmus stands about six foot three. Under brown hair that is fast turning gray, a pair of blue eyes expresses the unusual union of keen business ability with pure scientific excellence. Perhaps as a result of this his suits are always pressed, his words always precise. Conservative in taste, he favors blue, black, and gray color schemes, plays golf, and is absorbed in Technicolor. At the same time, his personality has its lyric side, developed by years at sea as a boy before working his way through M. I. T., where he graduated in 1904. For lyric satisfaction he listens to music, composes on the piano for his own amusement, owns the home of an old sea captain in Centerville, Massachusetts, and eighty acres of wooded land on Cape Cod, where he and Mrs. Kalmus camp and rest. Lovely Mrs. Kalmus with titian hair is in charge of the Technicolor art department and used to pose for early Technicolor experiments in Florida. Thus is the entire family absorbed in the development of this most modern of arts, Dr. Kalmus having started his researches in 1915 and now being both president and general manager of the Technicolor Motion Picture Corporation. In 1912 he was head of the Research Laboratory of Electrochemistry and Metallurgy for the Canadian Government.

For fifteen years he had had only one occupation: to make color movies. Ten years ago he produced in the laboratory colored movies as good as or better than any we have seen in the theatres. But the gap from laboratory to theatre was immense. The first real opportunity came in 1922 through the Brothers Schenck; Joseph M. loaned to Technicolor the facilities of the United Artists studio to make *Toll of the Sea,* starring Anna May Wong, and Nicholas M. distributed the picture through Metro-Goldwyn-Mayer. Paid for by Technicolor, this was the first all-color movie except for two sporadic attempts by other methods seventeen years before. M-G-M gave color a further boost by being the first to use it for a few scenes in their own big pictures (*Ben Hur, The Merry Widow*). Jesse Lasky of Paramount was the first producer to gamble an extra $100,000 on an all-color movie (*Wanderer of the Wasteland,* 1924), and Douglas Fairbanks followed with *The Black Pirate.* But it was the Warner Brothers who took the first real gamble on color, just as they were the first to gamble in sound. Having scooped the world in 1927 with sound, they undertook a color scoop in 1929 by contracting with Technicolor for no less than forty all-color pictures.

He who has seen a camera which will take color movies has seen a rare sight. There are only about fifty of them in the world—two years ago there were less than ten. Each costs about $4,000 as against several hundred dollars for non-color cameras. The actual photography of a color-movie is done from beginning to end by Technicolor crew—not by a producer's own cameramen. When the picture is taken, the master negative is sent to Boston, where with infinite care and patience the positive prints are made. For this complete photographic service Technicolor is paid about eight cents a foot by the producer, as against about two cents a foot which black and white photography costs the producer. This difference in mere photographic cost would stop anybody but a showman. A black and white feature picture contains about 7,000 feet of film and 200 prints will be required, making 1,400,000 feet in all. At two cents each, that is $28,000. The same picture in color, at eight cents a foot, will cost $112,000. Thus, simply for photography, a color picture raises the gamble by some $84,000. But far more than that is spent in the extra time consumed in making a color picture. Roughly, we may say that the same picture which would cost $750,000 in black and white will cost at least $1,000,000 in color. Let us hasten also to say that except for years of struggle in solving practical production problems, such a color picture would cost nearer $2,000,000 if it could be made at all. Here we must also note that there are many other color processes in competition with Technicolor. But however fine their laboratory product may be, none of them can be taken seriously until it has actually taken a full-length picture under Hollywood conditions and at a price somewhere near eight cents a foot. Paramount is experimenting; Fox has built a plant since abandoned. Howard Hughes has Multicolor, with a plant in Hollywood, while perhaps most advanced of Technicolor rivals is the Colorcraft Corporation, with a new plant on Long Island scheduled to be in production this fall.

COLOR AND COMPETITION

Now the producer is naturally reluctant to add $250,000 to his ante on a special production or $100,000 to his ante on the regular program picture. If there were only one producer in Hollywood, he would probably consign all color processes to the bottom of the sea, because it is scarcely arguable that color will materially increase the total "consumption" of movies. But competition being what it is, the producer must ask himself: will color develop to a point where black and white will fail to produce the illusion it always has produced? And therefore, will color, this season or next, or next, replace black and white? That is the question.

A year ago the answer seemed to be: "Yes—and soon." The talkie revolution had come in 1928 so much faster than anyone could have foreseen that in 1929 all the producers, afraid of being scooped again, followed Warner's lead in making huge non-cancellable part cash in advance contracts for color in 1929–30—nearly all, of course, with Technicolor. And they were, of course, wrong. For two reasons: (1) because, as aforesaid, the importance of color to drama is as nothing compared to the importance of voice; (2) because imperfect color is far more noticeable than imperfect sound (our eyes are many times more sensitive than our ears). For these reasons, color caused practically no sensation (few people realize how many 1929–30 pictures were made in color), and as for black and white pictures being obsolete in contrast with color pictures—that simply did not occur to the movie public. So for 1930–31 the trend seems definitely in the direction of less, rather than more, color. First National and Warner Brothers are postponing the fulfillment of their contracts with Technicolor—a procedure which was in any case necessary, since Technicolor simply could not print the pictures as fast as Hollywood thought it wanted them a year ago. So far has the color wave declined after its tidal sweep last winter that some movie executives have pronounced it of small importance. But in this they are likely to be quite wrong again. To be specific, there are two kinds of film plays for which color will almost certainly become essential: the musical comedy and the costume or spectacle drama. Both these types will rise and fall in popularity, but they will always be a big factor in the business. The talkies definitely added the musical comedy to the movie repertoire. From now on it seems likely that this type will increasingly become associated in the public mind with color, so that a film musical without color will not seem like a film musical at all. A similar mental association will not occur so definitely in the spectacle drama, but anyone who saw *Song of the Flame* or *The Rogue Song* will realize that if a producer is offering the spectacular he can hardly afford to omit the spectacular qualities of red and gold and purple. A public accustomed to red torches flaming in the night will not accept a parade of ghostly candles without the ghosts.

However, all of this sort of stuff is *not* the backbone, the meat and drink, of the movies. The big elaborate or sensational pictures are essential to the movie business, but they do *not* account for the bulk of the box office receipts. People go to the movies primarily to watch and to hear two or three human beings collide with each other in what is represented to be life. With the silent, and now more than ever with the talkie, the play is the thing. So, after allowing that 20 per cent or even 30 per cent of the movies must be in color for the special reasons just indicated, the great question is: is the time near when the ordinary play of love or adventure must be made in color?

Certainly the time has not yet arrived; it is probably several years and perhaps a decade away. Simply put, the reason comes down to this: to the degree that we are aware of the imperfection of color it is a distraction and consequently hinders rather than promotes dramatic action. To cease to be a distraction, color must be so perfect as to be *unnoticeable* except by contrast with absence of color. Or, what is more likely, we must become so accustomed to the imperfections of color as not to be distracted by it. Such perfection or such psychological adaptation is in all probability many, many years away. As for perfection, it is almost certain that an entirely different scientific principle must be employed before it can be expected. As for psychological adaptation, the more imperfect color we see, the less it will distract us until finally we will accept it as a convention and will be distracted when it is absent. Ultimately *all* movies are likely to be in color; until then every producer will be on his guard against failure to keep up with the color convention.

Meanwhile, technical improvement, however slow, may be expected. And almost as important as technical advance will be advance in the film theatre use of color. Two examples: use color to lengthen the life of favorite stars, for color hides the wrinkles; use it more soberly and hence less distractingly—green lawns, green trees instead of a continued riot of roses.

Historic Date

Undoubtedly producers jumped too fast at color this year. But to understand why they have good reason to jump at *any* new offering of invention, it is necessary only to grasp a few dates in the history of sound. These are dates in what we have already described as by all odds the most remarkable single revolution in industrial annals. Sound came so fast (it became "natural" so soon) that practically nobody (and least of all the movie critics) realized what was happening until it happened. Even the producers were in the condition of learning on Tuesday that what they thought might occur a year from Tuesday had actually happened a week ago Monday. In April, 1929, Fox's Mr. Sheehan, simultaneously with his company's complete surrender to the talkie, boldly predicted that by January 1, 1931, there would be 3,000 theatres wired for sound. There are today 10,000 such theatres. . . . Consider Paramount. In 1928 it released seventy-eight silent pictures, no talkies. In 1929 it released twenty silents and forty-seven talkies. In 1930 it released sixty-five talkies, no silents. (These are full-length pictures and do not count news reels, comedies, cartoons, etc.)

So great was the public's infatuation that in 1929 every producer made big money and, far more remarkable, nearly every single talkie made money. Net profits for leading concerns:

	1929	1928
Warner	$17,271,805	$2,044,842
Fox	9,469,050	5,957,217
Paramount	15,544,544	8,713,063
Loew's	11,756,956	8,568,162

But now . . . the first golden harvest is past; the public is taking its talkies critically. And meanwhile, new problems present themselves, the most obvious being that of foreign markets. In its Paris studios, Paramount is making each picture in four or five different languages, each with a different cast. Where the original English picture cost $400,000 or $500,000, the "translations" cost $50,000 or $75,000 each. The Spanish version may well repay the extra cost from the South American market. But it does not pay to make a version in Czechoslovakian. Thus, while the revolution in the greatest of all show businesses is a completely accomplished fact, there remain the resultant problems otherwise known as "gambles." . . .

■ ■ ■ ■

Hollywood Horizons (1930), Maurice L. Ahern

This article from the 21 May 1930 issue of *Commonweal* recounts the transition from silent-film stars to sound-film stars in Hollywood.

To affirm that America became air-minded and ear-conscious at precisely the same time would scarcely be an exaggeration in the light of recent history. The lone eagle was still flashing through the mid-Atlantic heavens when an amazed audience at the Roxy theatre in New York saw and heard his departure revivified on the sound screen. May 20, 1927, is thus doubly significant for it was on that day that Lindbergh soared from Mitchell field and the march of the microphones began.

Sound lost no time in fortifying its position. Each and every day that the Los Angeles limited pulled wearily into the Hollywood station scores of strange, keen-eyed men debouched upon the platform and, locust fashion, swarmed blithely over everything sacred in filmland. Engineers, statisticians, sound men, architects and technicians of every ilk labored with the speed of thought and the zeal of pioneers. A twenty-acre steel and concrete plant built exclusively for sound pictures arose in ninety days. The old studios were converted as fast as unlimited money and man power could do the trick. Phrases such as "mike fright," "voice test," "sound man," "movietone" and "synchronous" became glibly current throughout the land. In an incredibly short time the stage was set for a new act in the picture play.

Actors popped out of the ground like crocuses in April but they were actors of a breed that had rarely been seen in Hollywood before. Ladies and gentlemen of the legitimate stage, they were the elect of the new

"Hollywood Horizons," by Maurice L. Ahern, is from the 21 May 1930 issue of *Commonweal*.

medium. The players of the formerly silent screen openly resented the intrusion of the aliens and the issue of the struggle that ensued, brief as it was, forms an interesting interlude in the annals of the world's most popular entertainment.

It is but a little more than two years since the great sound migration westward. The southern California sun continues to beat down as it did then upon the picture city by the Pacific yet how different is the aspect of the multitude scurrying hatless in its warmth. There exists no longer a smug, carefree, strenuously sophisticated movie colony. In its place are two serious groups; one, the invaders from the Broadway stage; the other, a remnant of the once happy horde of picture actors standing now with their backs to the brink of oblivion.

Many of the latter will never again hold the centre of the screen. Some of them were just ascending the hill of fame when the sound wave engulfed them. Others had already passed over the crest. Irrespective of the degree of their past prestige they are melting quietly from the public gaze and hearing largely because they cannot talk suitably. In the past the tricks of kindly cameras could successfully disguise even physical defects but no instrument on earth can change into dulcet tones voices that are as cracked reeds. Milady of nineteen-thirty shadowland must not only be lovely as the dawn but must speak like tinkling bells at sunset or forever hold her peace.

In the older order of things the candidate for screen honors had virtually no chance of success unless he or she had "it." The lack of almost every other desirable attribute could be condoned if that one intangible quality were present. In the shadows and subtle silences of the "old-time" movie, "it" needed no voice other than that supplied by the imagination of the flappers and sheiks and their sisters and their cousins and their aunts.

Sound has changed all that. "It" has been supplanted by personality. The fanciful has given way to the real. The public can no longer be fooled and so droves of heavy lovers and impassioned ladies of the premicrophone days are drifting back to the overalls of the filling station and the apron of the cafeteria. They were like strutting peacocks; beautiful to gaze upon, terrible to hear.

Not all the mimes of other cinema days were brainless beauties with unpleasant voices. There is a goodly group upon whom sound has had the same effect as sun and rain on spring flowers. The glorious Garbo seems even more so as one listens to her throaty, accented speech. Lois Moran's personality has become vividly defined and given a vibrant quality through Movietone. Janet Gaynor's voice fully verifies the winsome personality we had always associated with her. Joan Crawford,

Edmund Lowe, Nancy Carroll, William Powell, Warner Baxter, Norma Shearer, Clive Brook and Ronald Colman are among those Hollywood fortunates who do not shudder as they face the microphone. Some, relegated almost to the limbo of bit players long before the age of microphone have, through the suitability of their voices, regained the eminence that once was theirs. Betty Compson, Bessie Love, Louise Dresser, Henry B. Walthall, Lila Lee, Irene Rich and Conrad Nagel are now firm believers that it is never too late to have luck.

Notwithstanding these exceptions it is sad but true that silent players by and large, have been most decidedly failures in the new spoken drama of the screen. The high have suffered as sadly as the low in spite of efforts to force them on the public because of a previous box-office value built up over a period of years. But with each syllable they utter a friendly fan is lost to them. Lloyd has added nothing to his fame in his first "talkie." Mary Pickford, Norma Talmadge and Douglas Fairbanks have not found dialogue in any way helpful to stem the ebb tide of popularity. Jannings has fled back to Germany. Chaplin sulks in his tent, apparently fearful to attempt a dialogue picture. In many a Hollywood hacienda the silence that was golden is mourned with sullen bitterness.

In the beginning of the sound era an obvious catch line presented itself to the eager, motion-picture publicity men and they made use of it ad nauseam. "The silent screen has found its voice." Clever and placidly pretty giving the impression that the movies woke up one fine morning and over the second cup of coffee and just before starting the second news section of the Times yawned and said "Dear me, there can be no doubt about it. Unquestionably this new feeling I have had for months must mean I can talk." No impression of what happened could be more wrong. As a matter of bald fact, for a time a near-panic reigned in filmland. The men behind the scenes suddenly found not that the movies had a voice but rather that the movies could use profitably a great many voices. Yet diligent and rapid, almost frantic, search revealed precious few voices in their own home town. In such an emergency the production executives did exactly what any good business men would have done. Needing voice and dramatic technique they went to the source for material to fill the sudden need. The clarion call went out. The response was eager. Broadway moved en masse to Hollywood and its hungry hordes waxed fat among the orange groves.

The course of events in the past two years has shown conclusively that success has crowned their efforts. The records of the three leading picture companies whose product accounts for over 60 percent of the entire yearly business of the industry show that three-quarters of the featured players under contract to them were engaged from the legitimate stage expressly for the purposes of Movietone and Vitaphone. Some of these players it is true have appeared only at the eastern studios of these companies, but that does not alter the main fact that they are of the stage and not the movies. George Arliss, Ruth Chatterton, John McCormack, Ann Harding, Al Jolson, Beatrice Lillie, Maurice Chevalier, Lenore Ulric, Dennis King, Marilyn Miller, Lawrence Tibbett. These and many others of equal prominence have seen their names that formerly only glittered before a comparatively few legitimate playhouses now blazoned forth on the gaudy marquees of 50,000 motion picture theatres at home and abroad. They have become the personal favorites of hundreds of millions as compared with a former following of a few hundred thousand. They have not failed in the new field of endeavor. On the contrary they have really made good in a trying situation and to the contentment that comes with achievement has been added the realization of a dream which has smoldered in the breast of every knight of the buskin since Aeschylus's day.

Success in the moving picture capital means working fifty-two weeks a year in the daytime like every other human being. It means having one's own home close to work in one of the world's beauty spots; a bungalow with a garden. There are frequent changes of rôle in the "talkies" and therefore no monotony; no cheap hotels, no Pullman cars and no one-night stands. And, most cogent happiness factor of all, Hollywood means filthy lucre in quantities that formerly seemed fantastic even to Broadway's best. The strolling players of Shakespeare's day must turn over in their graves at the thought of actors actually leading regular peaceful lives in common with other men and women. Yet that is precisely one of the rewards that Hollywood and the talking pictures have given to those who answered their siren call.

In passing it might not be amiss to mention briefly a third class of actors who do not really belong to either the silent or the stage classification. They are neither Hollywood fish nor Broadway fowl because they have been identified with both alternately for a long time and are thoroughly familiar with the technique of the stage and screen. Will Rogers, the Barrymores, Robert Edeson and others. The talkies are child's play for such as these. They are great but few and may safely be classed as neutrals.

Talking pictures are with us permanently for weal or woe. George Bernard Shaw admits it. King George, Mussolini, Foch, Clemenceau and Hindenburg have gladly posed for them. Even John D. Rockefeller recently went for his first airplane ride in Florida so that the sound camera could record the epochal event. To this tacit or outspoken approval by the leaders has been added the acclaim of the hoi polloi. The sales managers of all big companies declare emphatically that theatre owners just won't buy silent pictures any more because their customers won't come to see them. Yet Will Hays speaking for the Associated Motion Picture Producers of America makes an official report of an increase of 15,000,000 motion picture patrons during the past year. From these two facts alone the extent of the talkies' popularity may be judged.

There is the only fly in the ointment, for the public is fickle in such matters and what it has set up it can also very quickly cast down. Hollywood must hustle as it never did before to hold its sudden gains. As Robert Sherwood puts it, "It is one thing to persuade an audience to pay attention and quite another to give them something worthy of notice." The technique and style that would have been applauded in the silents is now frowned upon by the most illiterate fan who already regards the screen entertainment of four years ago as antique.

The talkies have engendered, in consequence, new criteria of craftsmanship and these in turn imply new responsibilities and standards in the artistic endeavors of those who make the talkies. It is no longer sufficient that they offer merely marvelous examples of the photographic art or the scenarist's facile pen or a pantomimist's subtleties. The success of a talkie depends ultimately and to the greatest degree upon the actors' skill in voice, posture and movement, all restrained to compensate for the exaggeration produced by the camera lens.

Who will play the parts in the talkies of the future—silent players who have survived the present cataclysm or imported players from the legitimate stage? The answer is, neither. Both classes are but strange branches temporarily grafted on a vigorous tree which is bent on producing foliage of its own although appreciative of the assistance received in its infancy. The talkies are new. They are very much alive and different and they must therefore have protagonists of their own fibre. And so, almost unnoticed, there has already grown up in Hollywood a type of actor essentially of the motion picture yet broadened and polished by contact with the histrionic experience of the veterans of the stage who have been his mentors for the past two years.

Frank Albertson, Sue Carol, Anita Page, John Boles, Bernice Claire, Joan Bennett, Gary Cooper, Dixie Lee, Richard Arlen, Helen Chandler, John Garrick, Charles Bickford, Mary Brian, Fay Wray, Jack Oakie, Mary Nolan, Regis Toomey and Mona Maris: these and their type will dominate the pictures of the future because they are talking picture actors bound, if at all, by only the slimmest of ties to other classifications of players. They cannot be classed as picture actors in the old sense because practically all their experience has been in talkies; on the other hand they cannot be herded with the clan of the legitimate stage because they never trod the boards nor faced an actual audience.

They are pictorial youth with a voice.

They are the children of the talking picture. This new form of entertainment may be the result of many different factors but it has its own individuality just the same. It is most emphatically not a photographed stage play nor is it a silent picture with dialogue added. Far from being a mere gathering together of various elements it is a fusion of those elements into something totally new.

So too are its children. They are a new race: a genus to themselves. Bred in Hollywood under the tutelage of Broadway they owe allegiance to neither but to sound whose symbol is the microphone.

■ ■ ■ ■

HOORAY FOR HOLLYWOOD

Hooray for Hollywood!
That screwy, ballyhooey Hollywood!
Where any office boy or young mechanic
Can be a panic
With just a good-looking pan.
And any shop-girl
Can be a top girl,
If she pleases the tired businessman.

Hooray for Hollywood!
You may be homely in your neighborhood.
But if you really want to be an actor
See Mr. Factor
He'll make your kisser look good.
In less than half an hour
You'll look like Tyrone Power.
Hooray for Hollywood!

Hooray for Hollywood!
That bully, wild-and-woolly Hollywood!
They hire cowboys and they hang their chaps up
And doll their maps up
And give them all that they lack.
Now aint it funny,
They pay them money—
Shows what you can do if your hoss can act.

Hooray for Hollywood!
They hire fellows whose physiques are good,
And then they tell them they're perfect shaped-men
To act like ape-men
And they convince them they should.
They make them bend and yell
And people think they're swell.
Hooray for Hollywood!

Music by Richard Whiting, lyric by Johnny Mercer;
from the motion picture *Hollywood Hotel*, 1937.

5

The Thirties
(1931–1940)

The decade from 1930 to 1940 was the Golden Age of the American Studio Movie. It was the decade of the great movie stars—Bette Davis, Katharine Hepburn, Greta Garbo, Marlene Dietrich, Clark Gable, James Cagney, Cary Grant, Gary Cooper. It was the decade of the great movie genres—the gangster cycle, the backstage musical, the screwball comedy. It was the decade of the great movie studios—MGM, Paramount, Warner Brothers, RKO, Twentieth Century–Fox, Columbia, Universal. And it was the decade of the great studio directors—Ernst Lubitsch, Josef von Sternberg, John Ford, Howard Hawks, George Cukor, Mervyn LeRoy, Frank Capra, Mitchell Leisen, William Wellman. In no other decade (perhaps in no other art) have art and commerce served one another so richly, fully, and energetically.

The decade was also a significant one in shaping Hollywood's relationship to American cultural life as a whole. The most famous social institution of the decade was the writing, adopting, and enforcing of the Hollywood Production Code. A combination of the industry's commercial instincts and the moral pressure of outside religious groups led to the industry's exercising a greater degre of control over the content of its product than it had ever exercised before. The adopting of the Production Code culminated over twenty-five years of agitation against the potentially licentious content of motion pictures. From this point of strictest control, the future of the movies would lie in a steady loosening and stretching of such moral regulations (see pages 693–715).

The decade was also one in which social scientists began to take a serious interest in Hollywood's relationship to American life. The Payne Fund Studies, published in 1933, attempted to assess the pervasiveness of the movies in shaping American attitudes, character, and conduct. Because the spirit to produce these studies was generally biased against movies and the kind of entertainment they provided, the conclusions of some of them lacked scientific integrity and sufficent data. Of course the conclusions of the least adequate Payne Fund Studies were attacked by both the film industry and other American thinkers for being biased, unfounded, and invalid. There were also serious economic studies of the financial bases and control of the industry as well as sociological studies of the characteristics of daily life in Hollywood.

Despite such studies, such controversies, and such semicensorship, the overwhelming fact about the American movie in the decade is that it had become central to American life and thought. Its plots reflected the ideals and aspirations of American society, its shifting cycles provided insights into the shifting attitudes of Americans toward important issues, and even its most escaptist art both mirrored and shaped the way that its audiences thought and felt.

■ ■ ■ ■

The Birth of the Production Code (1945), Raymond Moley
The Motion Picture Production Code of 1930, Motion Picture Producers and Distributors of America

Raymond Moley, a professional lawyer and amateur sociologist, had been chosen by the "Hays Office" as its official historian—primarily because of Moley's able defense of the industry against the Payne Fund attack (see pages 359–65). This chapter from his authorized history, *The Hays Office,* summarizes the events and attitudes that led to the writing of the Code.

The Birth of the Production Code

With the advent of 1930, Hays was approaching the end of his eighth year of his unprecedented job. He had discovered in those years how difficult it was to bring to a bright reality the repeated assurance of his directors that the creation of the Hays Office was to help in "establishing and maintaining the highest possible moral and artistic standards in motion-picture production." There had been marked progress in artistic and mechanical standards. There had been some improvement in moral standards. But the complications effected by the making of sound pictures and the increase in attendance that the coming of sound brought had made the moral quality of the product increasingly important. And now, after the stock-market crash in late 1929, it was apparent that the competitive spirit among the companies would give great impetus to the companies' tendency to seek short cuts to public patronage. And short cuts had always meant a drift to sensationalism and lower moral standards. Criticism was mounting, and no one knew this better than Hays, since his office was the clearinghouse for complaints by the citizenry.

Meanwhile, Hays was struggling with the problem of improving the

"The Birth of the Production Code" is from *The Hays Office,* by Raymond Moley (Bobbs-Merrill, 1945; Ozer, 1971).

administration of the studio-relations committee. The difficulty there was twofold. His system of policing the moral standards of pictures was not strong, but more important, neither was his system of law definite and adequate. The "Don'ts and Be Carefuls" could never be a satisfactory means of guiding the production of pictures because they were susceptible to an infinite number of interpretations. Even had Colonel Joy's setup been strong and direct, the absence of a definite industry-law would have prevented its success. During this period Hays was receiving many suggestions for improving things, and he was giving thoughtful consideration to them all. But they were, for the most part, outside suggestions backed by little intimate knowledge of picture making.

At this point there enters this story another man whose influence was to be vitally important in the motion-picture revolution which was just around the corner. Martin Quigley, the publisher of a number of trade papers and magazines, including *The Motion Picture Herald*, enjoyed the respect of every constructive person in the industry.[1] His active and professional interest in the industry began in 1915, when he established *The Exhibitors' Herald*. In all his years as an editor and publisher, he had never yielded to the temptation to offer mere lip service to motion pictures or to those who produced them. The dedication of his career to the publishing side of the motion-picture industry indicated his recognition of the film as a great and growing force. But from the beginning he also saw that the motion picture was subject to serious abuses. His detachment from the production and distribution sides of the picture business made it possible for him to offer public criticism. Over a period of fifteen years he had wielded a stinging whip. The people in the industry were sensitive to his judgments and, for the most part, were compelled to admit his steadfast championship of the motion picture as an institution. His consistent theme was the obligation of the industry to the public and he was constantly at pains to point out to the industry that unless it took a broader view of the public interest, the industry itself could not survive.

Quigley was a distinguished Catholic layman. His more advanced education had been in Catholic institutions, where he learned not only that his Church made the advancement of morality a prime part of its mission, but that, over the years, it had embodied its moral strictures in a highly specific code of ethical conduct.

He had seen evidence that powerful people in the motion-picture industry were deeply desirous of raising and maintaining standards. He was also convinced of Hays's sincerity. He had hailed with enthusiasm

1. Ed. Note: Quigley's moral principles and rhetoric become clear in the excerpt from his book, *Decency in Motion Pictures,* on pages 340–44.

the creation of the M.P.P.D.A. and had consistently supported Hays. But now, after nearly eight years, he had reached the conclusion that whatever might be the will of the industry to save itself, the existing machinery and procedures were not doing the job. His conclusion was that what was necessary was not merely a set of rules but rather an exposition of the philosophy of morality as applied to public entertainment; in short, not only rules, but reasons which might enable producers to give the rules more intelligent and broader application.

Hays knew Quigley well and fully respected and trusted him. Over the years they had conferred frequently on the problem with which they were both profoundly concerned—the elimination of the undesirable in pictures and the creation of better pictures. Late in 1929 Quigley conferred with Hays and told him that he was working on a plan that might meet the problem of enforcing morality in the making of pictures and outlined the nature of his idea. Hays indicated his great interest. The Quigley idea appealed to him, he says, because he saw at once that the Quigley plan offered a pattern which, in time, would become part of the psychological approach of producers to questions of propriety and morality. In this respect the plan offered something more than the many other ideas which had come from people in all parts of the country.

Thus encouraged, Quigley set himself to the task of creating a draft code. After conferring with Hays, he called to his assistance a man who was not only learned in the science of systematic ethics, but who had a wide knowledge of the drama and the motion picture. He was Daniel J. Lord, S. J., Professor of Dramatics at the University of St. Louis. Father Lord was no stranger to the motion-picture industry. Some years before, he had served in an advisory capacity to the producer of *The King of Kings*. He was the editor of a religious magazine, *The Queen's Work*, which gave considerable attention to motion pictures. He had written books and plays himself and, in his writing, had been a friendly and constructive critic of motion pictures. Hays and many of the producers knew Lord and respected his judgment.

The result of the Quigley-Lord collaboration was a proposed code which was first shown to Hays and later submitted to the producers in Hollywood.

In early January 1930 Hays went to Hollywood to prepare the way for a consideration by the producers of the Quigley-Lord proposal. He arranged a meeting of the producers, and Quigley presented the proposed code. Quigley discussed it and answered questions through three long sessions. Father Lord was sent for and, at a meeting a week later, discussed the draft code further with the producers. Shortly after, on February 17, 1930, the producers accepted the Code and on March 31 at a formal meeting of the directors of the M.P.P.D.A. the acceptance of the Code was made official.

It is very important to note that the Code is in two parts. The first is called the "Code"; the second is called the "Reasons." Both were formally adopted and both have the status of enforceable industry-law under the resolution of March 31, 1930.

The reason for the division of the Code into two parts is that in the course of the Hollywood discussions, it occurred to Hays that, in the interest of simplicity, it might be well to have a brief summary of the prohibitions of the Code. Hence, he asked Father Lord to prepare such a summary. That summary is what is now called the "Code." The original Quigley-Lord draft is virtually identical with the document known as the "Reasons."

The Code is, in the main, a list of prohibitions. The Reasons illuminate the prohibitions with a rational discussion of basic principles to be followed in making morally constructive pictures.

In the summary "Code" there appear provisions not mentioned in the original Quigley-Lord draft. These are not strictly within the code of morality as interpreted by Mr. Quigley and Father Lord. These are the prohibitions concerning "Methods of Crime," "The Use of Liquor," "Miscegenation," "National Feelings" and "Repellent Subjects." In the main these were added by Hays in the course of the discussions in 1930. Some of them come from the old "Don'ts and Be Carefuls," and from Hays's long experience in their application. . . .

Hays was the master of the operation from the time he approved of Quigley's idea of a code until the Code was formally adopted. During the discussions which preceded its adoption, there were many suggestions by the representatives of the producing companies. Subcommittees studied the Code and made reports. Thus the Code as it emerged and as it stands fourteen years later is the definitive expression of the will of the members of the industry. It is their own expression of the moral principles which should govern their product. And it is, therefore, the legitimate embodiment of their resolution of 1922 that moral principles would be observed in all pictures made by them.

It is important to note that the basic moral principles upon which Quigley and Father Lord worked in creating a systematic code did not involve matters of theology, concerning which there are differences among the religions of the Western world. The basic moral prohibitions in all these religions go back to the Ten Commandments. The moral principles observed in drafting the Code were based upon the Ten Commandments. For that reason, the Code, while originally drafted by members of the Catholic religion, was universally acceptable by the members of all Western religions. There was no other common ground upon which all who were concerned could stand. So the Code suggests the basic moral unity of Western civilization. . . .

THE MOTION PICTURE PRODUCTION CODE OF 1930

FIRST SECTION
GENERAL PRINCIPLES

I. Theatrical motion pictures, that is, pictures intended for the theatre as distinct from pictures intended for churches, schools, lecture halls, educational movements, social reform movements, etc., are primarily to be regarded as *Entertainment*.

Mankind has always recognized the importance of entertainment and its value in rebuilding the bodies and souls of human beings.

But it has always recognized that entertainment can be of a character *harmful* to the human race, and, in consequence, has clearly distinguished between:

> *Entertainment which tends to improve* the race, or, at least, to recreate and rebuild human beings exhausted with the realities of life; and
>
> *Entertainment which tends to degrade human beings,* or to lower their standards of life and living.

Hence the *moral importance* of entertainment is something which has been universally recognized. It enters intimately into the lives of men and women and affects them closely; it occupies their minds and affections during leisure hours, and ultimately touches the whole of their lives. A man may be judged by his standard of entertainment as easily as by the standard of his work.

> So *correct entertainment raises* the whole standard of a nation.
>
> *Wrong entertainment lowers* the whole living condition and moral ideals of a race.
>
> NOTE, for example, the healthy reactions to healthful moral sports like baseball, golf; the unhealthy reactions to sports like cockfighting, bullfighting, bear-baiting, etc. Note, too, the effect on a nation of gladiatorial combats, the obscene plays of Roman times, etc.

"The Motion Picture Production Code of 1930," by the Motion Picture Producers and Distributors of America, is taken from Olga J. Martin's *Hollywood's Movie Commandments* (H. W. Wilson, 1937).

II. Motion pictures are very important as *Art*.

Though a new art, possibly a combination art, it has the same object as the other arts, the presentation of human thoughts, emotions and experiences, in terms of an appeal to the soul thru the senses.

Here, as in entertainment:

Art *enters intimately* into the lives of human beings.

Art can be *morally good*, lifting men to higher levels. This has been done thru good music, great painting, authentic fiction, poetry, drama.

Art can be morally evil in its effects. This is the case clearly enough with unclean art, indecent books, suggestive drama. The effect on the lives of men and women is obvious.

NOTE: It has often been argued that art in itself is unmoral, neither good nor bad. This is perhaps true of the *thing* which is music, painting, poetry, etc. But the thing is the *product* of some person's mind, and that mind was either good or bad morally when it produced the thing. And the thing has its *effect* upon those who come into contact with it. In both these ways, as a product and the cause of definite effects, it has a deep moral significance and an unmistakable moral quality.

HENCE: The motion pictures which are the most popular of modern arts for the masses, have their moral quality from the minds which produce them and from their effects on the moral lives and reactions of their audiences. This gives them a most important morality.

1) They *reproduce* the morality of the men who use the pictures as a medium for the expression of their ideas and ideals;

2) They *affect* the moral standards of those who thru the screen take in these ideas and ideals.

In the case of the motion pictures, this effect may be particularly emphasized because no art has so quick and so widespread an appeal to the masses. It has become in an incredibly short period, *the art of the multitudes*.

III. The motion picture has special *Moral obligations:*

A) Most arts appeal to the mature. This art appeals at once to every class—mature, immature, developed, undeveloped, law-abiding, criminal. Music has its grades for different classes; so has literature and drama. This art of the motion picture, combining as it does the two fundamental appeals of looking at a picture and listening to a story, at once reaches every class of society.

B) Because of the mobility of a film and the ease of picture distribution, and because of the possibility of duplicating positives in large quantities, this art *reaches places* unpenetrated by other forms of art.

C) Because of these two facts, it is difficult to produce films intended for only *certain classes of people*. The exhibitor's theatres are for the masses, for the cultivated and the rude, mature and immature, self-restrained and inflammatory, young and old, law-respecting and criminal. Films, unlike books and music, can with difficulty be confined to certain selected groups.

D) The latitude given to film material cannot, in consequence, be as wide as the latitude given to *book material*. In addition:

   (a) A book describes; a film vividly presents.

   (b) A book reaches the mind thru words merely; a film reaches the eyes and ears thru the reproduction of actual events.

   (c) The reaction of a reader to a book depends largely on the keenness of the reader; the reaction to a film depends on the vividness of presentation.

E) This is also true when comparing the film with the newspapers. Newspapers present by description, films by actual presentation. Newspapers are after the fact and present things that have taken place; the film gives the events in the process of enactment and with apparent reality of life.

F) Everything possible in a *play* is not possible in a film.

   (a) Because of the larger audience of the film, and its consequently mixed character. Psychologically, the larger the audience, the lower the moral mass resistance to suggestion.

   (b) Because thru light, enlargement of character presentation, scenic emphasis, etc., the screen story is brought closer to the audience than the play.

   (c) The enthusiasm for and interest in the film *actors* and *actresses*, developed beyond anything of the sort in history, makes the audience largely sympathetic toward the characters they portray and the stories in which they figure. Hence they are more ready to confuse the actor and character, and they are most receptive of the emotions and ideals portrayed and presented by their favorite stars.

G) Small communities, remote from sophistication and from the hardening process which often takes place in the ethical and moral standards of larger cities, are easily and readily reached by any sort of film.

H) The grandeur of mass meetings, large action, spectacular features, etc., affects and arouses more intensely the emotional side of the audience.

IN GENERAL: The mobility, popularity, accessibility, emotional appeal, vividness, straight-forward presentation of fact in the films makes for intimate contact on a larger audience and greater emotional appeal.

Hence the larger moral responsibiliites of the motion pictures.

SECOND SECTION

WORKING PRINCIPLES

I. No picture should lower the moral standards of those who see it. This is done:

    (a) When evil is made to appear *attractive,* and good is made to appear *unattractive.*

    (b) When the *sympathy* of the audience is thrown on the side of crime, wrong-doing, evil, sin. The same thing is true of a film that would throw sympathy against goodness, honor, innocence, purity, honesty.

NOTE: *Sympathy with a person who sins,* is not the same as sympathy with the sin or crime of which he is guilty. We may feel sorry for the plight of the murderer or even understand the circumstances which led him to his crime; we may not feel sympathy with the wrong which he has done.

The presentation of evil is often essential for art, or fiction, or drama. This in itself is not wrong, provided:

    (a) That evil is *not presented alluringly.* Even if later on the evil is condemned or punished, it must not be allowed to appear so attractive that the emotions are drawn to desire or approve so strongly that later they forget the condemnation and remember only the apparent joy of the sin.

    (b) That thruout the presentation, *evil and good are never confused* and that evil is always recognized clearly as evil.

    (c) That in the end the audience feels that *evil is wrong* and *good is right.*

II. Law, natural or divine, must not be belittled, ridiculed, nor must a sentiment be created against it.

  A) The *presentation of crimes* against the law, human or divine, is often necessary for the carrying out of the plot. But the presentation must not throw sympathy with the criminal as against the law, nor with the crime as against those who punish it.

  B) The *courts* of the land should not be presented as *unjust.*

III. As far as possible, life should not be misrepresented, at least not in such a way as to place in the mind of youth false values on life.

  NOTE: This subject is touched just in passing. The attention of the producers is called, however, to the magnificent possibilities of the screen for character development, the building of right ideals, the inculcation in story-form of right principles. If motion pictures consistently held up high types of character, presented stories that would affect lives for the better, they could become the greatest natural force for the improvement of mankind.

PRINCIPLES OF PLOT

In accordance with the general principles laid down:

1) No plot or theme should definitely side *with evil and against good.*
2) Comedies and farces *should not make fun* of good, innocence, morality or justice.
3) No plot should be constructed as to leave the question of *right or wrong in doubt or fogged.*
4) No plot should by its treatment *throw the sympathy* of the audience with sin, crime, wrong-doing or evil.
5) No plot should present evil *alluringly.*

Serious Film Drama

I. As stated in the general principles, *sin and evil* enter into the story of human beings, and hence in themselves are dramatic material.

II. In the use of this material, it must be distinguished between *sin* which by its very nature *repels,* and *sin* which by its very nature *attracts.*

    (a) In the first class comes murder, most theft, most legal crimes, lying, hypocrisy, cruelty, etc.

    (b) In the second class come sex sins, sins and crimes of apparent heroism, such as banditry, daring thefts, leadership in evil, organized crime, revenge, etc.

A) The first class needs little care in handling, as sins and crimes of this class naturally are unattractive. The audience instinctively condemns and is repelled. Hence the one objective must be to avoid the *hardening* of the audiences, especially of those who are young and impressionable, to the thought and the fact of crime. People can become accustomed even to murder, cruelty, brutality and repellent crimes.

B) The second class needs real care in handling, as the response of human natures to their appeal is obvious. This is treated more fully below.

III. A careful distinction can be made between films intended for *general distribution,* and films intended for use in theatres restricted to a *limited audience.* Themes and plots quite appropriate for the latter would be altogether out of place and dangerous in the former.

NOTE: In general, the practice of using a general theatre and limiting the patronage during the showing of a certain film to "adults only" is not completely satisfactory and is only partially effective.

However, maturer minds may easily understand and accept without harm subject matter in plots which does younger people positive harm.

HENCE: If there should be created a special type of theatre, catering exclusively to an adult audience, for plays of this character (plays with problem themes, difficult discussions and maturer treatment) it would seem to afford an outlet, which does not now exist, for pictures unsuitable for general distribution but permissible for exhibitions to a restricted audience.

PLOT MATERIAL

1) *The triangle,* that is, the love of a third party by one already married, needs careful handling, if marriage, the sanctity of the home, and sex morality are not to be imperilled.

2) *Adultery* as a subject should be avoided:

   (a) It is *never* a fit subject for *comedy.* Thru comedy of this sort, ridicule is thrown on the essential relationships of home and family and marriage, and illicit relationships are made to seem permissible, and either delightful or daring.

   (b) Sometimes adultery must be counted on as material occuring in serious drama.

   In this case:

   (1) It should not appear to be justified;

   (2) It should not be used to weaken respect for marriage;

   (3) It should not be presented as attractive or alluring.

3) *Seduction and rape* are difficult subjects and bad material from the viewpoint of the general audience in the theatre.

   (a) They should never be introduced as subject matter *unless* absolutely essential to the plot.

   (b) They should *never* be treated as comedy.

   (c) Where essential to the plot, they must not be more than *suggested.*

   (d) Even the struggles preceding rape should not be shown.

   (e) The *methods* by which seduction, essential to the plot, is attained should not be explicit or represented in detail where there is likelihood of arousing wrongful emotions on the part of the audience.

4) *Scenes of passion* are sometimes necessary for the plot. However:

(a) They should appear only where necessary and *not* as an added stimulus to the emotions of the audience.

(b) *When not essential to the plot,* they should not occur.

(c) They must *not* be *explicit* in action nor vivid in method, e.g. by handling of the body, by lustful and prolonged kissing, by evidently lustful embraces, by positions which strongly arouse passions.

(d) In general, where essential to the plot, scenes of passion should *not* be presented in such a way as to *arouse or excite the passions of the ordinary spectator.*

5) *Sexual immorality* is sometimes necessary for the plot. It is subject to the following:

GENERAL PRINCIPLES—regarding plots dealing with sex, passion, and incidents relating to them:

All legislators have recognized clearly that there are in normal human beings emotions which react naturally and spontaneously to the presentation of certain definite manifestations of sex and passion.

(a) The presentation of scenes, episodes, plots, etc., which are deliberately meant to excite these manifestations on the part of the audience is always wrong, is subversive to the interest of society, and a peril to the human race.

(b) Sex and passion exist and consequently must *sometimes enter* into the stories which deal with human beings.

   (1) *Pure love,* the love of a man for a woman permitted by the law of God and man, is the rightful subject of plots. The passion arising from this love is not the subject for plots.

   (2) *Impure love,* the love of man and woman forbidden by human and divine law, must be presented in such a way that:

      a) It is clearly known by the audience to be wrong;

      b) Its presentation does not excite sexual reactions, mental or physical, in an ordinary audience;

      c) It is not treated as matter for comedy.

HENCE: *Even within the limits of pure love,* certain facts have been universally regarded by lawmakers as outside the limits of safe presentation. These are the manifestations of passion and the sacred intimacies of private life:

(1) Either before marriage in the courtship of decent people;

(2) Or after marriage, as is perfectly clear.

In the case of pure love, the difficulty is not so much about what details are permitted for presentation. This is perfectly clear in most cases. The difficulty concerns itself with the tact, delicacy, and general regard for propriety manifested in their presentation.

But in the case of impure love, the love which society has always regarded as wrong and which has been banned by divine law, the following are important:

(1) It must not be the subject of comedy or farce or treated as the material for laughter;

(2) It must not be presented as attractive and beautiful;

(3) It must not be presented in such a way as to arouse passion or morbid curiosity on the part of the audience;

(4) It must not be made to seem right and permissible;

(5) In general, it must not be detailed in method or manner.

6) *The presentation of murder* is often necessary for the carrying out of the plot. However:

(a) Frequent presentation of *murder* tends to lessen regard for the sacredness of life.

(b) *Brutal killings* should not be presented in detail.

(c) *Killings for revenge* should not be justified, i.e., the hero should not take justice into his own hands in such a way as to make his killing seem justified. This does not refer to killings in self-defense.

(d) *Dueling* should not be presented as right or just.

7) *Crimes against the law* naturally occur in the course of film stories. However:

(a) *Criminals* should not be made heroes, even if they are historical criminals.

(b) *Law and justice* must not by the treatment they receive from criminals be made to seem wrong or ridiculous.

(c) *Methods of committing crime,* e.g., burglary, should not be so explicit as to teach the audience how crime can be committed; that is, the film should not serve as a possible school in crime methods for those who seeing the methods might use them.

(d) Crime need *not always be punished,* as long as the audience is made to know that it is wrong.

DETAILS OF PLOT, EPISODE, AND TREATMENT

Vulgarity

Vulgarity may be carefully distinguished from obscenity. Vulgarity is the treatment of low, disgusting, unpleasant subjects which decent society considers outlawed from normal conversation.

Vulgarity in the motion pictures is limited in precisely the same way as in decent groups of men and women by the dictates of good taste and civilized usage, and by the effect of shock, scandal, and harm on those coming in contact with this vulgarity.

(1) *Oaths* should never be used as a comedy element. Where required by the plot, the less offensive oaths may be permitted.

(2) *Vulgar expressions* come under the same treatment as vulgarity in general. Where women and children are to see the film, vulgar expressions (and oaths) should be cut to the absolute essentials required by the situation.

(3) The name of *Jesus Christ* should never be used except in reverence.

Obscenity

Obscenity is concerned with immorality, but has the additional connotation of being common, vulgar and coarse.

(1) *Obscenity in fact,* that is, in spoken word, gesture, episode, plot, is against divine and human law, and hence altogether outside the range of subject matter or treatment.

(2) Obscenity should *not be suggested* by gesture, manner, etc.

(3) An obscene reference, even if it is expected to be understandable to only the more sophisticated part of the audience, should not be introduced.

(4) *Obscene language* is treated as all obscenity.

Costume

GENERAL PRINCIPLES:

(1) The effect of nudity or semi-nudity upon the normal man or woman, and much more upon the young person, has been honestly recognized by all lawmakers and moralists.

(2) Hence the fact that the nude or semi-nude body may be *beautiful* does not make its use in the films moral. For in addition to its beauty, the effects of the nude or semi-nude body on the normal individual must be taken into consideration.

(3) Nudity or semi-nudity used simply to put a "punch" into a picture comes under the head of immoral actions as treated above. It is immoral in its effect upon the average audience.

(4) Nudity or semi-nudity is sometimes apparently necessary for the plot. *Nudity is never permitted.* Semi-nudity may be permitted under conditions.

PARTICULAR PRINCIPLES:

(1) *The more intimate parts of the human body* are male and female organs and the breasts of a woman.
   (a) They should *never be uncovered.*

(b) They should *not* be covered with *transparent* or *translucent* material.

(c) They should not be clearly and umistakably *outlined* by the garment.

(2) *The less intimate parts of the body,* the legs, arms, shoulders and back, are less certain of causing reactions on the part of the audience. Hence:

(a) Exposure *necessary for the plot* or action is permitted.

(b) Exposure *for the sake of exposure* or the "punch" is wrong.

(c) *Scenes of undressing* should be avoided. When necessary for the plot, they should be kept within the limits of decency. When not necessary for the plot, they are to be avoided, as their effect on the ordinary spectator is harmful.

(d) *The manner or treatment of exposure* should not be suggestive or indecent.

(e) The following is important in connection with *dancing costumes:*

1. Dancing costumes cut to permit *grace* or freedom of movement, provided they remain within the limits of decency indicated are permissible.

2. Dancing costumes cut to *permit indecent actions* or movements or to make possible during the dance indecent exposure, are wrong, especially when permitting:

a) Movements of the breasts;

b) Movements or sexual suggestions of the intimate parts of the body;

c) Suggestion of nudity.

Dancing

(1) Dancing in general is recognized as an *art* and a *beautiful* form of expressing human emotion.

(2) *Obscene dances are those:*

(a) Which suggest or represent sexual actions, whether performed solo or with two or more;

(b) Which are designed to excite an audience, to arouse passions, or to cause physical excitement.

HENCE: Dances of the type known as "Kooch," or "Can-Can," since they violate decency in these two ways, are wrong.

Dances with movements of the breasts, excessive body movement while the feet remain stationary, the so-called "belly dances"—these dances are immoral, obscene, and hence altogether wrong.

Locations

Certain places are so closely and thoroly associated with sexual life or with sexual sin that their use must be carefully limited.

(1) *Brothels and houses of ill-fame*, no matter of what country, are *not* proper locations for drama. They suggest to the average person at once sex sin, or they excite an unwholesome and morbid curiosity in the minds of youth.

IN GENERAL: They are dangerous and bad dramatic locations.

(2) *Bedrooms*. In themselves they are perfectly innocent. Their suggestion may be kept innocent. However, under certain situations they are bad dramatic locations.

(a) Their use in a comedy or farce (on the principle of the so-called bedroom farce) is wrong, because they suggest sex laxity and obscenity.

(b) In serious drama, their use should, where sex is suggested, be confined to absolute essentials, in accordance with the principles laid down above.

Religion

(1) No film or episode in a film should be allowed to *throw ridicule* on any religious faith honestly maintained.

(2) *Ministers of religion* in their characters of ministers should not be used in comedy, as villains, or as unpleasant persons.

NOTE: The reason for this is not that there are not such ministers of religion, but because the attitude toward them tends to be an attitude toward religion in general.

Religion is lowered in the minds of the audience because it lowers their respect for the ministers.

(3) *Ceremonies* of any definite religion should be supervised by someone thoroly conversant with that religion.

PARTICULAR APPLICATIONS

I. *Crimes against the law:*

These shall never be presented in such a way as to throw sympathy with the crime as against law and justice or to inspire others with a desire for imitation:

The treatment of crimes against the law must not:

a. Teach methods of crime.

b. Inspire potential criminals with a desire for imitation.

c. Make criminals seem heroic and justified.

1. MURDER
    a. *The technique of murder* must be presented in a way that will *not* inspire imitation.
    b. *Brutal killings* are not to be presented in detail.
    c. *Revenge* in modern times shall not be justified. In lands and ages of less developed civilization and moral principles, revenge may sometimes be presented. This would be the case especially in places where no law exists to cover the crime because of which revenge is committed.
2. METHODS OF CRIME shall not be explicitly presented.
    a. *Theft, robbery, safe-cracking,* and *dynamiting* of trains, mines, buildings,etc., should not be detailed in method.
    b. *Arson* must be subject to the same safeguards.
    c. *The use of firearms* should be restricted to essentials.
    d. *Methods of smuggling* should not be presented.
3. ILLEGAL DRUG TRAFFIC must never be presented.
    Because of its evil consequences, the drug traffic should never be presented in any form. The existence of the trade should not be brought to the attention of audiences.
4. THE USE OF LIQUOR in American life, when not required by the plot or for proper characterization, should not be shown.
    The use of liquor should never be *excessively* presented even in picturing countries where its use is legal. In scenes from American life, the necessities of plot and proper characterization alone justify its use. And in this case, it should be shown with moderation.

II. *Sex*

The sanctity of the institution of marriage and the home shall be upheld. Pictures shall not infer that low forms of sex relationship are the accepted or common thing.

1. ADULTERY, sometimes necessary plot material, must not be explicitly treated, or justified, or presented attractively. Out of regard for the sanctity of marriage and the home, the *triangle,* that is, the love of a third party for one already married, needs careful handling. The treatment should not throw sympathy against marriage as an institution.
2. SCENES OF PASSION must be treated with an honest acknowledgment of human nature and its normal reactions. Many scenes cannot be presented without arousing dangerous emotions on the part of the immature, the young or the criminal classes.
    a. They should not be introduced when not essential to the plot.

  b. Excessive and lustful kissing, lustful embraces, suggestive postures and gestures, are not to be shown.
  c. In general, passion should be so treated that these scenes do
   not stimulate the lower and baser element.
 3. SEDUCTION OR RAPE
  a. They should never be more than suggested, and only when
   essential for the plot, and even then never shown by explicit
   method.
  b. They are never the proper subject for comedy.
 4. SEX PERVERSION or any inference to it is forbidden.
 5. WHITE SLAVERY shall not be treated.
 6. MISCEGENATION (sex relationship between the white and black
  races) is forbidden.
 7. SEX HYGIENE AND VENEREAL DISEASES are not subjects for motion
  pictures.
 8. SCENES OF ACTUAL CHILDBIRTH, in fact or in silhouette, are never
  to be presented.
 9. CHILDREN'S SEX ORGANS are never to be exposed. . . .

■ ■ ■ ■

THE LEGION OF DECENCY CAMPAIGN (1937), Olga J. Martin

Over four years elapsed between the industry's acceptance of the Code
(31 March 1930) and the appointment of Joseph Breen (12 July 1934) to
administer the Production Code Administration (at which time the Code
became a functioning document). Between these two dates came a
concerted campaign by the Catholic Legion of Decency against movie
immorality. Olga Martin's book, *Hollywood's Movie Commandments*,
was another authorized history of "Hays Office" activities, published
in 1937 more as pro-industry publicity than as a disinterested chronicle
of events. This chapter from the book reveals the way the "Hays Office"
perceived the Legion of Decency Campaign.

In October, 1933, the first impetus was given to the birth of the Legion
of Decency. The Most Rev. Amleto Giovanni Cicognani, Apostolic Delegate before the Charities Convention in New York, Archbishop of Laod-

 "The Legion of Decency Campaign" is from *Hollywood's Movie Commandments*,
by Olga J. Martin (H. W. Wilson, 1937).

icea in Phrygia, may be credited with having put the torch of religious fervor to the dry tinder of public disgust. The fire spread rapidly.

Hardly a month passed before an Episcopal Committee on Motion Pictures was appointed by the American Bishops at their annual meeting in Cincinnati of November, 1933. This Committee was composed of the Most Rev. John T. McNicholas, O.P., Archbishop of Cincinnati, Ohio (Chairman); The Most Rev. John J. Cantwell, Archbishop of Los Angeles, Calif.; the Most Rev. John F. Noll, Bishop of Fort Wayne, Ind.; and the Most Rev. Hugh C. Boyle, Bishop of Pittsburgh, Pa. That fall and winter the plans for a comprehensive campaign were carefully and painstakingly worked out. In April, 1934, this Committee declared war on the films thru the Legion of Decency, with its headquarters in New York City.

The far-reaching effect of the Legion of Decency boycott in which Protestant and Jewish groups joined, may be traced in the press reports of those days:

CATHOLIC BOYCOTT

CHICAGO DAILY TRIBUNE, June 5, 1934. "Urging that 'some censorship of morals' be put upon the motion picture industry, Cardinal Mundelein formally brought the Chicago Diocese yesterday into the nation-wide fight now being waged by the Catholic Church against indecent films coming out of Hollywood."

PROTESTANTS JOIN

CHICAGO DAILY TRIBUNE, June 6, 1934. "Protestant leaders praised the leadership taken by Cardinal Mundelein. . . . They announced their delight in the broad form of the Catholic campaign in which, they said, Protestants, Catholics and Jews will be able to join wholeheartedly. . . ."

The accuracy of the prediction of united action may be judged by the press notices of the following month.

The Catholic drive had manifested itself in fifty dioceses. Some estimates placed the number who had signed the pledge of the Legion of Decency (which was a pledge to boycott offensive films) at 2,000,000, with every likelihood of a 5,000,000 total within a short time (NOTE: the total eventually reached 11,000,000 at the height of the campaign). In Massachusetts, plans for a specific boycott of indecent pictures by cooperation of 1,695,000 Catholics received the approval of the Archbishop of Boston, William Cardinal O'Connell. The Dallas Diocese joined the fight. Fifteen thousand members of the Holy Name Society pledged their support in San Pedro, Calif.

Dr. Harold G. Campbell, Superintendent of City Schools of New York City, ordered an immediate investigation of pictures shown to school children. Dr. M. E. Dodd, President of the Southern Baptist Convention, called upon 12,000 Baptist ministers to join the crusade. The committee of ten of the Chicago Church Foundation, a Protestant group, pledged cooperation. Support was ordered by the United Presbyterian Assembly, the Massachusetts Civic League, the Christian Endeavor Union, the Oregon Methodist Conference, and the National Conference of Jews and Christians.

The Legion of Decency boycott exerted an irresistible economic pressure. This pressure came at a time when the movie industry was practically bankrupt; when each ticket at the box-office counted in the balance. Millions of movie-goers no longer appeared at theatre box-offices, and thus it came about that the producers, again for economic reasons, were ready to accept the motion picture Production Code set up for the industry in 1930.

Things began to happen in Hollywood with amazing suddenness. On July 12, 1934, Will H. Hays and the Board of Directors of the Association of Motion Picture Producers, Inc., at Hollywood, concluded action amending and amplifying the Production Code Administration. The Production Code Administration came into vital being with a fighting Irishman, Joseph I. Breen, at its head. What his appointment meant may be gathered from press comments:

A FIGHTING IRISHMAN COMES TO HOLLYWOOD

TERRE HAUTE (Indiana) STAR, July 17, 1934. "Something is being done about it now out in Hollywood, be sure of that. Joe Breen, the two-fisted assistant to Mr. Hays, once of the Philadelphia *North American,* and at heart a good newspaper man, now has his coat off and what he is saying about what is fit and what is unfit for the screen carries a terrific punch to the cowering, found-out direction and script-writing ilk. For years they have been scoffing at the Hays rule. . . . Mr. Breen has been appointed umpire of the movies, assigned to preview every picture and to order the product cut, remade, or discarded. He will be guided by a code that for four years has been available to producers and accepted by them, but latterly regarded by many directors as irksome and in the way of progress and profit. . . . Smut, glossed vice, faked romance, unhealthy sex appeal, will not pass Joe Breen if he can spot them. He is that kind of an editor."

Under the new arrangement, the presidents of all the producing companies accepted full responsibility for pictures exhibited, and no company was to exhibit any picture not approved by the Production Code Administration, such approval being printed on the film.

The Producer Appeals Board was abolished. The notice of this change appeared in the trade paper *Variety* (Hollywood) on June 15, 1934:

"Producers' Appeals Board is abolished. Joe Breen is supreme pontiff of picture morals from now on. Only appeal from Breen ruling is to the Hays directorate in New York.

"This is the unanimous dictum of the major companies after long sessions in the Hays office deliberating over means to satisfy church pressure.

". . . Switch of all moral problems from the West to the East is revealed to have been motivated by an understanding that the crusaders have lost patience with the studio heads, but still believe in the judgment and good intentions of the Eastern executives. Inference is also being broadly drawn that there will be comparatively few reversals of Breen's future judgment. Haysites tonight describe Breen as in a position where his word from now on will be the industry's law. . . ."

Said Mr. Hays, as this new control emerged out of the war waged on the films:

"It is recognized that the solution of the problem of the right kind of screen entertainment rests solely with the quality of the product and these strengthened arrangements are directed to discharging that responsibility more effectively."

With all of these radical changes going into effect, the Bishops decided to give the industry one more chance to fulfill its promises of Code enforcement, and, pending further action by the Hays office, called off the boycott on June 21, 1934, just two and one-half months after it went into effect.

In conference with the Bishops were Mr. Breen and Mr. Martin Quigley who convinced the Episcopal Committee, under the leadership of Bishop McNicholas that the new machinery for control would function effectively. The Committee expressed its confidence, thru the press, in these words:

"The Episcopal Committee views with favor the renewed efforts of the organized industry to discharge its responsibility of issuing only such motion pictures as may conform with reasonable moral standards. The Committee believes that the Production Code, if given enforcement, will materially and constructively influence the character of screen entertainment. Hence it is disposed to render encouragement and cooperation to these efforts which it hopes will achieve the promised results."—*Los Angeles Times,* June 22, 1934

The Protestant groups, too, expressed their willingness to give Mr. Breen a chance to show what he could do. Dr. Worth M. Tippy, Secretary of the Church and Social Service Department of the Federal Council of the Churches of Christ in America stated in a press comment:

"The future of this decency drive, so far as Protestants are concerned, can be determined only by what takes place at Hollywood. If Mr. Breen succeeds and the producers support him, and what is done is not a temporary effect, there will be no more drastic action. We would like to see Mr. Breen succeed."—Hollywood *Citizen-News,* July 26, 1934.

The Federal Council expressed confidence in Breen's ability to raise film standards to the level demanded by the churches.

This time there was no back-sliding by the industry. A slip at that time would have meant its annihilation. That the efforts of Joseph I. Breen exceeded the hopes of everyone concerned, and that the Production Code was an effective instrument, is markedly apparent from a statement appearing in *Harrison's Reports* (a trade paper devoted to the interests of exhibitors), on December 15, 1934 by Pete Harrison known in the industry as one of its most outspoken gentlemen. Said Mr. Harrison:

"In the last few months the moral tone of pictures has improved to an almost unbelievable degree. Along with the moral tone, *there has been a great improvement also in their entertainment values.*

"The person who is responsible for this improvement is none other than Joseph I. Breen, the unofficial representative of the self-regulated censorship system which has been adopted by the producers as the result of the pressure brought on the industry by the Legion of Decency. The obscenity that was found in four out of five pictures before last June has disappeared in the pictures that have been released since August.

". . . Since July 15th he has approved 217 pictures; 176 of these were passed by the censorship boards throughout the country without eliminations. Compare this record with the record prior to July of this year and you will realize the improvement that has been made in the moral tone of the pictures in so short a time."

At this point it is interesting to observe that there were no reversals of Mr. Breen's decision by the Board of Directors in New York on the few occasions in which an appeal from the Code ruling was made. It is also of interest to observe that the entertainment value of pictures has increased with the continued enforcement of the Production Code.

Further evidence of complete satisfaction with the work of the Production Code Administration appeared in the *Brooklyn Tablet* of March 16, 1935 indicating that the good work was continuing. In this statement issued by the Most Reverend John T. McNicholas, the Episcopal Committee on Motion Pictures took the opportunity to express its gratification for the marked improvement in films, and to encourage all those who realize the menace of immoral films to continue their vigilance so that the ground gained might not be lost.

The final acclaim, however, came thru the Encyclical on Motion Pictures, published in the *Los Angeles Times* on July 3, 1936, in which recognition of the success of the Legion of Decency campaign was expressed by Pope Pius XI in these words:

> "It is an exceedingly great comfort to us to note the outstanding success of the crusade. Because of your vigilance and because of the pressure which has been brought to bear by public opinion, the motion picture has shown improvement from the moral standpoint; crime and vice are portrayed less frequently; sin no longer is so openly approved or acclaimed; false ideals of life no longer are presented in so flagrant a manner to the impressionable minds of youth.
>
> ". . . In particular, you, venerable brethren of the United States, will be able to insist with justice that the industry in your country has recognized and accepted its responsibility before society."

The *Motion Picture Herald* recorded in an editorial by Terry Ramsaye the significance of the Encyclical to the motion picture industry, in its issue of July 11, 1936. He says:

> "Signal success in the greatest of the social adjustments of the motion picture, achieved for it by the American industry in its adoption of and operation under the Production Code, is recorded in terms destined to become historic in the encyclical letter discussing the screen by Pope Pius XI.
>
> "The encyclical was given to the press of the world from Rome July 2, and is presented in full in its official English translation in this issue of *Motion Picture Herald*. . . .
>
> "Within the motion picture industry, the encyclical is to be seen as of significant recognition, and approval, of the Production Code adopted in March of 1930, concerning which the letter observes: 'It is promised in this agreement that no film which lowers the moral standard of spectators, which casts discredit on natural or human law or arouses sympathy for their violation will be produced.'
>
> "And this judged by His Holiness as 'a wise and spontaneously taken decision'. . .
>
> "In substance the organized American industry's system of operation under the Production Code is held before the world by Pope Pius as an example for study and guidance.
>
> "It is not, however, to be gathered that there is any declaration of a state of perfection, and the encyclical sets forth to the churchmen of the world, including the American Bishops first addressed, the importance of an unrelenting vigilance against invasions of the purposes embodied in the Code, and includes provisions for the expression of the moral pressures indicated. Provision for reviewing com-

mittees and the issuance of lists of approved product, in the general manner of the Legion of Decency operation, is indicated. . . .

" *'Vigilant care'* is the title of and are among the most emphatic words of the encyclical."

The plea for "Vigilant care" is not voiced alone by the Catholic groups. The Protestant groups, too, demand continued vigilance. While they have confidence in the Hays Office, they have no illusions regarding the ability of that organization to enforce its self-regulatory measures unaided by forceful public opinion. As Dr. Fred Eastman states in his pamphlet:[1]

"How long the present trend in pictures will last, no one knows— probably only so long as public pressure lasts. The producers have not been converted. . . . When public pressure lets up they may again flood their theaters with pictures that harm character."

Dr. Eastman then goes on to suggest a program which will assure the continuance of better pictures for the future. In this connection he says:

". . . The effectiveness and permanence of Mr. Breen's office depend upon public support. . . . It is equally essential that the public be educated concerning the whole history and process of motion pictures and their social effects."

Here are some of the main points advocated by the Protestant groups:

1) Join the Legion of Decency by signing its pledge. Boycott bad pictures and continue to support the good ones.
2) Help your children select the pictures they see.
3) Cooperate with others throughout the country who are working in this cause.
4) Educate your community by providing for the holding of forums and discussions in civic and religious organizations.

The *Christian Century* and the Motion Picture Research Council also advocate federal control of motion picture distribution and booking, as an objective to insure better pictures. In regard to this question, Dr. Worth M. Tippy of the Federal Council of the Churches of Christ in America, made the statement, according to press reports, that the Federal Council would conduct no boycotts or censorships "except against unsatisfactory films." Dr. Tippy added, however, that "if this effort to clean up the screen proves futile, the industry can count upon a tremendous move for federal control which inevitably will include some form of censorship." . . .

1. *Better Motion Pictures,* by Fred Eastman and Edward Ouellette (Pilgrim Press, 1936, Boston).

■ ■ ■ ■

DECENCY IN MOTION PICTURES (1937), Martin Quigley

Martin Quigley was one of the key figures in shaping and enforcing the Production Code. The publisher of the *Motion Picture Herald*, Quigley was one of the original authors of the Code. A devout Catholic, he also served as the industry's troubleshooter during the Legion of Decency campaign—assuring the Legion that the industry was sincere about reforming its fare and, in turn, pressuring the industry to appoint someone tough like Joseph Breen to administer the Code. In later years, Quigley became increasingly irritated by the steady loosening of the Code's moral restrictions, yet it was Quigley who apparently helped the controversial *Lolita* get its Code Seal in 1961 (see Jack Vizzard's *See No Evil*). His book, *Decency in Motion Pictures*, was published in 1937, the same year as Olga Martin's, and, given Quigley's timely title, it was also intended for the same public-relations purposes as Ms. Martin's. These passages reveal Quigley's general (and highly questionable) views of art as well as his specific condemnations of several previous Hollywood films. Interestingly, his condemnations seem strikingly similar in style and tone to those of Ellis Paxson Oberholtzer in that book of fifteen years earlier (see pages 194–200). Oberholtzer's capsule reviews of offending films may well have served as Quigley's model.

THE FUNCTION OF ART

The function of art is to ennoble. Art is as much a servant and tool of civilization as science. Its utility, especially to youth, is as vicarious experience, food for imaginative stimulus—and who will argue for the education of youth by evil adventure and stimulus, no matter how real in fact or realistic in artistic representation?

One may reiterate here the responsibility of the artist to his function of selection in the interpretive recording of experience. There is, it is to be feared, much confusion between literalism and the proper realism of art. For instance, to select an example neutral and remote, the Congressional Record is literal, realistic, too, but it is neither literature nor art. Art was born of recording, but it grew great and powerful by selection of what is recorded. The argument for complete, literal recording, if that is what is meant by Mr. James Joyce and Mr. Ernest Hemingway, must

Decency in Motion Pictures, by Martin Quigley, was published by Macmillan in 1937 and reissued by Ozer in 1971.

presume a discriminatory approach by the audience that is not to be presumed of the commonality.

If selectivity is not to obtain the artist is without function.

The least that may be expected of art is that it shall not debase. It may serve as relaxation and diversion if it is only negative in its moral effect, but its higher purposes consist of the presentation and encouragement of right ideals and right conduct in life and living. This, of course, is not to be accomplished through the depiction of an unreal world of men and affairs. Good and evil may be contrasted; wrong motives as well as right motives may be presented, and there is no need of tiresome insistence that virtue is its own reward. But good and evil must not be confused; good must be presented as good and evil as evil.

There is reason and justification for the presentation of sin, crime, evil and sordidness provided that these elements are given right values in the moral scale and that their use is for legitimate dramatic purposes. *There is a grave difference between a presentation of what is wrong when the effect is only to acquaint the audience with the wrong and a presentation of wrong which encourages approval.* The over-all effect of the depiction of evil must be weighed, insuring that the end results in audience reaction will not amount to an invasion of the ideas and ideals of morality which the audience entertains.

ACCEPTED STANDARDS

There are many facts of life which simply because of their nature are unavailable for theatrical presentation. The theatre's very presentation bears to the typical patron implication of acceptance. There are realistic words of ancient lineage which are not put into dictionaries for general circulation because these words cannot be given institutional acceptance. This is not based on any fanciful notion that by ignoring facts their reality is destroyed or their influence conquered. Rather it is because their presentation and discussion serve not to destroy but to encourage; not to safeguard an audience but rather to callous its sensibilities, thus opening the door to tolerance and eventual acceptance. Such is the nature of man, as the accumulated wisdom of centuries amply attests.

Those who proclaim for realism ought, indeed, be realistic in their recognition of these facts. It is naive and unreal to deny that many things which the theatre is capable of presenting cause audience reaction which creates ideas and stimulates desires that tend toward a violation of traditional standards of morality.

There is a parallel between the political idea of state deification and the thesis of art for art's sake. The state's true function is to be servant to the citizenry; art's true function is to be servant to mankind. Those who assert that art has privileges and prerogatives which may be indulged in, even to the moral and spiritual injury of the race, are proclaiming a theory which is identical in essence with that which says that the citizen should serve the state and not that the state should serve the citizen. Both are abominable.

It is freely acknowledged and, in fact, insisted upon that all is chaos and confusion in theatrical entertainment and elsewhere if the traditional standards of morality are denied and rejected. The viewpoint expressed in these notes, as previously indicated, is predicated on an acceptance of these standards. It is not the present purpose to account for these standards or to defend them. There are and must be rules to every game and these are the rules in the game of life which since the dawn of civilization —and still—have the acceptance of an overwhelming proportion of mankind. They are recognized by mankind everywhere in the familiar words of the Ten Commandments. The experience of the race and the wisdom of the ages have led to no responsible rejection. These rules are insurmountable injunctions which cannot be successfully circumvented by anyone who would absorb in the theatres the concentrated attention of a vast public, thereby conveying to this public ideas and ideals which influence their habits of thought and conduct. . . .

PICTURES TYPICAL OF WRONG STANDARDS

The following are released pictures which are held to be typical of wrong standards in motion picture entertainment:

THE AFFAIRS OF CELLINI (The Firebrand). This production presents the amatory exploits of an historical character. It conveys no real knowledge of the character nor of the times in which he lived. The historical research involved apparently availed itself only of the costumes and physical appointments of the period. To these is added a story which recites the feminine conquests of the attractive and debonair leading character. The presentation serves to condone moral laxity and to encourage imitation. It lies distinctly outside the bounds of material suitable for mass entertainment. *Released August, 1934*

BACK STREET. A story which sympathetically portrays the character of a kept woman. It condones and justifies adultery. The influence is to incline an audience in favor of the mistress, conveying an approval of extramarital relationship, thereby reflecting adversely on the institution of marriage and belittling its obligations. The story makes an emotional appeal for audience acceptance of a false moral standard. *Released September, 1932.*

DESIGN FOR LIVING. A partial cleansing for the screen of a stage story notorious for its wealth and variety of moral code infractions. Even in its comparatively refined status it is an evil influence because it presents conduct on the part of attractive and likeable people which indicates denial and contempt of traditional moral standards, presenting, charmingly, wrong conduct as if it were right conduct. *Released December, 1933.*

FREAKS. This picture is selected for mention not because it may be said definitely to be in violation of one or more principles of morality but rather because it represents a type that provokes apprehension. It is a story concerned with the life and loves of circus freaks and because of the human abnormalities involved its unwholesome shockery creates morbid audience reactions. It is a skillfully presented production but of a character which in consideration of the susceptibilities of mass audiences should be avoided. Represented in this picture and appearing in some degree in many others is the horror element—this growing out of the procedure of the melodramatic mystery play. This element may not be considered as unreservedly objectionable but its use must be governed by reasonable judgment as to the character of the material, the degree of detail and emphasis given to it and a commonsense understanding of mass audience psychology. *Released February, 1932.*

I'M NO ANGEL. A vehicle for a notorious characterization of a scarlet woman whose amatory instincts are confined exclusively to the physical. There is no more pretense here of romance than on a stud-farm. The designed atmosphere is suggestive and bawdy. It is not without humor but the humor partakes of the burlesque theatre. Considered as entertainment for the mass theatre audience of the United States it is vulgar and degrading. It is morally objectionable because it is generally of low moral tone and because specifically its sportive wise-cracking tends to create tolerance if not acceptance of things essentially evil. *Released October, 1933.*

QUEEN CHRISTINA. A re-writing of history that transcends dramatic license, presenting among other objectionable incidents a bedroom sequence which registers with voluminous and unnecessary detail the fact of a sex affair. The sequence is emphasized and dwelt upon beyond all purposes legitimate to the telling of the story, thereby assuming a pornographic character. Its portrayal of the queen is dangerous because queens have authority, acceptance. *Released February, 1934.*

SCARFACE. A gangster picture which presents heroically the exploits of a criminal, showing him as rich, courageous and cunning against contrasting characteristics on the part of the guardians of the law. It glorifies crime, presents methods of crime and familiarizes the audience with them. Even though the criminal is brought to justice in the final scenes it is an influence against law and order and an incitement to impressionable minds to follow vicious practices. *Released March, 1932.*

THE SIGN OF THE CROSS. A conspicuous incident is a dance scene of a suggestive, erotic character. It is played principally by two persons, a lewd pagan dancer and an innocent Christian girl. The apparent dramatic intention is to contrast the evil character of the dancer and the innocence of the girl. The scene is objectionable because it transgresses the limits of legitimate dramatic requirements and becomes an incident liable to an evil audience effect. *Released December, 1932.*

■ ■ ■ ■

CODE SEAL AND LETTER, Production Code Administration

DEAR MR. ――――:

The attached certificate of approval is issued upon the condition that its acceptance by you, binds you, as producer and/or your distributor, and any and all other agents of yours; and your assigns, and successors, to the following terms and conditions:

(1) That all prints of the above picture to be released with the above title, shall be exact copies of the picture, hereby approved; and that no scene shall be added or removed from such picture, without the written approval of the Production Code Administration, except when required by any duly constituted public official or public authority, nor shall the title be changed without the written approval of this Association; and

(2) That all applicable regulations and penalties, promulgated by the Board of Directors of the Motion Picture Producers and Distributors of America, Inc., [now the Motion Picture Association] relative to the issuance and display of the seal of the Production Code Administration, are and shall remain in full force as to the certificate issued herewith; and

(3) That any and all advertising and publicity matter, including material for press books, still photographs, poster and lobby card designs, and trailers, used in any manner in connection with the advertising and exploitation of this picture, shall be submitted for approval to the Advertising Council of the Motion Picture Producers and Distributors of America, Inc., [now the Motion Picture Association] and that only such advertising or publicity material or trailers, approved by such Council shall be used in advertising and exploiting the picture hereby approved; and

(4) That, in addition to any other applicable penalties, the Production

Code Administration reserves the right to void this Certificate, at any time hereafter, for any violation of the conditions set forth herein and/or of the violation of any of the rules and regulations promulgated by the Board of Directors of the Motion Picture Producers and Distributors of America, Inc. [now the Motion Picture Association]. When any Certificate is voided, such Certificate shall be surrendered to the Production Code Administration immediately upon request, and the Seal removed from all prints within seven (7) days thereafter; but the voiding of the Certificate shall not relieve the Producer, who has violated the rules and regulations, from any other applicable penalties that may be imposed for their violation.

PRODUCTION CODE ADMINISTRATION
By: ———

■ ■ ■ ■

OUR MOVIE MADE CHILDREN (1933), Henry James Forman

In 1928, the Motion Picture Council, a group hostile to the movies who wished to demonstrate the ill effects of films on children and adolescents, received a $200,000 grant from the Payne Fund to prepare a series of studies of this topic. Under the direction of Professor W. W. Charters of Ohio State University the studies were prepared by professional social scientists, psychologists, and educators from some of the country's leading universities. The titles in the series were

Motion Pictures and Youth, by Charters
Movies and Conduct, by Herbert Blumer
Movies, Delinquency, and Crime, by Blumer and Philip M. Hauser
Children's Attendance at Motion Pictures, by Edgar Dale
The Content of Motion Pictures, by Dale
How to Appreciate Motion Pictures, by Dale
The Emotional Responses of Children to the Motion Picture Situation,
    by Wendell S. Dysinger and Christian A. Ruckmick
Getting Ideas from the Movies, by Perry W. Holaday and George D.
    Stoddard
Motion Pictures and Standards of Morality, by Charles C. Peters
Motion Pictures and the Social Attitudes of Children, by Ruth Peterson
    and L. I. Thurstone
Children's Sleep, by Samuel Renshaw, Vernon L. Miller, and Dorothy
    P. Marquis

The Social Conduct and Attitudes of Movies Fans, by Frank K. Shuttleworth and Mark A. May

Although several of these studies suffered from severe scientific deficiencies
(some of the titles forecast the results), the most widely read and controversial book in the series was the popularized summary of all of them,
Our Movie Made Children, by Henry James Forman. Forman's summary
was denounced as inflammatory and unscientific, but the idea of producing such a popularized account of these academic studies had been built
into the grant from the beginning, and Forman's book bears the approval
of Charters himself in its introduction. These passages from the 1933
book (the first of the series to appear in print) reveal not only Forman's
rhetoric but the attitudes of those Americans who assumed the worst
about the emotional effects of the movie art.

WHAT DO THEY SEE?

"Let's go to the movies."

"All right, let's. What shall we see?"

"I don't know, but there's a new show at the Palace and the poster is
a honey."

Jack, schoolmate and friend of your daughter Joan, has come on
pleasure bent. They are not exactly sure what they are going to see at
the movies, because titles are so numerous as to be confusing. But Jack
has seen what he calls a honey of a poster, which is almost certain to be a
highly colored lithograph of a man embracing and kissing a girl. As to
what the movie is about, neither of the children has any clear notion,
but the chances are seventy-five in a hundred that it will deal with love,
sex or crime.

Both Jack and Joan are lovely children, for are they not yours and
your neighbors? You want them to enjoy themselves, and doubtless they
will enjoy themselves, but there may be just a faint uneasiness in your
mind. Those movies! You cannot help wondering whether they are wholly
good or wholly profitable for the young people. Of course, you yourself
go to the movies, but then you are a mature adult and understand that
much of the stuff is just so much hokum. It is different with the children,
so eager and so naïve, so inexperienced in life. Many movies, we know, are
based upon stage plays. It never occurs to us to let our children see every
play presented, but somehow it seems different with the screen. These
movies must fill their heads with all sorts of queer ideas.

Our Movie Made Children, by Henry James Forman, was published by Macmillan
in 1933.

Right. They do. And so that you and I, and all of us, may clarify our minds of precisely that vagueness as to what the run of movies contain and deal with, certain investigators went to considerable pains to analyze, classify and sort out the contents of the vast and ceaseless output of Hollywood. It was no easy job. Dr. Edgar Dale undertook this task of sorting out, classifying and analyzing some 1500 movies and their contents. Without going into the details of laboratory technique, it will suffice to say that he took 500 pictures, output of each of the years 1920, 1925, and 1930. This included all the feature pictures produced by the leading companies in those years and, as we can readily see, gave him large samples to work with. With the utmost care he first of all classified them under headings running something like this: crime, sex, love, mystery, war, history, children, travel and geography, animals, comedy and social problems. Considerable diversity in these headings, as we see. What he found was that out of 500 pictures in 1920, eighty-two per cent dealt with the three major themes of crime, sex and love; in 1925, seventy-nine per cents were preoccupied with these themes, and in 1930, seventy-two per cent. In that year, however, mystery and war pictures, which often included crime, or, at all events, violence, rose from small figures to nine per cent, which goes to swell the above totals. In other words, somewhere between seventy-five and eighty per cent of all pictures dealt with love, sex, crime or mystery films.

That, in any case, should clear our minds as to what Jack and Joan are likely to see at the pictures. The chances are three out of four that every time they go to the movies they will see some story unfolding a plot dealing with the three major preoccupations—love, sex or crime. This probably explains why foreigners viewing this particular mirror of American life, so frequently conclude that we must be a highly erotic and criminal nation.

Let us for one moment think what all this means in terms of children. Granting, as we have found, that a child attends at least one picture program a week, or fifty-two a year, it means that at least thirty-nine of the feature pictures he sees will have for their themes crime, sex and love—the inescapable themes. But what is their effect upon young boys and girls? Imagine a visitor from another planet arriving for a survey of our manner of life, and finding that this is what we allow them, apparently without any effective objection on our part, to feast their eyes and minds upon week in, week out, through the years. Could he conclude otherwise than that we have fallen into a way of exaggerating those themes out of all proportion?

The classification "love" includes romantic love stories. Many of these are beautiful; some of them, clearly, are not meant for children; others, however, are quite harmless, even charming. In 1920, Dr. Dale finds, about forty-five per cent of all pictures could be classified under love. By 1925 this class of pictures had fallen to thirty-three per cent; by 1930 it was only thirty per cent. Primarily this shift was made from what is called straight love pictures to comedies, crime and sex pictures. As to children's pictures, those, that is, especially designed for children or in which children are the central characters, there were only four in 1925, and only one out of 500 in 1930. If children go to the movies they must see the regular run-of-the-mill output of love, sex and crime. . . .

We shall therefore glance a little more closely at the content of the average motion picture. Bearing in mind that in, say, 1930 there were among 500 pictures 137 dealing with crime and, in addition, 43 dealing with mystery and war, we arrive at the conclusion that thirty-six per cent of all the pictures were loaded with scenes of either crime or violence. Now, let us face the problem squarely. Do we mean to imply that crime is never to figure on the screen at all? Dr. Dale quotes Mr. Will Hays, as saying:

"The proper treatment of crime as a social fact or as a dramatic motive is the inalienable right of a free press, of free speech and of an unshackled stage or screen."

With this opinion there is no quarrel whatever. The key to the situation, however, lies in his second word—"proper." That crime is a social fact in this country, and in virtually all countries, there is no doubt. That it is emphasized on the screen out of all proportion to its place in the national life is equally clear of doubt, indeed, glaringly obvious. Were crime to receive similar emphasis in the life of any one of us as individuals, we should properly expect to be either in jail or in an insane asylum. Dr. Dale puts it conservatively when he says that this preoccupation with crime "robs the screen of pictures of beauty, idealism and imaginative charm." A screen on which nearly 400 out of 500 pictures are occupied with love, sex and crime is barren of so much else that would serve as inspiration and enlightenment in life, that the very inquiry upon which this volume is based is a sign of the uneasiness felt by all of us. Practically it is a sign of the alarm we feel that our children should be exposed to a screen product of which between forty and fifty per cent is occupied with crime and sex.

No one can intelligently defend the complete exclusion of the fundamental and adequate treatment of crime from the screen. But to give crime and sex so large a representation in the motion picture is surely to threaten the morals and characters of our children and youth. Now, as has already been foreshadowed and as we shall presently see in greater detail, pictures leave some impress upon the mind of every individual. If we believe that good pictures have a beneficent effect, it is clearly useless to say my child is proof against adverse influence, or that this crime picture will not count, or that that gangster picture or sex picture will make no impression upon any particular child or some especially favored boy or girl. In any such optimistic temporizing psychology is dead against us. As the late William James, in his book, *Psychology*, puts it:

"The drunken Rip Van Winkle, in Jefferson's play, excuses himself for every fresh dereliction by saying, 'I won't count this time!' Well! he may not count it, and a kind Heaven may not count it; but it is being counted none the less. Down among his nerve-cells and fibres the molecules are counting it, registering and storing it up to be used against him when the next temptation comes."

We certainly hope that the good influences count. Can anyone, then, conceivably imagine that the constant iteration of the crime theme in motion pictures, which during 1929 were attended weekly by 11,000,000 children of thirteen years of age or under, will in the slightest degree help the solution of the crime problem? Some producers, as we know, maintain that pictures of crime will lessen crime, and possibly for that reason produce so many pictures of crime. The film critic of *The Nation*, however, Alexander Bakshy, disagrees with them. Recently he wrote:

"Gangsters and racketeers play so prominent a part in the American life of today that it would be little short of a miracle if their exploits were ignored by the movies. Nor are they. In fact, the number of films dealing with the underworld and its criminal activities is altogether too great."

"Too great"—let us see. In 115 pictures taken at random from recent productions and analyzed by Dr. Dale, there are 59 in which murders and homicides are either attempted or committed. Seventy-one deaths by violence actually occur in fifty-four of the pictures. The hero, being a hero, is responsible for only twenty-one per cent of them; forty per cent fall to the villain's share, and the rest are variously distributed. The Bureau of Child Research of the University of Kansas not long ago presented a questionnaire to children between the ages of nine and thirteen, as to why, if for any reason, they dislike motion pictures. Following are brief summaries made by Dale of some of their answers, showing that even young children feel the excessive and inartistic overloading of pictures with crime:

Nine-year-old boys: Killing—don't like to see people killed. Don't like to look at them.

Nine-year-old girls: Danger and killing. Looks "offel." Not good for your mind. Scares me. I pity the people.

Ten-year-old boys: Killing—makes you too excited. Makes me sad. Wild west not good.

Ten-year-old girls: Killing—hate to see people killed. Don't like it. Makes me feel it's true. Scary. Bloody ones make me sick. Show you how to kill. Sad.

Eleven-year-old boys: Killing makes you have bad habits. Don't like blood. Like to laugh.

Eleven-year-old girls: Shooting and killing bad. Makes me scared to go anywhere after night. Hard on the eyes and mind. Too tiresome. Too exciting. Hate to see people suffer. Not good for children.

Twelve-year-old boys: Killing reacts on the nervous system too much. Too sad.

Twelve-year-old girls: Shooting and killing makes me sick. It looks so awful to see people killed, and do not think it is right. Scares me. Not interested. Not good for children.

Thirteen-year-old boys: Too much killing—learn to do wrong things. Learn you to do stealing.

Killing and killing and more killing—that is the impression left upon these children. Their nerves ravaged and their nascent consciousness of the glorious new world into which they are being initiated marred and shocked by foolishly excessive violence. Of course, these are other people's children, but to other people our Jack and Joan are also other people's children. In his analysis of 115 pictures to determine the most frequent crime committed in them (he did not include bad art) Dr. Dale arrived at some fascinating figures. They are, as these Kansas children indicate, "bloody," "gory," "offel."

The heroes, those handsome and debonair heroes of the screen, are alone responsible for thirteen good sound murders; the villains and villainesses for thirty. Heroines who, according to the axioms of the trade, must not be robbed of sympathy, are still kept comparatively unstained, with only one murder to their credit in the lot. Altogether some fifty-four murders are committed, to say nothing of fifty-nine cases of mere assault and battery. Thirty-six hold-ups are portrayed and twenty-one kidnappings, numerous other crimes scattering. The score, on the whole, is remarkable; forty-three crimes are attempted, and 406 crimes are actually committed, a total of 449. All in 115 pictures! When we consider the universality of a picture, its permeation of the entire country, its penetration into the smallest towns and even hamlets, how otherwise can this scarlet procession of criminal acts or attempts be described than as a veritable school for crime—especially to certain types of boys and girls?

Immediately someone calls me to task in rebuttal. Is not the criminal portrayed as unattractive, and does he not therefore serve as a horrible example to the youth of the land? Frequently he is in effect so portrayed. But not always. . . .

With the idea that screen criminals are alleged to present "horrible examples" to the young spectator, Dr. Dale asked this question of the movies: What are the consequences of the criminal's acts to the criminal himself? A detailed analysis of forty pictures, in which no less than fifty-seven criminals committed sixty-two crimes, gave him the answer:

Three of the fifty-seven criminals were arrested and held; four were arrested but released; another four, after being arrested, escaped; seven were arrested and their punishment was implied. In one group of five, three were arrested, one gave himself up, another's arrest was allowed to be inferred and all were legally punished. Twenty-four criminals were punished by what may be described as extra-legal methods—by their own henchmen, other gangsters and in a variety of ways with which the law had nothing to do. In seventeen cases the punishment was primarily accidental, and fifteen criminals went wholly unpunished. Some of the unpunished crimes were, murder by the hero, as in "Rogue Song"; kidnapping by the hero, as in "Devil May Care"; kidnapping by the villain, as in "Sea Legs"; stealing by the hero, as in "Along Came Youth"; embezzlement by the hero, as in "Six-Cylinder Love"; embezzlement by the heroine, as in "Miracle Woman", and house-breaking by the hero in the same picture.

The immediate answer is that the movies are, after all, a make-believe world, two-dimensional, in which the characters are not real, mere shadows on the screen. Evidence, however, will presently appear that to many young people and particularly to the younger children the world of the movies is not less real than life itself; the emotions and responses of the young to the fevered life of the screen are much the same as to those in actual life. Consider, if only one-fifth of the criminals in motion pictures are shown as receiving legal punishment and many going scot-free, is there any doubt but that such facts are infallibly registered within the youthful minds? "Surely," pleads Dr. Dale, "children and youth need assistance in interpreting such motion pictures. Many parents believe that they should not be seen at all."

For not only is this amazing and morbid preoccupation with criminals untrue to life, but the screen criminals themselves are untrue to life. They appear, as Dr. Dale points out, ready-made, with no future and almost no past. Minerva-like, they spring from the head of Jupiter, full-grown and more than fully armed. In the forty pictures analyzed in more minute detail, it was only rarely that he found the slightest indication that criminal patterns of behavior developed as a product of a long process of interaction between the individual and the successive social situations in which he lives. A feature picture seldom takes more than an hour and a quarter to show. This brevity of unfoldment makes it difficult if not impossible to portray a comprehensive development of character, with the social and psychological factors bearing upon it and making it what it is. Here of course the novel has a great advantage. European pictures, however, are frequently better than ours in this respect. Charlie Chaplin's pictures were often superior upon this point of character development.

The failure to portray the continuity of experience which produces the criminal is one of the worst features of crime pictures and goes far toward nullifying their claim, often made, of being an aid in the cure of crime. Their realism is a pseudo-realism, such as the showing of blood spurting from a wound, gun battles with the police, or the gallows upon which the criminal is to swing. The true causes of crime, such as insecurity and unemployment, disorganized homes or a chaotic social environment are almost never shown. Where they are shown, they are usually inadequate. In the film, "Scarface," for instance, the conclusion reached by the picture is that the individual citizens must see that more laws are passed and that they are obeyed, and that gangsters who are not citizens must be deported. And in this fashion the crime problem will be solved. After the examination of the plots of many crime pictures, this appears to be a fair specimen of movie criminology.

It is not, however, in the matter of crime alone that motion pictures depart from reality by exaggerated presentation and superficial solution. The range of reality to which they confine themselves is so narrow that they succeed in producing a distortion of life, its occupations and preoccupations.

"We are going to write, subject to our own limitations, about the whole of human life," is the way H. G. Wells outlines the scope of the novel. Yet, notwithstanding the almost fabulous opportunities of the motion pictures for the widest possible scope and the highest ideals, they concentrate upon a narrow range of themes, mostly trivial, in a regrettable dwelling upon crime and a preoccupation with sex that has aroused the complaint of all except possibly the least intelligent sections of the public.

Nor is that the only type of distortion. Thirty-three per cent of the heroes, for instance, and forty-four per cent of the heroines, fifty-four per cent of the villains and sixty-three per cent of the villainesses in 115 pictures—all these prominent protagonists, are either wealthy or ultra-wealthy. Of leading characters who are poor the run is only between five and fifteen per cent. The largest single class of occupations for heroes on the screen, in Dr. Dale's analysis, is "professional." The largest classification for all characters combined, including women, is "no occupation." Ninety characters in 115 pictures, the second largest group, may be labeled as "commercial." Well, commerce is, or was, one of the dominant occupations. The next two groups, however, with eighty characters in each, come under the headings of "occupation unknown" and "illegal occupation," including such trades as gangster, bootlegger, smuggler, thief, bandit, blackmailer and prostitute. The next largest grouping, "theatrical," with seventy-six representatives, may be excused on the ground that the majority of scenarists live in Hollywood. Servants and "high society" characters follow next numerically in this curiously arranged world of moviedom. All of these groupings together account for some six hundred and forty characters out of a total of eight hundred and eighty-three. The remaining quarter of this crazily assorted population is scattered among many callings, notable in that common labor is not included in them at all. A few agricultural laborers exist only because there are western ranches in the pictures. Were the population of the United States, the population of globe itself, so arranged and distributed, there would be no farming, no manufacturing, almost no industry; no vital statistics (excepting murders), almost no science, no economic problems and no economics. Such a world would speedily starve to death.

The movie world is built upon Oslerian lines. Apparently, almost every human being over forty in screenland has been chloroformed. Most of us admittedly like to see young people on stage and screen, but when sixty-seven per cent of all the characters are between the ages of nineteen and forty, the favored age being from twenty-three to twenty-six, it becomes obvious how remote all this is from life. Of those over forty, only a mere twenty-six per cent is left, and nearly half of the majority does not exceed the age of thirty.

Yet, though perilously treading on the verge of extinction in that world, where few toil and none spin, these movie characters play their rôles preponderantly in full accoutrements of formal dress. In seventy-three per cent of the films formal attire figures tremendously, and sixty-eight per cent of the men and women are doomed sooner or later to appear in it in the course of the picture. The silk hat, relic of Victorianism, is still prominent in the wardrobe of this strange people and the morning coat looms large. As to the dinner coat, it appears more essential than underclothes, so ubiquitous is it. Even a gang leader in his office cannot do without it. The very manikin in one picture plies his trade in full dress, and the tailor who employs him to extol his confections is similarly modish. And yet so many of these characters lack occupation that in a real world they might well be a concern to the police as having no visible means of support. They nearly all smoke, of course, to the number of eighty-seven and a half per cent. That one fact, one would think, is strictly true to life. As to drinking, of the 115 pictures sixty-three per cent show it and forty-three per cent exhibit intoxication. Seventy-eight per cent of all pictures contain liquor situations.

No medium has ever been blessed with a greater freedom from limitation in its choice of scenes and settings than are the movies. Yet with the entire world as their range, the interior of a bedroom figures in forty-nine of the 115 pictures, or forty-three per cent of the total, the largest single heading under a classification of "settings." The living-room and the office come next in point of frequency of settings used, but the bedroom triumphs over all.

As one sums up the people of the screen, always remembering that fine pictures have included many splendid characters, exhibiting fine manners and beautiful clothes, the total impression that survives, after reading the Dale analysis, is of a tawdry population, often absurdly over-dressed, often shady in character, much given to crime and sex, with little desire or need, apparently, of supporting themselves on this difficult planet. A people whom, for the most part, we should not want to know or live amongst. Poor be-glamoured, unprepared adolescents, however, may be moved to imitate them. . . .

THE PATH TO DELINQUENCY

We are all of us, it has been said, potential criminals, and the movies, some psycho-analysts believe, provide the spectators with opportunities for vicarious killing. It follows that the young, being more malleable, are likely to be more subject to influences than the adults. In the back of all our heads there has for some time been a vague notion that in some manner movies have a relationship to delinquency and crime. Substantial data upon this subject have been gathered and will presently, at least in part, be set forth. But even if we went no farther than this point, would it not suggest itself, in view of what has already been said, that, if the motion pictures analyzed by Dr. Dale did nothing else, they would, by sheer force of iteration, at least make young people more tolerant toward crime and delinquency? Even adults must come under such influence in view of the endless play upon these themes. The question is, then, how much effect and what manner of effect do the motion pictures have in influencing tendencies toward delinquency?

Delinquency is no new thing; it has always existed. It would be absurd to say even now that Al Capone and his organization are products solely of the movies. Numerous forces of present-day civilization play constantly upon characters and tendencies of youth, of which the movies are doubtless one, and movies are what we are here considering. What do

the movies contribute to an alarming condition? Through facility of seeing them is created a tolerance of criminal patterns and a ready stimulation to those either predisposed to delinquency and crime or to those
whose environment is too heavily weighted against them. The seed is
supplied all too lavishly to the fertile ground.

Before proceeding to the study of actual delinquency and criminals,
Professor Blumer and Mr. Hauser endeavored to find out to what extent
the usual run of boys and girls are made more tolerant of crime and
criminality by the pictures dealing in those subjects. They found that high-
school boys and girls often not only expressed sympathy for the criminal,
but that a few drew the conclusion that mere hard, plodding work is not
desirable. Sympathy for the criminal, it is the present writer's observation,
often implicit in the plots of motion pictures, is naturally quite common
among the young. To cite some of the cases listed by Blumer and Hauser,
a sixteen-year-old girl writes:

"Movies have made me less critical of criminals when I consider that
all are not as fortunate as we. Starvation has been the cause of more crime
than anything else as I see it in the movies. As a result, I believe crime
should be corrected instead of being punished for the latter encourages
more crime." "Usually," says another, "crime pictures make me feel sorry
for the criminals because the criminals probably do not get the right start."

"A lot of crime movies I have seen," declares a sixteen-year-old boy,
"made me feel favorable towards crime by depicting the criminal as a
hero who dies protecting his best friend against the police, or some movies
show them as a debonair gentleman who robs at will from the rich and
spares the poor. I have thought I would like to be a Robin Hood." "Many
times o'er," one lad poetically phrases it, "I have desired to become a
crook—and my ideal is Rob Roy, Scotland's greatest honorable crook,
with Robin Hood close behind him." Even young girls assert that motion
pictures create desires in them to become "benevolent criminals." "I have
always felt," announces a fifteen-year-old miss, "that being a character
like Robin Hood would be *the* life." . . .

Now, the boy who stated that films depicted the criminal as a hero and
made him more favorable toward crime has perhaps unwittingly put his
finger on one of the most important bearings touching this point. Herein,
to the mind of the present writer, lies much of the danger of crime movies
to the young. Life, it is true, is not geometrical in its patterns. It is difficult
to draw lines sharply and clearly between good and evil. The world, however, has agreed that for the young a certain austerity of conduct is indispensable. Otherwise, if that austerity is blurred or waived, if the child
or adolescent is treated as though he were the mature philosopher, or at

least the mature adult, there are certain to follow the irresponsibility, the bewilderment, the confusion so characteristic of our day. Many an educator has declared that the college generation of today is more responsible in various respects than were the generations of his forebears in the same institutions. But even if this be true, we must not forget that the total college population is but a small portion of the total minor movie population of 28,000,000.

"Quod licet Jovi," said the medieval schoolmen, *"non licet bovi"*—a Latin jingle, simple enough, expressing merely that what may be suitable for some is not suitable for others.

One of the easiest gateways to blurred and confused conduct is the ready assumption, frequently derived by the young from the movies, that luxury, extravagance, easy money are the inalienable right of everyone. The recent economic depression has shown us one result of an almost universally accepted concept that wealth is easily attainable. The study of the case of various young delinquents shows to what an extent the same concept derived from the movies has played havoc with the youthful lives.

"The creation of desires for riches and suggestions for easily realizing them," observe Blumer and Hauser, "may dispose many, and lead some, to criminal behavior." In his study Blumer found that among criminals, delinquents and what they call "marginal delinquents," the appeal of a life of ease plays a markedly important rôle. A fourteen-year-old boy in a Chicago area where delinquency runs high, expresses these influences briefly thus:

"No Limit" is a picture about gangsters. They always played dice and held people up and took the people's money. I felt like I was one of those and was getting some of the riches they had." Another, two years older, from the same area, declared, "Seeing gangsters having lots of money and big cars and being big shots makes a fellow want them. . . ."

These boys, however, are still only aspirants and their expression is as yet no more than a pious hope. The maturer tendency toward realization is exhibited in the terse statements of some reformatory inmates, sentenced for various crimes, who have already done and dared and come within the range of the Blumer-Hauser survey:

"As I became older," bluntly admits a lad convicted of robbery, "the luxuries of life showed in the movies, partly, made me want to possess them. I could not on the salary I was earning." Another, working off a burglary sentence, is even more explicit:

"The ideas that I got from the movies about easy money were from watching pictures where the hero never worked, but seemed always to have lots of money to spend. All the women would be after him. . . . I thought it would be great to lead that kind of life. To always have plenty of money and ride around in swell machines, wear good clothes, and grab off a girl whenever you wanted to. I still think it would be a great life."

A great life!—the ideal held up to view in so much of our public entertainment—"lots of money to spend"—"swell machines"—"women"—the cheapest and the shoddiest vulgarity even when it is not criminal. A large percentage of movie characters, as Dale has shown us, have either illegal occupations or no occupations—patterns tending to sensitize such material as these boys to suggestions of a similar life.

"The pictures that they show of this sort," mouths a young robber, "shows how the man that is a crook gets his money and how he outsmarts the law and it looks very easy."

But these, someone may object, are young criminals. True, they are young—but once they were not criminals, although many of them doubtless came from delinquent areas or unsuccessful homes. Even in a good neighborhood one-fifth of the boys examined, indicated on a questionnaire response that motion pictures moved them to the desire of making "a lot of money easily." In a high-rate delinquency area, that is, an area where there are frequent arrests, the percentage of such flashy ambitions rises to thirty-nine or nearly double the percentage of the other boys, while among the truant or behavior problem boys, it runs up to forty-five per cent. The conclusion appears inescapable that to show certain types of pictures—so numerous in the current output—in what are known as high-rate delinquency areas, in cities, is in some measure like selling whiskey to the Indians, against which there are quite justly severe laws and sharp penalties.

The natural protest would be that in that case no film depicting wealth, no so-called "society" drama could ever be shown upon the screen, since it might move many young people to yearn for easily acquired money. Upon investigation, however, it was found that it was not the society dramas, but the "gangster" or "crook" type of picture that caused the trouble. In a high-delinquency area, as Professor Thrasher and Mr. Cressey found, it is the gangster picture that points the way to wealth, and thereby the way to "high society." The themes and characters of such pictures are more familiar to the people concerned, the atmosphere more natural and kindred to their environment and interests, and as Thrasher puts it, "the boy of this community can with ease identify himself with the character portrayed." They exhale possibility within reach of the aspiring among themselves, whereas the film of wealth and fashion embodies a world remote and alien, in the realm of the unattainable.

The Blumer-Hauser investigation showed that more than one-half of the truant and behavior problem boys examined, fifty-five per cent, indicated that pictures dealing with gangsters and gun-play stirred in them desires for wanting "to make a lot of money easily." Only five per cent, however, believe that the wealthy type of picture, or the type indicating a wealthy social background, provoke in them the desire "to make lots of money easily." The crook pictures are the sort that suggest direct and comprehensible ways of making easy money. Twenty-five per cent of a sampling of 110 boys in a penal institution mention "hold-ups" as the high revelation they gleaned. Eleven per cent cite stealing, and twenty per cent give the vague but all-embracing "crime" as the royal road to fortune brought to them by the message of the pictures.

To some of them the themes and plots of such pictures bring an appeal and an urge all but irresistible. The kind of poverty that used to be called "decent" is not fashionable in the pictures. Instead there are those engaging characters found by Dr. Dale of "illegal occupation," or "no occupation." An eighteen-year-old lad in a reformatory, sentenced for robbery and rape, virtually traces his own derivation from such pictures:

"I would see the 'Big Shot' come in a cabaret. Everyone would greet him with a smile. The girls would all crowd around him. He would order wine and food for the girls. Tip the waiter $50.00 or more. After dining and dancing he would give the girls diamond bracelets, rings and fur coats. Then he would leave and go to meet his gang. They would all bow to him and give him the dough that was taken from different rackets. When I would see pictures like this I would go wild and say that some day I would be a Big Shot that everyone would be afraid of, and have big dough. Live like a king, without doing any work."

In a nut-shell, the above is the most striking anatomy of the "gangster" or "racket" picture and of its influence upon such as that boy, and, to many of us, one of the answers to the question of why crime is so prevalent in our cities. Dale has shown us how considerable is the percentage of crime pictures in the total. Compared with their continuous production, the sale of whiskey to reservation Indians is a trivial offense.

The Big Shot! Symbol of the spread of vulgarity in our troubled age, that seems to grope for solutions of its difficulties in all directions except the right ones. It will spend billions for frantically attempted "cures" and nostrums, but, in the domain of social malady, hardly anything for prevention. It is safe to say that not even Imperial Rome at its most decadent held up such symbols or images for its young to ape and copy. Even very young grade-school boys of ten and eleven in certain areas of cities actually crackle with bravado when they refer to some of their cinema obsessions.

"De 'Big House,'" says a ten-year-old lad, "made me feel like I was a big tough guy. I felt just like Machine Gun Butch." And an eleven-year-old Italian boy chortles, "When I saw Jack Oakie in 'The Gang Buster' I felt like a big gangster." "I feel like the big shot that knows schemes and hiding places," confessed another, "and knows how to kill and capture cops and get a lot of money." . . .

When they testify, as does one boy, that "pictures about gangsters enabled me to become one," or, as another, a reformatory inmate, puts it—"A picture that is pretty exciting and adventurous makes me want to do something and when I come out of a show . . . I would go with another fellow and break in some store that looked like it had a few dollars in it"—when pictures produce particularly significant effects like this, it would appear high time that protest and responsibility take the place of apathy and irresponsibility.

"If," conclude Blumer and Hauser, "it is true that in much delinquency and crime there is a spirit of bravado, boldness and 'toughness,' it seems to be a not unreasonable assumption that the inducement of this spirit by motion pictures may help to initiate or reinforce criminal activity. The declaration by some delinquents and criminals that this has been true in their cases suggests that it may be true in others." . . .

■ ■ ■ ■

Mr. Forman Goes to Town (1938), Raymond Moley

Raymond Moley wrote the industry's official response to Forman's charges in his book *Are We Movie Made?* To some extent Moley's book, like Forman's, was a popularization of more complex, academic work. Moley based much of his argument on Mortimer J. Adler's *Art and Prudence* (an excerpt from which follows Moley's piece), although Moley was more interested in exposing the specific fallacies of Forman and company than in inquiring into the abstract relationship between art and social utility—as Adler was. This section from Moley's book is his specific response to the Forman popularization.

The authors of the Payne Fund studies, with notable exceptions, distilled a mass of inadequate data into the expression of personal opinion. Mr. Forman's book, "Our Movie Made Children" (Macmillan Co., New York, 1933) is a process of double-distilling. Mr. Forman takes the con-

"Mr. Forman Goes to Town" is from Raymond Moley's *Are We Movie Made?* (Macy-Masius, 1938).

clusions of the authors, unsupported and confused with moral judgments as some of them are, and transforms them with even greater inaccuracy and confusion into conclusions of his own.

Mr. Forman's book originated in the desire of those responsible for the Payne Fund studies to popularize their findings. Mr. Forman's qualifications for this job do not readily appear. Perhaps they lie in the fact that he enjoyed some experience in writing and was the author of "The Rembrandt Murder," "The Pony Express," "Guilt," "The Enchanted Garden" and other literary efforts. At any rate, he was turned loose to ballyhoo the reports.

As a result, we have a book consisting of 284 pages of unrelieved condemnation. It is true that Mr. Forman mentions a few pictures that he liked, to which I shall refer presently. But aside from that, the book is a series of hysterical outcries. There is no evidence of an attempt to give equal weight to studies of the motion picture whose conclusions were not condemnatory. Nowhere does the book recognize that the motion picture industry had been working, within itself, to improve its product for a good many years before Mr. Forman got around to serious writing on the subject. Mr. Forman leaves the impression that no one had ever thought of improving the motion picture before Dr. Dale et al. began their examinations.

Mr. Forman says he is presenting facts: "The aim of all the studies upon which the present book is based, as well as of the book itself, is to bring us face to face with the facts—and they are grave. Once in possession of the facts, the public, it is hoped, will find the remedies. . . ." But in spite of this categorical statement, Mr. Forman indicates a complete lack of confidence in the ability of the public to draw conclusions by offering reckless conclusions of his own at every point, whether or not they are supported by the facts in the studies. For example: "With straws like this to show the direction of the wind, the question occurs to the present writer, even though none of the investigators touches upon it: Does not the exhibition of gangster pictures in the so-called high delinquency neighborhoods amount to the diffusion of poison?"

The book, in short, is simply a congeries of Mr. Forman's quotations of opinions—sometimes supported by fact and sometimes not—and a series of unadulterated Formanesqueries. These, in turn, he supports by data indiscriminately pulled out, now from one, now from another of the studies which he purports to be summarizing. Obviously, his book is not a genuine summary, though it was, by innuendo, presented as such to the public.

There can be no question that it was the intention of both Mr. Forman and Dr. Charters, director of the Payne Fund studies on the motion picture, that "Our Movie Made Children" should be regarded as a popular summary of the Payne Fund studies. Professor Charters helped the good work along by contributing, in his introduction to the book, a statement which seems calculated to approve the book without actually endorsing it. "I have examined Mr. Forman's manuscript," he said. "He shows a thorough grasp of the facts in the complicated materials presented in the nearly 3,000 pages which constitute the report of the 12 studies."

It is true that Dr. Charters then attempted to slide out from under by adding quietly that Mr. Forman himself was entirely responsible for the interpretation of the materials. But the fact remains that commentators were led by Dr. Charters' introduction and Mr. Forman's presentation to regard the book as a summary of the Payne Fund studies. And it is the further fact that when this assertion was later questioned, Mr. Forman rose to his own defense on December 2, 1935, in the *Christian Science Monitor,* as follows:

"After digesting and arranging the data of the monographs, some of which were already in type, but awaiting publication as a matter of publisher's policy, I wrote a first draft of which a dozen copies were made, one going to the head of each research problem in the different universities for criticism, suggestion or correction, if any, of my facts and statements. When these were returned, I prepared a second draft. A similar number of copies was made, for final scrutiny on the part of the research personnel, to the closest detail, including even shades of interpretation of meaning.

"With these rechecked manuscripts in hand, I spent several days with Dr. Charters at Ohio State University in Columbus weighing virtually every word, let alone every statement. After that I wrote the final draft, which Dr. Charters, on behalf of the research body, O.K.'d both to the publishers and to myself. The book was then published."

Evidently Dr. Charters went a good deal further than he liked to admit, if we accept this statement of Mr. Forman. But, even if he did not, his enlisting of Mr. Forman as a popularizer of studies made under his reputedly scientific direction and his implied approval of Mr. Forman's unrestrained editorializing, constitute, to my mind, at any rate, a grave departure from scientific procedure. What would be the present reputation of Banting if he had enlisted the aid of a writer without scientific training to ballyhoo the discovery of insulin to the public and proclaim it not only as a specific for the treatment of diabetes, but as a cure for tuberculosis, infantile paralysis and cancer?

It was to have been expected that Mr. Forman's reactions to methods and materials with which he was unfamiliar would be naïve, although such instances as the following may strain the credulity of those who have not read his book. For example, he says there were "no established means of finding out" what a child remembers of a movie and that therefore Dr. Holaday proceeded to devise such means. He says again that Renshaw, Miller and Marquis had no apparatus at hand to study motility, but "they proceeded to perfect one." At one point he says that Dr. Blumer was the *only* investigator in the research who sought facts *pro and con* about children's being frightened by pictures, not realizing, of course, that he thus unwittingly let the cat out of the bag; that he inadvertently put his finger upon the most vulnerable aspect of almost the entire series of Payne movie studies; that the absence of "controls," or comparative data makes most of them almost valueless as "scientific" materials. At another point he declares that "after noting the care of the investigators in getting their material, I must conclude that, as part of a large picture, their data are substantially correct." In other words, naïveté leads him to state that a scientist's results are to be judged by considerations of how hard he works, and not by a clear-cut analysis of his materials.

But if naïveté were all! It was not too much to ask that, as an experienced reporter and sometime editor, Mr. Forman confine himself to the presentation of the conclusions of the "scientists" whose work he was summarizing, however untenable they might be. Yet Mr. Forman has embellished his book with conclusions which those who did the research did not make.

Mr. Forman's book was characterized thus even by Professor Kimball Young, who swallowed much of the nonsense in the reports themselves: It is, he said, "by an apparently prejudiced writer" and has the effect of "giving a totally false impression to the American public regarding the findings of the research workers. It was distinctly unfair to them and distinctly misleading to the American people. I think it was a rather serious mistake to give the public such a biased view of the movies based upon alleged scientific works, when the monographs do not actually support the treatment in this popularized account."

Whenever other missiles are not at hand, Mr. Forman contributes the generalization that love, sex and crime are present in the movies to an excessive degree. He accompanies this generalization, at one place, with mention of three desirable motion pictures—all of which include portrayals of these three aspects of life. Among them, he particularly admires the play "Sorrell and Son," which, in addition, contains a sequence that would probably not be permitted under the Production Code as now administered, because it presents a "mercy killing" in a way that would tend to justify it.

Elsewhere, Mr. Forman says that the movies' preoccupation with crime is not true to life. He then cites some statistics designed to show the extent to which the motion picture "misrepresents" the punishment for crime. He says that 57 criminals in 40 pictures committeed 62 crimes. Of the 57 criminals, three were arrested and held, four were arrested but released, four escaped after being arrested, and seven were arrested and the punishment was implied. Let us assume that these figures, drawn from 40 pictures, are representative of all pictures. If they are, then the movies show a very much higher proportion of punishment than exists in real life. Compare these figures with the actual record of a typical American city, neither the best nor the worst in its record of law enforcement. For the single crime of murder there was in one year only one conviction for every seven crimes. Punishment for crime in real life, according to dozens of accurate statistical studies, is several times less frequent than Mr. Forman says it is in the world of the motion picture.

Nearly half of Mr. Forman's book is devoted to the thesis that the motion picture is a factor in causing delinquency and crime. It is apparent that Mr. Forman held forth on this subject despite his almost total ignorance of the existence of a great mass of data relating to this question—data gathered by men with a profound regard for the objective use of scientific technique. Had he familiarized himself with these data, he would have come face to face with the utterly negative results of those who have tried to isolate the causes of delinquency. He would have found that no scientific methods have been evolved to unravel the mystery of what factors specifically cause criminal conduct. More important still, he would have found that there is good conduct in the world as well as bad, and that the movies, as well as many other things, may cause good conduct. He would have written less sensationally and more judicially, probably reaching some such conclusion as that expressed by Sir Herbert Samuel, one of the wisest Home Secretaries ever to sit in a British Cabinet, after the British Film Commission reported to him in 1932: "My very expert and experienced advisers at the Home Office are of the opinion that on the whole the cinema conduces more to the prevention of crime than to its commission." Or perhaps he might have reached the conclusion of England's Lord Chief Justice, Lord Hewart, who said on December 14, 1936: "If virtue triumphed in actual life as on the films this world might be an easier place both to police and to understand. . . . Generations of men have in their youth read hair-raising stories of detection and adventure. . . . Yet it is seldom suggested that children who read works of this kind—many of them to be numbered among the classics of literature—are thereby encouraged to entertain evil designs or indulge in criminal practices. On what other grounds than prejudice can you base the view that the cinema makes criminals of young persons? . . ."

This does not mean, of course, that there are not situations in motion pictures that wise men, without benefit of science, believe are undesirable. Efforts have been made for many years to eliminate them—efforts of which Mr. Forman is apparently ignorant. Wise men and women know also, without benefit of science, that other factors in motion pictures build good conduct. This whole side of the picture is either unknown to Mr. Forman or has been omitted from his calculations.

Let us examine one of Mr. Forman's chapters as an example of his method—a chapter with the lurid title "Movie Made Criminals." First Mr. Forman says what everybody knows—that there is a lot of crime in the United States. (Incidentally, he here uses figures which were eleven years old when he wrote.) Then he confesses that, despite all the leading questions and all of the biased technique employed, only 17 percent of the delinquents questioned said that the motion picture "induced them to do something wrong." But Mr. Forman decides to chuck Blumer and Hauser overboard at this point. Their figures, bad as they are, are not bad enough for Mr. Forman. The figure is "conservative." He then "proves" his premise by selecting quotations from thirteen delinquents— flamboyant quotations, of course. These he flavors with sharp comment of his own. Finally, he concludes, the motion picture is a maker of criminals.

Note his logic: There are many crimes in America. Seventy-seven million people (his figure) go weekly to movies. Thirteen delinquent witnesses testify that movies taught them criminal ways. Ergo criminals are "movie-made."

At this point it ought to be made clear that those familiar with the minds and habits of criminals and delinquents know that a prison or reformatory is a veritable hot-house for imaginative stories. Criminals tell with great plausibility of the misdeeds of public men of all sorts: this judge, or that prosecutor, or that chief of police or that mayor did all manner of heinous wrongs. Wardens and keepers know how to evaluate such stuff. They know that only once in hundreds of instances is there truth in such tales. But the authors of some of these reports and Mr. Forman, subsequently, have taken down great masses of material like this and published it as a guide to parents, teachers and legislators. They have presented it as "scientific" material to condemn the motion picture.

Here and there vague and indirect statements seem to indicate that Mr. Forman is offering constructive suggestions to correct the "evils" of which he speaks. There is a hint of the need for a public subsidy in one place, the hint of the need for censorship in another.

Yet nowhere does Mr. Forman answer the basic question that he unwittingly raises. He has been at great pains to buttress his belief that, among *all* the motion pictures produced, *some* contain sequences which *might* hurt *some* children. The question thus raised is whether *all* movies should be leveled down to the point at which they will assuredly hurt no children at all—even the most impressionable. Does Mr. Forman mean that this should be done or does he not? He is silent on this point.

Instead of coming down to specifications, he gallops away at the end in a cloud of dust. He says that the Motion Picture Council "even possibly, may, propose remedies." That august body, apparently completely taken in by the inadequate Payne studies, gave wide publicity to Mr. Forman's unfair book. Maybe that is all he hoped for.

Thus Mr. Forman. His book went forth with the endorsement of a scientific fund. It "summarized," with lurid detail and an interpretation all Mr. Forman's own, materials gathered under the direction of a man who convicts himself of prejudice, by "experts" who, with notable exceptions, were superficial in their work, uncritical of their material and gratuitous in offering unsupported guesses as to the meaning of their work. The whole procedure reminds me of nothing so much as the story of the blind man, looking in a dark room for a black hat that wasn't there.

I offer this additional consideration: such a man may not find the hat; but the danger that he will smash something precious is exceedingly great. This consideration is what prevents the labors of Messrs. Charters, Forman, Blumer, Hauser, Dale, Dysinger, Ruckmick, Peters, Renshaw, Miller and Miss Marquis from attaining rank as immortal comedy. . . .

■ ■ ■ ■

ART AND PRUDENCE (1937), Mortimer J. Adler

Dr. Mortimer J. Adler, although originally a legal scholar and faculty member of the University of Chicago Law School, has become famous as the founder and prime mover of the Great Books philosophy that was later associated with that university and its president, Robert M. Hutchins. *Art and Prudence* was a lengthy (perhaps 300,000-word), complicated theoretical study, inspired by the Payne Fund series. As is typical of Adler, he is not interested in merely proving or disproving the scientific data but in tracing and establishing the meaning of the arguments to which the data have been applied. Adler makes a fundamental distinction between Art (the abstract impulse to create a thing of beauty whose only responsibility is to itself) and Prudence (the utilitarian impulse to create only things that are useful, good, and valuable for society). Adler sees these

Art and Prudence, by Mortimer J. Adler, was published by Longmans in 1937.

two impulses as necessarily contradictory (tracing the origins of the conflict back to Aristotle and Plato, the one who saw art as a matter of
Poetics not of Ethics and the other who banished artists from the Republic
because they could not be depended upon to tell "the truth"). For Adler,
the prudent person would only take an action against art if he *knew* the art
to be harmful (an implication of the Payne Fund Studies). So Adler seeks
to determine how much *knowledge* the Payne Fund Studies provide. The
following passages reveal, first, one of Adler's many theoretical outlines
of *what it means* to make some kind of moral claim and, second, his summary opinions of the specific "knowledge" that the Payne Fund Studies
provide. (Parenthetically, Adler's arguments might apply equally well today to the controversy over the effects of television on children.)

THE CONTEMPORARY ISSUE

I. INTERPRETATION OF THE CHARGE THAT SOME MOTION PICTURES ARE IM-
MORAL.
   A. The word "immoral" must not be understood here in the same sense
      in which it is said that some men are immoral.
      1. Strictly, only men are moral beings, only men can be immoral.
      2. The word is, therefore, being used analogically. A work of art
         can be called moral or immoral only in relation to the morality
         of men, as food is called healthy or unhealthy only in relation
         to the health of men. (This explains why those who insist upon
         considering art for art's sake can never understand questions
         about the morality of art. It is only when art is not considered
         for its own sake that it comes within the field of morals.)
      3. If a work of art can be spoken of as immoral only in its relation
         to man, the nature of this relation must be further determined.
         a. It is either the way in which the work of art influences human
            acts, or some other type of relation.
         b. If the only relation of art to man is of the first sort, then this
            first charge cannot be distinguished from the second charge,
            which is to follow.
         c. Therefore, if this first charge is to be distinguished, the im-
            morality here spoken of must be interpreted as referring to
            the content of motion pictures, *apart from their influence on
            human behavior:*
            (1) Either as that content is offensive to moral sensibilities;
            (2) Or as that content violates moral principles;
            (3) Or as that content betrays the immorality of the artist.
                (We need not consider this point here. It is discussed
                later.)

B. A work of art may be called immoral because it offends the moral
   sensibilities of its audience in a manner analogous to the way in
   which ugliness offends our aesthetic sensibilities, or even in the way
   in which unpleasant and painful objects offend our sense-organs.

   1. But there is a difference between a sense-organ and the moral
      sense. The former is biologically determined. The latter is con-
      stituted, in part, by accepted moral standards.

      a. The moral standards involved are usually those expressed in
         terms of the prevailing conventions of decency and propriety
         in public manners. (Thus, for example, not so very long ago
         the picture of women smoking or standing at a bar was of-
         fensive to any audience which accepted the prevailing *mores*
         in regard to such matters.)

      b. It does not matter that the standards are local, that they have
         not always been the same nor always will be, that they are
         not now the same in all countries.

         (1) Manners are necessarily conventional, but they are not
             merely or arbitrarily conventional. They are conventional
             determinations of more general moral considerations
             which formulate the principles of right and wrong con-
             duct.

         (2) The manners which we adopt at any time, the prevailing
             mores, are thus particular determinations of morality,
             just as human laws are particular determinations of
             justice.[1]

         (3) Transgressions of the *mores* are, therefore, offensive to
             our moral sensibilities.

   2. There is no question that that which is offensive in this way is
      undesirable.

      a. That which offends us is unpleasant and we obviously avoid
         the offensive.

      b. We do not willingly submit to the offensive in the field of our
         moral sensibilities, any more than we seek out ugliness or
         expose ourselves to unpleasant odors.

   3. But there is the question: To whom are particular works of art
      offensive in this way? There are two possibilities: they are offen-
      sive (1) either to the audience which they entertain, or (2) to
      others.

      a. But the first is impossible over a long period of time, unless
         the offense is so slight as to be negligible. Thus, if the movies
         were gravely offensive to their audience, they would soon

1. Cf. St. Thomas Aquinas, *Summa Theologica,* I-II, Q. 95, AA. 2, 4.

    lose it. An art cannot succeed as a popular amusement and at the same time be seriously offensive to its public.

b. The second alternative, then, must be the case; that is, individuals or groups in society who are not the regular patrons of an art must be offended by it and protest because they, too, would enjoy the art were its offensiveness lessened or eliminated; or because they maintain that the part of the public which does not seem to be offended, *should* be offended.

Digression

Although the basic principles of morality are everywhere the same, the *mores* or conventions not only are not the same at different times and places, but are not even the same in the same country at a given time. One of the chief differences between what are called primitive societies and what are called civilized ones is that in the former there is a much greater uniformity in the *mores* at a given time. In modern societies particularly we find the phenomenon of conflicting *mores* due to the presence of different social groups having different standards and manners. This fact makes the charge that the movies are offensive to moral sensibilities extremely difficult to interpret. The question is whose, and further, whether there is any clear ground for choosing among alternative and conflicting conventions.

    The charge of immorality, thus interpreted, is an old one. Plato made it against certain passages in Greek literature which offended his moral sensibilities and those which he thought *ought* to prevail in the population of an ideal state. Whether they actually did prevail in Greek society is a point of history. If they did not, the passages in question could hardly have been offensive to the audience which enjoyed that literature. The early Christian attack upon pagan literature, and upon the theatre especially, is partly this: these arts are offensive to a good Christian in so far as they present transgressions of Christian values and manners. But Christian manners are no less conventional than other manners.[2] They have changed from time to time, although essentially always remaining expressions of Christian morality, since as conventions they are determinations of the principles of that morality. What Christians find offensive has, therefore, changed in the course of centuries. The pros and cons of the Collier controversy in the seventeenth century are thus to be understood. The Restoration comedy was not offensive to the moral sensibilities of the particular audience which enjoyed it, though the fact that it existed and

---

    2. In his recent encyclical, Pope Pius recognized this difficulty: "circumstances, usages and forms vary from country to country; so it does not seem practical to have a single list for all the world."

was enjoyed by the gentry and the court gave offense to the moral sensibilities of a large class in the population, the Puritans. When this class became politically dominant and when, after the accession of William and Mary, its *mores* reigned, the theatre which could only succeed by pleasing its audience could no longer afford to give offense to the people who had became its patrons.

It is clear, then, that an art is never greatly offensive to the moral sensibilities of its persistent patrons. The extent of the patronage, the degree of popularity of an art, is thus some measure of prevailing manners. It is able to indicate the conventions and standards of the majority, or of a large group, in a society in which there are conflicting codes. Moreover, it indicates the relativity of these conventions to place and time. The plays of Shakespeare can contain parts that are offensive to the moral sensibilities of Robert Bridges and persons like him, although they were not similarly offensive to the thousands upon thousands of their Elizabethan audience.

The first interpretation of the charge that some movies are immoral requires no further discussion. If it be said further that the movies are not offensive to a large portion of the population because they have degraded the moral sensibilities of their audience, then we pass to another consideration, namely, the influence of the movies upon human behavior and consequently upon manners and standards generally. This matter will be examined later; it is part of the second charge. It is not relevant here because we are considering whether the movies are offensive and to whom, and not why they are *not* offensive to the audience which enjoys them.

C. A work of art may be called immoral because it violates moral principles. It can violate moral principles only if it be somehow construed as *asserting* their contraries. Thus, if a narrative be construed as asserting that men achieve happiness by vicious deeds or that men seek evil knowingly rather than good, it is immoral *as so construed*. (We need not stop here to discuss the necessity of the qualifying phrase "as so construed," beyond saying that works of art do not of themselves *assert* anything.) The charge that some movies are immoral can be interpreted in this sense.

    1. They are said, for example, to violate the canon of poetic justice as that has been traditionally formulated in English literary criticism.

        a. The doctrine of poetic justice says that vice and crime should always be rewarded by obvious failure and punishment, and virtue and lawfulness should always be obviously rewarded by success in some clearly recognized form, which usually means external prosperity and contentment.

    b. It does not require that narratives confine themselves only to good men and good deeds.

2. But as we have seen, this doctrine is a confusion of moral and aesthetic principles and is intrinsically pernicious.

    a. This does not mean that criminals should not be punished by the state or that those who are known to be vicious should not be despised, or perhaps pitied, for their weakness.

    b. But to try to teach a moral lesson by showing virtue always outwardly triumphant and vice always ending in the gutter or on the gallows is to distort the truth and pervert the moral lesson. History is full of contrary examples of vice prospering in all the external circumstances of life.

3. It may be objected nevertheless that the application of the principle of poetic justice to the movies is justified, even though it is intrinsically unsound.

    a. On the ground that unless the story abides by the canon of poetic justice, the influence upon the behavior and character of the movie audience is harmful.

    b. But this raises a question of fact: Is it the case that, despite the abundant evidence which history and life itself provide to the contrary, the outward triumph of virtue and the punishment of vice must be shown in motion pictures in order to help men, for morally pernicious reasons, to lead morally good lives? (Since the reasons are wrong, only the appearance of virtue can be thus achieved.)

Digression

It should be mentioned as a relevant fact that for the most part the movies have followed the principle of poetic justice, not only because it has been thought that that is the way to teach a moral lesson, but also because that is the way stories must be told to achieve their proper poetic effects. Despite the fact that almost all movies are so written and produced, their critics have many times insisted that the right ending does not prevent the movie from having insidious effects because of incidental elements in the plot. This raises an obvious question of fact about whether such is the case. In any event, the point raised nullifies the demand for poetic justice as a device for inculcating morals which, superficially formed for wrong reasons, must ultimately be worse than no morals at all.

    D. There is one further interpretation of the charge that some movies are immoral, namely, that they are obscene. We must ask whether this interpretation of the charge adds anything to the two preceding interpretations.

1. We must first attempt to define obscenity. Obscenity is usually a transgression of the *mores* with respect to sex, although it may also involve other matters connected with the exposure of the body, the customs governing the performance of certain bodily functions, the use of language of a certain sort, and so forth.

    a. It would thus appear that obscenity is the same as indecency and is objectionable to persons who are outraged by it.

    b. The standards by which obscenity is judged are conventional and local, just as all other standards of decency and propriety are. But that they are conventional makes no difference to the point. It does not lessen the shock of outrage which some people are made to suffer.

    c. So far the charge that some movies are obscene adds nothing to the charge that they offend moral sensibilities. But additional grounds may be offered for the objection to obscenity, particularly sexual obscenity.

        (1) It is not merely that some persons are outraged by such indecent manifestations.

        (2) Those who criticize an art for indulging in sexual obscenities have grounds for doing so, even though the large popular audience of that art may not be in any way shocked or offended.

2. The first of these reasons is the same as that which underlies the objection to pornography. It is the moral condemnation of sensuality as such.

    a. As St. Thomas said, man cannot live without pleasure; and unless he is provided higher pleasures, he will seek lower ones. The distinction which St. Thomas has in mind here is between sensual pleasures and the intellectual pleasures of contemplation.

    b. The pleasure which is appropriate to a work of art is, of course, the latter. Any sensual pleasure which a work of art may give is thoroughly accidental to its nature.

    c. But if a work is intentionally obscene, it aims to give sensual pleasure to its audience, and to this extent is not a work of art but a piece of pornography.

        (1) It may be that not all members of an audience will be responsive to the obscenity, but this makes no difference to the point of criticism if, according to prevailing standards of sexual morality, it is highly probable that the obscenity of the artist will gratify the desire for pornog-

raphy and the lust for sensual pleasure in a large number of people.

(2) Nor does it make any difference whether the obscenity
is or is not intentional, if the words, acts or spectacles in
question are, by the customs of the community, such that
they will probably be received as obscene.

Digression

There are some liberals who are never able to understand the objection
to sexual obscenity or pornography in any terms. This can only be because they do not accept Christian standards of sexual behavior or, for
that matter, any other code which predominates in their own society. They
would be unwilling to admit the distinction between higher and lower
pleasures, which is Greek as well as Christian and, curiously enough for
modern hedonists, Epicurean as well as Stoic. They sometimes recognize
the justification of laws which prohibit and punish pornography, but hide
in ostrich fashion behind a distinction impossible to make between the
obscene and the pornographic. They treat the question of obscenity and
pornography as if it were a curiously Christian foible, utterly forgetting
or ignoring that sexual taboos are both more complicated and more rigid
among primitive peoples and that the punishment of their transgression
in life or in art is universal. It is not necessary to deal with them further.
In the same sense that society is justified in legally prohibiting pornography, the precise nature of which must be determined according to the
standards held at the given time and place, so it is justified in protesting
against sexual obscenity in motion pictures and in advocating censorship
or other means to prevent it. In their code of self-regulation the motion
picture producers have fully recognized the objection to obscenity.

Consider the wisdom of Maritain's position in contrast: "There are,
says St. Paul, some things which must not be so much as mentioned
among you. Yet he immediately mentions them himself. What does that
mean? Nothing by *its kind alone* is a forbidden nutriment for art, like unclean animals to the Hebrews. From this point of view art can mention
them all, as St. Paul mentions avarice and lechery. But on condition that,
in the particular case and *in relation to the people* it is aiming at and with
whom it comes in contact, the work does not soil the mind and the heart.
From this point of view if there are certain things which the artist is not
strong enough or pure enough to mention without conniving with evil,
he has no right to mention them." And Maritain adds in a note: "In practice, printing and modern methods of vulgarization, by confusing different publics more and more in one shapeless mass, run the risk of making a problem already singularly difficult well-nigh impossible."

    d. Thus understood, the charge that some movies are obscene raises two questions of fact.

        (1) Are the standards by which the obscenity of any particular movie is judged standards which the community generally accepts, such as the standards of Christianity and of contemporary American life?

        (2) What proportion of motion pictures are obscene, and to what extent is any particular motion picture obscene, as judged by such standards?

3. The second reason for the objection to obscenity is that such matter tends to arouse the passion of lust in any of its myriad forms.

    a. Mere sensuality or sensual pleasure is distinguished from the passion of lust in that the latter is a movement of the appetite. It is a natural consequence of sensuality. In other words, the second reason adds to the first an objection to obscenity on the ground that it stimulates desires and initiates types of behavior which are condemnable.

    b. It is no answer to this objection to say that if art arouses such passions, it also purges them; because an art may arouse the passions so excessively that it fails to effect a sufficient catharsis, in which case man's burden of concupiscence is made heavier rather than lighter.

        (1) Whatever in a work of art arouses lust or concupiscence to such an extent that the correlative purgation is inadequate is obscene.

        (2) It must be admitted, however, that to whatever extent a work of art arouses and purges lust, it is not only not obscene in this sense, but serves a positively good end which ancient psychology called catharsis and modern psychology calls sublimation.

    c. Understood in this way, the second objection to obscenity raises a question of fact about the influence of motion pictures upon human behavior, upon the desires and actions of men.

        (1) If some movies are objectionably obscene only to the extent that they fail adequately to purge the lust which they excessively arouse, the question of fact can be answered only if the unpurged passion has some determinable effect upon behavior or character.

        (2) Furthermore, since the unpurged passion may cause action of a sort which either conforms to or transgresses the sexual *mores* of the community, the determination of

obscenity rests upon this additional question of fact.

(3) These questions of fact indicate that, on the second meaning of obscenity, the charge we are here considering reduces to the charge that some movies influence human character or conduct in ways that are undesirable. That is the second major charge presently to be considered.

Digression

This charge is the ancient Christian objection to the theatre as essentially obscene: it intensifies the carnal concupiscence which is a heavy burden of potential sin in man's corrupt nature. The objection has been many times repeated, notably by Prynne and Collier, by Bossuet and Rousseau. It is much emphasized in the recurrent disapproval of the movies by the churches.

THE PROBLEM IN PRACTICAL PHILOSOPHY

1. A brief recapitulation is necessary here. We have analyzed the nature of practical problems in general. We have applied that analysis to the formulation of the particular practical problem with which we are here concerned, the problem of the arts in the state. Three basic alternatives were indicated: inaction, regulation, extirpation. In the case of each of these alternatives, a number of questions required to be answered before a prudent man would feel justified in proceeding, questions of fact about the influence of the art under consideration and questions of evaluation directed toward weighing the positive and negative values involved. At other times in the history of this problem, the issue has been formulated in terms of extirpation; but in the current instance of the problem, concerning the motion picture, the issue is between the alternatives of inaction and some type of regulation or control. That the issue is formulated in this way acknowledges that there is a balance of positive and negative values. It would be better to leave the art alone if any sort of action would substantially diminish the good without proportionally lessening the evil. A policy of regulation or control can be justified only by the assurance that action of a given sort would minimize the regrettable influences of the art without impairing or destroying its contribution to human welfare. A sound practical decision here must be guided not only by a consideration of the probable effectiveness of different courses of action in view of all their probable consequences, but also by a consideration of the various effects of the art upon its audience.

Our review of all the questions which a prudent man must face indicated the need for knowledge and, more than that, the need for a distinction between knowledge and opinion. Since practical problems are concerned with contingent matters, and since the distinction between knowledge and opinion turns upon the criterion of necessity and contingency, it was seen to follow that the prudent man must depend upon opinion for the solution of practical problems. Though there is some knowledge of contingent matters, it is possible only by abstracting from their contingency. Though there is some knowledge that is relevant to practical problems, it is always of great generality. It provides the basic principles, but these are always insufficient for casuistry. The prudent man must deliberate about the contingent circumstances of the particular case, and in order to supplement the principles he must, therefore, take counsel from prevailing opinions. His task is easy if common or expert opinion is relatively clear and definite on one side of the issue; it is difficult in proportion as there is unclarity and conflict in the field of opinion which he must consult.

In the contemporary world, the situation is complicated by the existence of empirical or investigative science which claims to be better than opinion. We have seen that it is, that science is a mean between knowledge and opinion, sharing in some part the traits of both.[3] But we have also seen that there is a radical difference between the natural sciences and that part of empirical psychology and social research which seeks to be a science of human behavior. Whereas scientific knowledge about natural phenomena is clearly better than opinion, largely by addition rather than correction, what claims to be scientific knowledge about human affairs seldom adds to or corrects the prevailing opinion about these matters. From the practical point of view, the value of scientific research about human behavior depends upon its superiority to opinion, either through novelty, or by greater definiteness and higher probability, or in resolving oppositions by adding the weight of scientific evidence to one or another side. It is always necessary to test the claims of scientific research by such criteria, as well as by the common standards of reliability, accuracy and inference in scientific method. To make this test, we examined the attempts at scientific research about motion pictures in relation to human behavior, in the light of a survey of existing opinion on the subject. We are now prepared to summarize the results of that critical review and to state whether the position of the prudent man has been altered by the efforts of science.

2. We divided the problem into two parts by distinguishing between the mature and the immature, because we found good analytical reasons for supposing that the influence of an art, both in extent and character, is different for these two elements in its audience. The analytical point is

3. *I.e.,* in the field of human behavior.

further supported by a survey of existing opinion concerning motion pictures. In the case of the mature, there is no settled common opinion. The clear fact is conflict, both in opinions commonly held and among experts. But in the case of the immature, there seems to be a predominance of common, and even of expert, opinion, on the affirmative side. i.e., that motion pictures have a somewhat undesirable influence on children and youth. This predominance of opinion can, perhaps, be most accurately described as a *fear* or *concern* about the physical, intellectual and moral effects of motion pictures on the young. Even if there were no scientific research, the prevalence of this feeling might move the prudent man to consider whether action of some sort might not be desirable. He would not be similarly moved if the audience of motion pictures comprised adults only. *That he is moved to such consideration indicates nothing about the sort of action to be taken, if any.* But before we proceed further with the analysis of the practical problem, as it thus arises, let us determine whether scientific research has made any difference whatsoever. . . .

It will be interesting here to begin by considering the three conclusions which Professor Charters thinks follow inevitably from the Payne Fund studies on motion pictures and youth. (1) The motion picture is "a potent medium of education."[4] The evidence of this influence, which Charters thinks is "massive and irrefutable," consists of the Holaday-Stoddard finding about the amount that children learn and remember from witnessing movies, the Thurstone-Peterson finding about the formation of attitudes, the Dysinger-Ruckmick finding that children are emotionally excited by movies, and Blumer's autobiographical materials. It is difficult to see how anything but Holaday and Stoddard's work bears upon intellectual education. Their conclusion was generally favorable to the movies as an informal educational device, qualified only by the finding that factual errors as well as correct information are learned. The rest of the massive and irrefutable evidence must be related to moral education, and here it is absolutely impossible to interpret the studies cited to support an evaluation of the movies as a factor in the training of character. (2) "For children the content of motion pictures is not *good*. There is too *much* sex and crime and love for a balanced diet for children." (Italics mine.) Whereas the studies mentioned above indicated the power of motion pictures, here the investigations of Dale, Blumer, Thrasher, Peters and their associates "clearly indicate that the power flows *too much in dangerous directions*." (Italics mine.) We have already seen that the data collected—to whatever extent they are reliable—show nothing of the sort.

4. *Motion Pictures and Youth: A Summary*, New York, 1933: p. 60.

The work cited cannot be made the basis of the moral evaluation which Charters states as its conclusion. (3) "The motion picture situation is very complicated. It is one among many influences which mold the experience of children. How powerful this is in relation to the influence of the ideals taught in the home, in the school and in the church, by street life and companions or by community customs, *these studies have not canvassed.*" (Italics mine.) The negative finding of May and Shuttleworth is then cited, but Charters adds the findings of Holaday-Stoddard and Thurstone-Peterson, as if they were inconsistent with it. That is not the case. All three pieces of research indicate what Charters calls the complexity of "the motion picture situation." In any event, this third conclusion curiously undermines the significance of the other two, even if we do not question their validity independently. If the movies exert any influence upon the characters of children, they must do so in conjunction with or in opposition to other leading forces, such as home, school, church, friends, books. If the relation of these factors is not known; if, as Charters admits, a simple cause and effect relationship cannot be said to prevail, it does not follow, as Charters elsewhere tries to insist, that the lover of children should be "concerned with the question of how well the commercial motion picture plays its individual part in the education of children and not with whether it is more or less important than another instrument." Those interested in the welfare of children may well be concerned with this question, but that concern is not augmented or given definite direction by the results of scientific research.

For the sake of contrast and also to present a more accurate picture of scientific findings, I offer the following summary. (1) In the matter of juvenile delinquency, as in the case of adult criminality, there is a balance of affirmative and negative opinion. So far as there are any scientific data even remotely relevant to this point, they are extremely unreliable and plainly inconsistent: the autobiographical materials Blumer collected and supplemented by his own opinions, on the one hand, and the data and opinions of English investigators, the autobiographical materials of Mrs. Mitchell, and the findings of May and Shuttleworth, on the other. (2) In the matter of moral influence, the relevance of the scientific data is questionable. To whatever extent they are relevant and can be considered as reliable, the findings are inconsistent and tend to be negative. There is only, *on the one hand,* the autobiographical material of Blumer with regard to emotional experience and the formation of ideas, supported by the measurement of emotional responses by Dysinger and Ruckmick, and the finding of Holaday-Stoddard about how much children learn. This is certainly not a showing that the movies corrupt the moral character of the immature. Nor is it made so by Dale's survey of the major themes of motion pictures and his amazing discovery that stories of love, sex and crime predominate, because, *on the other hand,* the finding of Holaday-Stoddard, supported by the English reports, show that children learn little from the movies that they are not already prepared for by prior experience. Furthermore, the finding of May-Shuttleworth shows that for the most part there are no significant differences in moral attitudies, etc., between children who frequent and children who abstain from the movies; the finding of Thurstone-Peterson shows that the attitudes of children may be formed by movies in opposite directions, either *or* both of which may be desirable *or* undesirable; and the finding of Peters that the movies either conform to the mores as they are practised or, for the most part, are "better" than such practices. If all of this has any significance, after unreliability of methods and data have been taken into account and inconsistencies nullify each other, it tends to cast some doubt upon the popular concern about the moral influence of motion pictures upon the immature.

(3) In the matter of health, fears rather than opinions predominate. Parents have been generally concerned about the injury that may be done by violent emotional disturbances, especially the anxieties and panics, which movies seem to produce in some children. Their worry is not clearly supported by the physiological measurements of Dysinger and Ruckmick, since the physiological significance of the size of a psychogalvanic response is not known, nor can its bearing on general health be guessed. The experimental evidence here, furthermore, shows marked individual differences and inconsistent emotional effects. The autobiographical materials of Blumer merely confirm what most parents already know: that *some* children are violently excited by *some* motion pictures. But they also indicate that, for the most part, these emotional experiences are extremely short-lived. Even when they are not transient, the autobiographical data do not show whether they are harmful or beneficial. Finally, there is some experimental data to show that exposure to movies may disturb sleep either in the direction of increased or decreased motility, but again there are marked individual differences and there is no sound experimental or theoretical basis for the interpretation of these changes in motility as bearing on health. (4) In the matter of intellectual education, the opinion of teachers is predominantly against the movies, as an impediment to study and school work, and this seems to be supported by the May-Shuttleworth finding that children who frequently attend the movies have lower scholastic standing than those who do not. But neither the opinions of teachers nor the scientific data can be made the basis for a causal conclusion. *If* there is a reliably determined relationship between frequency of movie attendance and school grades, the correlation does

not mean that either one is the cause of the other. On the other hand, the findings of Holaday and Stoddard, supported by the autobiographical materials of Blumer, show that the movies contribute substantially to the information and ideas of their juvenile audience. But this evidence does not indicate what evaluation should be made of the educational worth of this contribution, even though it is discovered that in some proportion erroneous and misleading information is acquired.

In short, the scientific work that has been done is of little or no practical value to the prudent man. On the crucial point—the influence of motion pictures on moral character and conduct—science has not improved or altered the state of existing opinion. In those few instances in which the scientific work has been well done and reported with proper scientific restraint—the researches of Thurstone-Peterson and Holaday-Stoddard—the findings do not warrant any moral judgments about the effects discovered. We must proceed, therefore, without the benefit of science.

■ ■ ■ ■

The Movies, the Actor, and the Public Morals (1936), Edward G. Robinson

The actors also took part in the debate on the moral and social responsibility of the movies. In this essay, originally published in a 1936 anthology, *The Movies on Trial,* edited by William Perlman, Robinson argues that the artist's only responsibility is to his art (in Mortimer Adler's terms). Although a controversial figure in the 1930s because of the famous and immoral gangster he played in *Little Caesar,* Robinson would find himself in greater personal difficulties a decade or so later during the Blacklist period because of his intelligent, articulate, and vocal defense of liberal political causes.

The actor who takes himself and his work seriously is not concerned with morals. In view of the fact that morality is usually applied to "the conduct of other people," it already has more watch dogs than necessary for its preservation. It is the exclusive business of reformers, preachers, grammarians and legislators. And therein, perhaps, lies the root of all evil. The cry for cleaner pictures, for cleaner stage, art and literature, has been made a business of. The actor, not unlike all true artists, is

"The Movies, the Actor, and the Public Morals," by Edward G. Robinson, is from *The Movies on Trial,* edited by William Perlman (Macmillan, 1936).

primarily interested in rendering a faithful portrayal of the part he undertakes. If he is called upon to interpret the role of a villain, he must not shrink from accentuating the propensities or idiosyncracies of that particular character no matter how hideous or despicable. To impersonate an underworld character requires as much histrionic ability as to enact the part of saint or nobleman. Most important is to render the character lifelike and human, and if necessary, repulsive and grotesque. . . .

The moralist's objection to "Little Caesar," and to pictures of a similar *genre,* was that a hero has been made out of a rapscallion, that an enemy of society has been endowed with certain redeeming features, with certain laudatory traits, and that when he met the doom he so justly deserved, he evoked a sympathetic response from the human breast. That may be true. But there is no gainsaying that "Little Caesar," and many of his phototypes in the underworld, have a code of morals of their own. They evince a loyalty among themselves seldom encountered among men in our so-called upper strata of society. A dangerous assertion for a respectable citizen to make, no doubt; but to state a fact does not necessarily mean its endorsement. It is a well known fact that Arnold Rothstein and "Legs" Diamond and many other notorious criminals had met death at the hands of their own henchmen; and yet, when questioned by the police before they died, these victims had steadfastly refused to divulge the names of their assailants, though they knew the hand that had pulled the trigger.

"Little Caesar" was, in the parlance of gangdom "a square shooter." His ambition was to become czar of his immediate underworld. In the light of the milieu to which he belonged and, perhaps, even in our own light, he was kind, generous, and on the level,—a real pal to his faithful hangers on. But woe to him who double crossed him. Born and bred in a different environment, he probably would have turned out to be a useful member of society. However, be that as it may. It is unreasonable to assume that the character of "Little Caesar" was glorified in any form, shape or manner. His miserable end precluded any such conclusion. He died like a rat. The picture pointed to a definite moral: He who lives by the sword shall died by it, or, the wages of sin is death.

In my opinion, the success of "Little Caesar" was due to the fact that the character was truly conceived and drawn by the author. If he were not human and lifelike he would have not appealed to the multitudes. The vogue of any novel, play or movie, depends entirely upon the human elements with which the protagonist has been invested. Life is, for the most part, drab and monotonous. People read books and go to the theatre to temporarily forget their immediate surroundings—house, duties, children, husbands, wives, responsibilities. By following the exploits of the hero or heroine of a good story we experience a vicarious thrill. If the characters are faithfully drawn we often change places with them. How many of us wanted but lacked the courage to emulate the pleasant wickedness of the characters flashed before us on the screen? We are fed up with being constantly good. Virtue may have its reward in heaven, but why wait so long if vice has its own charms and pays dividends here and now?

If we do not follow the paths of "Little Caesar," it is not because we are virtuous but because we are intelligent, or, maybe, because we fear the policeman, or St. Peter, or our own conscience. Secretly most of us applaud those who dare and do. To illustrate this unconsciously hidden admiration each and every one has for the delinquents of society, I can do no better than to relate the following story:

One day, as I walked out of a picture house (yes, I go to the movies quite often, and not always to see the pictures in which I appear), I was confronted by an elderly woman who was leading a seven or eight year old boy by the hand. She asked me if I was Edward G. Robinson, I admitted my identity.

"So it's you who played 'Little Caesar' and so many other bad men?" She said more in the form of reproof than seeking information.

I pleaded guilty to the accusation.

"Well, I'm glad I have this opportunity of telling you to your face what a bad influence your pictures have had on our young people."

"What makes you think so?" I asked her.

"I ought to know," she replied quite sure of her ground, "I've taken my grandchild to see 'Little Caesar' eight times."

I sincerely hope that all the sins committed by the "bad men" I have played will not be chalked up against me. Nor do I want it understood that I am particularly fond of, or hold a brief for, gangsters, killers and the vanishing bootlegger. My neighbors will vouch that I am a peaceful citizen and an honest taxpayer. I even observe all traffic regulations. Nevertheless, I would like to know and understand the psychology of the criminals that fill our prisons. I would like to probe the mainsprings of the human soul that make one a saint and another a sinner. Freud blames our anti-social vagaries on the "infantile" and "primitive" instincts forever lurking in the "subconscious," and waiting for the opportunity to overpower us. We never can tell when these monsters might break loose and turn us into criminals.

It is all too engrossing a subject, criminology is. And my interest in it is purely professional. I believe that it is impossible for any actor to render a true portrayal of character unless he can fathom the psychology that prompts a man to do the stupidest things.

I have often wondered why it is that our moral preachers, forever trying to reform this sinful world of ours, have never turned their broadside against the press. The fables presentedon the screen are Sunday School sermons compared to some of the stories featured in our dailies. As an example, let us glance at the records dealing with the shooting of John Dillinger.

That that event was an important news item is undeniable; and no one can take exception to the detailed description of the various incidents leading to the apprehension and killing of Public Enemy Number 1 featured in the newspapers. It was a fine piece of detective work—intelligent, daring, well-planned and well-executed. But was it necessary to go into detail about Dillinger's life, his habits, his criminal exploits, his love affairs and his burial? Column after column was devoted to the gunman even for days after the shooting. If a movie were made of the actual newspaper records, our moralists would have denounced it as indecent, tending to corrupt the morals of the young. But an even more egregious breach of good taste committed by the press and condoned by the champions of public morals is still fresh in our memory.

No event in the annals of recent history has been more publicized than the Hauptmann case. No details of the court proceedings, fit or unfit for public consumption, were omitted. Every bit of testimony was faithfully recorded. Full page photographs of all the *dramatis personæ* connected with the trial were displayed. Every prominent newspaper featured special articles by specially assigned correspondents. The world's literati were gathered in the courtroom at Flemington, N.J. Every move and gesture of the defendant were dwelt upon. How and what he ate, how he slept, and the mood he was in at the various stages of the trial. In addition to all these minutae covered by the press, every radio station had special commentators analyzing and dissecting the evidence. Motion pictures, showing the defendant on the witness stand, were surreptitiously taken and shown on the screen twenty-four hours later: If ever an arch criminal was lionized it was Hauptmann.

Turn to the pages of the tabloids, the circulation of which, in round numbers, rivals the movie-going public. How much space do they devote to politics, to international affairs, to scientific discoveries, to civic and cultural progress? Hardly any. But a mere rumor that a Hollywood star is about to be divorced will be featured in type a foot high.

The tendency of the press to stress the sensational may be multiplied *an infinitum*. Gruesome stories of murder, arson and rape, salacious accounts of divorce cases and breach of promise suits, so boldly related as to leave nothing to the imagination, have always been featured by the newspapers. Let us turn to the newspaper files of bygone years and note the news items that were given prominence: The homicide trials of Harry Thaw, Nan Patterson, Rolland Molyneux, the Becker case, Ruth Snyder.

City editors know their business. They know the importance of news value. They know that their readers love melodrama. And what is more melodramatic than a man or woman being tried for murder?

The advocates of movie censorship maintain that the general, present day disregard for law and order has been enhanced by the screen's exploitation of scandalous and unsavory topics. Are we then to assume that the sordid stories flashed on the front pages of our dailies exert a more benign influence than the fictitious and highly romantic tales flashed on the screen? That is hardly conceivable.

Apparently, the attitude of our moralists towards the press, on the one hand, and the movies, on the other, is somewhat paradoxical. And there is only one plausible explanation for this paradox. The Fourth Estate is too dangerous, and a much too powerful organization to attack. The movies provide a less dangerous target. And besides, even reformers crave publicity. It would not do to war against the press.

In my opinion, neither the movies nor the press can be held reprehensible for the widespread of lawlessness and the laxity of morals. If our would be censors were better sociologists, and more concerned with truth than with morals, they would experience no difficulty in giving us a correct diagnosis of the symptoms. . . .

■ ■ ■ ■

The Motion Picture Industry Today (1944), Mae D. Huettig

Much more to the credit of academic research than the Payne Fund Studies were several careful and rigorous examinations of the economic bases of the motion picture industry. Mae Huettig's book, *Economic Control of the Motion Picture Industry,* was published by a university press (Pennsylvania) in 1944. This section from the book examines the economic structure of the industry as a whole and the corporate structure of the major companies during Hollywood's Golden Years.

Some Questions to Be Answered

Despite the glamour of Hollywood, the crux of the motion picture industry is the theatre. It is in the brick-and-mortar branch of the industry

"The Motion Picture Industry Today" is from *Economic Control of the Motion Picture Industry,* by Mae D. Huettig (University of Pennsylvania Press, 1944; Ozer, 1971).

that most of the money is invested and made. Without understanding this fact, devotees of the film are likely to remain forever baffled by some characteristics of an industry which is in turn exciting, perplexing, and irritating. Emphasis on the economic role of the theatre is not meant to belittle the film itself. Obviously it is the film which draws people to the theatre. Nevertheless, the structure of the motion picture industry (a large inverted pyramid, top-heavy with real estate and theatres, resting on a narrow base of the intangibles which constitute films) has had far-reaching effects on the film itself.

This may seem farfetched. Most writers on the motion picture industry rather studiously avoid its duller aspects, i.e., those dealing with the trade practices, financial policies, intercorporate relationships, etc. But the facts indicate clearly that there is a connection between the form taken by the film and the mechanics of the business, even if the connection is somewhat obscure. It is true, as one student has pointed out, that "the issues involved are not peculiar to the motion picture history."[1] Despite this lack of uniqueness, the problems of organization, intercorporate relationships, and financial policy in the motion picture industry deserve more than passing mention. The attitude of the industry itself toward discussion of these problems has not been completely candid. A great reluctance to disclose factual information with respect to its operations has unfortunately characterized most of the leaders of the industry.

Among the many questions which lack a reliable answer are: How many people attend movies? How often? How large is the industry in terms of invested capital and volume of business? What is the annual income of all theatres? How many theatres are owned by what groups? What type of film is most uniformly successful? What is the relationship between the cost of films and their drawing power? Little is known of the industry's place in the broader pattern of American industry, or its method of solving the specialized problems of commercial entertainment. There are few reliable statistics available (and of these none is compiled by the industry itself) with regard to these questions.

WHAT IS THE ECONOMIC IMPORTANCE OF THE INDUSTRY?

There are various ways of measuring the role of an industry in our economy. The indices most commonly used are: (1) volume of business, (2) invested capital, and (3) number of employees. The value of such criteria is limited, since comparison between all types of industries produces results too general to be significant. However, in the case of the motion picture industry, these indices are valuable as a means of delimiting its economic importance and recording some basic information re-

1. Howard T. Lewis, *The Motion Picture Industry,* p. 13.

garding its size. This question assumes importance partly because the industry itself seems to be under some misapprehension with respect to
the answer. It may well be true, as Will Hays frequently says, that the motion picture is a great social necessity, an integral part of human life in
the whole civilized world, but this value is in no way minimized by an
accurate statement as to the industry's economic importance. "Standing
well among the first ten (or the first four) industries in this country," has
so often prefaced the remarks of industry spokesmen as to indicate that
the facts are not generally known.

Here, then, let it be noted that in so far as size of industry is measured
by dollar volume of business, the motion picture industry is not only
not among the first ten, it is not even among the first forty. It is surpassed
by such industries, to name only a few, as laundries, hotels, restaurants,
loan companies, investment trusts, liquor, tobacco, and musical instrument. . . .

Viewed thus as a part of our national economy, the motion picture industry is not a major bulwark. There are forty-four other industries, out
of the total of ninety-four industrial groups enumerated by *Statistics of
Income* (Bureau of Internal Revenue), that reported a larger gross income
in 1937 than did the combined motion picture producing and exhibition
corporations. In terms of employment, the motion picture industry accounts for somewhat fewer than 200,000 persons in all three branches
of production, distribution, and exhibition. . . .

When motion picture corporations are compared with those in other
branches of the entertainment field, another story is presented. The entire field of commercial amusement, including billiard halls, bowling
alleys, dance halls, etc., is dominated by the motion picture industry. Motion picture corporations, constituting 44 per cent of the total number of
amusement corporations in 1937, accounted for 78 per cent of the gross
income and 92 per cent of the total net income of the group. This should
prove what has long been suspected and probably needs little proof:
that movies are the favorite form of entertainment for most Americans.

Production versus Exhibition

From the point of view of the movie-going public, one of the most important questions about the industry is: Who decides what films are made;
or as it is more commonly put, why are films what they are? From the
industry's point of view, too, this question of the kind of product released
is ultimately its most important single problem. Quality of product is increasingly vital now that the motion picture business is settling down
into a semblance of middle age, devoid of the novelty appeal it formerly
had.

The answer to the question posed above is in the relationship between the various branches of the industry. By virtue of the division of labor within the business, film distributors and exhibitors are much more closely in touch with the movie-going public than are the producers, and they trade heavily on their advantageous positions. From their seat in the box office they announce that so-and-so is "poison at the box office," that what the public wants is musicals or blood-and-thunder westerns, that English stars murder business, and that sophisticated farce comedies leave their audiences completely cold.

Broadly speaking, and omitting the relatively unimportant independent producers, the relationship between the three branches of the industry may be described in two ways. First, there is the relationship between a major producer and theatre operators not affliated with his company. Secondly, there is the relationship *within* a major company between the various departments of production, distribution, and exhibition. The intra-company relationship is the more important with respect to the kind of films made, since contact within the organization is much closer than contact between the unaffiliated exhibitors and producers. The unaffiliated exhibitors are not generally consulted by producers with respect to the nature of the films to be made. However, they occasionally make their views known through advertisements in the trade press and probably express their opinions quite freely in talking with the sales representatives of the producers. Most of their arguments are ex post facto, however, and affect the future line-up of product negatively, or not at all.

On the other hand, the sales and theatre people *within* the integrated companies are extremely important in determining the type of picture to be made, the number of pictures in each cost class, the type of story, etc. It is not intended to give here a detailed account of the manner in which these decisions are reached, but in general the procedure is as follows: The person in charge of distribution announces the number of films wanted for the following season. This figure is presumably based on some estimate of what can be profitably sold, but it is also related to the needs of the company's own theatres for product. The chief executive announces the amount of money available for the total product. The amounts vary among the individual companies from $7 or $8 million for the smaller companies to $28 million for Loew's. The next step is the division and allocation of the total amount to groups of pictures. The names given these classes vary, but the grouping is in accordance with the quality to be aimed at as defined by the amount of money to be spent. That is, there are the "specials" and the more ordinary "program" features. There are "A" pictures and "B" pictures. The latter are designed, more or less frankly, to meet the need for the lesser half of the double-feature program. Once the allocation of production funds is made, the next step is that of determining the budgets for the individual pictures within each group. The amount spent on a given picture is presumably related in some way to the anticipated drawing power of the particular combination of talent and production values planned for the given picture. After the detailed budget is worked out, a tentative release schedule is prepared for the use of the sales force (distribution). From this point on the problems belong primarily to the production department.

Note what this cursory outline reveals. Company executives, i.e., theatre, sales, and production people, determine the following: the number of pictures to be made, the total amount of money to be spent, the distribution of the funds between the various classes of pictures, the budgets of the individual pictures, and the dates when the pictures are to be finished.

It is not meant that all such issues are decided by ukase and handed down from the front office to the production staff. The interdepartmental conference technique is customary, with every department chief valiantly defending his own position. At work are all the usual subterranean factors which determine where power ultimately rests. There are, however, certain objective factors which are present to some degree in each of the five large majors. These tend to give decisive policy-making power regarding the kind of films made to the groups farthest removed from production itself, i.e., the men in distribution and theatre management.

The objective factors are found in a prosaic listing of the various sources of income to the five principal companies. In approximate order of importance, they are: (1) theatre admissions, (2) film rentals, (3) the sale of film accessories, and (4) dividends from affiliated companies. The relative importance of each source varies for the individual majors, but in almost every instance the chief single source of income is theatre admissions. Although there is an inseparable connection between the quality of films and company earnings from film rentals and theatres, the division of functions within the company structure operates to give the preponderance of power to those nearest the principal source of income, i.e., the theatres. Furthermore, the earning power of a given chain of theatres depends not so much upon the quality of films made by its parent company as on the quality of films in general. If successful films are available, the dominant group of affiliated theatres in a given area generally has preferential access to them, regardless of which major produced them. In other words, the successful theatre operations of each of the majors depend largely on the return from the theatres. But successful theatre operation for a major company is not directly dependent on the quality of its own pictures, although this contributes of course. By virtue of the regional division of the theatre market, there is in effect a pooling of the product;

the affiliated theatres in their separate areas have access to the best pictures available. Consequently, competition in the production of pictures has no real parallel in the theatre organization. A good picture, i.e., one successful at the box office, redounds to the benefit of each of the theatre-owning majors since each shares in the box office. This interdependence seems a unique characteristic of the motion picture business. In other industries, an exceptionally good product is feared and disliked by other producers or sellers of similiar goods. But of the small group of dominant movie companies, it is really true that the good of one is the good of all.

The production and exhibition phases of the business behave toward each other like a chronically quarrelsome but firmly married couple and not without reason. The exhibitor group controls the purse-strings; it accounts for more than nine-tenths of the invested capital and approximately two-thirds of the industry's income. Nevertheless, it requires films. Consequently, the conflict between the two groups more nearly resembles a family quarrel than is ordinarily true of trade disputes, since the essential interdependence between production and exhibition is recognized by all. To a theatre operator there is no substitute for "celluloid." Conversely, the producers of movies have no real alternative to the theatres as outlets for their product. The normal interdependency between supplier and customer is accentuated in the motion picture industry by the combination of functions within the same corporate framework. But difficulty results from the fact that while the selling of entertainment is a commercial process, making films is largely creative and artistic in nature. Movie-makers, like artists in other fields, are generally inclined to experiment with new techniques and are not above wanting to interpret or affect their surroundings. Exhibitors, on the other hand, may not know much about the art of the film, but they know what has been good box office before. Consequently, theirs is the conservative influence; they are the traditionalists of the trade, exerting their influence in the direction of the safe-and-sound in film making. . . .

THE MAJORS

The best single source of information about the major motion picture companies is the Securities and Exchange Commission with which registration statements and annual reports are filed. These provide considerably more factual data than have ever before been available to outsiders, making it possible to delineate the structure of the companies and their relationship to each other with respect to size, volume of business, their financial policies, profitability, executive remuneration.

Examination of the list of subsidiaries reported by any one of the five large companies indicates that the production of films is merely one of many activities and not necessarily the most important. Warner Brothers Pictures, Inc., for example, lists 108 subsidiaries. They include the following: a film laboratory, Brunswick Radio Corporation, and a radio manufacturing subsidiary, a lithographing concern, a concern that makes theatre accessories, 10 music publishing houses, real estate companies, booking agencies, several broadcasting corporations, a company called Warner Brothers Cellulose Products, Inc., theatre management companies, recording studios, and a television company—all this in addition to a film-producing unit and numerous theatre subsidiaries, controlling approximately 507 theatres.

Loew's, Inc., consists of approximately 73 subsidiaries controlled more than 50 per cent, plus 20 additional corporations in which effective control was disclaimed. The subsidiaries are primarily theatre concerns, but include distribution companies, vaudeville booking agencies, music publishing houses, and several realty concerns. In fact, three of Loew's most important subsidiaries are registered with the S.E.C. as real-estate corporations. Control without majority ownership of the stock in many of the theatre subsidiaries operates either through written agreements or through acquiescence of the remaining stockholders. In practice, this generally means that the owners of the theatre have agreed to share control with Loew's in exchange for a franchise to exhibit Loew's pictures.

Paramount Pictures, Inc., is the most complex of the five, although its activities are apparently less ramified than Warner Brothers. Whereas it originally bought out entire circuits of theatres, financing most of the purchases with bonds, reorganization in 1935 brought with it many changes in policy and structure. Today, most of its theatre enterprises are partnerships; Paramount participates but does not exercise complete control. This is borne out by the fact that only 95 of its 203 subsidiaries are controlled 50 per cent or more. Decentralized theatre operations have been the approved policy at Paramount since the failure in 1933 of an attempt to manage in detail some 1,600 theatres from New York. It is estimated that at least half of Paramount's theatres are now run by their original owners on a part-ownership and contract basis, and that Paramount's average interest in its theatres is somewhat less than 70 per cent.

The smaller producing companies are less complicated in structure and less far-flung in their activities. However, even concerns like Columbia Pictures and Universal Pictures operate twenty-eight and thirty-four subsidiaries respectively. Most of these are distribution units. Universal Pictures Corporation is itself a subsidiary of Universal Corporation, a holding company which controls almost all its common stock. Both Universal Corporation and Columbia Pictures Corporation are managed by voting trusts.

The diversity of functions demonstrated by the large movie companies is reflected in the executive personnel, that is, the directors and officers of the companies. If the production of movies is but one aspect of the corporate existence, it follows that representation will be given to the other activities in some proportion to their importance. Take Paramount, for instance. Its board of directors includes the following: Harvey D. Gibson, banker, affiliated with the New York Trust Company, Manufacturers' Trust Company, the Textile Banking Company, etc.; A. Conger Goodyear, manufacturer and financier; John D. Hertz, partner in Lehman Brothers, founder of the Yellow Cab Company; Maurice Newton, partner in Hallgarten and Company, investment banker with diverse interests in tobacco, rubber, petroleum, and real estate. The president of Paramount is Barney Balaban, a Chicago theatre man; vice-president is Frank Freeman, also originally a theatre operator. Chairman of the executive committee is Stanton Griffis, broker and partner in Hemphill, Noyes. Mr. Adolph Zukor, the company's founder, occupies the somewhat honorific post of chairman of the board of directors.

The executive group of Radio-Keith-Orpheum presents a similar concentration of non-theatrical personnel. Chairman of the board is Richard C. Patterson. Atlas Corporation is represented by Peter Rathvon, chairman of the excutive committee, and W. Mallard, described in the company's registration statement with the S.E.C. as an independent consultant on reorganization. Of the five principal executive officers, only two have had any previous experience in the motion picture industry: George Schaefer, president of the company, and Ned E. Depinet, vice-president, had both previously been concerned with distribution. Neither is primarily a production person. The board of directors includes Floyd Odlum, president of Atlas Corporation; William Hamilton, a partner of J. P. Morgan; James G. Harbord, formerly chairman of the board of Radio Corporation of America; and Lumford P. Yandell, also associated with R.C.A.

Universal Corporation, the parent company of Universal Pictures, is controlled by seven voting trustees, only one of whom is a motion picture person. The production company itself is operated by a group of men thoroughly familiar with the theatre business but relatively new to problems of production.

The structure of the major companies is important because there is a real and direct connection between the way in which they are set up, the kind of people who run them, and the kind of films produced. This is the reason for emphasis on the fact that the capital assets of the dominant companies are so largely land, buildings, and real estate. Where the investment takes this form, it is not surprising that the executive personnel should consist of men skilled primarily in the art of selecting theatre sites, managing real estate, and financing operations, rather than of talented producers.

The balance sheets of the five theatre-owning majors show that from half to three-quarters of their total assets are "land, buildings, and equipment." On the other hand, for the two producing-distributing companies (Universal and Columbia), this proportion is under 15 per cent. . . .

In itself, the fact that the majors' assets are chiefly theatres, i.e., real estate, might have little significance. However, most of the theatres were acquired with the aid of bonds and other forms of long-term debt. The policy of debt financing has been of great importance in the history of the industry. More than 30 per cent of the total invested capital in the seven major motion picture companies is borrowed. The case of several individual companies is even more extreme. Nearly half of the total capital of Warner Brothers and Paramount, for example, is borrowed. Thus, it is no accident that the principal corporate officers of four out of the five big majors are bondholders or their representatives. Debt financing has had many important ramifications affecting the stockholders, dividend policies, and internal corporate practices. Most important, however, to the movie-goer, is this fact: The production of films, essentially fluid and experimental as a process, is harnessed to a form of organization which can rarely afford to be either experimental or speculative because of the regularity with which heavy fixed charges must be met.

Originally, the motive behind the acquisition of theatres by producing companies may have been the need for the security represented by assured first-run exhibition for their films. Today, however, the majors derive most of their income from their theatres, and production is less important as a source of revenue than exhibition. In fact, the chief advantage of continued control over production and distribution is that it enables them to maintain their advantageous position as favored theatre operators. Thus, the production of films by the major companies is not really an end in itself, on the success or failure of which the company's existence depends; it is an instrument directed toward the accomplishment of a larger end, i.e., domination of the theatre market. This does not mean that there is no attempt to make successful films or that film production is itself unprofitable (although three of the five largest major companies have regularly incurred losses in production); it means simply that the principal concern of the men who run the major companies is their theatres. . . .

■ ■ ■ ■

LOEW'S INC. (1939)

The increasing interest of the business world in the motion picture in-dustry was indicated by a series of articles in *Fortune* magazine during the decade, each devoted to a single film company. Ms. Huettig's chapter reprinted above examines the potentially conflicting interests of producing films and exhibiting them. The article reprinted below, which appeared in the *Fortune* series, also alludes to the tension between East Coast (the offices of Loew's Inc.) and West (the studio of MGM). Examining the richest and most successful company of them all, the piece stands at an in-teresting point in the economic history of Hollywood. Despite the wealth of the past and present, the troubles that would erode Hollywood's eco-nomic future were already visible (particularly the government litigation that would divorce studios from theaters—that would, in effect, divorce MGM from Loew's Inc.). The editors' prediction—that Loew's would keep its studio and sell its theaters—would turn out to be temporarily true. Eventually, Loew's would dump both to make its money from hotels.

Mr. Nicholas M. Schenck, for the last twelve years President of Loew's Inc., is the author of that optimistic saying, "There is nothing wrong with this industry that good pictures cannot cure." It has been the easier for Mr. Schenck to say that about the movie business because Loew's picture-making unit, Metro-Goldwyn-Mayer, has for at least eight years made far and away the best pictures of any studio in Hollywood. Metro's gross revenue from film rentals has been consistently higher than that of other studios, and as a result Loew's Inc. has been and still is the most profitable movie company in the world. So vital are Metro pictures to Loew's earnings that whereas Mr. Schenck, the undisputed boss of the whole shebang, received some $220,000 from his profit-sharing contract last year (over and above a salary of $2,500 a week), Mr. Louis B. Mayer, the employee who runs Metro, received $763,0000 on his profit-sharing con-tract, over and above a salary of $3,000 a week. That's what Mr. Schenck and his Board of Directors are willing to pay for "good pictures."

When FORTUNE looked at Loew's in December, 1932, the whole story was devoted to Mr. Mayer's fabulous studio, and Mr. Schenck's parent company was relegated to an appendix. Today, however, Mr. Schenck is faced with one or two problems, not then anticipated, which Mr. Mayer may not be able to solve for him singlehanded. The chief one is the anti-

"Loew's Inc." is from the August 1939 issue of *Fortune*.

trust suit that the Department of Justice brought against Loew's and seven other major units of the movie industry in July, 1938. Loew's, like its four biggest competitors, is engaged in selling and exhibiting, as well as in making pictures; and the government, on behalf of the small producers and independent theatre owners who feel squeezed by this vertical trustification, seems resolved to break it into halves. The fight is proceeding to trial very, very slowly, but only the vagaries of the law, and not good pictures, will ultimately end it.

Another thing in the back of Mr. Schenck's mind is the fact that Metro pictures, while still possibly the most successful in the world, have recently been failing to make their customary splash in the trade. The absence of splash was loudly heard last fall, when the expensive super-specials *Marie Antoinette* and *The Great Waltz* were presented to an American public that has not even yet shown any inclination to return to Metro their negative costs. Jeanette MacDonald's *Broadway Serenade* and Joan Crawford's *Ice Follies of 1939*, coming along in the spring, helped to confirm the impression that Metro had struck a slump; so did the news that the touted *I Take This Woman* (Spencer Tracy and Hedy Lamarr) has been indefinitely postponed. In a company that had grown used to releasing a *Grand Hotel, Mutiny on the Bounty, Thin Man, Test Pilot, Boys' Town, Captains Courageous,* or their box-office equivalents every month or so, the recent Metro crop of turkeys has not been reassuring. In so far as this constitutes a problem for Mr. Schenck, he can hardly turn solely to Mr. Mayer, for it might be Mr. Mayer's fault. It is certainly Mr. Mayer's responsibility. But it has not been costing Mr. Schenck any sleep. The fact is that Metro's gross picture rentals, which reflect the average popularity of the studio's entire product of fifty or so pictures a year, are ahead of the 1938 gross to date by some $2,000,000. The number of exhibitors who are buying the product has also been steadily climbing. Hence if Metro is indeed in a serious slump, the only measure thereof is the volatile thermometer of Hollywood gossip. To be sure, Hollywood gossip is itself sometimes a hard business factor, in its effect on people in the industry.

The antitrust problem, though more tangible than the studio problem, has not troubled any Schenck sleep yet either. He believes that Loew's cause is just, and that the government will either drop its suit (which Assistant Attorney General Thurman Arnold denies) or lose it. Some people say that even if the five big chains were to be divorced from the five big studios, the effect might be to stimulate Loew's profits rather than to stop them. It would be a different sort of picture business from the one Mr. Schenck knows, however. A trust is a delicate thing to monkey with, and not even Trust-Buster Arnold dares envision the result if he should bust this one. We can best tell what both he and Mr. Schenck are up against by looking at Loew's as a whole, to see how the richest of the movie trusts gets its ephemeral product made, distributed, exhibited, and turned into such surprising quantities of cash.

Although Loew's assets, some $144,000,000 are exceeded by those of Warner Bros., its profits have for eight years been well ahead of those of any rival. Its gross revenues are also larger. In 1930 and 1937, on grosses of $129,500,000 and $121,800,000 respectively, it earned some $14,500,000. Last year, on a gross of $122,700,000, it earned just under $10,000,000; and even in 1933, the poorest movie year since sound, its profits were $4,000,000. With the somewhat special exception of Warner Bros. (FORTUNE, December, 1937), Loew's was the only one of the five integrated "majors" to weather the depression without bankruptcy, re-organization, or shake-up of any kind.

For a company with such a record, the home offices over the State Theatre at Broadway and Forty-fifth Street, New York, are modest to the point of dinginess. Overshadowed by the Paramount Building and by many a flyspecked Times Square hotel, the sixteen-story Loew's build-ing gives no hint of the size of the checks that are signed on its seventh floor. The executives, too, present what is for Broadway an almost con-servative front. There are no fluted vests, but they are all well fed and healthy looking with Florida tans, and are mostly free from that appre-hensive quickness of speech and gesture that the uncertainties of show business stamp on so many of its votaries. For Loew's men, show business is not uncertain at all. And a surprising number count their service to Loew's in decades, not in years. Mr. Schenck himself, for example, has not worked for anyone else since 1906, and being a quiet, imperturbable, almost diffident man, he has succeeded in holding the loyalty and affec-tion, as well as the services, of his executives. He still talks with an ac-cent carried all the way from central Russia, which he left when he was nine, but it is unaccompanied by the bombast, the flailing gestures, the arrogance commonly associated with men who have reached large posi-tions in pictures. Mr. Schenck has an uncanny eye for profitable pictures, and a genius for building theatres in the correct places. But he eschews any self-glorification. He plays the ponies for a profit as well as for fun, and keeps a fast speedboat and an unpretentious yacht on Long Island Sound. The speedboat he uses mainly for commuting between Manhat-tan and his estate next to Walter Chrysler's at Greak Neck. The estate is inhabited by Mr. Schenck, Mrs. Schenck (nee Pansy Wilcox of Morgan-town, West Virginia), and three daughters, who are their father's main interest in life. The Schenck ménage is a gracious place of unobtrusive luxuriousness, resembling an English country house in mood and having only one boisterous detail—a set of tremendous brass cuspidors labeled "Great Expectorations" in the bar. . . .

Marcus Loew died in 1927, leaving an estate of more than $10,000,000 and a staff of executives trained for years in his conservative—for the picture industry—methods. During the late twenties, when Paramount, Fox, and Warner Bros. were borrowing money to buy or build as many theatres as they could get, Loew's sat tight with its chain of ten dozen or so high-class houses. "The day of reckoning will come," Mr. Schenck kept saying, resisting the pressure to join his competitors' spree. Indeed it did. When box-office receipts dropped in the depression, Fox, Paramount, and the others were left holding a bagful of inflated real estate and debt. The greater part of the industry went down in a dismal heap of bankruptcies, lawsuits, shake-ups, and reorganizations, in which control passed largely to Wall Street. Loew's, however, stood like Gibraltar, keeping its theatres and its financial independence as well.

There was a period, to be sure, when Loew's independence was in serious doubt. In 1929 William Fox bought a 45 per cent interest in the company, obtained mainly through purchase of stock from the Loew estate, Nicholas Schenck, and other executives. There was some idea of eventual merger, and Fox put a couple of Directors on the Board. But he never got around to interfering with the Schenck management. Before he had the chance, his own huge chain of theatres was in the most absorbing difficulties, and on top of that the government as an antitrust measure sued to restrain him from voting his Loew's stock. The stock was sequestered and three Directors "in the public interest" went on the Board. After Fox was dethroned from his own company, his Loew's stock reverted to the Chase Bank and other creditors, and has since been disposed of gradually in the open market. Nobody owns so much as 10 per cent of Loew's 1,600,000 shares of common or 137,000 shares of preferred today.

Loew's strength in the depression—a dividend was paid in every year —was only partly due to Mr. Schenck's caution in the matter of the theatres. There was only one year, 1932, when the profits from the theatres ($5,000,000 that year) exceeded the profits from the studio ($3,000,000). The rest of the time it was just the other way around. For while the theatre chain had been keeping itself within handy and profitable limits, Metro-Goldwyn-Mayer had been setting the industry by the ears. Getting off to a good start after 1924 with *He Who Gets Slapped, The Big Parade,* and the Garbo-Gilbert silents, the new sixty-three-acre studio at Culver City rapidly became encrusted with more stars and triumphs than Hollywood had seen in one place since the great Wallace

Reid days of the old Paramount lot. And Culver City had something else that Paramount had never had. This was a studio chief whom all Hollywood united in calling a production "genius," the small, pale, nervous youth named Irving Thalberg. To his golden touch with stars and stories Metro's amazing profits were almost universally ascribed. Thalberg, by attempting with a good deal of success to oversee every consequential production on the lot, drove himself to a physical breakdown, and although he tooks things a little easier thereafter, he died three years later, in September, 1936. In examining the Loew's of 1939, it is logical to begin with the rich heritage of Culver City that Thalberg left behind.

STAR FACTORY

"They won't miss him today or tomorrow or six months from now or a year from now," a studio executive remarked at Thalberg's funeral. "But two years from now they'll begin to feel the squeeze." With the release of *Goodbye, Mr. Chips,* M-G-M parted with the last picture that Irving Thalberg had anything to do with, and his admirers, a group that includes many who never knew him, have been pointing out symptoms of the squeeze for about a year. After his illness there was, of course, a determined effort to fill his shoes. There has been a long parade of would-bes— David Selznick (*David Copperfield, Tale of Two Cities*), Hunt Stromberg (*Maytime, The Thin Man*), and Mervyn LeRoy (*Wizard of Oz*), among others—and the Culver City lot today burgeons with characters who believe themselves to be undiscovered second Thalbergs. Thalberg is almost as pervasive an influence at Culver City today as he was in his lifetime. Recent errors of executive judgment are ridiculed in his name, and compared with the master's performance in similar situations. During his illness, Deanna Durbin and Fred Astaire were tested at Culver City, and turned down. On the subject of Astaire, some hapless underling scrawled on his report card, "Can't act; slightly bald; can dance a little." The Irving Thalberg Building, which harbors the executives, is super-air-conditioned and hermetically sealed. This, the wags allege, is so that the ghost of Thalberg can't get in to see what his successors are doing.

But if M-G-M no longer has a Thalberg, it still has a weekly studio payroll of $615,000 and a production force of 6,000 people. Among these are the twenty-six M-G-M stars, which the trade has been told are "more stars than there are in heaven." They are headed by the veterans Crawford, Shearer, William Powell, Garbo, and Gable, and include Loy, Donat, Spencer Tracy, Eddie Cantor, the Marx brothers, Robert Taylor, James Stewart, Rosalind Russell, Jeanette MacDonald, Nelson Eddy, Hedy Lamarr, Mickey Rooney, Wallace Beery, and Lionel Barrymore. There are fifty-odd featured players; eighty writers, among them F. Scott Fitzgerald, Ben Hecht, Anita Loos, and Laurence Stallings; the Class I directors, like Jack Conway, Victor Fleming, W. S. Van Dyke, Robert Z. Leonard, King Vidor, Sam Wood, Frank Borzage, H. S. Bucquet (a graduate of the shorts department and the current white hope of the studio), Norman Taurog, Clarence Brown, and George Cukor. There are the usual host of grips, maids, artists, flacks, and other proletariat, among them such unclassifiables as the man who, during the recent making of *The Wizard of Oz,* stood by the men's room to make sure that none of the many midgets employed in the picture fell into the full-sized commodes. There are also the executives.

Chief of these, of course, is Mr. Louis B. Mayer himself. Now fifty-four, Mr. Mayer is essentially a businessman, although in that capacity he does a good deal of informal acting and is sometimes known as Lionel Barrymore Mayer. In an effort to induce Jeanette MacDonald to unfreeze for her songs in *Maytime,* for example, he called her to his office and sang *Eli Eli* to her on the spot. He is also a tireless pinochle player and rumba dancer, and the possessor of a tough and energetic physique. A hard-shell Republican, he got a lot of kudos in the old days through his friendship with Hoover, which no doubt helped to reconcile the inner Mayer to sharing so much of the credit for Metro pictures with Thalberg. Perhaps he misses these kudos today. But being a good businessman, he has not tried to fill Thalberg's shoes himself. His job remains what it was, to oversee the entire studio, to handle the delicate diplomacy of contract negotiations, and to refer the tougher problems to Mr. Schenck, whom he calls "The General" and with whom he talks on the telephone two or three times a day. Mr. Mayer, perhaps the most feared man in Hollywood, is also responsible for the general lines along which Metro pictures are constructed. Unlike the rest of the world, these have not changed since the days when Mr. Mayer was a White House guest.

The chief of these policies is a ringing faith in the star system. Metro has created most of its own stars, and has even recreated a few (William Powell, Wallace Beery) whom other studios had virtually given up. How costly the making of a star can be is illustrated by *I Take This Woman,* already mentioned as having been shelved after considerable production expense. Because Hedy Lamarr is potentially a very valuable property, Metro dropped the money rather than get her off to a bad start. (Of course, the picture may yet be completed and titled, say the wags, *I Retake This Woman.*) But the making of a star, although it calls for a judicious selection of material to begin with, also imposes penalties on the star's casting thereafter. Metro pictures are more often vehicles than stories. Mr. Rubin and his aides are constantly combing the world for creative matter of all kinds, and they pay the best prices for it, but many of their best story buys are twisted out of recognition to fit expensive reputations. Even history can be bent to Metro's purpose, the most conspicuous recent example being Norma Shearer's *Marie Antoinette*. The "let 'em eat cake" line was deleted, and the queenly nincompoop became a brave and sympathetic heroine for the sake of Shearer's fans. This gingerly handling of stars has certainly paid in the past, and is almost essential to a studio that has such a huge investment in the precarious intangible of star power. But other, less plush-lined studios like Warner and Twentieth Century-Fox have lately been proving that a good story idea with an inexpensive cast can make money too, and the trend seems to lie in their direction.

Led by Warner, another advance in picture technique finds Metro even further behind. This is the handling of controversial or newsy themes, which are regarded as sure poison in the Metro front office. Sinclair Lewis's *It Can't Happen Here,* which Metro bought for $50,000, has been scheduled for two seasons, withdrawn both times, and is now for sale. *The Forty Days of Musa Dagh* has also been abandoned, owing to the harm it might do modern Turkey. Occasionally a producer slips a hot topic through (Joe Mankiewicz's *Fury* is the best example), but Mr. Mayer and his associates make no bones about the fact that they are conservative in their choice of subject matter. When *Fury* was being edited, an executive said to Fritz Lang, "It's all very well for you directors to want to make pictures with messages in them, but just remember that Cinderella paid this company $8,000,000 last year—and $8,000,000 can't be wrong." If Metro prefers one story to another, to all others, Cinderella is it.

Naturally there is no issue of taste or social conscience to be raised by this timidity; but there is a question of studio morale. Since the ingredients of a successful picture are nothing but people and ideas, an atmosphere of courage and inventiveness can be just as vital to a studio as a chestful of contracts for stories and stars. Many Hollywood gossips believe that the recent series of Metro fiascos can be traced to a decline in morale. In spite of the slogan on the executive walls—"Don't let Metro's success go to your head"—a good deal of complacence can be sniffed in the Culver City air. Mr. Mayer's executive staff—Eddie Mannix, Sam Katz, Ben Thau, Joe Cohn, and Al Lichtman—is an honest and competent group, but, like Mr. Mayer himself, some of them have been there an awfully long time. The studio manager is sufficiently unpopular to convince Mr. Schenck that he must be a good one, but he happens to be Louis Mayer's brother. Not that Mr. Mayer practices nepotism as extravagantly as some other studio heads, even if—having a nephew and two nieces on the payroll—somewhat more literally. But the gossips agree that a lot of the energy that used to go into good pictures seems to be going somewhere else. Leaving some rushes of his last picture, one of the twenty-three Metro producers yawned. "Really," he was heard to say, as he made for a telephone to see how they were running at Santa Anita, "really, I suppose I've got to find a production I can really interest myself in."

But we are here dealing with intangibles; and there is obviously no good evidence yet that Metro, like Paramount before it, has passed its prime. It should be pointed out that all studios have suffered and survived slumps, including Metro itself. And the tangible evidence of the whole product shows no slump at all. Metro has figured about as heavily in the annual Academy awards in the last two years as it ever did, and in 1938 it produced four of the "Ten Best Pictures" (*Boys' Town, Marie Antoinette, The Citadel,* and *Love Finds Andy Hardy*) selected by *Film Daily*'s poll vote of critics all over the country. For the coming season about fifty pictures are scheduled on a studio budget of $42,000,000. This, as usual with Metro, is the highest per-picture budget in the industry, and probably the proportion of hits, duds, and break-evens will not change very much. This summer (always a movie low spot) Metro has already released a big hit in *Goodbye, Mr. Chips,* made in its English studio. *Tarzan Finds a Son* also looks like a big grosser, as do the forthcoming *Lady of the Tropics, Wizard of Oz,* and—to be sold by Metro, though made by David O. Selznick—*Gone With the Wind.* Meanwhile the studio is getting from three to five times the negative cost out of its Dr. Kildare and Hardy Family series, which are produced for less than $300,000 apiece and have struck a new note in screen fare by being quiet, homely, pleasant, and increasingly successful. . . .

PIG IN A POKE

The trouble with the movie business, say statisticians, is that it is overseated and underproduced. The 16,250 theatres now open in the U.S. can seat about 10,000,000 people at once, whereas the average attendance in 1938 was only 80,000,000 a week. The average seat is thus occupied only two or three hours a day. But the first-run houses are nearly full most of the time, which means that the others are proportionately empty. Moreover, so many theatres change bills twice a week or more, and double features at that, that the 400 features or less turned out by all eight major studios in the course of a year are scarcely enough to keep all the theatres going. In order to assure himself of "product," every exhibitor therefore has to make an annual contract for a steady supply of pictures. The studios, on their part, try to sell only to those exhibitors who will give them the fullest representation in each town. As a result there has grown up a bargaining system that makes the process of getting the pictures into theatres the most confusing part of show business. Over Loew's part in this confusion sits one William Rodgers, who took the job in 1936.

To call on the 11,000 theatres with which Loew's is able and willing to deal, Mr. Rodgers sends out his 150 salesmen early every summer, when the selling season begins. In trying to make annual contracts, the salesmen are under some handicap because, while they talk freely about Culver City's plans, they can guarantee nothing, not even a definite number of pictures. They used to guarantee a certain number of Gables, Crawfords, and perhaps one Marx Brothers, but Loew's found itself with so many unfulfilled contracts that Mr. Rodgers changed that. Now the sale is made on the basis of the previous season's performance, or what Mr. Rodgers calls "the integrity of our company." The salesmen don't have a price list either. What they offer, with wide variations depending on the strategic importance of the account, are four unnamed superspecials on which they want about 40 per cent; perhaps ten lesser bombshells at about 35 per cent; another ten at around 30 percent; and a residue of twelve or more program pictures—the "B's"—mostly at flat rentals. But the salesman's object is clear: to get the best available house in each neighborhood to contract for as many pictures as possible. If he can, the salesman insists on the exhibitor's taking the whole line; well over half of Metro's contracts are on that basis. Robert Benchley, Pete Smith novelties, and other shorts also figure in the deal. Through a slit in this poke can be seen a tip of the pig's ear. This is the cancellation clause, which permits the exhibitor to cancel up to 10 per cent of the pictures after he has read the reviews.

This system, called block booking and blind selling, has of course been roundly attacked. The Neely bill now before the Senate would bar it altogether, and Claude Fuess, the headmaster of Andover, is one of the high-minded people who have written in support of such a measure, presumably from his experience as a picture buyer for the Saturday-night shows in the auditorium. Many an independent exhibitor objects to block booking too. But the chain exhibitors apparently do not. It would seem more of an evil, perhaps, if the average exhibitor did not need two or three hundred pictures a year anyway, a number that could not represent much intelligent winnowing on his part even under the most favorable circumstances. And indeed the loudest exhibitor complaints are directed not at block booking as such, but at questions of priority rights to good releases, "clearance" (how soon afterward what rival gets what picture), and the percentage brackets to which the various releases are applied.

The blocked deals made by Mr. Rodgers' salesmen are mainly limited to five or six thousand independent theatres. These theatres account for about 40 per cent of Metro's gross. There are also the deals made with the large independent chains (10 to 15 per cent), and still more vital are those made with the five big chains of the "trusts." These deals Mr. Rodgers himself gets in on. Some 48 per cent of the Metro gross comes from Mr. Rodgers' deals with Loews, Paramount, Warner, RKO, and National Theatres (affiliated with Twentieth Century-Fox). The Loew chain alone, small as it is, accounts for 15 per cent of Mr. Rodgers' gross. An interesting fact about the chains, which the government pointed out in its opening petition in the antitrust suit, is that except in metropolitan areas (the downtown de luxe theatres) they tend to complement rather than compete with each other. Loew is concentrated in New York state, Paramount in Canada, New England, and the South, Warner in Pennsylvania and New Jersey, Fox on the West Coast, and so on.

In such a setup, the big studios obviously need each other's chains very badly in order to get national distribution for their pictures. Mr. Rodgers makes the best deal he can with Joe Bernhard, head of the Warner chain, while Warner's sales manager Gradwell Sears is talking to Joe Vogel and Charlie Moskowitz. When you add up all these Big Five deals, multiply them by repeated quarrels over preferred showing, clearance, percentages, and the dozen other points raised by each release, you get a very complicated situation indeed. It is so complicated that it is only natural to suppose that the boys would like to sit down together, all at the same table.

Although the government has been bloodhounding the industry for many years, nobody has ever yet found such a table. Nor is there any positive evidence that any sales manager, aggrieved by bad representation in a competitor's town, ever tries to use his own company's theatres as a club—that would be illegal too. What probably happens is that the bargaining strength of the various chains all cancel each other. At any rate, the battle for the best showings is settled in the long run by the comparative drawing powers of the different studio products. If the Loew chain were twice as big as it is, the gross revenues of Metro pictures would probably not be any bigger than they are.

The government claims that Mr. Rodgers sells his pictures to the big chains on terms more favorable than he gives to the independent exhibitors. Mr. Rodgers says it is the other way around. The considerations of priority and clearance are so shaded and complex that either claim would probably be impossible to prove. Naturally Mr. Rodgers gives theatres in the Loew chain a certain edge, which helps account for the Loew chain's impressive contribution to the Metro gross; and this may put *some* independent exhibitors at a disadvantage. But Mr. Schenck will challenge you to find a single independent who has been forced out of business by chain competition. And industry figures show that while the number of Big Five chain theatres in operation has been standing still, the number of independent theatres—especially the number affiliated with independent chains—has been increasing. Meanwhile Mr. Rodgers has been doing his bit to stave off the Neely bill and similar symptoms of "indie" agitation by a long-range appeasement program, instituted in 1936. Metro, the hard-dealing company that first broke the Balaban & Katz refusal to make percentage deals in the Chicago area, now advertises itself to the trade as "the Friendly Company," and goes to great lengths to the end that no exhibitor can blame his losses on a Metro deal. Each of Mr. Rodgers' sales or district managers has a fund from which he can rebate on the spot to any exhibitor whose books show an unjust deal; Metro turns back several hundred thousand dollars a year on this account. Mr. Rodgers is also chairman of the industry's code committee, which is busy drawing up new trade practices, including a 20 per cent cancellation clause.

The concentration of economic strength in Loew and its rival trusts is probably not very different from that observable in many other industries, and can certainly have happened without collusion. But the government, besides wishing to divorce the chains from the studios, brings the further claim that the big studios are not really competing with each other at all. This complaint takes us back to Hollywood. One of the commonest practices out there is the renting of stars by one studio to another. The lending studio usually charges about 75 per cent more than the star's salary, as a contribution to the lender's burden of idle star time. For its part the borrowing studio gets the star it wants for no longer than it wants. An especially frequent borrower from Metro's opulent star stable has been Twentieth Century-Fox, of which Joseph M. Schenck, Nick's massive brother, is Chairman of the Board. The far tentacled Mr. Mayer is also related to the Fox studio, through his son-in-law William Goetz. It is undoubtedly easier for Fox to borrow Spencer Tracy than it would be for an independent studio like, say, Republic; but that is not because of the managerial kinship. Both Metro and Spencer Tracy would certainly feel safer with Darryl Zanuck in charge, even if Republic paid in advance. And Mr. Mayer can still gnash his teeth when Darryl Zanuck produces a hit and gloat when he lays an egg—provided, of course, a Metro star isn't in it. At any rate, the practice of star pooling has proved so useful to Hollywood that it is difficult to envision the making of pictures without it.

A similar fogginess, indeed, envelops the vision of any part of the movie business in which the government's suit may be successful. Astronomical budgets, which give Metro pictures their high commercial gloss if nothing else, can be supported only by a nation-wide (plus an international) market, and that means that the pictures must be sold to some kind of chains. On the other hand, a strong theatre chain that could get nothing but a shoestringer's pictures, however artistic, would soon be financing another Lasky, Zukor, Goldwyn, or other successfully extravagant showman, and start the cycle all over again. The problem is so complicated that Mr. Arnold himself has no suggestions as to how his suit will improve matters, or what shape an ideal picture industry ought to take. But if a cleavage comes, and Mr. Schenck must decide between his theatres and his pictures, the theatres would presumably be sold. Steady earners though they are, they haven't the golden possibilities that Metro still has. It would then become Mr. Schenck's even more urgent duty to keep Metro ahead of the field with "good pictures." Perhaps his aphorism is the answer to this problem after all.

■ ■ ■ ■

THE MOVIE COLONY (1941), Leo C. Rosten

The first serious, detailed statistical study of Hollywood as a separate and unique culture was Leo Rosten's *Hollywood: The Movie Colony*, which examined the realities rather than the myths of Hollywood life and the people who lived there: salaries, educational backgrounds, age-groups, national origins, career goals, serious dissatisfactions, hobbies, and so forth. In particular, Rosten (who would become famous for such later books as *The Joys of Yiddish* and *The Education of H*Y*M*A*N K*A*P*L*A*N*) believed that Hollywood was simply another manifestation of the opulent, nouveau riche American pattern of excess—not very different from that of the eastern steel, oil, railroad, and financial tycoons of the "Gilded Age." This early chapter from the book reveals some of Rosten's general conclusions.

It is often said that Hollywood has no sense of reality, and spins its fables in some Nirvana out of space and time. One of the less original aphorisms with which we are all familiar is "Hollywood is only a state of mind." Hollywood is in the southwestern nook of the United States, only a hundred odd miles from Mexico. But it is 2,741 miles from Washington, 2,901 miles from New York, 2,219 miles from Chicago, 1,925 miles from St. Louis, 1,938 miles from New Orleans.

These are not simply figures; they are signs of psychological as well as

"The Movie Colony" is from Leo C. Rosten's book *Hollywood: The Movie Colony* (Harcourt, Brace, 1941).

geographical distance. The climate of Hollywood is like that of Capri or the Riviera, not the East or the South or the Middle West; and the mental climate complements the weather. Upheavals in Washington, droughts in Kansas, convulsions in Wall Street, seem muffled and remote in a town where the sun is felicitous and the houses are brightly colored, a town where the daily energy is exhausted in slashing at the Gordian knot of a fictitious Story. The Los Angeles papers offer scanty international news compared with the newspapers of the East, and New York newspapers and national political journals arrive in Hollywood four to five days late. Even the radio is less immediate in its impact; some national programs do not come through at all; others are rebroadcast from disks at inconvenient hours. The salubrious climate and the pervading sense of isolation led one melancholy screen writer to say, "Hollywood is a warm Siberia."

There are other reasons for the antipodean character of the movie colony. Hollywood is a one-industry town. Its people sleep, eat, talk, and think movies. They are engaged in the creation of symbols rather than of material goods. Movie making is one prolonged, involuted fantasy. It is often said that the movies are an escape for the masses; it is rarely suggested that they are also an escape for the movie makers. When a movie producer or actor, director or writer, goes to sleep he leaves the world of fantasy and enters the world of reality.

It is stories, roles, dramatic artifices, which tyrannize Hollwood's attention, not goods or crops or machines. And this preoccupation with the fanciful must tend to blur perceptions of the real. To personalities lost in fantasy, reality passes through a distorted receiver; either it ceases to seem as threatening as it ought to, as in the case of children, or it becomes absurdly ominous, as in the case of psychotics. In either case, the real world—of men and things and events—loses its proper proportion and becomes exaggerated at an extreme. The singular anxiety of some of the movie makers, and the singular indifferentism of others, are end points on Hollywood's psychological horizon. If Hollywood is a community of people who work and live in fantasy, then it is to be expected that their life should take on the attributes of the fantastic. The greater wonder, one visitor exclaimed to this writer, is that Hollywood is sane.

The movie colony's intense engrossment in its work gives Hollywood a feverish, self-fascinated quality, and lends a despotic priority to its own values. This can be illustrated by a few classic examples. When Tom Mooney was released from San Quentin—an event which was front-page news on the seven continents—a columnist in the *Hollywood Reporter* solemnly announced: "The labor activities of Tom Mooney have very likely cost him a picture contract." When Mussolini's legions marched into Ethiopia and the world waited for the League of Nations to act, a producer was asked by a breathless friend, "Have you heard any late news?" To which that child of Hollywood replied hotly, "Italy just banned *Marie Antoinette!*" And in the week in which Mussolini raped Albania, Louella Parsons, correspondent for all the Hearst papers and dean of Hollywood's gossip writers, began one of her extraordinary columns: "The deadly dullness of the past week was lifted today when Darryl Zanuck announced he had bought all rights to *The Bluebird* for Shirley Temple."[1]

Let us examine this escapist haven more closely.

Hollywood is young. The movie colony itself is barely thirty years old, and its people are young—not as young as the public seems to think, or as the publicity would have it. But compared with other industries or professional groups, Hollywood would probably show a marked youthfulness. An analysis of 707 cases[2] showed that 46.2 percent of the movie colony are under 40 years of age; over a third are between 30 and 40. If we break the data into groups, we find:

Producers: Over a fourth are under 40; over half (52.6 percent) are under 45; three-fourths are under 50. The median average age is 43.

Directors: Over a third are under 40; over two-thirds are under 45; less than a tenth are 50 or over. The median age is 42.

Actors: Almost a third are under 35; 37.6 percent of the actresses are under 30 and over a fifth are under 25. The median age for actresses is 34, for actors (including veteran "character" players) 46, for both, 42.

Writers: 31.7 percent are under 35, well over half (57.6 percent) are under 40; 70.9 percent are under 45, and 84.2 percent are under 50. The median age is 37.

Assistant Directors: Over a third are under 35; almost two-thirds are under 40. The median age is 37.

First Film Editors (cutters): Over 85 percent are under 45. The median age is 37.

There is more striking evidence of the role of youth in Hollywood. The history of the movie colony and the motion picture industry is crammed

1. Miss Parsons, called by one commentator "the most consistently inaccurate reporter who ever lived to draw $600 a week," announced on various occasions that RKO was in the process of negotiating with W. H. Hudson to do a screen version of *Green Mansions;* that Paramount intended to remake *Peter Ibbetson,* "by Henrik Ibsen"; and that D'Annunzio's inamorata was a famous Italian actress named Il Duse. She (Miss Parsons) once burst into verse in her column with this line: "Oh, to be in England now that it's May," and lightly corrected the *faux pas* the next day by writing: "Oh, to be in England now that May is here."

2. 271 actors and actresses, 92 producers, 20 executives, 66 directors, 120 writers, 79 assistant directors, 41 first film editors, 18 directors of photography.

with the saga of "boy geniuses." Movie production at the studios, involving the millions of dollars that were cited earlier, is often placed in the hands of very young men. In few other industries are comparable power and freedom delivered into such callow (and gifted) hands. The late Irving Thalberg, for instance, was in his twenties when he began to soar through the movie firmament and was breaking precedents and box-office records before he was thirty. At 22, Darryl F. Zanuck was writing scenarios for Rin Tin Tin; but at 26 he became the head producer at the big Warner Brothers plant; and at 30 he was one of the most influential figures in Hollywood, tore up his $5,000-a-week contract, and within a year was put into the top production chair at Twentieth Century-Fox as vice-president. David O. Selznick was vice-president in charge of production at RKO when he was 29; he was a vice-president and producer at MGM when he was 31. Hal B. Wallis stepped into the chief executive-producer post at Warner Brothers when he was 32. Matthew Fox became assistant to the president of Universal when he was 29. Pandro Berman took over the reins at RKO when he was less than 32. And a 26-year-old like Garson Kanin directed top-flight pictures, the budgets for which were around $750,000. Youth is at a premium in Hollywood, and those who are not so young spend a conspicuous amount of effort in offering visible indications of their rejuvenescence.

The emphatic youthfulness of many of Hollywood's central personalities brings up a point which is not generally given the attention it deserves: The movie people—famous, pampered, rich—are very young to be so famous, so pampered, and so rich. Probably never in history has so immature a group been accorded such luster, such sanctions, and such incomes. "Youth on the prow, and Pleasure at the helm . . ."

Hollywood's wealth is first-generation wealth, possessed by people who have not inherited it, spent by people who have not been accustomed to handling it, earned as a reward for talent (or luck) rather than heritage. It is not surprising that the movie colony has not achieved stability or integration: it is too young, too new, and too uncertain. The people of the movie colony are characterized by showmanship, not breeding; glibness, not wisdom; audacity, not poise. Of Hollywood it might be written, as was written of the America of the 1880s, here is "a society that for the first time found its opportunities equal to its desires, a youthful society that accounted the world its oyster and wanted no restrictions laid on its will."

In a professional community which is itself young, and whose population is weighted towards youth in its composition, one would expect optimism to flourish; and when the dominant industry in that community demands buoyant, creative types, then we would expect optimism to be at a maximum. Hollywood is optimistic. Hollywood demands optimism. Hollywood's restaurants, parties, and offices are characterized by much levity and verbal horseplay. Despite the perennial crises in the motion picture industry (labor strife, wholesale lay-offs, shrinking box-office receipts) Hollywood possesses a sense of insulation from the electrical displays of our economy.

To Hollywood, economic reversals seem to be but passing fevers. The long trend of the movie business has been one of phenomenal prosperity and expansion, with greater and greater profits to the industry and higher and higher rewards to most of its personnel.[3] The Hollywoodian therefore suspects that when a producer complains that business is not good he means that it isn't as superlatively good as he had hoped it would be, or that it isn't as good as it was last year (when it was usually good), or that although it is fine at the moment it *may* get worse. And, secretly, the producer generally does not believe his own lamentations either; his mind is focused on a smash hit just around the corner.

"You've got to be an optimist to be in pictures," a New York film executive told this writer. "It is wild, unbeatable optimism that built the industry. The way Hollywood makes pictures and the fortunes they cost would terrify ordinary businessmen—but Hollywood makes profits. Enthusiasm pays huge dividends in the motion picture industry."

Wherever optimism is too conspicuous and too determined, the observer has reason to doubt its appearance. Along with the insistent optimism, there is in Hollywood a vague, restless fear that "it can't go on," that the mighty structure is impermanent, that its foundations are unsound. From many choirs in the movie colony this uneasy refrain ascends: "It can't last. Pictures cost too much; producers get too much; actors ask too much; writers earn too much; directors make too much. It *can't* go on this way."

> [Hollywood] is a serene principality on its surface, but one need not scratch deep to discover that it is afraid of its shadow, still more afraid of the shadow it casts upon the world's screens. Fear is behind its production code, a fear of giving offense which might, in turn, produce an offensive onslaught on the box-office. Fear is behind its players, writers, and directors—a fear that one bad picture will wipe out the memory of all their good ones. Fear is what makes [Hollywood] the unreal world that it is, fear far more than glamour, far more than wealth and beauty and the Southern California sunshine.

3. A studio such as MGM has made net earnings well over seven million dollars a year in each and every year from 1935 to the present date (1941). In one year, 1937, the net earnings were $14,334,000.

Optimism and insecurity run through the movie colony side by side. This is no paradox, for optimism is often a narcotic to deaden anxiety, and in Hollywood anxiety serves as a restraint on excessive elation and as a kind of penance for extravagances of income, spending, conduct, or business operations. There seems to be an unconscious *need* for anxiety in the movie colony, and anxiety is provoked, nursed, and kept alive (note the popularity of gambling, for example) in a manner which suggests self-punishment for obscure and disturbing guilts.

Hollywood tries to resolve its anxieties by keeping other people anxious about the same things. It is for this reason that conclaves in the movie colony—whether at the Brown Derby or a Guild meeting—tend to keep attention focussed on a threatening future. "Something's going to crack up at MGM. . . . Such-and-such a studio is headed right for bankruptcy. . . . It can't last. . . ." These points help to explain the constant "suffering" of Hollywood, the morbidity and self-deprecation which the movie people cultivate—and, if you please, enjoy. Optimism is the desideratum of Hollywood, but Cassandra is its prophet.

Hollywood's chronic dissatisfaction has impressed many visitors. The comedians want to play parts with social significance; the tragedians yearn for a chance at farce; the directors complain about their scripts; the writers fondle dreams of the Great American Novel. One columnist, impressed by Hollywood's variations on the lachrymose theme, exclaimed:

> I doubt if any town in history ever had as many carpers, cry babies, belly-achers, and habitual self-pitiers as does this "gay and glittering" city of Hollywood. To tour a studio, one must wade through a sea of tears. My desk is piled high with letters, my telephone is kept buzzing with calls and my reception room is crowded with visitors—all with complaints. . . .

There are many reasons for the perennial complaints, as we shall see. One of the most important is that dissatisfaction is inevitable in a place where there are *no fixed goals*. It is natural for the actress who earns $20,000 a year to envy the actress making $50,000, who envies the actress getting $100,000. In a community where one can make $350,000 a year, $75,000 is not especially impressive—either to the group or the self. Where there is no reasonable point at which to fix "success," where salaries are as well known and as widely discussed as they are in Hollywood, where the scale of rewards against which people measure their success and their prestige is so long and so extensible—there the ego suffers many rebuffs. In the movie colony, there are few places for the ego to rest in peace, except at the very top—and the top in Hollywood is very high. "In this town," one unhardened soul said, "I'm snubbed socially because I only get a thousand a week. That hurts."

The personalities who make pictures are impulsive, volatile, and creative. They always will be; movies can't be made by punch-press operators. And the fact that the movies, as a business, are exposed to a daily ballot of dimes and quarters means that the expectations of months can be smashed or galvanized by the box-office returns of a day. The vicissitudes of movie studios can be illustrated by a few striking examples:

The net earnings of Paramount skyrocketed 820 percent in one year (1935–36).

The net earnings of RKO plummeted 110 percent in one year (1938–39).

The *deficit* of Warner Brothers was $7,918,605 in 1931, and $14,095,054 in 1932; in 1935 the *net earnings* were $674,150; in 1936 they were $3,177,313 (a jump of 371 percent); in 1937 they had jumped to $5,876,183, and in 1939 they had dropped to $1,741,000.

The record of many movie individuals reflects the record of the motion picture companies. In Hollywood, men who have earned several thousand dollars a week can go unemployed for years. The writers of several pictures which won Academy Awards were not able to get jobs a week later. Actors who enjoy majestic salaries may become "box-office poison" before they quite understand what has happened. Mae West earned $326,500 in one year, but found it difficult to get a contract the next. The late John Gilbert's career collapsed overnight, when sound pictures came in; so did Ramon Novarro's. Luise Rainer won two Academy Awards and the fame which attends them, then dropped out of movies because her drawing power had vanished. The rolls of the Motion Picture Relief Fund and of the Los Angeles bankruptcy courts are studded with once dazzling names.

There are few places in our economy where fluctuations in earnings and security can be as violent and unpredictable as they are in Hollywood. We have heard of the startling rapidity of movie success. (One actor, for example, received a weekly salary of $100 and earned $3,100 in 1928; the next year his salary jumped to $1,000 a week; and in 1939 he got $3,000 a week and earned $180,000 for the year.) But there are ample cases to illustrate the rapidity of the collapse of movie careers. Note the earnings of the following movie directors, for example:[4]

	1936	1937	1938
A.	$30,000	$75,000	none
B.	80,000	40,000	$7,000
C.	15,000	4,500	1,500
D.	63,000	42,000	none

4. The cases are taken from replies to questionnaires.

The volatility of fortune in Hollywood subjects its personalities to a severe and persistent strain. "You're only as good as your last picture" is a by-word in the movie colony, and an hour after a picture is previewed the solemn consensus that "Griffiths is slipping" or "Rogers is through" races through the town. This is scarcely a climate conducive to psychological serenity or efficient digestion. The movies require creative—hence temperamental—personalities; the objective conditions of the business are hazardous; and the combination of an erratic milieu and quivering personalities intensifies the insecurity of both.

> The pace is too swift, things change too fast, success and failure are too close together. You can't expect people to gait their lives to the pace of the world outside. Normally a man builds all his life; he may succeed, enjoy a few easy years, and then he is ready to retire. Here success may come overnight and vanish overnight. How can you have that happen and expect to find people living as they do elsewhere?

The movie colony gets a curious satisfaction out of drumming these facts home—to itself. The stories which begin, "You see that man over there—the one in the shiny serge suit? Well, two years ago . . ." serve to remind the movie makers of the precarious foundation of their careers. The movie makers frighten themselves into caution. They also feel less frightened when they see someone more frightened. They also keep anxiety alive by their identification with the sad fate of others.

The reckless and flamboyant acts for which the movie makers are renowned betray their abysmal insecurity. Bravado typifies Hollywood, bravado in its publicity, its manners, its romances. And bravado is a revealing trait, for it is an attempt—like whistling in the dark—to cover up uncertainty. If Hollywood is afraid "It can't last . . ." then the defiant conduct and compulsive spending of the movie makers represent an effort to act as if it *will* last. The psychic game of "as if" is played by those who are haunted by a suspicion that their extraordinary fortune is unreal or undeserved, subject, in any event, to the caprices of luck; they act *as if* it will last. This kind of behavior is partly designed to negate doubt; it is also a form of magical thinking, an effort to make reality conform to wish. The bravado which is rooted in deep-seated fears drives the movie people to commit acts which, to the outsider, seem to defy the fates, and these are another manifestation of the effort to impress, to spur, to challenge the self: "Now that I've bought this big house (or built this big swimming pool), I'll *have* to do better work, I'll *have* to succeed, I'll *have* to get a higher salary and a long-term contract . . ."

Hollywood is famed for its "individuality" and "temperament," and these, too, spring from the bravado which shields the ego. There is a

juvenile tone in the extremes to which the movie colony resorts in order
to flaunt its individuality. One actor for years won attention by wearing
a sweat shirt to formal parties. Another actor followed the quaint whim
of driving to the studio in a cavalcade of seven Cadillacs, each chauf-
feured, and with a secretary, maid, hair-dresser, and trainer esconced
in station. The director who dresses like a cross between an African ex-
plorer and a polo player is familiar to the public. These puerilities are
symptomatic of several things: the desire to attract attention and gain
exhibitionistic gratification; the urge to "show them"; and the need to
release the rebelliousness in which so many of Hollywood's personalities
are steeped. The psychological protests of the movie colony are often
expressed in the violation of unimportant customs—especially in garb
and deportment. The movie makers are given to acts of pointless defiance
—but the meaning is not to be found on the surface of their acts. Like
children, who assume that age brings peace and maturity, the movie
makers are disturbed when they discover that getting older does not mean
getting more adult.

The movie makers are engaged in an endless search for deference—
from the world, their colleagues, themselves. They seem to be lost in a
long, unhappy effort to win respect from symbolic juries. The hunger
for praise is marked in Hollywood, and the hunger for orientation amidst
the confusion of the world. In an epoch charged with catastrophic crisis
and violent social change, the people who play the game of movie making are periodically overcome by the urge to "do something important."
For Hollywood is plagued by a vague contempt for itself, a revulsion
against the make-believe of its life and work. The movie makers always
devalue what they have achieved, and continue to set greater and greater
goals for their talents. This perennial dissatisfaction, this relentless comparison of what they are or what they are doing with utterly utopian desires heightens the discontent in which they are lost. People of this type
are driven to surround themselves with a human and indulgent environment, because they demand constant response—to maintain their inner
security and their professional output.

This helps to explain the profusion of "yes-men" in the movie colony.
To say that "yes-men" are unnecessary in Hollywood is like saying that
gondoliers are unnecessary in Venice. The "yes-men" are quite necessary to those executives and producers who cannot function without consistent admiration. The "yes-man" buttresses the ego and the confidence
of his superiors; he shields them from doubt and indecision. The "yes-
man" is not really superfluous; he is simply overpaid. There is a functional
niche in Hollywood for those who carry the banner of confidence and
forever cry: "Swell! That's great! It'll roll them in the aisles!" They may

be wrong, and generally are; but they counterbalance the congenital uncertainty with which Hollywood's creators are cursed. They pour ebullience into those who cannot create without it.

Hollywood needs face-to-face stimulation. The movie colony is highly gregarious. The craving for company at almost every hour of day or night exposes the great loneliness which lives under Hollywood's façade of gaiety. The movie makers make a career out of their neuroses and their anxiety. They are overcome by depression when they are alone; hence they do not like to be alone. Anxiety, like misery, loves company. . . .

When Orson Welles (of whom someone said, "There, but for the grace of God, goes God") was first shown through a studio he exclaimed, "This is the biggest electric train any boy ever had!" The remark is acute and revealing. Movie making is a game; the movie makers play it with great zest and, as in all games, the players surrender to periodic impatience with the game's illusory significance. An interesting refrain runs through Hollywood: "This is a crazy business. It ruins your digestion. It undermines your self-respect. It drives you nuts. But I wouldn't be doing anything else for the world!" This hymn of woe, which might be dubbed the Hollywood Lament, always ends with an emphatic, "I wouldn't be doing anything else for the world!"

The movie makers love their work. The actors complain about their stories and their directors; the directors complain about the producers and the scripts; the producers complain about their directors and their writers; the writers complain about the producers, the directors, the actors, and the industry. But they all love making movies.[5] There is no tedium in making pictures, except for the repetitive "shooting" on sound stages. There is no serenity, either. Hollywood takes immense nervous energy out of those caught in the controlled delirium of movie making. Weeks of tension follow weeks of semi-indolence; there is no encompassing routine into which life can fall, no certain progression in which personalities can find long-range equilibrium.

The movie people cannot stay away from Hollywood without falling into boredom and uneasiness. Time and again a producer or a director will announce that he is going away for a six months' vacation—and is back in Hollywood within six weeks. The movie makers do not seem to be able to endure extended residence in the world outside the movie colony. This can be understood; what other environments are as in-

5. The antagonisms of the movie makers, their complaints and suggestions, were analyzed from replies to questionnaires which contained several questions intended to encourage the expression of grievances: "What are your chief complaints about working as a [director, writer, etc.]?" "In what specific ways could your working relationship be improved?"

dulgent as Hollywood's, or as variegated, or as distracting? What other places offer such exhilarating conflicts, such opportunities for self-dramatization? Where else are there so many aggressive people who by their hostility excuse counter-hostility? Where else can narcissism be so richly fed? "I always bragged of the fact that no second of those contained in the twenty-four hours ever passed but that the name of William Fox was on the screen, being exhibited in some theatre in some part of the world." A movie director confessed: "When the credits dissolve on that screen and the music comes up and it says 'Directed by'—I get a lump in my throat."

The movie makers enjoy making movies and, for the most part, they like the jobs they hold. Sample comments from several hundred answers to questionnaires illustrate the point:

I feel happier at directing than anything else.
No two days are alike.
I actually enjoy the work.
Greatest medium of self-expression.
Thrilling, exciting.
Most creative of all branches.
I love the work.

This presents a point of the utmost importance. Most Americans live in two separate universes, the world of work and the world of play. Our schools, our churches, stress the idea that play *follows* work, that work is something unpleasant which sanctions play. But in Hollywood the work is a form of play, and the people love their work, and they are paid handsomely for having fun. The movie makers are paid to dream their dreams and exploit their reveries. They are paid for doing things which other people would like to do without being paid. Is it any wonder that the movie makers are plagued by ambiguous guilts? In a society where work means sacrifice or the performance of distasteful routines, those who are rewarded for having fun may be expected to be ridden by remorse. And where the rewards are as high as they are in Hollywood, and, in addition, are coupled with adulation from the populace, the guilts would be all the greater. Is it for this reason that so many people in the movie colony jump at the chance to impress the listener with how hard they work? They seem to be defending themselves. They seem to be trying to convince themselves. They seem to think that no one believes that they do work hard; and they themselves, when they look at their bank books and their homes, their press clippings and their social calendars, can't believe that they worked *that* hard.

Love of work is especially noteworthy in a society in which work has become increasingly dull, routinized, and mechanistic. The best comment on the morale of the movie factories is that they have the atmosphere of a high-school dramatic club. The joy of craftsmanship, which characterized prefactory work and was swept away by the Industrial Revolution, still thrives in Hollywood's plants.[6] The movie maker gets personal attention and individual approbation; in few other fields are men so encouraged to "express yourself," in few other fields does the ego receive such sustained and deferential rewards. Psychological income is high in Hollywood.

No one retires voluntarily in Hollywood. There is no precedent or expectancy that the attainment of a given age or a certain estate will be followed by professional retirement and a life of leisure. This is partly because of the absence of fixed goals, partly because movie making is forever fascinating, partly because the kind of people who make movies can never rest in the effort to prove their skill and potency to the world, and partly because the expiation of guilts is a lifelong proposition. Those who retire from Hollywood are forced to retire and those who have been forced out plan desperately to get back. In the movie colony, the champ never retires undefeated; if he did, everyone would say knowingly, "No wonder . . . he was going blind!"

The ex-romantic star tries character parts; the ex-glamour girl accepts matron roles; the producer organizes a small company; the director takes less attractive jobs. The simplest explanation is that the comparative inaction and anonymity of the world outside are intolerable after the exhilarating work and life of Hollywood. True enough—but there are more penetrating reasons. The movie makers depend upon praise for their inner security; they are driven by an urgency to keep on working; their need for testimonials to their talent is bottomless; their need for support to their ego is infinite; their need to remain preoccupied with problems outside themselves is ubiquitous. Hollywood is almost Japanese in the value it places upon "face," and saving face is a double-sided matter—the preservation of prestige in the eyes of the community, and the retention of a sense of value by the self.

So it is that the aging Adolph Zukor, once the most powerful man in films, and more recently relegated to positions of high-sounding vacuity, continues to fight for activity and power in the Paramount plant. Harold Lloyd, who could retire for life, produces pictures now that he has passed

6. Even the carpenters, property men, and messenger boys get a certain amount of awe from their wives and friends because of their proximity to the wonders and demigods of the sound stage. Such envy is not accorded to most laborers in our society. Two union leaders told this writer that studio painters and electricians feel quite superior to painters and electricians in the Los Angeles locals.

the apex of his popularity as a comedian. Gloria Swanson and Richard Barthelmess, after years of retirement and travel, have embarked on comeback careers. Mary Pickford continues to plan productions which she will finance, and yearns for a chance to act. Winfield Sheehan, once head of the Fox studio, drifts in and out of studios in secondary production capacities. Dozens of men and women in the movie colony who have ample money and fat scrapbooks cannot face the prospect of life outside the gratifying realm of movie making.

> No one ever retires on his laurels. . . . The minute that a man is no longer an active participant he loses all standing in the community and may even be taunted with the fact that he was once a big man. . . .
>
> The only recognized, valid motivation . . . is the desire to succeed and to continue to succeed. A successful man must always continue the game, which is played for no fixed prize. Retirement is without honor, and means that such an individual is henceforth to be ignored as a non-entity. The whole of the social life is integrated into this one pattern; no field of social life is exempted from it.

This quotation, so pertinent to Hollywood, was written by Dr. Margaret Mead—about the Manus tribe in the Admiralty Islands.

Hollywood is cosmopolitan. A random inspection of movie biographies disclosed actors from Tasmania, Brooklyn, Stockholm; directors from Pasadena, Tiflis, Sicily; writers from Budapest to Wapakoneta, Ohio; cameramen from China to New York; producers from Minsk to Wahoo, Nebraska. The largest collection of Indians outside of a government reservation is said to reside in Hollywood. On the social margins of the movie colony there are such fugitive groups as the Indian Actors Association, the Latin Writers Association, the Malayan-Filipino Club, the Chinese Screen Actors Association, the Hawaiian Actors Association and others.

The endless search for new faces and rare skills has brought people to Hollywood from the unnumbered places of the world. There are almost as many accents in Hollywood as in Shanghai, and the assemblage of skills surpasses the collection of nationalities. Within the circumference of the movie colony one has no difficulty in finding deep-sea divers, snake charmers, hog callers, dust manufacturers, walrus trainers, glass blowers, Cossacks, Yogis, Foreign Legionnaires, and so on and on.

The potency of "Hollywood" as a symbol of quick opportunities and lavish rewards, like the symbol of "America" a generation earlier, has become a giant magnet to the world. The stream of actors, technical advisers, movie hopefuls, and tourists, the swarm of new faces and new careers, the sporadic changes in personnel, give Hollywood (as Washington) the character of a hotel lobby. In the movie colony, everyone seems to be from somewhere else.

In the days of silent pictures, a foreign accent may have presented a problem on Broadway, but not in Hollywood. The dislocations of post-war Europe impelled many entertainers and movie technicians to migrate to Hollywood, and the catastrophic impact of Hitler over Europe drove hundreds of artists off the continent, to strike out for new careers in South and North America.

How large a proportion of the movie makers are foreign-born? An analysis of 555 cases (producers, actors, directors, writers) showed that 78.2 percent were born in the United States and 21.8 percent outside the United States.[7] (80.2 per cent were born in the United States and Canada.) About a fifth of the four major skill groups in Hollywood, therefore, were born outside of the United States. Foreign birth does not, of course, imply alien status. Many of the movie makers who were born abroad, like many other Americans, came to the United States at a tender age and were raised and educated here. By countries, the origins of the movie makers are:

		PERCENT
United States		78.20
Great Britain and Dominions		12.25
Great Britain	7.03	
Canada	1.98	
Ireland	1.98	
Union of South Africa	.54	
Australia	.36	
India	.18	
British West Indies	.18	
Russia		2.53
Germany		1.98
Hungary		1.26
Austria		1.08
France		.72

Under one-half of one percent each: Sweden, Poland, Japan, Italy, China, Mexico, Norway.

---

7. 221 actors and actresses, 132 producers and executives, 108 writers, 94 directors. The percentage of foreign-born whites 21 years old and over in the United States is 11.6. The 21.8 percent foreign-born of Hollywood's movie makers is a smaller proportion than the foreign-born whites in the following cities: Boston (29.4), Cambridge, Mass. (28.4), Waterbury, Conn. (27.8), Providence, R. I. (25.5), Detroit (25.5), San Francisco (24.2), Rockford, Ill. (21.2), and so on (1930 census figures). But the concentration within one area, one profession, one general social group, and one field of identification, gives the movie colony a more cosmopolitan flavor than is found in the cities mentioned.

The distribution of foreign-born among the four major groups offers a little surprise:

	PERCENT
Directors	28.7
Actors and actresses	25.3
Producers	17.4
Writers	13.9

The high proportion of movie directors of foreign birth is explicable by the fact that European directors were more expert and inventive than other film groups on the Continent; they found a readier market in Hollywood for their experience and skills. Besides, the director, unlike the actor or writer, needs little command of English; he works with visual rather than verbal techniques.

It was Dorothy Parker who said, "Authors and actors and artists and such, never know nothing and never know much." The educational background of Hollywood presents another surprise to those who hold the impression of widespread illiteracy in the movie colony. An analysis of 706 cases,[8] ranging from executives and actors to film editors and cinematographers, showed:

57.1 percent went to college
38.5 percent went to high school but not to college
 9.2 percent undertook postgraduate work beyond the four-year college level
 4.4 percent did not go to high school . . . .

Hollywood is characterized by sudden wealth and sudden success; it is typified by brash personalities and assertive behavior; it seems dedicated to ostentation and self-indulgence.

> With all the opulence and splendor of this city, there is very little good breeding to be found. I have not seen one real gentleman, one well-bred man, since I came to town. At their entertainments there is no conversation that is agreeable; there is no modesty, no attention to one another. They talk very loud, very fast, and all together.

This statement, oddly enough, was not made of Hollywood. It was made by John Adams, second President of the United States, and he was referring to the Society of eighteenth-century New York. It is a particularly fitting quotation here, since it epitomizes the reaction of the Brahmin to persons who lack lineage and decorum. Hollywood—new, thriving, so-

---

8. 251 actors and actresses, 121 producers and executives, 133 writers, 66 directors, 17 directors of photography, 79 assistant directors, 39 first film editors.

Production stills from early Paramount talkies included the dialogue as captions:
Jeannette Macdonald and Maurice Chevalier in *The Love Parade;*
Gary Cooper and Carole Lombard in *I Take This Woman.*

cially ambitious—lacks both. The disdain with which Hollywood is customarily regarded is, in its essence, similar to the scorn which Cabot Lodge cast upon the vulgarity and intellectual poverty of the elite of the Nineties. It is similar to the icy contempt which the patricians of Southampton held toward Newport (!) because that celebrated spa worshipped "cash rather than culture, arrogance rather than aristocracy." The condescension with which the movie colony is generally discussed is, it would seem, a contemporary version of an ancient snobbery. Hollywood lacks urbanity. Its people are characterized by notoriety, not pedigree; its position rests on money, not birth; its fame depends on publicity, not ancestry. To paraphrase the words of a *grande dame* who despised the merchant princes of her day, Society represents a wealthy aristocracy, but Hollywood represents an aristocracy of wealth.

For Hollywood is *nouveau riche*. Its magnificos are young, untrained in the art of the good life, untempered by old codes of behavior. In the movie colony there is being formed an amusement-aristocracy, to use Miriam Beard's phrase, and Hollywood is assuming the social function of European royalty—"that of luxuriously diverting itself in public and diverting others . . . In such an elite, gradually enlarged and diversified . . . the people sees itself mirrored and seeks its models."

■ ■ ■ ■
_____

WHEN THE MOVIES REALLY COUNTED (1963), Arthur Schlesinger, Jr.

The distinguished American historian Arthur Schlesinger, Jr., also served briefly as film critic for *Vogue* and the short-lived *Show* magazine. In this essay for the first issue of *Show* (April 1963), Schlesinger compares the importance of movies to their audiences in the 1930s with their dwindling importance and audiences in the 1960s, tracing the connections between American film history and American social history.

_____

One of the melancholy casualties of progress has been the American motion picture. Oh, I know that the industry still exists and that it occasionally turns out some quite good films. But the old enchantment has faded away. A quarter of a century ago, Hollywood possessed the nation. It formed our images and shaped our dreams. It was a magical com-

Arthur Schlesinger's article "When the Movies Really Counted" appeared in the April 1963 issue of *Show*.

munity, fixed in the national mind as mingling the more celebrated features of Elizabethan London, the Riviera, Greenwich Village, Broadway, Red Square and Mecca. Today it is in comparison a ghost town, a place of pilgrimage for aging and desolate tourists, a sad city where sad men grind out television shows. There was a moment of miracle, but the miracle is over.

During that moment, films mattered in American life. The announcement of new movies created anticipation and suspense. The art was bursting with ideas and vitality and point. Young men sauntered down the street like James Cagney, wisecracked like William Powell, cursed like Humphrey Bogart and wooed like Clark Gable; young women laughed like Lombard and sighed like Garbo and looked (or tried to look) like Hedy Lamarr. Hollywood today has its valiant writers and directors and actors; but mostly it seems filled with indistinguishable young men named Rock or Tab or Rory and indistinguishable young women named Debbie.

I am not talking about the decline of fan clubs or of fan magazines; I am talking about the decline of fans. A great popular art requires a committed popular audience. That is what existed in the United States in the Thirties. In 1937, 61 percent of the population went to the movies each week (today it is about 23 percent). The film had for a moment a vital connection with American emotions—more, I think, than it ever had before; more certainly than it has had since. The movies were near the operative center of the nation's consciousness. They played an indispensable role in sustaining and stimulating the national imagination. That is why those who went to the movies in the Thirties remember the movies they saw with so much greater vividness than those who went earlier and those who went later—why scenes and faces and lines and credits still linger in our minds with a peculiar exactness and intensity—why, as Roger Angel put it in a brilliant paragraph in a recent *New Yorker,* those who went to the movies in the Thirties are forever and uniquely members of the Movie Generation.

It is not that Hollywood necessarily made its best pictures in the Thirties. A strong argument can be made that great silent films have never been surpassed; and no one can deny that distinguished and powerful films have been made in the Forties and Fifties and Sixties. But the link between the films and the nation was far more intimate in the Thirties, the experience of film-going more crucial, the impact more piercing.

The Thirties represented America's first great crisis of confidence. For nearly a century and a half, the Republic had lived and grown without serious doubts about its future. "All the conditions of American life," as Herbert Croly wrote in 1909, "have tended to encourage an easy, generous, and irresponsible optimism." The rivers could always be forded,

the mountains climbed, the wilderness domesticated, the Indians subdued. The national belief was in the omnipotence of the happy ending.

The First World War disturbed this confidence for a moment, but only
for a moment. Then came the crash of 1929, and suddenly the party was
unmistakably over. Instead came the collapse of a supposedly infallible
system, unemployment and misery, an unprecedented series of blows to
the national morale, dwindling belief in the national capacity to deal with
the future. The birth rate precisely registered the decay of national faith;
the country's population increase in the Thirties was only half of what
it had been in the Twenties.

Doubt, discouragement, despair generated the psychological imperatives which gave the movies a new role in the nation's emotional economy. It was not just a need for distraction and entertainment. It was a
need for reassurance and hope. With the American dream in apparent
ruins, with the American people struck down by circumstances beyond
their individual control, with the very idea of the individual threatened
by anonymous and impenetrable economic forces, people longed to hear
again an affirmation of individual identity, to see again a chance for
individual possibility, to feel again a sense of individual potency.

The movies were by no means the only method of therapy. The deeds
which began to restore the national confidence took place, first of all,
in Washington, where a strong President showed that the nation did not
have to lie down and take it, the impotent victim of inexorable economic
fatality. The combination of the Depression and the New Deal gave the
Hollywood of the Thirties its particular audience—an audience which
was at once demoralized by the downfall of the system, exhilarated by
the promise of action and deeply responsive to images of purpose and
freedom.

Nothing expressed the change from the Twenties to the Thirties more
vividly than comedy. In the confident optimism of the Twenties, comedy
sprang from frustration, defeat, passivity. The characteristic figures were
Little Men pushed around by Big Men—Chaplin, Lloyd, Keaton, Laurel
and Hardy, forever buffeted, forever beset; retaining shreds of dignity
in the face of overwhelming tribulation. The Depression saw a critical
shift from the comedy of pathos to the comedy of aggression. The great
comedians of the Thirties were impatient, domineering figures, free and
fearless, openly derisive of the folkways to which Chaplin, Lloyd and
Keaton had tried so unavailingly to conform.

No one could ever call Groucho Marx a Little Man. The Marx
Brothers, in their classic period at Paramount in the early Thirties, represented the polar opposite of the film comedy of the Twenties. The world
was their oyster, to be swallowed and regurgitated with total indifference

to the pieties and the verities. The Brothers had the imagination of anarchy; whatever existed was there not for deference but for destruction. Society matrons were to be assaulted, blondes to be chased, social conventions to be punned and pummeled out of existence. The first two Marx Brothers films, "The Cocoanuts" and "Animal Crackers," were adapted from the stage and, though diabolical, suffered from certain constraints of format. With "Horse Feathers" and "Monkey Business," the Brothers came into their own in the movies. No aspect of the Establishment escaped unscathed, whether the tycoon, the judge, the college president or even the gangster. Groucho's contemptuous passion for the glorious Margaret Dumont summed up the relation between the Marxes and respectability. In "Duck Soup," they turned to international affairs and Surrealism, carrying their precarious logic almost beyond the point of no return. This drastic experiment must have exhausted the vein. The Brothers passed on to Metro-Goldwyn-Mayer, executed the glossier and more conventional "A Night at the Opera" and "A Day at the Races" and eventually, defeated by the revival of national confidence, made their peace with the new America as quizmasters, bandleaders and friends of Alexander Woollcott.

W. C. Fields, though more of a transition figure than the Marx Brothers, immersed himself equally in the destructive element. Like his colleagues of the Twenties, he bore with fortitude the persecution of wives, children, bill collectors, bank investigators and the law. But what created the delicious tensions in the Fields films was the sense of violence lurking underneath—the anticipated joy of the moment when he would kick Baby LeRoy or, as in "If I Had a Million," use his new-found fortune to bash in the automobiles of the reckless drivers who had dented his own cherished jalopy. In time, the full-fledged Fields arose—a cunning, swaggering figure, capable of exploiting every opening and mastering every crisis. "Never Give a Sucker an Even Break" was the title of one of his films; it crystallized the new mood in movie comedy. Fields's pictures were scratchy and patchy, but I do not think anyone has been so funny since.

An associated phenomenon was the satiric woman. In part, this was nothing new; the wisecracking female had often been seen before, but typically as a second lead. Hollywood in the Thirties now brought about a spectacular merger between humor and sex. The new heroine was not only seductive but funny. Thus Jean Harlow, who began in "Hell's Angels" as the incarnation of solemn sexuality, rapidly developed into an astute and fetching comedienne. Her ripened talent can be seen in Victor Fleming's "Blonde Bombshell," one of the best of the Hollywood self-satires, in which she performed superbly with the support of an unbeatable troupe of pros—Lee Tracy, Pat O'Brien, Franchot Tone, Frank Morgan and Ted Healy.

Miss Harlow died in 1937, but the type she played so well was already acquiring new charm and finesse in the hands of Carole Lombard. Miss Lombard was beautiful, deft, alert, ready for love but with her capacity for romance always tripped up by her unquenchable instinct for reality. She played against some of the best male comedians of the time—William Powell, John Barrymore, Fred MacMurray—and brilliantly dominated a remarkable series of films—Howard Hawks's "Twentieth Century," Gregory La Cava's "My Man Godfrey," William Wellman's "Nothing Sacred," Wesley Ruggles' "True Confession." She also died prematurely. In our own time, the tradition was wonderfully sustained by Marilyn Monroe. Why is it that so many of these satiric women, from Harlow and Thelma Todd, who was a great foil for Groucho Marx, through Lombard and Carole Landis, to Monroe and Kay Kendall, have died suddenly at the top of their careers?

The satiric woman cheered everybody with her affirmation both of identity and of competence. In Mae West, the type satirized itself. In Myrna Loy and Jean Arthur, it was transmuted from farce to drama and furthered the impression that the liberated female could cope with anything. But the main burden of renewing a sense of the potency of the individual fell to the male movie stars. At the very least, one could face catastrophe with the gleeful urbanity of William Powell, whose unlimited resourcefulness could discover a way out of any dilemma. And Hollywood was prepared to go further than this. To console an age in which the individual felt himself helpless in an inaccessible world, the film now turned out a gallery of bold and strong men who, when they could not order their environment, could at least take revenge upon it.

The gangster film became the protracted parable of man's relationship to a hostile society. In the early Thirties, the gangster was the man who rejected the social order—who, almost alone in the stricken country, seemed able to live in luxury, drive in swift and silent motorcars, ignore the employment agency and bread line and be the master of his destiny. He was the free man who, by carrying freedom to excess, invited destruction; but the symbolism remained compelling. Who in the Movie Generation can ever forget Paul Muni in "Scarface," with George Raft flipping his coin in the corner, or Edward G. Robinson in "Little Caesar" or James Cagney in "The Public Enemy"? Richard Schickel, in his admirable new book "The Stars," describes Cagney's crook as "the first existential antihero of the American films. Totally lacking in ideals, supremely contemptuous of conventional morality, he was interested only in the destruction of the world he never made. In every sense, he was the man alone, responding to the world's absurdity with a deadly and magnificent display of chillingly humorous destructiveness."

The gangster film was the culmination of a style of brisk journalistic notation deriving from such plays of the Twenties as the Abbott-Dunning "Broadway" and the Hecht-MacArthur "The Front Page." Lewis Milestone's remarkable film of "The Front Page" in 1931 pointed the way, with the unsurpassed fluidity and audacity of the camera, the staccato bursts of dialogue and the highly charged performances of Pat O'Brien and Adolphe Menjou. The gangster film extended these conventions to studies of brutality, greed and murder. The new genre was swift and cold; the dialogue went off like Chinese firecrackers; the settings were realistic and unadorned; the photography stark and truthful. The influence of the gangster film spread in many directions. Warner Brothers specialized in all the variations; and the so-called Warner Brothers stock company of the Thirties—including two splendid satiric women, Joan Blondell and Ann Sheridan, and a notable collection of character actors and comics, such as Allen Jenkins, Frank McHugh, Glenda Farrell, Ned Sparks and Hugh Herbert—made a long series of pictures putting a comic or melodramatic shine on the familiar surfaces of American life.

The classic gangster film was the product of the early Thirties. As the national mood improved, the gangster genre lost its original necessity and bite. In time, even the gangster heroes began to go legitimate. Paul Muni, after impressive performances in "I Am a Fugitive From a Chain Gang" and "Black Fury," turned into *Mr.* Paul Muni, the eminent impersonator of historical figures. Cagney went on to comedy and derring-do; Edward G. Robinson first parodied himself marvelously in "A Slight Case of Murder" and then joined the opposition. By 1939, when Robinson appeared about a third of the way along as an FBI man in "Confessions of a Nazi Spy," the audience was able to breathe a huge sigh of relief, knowing that the hitherto invincible Nazi agents would at last be brought to justice.

Yet the symbolism persisted and found a new embodiment in the private detective. This shift from the gangster to the private eye was conducted by the most penetrating and evocative of all the actors of the Thirties, Humphrey Bogart. Bogart began as a gangster in "The Petrified Forest," and in the Raoul Walsh–John Huston "High Sierra," one of the last and best of the gangster films, he supplied the definitive rendition of the gangster stance of desperation and contempt. But, as social stresses relaxed, it was increasingly possible and even desirable to be at once alienated from society and on the side of order. Dashiell Hammett and Raymond Chandler had already created the hero to replace the antihero. Sam Spade and Philip Marlowe had the loneliness, the toughness and the disdain of the gangster; but they had too an absurd sense of honor which kept them honest in a squalid world. Above all, unlike the gangster, they were supremely realistic, without hope and without illusion. "If being in revolt against a corrupt society constitutes being immature," Chandler once wrote, "then Philip Marlowe is extremely immature. If seeing dirt where there is dirt constitutes an inadequate social adjustment, then Philip Marlowe has inadequate social adjustment. Of course, Marlowe is a failure and he knows it." For the private eye, success lay in the fulfillment of his own harsh standards.

William Powell's Nick Charles in the W. S. Van Dyke series of "The Thin Man" films provided an amiable foretaste, as did Warren William's Perry Mason for Warner Brothers; but the classic definition of the new pattern came in 1941 with John Huston's version of Hammett's "The Maltese Falcon." In this orgy of double-dealing, only Bogart, the private eye, remained lucid and dispassionate, even to the point of turning in the girl he loved. More and more, Bogart became a mythic figure, with his harrowed face, sharp, expressionless eyes, twisted mouth, weary walk; a figure mingling cynicism and duty as the moral man in an immoral society and soon finding, in the films and in life, a perfect companion in Lauren Bacall, raucous and lovely, one of the best of the satiric women. The spell continues; the French gangster film of a year or two back, "Breathless," showed its hero pausing as if in a moment of rededication before a photograph of Bogart outside a Paris movie theater.

This was a decade where America recovered in fantasy the sense of individual identity and purpose it feared it was losing in actuality. They were all *men* then—Gary Cooper, the Barrymores, Lee Tracy, Walter Huston, Chester Morris, Victor McLaglen, Fredric March, John Garfield, Henry Fonda, Cary Grant, Spencer Tracy—sharply defined individuals rather than interchangeable parts. And the women too—Bette Davis, the queen of jangled nerves, Margaret Sullavan, Katharine Hepburn, Miriam Hopkins, Barbara Stanwyck, Joan Fontaine. And, because I have been writing about American images and American performers, I have not mentioned the great Hollywood films in the Continental manner, especially the stylish and bewitching comedies of Ernst Lubitsch, or the great Continental players—Dietrich, Boyer and, above all, the greatest actress and the most magical personality known to the Thirties or to any other decade of the movies, Garbo.

It is hard to know how much nostalgia falsifies the past. One can say with more confidence that movies counted to Americans in the Thirties than one can say that the movies which counted were better than the movies of today. Yet, as I observed the struggle of American critics to name the ten best films of 1961, and noted that they so often ended up with more French, Italian and English than American films on their lists, I thought how much easier things were in years like 1934. In that year the American film industry turned out "Twentieth Century"; "The Thin Man"; Capra's "It Happened One Night"; Bette Davis and Leslie Howard in "Of Human Bondage"; John Ford's strong suspense film "The Lost Patrol"; the Hecht-MacArthur shocker "Crime Without Passion"; the incomparable Fred Astaire in "The Gay Divorcee"; King Vidor's Depression film "Our Daily Bread." When one reflects further that "Duck Soup," "Blonde Bombshell," Rouben Mamoulian's "Queen Christina" with Garbo, Lowell Sherman's "She Done Him Wrong" with Mae West, "42nd Street," "King Kong," Frank Lloyd's "Cavalcade" and Lubitsch's "Design for Living" came out the year before, and Ford's "The Informer," Astaire's "Top Hat" and "Roberta," Lloyd's "Mutiny on the Bounty" with Laughton, Gable and Tone, "A Night at the Opera," "Black Fury," Leo McCarey's "Ruggles of Red Gap," Cagney's "The G-Men," Henry Hathaway's "Lives of a Bengal Lancer" and the Hecht-MacArthur "The Scoundrel," with Noel Coward, came out the year after, one can understand the zest, creativity and excitement of Hollywood 30 years ago.

What happened? What severed the link between the American audience and the American film? The first blow came with the rise of self-censorship in the middle Thirties. The Motion Picture Code imposed on film-making a set of rigid requirements and taboos which would have destroyed Shakespeare, Ibsen and Shaw and which the lesser talents of Hollywood could not overcome. However satisfying the Code might have been to the guardians of public morality, it began the process of cutting the films off from the realities of American experience.

Then, as political action and economic improvement began to replenish the sense of national confidence in the course of the decade, the need for cinematic reassurance became less intense. The Second World War speeded the process by which the movies were reduced from a necessity to a diversion. War not only monopolized the national attention; it also compelled the individual to test out his own identity in direct rather than vicarious experience. After the war, the country went into a period of comparative prosperity. The emotional imperatives which had given films their role in the psychological equilibrium of the Thirties subsided. The great postwar films were exercises in recapitulation rather than discovery, like Fred Zinneman's "High Noon" and George Stevens' "Shane," which distilled out of the Western (a neglected genre in the Thirties) the quality of existential or historical myth. When television came along in the Fifties, it did not kill the American movie; it only administered the *coup de grâce* to an industry and art which had lost its roots and nourishment in its own audience. . . .

■ ■ ■ ■

THE MOVIES IN PERIL (1935), Gilbert Seldes

Gilbert Seldes, always the astute oberver and chronicler of popular taste,
foresaw the Hollywood movie's danger of losing its audience. His article
was to prove prophetic in several senses. First, the remedy he proposes,
the need to create *character* in movies, might be described as precisely
the choice Hollywood made in the years that followed the first six years
of the talkies which Seldes summarizes. Second, even that solution failed
to save the movies from the principal danger which Seldes foresaw—
television.

It is now five full years since the moving picture found its tongue, long
enough in movie terms for a rough judgment. I think that most observers
would divide that judgment into two parts and their prejudice would
be shown only by the one they chose to emphasize. As my prejudice is in
favor of the movies, I place the favorable one first:

The talking picture has utterly confounded the pessimists and won
over the die-hard enthusiasts for the silent moving pictures; the entertainment it provides is more varied and more intelligent than that of the silent
picture; and it has a vitality and an obscure faith which makes it often
superior to the stage. Yet—

In five years the talking picture has not produced a single work of the
highest order of importance; it has floundered in ignorance of its own
capacities; and at the present moment it is in grave danger of sinking to
a level of monotonous, moderately satisfactory production.

In these five years, four of which witnessed the progressive impoverish-
ment of the American people, some 5 billion dollars have been paid at box
offices by audiences which varied from 60 to 100 million individuals a
week, at 12,000 theaters which showed some 3000 full-length pictures,
made in Hollywood at annual costs ranging from 100 to 150 million
dollars. To counteract the natural enthusiasm of all those connected with
the moving-picture industry I have used minimums wherever exact figures
were not available, and find the totals impressive. Less significant, although more often noted, are salaries of individuals: the notorious $30,000
a week paid for several weeks to an actress who has never been the most
popular or the most talented player in Hollywood and the well-earned
half-million a year wage of a young producer.

The talking picture could not have held itself at these financial levels,

"The Movies in Peril," by Gilbert Seldes, appeared in the February 1935 issue of
Scribner's Magazine.

which accurately represent the favor of the multiude, if it had not rapidly perfected the mechanism and, a little more slowly, retreated from its first error, which was the belief that the talking mechanism was the important thing in a picture. The improvements in sound and in articulation came quickly and the pictures were aided by their only real rival in public entertainment, the radio, because the radio accustomed people to the loudness, volume, and fuzzy contours of human speech as it issues from the microphone or the screen. A certain amount of braying still takes the place of human utterance, but it is no longer disagreeable; within the past year a natural, quiet voice has sometimes been heard, but if more progress is not made, if the necessities of large auditoriums continue to influence the production of sound, it is quite likely that we will all begin to imitate the microphone in our daily conversation.

Enchanted with "the mike" in the early days of the talking picture, producers and directors forgot one of the prime values of their older instrument—the mobility of the camera—and trained the lens on the face, and often down the gullet, of the person who spoke or sang. I do not think I was alone among critics when I suggested in 1929 that the person to whom a thing is said—"I am going to kill you"—is as important, pictorially, as the person who spoke; but it was nearly two years before the camera detached itself from the speaker. The directors seemed actually to forget, at times, that they had a camera at all, as in the case of the movie made from the stage-play, *Broadway*, where an attempted murder in a taxi-cab was shown on the screen and instantly, the victim of the attempt entered the speakeasy and described the scene (in the words used in the stage production where, of course, the event had not been witnessed by the audience). In brief, during the early days of the new mechanism, the moving picture ceased to move. Yet, while audiences sat spellbound at the miracle of sound issuing from the screen (which was only the miracle of the phonograph synchronized to screen movements), the critics kept insisting that the picture must keep moving and that wherever sound interfered with action, sound must be sacrificed. It is perhaps the critics' only great contribution to the cinematic art and they have not yet been adequately thanked. The reason is that directors, of themselves, went back to the camera and, as technical improvements created a mobile microphone, the conflict between the two mechanisms abated. The victory, however, was definitely in favor of the camera and the proof is that no new name for the talking pictures was ever accepted: they are still "the movies."

In spite of this victory the movie is still in danger, and, with the continued threat of television escaping from the research laboratories, the urgency of reforming the battle lines is great. Where the danger lies can best be seen after the accomplishments of the talking pictures have been noted.

The least interesting (although highly successful) thing the talking movie has done is the musical show, and the speed at which popular art moves in America can be measured by the fact that in five years this type has not only been exhausted and discarded, but has been welcomed back again and is on its way to a second oblivion. It happened that one of the first great successes was *Broadway Melody;* so many back-stage plots, contrasting private agony with the gaiety of a musical production, followed, that the theme became tiresome and "musicals" were condemned. Four years later they return with only vestiges of plot, and even with burlesques of the plot, and are frankly presented as happenings on the musical comedy stage which sometimes enlarges itself to show half a mile of a river and always presents dancers in brilliant mass formations seen as no theater-goer ever saw them, from the air and at the bottom of the sea, multiplied or divided by tricks of the camera, a little stupefying and not important.

The cycle which followed was by all odds the best the talkie has done so far: the epic of the gangsters. It is quite probable, as Mr. Alva Johnston said in his *New Yorker* profile of Darryl Zanuck, that the films accomplished what laws and commissions failed to do: they stirred the public to resentment against the crimes of prohibition and made murder a matter of public concern. As movies they were important because most of the best ones were not drawn from books and plays, but were created specifically for the screen, they brought a sense of actuality and a rude male vigor to an art given to prettiness and sentimentality, they shifted emphasis from women to men and created stars who were neither clothes models nor movie actors, but players in a new medium. The moving picture, vocal or silent, has always been skilful in exploiting a passing interest, but in most cases it has used the war or transcontinental bus travel or a championship prizefight as mere background for its single absorption in the separation and return of young lovers. In the gangster pictures the rackets themselves took first place and for the first time people felt that the moving picture was interested in them and their daily affairs. These pictures corresponded in a way to the dime novel, but the pathos of distance was lacking, and they were all harsh, menacing, and tough. Of the dozens which spoke in these new accents, three easily led the field: *Scarface, Little Cæsar,* and preeminently, *Public Enemy.* Produced by Zanuck, it established James Cagney as a new star, brought Kubec Glasmon and John Bright to Hollywood as screen writers, and brought fresh honor to the director, William A. Wellman.

No group or cycle of feature films, in either the silent or talking movies, has been as satisfactory as these gangster and racket pictures. Against them rose a great clamor that they glorified the criminal, gave a false impression of American life, and corrupted the young. It was perfectly natural that the defenders of prohibition should raise this outcry; rather startling is the comment of Will H. Hays, who singled out, among others, *Broken Lullaby, The Champ, Skippy, Sooky, Tarzan, Shanghai Express, Ladies of the Jury,* and *The Spirit of Notre Dame* as pictures showing improvement in the screen, but mentioned not one of the gangster films by name, and repeated what he had said in March, 1931: "I took occasion to re-emphasize the suggestion . . . that with the growing indignation against gangster rule, public interest in such themes in literature, on the stage, and the films was waning . . ."

That public interest was waning while public indignation grew, happened not to be so; Mr. Hays is not paid to prophesy and his attempt was ludicrous, for it was after this judgment had been delivered that the most successful gangster pictures were released. Mr. Hays did say that "the screen has done much . . . to 'debunk' the gangster by removing his mask of mock-heroism . . . Nevertheless . . . to over-emphasize the gangster's rôle in American life was undesirable . . . Public taste . . . demanded a more inspiring type of entertainment. . . ." And, the following year, Mr. Hays was pleased to discover that "the gangster theme was practically eliminated by . . . wholesome travesties. . . ."

What took their place? The five pictures of the next year which brought in more than a million dollars in rentals were: *Grand Hotel, Emma, Bring 'Em Back Alive, Dr. Jekyll and Mr. Hyde,* and *Arrowsmith;* and *The Champ* which was released in December of 1931 may be counted in for good measure. All except the animal picture, *Bring 'Em Back Alive,* were chosen by some 300 moving-picture critics as among the ten best pictures of the year; the other five were: *The Guardsman, Smilin' Through, Bill of Divorcement, Back Street,* and—as if to spite Mr. Hays—*Scarface.* The balance between serious and light plays, between deep emotion and sentimentality, between the cinematic adult and the universal infantile, is equal in this selection, and the list is so varied that no conclusions can be drawn. By 1933, however, it was possible to say what had taken the place of the gangster film. The pictures which reached the million mark were: *Cavalcade, I'm No Angel, Little Women, She Done Him Wrong, State Fair,* and *Footlight Parade.* Nearly 400 critics chose the first, fourth, and fifth of these for the best ten (and *Little Women,* which was a late release, will probably be among those chosen for 1934). The others were: *42nd Street, Private Life of Henry VIII, Lady for a Day, Farewell to Arms, I am a Fugitive from a Chain Gang, Maedchen in Uniform,* and *Rasputin and the Empress.* Here we have two historical films of the distant past; two recaptures of the immediate past; two Mae West films; a love story of the World War; two musical shows; a sentimental story of the past and one of the present; a moderately realistic version of a social disgrace; and an importation from Germany which escapes classification. In addition to some of those mentioned, the Committee on Exceptional Photoplays of the National Board of Review chose *Berkeley Square* (pathos of the past); *Three Cornered Moon* (fantasy); *Zoo in Budapest* (fantasy and young love), and above all these, *Topaze,* a supremely well-done comedy of financial chicane. Not one of the leading pictures was concerned with any subject of immediate interest to the average man. They were films providing escape from every-day life.

THE TEN BEST TALKING PICTURES

1929	*Disraeli*	
	Broadway Melody	
1930	*All Quiet on the Western Front*	
	Abraham Lincoln	
1931	*Cimarron*	
	Street Scene	
1932	*Grand Hotel*	
	The Champ	
1933	*Cavalcade*	
	42nd Street	
1934	(see footnote)	

Each year *The Film Daily* asks several hundred motion-picture critics of America to name the ten best pictures. The accompanying list is made up of the first two choices of each of the past five years. It is quite possible that the same critics would not omit some of their earlier choices. These, in any case, were considered the most important pictures of their times. The Year Book issued by *The Film Daily* is the source for statistics used herewith, except for the figures on box-office rentals which were compiled by *The Motion Picture Herald*. Seven of the ten pictures made more than $1,500,000 (*Disraeli, Abraham Lincoln* and *Street Scene* excepted). Pictures which gross more than a million dollars in rentals constitute the financial honor roll of the industry.

Note: The list of the ten best talking pictures for 1934 is just published by *The Film Daily* as this magazine goes to press. A discussion of these pictures as a group is not therefore included in this article. The 1934 list follows: *The Barretts of Wimpole Street, The House of Rothschild, It Happened One Night, One Night of Love, Little Women, The Thin Man, Viva Villa, Dinner at Eight, The Count of Monte Cristo, Berkeley Square.*

Nonetheless, the influence of the gangster films has worked through the whole business of making pictures, so that in nearly every picture the adult and intelligent observer catches a glimpse of its factual rudeness; in nearly every one there is a character who drastically or sourly says what human beings really think, or mocks at heroics, or deflates pretensions. In the gangster cycle, the movies came down to earth and have had a new saltiness and vigor ever since.

One other type of picture has had an influence outside of its own immediate radius; that is the *Grand Hotel* type, the picture in which a group of unrelated individuals are brought together in one place and their lives set to impinge one upon the other. Inspired by the success of *Grand Hotel* on the stage, the movies made this type even before they made *Grand Hotel*, placing their characters in railway stations, transcontinental busses, trains, and, above all, on board ship. There could hardly be a dominating plot in these pictures, and there had to be half a dozen more or less developed personalities. The result was that many excellent minor actors became interesting for themselves, and not for the support they gave to stars, and the movies began to develop quirks and oddities of action and expression. Eccentric characters were used for their comic value, and the pictures inevitably had more of the surprise and variety of life than those of the stricter order. The pursuit of these by-paths is natural to the camera technic, and today you may find traces of the method, even in highly dramatic pictures, corresponding more or less to the injection of sub-plots and unrelated characters in the old Elizabethan drama.

It is the distinction of Miss Mae West that she has not only created a movie cycle but, it would appear, has completed it all by herself. It took five years for the moving-picture producers to recognize the shrewdness of the few critics who told them that Miss West was a remarkable actress, but when the movies got around to this phenomenal woman, they did remarkably well by her, giving her her head, to say the least, and allowing her to create herself on the screen. She has had directors, but the style is still the style of Mae West; she has written her own stories; she broke down the two artificial screen concepts of love as a mystery and as a sin; she made, in less than one year, two films which grossed more than two million dollars each in rentals—*i.e.*, money paid by the exhibitors to the producing company—a unique record, all the more pleasing to Paramount because hers are the only pictures bearing that name which are in the "smash hit" class for the dolorous year of 1933; and in all probability she was the chief cause of the most violent outbreak of hostility against the movies in the present generation.

To understand why, it is necessary to recall the three preceding types of sexual allurement exploited by the movies: the vamp (Theda Bara); the It girl (Clara Bow); the Pained Lady (Greta Garbo). I have put in parenthesis the names of the most famous exemplars; each had dozens of rivals, imitators, or followers. Parallel to the exploitation of each of these types, there ran the permanent moving-picture theme that while human beings, chiefly under the age of twenty fell in love, they did not make love, and, if slightly older but still attractive men and women had lovers, the sexual passion did not exist for them. I do not note these circumstances in behalf of any thesis about Americans and love, considering that all the theses so far advanced have been peculiarly short-sighted. The thing to bear in mind, in this connection, is that the movies from the beginning were made for the sole purpose of universal light entertainment; obviously (and perhaps correctly) the full impact of the sexual passion was considered inappropriate to this purpose.

However, the three types mentioned did exist, and if they did not represent the truth of desire, they offered a dosage of sex. The first was foreign: the slinky seductress, the sort of thing one read about in French novels and French murder cases; the second was entirely American, perhaps the strangest phenomenon in the entire history of the screen. For it glorified the sex appeal of the sexless. The fairly attractive Miss Bow was a hoyden and madcap in most of her pictures, athletic, a good pal, an ever so healthy and mildly necking adolescent female. There is nothing to indicate the captain of the girl's basketball team in a mid-western high school is the ideal mistress of the American man; her appearance on the screen may be analyzed according to Freud or according to Marx, and I am afraid it will not make much sense in either case. Incidentally it should be noted that the movies heavily overcapitalized Sex Appeal; none of the great money makers of that period is an It film, and the great names (Chaplin, Fairbanks, Pickford, Tom Mix's Horse, and Rin-tin-tin) are innocent of S. A.

The third, or Pained Lady, type arrived at perfection with the coming of speech. In it women with mysterious profundities of soul and equally mysterious aspirations to something beyond sex, play hob with gentlemen whose objects, however matrimonial, are a little fleshly. To the Garbos, Shearers, Crawfords, and many less distinguished, speech, especially when it was witty speech, afforded a new instrument of defense against the brutal advances of men. In the end love triumphed, but it was love compromised with the intellect, leading to marriage in the manner of a Long Island house-party comedy.

All these folderols vanished before the simple statement which is the essence of all of Miss West's pictures, that the practice of love by a man and a woman is the occasion of *mutual* delight. To the endless repetition of this statement all the murmurs and shrugs and wags and glances of her technic minister; her plots are nothing; her characters nothing; her settings are slightly beglamored, so that the common reality of what she is saying is never too instant and harsh. Her characteristic title is the one which her company abandoned after the midsummer threat of boycott: "It Ain't No Sin." To be candid, her films are hardly vulgar. As for high impropriety, the films had been playing with homosexuality, as comedy relief, for years—it is definitely suggested in one of Chaplin's early comedies; and in recent months the musical films had been full of smirks and a dull innuendo, with oblique references to sex and digestion which were stupidly vulgar. The crime of Mae West was that she annihilated all the artificial approaches to sex, that she made no approach in that sense at all, but simply was sex. It is not surprising that the moralists fell upon her.

In several ways the talking picture was more offensive to the moralist than the silent picture had been. In the old movies a prolonged or too passionate kiss brought objection, but the commercial feature picture never allowed itself a downright indecency of gesture. Speech brought the opportunity for circumlocution, for hinting at improprieties and, even more, for silence. The moment a man and a woman stopped talking, and the scene faded, the worst was apprehended, and audiences whistled appreciatively. I recall a neat trick: James Cagney picking up a forward young woman, whom he disliked in spite of her passion for him, and carrying her to her bedroom, depositing her upon her bed. "What are you going to do?" she asked. The reply was, more or less, "I'm going to give you an experience you will never forget." And with that, he slammed the door upon her and departed. But that was comedy. In the films of passion, the action was not visible—all was presumed to be different. Moreover, with speech, the picture could take over the more sophisticated product of the stage, and although screen versions were purified, *Design for Living, Strange Interlude,* and *The Guardsman* appeared. And from another field of legitimate production, the smutty black-out of musical shows was reproduced.

Speech added subtlety to the moving picture. In silence, you could do anything and trust to a written caption to cover up inconsistencies, but speech demanded at least a minimum of logic and, in serious plays, some consideration of human motives. The intellectual content of the pictures, still not too great, has increased.

The increase has not, however, included in any serious way the economic problems of the depression. Roused by Russian films exploiting the grandeurs of the Soviet régime, critics have complained that Hollywood lags behind the times or goes fascist (in the sense that every film which provides escape from contemporary problems helps maintain the established order). In this complaint it is forgotten that Russia is ascendant and America, for the first time in generations, is temporarily descendant, and that in neither country do films attack the prevailing system. Entertainment always lags behind events and the remarkable thing is only that Hollwood has not produced highly successful films based on the psychological revolution accomplished by President Roosevelt in 1933. King

Vidor's *Our Daily Bread* chose a minute item in Recovery for its theme. Even Repeal and the weathering of the banking storm brought only minor pictures, and *Gabriel over the White House,* a melodrama of dictatorship, was not an exceptional success. For the past year the producers, scenting a good topic, have been trying to find a way to make the munitions business acceptable to the bankers who control the movies and to the foreign countries which are still important buyers of the Hollywood product.

Leaving the feature film, I come now to the great disaster and to the great triumph of the talking picture. The disaster is the newsreel which has lost its prime quality: that it was a record of actuality. Events are occasionally recorded as they happened: the riot at Ambridge, Pennsylvania, the later stage of the *Morro Castle* disaster, and the assassination of King Alexander are instances. But far too many events are rehearsed and taken, or are taken after the actual event, sometimes with "improvements." The camera can be concealed, but the microphone cannot; and the self-consciousness of public figures is obvious. I have not myself come across

---

SUCCESSFUL PICTURES AND "FLOPS"

In November of last year, Douglas W. Churchill reported to *The New York Times* the results of a poll of four hundred theater managers, which indicated the comparative success and failure of the leading films of all companies. The most striking feature of this report is that several heavily publicized large-scale productions are listed as failures; on the other hand, half a dozen of the most meritorious films made in the year were successful. That dozens of totally insignificant pictures made money was to be expected; and this list, of course, made no mention of hundreds of films which brought in meager returns, but apparently were not expected to do any better.

Among the successes and failures are:

SUCCESSFUL FILMS	UNSUCCESSFUL FILMS
It Happened One Night	*Twentieth Century*
Five pictures starring Will Rogers	*Berkeley Square*
Dinner at Eight	*Treasure Island*
The Thin Man	*Queen Christina*
Viva Villa	(with Greta Garbo)
Dancing Lady	*Design for Living*
I'm No Angel	*Death Takes a Holiday*
The pictures with Shirley Temple	*Nana*
Little Women	*Counsellor at Law*
The House of Rothschild	*Little Man What Now?*
Footlight Parade	*George White's Scandals*
	The Song of Songs
	(with Marlene Dietrich)

serious falsification—that is usually left to the commentators whose introductions are often totally hostile to the shown event. But the sense of the real and the unpremeditated which made the old newsreel a relief and a delight, after the mannered feature picture, has gone. As these reels will eventually form the raw material of history, this is a grave misfortune.

The corresponding triumph is Walt Disney's. Just as the old Keystone comedies were always the best part of the average movie show, the Silly Symphonies today tower over all but the most exceptional feature pictures. Beginning with *Mickey Mouse,* Mr. Disney instantly discovered what to do with sound—that is, he reduced it to an accompaniment of action and, as far as he was able, made it as unreal and fantastic as his action. With color added to the Silly Symphonies he achieved perfection. Technical limitations on the color spectrum turned out an advantage, the Symphonies appearing in a sort of wash or pastel which recalls the old magic lantern and something of the Christmas card. Speech is cut to a minimum; what might be said is usually sung; the Silly Symphonies are completely satisfactory to every sense. They are successful, of course, because of their charm, their humor, their ingenuity, their simplicity— but of these things I need not write. They are universally known.

I said near the beginning that the talking movie was in danger, and by that I did not mean the danger of being disliked by a few intellectuals. It is the practical financial danger which threatens every form of popular entertainment which fails to change and develop—the danger which finally destroyed the minstrel show, burlesque, and vaudeville; the danger averted to an extent by musical shows when they turned satirical; the danger from which the old movie was saved at the last moment by talk. The danger may be summarized in this way: with the introduction of speech, the movie has lost magic and has failed to create the one element which could take the place of magic, *i.e.,* character.

The loss of magic is baffling; it ought not to have happened when she mystery of speech was added to the mystery of motion on the screen. I do not think it has, so far, touched the movies' audiences who are diminished in number not because they dislike the movies, but because they do like the virtually free radio and have less money to spend. But the kind of elation which the old movie gave has disappeared and we are all too familiar with the movies now to fall completely under their spell. It is not the microphone, but the wrong use of it which is to blame. Technically, as I said, the mobile camera defeated the static mike; but in the creation of pictures as a whole, the realistic microphone still dominates; there is too much dialogue (which is seldom the conversation of human beings) and too little imagination, and every time a person speaks, he shatters the created illusion which the picture can give.

This belief in speech could be destroyed instantly if the producers of movies would ask their audiences, seriously, what they remember of their favorite films. Of an exceptionally bright film, *It Happened One Night*, one spectator, without prompting, recalled Claudette Colbert toying with her garter to attract attention when Clark Gable's thumbing had failed to get them a ride. Of *Public Enemy* every one I have asked remembers the bandaged corpse of the gangster falling through the door. Of *Caval-cade* it is the moment when the lifebelt, before which the lovers have sworn eternal fidelity, is seen to bear the name of the *Titanic;* of *All Quiet on the Western Front* it is the faces of marching men or a battle scene; of *Queen Christina* it is the face and form of Greta Garbo, flaw-lessly beautiful. Always it is something seen, not something heard. Even in *The Thin Man,* one of the wittiest films made, one remembers walking the dog more than the badinage.

Lubitsch, Vidor, Van Dyke, Capra, Milestone, and one or two other directors, are aware of this and often let movement and gesture tell more than words. To others, the only movement is a man walking one of those endless Hollywood marches from one room to another, between conver-sations. None has yet created a style of production in which the movie has its own kind of talk, a kind which should be as different from that of the stage as that of the stage is from the talk in musical shows. Until that is done, the talking movie will remain a hybrid. It must create speech with a rhythm, accent, economy, and reference to action all appropriate to the movie—and to nothing else. That this will restore magic to the films, I cannot say. I am only sure that this has to be done first.

Even if it is done, and certainly if it is not, the movie has to go into the business of creating characters if it wants to save its neck. Again the rea-son is practical. There are few plots in the world and the movie exhausts local color and new fads rapidly; the third time a husband, wife, and lover are seen in a submerged submarine, an effect of boredom obtains and even if the next time you see them in the bowels of an active volcano, it isn't all fresh and exciting. Even in the most ingenious of films, connecting links between episodes of the story are weak, and the usual method is to strengthen them with comedy—which also is not unlimited in supply. The one matrix in which plot can be safely embedded is human character. If you are interested in a character, your absorption makes you immune to boredom. And the contemporary movie almost always ignores character. It presents individuals with queer traits or habits or looks; it offers easily identified types; and it is overpopulated with actors and actresses. But ask ,"What character played by your favorite player did you like best and how did it differ from any other character?" and you discover that characters, in the ordinary sense, as we speak of characters on the stage or in fiction, hardly exist. The producers reply that their audiences demand what they get, refusing to allow ZaSu Pitts to play anything but the comic distracted figure of fun; but that is a confusion of ideas. Marie Dressler was always the familiar Marie Dressler, but nearly always created character; Roland Young is recognizably himself, but always creative; so is Charles Laughton; Bette Davis created a remarkable character in *Of Human Bondage,* but seldom before; W. C. Fields creates character and Jimmie Durante doesn't—and apparently doesn't need to. The moving-picture "character" as now exploited is briefly remembered for what he or she did, not for what he or she was. That is why they are soon forgotten.

And if a producer were to say to me, more frankly than usual, "What of it? We are not in the business of making imperishable masterpieces. We make them to be forgotten, so that next month's releases will take their place—" I would have to answer that when enough individual movies are forgotten, the movies as a whole will be forgotten. That is the danger. The movies have never played for the long run. In the beginning, they didn't have to—almost anything made money. Again, when the movies began to talk, the gold rush was on. Now, under financial pressure, the producers naturally cling to the old favorites, the old methods; they must show a profit each quarter; they dare not experiment; they cannot think five years ahead.

I am not hopelessly prophesying disaster. The moving picture has such a natural and universal appeal, that it can count on attracting a large number of the two million children who reach the movie age every year. But it needs 100 million attendants a week, which means that it must establish and nourish the habit of going to the movies, which can only be done by continuing interest. It does not need to satisfy the intellectuals, but the producers might note that of the seventy-three films with the highest box-office returns, at least thirty-five were satisfactory to a critical taste. You can get instant popularity by a cheap exploitation of any temporary interest; the long run requires only good movie craftsmanship.

Greater commercial empires than that of Hollywood have crumbled and sunk beneath the sea. By thinking boldly and experimenting freely, the movies can insure themselves against oblivion. And not otherwise.

■ ■ ■ ■

No Love, No Nothin'

I'm just about as solitary
As anyone could be.
Of course my life is not so merry,
But that's all right with me.

No Love, No Nothin',
Until my baby comes home.
No Sir! No nothin',
As long as baby must roam.
I promised him I'd wait for him
Till even Hades froze.
I'm lonesome, heaven knows,
But what I said still goes.

No Love, No Nothin',
And that's a promise I'll keep.
No fun with no one,
I'm getting plenty of sleep.
My heart's on strike
And tho' it's like
An empty honey comb,
No Love, no Sir! No Nothin' 'till my baby comes home.

Lyric by Leo Robin, music by Harry Warren;
from the motion picture *The Gang's All Here*, 1943.

6

The War Abroad, a War at Home

(1941–1952)

The four years of war provided the occasion for the motion picture industry's greatest era of concerted social purpose, its greatest period of service to the nation as a whole. The industry continued to make entertainment films, for entertainment was as vital to the war effort as guns and butter. Both workers at home and soldiers overseas watched movies as one of their major rewards for a day's work well done. In addition, motion pictures were necessary for many kinds of "educational" purposes—to teach soldiers how to perform their tasks, to teach the public the issues for which we were fighting, to inform Americans both how the fight was going and why it was going as it was.

During the war years the movies themselves became conscious of the potential seriousness of film content. Even the most escapist, entertaining films contained "ideas," "propaganda" of some kind or other. Some criticized Hollywood's wartime films for lacking the seriousness and sense of purpose of those films made by the other countries at war (for example, Great Britain). Others criticized Hollywood's entertainment films for having any ideas at all, for not sticking to the business of "pure entertainment." Such attacks on Hollywood as a propaganda mill were infrequent during the war—primarily because its propaganda was consistent with American interests and policy.

Just before America entered the war, however, a Senate investigation probed the reasons for Hollywood's refusal to remain neutral, for siding with England and the Allies, against Germany and the Axis. Although the bombing of Pearl Harbor put an end to this investigation, the Senate hearings were to be a preview of things to come.

If America and Hollywood went off to war together in the first half of the 1940s, they went to war against each other in the second half of the decade. The six years that followed the Second World War were the most troublesome, the most divisive, and the most devastating in the entire cultural history of the motion picture in America. By the end of this era the entire relationship of the movies to American cultural life as a whole had been fundamentally and irrevocably changed. A simple "box score" of the major events of this six-year period is itself indicative: two damaging congressional investigations of subversion in motion pictures; two troublesome Supreme Court decisions; one new competitor for the entertainment dollar that stole the audience from the movies because it was cheaper and easier to get—the same reason that the movies came to commercial power fifty years earlier.

The first nationally publicized investigation of the House Un-American Activities Committee (HUAC) into the political practices, beliefs, and loyalties of the motion picture industry came in 1947. The witnesses for the industry entered these hearings confidently; there was broad public support for the rights of those already named as "unfriendly witnesses" to speak freely. Those "unfriendly witnesses" were so unfriendly, so hostile to their accusers, that the conclusion of the two-week hearings left the industry's confidence in itself and its commitment to freedom of speech in a shambles. The first ten "unfriendly witnesses"—Alvah Bessie, Herbert Biberman, Lester Cole, Edward Dmytryk, Ring Lardner, Jr., John Howard Lawson, Albert Maltz, Samuel Ornitz, Adrian Scott, and Dalton Trumbo—served a year in prison for contempt of Congress. Shortly after the hearings, the official spokesman for the industry, Eric Johnston, who had succeeded the retired Will Hays as president of the Motion Picture Producers and Distributors of America, informed the American people that no known or suspected Communist would be permitted to work in Hollywood films. The Blacklist had begun.

The second set of HUAC hearings of testimony about the motion picture industry (1951–52) were longer, quieter, duller, and sadder. The industry was clearly in retreat. Given the example of the "Hollywood Ten," the witnesses this time were careful to avoid the same punishment. These "unfriendly" witnesses had two ways to avoid being cited for contempt of Congress. The first was to admit former membership in the Communist party and then to name in the public presence of the

committe and the press all those with whom the confessed former
Communist had ever been associated in his or her Party past. The second
was to refuse to answer any questions at all on the grounds of the
Constitution's guarantee against self-incrimination ("standing on the
Fifth Amendment," or "taking the Fifth," as this practice was colloquially
called). Although no one went to jail as a result of these hearings,
neither the individual witness nor the industry as a whole benefited
from either kind of answer.

The first major Supreme Court decision to work against the industry
came in 1948 in the final settlement of the *United States v. Paramount
Pictures* after ten years of litigation. The effect of the settlement was to
divorce the film-producing companies from their theaters which showed
the films, a result that further aggravated the increasing financial
difficulties of the major companies. The decision began the dismantling
of the entire studio system, which had been the basis of the American
film industry for over thirty years, in favor of the independent producers
and the smaller companies.

Although a second landmark Supreme Court decision did not work
specifically against the industry, the controversy it generated did not help
the film business. In 1952 the Supreme Court decided that films were
entitled to the First Amendment protection of the Constitution. The
specific catalyst of the case—*Joseph Burstyn v. Wilson*—was a short
Italian film by Roberto Rossellini, *The Miracle,* which was condemned
as sacrilegious by many Catholic groups and priests (including Francis
Cardinal Spellman of New York). Although motion pictures had won
the official right to speak freely, they were too commercially battered, too
financially frightened to exercise the right.

As disturbing as this social agitation might have been at any other
time, it was even more disturbing to an industry that was steadily losing
its audience to television. Just as in 1934, when the film industry began
to enforce the Production Code, the industry was most sensitive to social
pressure in periods of financial decline. The industry probably instituted
its blacklist of possible Communists out of the fear that without such a
public-relations move the movies would lose even more of its audience
even more rapidly.

By the end of this bitter era, the motion picture industry was in spiritual
and commercial chaos. It had lost the affection of much of its audience;
it was uncertain how to retrieve those it had lost or retain those it had
not; its commercial structures for manufacturing and marketing its
wares were no longer legal and, worse, no longer even functional. With
fewer Americans in the audience (and with increasing European quotas
on the number of American movies that could be shown on foreign

screens), the film industry required fewer films. Fewer films meant fewer places to make them and show them, which meant fewer people to work in them and on them. The financial boom years that followed the war for most other industries were bust years for the movies. And the future did not look as if it could or would be any better.

■ ■ ■ ■

War in the World of Make Believe (1942), Frederick C. Othman

This article from the *Saturday Evening Post* describes Hollywood's
wartime difficulties in carrying on its day-to-day business—the shortage
of materials, the improvisation necessitated by rationing, the dwindling
supply of male actors.

Chinese coolies run to cover. Mechanics spin the props of the P-40's and
one after another of the mighty planes with the sharks' teeth painted on
their bellies roar to life. Pilots in the uniforms of the Flying Tigers gun
their motors and the ships race down the hidden flying field, in San Fernando Valley in Southern California, where planes, save those of the
United States air forces, simply are not allowed.

The motors of five of these planes scream like so many furies. The
sixth makes no sound whatever as its whirling propeller sends it bouncing down the field. There's something strange about these ships. There
certainly is.

They're built of plywood and paint and stickum. They taxi down the
meadow, and roar, and kick up dust, but they won't fly. They're powered
by old automobile engines, except one, which contains an electric motor,
so the voices of Pilots John Wayne and John Carroll won't be drowned
out. They're movie planes, built to order at a cost of $20,000 in the
property shops of Republic Studios, because the picture makers can no
longer pick up the phone and rent a fleet of airplanes.

War has come to Hollywood in the form of shortages in almost everything the movies use, from leading men to rubber ears, and from spun-
sugar windowpanes to Chinese actors who'll play Japs. The fact that
films are still being made is a tribute to the gentlemen who have made
a fine art of fakery for the last quarter century.

One good thing the war has done for the movie capital—provided

"War in the World of Make Believe," by Frederick C. Othman, is reprinted from the
17 October 1942 issue of *Saturday Evening Post* (© 1941 The Curtis Publishing Company).

plenty of villains, Germans, Italians, Japanese, and even an occasional
Finn. The Nazis make heavy heavies, the Italians light heavies, the Japs
the cruelest of all.

But there is not a genuine Japanese left in Hollywood. They're all in
the Government relocation centers. It is a relatively simple matter to
make a Chinese actor look like a Japanese. Straighten the hair line across
his forehead, comb his hair straight back, accent and turn down his eye-
brows and build out his mouth and you've turned the native of Chungking
into a son of Tokyo. What is not so simple is persuading a Chinese actor
to play a Jap. Mostly it can't be done.

Consider Keye Luke, who was Charlie Chan's No. 1 son until the death
of Warner Oland. Luke refuses to look like a Jap. He'd rather starve. He
is eating regularly, nonetheless. Chinese heroes fight in every movie concerning Japanese villains, and Luke is perhaps the busiest actor in
Hollywood.

The man-power problem has the picture producers biting their fingernails. A year ago they'd have been pulling out their telephones by the
roots. Now they dare not. Hollywood, which used to wreck more telephones per capita than any other city, ruins them no more. The phone
company cannot replace the broken pieces. The onetime phone smasher
has now become, by necessity, a fingernail gnawer.

The gnawing concerns each succeeding movie star who joins the armed
services. The list is assuming nightmarish proportions to the men who
must continue making films about handsome heroes rescuing beauteous
ladies from fates worse than death. How can you make such pictures, they
ask, when you've lost most of your top-flight stars?

Clark Gable, Rudy Vallee, Gene Autry, Victor Mature, Tyrone Power,
Ronald Reagan, Gene Raymond, George O'Brien, Wayne Morris, Burgess
Meredith, James Stewart, Jackie Coogan, Douglas Fairbanks, Jr., Patric
Knowles, Jeffrey Lynn, Robert Montgomery—to mention only a few of
the best—have gone to the wars. So have dozens of lesser lights.

The resultant problem is critical. Universal studios have scheduled a
picture with an all-woman cast. Dance Director Dave Gould is dressing
tall chorus girls in men's clothes to replace drafted chorus men. Twentieth
Century–Fox has made one film in which the males either are twelve
years old, or fifty, like Monte (The Beard) Woolley, the hero.

Walter Wanger, leading producer and president of the Motion Picture
Academy, believes that the only solution is to borrow back leading men
from the Army.

"The British Army has lent actors to the studios in England," he says.
"Our Army must do the same if the picture industry is to continue."

Until the Army does decide to give movie actors furloughs before the cameras, older actors are being called back and told to cover their bald spots with hair pieces.

Where will they get them? Hair for wigs these many years has been a monopoly of the peasant women of Middle Europe, who grew the finest grades and cropped it off at regular intervals for pin money. Cheaper hair, which was split, bleached and otherwise processed before it went on the head of a glamour girl, came from China.

The European supply was cut off first. Make-up chieftains, like Jack Dawn, of Metro-Goldwyn-Mayer, began putting good hair in the front of wigs, where it showed, and processed hair in the back, where it didn't. Then the Chinese sources were shut off. There is not enough hair for wigs in town now for one good costume picture. Leading ladies at Universal have been ordered to let their hair grow long, so they won't need wigs. Extras on the Wild West sequences of the Mark Twain movie have been instructed by Producer Jesse L. Lasky to grow their own whiskers; he can't find fake ones.

The hair problem is critical, and yet, like so many of Hollywood's warborn crises, it has its brighter side. Dawn has invented and put into production the world's first synthetic wigs, made of material similar to present-day toothbrush bristles and spun out in long silky white strands. Inventor Dawn dyes these strands to suit, ties them thread by thread into hair-lace foundations and curls them under such heat as would sizzle genuine hair.

The result, he says, is the indestructible wig, with which an actress can walk through a flaming forest or swim the deepest river without ever getting a curl out of place.

His first synthetic hair will be visible this fall on the screen, as whiskers on such stalwarts as Van Heflin and Regis Toomey in a movie about Andrew Johnson.

Dawn also is the man who inadvertently got Hollywood in its current jam over false noses. It used to be that the make-up departments manufactured noses, ears, moles and scars of a material whose principal ingredient was glycerin. It looked like flesh and it worked beautifully, except for its tendency to melt. Many a lovely lady lost her face under the lights; many a plump cheek gradually dribbled down on the wearer's shirt front.

This problem Dawn solved by manufacturing faces of liquid latex. It was the perfect solution. Some of his competitors even used variations of this rubber solution for false bosoms and thigh pads for the lean-shanked. Hollywood was consuming almost as much latex as Akron. There's no rubber now, not a dribble, and the experts once again are trying to perfect glycerin flesh that won't melt.

In Paramount's Star-Spangled Rhythm,
Dotty Lamour fills the same sarong
used in a previous picture, to help solve
the budget problem

Vegetarian tiger! This penguin of the Hollywood air runs, but never flies. For its film, Flying Tigers, Republic substituted plywood planes, armored with shellac, for the real thing.

The war has provided plenty of villains for the movies. The Nazis make heavy heavies, the Italians light heavies, the Japs the cruelest of all.

Worries of the make-up men are legion. Take one little thing—the sponge. There was a shortage of sponges for applying face paint two years ago. One of the boys devised a silk sponge. Then there wasn't any silk. Another perfected a rubber sponge. Now he's trying again.

Lack of rubber is one of the real toughies. Cecil B. De Mille's celebrated octopus, with the brass valves for innards, has gone to President Roosevelt's rubber-conservation campaign. So has the 300-pound python that cost Alexander Korda $8000 before he got it to wriggle properly in his Jungle Book film. There'll be no more such terrifying beasts in the movies for the duration.

THE PASSING OF THE SIX-GUN

Tyrone Power's last film before he joined the Navy concerned buccaneers stealing gold and the lovely Miss Maureen O'Hara. It was the first pirate movie Hollywood ever made without mayhem. Producer-Director Henry King simply could not provide the rubber ears and noses for his pirates to slice off each other. There is no more rubber to make spiderwebs in horror pictures, knife blades in stabbing scenes, or paving blocks in explosion sequences.

The Wild Western movies received their biggest jolt when Gene Autry became a sergeant in the Army. They'd already had some others. Producer Harry Sherman, who'd made a reputation for presenting magnificent scenery along with his Injun slayings in the Hopalong Cassidy series, was forced by the tire shortage to abandon his location junkets and to make out with whatever scenery he could find in the Hollywood hills.

Republic Studios, specialists in the art of the singing cowboy, contributed the six-shooters of all its cow pokes to defense agencies and handed its heroes wooden guns. These do very well under the circumstances. They can't use real ones, because they can't buy blank cartridges. The villains in the sagas of the sagebrush now meet their fates at the hands of intrepid heroes who go after them with lassos or fists. If there's any gunfire, the explosions are dubbed in afterward by the sound departments.

Throughout Hollywood, writers are making last-minute changes in their scripts to eliminate automobile wrecks. They are trying especially to keep from ruining tires, on the theory that now is no time to irritate the customers by scraping rubber off of casings.

SPARE THAT TIRE!

This situation proved particularly embarrassing to Robert R. Crutcher, who had written a screen play for Twentieth Century–Fox which depended for its climax on Don Ameche shooting with a blunderbuss all four of the super de luxe, white-side-wall tires on Joan Bennett's limousine. In days past, the studio would have exploded these tires with dynamite caps and thought no more about it. Those days are past. Crutcher rewrote his scenario for Ameche to shoot only two tires.

Ameche refused. He said he'd worked hard in twenty-five movies to build himself up as a hero, and he didn't intend to make himself a heel in the twenty-sixth. Then, the producers asked, would he mind shooting one tire? Ameche said that was almost as bad, but that if it could be made to look accidental, he'd stumble, drop the gun, and let the tire blast.

He did exactly that, though the studio couldn't see itself ruining even one tire. It took a whole morning to fake the shooting of that tire, and cost approximately $1000 in actors' salaries.

The breakaway departments, which make it possible for stunt men to smash chair legs on each other's heads, throw bottles at one another and dive through plate-glass windows, are in a serious pickle.

Breakaway windows have been made of pure sugar candy for the last twenty-five years. An actor could jump through such a window, sending splinters in all directions, without ever suffering a scratch. The trouble now, according to A. G. Cook, of the Paramount property department, is that the Government can't see its way to issuing sugar-ration stamps for window-smashing use. Cook says even he can understand that.

The beer bottles and the vases which used to crash so regularly on the villains' heads are no more. They were composed of a resin obtainable only in the Balkans, while the chairs which crunched so many skulls were built of balsa wood from the Philippines. Experimentation lately with rolled newspapers for clubs hasn't turned out so well; the actors crumpled, instead of the weapons.

Looks like there'll be no more snow in the movies, either, until Hitler is crushed. It can be cold and the actors can shiver, but they can't brave blizzards. As Director William Wellman, who had to eliminate the snow scenes from the film he completed with Henry Fonda, points out, snow is made of untoasted cornflakes and gypsum. The cornflakes sift down from the rafters, while the gypsum drifts outside the heroine's front door. Cornflakes are used exclusively for eating purposes these days, while gypsum goes into a variety of war products.

"Even more important," Wellman says, "is the fact that snow wastes a lot of film. It ruins the lighting. Sometimes it sifts too close to the lens. It has been known to tickle an actor or make him sneeze. It always causes take after take."

Film is a precious commodity which must be conserved. Wellman and all other directors are attempting to banish unnecessary takes. The Screen

Actors Guild has promised to discipline any performer who habitually blows up in his lines, while the producers even now are seeking to skip the credit cards at the start of every film, which would save an estimated 1,000,000 feet of film per year.

Many more millions of feet could be saved, without sacrificing the quality of the movies an iota, simply by reducing the speed at which the print runs through the projectors. But that would entail adapters in every theater in America, which would run into many tons of critical metals. The idea has had to be abandoned.

Fred Gabourie, Metro-Goldwyn-Mayer construction superintendent, has invented the nail-straightening machine. It costs more to straighten old nails than buy new ones, but now that they can't be purchased, his gadget is paying dividends.

The Federal edict that no studio may spend more than $5000 for new material to go into the sets of any one movie has been no money saver; it has proved a tremendous expense to the picture makers. Cost of rebuilding old sets is higher than starting from scratch with new lumber, canvas and paint.

Before the ruling went into effect, Paramount had scheduled for production Ernest Hemingway's For Whom the Bell Tolls. The whole picture was to have been shot on the Marathon Avenue lot, where the water tower was to have been blacked out and the mountains of Spain recreated at a total cost of $140,000. Some 40 per cent of this sum had been allocated for new materials.

When the studio learned it could not spend more than $5000 for its mountains, it sent Director Sam Wood and a troupe of actors, including Gary Cooper and Vera Zorina, to the high Sierras, where mountains were free for the photographing. Cost sheets of this expedition have not yet been compiled, but probably will total twice what it would have cost to build the mountains in Hollywood.

The war has caused a boom in sea pictures. They used to be easy; the producers merely went to sea off the shore at Santa Monica and shot 'em. Now the ocean is closed to the movie makers. There are no boats to rent, even if the sea were available.

Several years ago the Warner Brothers built their own private ocean, almost the size of a football field. They equipped it, at a cost of $100,000, with a roof, a trick horizon, ripple-making machinery, hydraulic lifts to toss the boats in case of typhoons, and air conditioning to keep the actors comfortable. The Warners are prepared for stories of the sea. Most of the other studios are not. They must build their boats, up to and including battleships, on their sound stages, nail them to the hardwood floors, and provide the water through hocus-pocus photography.

One of these seagoing movies involves Sailors Pat O'Brien, George Murphy and Max Baer in a convoy fight in the North Atlantic on Stage 14 at RKO Pathé. The sailormen had to shoot a 4-inch naval gun from the deck of their freighter. Where to get the gun was the problem.

The property-department engineers drove a truck to a Los Angeles junk yard and spent twenty dollars for some old oil-well drilling machinery and the gears from the bread mixer of a bankrupt bakery. They built their gun to naval specifications, insofar as looks were concerned, from these materials and some paint. They were surprised later to discover that so many hours of labor were entailed that the bill for their gun amounted to nearly $6000. But it is a beautiful gun. It recoils with compressed air and spurts flame to Director Eddie Sutherland's order with acetylene gas.

The war has put a serious crimp in usual production methods, but Hollywood will continue to make movies at the same old stand because it still has three essentials in plentiful supply: 1, villains; 2, dollars; 3, brains. And if Paramount has to use a horse and wagon to haul film to the laboratory, because it is against the rules for a motor truck to return from a trip empty, the patrons never will know.

■ ■ ■ ■
_____

THE MOVIES (1946), Bosley Crowther

Bosley Crowther was film critic for the *New York Times* for almost thirty years (1941–68). This excellent summary of motion picture activity during the war years was published as one of the essays in *While You Were Gone*, edited by Jack Goodman, a collection especially designed to acquaint returning servicemen with what had been happening at home in their absence.
_____

Now let's go the movies and see where they came in. . . . .

To get this picture in focus, you have got to keep in mind that "movies," the way we use it, is a catch-all or baggage-car word. It embraces not only the products turned out by Hollywood—the star-spangled entertainments which are the standard of the American screen; the wishful-thinking fables so beloved by us romantic souls—but it includes other types of motion pictures that have become more conspicuous during the war: the

"The Movies," by Bosley Crowther, is from *While You Were Gone*, edited by Jack Goodman (Simon & Schuster, 1946; Da Capo, 1974).

newsreels, the "fact" films, the "teach" films, and, especially, the ones that help you think.

Also, that satchel word "movies" contains, in the visions it calls up, all of the glamorous people who are part of the mythos of our screen—the actors and actresses, directors, and those vaguely anonymous folks who make and convey the movies from the studios to you. They are the Movies Incarnate, the shadows reduced to flesh and blood. What were they doing in the war years? Where did they figure in? Take the Gables and Stewarts and Rooneys—the ones who got into uniform, along with some 12,000,000 other American guys and girls—or the Hopes and the Browns and the Crosbys who went out on entertainment tours and bucked up the kids with home-grown cornstarch in bivouacs all over the world. And then "the industry" in general: how did it give of itself with bond sales and war drives and whoop-la and free movies sent overseas? . . . This all makes a big, broad picture, and you've got to see it from the beginning and as a whole.

First things come first, however, and Hollywood's films are that. They have the top priority as the test of American movies during the war. They were seen by millions of people, both here and in foreign lands; they probably reached a vaster audience than any other form of visual stimuli. The masses swarmed to see them for refreshment, replenishment, release; next to mail, they were readily acknowledged as the serviceman's closest touch with "home." And so they had a responsibility—much greater than they had ever had before—to nourish the spirits of their patrons with the most bracing and satisfying food. How well they fulfilled it is the question. How successfully did they entertain? How nearly did they realize their potential for expanding men's hearts and minds?

This is an estimation in which most everyone is qualified to join—everyone, that is, who went to movies between 1941 and now. And that, of course, includes the fighting forces, which saw almost as many as folks back home. From the Main Street theatre in your own town to the "beachhead Bijou" wherever you were, the same films were shown, with some exceptions; the same images flickered on the screen. The only thing is that all of us didn't see them through precisely the same eyes. Some, such as fighters in the rest camps or weary war workers, say, looked to movies for utter diversion and judged them on how much they gave. Others, desiring more from them than music, wisecracks, and shapely girls, gauged them according to how much dramatic validity they had. And still others who felt that movies should have strived to clarify the real drama of this momentous era took a much different slant on what they saw.

It depends upon where you were sitting. But this you must understand: the making of movies is a business with the big boys in Hollywood—a business which the war, for all the obstacles that it placed in the way, did a great deal to boom. More people had more money during the war years than they had ever had before; more people were willing to spend it for entertainment, no matter what. Theatre box-office grosses reached unprecedented heights. It took a pretty crummy picture not to show a return. So the Hollywood nabobs, in the manner of good business people, inclined—with a few rather notable exceptions—to play their tickets safe. They didn't go in for bold experiments. They stuck generally to familiar routines. Remember, too, that Hollywood was never particularly famed for an accurate scan of life. Remember, because these facts have bearing upon the quality of Hollywood's wartime films.

You probably recall the general nature of our movies during 1941— the year before Pearl Harbor; the year that we sat on the fence. A none too profound comprehension of what was cooking showed in Hollywood's films. (A few previous anti-Nazi pictures had been more or less candidly made and had provoked senatorial isolationists to raise a ruction which soon came to naught.) The big and most popular pictures that year were *Kitty Foyle, Sergeant York, The Philadelphia Story, Citizen Kane,* and such as those. *Gone With the Wind* was still stirring considerable box-office dust. *How Green Was My Valley* had its premiere just six weeks before the Japs let fly.

Oh, sure—the war was distantly suggested in such fictions as *A Yank in the R.A.F., I Wanted Wings,* and *Dive Bomber* and a spate of so-called "service comedies." These latter were pictures which kidded the experiences of "selectees," and most memorable among them were Bud Abbott's and Lou Costello's *Buck Privates* and *In the Navy.* Out of England did come a few pictures such as *Target for Tonight* and that brilliant little fact film, *London Can Take It,* which told bravely of that city's trial by blitz. But, in general, the screens of our theatres were as peaceful as a bright summer day. Our movies were giving us pleasure in the familiar escapist groove.

Wham! Pearl Harbor! (Or BOOM! "December 7th"—as they flash it on the screen.) Hollywood rubbed its eyes one morning and heard we were in a war. The men who produce motion pictures were confronted with a fact which now put it up to them squarely: What is to be the function of the screen? Skipping, for the moment, the many forthright and direct things that Hollywood people did—their organizations for war activities, the enlistments, all of that—let's have a look at the consequences of the productive decisions the big boys made.

The best way to take them is in order. During the first year that we were in the war—and the first year, as a consequence, that some of you were away—a pretty strong smell of high explosives got into Hollywood's films. Indeed, the war figured somehow in about one out of every four. The fact that most of these pictures were begun at least a year in advance was evidence that the producers had been following the news headlines.

Mrs. Miniver was the first one that you would call a top-notch job. It came along in early summer, about the time that we were catching our breath. Although it was questioned in England as a silly representation of their case, it gave to secure Americans a sudden heart-shocking sense of total war. That wonderful English lady and her darling family! So *that's* how it was! (Of course, it really wasn't—but the effect, in movie idioms, was intense.)

Wake Island, which opened in September, when the papers were full of Guadalcanal, was likewise a sock in the kisser for such folks as were still rubbing their eyes. Sure, the fellows who had seen the real McCoy said it looked awfully phoney to them. But to us back here in the theatres, reading daily about the Marines and their fight on that other fuming island, it carried a credible punch. Also, *Joe Smith, American* brought the peril pretty close on the home front, and *Casablanca* and *Journey for Margaret* looked sharply behind some transatlantic scenes. At the year's end there also came from England Noel Coward's *In Which We Serve,* a moving saga of the British Navy, which was "limey" as all hell but solid stuff. (As it happened, the American public was strangely lukewarm towards it.)

On the other hand, there were such "war" films as *Eagle Squadron, Captains of the Clouds, To the Shores of Tripoli,* and *Desperate Journey* —sheer glamour-boy-in-uniform hoke, as far from realities as dreamland, as heroic as a Superman cartoon.

For straight entertainment, however, that first year of the war did bring some pretty sweet movies—*The Man Who Came to Dinner, Woman of the Year, Sullivan's Travels, Road to Morocco, The Pride of the Yankees,* and—the best of the lot—*Yankee Doodle Dandy,* in which Jim Cagney played George M. Cohan. It waved the flag like the mischief, but that kind of waving was good.

Now, let's see what sort of pictures Hollywood gave us in 1943—the year of the clean-up in North Africa, the beginning of the Italian show, and the big Pacific island hopping. You would think the producers, by now, would have been pretty well on the war beam. And, in their way, they were. The Warners' *Air Force*—and we mention especially that studio's name because it had a good record of honest, hard-hitting war films—began the year well with a tribute to the spirit of a B-17 crew. The same studio's *Action in the North Atlantic* was a tough film about the Merchant Marine (which, indeed, was shown to trainees as a picture of how things generally were), and its *Watch on the Rhine* won prizes as the best picture of that year. It was a drama of the peril of complacency towards fascist operators at large in the world.

As a matter of fact, Hollywood gave us a big bunch of war films that year—some of them good and some of them elaborately overdone. *Sahara* showed desert warfare in a mixture of realism and Hollywood. *Corvette K-225* was tough sea-fighting, laced rather tenderly with love. *Bataan* and *Guadalcanal Diary* were dubious dramatizations of those dirty shows. And *So Proudly We Hail* was strictly grease-paint, but people liked its story of nurses on Bataan. (Did you see it? Claudette Colbert, Paulette Goddard, and Veronica Lake were spectacularly brave.) *The Moon Is Down, This Land Is Mine, The North Star,* and *Commandoes Strike at Dawn* were various fictitious notions of resistance to the Nazis in occupied lands, shot through with platitudinous mouthings, but well-intentioned, at least.

But with strictly un-war-clouded movies, the boys did much in 1943. *The More the Merrier, Madame Curie, Best Foot Forward,* and *Coney Island* were their speed. Warners filmed *This Is the Army,* the famous Irving Berlin army show, and donated all the profits, plus a quarter million for screen rights, to Army Relief. And Sol Lesser made *Stage Door Canteen* with a large cast of free-talent stars and turned over most of the proceeds to the American Theatre Wing.

This is notable, however: two films of that year caused considerable argument and stir. (When a movie arouses indignation, that's a new twist on man biting dog.) Paramount's prettified version of Hemingway's novel *For Whom the Bell Tolls* got loud boos for reducing the issues in the Spanish Civil War (the thematic crux of the novel) to the vague perplexities of a mountaineers' feud. (Sam Wood, who produced and directed, claimed the "politics" didn't matter, anyhow.) And the Warners' uncommonly daring exegesis on current affairs—their idealized dramatization of *Mission to Moscow,* former Ambassador Joseph E. Davies' diary —got lots of people hot and bothered because it made Russia look like Paradise. It also skipped very politely over the details of the famous Moscow trials. *For Whom the Bell Tolls,* with Gary Cooper and Ingrid Bergman in the cast, was generally successful. *Mission to Moscow,* without star players, laid an egg.

(Incidentally, it might here be noted that the box-office headliner of that critical year, as picked in a poll of theatre operators, was Betty Grable. Does that prove anything?)

Came 1944 and Hollywood's product began to show a pronounced trend towards lighter and mellower diversion, away from the serious thoughts of war. The fact that the year's most popular picture was Bing

Crosby's *Going My Way*, the story of two priests in a New York parish, was just one manifestation of the trend. It touched a human note of spiritual triumph which was plainly gratifying in these times. *The Song of Bernadette*, also popular, was as much in the current of this trend as were Preston Sturges' howling satires, *Hail the Conquering Hero* and *The Miracle of Morgan's Creek*. *National Velvet* and *Meet Me in St. Louis*, *Home in Indiana* and *Cover Girl*, *See Here, Private Hargrove* and *Laura*—they were all significantly "escape."

It is interesting to note, psychologically, that there came along towards the year's end a run of elegant "shockers," of which *Laura* was a type. Among them were *Double Indemnity*, *The Woman in the Window*, and *Murder, My Sweet*—films of vicarious violence. And the public loved them. Now, figure that one out.

There were some notable war films, for all that—especially *Destination Tokyo*, *The Purple Heart*, *Gung Ho!*, *Thirty Seconds Over Tokyo*, and *A Wing and a Prayer*. All of them had their faults, obviously—glaring errors at which the serviceman could scoff. But they did show a steady development towards a more honest treatment of war. And Darryl Zanuck's production, *Wilson*, which told a story of our first World War President, was a courageous and timely dramatization of a personalized ideal of world accord. It was a rare contribution to public thinking—the sort that Hollywood usually avoids.

On the other hand, the picture *Lifeboat* was occasion for a bitter critical row. Based on a story by John Steinbeck and directed by Alfred Hitchcock, it told of a group of torpedoed Americans and Britishers adrift in a small boat with a Nazi submarine captain. It was widely accepted as a compelling drama of the sea, with the Allied men and women stacked up against the Nazi properly. But several critics and Dorothy Thompson, not to mention a lot of just plain folks, felt it made the Nazi out to be a champion and the democrats a bunch of bungling dopes. This writer concurred with that opinion. It seemed a strangely antidemocratic film, excusable on no basis, even in our enlightened society.

But, to get on with it—the trend towards lightness continued into 1945. Outside of *Objective Burma*, which had Errol Flynn doing a fine job on the Japs, there wasn't a fictional war film of any moment from Hollywood in the year's first half. *Counter-Attack* was a minor episode in which Paul Muni as a Russian guerrilla foxed the Huns, and *God Is My Co-Pilot* was a flamboyant and distasteful flying-hero film. Just after the Japanese capitulation, however, there did come along two very good Hollywood war films, *Pride of the Marines* and *The Story of G. I. Joe*. The former was an understanding study of a blinded veteran's readjustment, frankly based on the real-life experience of a marine who fought on Guadalcanal, Sergeant Al Schmid. And *The Story of G. I. Joe* was documented from the articles of Ernie Pyle. It was fully endorsed by veterans of the Italian campaign, who saw it in preview.

Otherwise, the top Hollywood pictures up to mid-1945 were such as *A Song to Remember,* a wistful musical about the composer Chopin; *A Tree Grows in Brooklyn, Without Love, The Valley of Decision,* and *Wonder Man.*

Looking back on the over-all record of Hollywood's films in the war, one might reach the dispassionate conclusion that it was neither as good nor as bad as it might have been. There is not the slightest question that it shows evidences of bad taste and occasionally horrible obtuseness. Such films as *Four Jills in a Jeep,* which showed four Hollywood actresses having the jolliest, romantic time touring war fronts; or *Hollywood Canteen,* a quite offensive display of self-esteem; or *Ladies Courageous,* in which the female ferry-pilots were saved by one brave dame; or *Keep Your Powder Dry,* a wretched fiction about three glamour girls in the WAC, were terrible. That's the only word for them.

Furthermore, it cannot be denied that the familiar "hero" pattern was unhappily overused. As he was from the beginning of movies, the individual two-fisted guy was too frequently winning for our side beyond a possible shadow of doubt. And he wasn't always a very pleasant fellow. He was either an elegant sort of snob who finally heard the stern call of duty, or he was a suddenly regenerated punk. The plainly fictitious warfare in which such characters engaged gave the public a dangerous conception of the real kind our men were up against.

And that is the sternest indictment to be drawn against Hollywood's films: they did not give a consistent or reliable impression of the wartime world. Many producers, underrating the public's intelligence as they often do, felt that their films were sufficient if they stated such platitudes as the Nazis are cruel, the Japs are fiendish, the Russians are nice and the Chinese are, too. They did not perceive that the chief thing was to give to audiences a sense of the immense and impersonal conflict into which all peoples have been collectively drawn.

Of course, there is always the question whether Hollywood could have been expected to make any broad and profound clarification of the drama that has baffled expert minds. To expect that it could is assuming an undemonstrated competence. If its films caught a surface indication of the physical nature of war, of the suffering and courage of peoples, then they did about as much as they could. The dramatic comprehension of deep conflicts and of the impersonal tragedy of war was a big bite for fellows in Hollywood who were trained in the mills of make-believe.

Furthermore, added to the confusions and limitations of the makers of Hollywood films there was always the pressure of exhibitors against serious and realistic films. Their periodic yammer was that "the public wants to be entertained," "the public is fed up with war films," and "the theatre is not the place for woe." This thesis, of course, was a bogey. The public did go for *good* war films, such as *Mrs. Miniver, Air Force,* and *Destination Tokyo.* But it was either indifferent or resentful towards the phony and mock-heroic ones. So the exhibitors, rather than take chances on the ratio of good war films to bad, and naturally anxious for fat pickings, said (generally), "Let's stick to 'escape.'"

Also exhibitor pressure on the makers of Hollywood films was supported by the argument that servicemen overseas weren't interested in realistic dramas about the war or anything else. "Just give 'em lots of girls and comedies"—that's what these stand-patters said. Hollywood, meshed in its anxiety to please everybody, took the cue.

But, for all that, our screens did get some "war" films of a real and persuasive sort—pictures that showed what actually happened in straight, photographic detail. These were the documentary pictures of the nation and its forces in action. They were movies, of course—emphatically *movies*—but very different from Hollywood's fiction films.

Again, to get the continuity, we must go back a bit and understand what was doing with "factual" films before the war. Pictures which showed realities had been familiar on the commercial screen ever since movies started flickering, in the shape of newsreels, travelogues, and filmed reports. But in the early 1930's there began to emerge a new school of actuality film-makers who took their cameras out and photographed real life, then composed this material into pictures aimed to catch the true drama of daily events.

These films, known as "documentaries," advanced more rapidly in England at first, gained some momentum on the Continent, and spread to the United States. The March of Time represented the first considerable effort in this line, with its monthly releases of short pictures which dramatized and discussed current happenings. Pare Lorentz made two pictures for government agencies, *The Plow That Broke the Plains* and *The River,* classics in this medium, which further developed the style. Numerous independent producers had made a variety of these fact films before the war, and even the Hollywood shorts departments had made a few interesting tries. But the documentary was still a stepchild on the commercial screen in 1941.

With the outbreak of war, however, it was immediately manifest to public-relations experts that films were a powerful medium for conveying to the people information and inspiration. They were labeled a "weapon of war." The old saw about a picture being worth 10,000 words could be multiplied by twenty when the picture moved, they said. So steps were forthwith taken to bring the movie medium into use. Most appropriate to the purpose was the documentary film.

It so happened that, long before Pearl Harbor—a year and a half before, in fact—the motion-picture industry (meaning the producers, distributors, and exhibitors of Hollywood films) had organized a committee —the Motion Picture Committee Co-operating for National Defense— designated to co-ordinate the industry with outside groups in the national emergency. Even before Pearl Harbor, this committee had helpfully arranged to give distribution in regular theatres to government-made information films—short pictures such as the National Defense Commission's *Power for Defense* and the Office of Emergency Management's *Bomber, Food for Freedom,* and *Women in Defense.*

Immediately after Pearl Harbor this group was renamed the War Activities Committee of the Motion Picture Industry, and a request was sent to President Roosevelt asking that he appoint a co-ordinator of government films. Six days later the President appointed Lowell Mellett, then serving as director of the Office of Government Reports, to fill this additional job. When the Office of War Information was established a few weeks later, Mr. Mellett was named chief of its Bureau of Films, through which were passed to the industry all government- and service-made films.

The relations of the War Activities Committee (or the WAC) with the OWI—and with the armed services for which it acted—could fill a whole chapter in this book. But it is enough to say that the industry, despite some painful groans, did give release to more than one hundred information and war-combat films. These ranged from films made specifically by the OWI's own producing unit—such films as *The World at War, Troop Train,* and *Manpower*—to such splendid combat pictures as *The Memphis Belle* and *With the Marines at Tarawa.* It included fact films made in England and sponsored by the OWI over here, films made by the Army for "orientation," and special films made in Hollywood. Among the latter was the excellent little cartoon which Walt Disney made for the Treasury, encouraging people to enjoy paying their income tax in 1942.

All of these films—most of which were made at the government's expense—were distributed free of charge by the industry to some 16,000 theatres. This was the number of houses that pledged themselves to show the films, and it is fair to assume that most of them abided by their pledges, more or less. The fact that some theatres took exception to the quality of some of these films—if, indeed, they weren't outright resistant to "war" pictures—occasions the doubt.

It is true that many of the items turned out by the OWI were not particularly impressive. They were hurriedly and sometimes haphazardly made. And they fitted no long-range pattern of information. They were made for "spot" jobs. But then the domestic film unit of the OWI was dropped by a congressional economy in the budget in July, 1943, and the making of information films thereafter was left to volunteers in Hollywood. The fact that they didn't do much better bespeaks an incompetence in this line.

However, the factual combat pictures which were made by the services, with their own combat photographers, were something else, when they came along. It was in these that the documentary method was put to excellent use. First of the lot was *The Battle of Midway,* made by Commander John Ford, former Hollywood director (*The Informer, The Grapes of Wrath*), which gave (with only a touch of "Hollywood" faking) a grim picture of the attack on that island. It was released in August, 1942, was in color, and was widely shown.

Less successful but still effective was the Signal Corps's *At the Front,* which described the initial phases of the North African campaign. It was made under the supervision of Darryl Zanuck (then a lieutenant colonel), it was in color, too, and it went out through the WAC to theatres early in 1943. Later that year *Report from the Aleutians* was sent through by the Signal Corps, and it gave a bang-up picture of the rugged conditions in that frozen combat zone. Captain (later Major) John Huston, another former Hollywood director, was in charge of its production. It was a significant finger-post.

For the real combat *documentaries* began coming in 1944, and they clearly manifested the new, realistic "shock" approach. *With the Marines at Tarawa,* made by that service's combat cameramen under the direction of Captain Louis Hayward, was a vivid and sobering illustration of the terrible cost of that little isle. *The Memphis Belle,* filmed by an Air Force Photo unit under Major William Wyler (also of Hollywood), gave a spectacular conception of a bombing mission over Germany. *Attack!— The Battle of New Britain* showed the Arawe Beach assault and the subsequent drive on Cape Gloucester in all its grueling jungle-fighting detail, while *Target Japan* and *The Battle for the Marianas* were brief but tough glimpses of the Pacific naval war.

This flow of vivid combat pictures continued—and, indeed, increased—in 1945. It included the Navy's *Brought to Action,* the Army's *The Enemy Strikes* (Battle of the Bulge), and the joint services' *Fury in the Pacific,* recounting the capture of Peleliu. It also included *The Fighting Lady,* a tremendous feature-length film put together by Louis de Rochemont of Twentieth Century-Fox from footage shot by navy cameras. It told the story of life on an aircraft carrier and was climaxed by spectacular combat scenes. Commercially released to theatres, it was one of the brilliant pictures of the war. (And, we might add, it was eminently successful.)

List, too, among the year's good combat films *To the Shores of Iwo Jima*, made by navy, marine, and coast guard cameramen; *Target Tokyo*, an Air Force picture recounting a B-29 raid; and the Navy's film of kamikaze resistance off Okinawa, *The Fleet That Came to Stay*. A little late but solemnly impressive was the Signal Corps's *San Pietro*, showing the action for that small town in Italy during the winter (1943) campaign. And the full-length review of the invasion of Europe, from the inception to the fall of Berlin—*The True Glory*—was a fine comprehension of that great effort, when it was shown in the early fall.

Widely exhibited in regular theatres, these films had a marked effect in bringing home to audiences the grim realities of war. Maybe the average movie-goer didn't see all of them; maybe he missed, for various reasons, all but five or six. But whichever and however many of them he happened to see, his knowledge and comprehension of the real thing was sharpened thereby. And, remember, the showing of these pictures was a public service of the industry.

This calls to mind a story recounted by a service cameraman who was going ashore in an assault boat during one of the Pacific island attacks. A rifleman, crouched next to him, tossed him a nasty crack about how he could be more helpful with a rifle than with that camera. "Look here, pal," said the cameraman, "do you ever write letters home?" "Sure," said the guy with the rifle. "And does the stuff that you write get through —I mean, the stuff about the fighting and the dying that you've already seen?" The rifleman looked at him coldly. "The censors cut it," he growled. "The folks back home have no idea what it's like." With that the cameraman smiled and tapped his camera: "That's what I've got this thing for—to show the people back home exactly what you're going through." From then on, he said, the rifleman was his most considerate friend. . . .

In addition to our own combat pictures, there were also shown on our screens similar films from other countries—the British-made *Desert Victory*, recounting the Eighth Army's fateful defeat of Rommel at El Alamein; *Moscow Strikes Back*, a splendid fact film of the Russian repulse of the Nazis at Moscow's gate; *The Siege of Leningrad*, a grim, cold document of that city's long and painful stand; and *The City That Stopped Hitler—Heroic Stalingrad*, another Russian film.

Mention should also be made here of the Army's famous "orientation" films which were put out for public showing through the OWI and the WAC. These were the "Why We Fight" pictures, which were officially required to be shown to every man in the Army before he went overseas.

There were seven films in the series, all made under the supervision of Lieutenant Colonel Frank Capra, another famous director from Hollywood and, incidentally, one of the foremost innovators with films during the war. Of the seven, only three—*Prelude to War, The Battle of Russia,* and *War Comes to America*—were publicly released. But, despite rather limited showing, they helped clarify the war's background. And the whole series marked a rare advancement in the use of films to reach men's minds.

As for the role of the newsreels during the war, it was adequate. No one, least of all the newsreel people, were entirely satisfied with it. In the first place, the newsreel companies were put under strict security; their cameramen were generally restricted overseas and all of their footage was "pooled." That is to say, whatever pictures one of them got were distributed to all—after passing the usual censorship. But the fact is that most of their stuff on the war and everything pertaining thereto was furnished to them by the services, share and share alike. As a consequence, the newsreels were dependent almost entirely upon the services for really important war coverage—a condition which plainly limited them. The length of the reels was also limited (by the War Production Board) to 750 feet for each release, but this limitation was politely winked at when the boys had something hot.

And they did get a few sensational stories. The navy footage from Tarawa, and the joint material from Peleliu and Anguar made up into fine, timely newsreels. The films of the liberation of Paris, most of them made by a regular newsreel man working with the resistance forces before the city's "release," were historic, as were the pictures of Manila's capture. Most impressive of all newsreel issues during the war, however, were the films showing the Nazi prison-camp atrocities, released after the fall of Germany. These films were so stark and unstinting that a few theatres declined to show them. But they did reach the public very widely, and were classics in news-film reportage.

The commercially made "think" pictures which were released periodically by the March of Time, the World in Action (Canadian National Film Board), and Pathé's This Is America series contributed, too, to the public's understanding of issues and problems during the war years. A great deal of attention was given in these factual films to the international scene—a healthy indication of broadening horizons on our screens.

And the *movies* still served other purposes—significant purposes—during the war, many of them in areas removed from the general public's eye. There were, of course, the elaborate programs of service training films—a vast new function of motion pictures developed during a few fateful years. (It is proper to note that the Hollywood studios assisted these programs in their initial stages by making many training films on order, before the services completed their own production units.)

There were the special-purpose films produced by Hollywood and other commercial studios—especially by Walt Disney's outfit—for release in Latin America by the Office of the Co-Ordinator of Inter-American Affairs; the films made by the Overseas Motion Picture Bureau of the OWI for exhibition to foreign audiences to acquaint them with our country and our ways. There were the fact films produced by the services and released non-theatrically by them for showing in schools and factories as part of large "industrial incentive" programs. And there were films put out for such occasions as bond and war-charity drives. No one can ever say that movies didn't win their service stripes in World War II.

Now, let's make a hasty survey of the participation of movie people in straight war work. First, of course, there were those who entered the services—some voluntarily, some by request—among them Clark Gable, James Stewart, Robert Montgomery, Douglas Fairbanks, Jr., Henry Fonda, Louis Hayward, Tyrone Power, Mickey Rooney, Victor Mature, David Niven, Wayne Morris, Gene Autry, and Lew Ayres. William Wyler, Frank Capra, John Ford, Anatole Litvak, Anthony Veillier, John Huston, and Gene Markey were among the writers and directors. These are just some of the "star" names. At least one-fourth of the male employees of Hollywood—and from other branches of the industry—went into uniform.

And those who stayed in "civvies" did much work, too. Three days after Pearl Harbor the Hollywood Victory Committee, a wartime outfit, was enthusiastically formed. This organization, embracing virtually all of the people of Hollywood, mobilized the colony's talents and energies for the many activities to which they were called—for bond rallies, camp entertainments, and USO tours overseas. Between the day of its formation and June 1, 1945, the Hollywood Victory Committee enlisted a total of 3,865 players for 47,300 free appearances in 6,810 events contributing to the purposes named above.

Or, to break those figures down into categories:

One hundred and thirty-eight artists played 9,187 days on entertainment tours overseas.

Three hundred and eighty-six personalities played 5,560 days in camps and hospitals in this country.

Two hundred and thirty-nine personalities played 2,919 days on 26 national tours, largely for the Treasury Department bond rallies.

Fifty-two personalities played 221 days on Canadian bond tours.

One thousand seven hundred and seventy-four performances were staged at West Coast embarkation points and staging areas to entertain men headed for the Pacific.

This is not to mention players provided for radio programs, transcriptions, and personal appearances at numerous other rallies.

These figures, of course, do not capture the personal drama and sometimes sacrifice involved. They do not reveal, for instance, that Carole Lombard lost her life in an airplane wreck during a bond tour; that Joe E. Brown made four lengthy trips into practically every war area in which American forces fought, from the Aleutians to North Africa; that Bob Hope and his company were out on the "foxhole circuit" for as many months, almost, as they were at home, or that hundreds of familiar—and unfamiliar—troupers gladly took discomfort in their stride to bring to our fighting forces (and to our wounded veterans) a measure of cheer and hope. If there were a few unfortunate incidents connected with their overseas tours, as occasionally reported, they were exceptions and may now be dismissed.

And the industry itself gave to our forces the most salubrious gift of all when it contributed *all* of its product for free showing at bases overseas. In February, 1942, the WAC presented on behalf of the industry to the Special Services Division of the War Department an initial gift of 1,200 prints on 16-mm. film of feature films released up to that time and assured the Army that any picture made thereafter might be taken for free showing overseas. In short, the Army was invited to take whatever pictures it desired.

The organization of the overseas facilities for distributing and showing films was, of course, the Army's responsibility, and it was a little slow in shaping at first. Reports came back that the pictures were old and were not widely shown. But the kinks had been pretty well ironed out by the summer of 1943, small projectors were abroad in large numbers, and four new features were going out every week.

Eventually the Army established twenty-one film exchanges overseas, supplying pictures for an average of 5,850 showings a night. A total of 982 different feature films had been sent abroad by mid-1945—or exactly 34,232 prints. It might be mentioned that the raw stock on which these films were printed was contributed free by manufacturers and that the industry, through its subsidiaries, was helpful in bringing it about that the Army had approximately 7,500 16-mm. projection machines available at all times for the showing of entertainment films throughout the world. Many of Hollywood's top pictures were exhibited to troops overseas long before they were released to theatres here at home. . . .

You may question now, in conclusion, what has been the total effect of the war upon American movies. Where do they stand now—and where do they go from here? Those are questions which even the film folks have not fully weighed and appraised. Time alone—and the public's own reactions in the postwar scheme—will answer them.

But this much is fairly obvious: the makers of entertainment films see a greater responsibility to society than they saw before the war. They know that the public—and particularly the fighters who return to civil life—have a broader concept of peoples and of the organization of this world. They know that the mind of the masses, awakened to sharp realities, will not henceforth be susceptible to unmitigated "escape." They know that our films of the future will have to come to a closer grip with life.

The fact that many film-makers have gained combat experience in this war and have seen a new function for movies beyond entertainment is good. These creative men will be anxious to make a richer type of film when they return. They will want to project their experience and their maturity in new dramatic terms. Add to this the fact that the techniques of the documentary have been so well advanced that the public is now accustomed to them and you have a whole new horizon. Films of the future should stimulate, not lull and delude, men's minds.

But that is the "coming attraction"—"next week at this theatre." Our job was to scan the current epic. And this is where we came in.

■ ■ ■ ■

So Proudly We Fail (1943), James Agee

James Agee, one of America's most perceptive, most literate, and most respected film critics, was appalled by the timidity and banality of Hollywood's war films. This article, which appeared in the *Nation* of 30 October 1943, compares the Hollywoodizing of the war with the honesty and power of the British documentaries.

We suffer—we vaguely realize—a unique and constantly intensifying schizophrenia which threatens no other nation involved in this war. Geography is the core of the disease. Those Americans who are doing the fighting are doing it in parts of the world which seem irrelevant to them; those who are not, remain untouched, virginal, prenatal, while every other considerable population on earth comes of age. In every bit of information

James Agee's "So Proudly We Fail" appeared in the 30 October 1943 *Nation*.

you can gather about breakdowns of American troops in combat, overseas, even in the camps, a sense of unutterable dislocation, dereliction,
absence of contact, trust, wholeness, and reference, in a kind and force
which no other soldiers have to suffer, clearly works at the root of the
disaster. Moreover, while this chasm widens and deepens daily between
our fighting and civilian populations and within each mind, another—
much deeper and wider than any which geography alone could impose
—forms and increases between this nation and the other key nations
of the world. Their experience of war is unprecedented in immediacy and
unanimity. Ours, even in the fraction which has the experience at all,
is essentially specialized, lonely, bitter, and sterile; our great majority
will emerge from the war almost as if it had never taken place; and not all
the lip-service in the world about internationalism will make that different. This, and more and worse, is all so obvious, so horrifying, and
so apparently unalterable that, being a peculiarly neurotic people, we
are the more liable to nod and pay it the least possible attention. That is
unfortunate. Our predicament is bad enough as it stands; the civil and
international prospect is unimaginably sinister.

Since it is beyond our power to involve ourselves as deeply in experience
as the people of Russia, England, China, Germany, Japan, we have to
make up the difference as well as we can at second hand. Granting that
knowledge at second hand, taken at a comfortable distance, is of itself
choked with new and terrible liabilities, I believe nevertheless that much
could be done to combat and reduce those liabilities, and that second-
hand knowledge is at least less dangerous than no knowledge at all. And
I think it is obvious that in imparting it, moving pictures could be match-
lessly useful. How we might use them, and how gruesomely we have
failed to, I lack room to say; but a good bit is suggested by a few films I
want to speak of now.

Even the Army Orientation films, through no fault intrinsic to them,
carry their load of poison, of failure. You can hear from every sort of soldier from the simplest to the most intricate what a valuable job they are
doing. But because they are doing it only for service men they serve inadvertently to widen the abyss between fighters and the civilians who need
just as urgently to see them. Civilians, however, get very little chance to
learn anything from moving pictures. We are not presumed to be brave
enough. And the tragic thing is that after a couple of decades of Hollywood and radio, we are used to accepting such deprivations and insults
quite docilely; often, indeed, we resent anyone who has the daring to try
to treat us as if we were human beings.

Just now it is a fought question whether numbers four and five of the
Orientation Series, "The Battle of Britain" and "The Battle of Russia,"

will get public distribution. Whether they do depends on what is laugh-
ingly called the Office of War Information and on what is uproariously
called the War Activities Committee. The OWI's poor little pictures, blue-
born with timidity from the start, have finally been sabotaged out of
existence; and judging by the performance to date of the WAC, it is not
very likely that we shall see these films. And if we do see them, it is more
than likely that we shall see them with roast albatrosses like "The Keeper
of the Flame" hung around their necks.

I can only urge you to write your Congressman, if he can read. For
these films are responsible, irreplaceable pieces of teaching. "Britain," one
hour's calculated hammering of the eye and ear, can tell you more about
that battle than you are ever likely otherwise to suspect, short of having
been there. "Russia," though it is a lucid piece of exposition, is cut
neither for fact nor for political needlepoint but purely, resourcefully, and
with immensely powerful effect, for emotion. It is by no means an ultimate handling of its material, but it is better than the Russian records
from which it was drawn, and next to the tearful magnificence of "The
Birth of a Nation" is, I believe, the best and most important war film
ever assembled in this country.

Beside it Samuel Goldwyn's "The North Star" is something to be seen
more in sorrow than in anger and more in the attitude of the diagnostician
than in any emotion at all. It represents to perfection some crucially
symptomatic characteristics of Hollywood and of the American people in
so far as Hollywood reflects, or is accepted by, the people. Hollywood's
noble, exciting, all but unprecedented intention here is to show the conduct of the inhabitants of a Russian border village during the first days
of their war; to show real people, involved in realities, encumbered by a
minimum of star-spotlighting or story. The carrying out of that intention
implies in every detail the hopeless mistrust in which Hollywood holds its
public. To call this "commercial" and to talk about lack of intelligence
and taste is, I think, wide of the main mark. The attitude is more nearly
that of the fatally misguided parent toward the already all but fatally
spoiled child. The result is one long orgy of meeching, sugaring, propitiation, which, as a matter of fact, enlists, develops, and infallibly corrupts
a good deal of intelligence, taste, courage, and disinterestedness. I am
sorry not to talk at length and in detail about this film. I can only urge you
to watch what happens in it: how every attempt to use a reality brings the
romantic juice and the annihilation of any possible reality pouring from
every gland. In its basic design Lillian Hellman's script could have become
a fine picture: but the characters are stock, their lines are tinny-literary,
their appearance and that of their village is scrubbed behind the ears
and "beautified"; the camera work is nearly all glossy and overcomposed;

the proudly complicated action sequences are stale from overtraining; even the best of Aaron Copland's score has no business ornamenting a film drowned in ornament: every resourcefulness appropriate to some kinds of screen romance, in short, is used to make palatable what is by no remote stretch of the mind romantic. I think the picture represents the utmost Hollywood can do, within its present decaying tradition, with a major theme. I am afraid the general public will swallow it whole. I insist, however, that that public must and can be trusted and reached with a kind of honesty difficult, in so mental-hospital a situation, to contrive; impossible, perhaps, among the complicated pressures and self-defensive virtuosities of the great studios.

The thing that so impresses me about the non-fiction films which keep coming over from England is the abounding evidence of just such a universal adulthood, intelligence, and trust as we lack. I lack space to mention them in detail (the new titles are "I Was a Fireman," "Before the Raid," and, even better, "ABCA" and the bleak, beautiful, and heartrending "Psychiatry in Action"), but I urge you to see every one that comes your way. They are free, as not even our Orientation films are entirely, of salesmanship; they are utterly innocent of our rampant disease of masked contempt and propitiation. It comes about simply enough: everyone, on and off screen and in the audience, clearly trusts and respects himself and others.

There is a lot of talk here about the need for "escape" pictures. To those who want to spend a few minutes in a decently ventilated and healthful world, where, if only for the duration, human beings are worthy of themselves and of each other, I recommend these British films almost with reverence as the finest "escapes" available.

■ ■ ■ ■

Is Hollywood Growing Up? (1945), Dorothy B. Jones

This article by Dorothy Jones appeared in the *Nation* on 3 February 1945, some fifteen months after Agee's condemnation of Hollywood's war films appeared there. Ms. Jones, who worked as the head of the Film Reviewing and Analysis Section of the Office of War Information, was less critical of Hollywood's wartime efforts. Further, the best American

"Is Hollywood Growing Up?" by Dorothy B. Jones, appeared in the *Nation* on 3 February 1945.

documentaries of the war had been released in the period between the appearance of the two articles.

In evaluating Hollywood's role in the war, one is faced with a curious paradox. On the one hand, a careful examination of the record shows that the motion-picture industry has contributed relatively little to the war effort through its feature films. On the other, there are many evidences of its rapidly increasing maturity during the war years. New attitudes toward the film have been spreading through all Hollywood—various talent groups have stepped forward to accept their social and political responsibilities toward the motion-picture colony and the country at large. Furthermore, the industry as a whole, like many other American industries, has achieved new unity as a result of the war. To explain this apparent paradox it is necessary to review some of the changes which have been taking place in the movie capital since America's entry into the war.

New Attitude toward Minority Groups

Traditionally, Hollywood has regarded the feature film as a fantasy medium with only one responsibility—to provide enjoyment or entertainment for its audiences. Consequently the average Hollywood film-maker has felt no special obligation toward his material. In order to make his story timely and thereby improve the box-office appeal of his picture, he has often dealt with important topics of the day, but out of confusion or ignorance he has adapted, twisted, or misinterpreted social and political facts. If greater integrity of presentation was urged upon him, the average producer usually insisted that after all "it's only a movie," only make-believe.

With the war, however, Hollywood producers have gradually become aware that a motion picture—even a purely "escapist" picture—is a social document which, regardless of the producer's intention, is certain to influence those who see it. For example, it was brought home to the industry that the time-worn portrayal of minority groups was no longer acceptable. The criticism of film reviewers and reports on the reactions of foreign audiences made it evident that the Negro could no longer be presented as a comic menial, the stupid, shiftless character common on the screen for many years; that during a war being fought, among other things, to stamp out fascist theories of racial superiority such portrayals supported the propaganda of our enemies. As a result the old Negro stereotype has appeared less frequently on the screen, and a new and refreshing picture of the Negro has replaced it. Dore Schary, in planning the film "Bataan" (MGM), deliberately waited until the story was completed before casting a Negro in one of the main roles so that the part would not be specially written for a Negro. The Sudanese Negro in "Sahara" (Columbia) is another example of the changed characterization of the Negro on the screen. Various films have given prominent roles to Negro players, roles which showed the Negro as an accepted member of society instead of as a type set apart by prejudice. The more frequent appearance of Negro faces in group or crowd scenes reflect the new attitude.

The Chinese laundryman or cook with his pidgin English, who was always good for a laugh in days gone by, appears less often. There has even been some effort to atone for the indignities inflicted in the past by portraying the positive virtues of the Chinese American. One example of this is the characterization of the young Chinese interne in the Dr. Kildare pictures. Similarly the stereotypes of the "dumb wop," the bearded Russian, the hysterical Frenchman, have tended to be replaced by human beings not unlike ourselves, toward whom audiences everywhere can feel sympathy or dislike, depending upon the role of such characters in the story rather than their nationality.

ADAPTING FILMS TO WORLD AUDIENCES

The war has brought to Hollywood a broadened concept of film audiences. Although before the war the industry derived from 30 to 40 per cent of its gross take from the foreign market, Hollywood movie-makers had long been accustomed to keeping their eye on the domestic box-office. It is true that most studios had set up foreign departments whose main function was to warn producers against the portrayal of incidents or customs which might prove offensive in some countries. Certain rules were established—no villain could be identified as a friendly national, Latin American women should not be shown as having loose morals, and so on—and violations of them were either eliminated from the script or cut from the export prints. But little thought was given to orienting entire films for the world market.

The idea that each script must be considered from the standpoint of world as well as domestic audiences has been firmly established in Hollywood by the daily conferences of producers and writers with the Overseas Branch of the Office of War Information. Hollywood filmmakers have been informed about the unfortunate use made of gangster films by our enemies. Pre-war gangster films had been reedited by the Nazis and shown in conquered countries as confirmation of their claims that this country was ruled by gangsters and thugs. And Hollywood gangster films had been cited by the Nazi short-wave radio as testimony that gangster-ruled America could not be relied upon by its allies or the peoples it promised to liberate. Having learned that Hollywood films are accepted overseas as documentary portrayals of the American scene, Hollywood producers now have a new understanding of the international importance of their product.

HOLLYWOOD WRITERS MOBILIZE FOR WAR

Hollywood writers were among the first to demand the more vital use of the film during the war. One week after Pearl Harbor they met to dedicate their talents to furnishing morale-building material. An organization called the Hollywood Writers' Mobilization was formed, representing eight different writers' groups. This organization has provided writing talent for government and other agencies engaged in war work. It has also had considerable influence, both direct and indirect, upon the work of script writers. The mobilization itself has furnished scripts for almost 150 film shorts, trailers, and documentaries for government agencies, the armed forces, and war charities. It has produced more than 800 radio scripts and spot announcements, almost as many sketches for camp and factory shows, hundreds of speeches, posters, and slogans, and innumerable brochures, feature articles, and songs.

In October, 1943, the Hollywood Writers' Mobilization, acting jointly with the University of California at Los Angeles, sponsored a Writers' Congress which was attended by 1,300 people. At general meetings and seminars writers, directors, and producers, together with university students and teachers, participated in discussions of how the motion picture and radio could best aid in the winning of the war and the peace. The congress gave great impetus to the growing realization that the Hollywood film could not remain isolated from social problems of the day but must assume its place in world thinking.

As a follow-up to the Writers' Congress, the Mobilization initiated a series of seminars in which writers discussed the problems involved in a more effective war-time use of the Hollywood film. The presentation of the returning service man and the portrayal of minority groups were among the topics considered. By and large, these seminars were well attended. They became not only a source of information and a stimulus to constructive thinking but also a new and vital type of story conference at which writers could clarify their own thinking about their current work.

AN ANTI-FASCIST HOLLYWOOD

There are other signs of Hollywood's growing maturity. Early in 1944 the Hollywood Motion Picture Alliance,[1] a labor-baiting organization of the America First variety, made its appearance. This organization,

1. Ed. Note: This "fascist," "labor-baiting" organization would be treated as Hollywood's patriotic model during the HUAC hearings two years later. (See pages 500–502.)

which claimed to speak for the entire film industry, sought to brand as "red" and "un-American" all progressive thinkers in the motion-picture colony and to thwart the progressive movement. Other Hollywood groups, led by the Writers' Mobilization, moved into action against it. Their opposition culminated in a meeting held on June 28, 1944, which was attended by about a thousand delegates representing seventeen guilds and unions and which called for unified action to protect the industry and its workers against anti-democratic and anti-labor acts. The meeting was a public rebuff to the Motion Picture Alliance and served notice that Hollywood would not tolerate a fascist-type organization which pretended to represent the industry and its workers. Subsequent to the meeting, the Screen Actors' Guild and the Federation of Musicians joined the protest group, which formed a Council of Hollywood Guilds and Unions representing 22,000 of the 30,000 workers in the motion-picture industry. An account of the meeting was published in a pamphlet entitled "The Truth About Hollywood," thousands of copies of which were distributed to guilds and unions throughout the country to show how one industry fought the attempt of a fascist group to organize in its midst and take over its representation. The incident marked a new high in social thought and action in the motion-picture colony.

No discussion of Hollywood's changing role in public affairs would be complete without some mention of the contribution of its talent groups in the election campaign. Writers, actors, musicians, cartoonists, and other artists gave generously of their time in dramatizing the issues. Humphrey Bogart, Orson Welles, Katharine Hepburn, Edward G. Robinson, the Warners, Walter Wanger, to name but a few of the top figures, as well as innumerable lesser persons, worked tirelessly for the reelection of President Roosevelt. Their progressive attitude is bound to be reflected in the future product of the industry.

NEW TECHNIQUES FROM THE BATTLE FRONTS

Probably one of the most important influences upon the future film will be that exerted by members of the industry who have actively participated in the war. Many Hollywood camera men, actors, writers, directors, and technicians have been under fire, recording battle action with camera and sound equipment. Others have worked behind the lines assembling and editing newsreel footage. Still others have made orientation or training films or prepared documentaries about America to follow our armed forces into the liberated areas. In doing these jobs Hollywood talent and technical groups have learned all kinds of new techniques. In fact, it is safe to say that their entire way of thinking about the film has been modified.

Most of these men will return to their civilian jobs when the war is over. Among their number are some outstanding Hollywood names—Frank Capra, John Ford, George Oppenheimer, Robert Riskin, Irving Reis, and many others. Their influence upon Hollywood's future product can scarcely be measured at this time. Certainly men who for the past several years have been making the film a dynamic weapon of war will not be content to produce exclusively escapist films which recognize no social or political responsibility.

THE POST-WAR OUTLOOK

The traditional ideas about film-making which have so long governed the motion-picture industry are slowly yielding before the progressive forces which have been gathering strength in the movie capital as elsewhere in the world. The gradual revision of the stereotyped characterization of minority groups, the new effort toward a more realistic portrayal of American life for foreign audiences are but two of many indications that a revolution is taking place in Hollywood. The fact that such films as "Sahara" (Col.), "Guadalcanal Diary" (20th), "Corvette K-225" (Univ.), "This Land Is Mine" (RKO), "Watch on the Rhine" (WB), "North Star" (Goldwyn), "Wilson" (20th), and similar pictures have come out of Hollywood and have been successful at the box-office offers further evidence that a new day is coming. The bulk of the Hollywood product will undoubtedly continue to be musicals, comedies, murder mysteries, and westerns. But the film which attempts a serious treatment of social and economic problems has become an accepted part of the product. Equally important, the average Hollywood musical or comedy, in so far as it touches upon current problems, will tend increasingly to reflect Hollywood's growing sense of responsibility to foreign as well as American audiences.

The changes which have come about in Hollywood as a result of the war are in no sense temporary ones which will vanish on V-Day. Organizations like the Hollywood Writers' Mobilization and the Council of Hollywood Guilds and Unions have already begun to plan their peacetime programs. The Writers' Mobilization, for instance, will function as a cultural center for motion-picture writers interested in the social and political implications of the film and will further the exchange of ideas with the script writers of other nations.

Nor will Hollywood's future influence be exerted, as in the past, solely through its output. The people who work in Hollywood have, through their war experience, gained immeasurably in social awareness and have learned how to act together in the interests of the American people and of people everywhere. With the best artistic talent of the country at its disposal, Hollywood may in time assume the progressive leadership of the nation.

■ ■ ■ ■

MOVING-PICTURE AND RADIO PROPAGANDA (1941), U.S. Senate, Subcommittee of the Committee on Interstate Commerce

That Ms. Jones's predictions for Hollywood's future never came true can be partially attributed to her inability to foresee a shift in American social attitudes toward the movies (a shift signaled by the reversal and redemption of the reputation of the Motion Picture Alliance). Although the causes for such a shift in attitudes may have been invisible in 1945, a somewhat forgotten, very short-lived, and seemingly unimportant congressional investigation into motion picture propaganda appears more significant now than it did in 1941. Congressional committees and subcommittees had previously investigated the commercial practices of the film industry (such as block-booking); and Martin Dies, the founder of the House Un-American Activities Committee, had indeed begun a 1940 investigation into movie subversion, but the brief hearings proved more embarrassing to the congressman than to the industry. The 1941 Senate hearings, however, marked the first time that the federal government held the ideology and attitudes of the motion picture industry up for public scrutiny and (by implication) censure. The official question that provoked the hearings was why did Hollywood films one-sidedly support the Allied cause in the European war. The odor of anti-Semitism attached itself to the hearings even before they had begun. The motion picture industry came through this first trial by government with renewed unity and strength (as they would not a half-decade later): the Hollywood spokesmen were so fervently sincere and committeed to their beliefs; the motives of their accusers were so suspicious; public and press opinion was as one-sided on the hearings as was the content of the movies on the war in Europe. Within three months, the question that had provoked the hearings had become moot.

The subcommittee met, pursuant to call, at 10:15 a.m., in the caucus room, Senate Office Building, Senator D. Worth Clark presiding.

The Senate Subcommittee of the Committee on Interstate Commerce hearings on *Moving-Picture and Radio Propaganda* began 9 September 1941.

Present: Senators Clark of Idaho (chairman of the subcommittee), Mc-Farland, Tobey, and Brooks. Senator Bone as a member was not present.

Present also: Senators Smith, Clark of Missouri, and Nye.

Senator CLARK of Idaho (chairman of the subcommittee). The subcommittee will please come to order, and also the members of the audience.

These hearings, which are about to begin, before a subcommittee of the Senate Committee on Interstate Commerce come on by virtue of Senate Resolution 152.

In view of the fact that there has been considerable comment in the press concerning this committee; and further, in view of the fact that there seems to be some misapprehension as to what these hearings are all about, both as to their legality and other characteristics, I think it proper that the chairman of the subcommittee make a brief preliminary statement.

On the 1st day of August 1941 Senator Nye and Senator Clark of Missouri introduced in the Senate of the United States, Senate Resolution 152. I will ask that that resolution be placed in the record of our hearings, but, first, it is short and I desire to read it:

RESOLUTION

Whereas the motion-picture and the radio are the most potent instruments of communication of ideas; and

Whereas numerous charges have been made that the motion picture and the radio have been extensively used for propaganda purposes designed to influence the public mind in the direction of participation in the European war; and

Whereas all of this propaganda has been directed to one side of the important debate now being held, not only in Congress, but throughout the country; and

Whereas this propaganda reaches weekly the eyes and ears of one hundred million people and is in the hands of groups interested in involving the United States in war: Therefore be it

Resolved, That the Committee, or any duly authorized subcommittee thereof, is authorized and directed to make, and to report to the Senate the results of, a thorough and complete investigation of any propaganda disseminated by motion pictures and radio or any other activity of the motion-picture industry to influence public sentiment in the direction of participation by the United States in the present European war . . . .

SENATOR NYE. All right. At the outset, I should like to point out that no contention can validly be raised that any investigation of propaganda in the movies, amounts to censorship of freedom of speech or freedom of the press. The fact is, and the law is, that the movies are not part of the press of this country, and are not protected by the first amendment to our Constitution. This has been held by the Supreme Court of the United States. In 1915, the Court was faced with the problem whether a State law censoring movies amounted to a violation of freedom of speech or of the press. The State which enacted that law had a constitutional provision similar to the first amendment to the United States Constitution, so far as freedom of speech and of the press are concerned. The Supreme Court held flatly that movies were not part of our press, and stated (I quote from the opinion in *Mutual Film Corp. v. Ohio Industrial Commission,* 236 U.S. 230):

> It cannot be put out of view that the exhibition of moving pictures is a business pure and simple, originated and conducted for profit, like other spectacles, not to be regarded, nor intended by the Ohio constitution, we think, as part of the press of the country or as organs of public opinion. They are mere representations of events, of ideas and sentiments published and known, vivid, useful and entertaining no doubt, but, as we have said, capable of evil, having power for it, the greater because of their attractiveness and manner of exhibition.

Laying aside this opinion and decision let me say I am not asking for any governmental interference with the freedom of the movies. I entertain no desire for moving-picture censorship. That is quite as undesirable as is press censorship. I entertain no sympathy toward any idea which would have the Government take over the movies or have the Government dictate what should be run in the pictures.

I do hope, however, that the industry will more largely recognize the obligation it owes our country and its people, and that in times of peace for our country, that industry will entertain that American courage which will boldly resist any effort by administration agents of our Government to dictate what kind of picture it shall or shall not make. The American public can afford the degree of censorship necessary to keep any semi-public agency functioning properly.

Mr. Chairman, I am sure that you and members of your committee are quite aware of the determined effort that has been put forth to convey to the public that the investigation asked is the result of a desire to serve the un-American, narrow cause of anti-Semitism. . . . I would like to refer first to Dr. John H. Sherman, president of Webber College, a college in Florida, who was made responsible for a nasty, colored news release dated August 9 and published in at least one interventionist newspaper, this release having to do with my address at St. Louis dealing with moving-picture propaganda. I am quoting now Dr. Sherman:

Sixteen years ago Adolf Hitler wrote in Mein Kampf that the paralysis of America preliminary to conquest would easily be accomplished. He went on to outline the means and the method by which, through utilizing the prejudices and hatreds of antagonistic groups within our heterogeneous population, he would destroy unity and paralyze governmental action. He particularly mentioned the probable power of a propaganda campaign of race hatred among us.

On Friday, August 1, 1941, the America First Committee threw off the last shred of disguise (except its misleading name) as it presented Gerald Nye to a howling mob in St. Louis. The crowd mob-howled at every slur upon American foreign policy, cheered reference to democratic nonsuccesses, and particularly shouted approval of Nye's principal effort of the evening.

It would be wrong to use Nye's official title here, because that principal effort was so low and un-American as to be a disgrace to the Senate of the United States, or to any Senator. His principal effort of the evening was a Hitleresque attack upon the American Jews. Deliberately, adroitly, with every trick of timing and inflection of voice, Nye accused the motion-picture industry of fostering pro-British sentiment, and then called a list of Jewish names associated with the motion-picture industry, drolly exaggerating their most Hebraic-sounding syllables, with pauses to encourage his inflamed hearers to shout and hiss.

I happened to be there, Mr. Chairman. I do not recall the slightest foundation for any such contention as this president of a college offers in this story. . . . Continuing to quote from Dr. Sherman's statement:

> He did not use a complete list, which would have included many honored gentiles. Nor did he mention the fact that some of our best and most convincing motion-picture appeals for peace have been produced by the men he named.

May I comment at this point to the extent of remarking that had I continued with the names of those in the motion-picture industry, using those of lesser consequence in the industry, the proportion of Jewish names would, if anything, have increased.

I continue reading from Dr. Sherman's article:

> His attack thus was not truly an attack on the motion-picture industry, as such, and not an attack on war advocates within the industry, but merely an attack upon Jews because they were Jews, in typical Nazi style.

Any person who has doubted that the America First Committee has a definite place and part to play in the Hitler campaign to disrupt America must surely have found the full answer in the Nye speech.

That un-American appeal to anti-Semitic prejudice was in the pattern of Goebbels, and shrewdly calculated to do maximum damage to the internal peace of our American people.

That is exactly what Hitler, 16 years ago, promised to accomplish among us. . . .

I bitterly resent, Mr. Chairman, this effort to misrepresent our purpose and to prejudice the public mind and your mind by dragging this racial issue to the front. I will not consent to its being used to cover the tracks of those who have been pushing our country on the way to war with their propaganda intended to inflame the American mind with hatred for one foreign cause and magnified respect and glorification for another foreign cause, until we shall come to feel that wars elsewhere in the world are really after all our wars.

Those primarily responsible for the propaganda pictures have a peculiar though natural interest prompting them in their work. They themselves may not be mindful of what they are doing, but this is not true of all of them.

Those primarily responsible for the propaganda pictures are born abroad. They came to our land and took citizenship here entertaining violent animosities toward certain causes abroad. Quite natural is their feeling and desire to aid those who are at war against the causes which so naturally antagonize them. If they lose sight of what some Americans might call the first interests of America in times like these, I can excuse them. But their prejudices by no means necessitate our closing our eyes to these interests and refraining from any undertaking to correct their error.

It was in this spirit that I acted on August 1 of this year when, after joining with Senator Clark of Missouri in introducing the pending resolution, I spoke at St. Louis. It was this action which brought down upon me the condemnation of many Jewish and other writers who were, no doubt, getting their cue from the moving-picture heads against whom my effort was extended and whom I had named in that address.

There would have been no differing approach by me to the subject had those primarily responsible for propaganda in the movies been in the main Methodists, Episcopalians, Catholics, or Mohammedans. The fact is that of those I named, not all were Jews as has been so often insinuated. However, if I had it to do over and were I determined to name those primarily responsible for propaganda in the moving-picture field, I would, in light of what I have since learned, confine myself to four names, each that of one of the Jewish faith, each except only one foreign-born. But I would do that without any spirit of prejudice and without prompting by any cause as foreign to my thinking as is anti-Semitism.

Mr. Chairman, such Jewish constituency as I have in my State can best testify to my mental make-up on this issue of anti-Semitism. They could reveal how I have rallied to their aid in their many efforts to free and bring loved ones from the horrible results of rampant anti-Semitism abroad. They could best afford the information concerning my activities in opening and trying to open the doors of medical schools to their sons who found university and college doors closed to Jewish medical students. They could best reveal my unqualified opposition to those who would let political decision and choice rest upon whether a candidate were a Jew or a Gentile.

However much my patience may be tried by such of the faith as would invite an anti-Semitic mind, I remain, as yet at least, bitterly opposed to the injection of anti-Semitism as a cause or issue in our American thinking and acting. It should have no place in our way of life. Opportunity for all, irrespective of faith, has been one of the foundation stones which has made our country both strong and great.

If the anti-Semitic issue is now raised for the moment, it is raised by those of the Jewish faith and those who would prejudice the issues in these studies; not by me, not by this committee. I shall not disguise the fact that it angers me no end, and since it is raised, I feel it must be met head-on, answered, then thrown aside to the end that there may be proceeding here in keeping with the spirit entertained by the authors of the pending resolution and the spirit of your committee.

I am not unmindful of the fact that there are those who would cast the suspicion of anti-Semitism upon some members of this committee as well as upon its authors. If even mere suspicion endures then this investigation cannot have the favor of such beneficial results as I believe can flow from it if it can be known that there is only broad, clean, and American interest involved in the study. We must not permit selfish causes to confuse the facts by dragging any "red herring" into the scene. . . .

I most emphatically deny, though this committee will not need this denial to know the truth, that there is any anti-Semitic cause served in the request which Senator Clark and I make for this investigation of propaganda.

I have splendid Jewish friends in and out of the moving-picture business. I dare to hope that I shall keep them as friends. . . .

SENATOR CLARK OF MISSOURI. Mr. Will Hays, who speaks for the organized moving-picture industry, and Mr. Wendell Willkie, who says that he represents the whole industry in a legal capacity (I hope that when he takes the stand, if he does that, he will set out in detail for the record the name of his clients) declare that this is an attempt to restrain the right of the motion-picture screen to present the problems of contemporary life without restraint from the Government. In other words, they begin —and I am sure we will hear a great deal more of it as we go along— with the effort to turn this inquiry into a great struggle by the movie magnates for freedom of speech.

I am willing and eager to meet these gentlemen on that ground. There are a great many naive souls who think that speech is free so long as political authority, particularly the Government, does not shackle it. They overlook the fact that there can be such a thing, particularly in our day, as the denial of speech when one individual or small collection of individuals can band together and get control of the instruments of speech and deny them to everybody but themselves. When our Constitution was adopted, freedom of speech meant pretty much a man's right to say what he wanted to his neighbor, or to express himself in his little newspaper, or to publish a pamphlet, or to hire a hall somewhere, or get out in a cow pasture, or up on a stile or a soap box, and express himself fully. Indeed, this was the rule until a few years ago.

The instruments of speech were a man's own tongue and lips and larynx, invented and constructed by Almighty God, or else his hand which could convey to type the product of his mind and heart. Every man had this equipment, use it as he might. A man could talk to as many people as he could reach with his unaided voice in a small hall or an open field. It was not a great many. Abraham Lincoln in his campaign for the Presidency talked to numerous crowds—great for that era—but most of them only a few thousand people, many of them only a few hundred. In his whole campaign it is doubtful that he reached the ears of more than 100,000 people.

William J. Bryan in 1896 made what up to that time was the most spectacular tour of the Nation. He made more than 200 speeches, some of them to crowds of 10,000, some to crowds less than 500. Added all together he did not talk to more than a million different people, and it took him 4 months' incessant travel and extraordinary physical stamina to do that, and, to reach that many, he had to be a candidate for the Presidency of the United States and had to have the appeal and glamour of his remarkable eloquence.

But today a hitherto unknown politician or newspaper columnist can go on the radio and in one night talk to four, five, or ten million people. I am told that when the President of the United States talks he is listened to by fifty or sixty million people, and he doesn't have to leave his study to reach them. That is because something new has happened in the world —this thing called technology. Science has invented the radio machine and the moving-picture machine. In the discussion of public affairs, therefore, there is no equal competition between the man whose equipment is just his tongue, lips, larynx, and lungs and the man who has in his possession or access to a radio microphone.

It comes down to this: That the man who owns that machine now exercises over the freedom of discussion a power which no government could ever exercise. To interfere with a man's speech the Government has to pass oppressive laws, organize a ruthless constabulary, must hound men and prosecute them and put them in jail and incur the difficulties of opposition and the possibility of revolution. But the man who owns the radio machine can cut off from discussion those who disagree with him by the simple expedient of saying "No." And who is that man? He is not a public official; he is not elected to office; he is not an authorized public censor; he is not chosen by the people. He is just a businessman who by virtue of his acquisitive talents has gotten possession of this little microphone.

Now, the same thing is true of the moving-picture machine, save that the moving-picture machine is even more powerful than the microphone. Any man or any group of men who can get control of the screen can reach every week in this country an audience of 80,000,000 people. If there is a great debate before the Nation involving its economic life or even its liberties, no man can get a syllable in the sound pictures save by the grace of the men who control the sound pictures. And I here formally and deliberately charge that a handful of men have gotten possession of both the radio microphone and the moving-picture screen, beside which all other forms of discussion are antique and feeble, and that men and women in America discussing the great problems of America can use these machines or not only by the grace of this small oligarchy.

When the Oklahoma City Council refuses to allow Senator Wheeler and Col. Charles Lindbergh to talk in the city auditorium because it doesn't agree with them, that is an outrageous performance. But it does not muzzle them, for they can go out in a cow pasture or a ball park and speak. If I can't hire one hall in my town I can usually hire another. I must say it is something new in this country, however, to have the owners of halls closing their doors to American citizens with whom they do not agree. I do not want to minimize the gravity of this phenomenon in which men who·have the brass to talk about bringing freedom of speech to Russia, China, Japan, and Germany, and Addis Ababa, think that they can do it by closing the halls of America to distinguished American citizens who are actually expressing the views of the vast majority of Americans who want to stay out of this war. But bad as that is—damnable as it is—the aggrieved victim of these repressions can usually find a hall some place else or go on the street corners or into the open fields of the countryside and talk.

But when a few men get possession of the radio and the moving picture and shut me off from that vast audience, while opening it up to the man who opposes me in public life, how can that man be so foolish as to say there is freedom of speech as to that question, vital as it may be to our national existence? And, above all, how can the men who do that have the impudence to come here before this committee and tell you that they are fighting for freedom of speech? They are fighting for the freedom to say what they want and the freedom to prevent those who disagree with them from uttering a syllable in opposition.

Talk about hiring a hall! There are 17,000 moving-picture theaters in the United States. They do not belong to a handful of men, of course, but the pictures that appear on the screens of those theaters are produced by a handful of men and that handful of men can open or close those 17,000 theaters to ideas at their sweet will. They hold the power of life and death over those motion-picture houses because by their block-booking system, blind-selling system, and other devices they can close almost any house that they please on any day and at any time.

At the present time they have opened those 17,000 theaters to the idea of war, to the glorification of war, to the glorification of England's imperialism, to the creation of hatred of the people of Germany and now of France, to the hatred of those in America who disagree with them. Does anyone see a pictorial representation of life in Russia under "Bloody Joe" Stalin? They do not. In other words, they are turning these 17,000 theaters into 17,000 daily and nightly mass meetings for war. I say that this is a monopoly. The rules which apply to freedom of speech among a hundred million Americans have nothing to do with the situation where the instrumentalities of speech have been seized and monopolized by a few men. . . .

Dozens of pictures, great features costing—some of them hundreds of thousands of dollars, some of them millions of dollars—are used to infect the minds of their audiences with hatred, to inflame them, to arouse their emotions, and make them clamor for war. And not one word on the side of the argument against war is heard. That is because the moving-picture industry is a monopoly controlled by half a dozen men and because most of those men are themselves dominated by these hatreds, and are determined, in order to wreak vengeance on Adolf Hitler, a ferocious beast, to plunge this Nation into war on behalf of another ferocious beast. And, unless they are restrained, unless the people of this country are at least warned about them, they will plunge the country into war and, if this country goes to war and if a million men pour out their blood on the battlefields of the world, then when it is all over and America is looking around for the men responsible for this infamy and the roll of the guilty is called, the names of the men who rule this industry must stand high on the list before the bar of public opinion in that angry America which will inevitably follow the war. . . .

TESTIMONY OF HARRY M. WARNER, PRESIDENT OF WARNER BROS. PICTURES, INC., HOLLYWOOD, CALIF.

SENATOR CLARK OF IDAHO. Will you give your full name to the committee reporter, please?

MR. WARNER. Harry M. Warner.

SENATOR CLARK OF IDAHO. Mr. Warner, I understand you have a prepared statement. Would you prefer to proceed to read it without interruption and then to submit to such questions as members of the subcommittee may desire to ask at the conclusion?

MR. WARNER. In fact, I would appreciate that very much.

SENATOR CLARK OF IDAHO. I am sure the subcommittee will be glad to extend to you the courtesy of allowing you to proceed without interruption until you have finished. I suggest that you get as close as possible to the microphone so that we may be able to hear you clearly. The acoustics in this room are not of the best.

MR. WARNER. I believe in trying things out. Could you hear that?

SENATOR CLARK OF IDAHO. Oh, yes; that is fine. You may proceed.

MR. WARNER. I have read in the public press the accusations made against the motion-picture industry by Senator Gerald Nye and others. I have also read the testimony of Senators Nye and Bennett C. Clark and others before your committee. After measuring my words, and speaking with full sincerity, I want the record to show immediately that I deny, with all the strength I have, these reckless and unfounded charges.

At various points in the charges, Warner Bros. and I have been mentioned specifically. The charges against my company and myself are untrue. The charges are either based on a lack of information or concocted from pure fancy. Yet the gossip has been widely disseminated.

I am opposed to nazi-ism. I abhor and detest every principle and practice of the Nazi movement. To me, nazi-ism typifies the very opposite of the kind of life every decent man, woman, and child wants to live. I believe nazi-ism is a world revolution whose ultimate objective is to destroy our democracy, wipe out all religion, and enslave our people—just as Germany has destroyed and enslaved Poland, Belgium, Holland, France, and all the other counrties. I am ready to give myself and all my personal resources to aid in the defeat of the Nazi menace to the American people.

I realize that my convictions, of themselves, are unimportant. However, I am proud of them. As as matter of fact, I have never made a secret of them. I have always believed that every citizen has the right to express his views. I have done so both among my friends and associates and publicly to the press. I stand on my public record of the last 8 years. But for the record of the hearing and to avoid misrepresentation, I should like to summarize my convictions. They are not newly found convictions. They are deep-rooted.

Shortly after Hitler came to power in Germany I became convinced that Hitlerism was an evil force designed to destroy free people, whether they were Catholics, Protestants, or Jews. I claim no credit as a prophet. Many appraised the Nazis in their true role, from the very day of Hitler's rise to power.

I have always been in accord with President Roosevelt's foreign policy. In September 1939, when the Second World War began, I believed, and I believe today, that the world struggle for freedom was in its final stage. I said publicly then, and I say today, that the freedom which this country fought England to obtain, we may have to fight with England to retain.

I am unequivocally in favor of giving England and her allies all supplies which our country can spare. I also support the President's doctrine of freedom of the seas, as recently explained to the public by him.

Frankly, I am not certain whether or not this country should enter the war in its own defense at the present time. The President knows the world situation and our country's problems better than any other man. I would follow his recommendation concerning a declaration of war.

If Hitler should be the victor abroad, the United States would be faced with a Nazi-dominated world. I believe—and I am sure that the sub-committee shares my feeling—that this would be a catastrophe for our country. I want to avoid such a catastrophe, as I know you do.

I have given my views to you frankly and honestly. They reduce themselves to my previous statement: I am opposed to nazi-ism. I abhor and detest every principle and practice of the Nazi movement. I am not alone in feeling this. I am sure that the overwhelming majority of our people and our Congress share the same views.

While I am opposed to nazi-ism, I deny that the pictures produced by my company are "propaganda," as has been alleged. Senator Nye has said that our picture Sergeant York is designed to create war hysteria. Senator Clark had added Confessions of a Nazi Spy to the isolationist blacklist. John T. Flynn, in turn, has added Underground. These witnesses have not seen these pictures, so I cannot imagine how they can judge them. On the other hand, millions of average citizens have paid to see these pictures. They have enjoyed wide popularity and have been profitable to our company. In short, these pictures have been judged by the public and the judgment has been favorable.

Sergeant York is a factual portrait of the life of one of the great heroes of the last war. If that is propaganda, we plead guilty. Confessions of a Nazi Spy is a factual portrayal of a Nazi spy ring that actually operated in New York City. If that is propaganda, we plead guilty.

So it is with each and every one of our pictures dealing with the world situation or with the national defense. These pictures were carefully prepared on the basis of factual happenings and they were not twisted to serve any ulterior purpose.

In truth, the only sin of which Warner Bros. is guilty is that of accurately recording on the screen the world as it is or as it has been. Unfortunately, we cannot change the facts in the world today. If the committee will permit, we will present witnesses to show that these pictures are true to life. I am certain that we can easily prove to you that Warner Bros. has not duped its patrons but has, in fact, kept its obligation to the movie-going public.

Apparently our accusers desire that we change our policy of picturing accurately world affairs and the national-defense program. This, Warner Bros. will never do. This, I am sure the Congress would not want us to do. This, I am certain the public would not tolerate. . . .

I want to be frank with this committee. . . . Our company has pioneered what, for a better phrase, I will call "action" pictures. By that I mean we have tried to portray on the screen current happenings of our times. We have tried to do this realistically and accurately, and over a long period we have discovered that the public is interested in and grateful for this type of picture. Perhaps I can explain what I mean better by listing a few of these pictures.

We produced I Am a Fugitive From a Chain Gang, which was a story of a chain gang. We produced British Agent, which was an exposé of communistic Russia based upon the book by Bruce Lockhart. We produced Black Fury, which was a factual portrayal of conditions in the coal-mining industry. We also produced many realistic biographies of such great world figures as Pasteur (the French scientist), Juarez (the Abraham Lincoln of Mexico), Dr. Ehrlich (the great German doctor), and Zola, who aroused the conscience of the world in behalf of Dreyfus—the victim of religious bigotry.

I have no apology to make to the committee for the fact that for many years Warner Bros. has been attempting to record history in the making. We discovered early in our career that our patrons wanted to see accurate stories of the world in which they lived. I know that I have shown to the satisfaction of the impartial observer that Warner Bros., long before there was a Nazi Germany, had been making pictures on topical subjects. It was only natural, therefore, with the new political movement, however horrible it may be, that we should make some pictures concerning the

Nazis. It was equally logical that we should produce motion pictures concerning national defense. . . .

If Warner Bros. had produced no pictures concerning the Nazi movement, our public would have had good reason to criticize. We would have been living in a dream world. Today 70 percent of the nonfiction books published deal with the Nazi menace. Today 10 percent of the fiction novels are anti-Nazi in theme. Today 10 percent of all material submitted to us for consideration is anti-Nazi in character. Today the newspapers and radio devote a good portion of their facilities to describing nazi-ism. Today there is a war involving all hemispheres except our own and touching the lives of all of us. . . .

I am an American citizen, and I bow to no one in my patriotism and devotion to my country. Our country has become great because it is, in truth, a land of freedom. No one can take these freedoms from the American people. The United States has always been a united nation of free people living in tolerance and faith in each other. We have been able to achieve this unity because of the freedoms of the individual.

In conclusion, I tell this committe honestly, I care nothing for any temporary advantage or profit that may be offered to me or my company. I will not censor the dramatization of the works of reputable and well-informed writers to conceal from the American people what is happening in the world. Freedom of speech, freedom of religion, and freedom of enterprise cannot be bought at the price of other people's rights. . . .

■ ■ ■ ■

FREEDOM OF THE MOVIES (1947), Ruth A. Inglis

In 1947, the Commission on Freedom of the Press presented its first (and last) study of ideological freedom in the motion pictures—*Freedom of the Movies,* by Ruth A. Inglis. Supported by grants from Time, Inc., and the *Encyclopaedia Britannica,* the Commission on Freedom of the Press was a research project administered by the University of Chicago which sought, in effect, to examine some practical applications of the theoretical questions which Mortimer Adler had raised in *Art and Prudence.* The study is significant, not only as an academic attempt to remedy the intellectually questionable procedures of some of the Payne Fund Studies, but also because the notion of "freedom" is probably the central issue of this turbulent social era. Ms. Inglis concentrated on the issues of artistic freedom

Ruth A. Inglis, *Freedom of the Movies* (University of Chicago Press, 1947).

in treating moral issues and the social responsibility of doing so (for which read Adler's "art" and "prudence"), little knowing that an era of political (rather than moral) suppression lay in the immediate future of the movies. In this section of her study, Ms. Inglis is able to see the potentially dangerous implications of the Senate hearings of 1941.

STATEMENT BY THE COMMISSION

Obliged to surmount great technical obstacles and at the same time to establish itself on a profit-making basis, the motion picture industry has not yet developed its full possibilities. These possibilities are threefold: to help the public to understand the issues that confront them as citizens of the United States and of the world; to raise standards of popular taste; and to foster creative ability on the part of the writers, actors, directors, musicians, and photographers who make the pictures. The accompanying study illuminates many of the difficulties in the way. Some result from the industry's highly concentrated business structure and the manufacture of films to attract mass audiences; others, from pressures exerted by outside bodies with axes to grind.

The Commission would emphasize the fact that the public service or educational function of the movies, so brilliantly demonstrated during the recent war, faces new opportunities and responsibilities in the years ahead. It is imperative that the motion picture industry rise to the occasion.

As means to that end the Commission offers the following general recommendations:

1. The constitutional guarantees of freedom of the press should be recognized as including motion pictures. The growing importance of the documentary film gives fresh emphasis to the need.

2. The government should use its antitrust powers to destroy monopolistic control of production, distribution, and theatrical outlets. A healthy competition within the industry conduces to that variety and quality of service which the public interest requires.

3. The motion picture industry, by its own action, should place increasing stress on its role as a civic and informational agency conscious of the evolving character of many political and social problems. The industry as a responsible member of the body politic cannot shirk its obligation to promote, so far as possible, an intelligent understanding of domestic and international affairs. It should guard against misrepresentation of social groups and foreign peoples. Newsreels, when fairly selected and adequately annotated, contribute to popular enlightenment; and the documentary film, if developed in the United States as in certain other countries, affords even greater promise in this direction. This service to good

citizenship is often good business as well. At all events, in a free society like ours, it is a duty.

4. The industry should be also constantly alert to opportunities to develop further the screen's artistic and intellectual possibilities. Such ventures involve financial risks, but may in the long run be expected to attract sizable audiences and yield remunerative returns. The industry should use part of its profits, as some units have already done, to promote experimental ventures.

5. The public itself should insist upon the highest attainable accomplishment by the movies. Too often inarticulate, or articulate only in private, the customers fail to exert their influence. Newspapers and magazines could help by adopting the practice, already followed by some, of devoting regular space to serious criticism. In addition, every community should maintain one or more citizens' committees, not to further narrow purposes, but to encourage worthy achievement. These committees should be broadly representative, including persons jealous for the artistic integrity of the screen. The public has an important role to play also in encouraging the movie outside the commercial theater. Educational institutions, public libraries, churches, business clubs, trade-unions, women's groups, and the like should co-operate in making available suitable films for nontheatrical audiences and in drawing on nation-wide sources for information and comment to indicate to producers the principal needs. All such efforts would be greatly strengthened if universities and foundations should pay appropriate attention to this new potential in American life. In particular, they should set up centers of advanced study and research, whose investigations and reports would incite both producers and public to higher standards.

6. Finally, the public should sponsor a national advisory board to review and propose changes from time to time in the Motion Picture Production and Advertising Codes. These regulations were devised at an early stage of the movies, and, however useful they may be, they do not encourage the screen in attaining its full stature as a civic and artistic medium. The national advisory board should represent diverse elements, including creative talent from within the industry as well as educators, religious leaders, and men of affairs. If any agency on freedom of the press is created, as recommended in our General Report, it would be a logical function of this body to appoint the national advisory board.

In short, the Commission believes that the movies can realize their full promise only by unremitting effort from all concerned: the government, the industry, and the public—each in its own sphere. It further believes that the industry, possessing most of the means, can, if it has the will, cure the most serious ills of its own motion.

> Robert M. Hutchins   Charles E. Merriam
> Zechariah Chafee, Jr.   Reinhold Niebuhr
> John M. Clark   Robert Redfield
> John Dickinson   Beardsley Ruml
> William F. Hocking   Arthur M. Schlesinger
> Harold D. Lasswell   George N. Shuster
> Archibald MacLeish

OPINION WITHIN THE INDUSTRY

The recent war brought to many in the industry a dramatic revelation of potentialities in the screen, and a new respect for the social responsibilities of the medium is growing in Hollywood.

The new public representative of the major producers and distributors, Eric Johnston, has acknowledged that the film is not solely a means of mass entertainment but is comparable to the radio and the printed word as an agency of mass communciation—a statement his predecessor, Will Hays, would never have made. "Honest exchange of information and ideas is the primary function of motion pictures as well as of newspapers and the radio," Jack L. Warner of Warner Brothers Pictures said recently. He did not mean to deny, however, that theatrical motion pictures, first of all, must be entertaining.

Murray Silverstone, president of Twentieth Century–Fox International Corporation, stated in *Variety* for January 9, 1946: "Our industry is today more aware than ever before that movies are one of the most powerful forms of expression and persuasion. There is, therefore, complete agreement that the motion picture must continue as an articulate force in the postwar world so that it can contribute vitally and validly to the development of permanent peace, prosperity, progress and security on a global basis. It means that the motion picture has definitely broadened its scope of activity to include many more themes which can be presented in dramatic and entertaining manner."

In the *New York Times Magazine* for April 22, 1945, Samuel Goldwyn declared that the two jobs of the screen are "to entertain and to educate" and that there is no conflict between them. "I think," he said, "the screen's responsibility is so great just because pictures are both vivid and subtle—because they teach when they are pretending not to." Barney Balaban, president of Paramount Pictures, recently urged a broadening of the scope of pictorial subject matter. "The screen," he declared, "can hope to do something more than to provide purely escapist entertainment."

The social role of the movies has not always been so broadly defined by the representatives of the motion picture industry. In the past the function of public enlightenment has been greatly overshadowed by the use of the film as a vehicle for entertainment. Even now the argument arises occasionally that films in theaters should offer "pure" entertainment, untainted by "propaganda." Some exhibitors point out that patrons pay their money for entertainment and that, if they get "propaganda" instead, they are being cheated and will not return.

At the outset, let us recognize that an abundance of relatively inexpensive entertainment is necessary to social morale and its social value is not to be underestimated. All the leaders of the industry quoted above stress that entertainment is essential—and we wholeheartedly concur. No one wants dull movies. We agree without reservation with Mr. Howard Dietz, vice-president of Loew's, that "a bad show on a lofty theme is far worse than a good show on a lesser one." Need this be the choice? The assumption that films must be lacking in public significance in order to be entertaining is erroneous.

The fundamental fallacy disappears when the nature of "propaganda" is clarified. Originally, the word was associated with the propagation of religious faith and was any form of proselyting, publicity, or education. During the first World War the term acquired the connotation of duplicity. In common usage it has degenerated into an epithet for whatever one does not like. If by "propaganda" is meant something deceitful or misleading, then, of course, the movie must have none of it.

If we mean by "propaganda" any content which might change the ideas, sentiments, or values of those exposed to it, the motion picture cannot in any conceivable way avoid being propagandistic. Movies necessarily carry images of people and implications regarding ideas and ideals which have relevance to the community at large. The solution to the difficult problem of using images wisely is not to be found by pretending that the problem does not exist; that is, that the movies are "merely pure entertainment" and should not or cannot have anything serious to say.

A correlative but less tenacious argument is that the screen must shun serious themes because audiences do not like them. To this there are several answers. In the first place, no one contemplates abolishing westerns and light musical comedies. They have their place on the screen and probably always will have. The fact that some people want more meaty film fare and are disgusted with meaninglessness keeps them away from the movies altogether. One of the most pressing tasks for producers is to determine more precisely the reasons why some people attend the movies frequently and the reasons why others do not.

Sometimes film-makers are surprised at the reception of their own pictures. *The Lost Weekend* is a good recent example. Paramount asked exhibitors to pay a higher rental for the picture than was originally agreed upon. The highly significant reasons are indicated in the following excerpts from a letter from Charles Reagan, Paramount distribution head, to the editor of the *Film Bulletin* as quoted by *Harrison's Reports* for February 16, 1946: "It is true that we are now selling 'The Lost Weekend' at a higher sales classification than was originally designated for it. . . . With the amazing box-office results of the first showings, *it was unquestionably plain that we had grossly underestimated the public enthusiasm for the picture.* . . . We are asking our customers to recognize voluntarily the unusual development on 'The Lost Weekend' and to agree to a revised deal in keeping with its performance."

In other words, *The Lost Weekend* was a "sleeper"; that is, a picture which received much better public reception than was anticipated. Incidentally, Mr. Reagan's letter was written before the Academy Award was given to the film. It may well be that the production of films of social and personal significance will prove to be not only a public service but also a source of profit to producers with vision. Such pictures may attract a new audience to the movies.

In the second place, the so-called serious films can be entertaining. *Mrs. Miniver*, for example, not only created new bonds of sympathy between Britons and Americans during a trying period of the war but was outstanding entertainment and attracted huge audiences. Years ago *Dead End* told a story which left the audience with an enlarged perception of one of the causes of juvenile crime. Its producer, Mr. Samuel Goldwyn, stated in the *New York Times Magazine* for April 22, 1945: "I made it to make money and to entertain people. It did both."

In defense of unadulterated frivolity it is usual to cite cases of "significant" films which failed at the box office. Such pictures, we agree with Mr. Darryl Zanuck, are, under present marketing conditions, a waste. Pictures are made to be seen and can do little good unless they reach an audience in keeping with the high cost of picture-making. This applies to films of "sheer entertainment" as well as to serious pictures; the former sometimes fail too.

The "significant failures," like the insignificant ones, often are not entertaining. Pictures loaded with dull speeches cannot be expected to amuse people. The usual factors of attractive titles, story values, and stars with proved box-office appeal must be weighed against total costs. Analyzed in these terms, *Mission to Moscow* and *Wilson* are not very good test cases.

Occasionally, extraneous factors influence the success of so-called significant pictures. In the past, they have not been marketed too intelligently. The pitfalls lie in two directions. If a picture is advertised wholly in terms of its social significance, fun-loving people will stay away in droves. On the other hand, there is little sense in advertising all pictures on the basis of romantic content. Those who go to the film to see the love life of Mr. and Mrs. Woodrow Wilson will be disappointed, and those who would normally be interested in other aspects of their lives will be repulsed.

Another variant of the negative point of view is that films in theaters should not deal with controversial public issues. James K. McGuinness, an executive of Metro-Goldwyn-Mayer, expressed this opinion on "The Town Meeting of the Air" program of September 6, 1945, devoted to the question "Should Hollywood make movies designed to influence public opinion?" Although he agreed that films do and should influence public opinion, he took the view that the film is not a good medium for political debate: each film must take sides, and film-making being what it is, approximately fifteen months are required to prepare a filmic rebuttal. . . .

The threat of governmental repression is sometimes given as a reason for not presenting controversial issues on the screen. This, for instance, is the claim of Darryl Zanuck in *Treasury for the Free World:* "Let me be blunt. The fear of political reprisal and persecution has been a millstone about the neck of the industry for many years. It has prevented free expression on the screen and retarded its development. The loss has not been merely our own. It has been the nation's and the world's. Few of us insiders can forget that shortly before Pearl Harbor the entire motion picture industry was called on the carpet in Washington by a Senate committee dominated by isolationists and asked to render an account of its activities. We were pilloried with the accusation that we were allegedly making anti-nazi films which might be offensive to Germany."

Mr. Zanuck's statement raises a number of important questions. Was the investigation a proper or desirable one for the United States Senate to make? Should the industry ever be asked to render an account of its activities? Did the investigation amount to political reprisal or persecution?

Although the Senate investigation was never completed, it started to determine whether films having to do with the war were all one-sided and why. Was it because the power of the federal government or monopolistic powers within the industry were being used to influence the content of films? The investigators did not challenge the right of any company to make anti-Nazi films. The fact that, although public opinion polls at the time showed approximately 80 percent of the people opposed the entry of the United States into the war, there were few films with a noninterventionist appeal made an inquiry into the question as to whether the anti-Nazi films had been produced because of pressures from the government or a too tightly controlled industry a pertinent one. The congressional subcommittee did not propose restrictive legislation; it was an investigative committee and as such was a legitimate Senate activity. Its purpose was to investigate "any propaganda disseminated by motion pictures and radio or any other activity of the motion picture industry to influence public sentiment in the direction of participation by the United States in the . . . European war."

This is not to deny that the authors of Senate Resolution 152, introduced August 1, 1941, authorizing the investigation, Senators Nye and Clark, vigorously opposed the intervention of this country in the second World War or that they intended the investigation to embarrass interventionists in the motion picture industry and in the Administration. Also, while the investigation was in progress, there were accusations and denials of anti-Semitism.

The investigation was abandoned, and no conclusions were reached regarding the existence or causes of interventionist propaganda in films. The incident is instructive, however, because it brings into sharp focus the requirements of responsibility in dealing with controversial ideas. We have urged that the movies should not shun controversy. This does not mean that they should use the film to promote their own partisan policies or special interests. The use of newsreels in opposition to the election of Upton Sinclair for governor of California in 1934, for example, was a disgrace to the industry. Staged pictures and actual shots of indigent bums arriving in California on boxcars in anticipation of the social benefits of a Sinclair victory were shown. The reels purported to be neutral and so were a breach of faith with the audience.

A politically free screen is one in which varying ideas—minority as well as majority—find expression. If films as a whole overwhelmingly take one side of an issue on which public opinion is divided, they should properly be called to an accounting. If the screen is free of governmental or monopolistic restraints, such a situation is not likely to result.

The Senate investigation is instructive on another count. For the first time in many years the industry vigorously defended its right to free expression. No longer did it hide behind the excuse of "pure entertainment." Although, unfortunately, irrelevant issues were introduced both by the committee and by the industry—especially by the trade press—the industry also prepared factual refutations of the charges. It officially recognized and defended the right of the screen to have something to say.

Occasionally, a genuine source of governmental interference with the political content of films is to be found in the activities of the various state and municipal censor boards. For example, *Of Greater Promise*, a Russian film, was banned in Ohio in 1937 because "the picture encourages social and racial equality, thereby stirring up racial hatred . . . all the above doctrines are contrary to accepted codes of American life."[1] Likewise *Spain in Flames*, a documentary film dealing with the civil war in Spain, was rejected by the Pennsylvania Censor Board with the suggestion that the film would be acceptable if the words "Fascist," "Nazi," "Italian," "Rome," "German," "Berlin," etc., were deleted. This decision was reversed by the courts on the grounds that the film dealt with current events and therefore was allowable in the state without examination by the censor board. Examples like the above, however, are rare, and often the decisions are rescinded if an issue is made of the case in court. The producer or exhibitor who fights a case of this kind is almost sure to win. . . .

■ ■ ■ ■

Hearings regarding the Communist Infiltration of the Motion-Picture-Industry Activities in the United States (1947), U.S. House of Representatives, Committee on Un-American Activities

The hearings began on 20 October 1947 with a week of testimony by witnesses who were "friendly" to the committee's work. These "friendly witnesses" included producers (Jack Warner, Louis B. Mayer), writers (Ayn Rand, Morrie Ryskind), actors (Adolph Menjou, Robert Taylor, Robert Montgomery, George Murphy, Ronald Reagan, Gary Cooper), directors (Sam Wood, Leo McCarey), critics (John Moffitt, Howard Rushmore), one mother (Mrs. Lela Rogers, mother of Ginger), one political science instructor (Oliver Carlson), and one animator-producer-director (Walt Disney).

The committee met at 10:30 a. m., Hon. J. Parnell Thomas (chairman) presiding.

THE CHAIRMAN. The meeting will come to order. The record will show that the following members are present: Mr. McDowell, Mr. Vail, Mr. Nixon, Mr. Thomas. A subcommittee is sitting.

1. See "Censorship in Motion Pictures," *Yale Law Journal*, November, 1939.

Conducted by the House Committee on Un-American Activities, the *Hearings regarding the Communist Infiltration of the Motion-Picture-Industry Activities in the United States* began 20 October 1947.

Staff members present: Mr. Robert E. Stripling, chief investigator; Messrs. Louis J. Russell, Robert B. Gaston, H. A. Smith, and A. B. Leckie, investigators; and Mr. Benjamin Mandel, director of research. Before this hearing gets under way, I would like to call attention to some of the basic principles by which the Committee on Un-American Activities is being guided in its investigation into alleged subversive influence in America's motion-picture industry.

The committee is well aware of the magnitude of the subject which it is investigating. The motion-picture business represents an investment of billions of dollars. It represents employment for thousands of workers, ranging from unskilled laborers to high-salaried actors and executives. And even more important, the motion-picture industry represents what is probably the largest single vehicle of entertainment for the American public—over 85,000,000 persons attend the movies each week.

However, it is the very magnitude of the scope of the motion-picture industry which makes this investigation so necessary. We all recognize, certainly, the tremendous effect which moving pictures have on their mass audiences, far removed from the Hollywood sets. We all recognize that what the citizen sees and hears in his neighborhood movie house carries a powerful impact on his thoughts and behavior.

With such vast influence over the lives of American citizens as the motion-picture industry exerts, it is not unnatural—in fact, it is very logical—that subversive and undemocratic forces should attempt to use this medium for un-American purposes.

I want to emphasize at the outset of these hearings that the fact that the Committee on Un-American Activities is investigating alleged Communist influence and infiltration in the motion-picture industry must not be considered or interpreted as an attack on the majority of persons associated with this great industry. I have every confidence that the vast majority of movie workers are patriotic and loyal Americans.

This committee, under its mandate from the House of Representatives, has the responsibility of exposing and spotlighting subversive elements wherever they may exist. As I have already pointed out, it is only to be expected that such elements would strive desperately to gain entry to the motion-picture industry, simply because the industry offers such a tremendous weapon for education and propaganda. That Communists have made such an attempt in Hollywood and with considerable success is already evident to this committee from its preliminary investigative work.

The problem of Communist infiltration is not limited to the movie industry. That even our Federal Government has not been immune from the menace is evidenced by the fact that $11,000,000 is now being spent to rid the Federal service of Communists. Communists are also firmly entrenched in control of a number of large and powerful labor unions in this country. Yet simply because there are Communist union leaders among the longshoremen or seamen, for example, one does not infer that the owners of the shipping industries are Communists and Communist sympathizers, or that the majority of workers in those industries hold to an un-American philosophy. So it is with the movie industry.

I cannot emphasize too strongly the seriousness of Communist infiltration, which we have found to be a mutual problem for many, many different fields of endeavor in the United States. Communists for years have been conducting an unrelentless "boring from within" campaign against America's democratic institutions. While never possessing a large numerical strength, the Communists, nevertheless have found that they could dominate the activities of unions or other mass enterprises in this country by capturing a few strategic positions of leadership.

This technique, I am sorry to say, has been amazingly profitable for the Communists. And they have been aided all along the line by non-Communists, who are either sympathetic to the aims of communism or are unwilling to recognize the danger in Communist infiltration.

The ultimate purpose of the Communists is a well-established fact. Despite sporadic statements made to the contrary for reasons of expediency, the Communist movement looks to the establishment of Soviet-dominated, totalitarian governments in all of the countries of the world, and the Communists are willing to use force and violence to achieve this aim if necessary.

The United States is one of the biggest obstacles to this movement. The fact was startlingly illustrated recently by the open announcement of the Communist International—a world-wide party organization dedicated to promoting world-wide Communist revolution, which previously operated underground.

The vituperation leveled at the United States by this new international Communist organization clearly indicated that America is considered the chief stumbling block in the Soviet plans for world domination and is therefore the chief target in what we might call the Soviet Union's ideological war against non-Soviet governments.

There is no question that there are Communists in Hollywood. We cannot minimize their importance there, and that their influence has already made itself felt has been evidenced by internal turmoil in the industry over the Communist issue. Prominent figures in the motion-picture business have been engaged in a sort of running battle over Communist infiltration for the last 4 or 5 years and a number of anti-Communist organizations have been set up within the industry in an attempt to combat this menace.

The question before this committee, therefore, and the scope of its present inquiry, will be to determine the extent of Communist infiltration in the Hollywood motion-picture industry. We want to know what strategic positions in the industry have been captured by these elements, whose loyalty is pledged in word and deed to the interests of a foreign power.

The committee is determined that the hearings shall be fair and impartial. We have subpenaed witnesses representing both sides of the question. All we are after are the facts. . . .

TESTIMONY OF SAMUEL GROSVENOR WOOD

MR. STRIPLING. Mr. Wood, will you please state your full name?

MR. WOOD. Samuel Grosvenor Wood.

MR. STRIPLING. What is your present occupation?

MR. WOOD. I am a motion-picture producer and director.

MR. STRIPLING. When and where were you born?

MR. WOOD. I was born in Philadelphia, Pa., 1883.

THE CHAIRMAN. Excuse me, Mr. Stripling.

Haven't you an attorney?

MR. WOOD. No.

THE CHAIRMAN. Go ahead.

MR. STRIPLING. Do you desire an attorney?

MR. WOOD. No. I am certainly satisfied.

MR. STRIPLING. How long have you been associated with the motion picture industry, Mr. Wood?

MR. WOOD. For over 30 years.

MR. STRIPLING. What are the various positions that you have held in the motion-picture industry?

MR. WOOD. Pardon me?

MR. STRIPLING. The various positions you have held. You have been producer, director—

MR. WOOD. I was first assistant director for a year and a half and then became a director; then I produced and directed my own pictures.

MR. STRIPLING. Would you name to the committee some of the films which you have produced and directed in recent years?

MR. WOOD. Well, Saratoga Trunk, Goodbye Mr. Chips, For Whom the Bell Tolls, Kitty Foyle, King's Row; the last picture was Ivy, with Joan Fontaine.

MR. STRIPLING. Are you a member of the Screen Directors Guild?

MR. WOOD. Yes, sir.

MR. STRIPLING. Would you explain to the committee what the Screen Directors Guild is?

MR. WOOD. Well, it is very similar to a union. I mean, we have banded together to protect our rights and have a uniform front on subjects that might come up with the executives or the studios.

MR. STRIPLING. Do you know how many members the Screen Directors Guild has?

MR. WOOD. I think we have two hundred and forty-some. I am not sure of that, but I think that is it.

MR. STRIPLING. Do you know whether or not the Screen Directors Guild has ever been infiltrated by the Communists?

MR. WOOD. They have tried.

MR. STRIPLING. Will you tell the committee of the efforts that you are aware of on the part of the Communists to infiltrate the Screen Directors Guild?

MR. WOOD. There is a constant effort to get control of the guild. In fact, there is an effort to get control of all unions and guilds in Hollywood. I think our most serious time was when George Stevens was president; he went in the service and another gentleman took his place, who died, and it was turned over to John Cromwell. Cromwell, with the assistance of three or four others, tried hard to steer us into the Red river, but we had a little too much weight for that.

MR. STRIPLING. Will you name the others?

MR. WOOD. Irving Pichel, Edward Dmytryk, Frank Tuttle, and—I am sorry, there is another name there. I forget.

MR. STRIPLING. If you think of it, will you give it for the record?

MR. WOOD. Yes.

MR. STRIPLING. Mr. Wood, are you a member of the Motion Picture Alliance for the Preservation of American Ideals?

MR. WOOD. I am. I was the first president.

MR. STRIPLING. Will you tell the committee the circumstances under which this organization was founded, and the reason why it was founded?

MR. WOOD. Well, the reason was very simple. We organized in self-defense. We felt that there was a definite effort by the Communist Party members, or Party travelers, to take over the unions and the guilds of Hollywood, and if they had the unions and guilds controlled, they would have the plum in their lap and they would move on to use it for Communist propaganda.

MR. STRIPLING. Do you recall the year that the alliance was established?

MR. WOOD. 1944.

MR. STRIPLING. I have here a copy of the statement of principles of the guild.

MR. WOOD. Yes, sir.

MR. STRIPLING. Without reading them into the record, could you briefly outline to the committee the purposes? I will hand you this.

MR. WOOD. I am sorry. I don't have my glasses. I was going to ask you to read it for me.

MR. STRIPLING (reading):

STATEMENT OF PRINCIPLES

We believe in, and like, the American way of life: the liberty and freedom which generations before us have fought to create and preserve; the freedom to speak, to think, to live, to worship, to work, and to govern ourselves as individuals, as free men; the right to succeed or fail as free men, according to the measure of our ability and our strength.

Believing in these things, we find ourselves in sharp revolt against a rising tide of communism, fascism, and kindred beliefs, that seek by subversive means to undermine and change this way of life; groups that have forfeited their right to exist in this country of ours, because they seek to achieve their change by means other than the vested procedure of the ballot and to deny the right of the majority opinion of the people to rule.

In our special field of motion pictures, we resent the growing impression that this industry is made of, and dominated by, Communists, radicals, and crackpots. We believe that we represent the vast majority of the people who serve this great medium of expression. But unfortunately it has been an unorganized majority. This has been almost inevitable. The very love of freedom, of the rights of the individual, make this great majority reluctant to organize. But now we must, or we shall meanly lose "the last, best hope on earth."

As Americans, we have no new plan to offer. We want no new plan, we want only to defend against its enemies that which is our priceless heritage; that freedom which has given man, in this country, the fullest life and the richest expression the world has ever known; that system which, in the present emergency, has fathered an effort that, more than any other single factor, will make possible the winning of this war.

As members of the motion-picture industry, we must face and accept an especial responsibility. Motion pictures are inescapably one of the world's greatest forces for influencing public thought and opinion, both at home and abroad. In this fact lies solemn obligation. We refuse to permit the effort of Communist, Fascist, and other totalitarian-minded groups to pervert this powerful medium into an instrument for the dissemination of un-American ideas and beliefs. We pledge ourselves to fight, with every means at our organized command, any effort of any group or individual, to divert the loyalty of the screen from the free America that give it birth. And to dedicate our work, in the fullest possible measure, to the presentation of the American scene, its standards and its freedoms, its beliefs and its ideals, as we know them and believe in them.

Mr. Wood, would you name some of the other individuals in Holly-wood who were associated with you in the formation of this organi-zation?

MR. WOOD. Maurice Riskin, Gary Cooper, Clark Gable, Bob Taylor, Jim McGuinness, Howard Emmett Rogers, Ralph Clair, Ben Martinez, Joe Touhy. Those last three men are labor leaders. When we first in-corporated, I think we had 50 to 100 people together to talk this over, and then we decided to organize. It is difficult to remember all the names. I don't know whether that is enough. Oh, there is Ginger Rogers.

MR. STRIPLING. Victor Fleming?

MR. WOOD. Victor Fleming. Clarence Brown.

MR. STRIPLING. Rupert Hughes?

MR. WOOD. Rupert Hughes.

MR. STRIPLING. They were people who were very prominent in the in-dustry?

MR. WOOD. Yes; very prominent.

MR. STRIPLING. The reason for forming this organization was to combat the inroads that the Communists were making or attempting to make within the industry?

MR. WOOD. Both the Communists and the Fascists. . . .

MR. STRIPLING. Mr. Wood, is it your opinion that the Communists do exercise some degree of influence in the making and production of motion pictures in Hollywood at the present time, or have in the past?

MR. WOOD. Well, at the present time—of course, they are always trying —but I think at the present time Hollywood is pretty well aware of them and I think the thing is watched pretty closely. It has really caused every-one to be a watch dog. They know pretty well. I think it was inexperience that any material crept through. Now that they are aware of it they kept a pretty good eye on them.

It isn't only what they get in the films, it is what they keep out. If a story has a good point, that sells the American way of living, that can be elim-inated and you wouldn't miss it. If you picture some official, or the banker, as a dirty "so and so," we can see that, and out it goes. Of course, they know me pretty well. In fact, I don't have any of them around. I don't want them.

MR. STRIPLING. You haven't had any trouble with any of the Commu-nists in your own productions?

MR. WOOD. No.

MR. STRIPLING. Why do you think that is?

MR. WOOD. Because I don't have them. Don't want them.

MR. STRIPLING. Is that true of all the studios in the motion-picture in-dustry?

MR. WOOD. I know the heads of most of the studios. I know Louis Mayer, Mrs. Schenk, Eddie Mannix, I know the Warners, Mr. Friedman, Mr. Ginsburg of Paramount, Mr. Yates of Republic. I could go on down the line. I don't think any of them would willingly permit propaganda, Communist propaganda, in their pictures. But it is impossible, utterly impossible for the heads of the studios to read the number of scripts they would have to read. There is the danger. They are always trying. So you have to be a watchdog.

MR. STRIPLING. What group in the industry must be watched more carefully than the rest?

MR. WOOD. The writers.

MR. STRIPLING. The writers?

MR. WOOD. Yes, sir.

MR. STRIPLING. Is it your opinion that there are Communist writers in the motion-picture industry?

MR. WOOD. Oh, yes. It is not my opinion, I know positively there are.

MR. STRIPLING. Would you care to name any that you know yourself to be Communist?

MR. WOOD. Well, I don't think there is any question about Dalton Trumbo; any question about Donald Ogden Stewart. The reporter asked the question of a great many writers, "Are you a member of the Communist Party," or "Are you a Communist?"

MR. STRIPLING. Did they deny it?

MR. WOOD. They didn't answer it.

MR. STRIPLING. Was John Howard Lawson one of those persons?

MR. WOOD. Oh, yes; he is active in every piece of Communist work going on.

MR. STRIPLING. Is there any question in your mind that John Howard Lawson is a Communist?

MR. WOOD. If there is, then I haven't any mind.

I suppose there are 19 gentlemen back there that say I haven't. . . .

MR. STRIPLING. Now, Mr. Wood, would you give the committee some of these examples in which the Communists have exerted influence in the motion-picture industry? In other words, how do they go about it, what is the mechanics of it?

MR. WOOD. There are a number of ways. I think the thing that is very important, and the thing I was most anxious about, is the pride of Americans in working. They are pretty subtle. For instance, a man gets a key position in the studio and has charge of the writers. When you, as a director or a producer, are ready for a writer you ask for a list and this man shows you a list. Well, if he is following the party line his pets are on top or the other people aren't on at all. If there is a particular man in there that has been opposing them they will leave his name off the list. Then if that man isn't employed for about 2 months they go to the head of the studio and say, "Nobody wants this man." The head is perfectly honest about it and says, "Nobody wants to use him, let him go." So a good American is let out. But it doesn't stop there. They point that out as an example and say, "You better fall in line, play ball, or else." And they go down the line on it.

MR. STRIPLING. That is true in the case of writers. Would you say it is true in any other branch of the industry?

MR. WOOD. I don't think, in any part of the business, they will use a party who is opposed to their ideas, if they can avoid it, and they can usually avoid it.

MR. STRIPLING. They operate as cliques, in other words?

MR. WOOD. Oh, yes; they have their meetings every night. They are together; they work for one purpose.

MR. STRIPLING. What is that purpose, Mr. Wood?

MR. WOOD. Well, I think they are agents of a foreign country, myself.

MR. STRIPLING. I see.

THE CHAIRMAN. Would you say that these persons you named here today were agents of a foreign country?

MR. WOOD. I think anyone following the party line, I think this particular party line, are agents of a foreign country. I think they are directed from a foreign country. . . .

Testimony of Louis B. Mayer

MR. SMITH. Mr. Mayer, since you have been in Hollywood, have you observed whether or not there are any efforts on behalf of Communists to infiltrate themselves into the motion-picture industry?

MR. MAYER. I have been told many times about Communists. I have never feared them. They can't get a single thing into our pictures or our studio under our set-up.

MR. SMITH. Why is that?

MR. MAYER. Because the only ones that I would have to worry about are the producers, the editors, the executives, because our scripts are read and re-read by so many of the executive force, producers and editors, that if you looked carefully at 1,200 or 1,500 pictures I produced with my people out at the studio you would be surprised how little you could possibly point to, even now, when we are on the lookout for it, particularly at this time.

MR. SMITH. Is it necessary to employ certain personnel to keep the Communists from trying to get information into the pictures?

MR. MAYER. No; we don't engage anybody. These men are supposed to figure out what will make a good picture. If they should find anything detrimental to the American Government or the Congress I would never allow anything against anybody in our Government or in our Congress, I would never allow them to have a laugh at such a serious price.

MR. SMITH. Are there any Communists, to your knowledge, in Metro-Goldwyn-Mayer?

MR. MAYER. They have mentioned two or three writers to me several times. There is no proof about it, except they mark them as Communists, and when I look at the pictures they have written for us I can't find once where they have written something like that. Whether they think they can't get away with it in our place, or what, I can't tell you, but there are the pictures and they will speak for themselves. I have as much contempt for them as anybody living in this world.

MR. SMITH. Who are these people they have named?

MR. MAYER. Trumbo and Lester Cole, they said. I think there was one other fellow, a third one.

MR. SMITH. Is that Dalton Trumbo you are speaking of?

MR. MAYER. Yes, sir.

MR. SMITH. And his position, please?

MR. MAYER. He is a writer.

MR. SMITH. And Lester Cole?

MR. MAYER. A writer.

MR. SMITH. Have you observed any efforts on their part to get Communist propaganda into their pictures?

MR. MAYER. I have never heard of any. . . .

MR. SMITH. The third individual you mentioned, would that be Donald Ogden Stewart?

MR. MAYER. Yes.

MR. SMITH. Do you know what salaries these men are paid?

MR. MAYER. I don't know offhand. Two of them are very high, Stewart and Trumbo.

MR. SMITH. Mr. Chairman, I have here, in answer to a subpena, the official records of the salaries paid Mr. Dalton Trumbo, Mr. Lester Cole, and Donald Ogden Stewart over a period of the last 5 years, which information I would like to submit at this time for the record.

THE CHAIRMAN. Without objection, so ordered.

MR. SMITH. Dalton Trumbo, during the year 1943, received $76,250; during 1944, $39,000; in 1945, $95,000; in 1946, $71,000; in 1947, to and including October 14, 1947, $85,000.

MR. MAYER. I don't think that is all, Mr. Smith. They work in other studios also during the same year.

MR. SMITH. This is from Metro-Goldwyn-Mayer.

MR. MAYER. Yes; but they probably earn much more than that during that same period.

MR. SMITH. On Lester Cole, who has not been employed at Metro-Goldwyn-Mayer for a period of 5 years, his record is 1945 to and including October 4, 1947. The record reflects that from Metro-Goldwyn-Mayer pictures in 1945 his salary was $33,491.67; in 1946, $53,666.67; in 1947, to and including October 4, $43,700.

Donald Ogden Stewart, in 1943, from Metro-Goldwyn-Mayer, $40,000; in 1944, $27,083.33; in 1946, $65,000; in 1947, to and including October 4, $17,500.

Mr. Mayer, these individuals that have been mentioned as being reported to you as Communists, do you think the studios should continue to employ those individuals?

MR. MAYER. I have asked counsel. They claim that unless you can prove they are Communists they could hold you for damages. Saturday when I arrived here I saw in the papers a case where the high court of New York State just held you could not even say a man was a Communist sympathizer without being liable if you cannot prove it.

THE CHAIRMAN. Mr. Smith, may I ask a question right there?

MR. SMITH. Yes, sir.

THE CHAIRMAN. If you were shown the Communist dues cards of any one of these three individuals, then would you continue to employ them?

MR. MAYER. No, sir.

MR. SMITH. By the same token, Mr. Mayer, would you employ a Bundist, a known member of the Bund?

MR. MAYER. I have probably had them; I wouldn't employ him knowingly; no, sir.

MR. SMITH. At the present time?

MR. MAYER. No, sir.

MR. SMITH. Is it correct from your testimony that a great effort or considerable effort is made by the studios to keep Communist writers or persons alleged to be Communist writers from injecting propaganda into the pictures? . . .

MR. MAYER. I am just hopeful . . . that perhaps out of this hearing will come a recommendation to the Congress for legislation on which there can be no question and they will give us a policy as to how to handle American citizens who do not deserve to be American citizens, and if they are Communists how to get them out of our place. . . .

TESTIMONY OF GARY COOPER

MR. STRIPLING. Mr. Cooper, will you state your full name and present address, please?

MR. COOPER. My name is Gary Cooper; I live in Los Angeles, Calif.

MR. STRIPLING. When and where were you born, Mr. Cooper?

MR. COOPER. I was born in Helena, Mont., in 1901.

MR. STRIPLING. What is your present occupation?

MR. COOPER. An actor.

MR. STRIPLING. Mr. Cooper, you are here in response to a subpena which was served upon you on September 26; are you not?

MR. COOPER. Yes; I am.

MR. STRIPLING. Mr. Chairman, the interrogation of Mr. Cooper will be done by Mr. Smith.

THE CHAIRMAN. Mr. Smith. We will have more order, please.

MR. SMITH. Mr. Cooper, how long have you been an actor?

MR. COOPER. I have been an actor since 1925.

MR. SMITH. And how long have you been in Hollywood?

MR. COOPER. Since 1924.

MR. SMITH. I believe you made many pictures, some of which pictures are Unconquered, Pride of the Yankees, Saratoga Trunk, Mr. Deeds Goes to Town, and you are presently making Good Sam; is that correct?

MR. COOPER. Yes.

THE CHAIRMAN. Mr. Smith and Mr. Cooper, will you please speak up?

MR. SMITH. Yes, sir.

MR. COOPER. Yes, sir.

MR. SMITH. Are you a member of the Screen Actors Guild?

MR. COOPER. Yes; I have been a member since the guild was organized.

MR. SMITH. During the time that you have been in Hollywood, have you ever observed any communistic influence in Hollywood or in the motion-picture industry?

MR. COOPER. I believe I have noticed some.

MR. SMITH. What do you believe the principal medium is that they use Hollywood or the industry to inject propaganda?

MR. COOPER. Well, I believe it is done through word of mouth—

THE CHAIRMAN. Will you speak louder, please, Mr. Cooper?

MR. COOPER. I believe it is done through word of mouth and through the medium of pamphleting—and writers, I suppose.

MR. SMITH. By word of mouth, what do you mean, Mr. Cooper?

MR. COOPER. Well, I mean sort of social gatherings.

MR. SMITH. That has been your observation?

MR. COOPER. That has been my only observation; yes.

MR. SMITH. Can you tell us some of the statements that you may have heard at these gatherings that you believe are communistic?

MR. COOPER. Well, I have heard quite a few, I think, from time to time over the years. Well, I have heard tossed around such statements as, "Don't you think the Constitution of the United States is about 150 years out of date?" and—oh, I don't know—I have heard people mention that, well, "Perhaps this would be a more efficient Government without a Congress" —which statements I think are very un-American.

MR. SMITH. Have you ever observed any communistic information in any script?

MR. COOPER. Well, I have turned down quite a few scripts because I thought they were tinged with communistic ideas.

MR. SMITH. Can you name any of those scripts?

MR. COOPER. No; I can't recall any of those scripts to mind.

MR. SMITH. Can you tell us—

MR. COOPER. The titles.

THE CHAIRMAN. Just a minute. Mr. Cooper, you haven't got that bad a memory.

MR. COOPER. I beg your pardon, sir?

THE CHAIRMAN. I say, you haven't got that bad a memory, have you? You must be able to remember some of those scripts your turned down because you thought they were Communist scripts.

MR. COOPER. Well, I can't actually give you a title to any of them; no.

THE CHAIRMAN. Will you think it over, then, and supply the committee with a list of those scripts?

MR. COOPER. I don't think I could, because most of the scripts I read at night, and if they don't look good to me I don't finish them or if I do finish them I send them back as soon as possible to their author.

THE CHAIRMAN. I understand. I didn't understand you before. Go ahead.

MR. MCDOWELL. That is the custom of most actors, most stars, Mr. Cooper?

MR. COOPER. Yes, I believe so; yes sir. As to the material, which is more important than the name of the script, I did turn back one script because the leading character in the play was a man whose life's ambition was to organize an army in the United States, an army of soldiers who would never fight to defend their country. I don't remember any more details of the play, but that was enough of a basic idea for me to send it back quickly to its author.

MR. SMITH. Mr. Cooper, have you ever had any personal experience where you feel the Communist Party may have attempted to use you?

MR. COOPER. They haven't attempted to use me, I don't think, because, apparently, they know that I am not very sympathetic to communism. Several years ago, when communism was more of a social chit-chatter in parties for offices, and so on, when communism didn't have the implications that it has now, discussion of communism was more open and I remember hearing statements from some folks to the effect that the communistic system had a great many features that were desirable, one of which would be desirable to us in the motion-picture business in that it offered the actors and artists—in other words, the creative people—a special place in Government where we would be somewhat immune from the ordinary leveling of income. And as I remember, some actor's name was mentioned to me who had a house in Moscow which was very large— he had three cars, and stuff, with his house being quite a bit larger than my house in Beverly Hills at the time—and it looked to me like a pretty phony come-on to us in the picture business. From that time on, I could never take any of this pinko mouthing very seriously, because I didn't feel it was on the level.

MR. SMITH. Mr. Chairman, we have several official documents that we have obtained through the State Department, which I believe clearly shows that the Communist Party attempts to use actors individually throughout the world to further their cause. With your permission, I would like to show one of these documents to Mr. Cooper and have him read it to the committee.

THE CHAIRMAN. Without objection, so ordered.

MR. SMITH. I would like to have you glance at this document, Mr. Cooper, and read to the committee from this document.

MR. COOPER. Ahem—

MR. SMITH. Just one moment, please, Mr. Cooper. This document from which Mr. Cooper is going to read was distributed in pamphlets in Italy during May of 1947.

MR. COOPER. Shall I read it?

MR. SMITH. By the Communist Party. Yes, sir; go ahead.

MR. COOPER. (reading):

Gary Cooper, who took part in the fights for the independence of Spain, held a speech before a crowd of 90,000 in Philadelphia on the occasion of the consecration of the banner of the Philadelphia Communist Federation.

Between other things, he said: "In our days it is the greatest honor to be a Communist. I wish the whole world to understand what we Communists really are. There could be nobody then who might say that we are enemies of mankind and peace. Those who want to discuss Communist ideas should first get to know them. Americans learn this with great difficulty. Millions of people from other continents regard America as a center of modern civilization, but only we Americans can see how false this opinion is. Let us be frank. Our country is a country of gold, silver, petrol, and great railways. But at the same time it is a country where Rockefeller, Ford, and Rothschild use tear gas against striking workers fighting for their legitimate rights. Our country is the fatherland of Lincoln and Roosevelt, but at the same time it is a country of men like Senator Bilbo and many of his type. It is a country where redskins were exterminated by arms and brandy."

MR. SMITH. Have you any comment on that, Mr. Cooper?

MR. COOPER. Well, sir —

THE CHAIRMAN. Excuse me a minute. Mr. Smith, you say this letter was distributed by the Communist Party in Italy?

MR. SMITH. In May of 1947, Mr. Chairman; yes, sir.

THE CHAIRMAN. And we got the letter from the State Department?

MR. SMITH. Yes, sir.

THE CHAIRMAN. Proceed, Mr. Cooper.

MR. SMITH. Were you ever in Philadelphia, Mr. Cooper?

MR. COOPER. No, sir; I was never in Philadelphia.

MR. SMITH. Do you have any comment to make regarding this letter?

MR. COOPER. Well, a 90,000 audience is a little tough to disregard, but it is not true.

THE CHAIRMAN. I want to help you along, Mr. Cooper—

MR. COOPER. No part of it is true, sir.

THE CHAIRMAN. I happen to know it is just a plain, ordinary, ruthless lie. We know that for a fact. So you don't have to worry any more about that.

MR. MCDOWELL. And also, Mr. Cooper, in order to get it into the record, don't you think there wouldn't be 90,000 people in Philadelphia who were Communists?

MR. COOPER. Well, I believe it was Mr. Smith here that said you would have a hard time getting 90,000 people out in Philadelphia for anything. I don't know about that.

MR. SMITH. Mr. Chairman, I have in my possession another similar document which I believe should be read, some portions of it should be read into the record. It was distributed on Saturday, July 19, 1947, by the Communist Party in Yugoslavia, in various cities therein, and with your permission I would like to read a few paragraphs therefrom.

THE CHAIRMAN. Without objection, so ordered.

MR. SMITH. (reading):

In the usual column on the sixth page entitled "Fascist Shooting on Broadway," appeared the following:

"In the middle of June, in Hollywood, Gary Cooper, Tyrone Power, and Alan Ladd, well-known film stars, were imprisoned because they were marked as leftists and denounced un-Americans, but before that happened, something else was going on, about which the American newspaper agencies did not speak, and that is very characteristic of conditions today in the United States.

"The film actor, Buster Crabbe, lost his life in a mysterious way. The background of this tragic and mysterious death of Buster Crabbe was set forth by the New York paper, Red Star. From the articles of Immy Stendaph, we can see that Buster Crabbe was very popular in the United States. He organized a movement in the Army to protest against the investigation of un-American activities against Cooper, Chaplin, and other film stars.

"The beginning of Buster Crabbe's tragedy was when he found valuable documents, through which documents he could give light and prove the criminal and aggressive plans of reactionary circles in America.

"* * * On May 31, Buster Crabbe came to the apartment of the well-known film actor, Spencer Tracy, also well-known as a leftist and they had a long talk in the presence of Tyrone Power.

"* * * On June 3, on Broadway, on the corner of Seventh Avenue, Crabbe was riddled with bullets from a machine gun from a closed car. This tragic death of Crabbe, provoked terrific unrest in Hollywood. At the funeral of Buster Crabbe, 150,000 men were present, and the coffin was carried by Comrades Gary Cooper, Tyrone Power"—

THE CHAIRMAN. I don't think we will have to have any more of that letter. But what I would like to have you do, Mr. Smith, is to identify, clearly identify the source.

MR. SMITH. Yes, sir; there is just one more paragraph.

THE CHAIRMAN. All right, read on, if you want to.

MR. SMITH (reading):

This case is very characteristic of the conditions which are now prevailing in the United States. This is the method of Fascist liquidation which this country of freedom and democracy is dealing with a political opponent. It is quite possible that this crime was committed by the KKK and inspired by the elements who were interested in Crabbe's disappearance—that he stop talking.

My point, Mr. Chairman, is to show not only in Hollywood, but throughout the world the extent to which the Communist Party can go to use an actor to further their cause. This particular document was distributed by the Communist Party in July 1947 in Yugoslavia. We have the official copy from the State Department for introduction into the record.

THE CHAIRMAN. Well, you see from that, Mr. Cooper, to what extent they will go.

MR. COOPER. Yes, sir.

THE CHAIRMAN. So when they used your name in that regard you can almost consider it a compliment.

MR. COOPER. Thank you.

MR. MCDOWELL. May I ask, Mr. Chairman, if Crabbe is living? Is Mr. Crabbe living?

MR. SMITH. So far as I know, he is living.

MR. COOPER. Mr. Crabbe is a very healthy specimen of American manhood.

MR. SMITH. I have no further questions, Mr. Chairman. . . .

■ ■ ■ ■

HEARINGS REGARDING THE COMMUNIST INFILTRATION OF THE MOTION-PICTURE-INDUSTRY ACTIVITIES IN THE UNITED STATES (SECOND WEEK) (1947), U.S. House of Representatives, Committee on Un-American Activities

Over the weekend recess, Chairman Thomas made a surprising change in his lineup for the next week's "unfriendly witnesses." Rather than beginning, as announced, with the judicious Eric Johnston (who was to make an impassioned plea for freedom of speech and tolerance of political differences) and Roy Brewer (an anti-Communist union leader who had cleaned up much of the Hollywood union mess), Chairman Thomas began with the belligerent John Howard Lawson, a screenwriter who had been president of the Screen Writers' Guild and who had already been identified as a Communist by several of the "friendly witnesses." Lawson's angry denunciation of the committee not only alienated the sympathies of the general public but also undercut the power and effect of Johnston's appeal, which immediately followed Lawson's turbulent ejection from the committee room.

TESTIMONY OF JOHN HOWARD LAWSON

MR. LAWSON. Mr. Chairman, I have a statement here which I wish to make—

THE CHAIRMAN. Well, all right; let me see your statement.

(Statement handed to the chairman.)

MR. STRIPLING. Do you have a copy of that?

MR. CRUM. We can get you copies.

THE CHAIRMAN. I don't care to read any more of the statement. The statement will not be read. I read the first line.

MR. LAWSON. You have spent 1 week vilifying me before the American public—

THE CHAIRMAN. Just a minute—

MR. LAWSON. And you refuse to allow me to make a statement on my rights as an American citizen.

THE CHAIRMAN. I refuse you to make the statement, because of the first sentence in your statement. That statement is not pertinent to the inquiry.

Now, this is a congressional committee a—congressional committee set up by law. We must have orderly procedure, and we are going to have orderly procedure.

Mr. Stripling, identify the witness.

MR. LAWSON. The rights of American citizens are important in this room here, and I intend to stand up for those rights, Congressman Thomas.

MR. STRIPLING. Mr. Lawson, will you state your full name, please?

MR. LAWSON. I wish to protest against the unwillingness of this committee to read a statement, when you permitted Mr. Warner, Mr. Mayer, and others to read statements in this room.

My name is John Howard Lawson.

MR. STRIPLING. What is your present address?

MR. LAWSON. 9354 Burnett Avenue, San Fernando, Calif.

MR. STRIPLING. When and where were you born?

MR. LAWSON. New York City.

MR. STRIPLING. What year?

MR. LAWSON. 1894.

MR. STRIPLING. Give us the exact date.

MR. LAWSON. September 25.

MR. STRIPLING. Mr. Lawson, you are here in response to a subpena which was served upon you on September 19, 1947; is that true?

MR. LAWSON. That is correct.

MR. STRIPLING. That subpena called for your appearance before the committee on October 23, at 10:30 a. m.; is that correct?

MR. LAWSON. That is correct.

MR. STRIPLING. Did you receive the following telegram on October 11, addressed to you, Mr. John Howard Lawson, 9354 Burnett Avenue, San Fernando, Calif.?

MR. LAWSON. I did.

MR. STRIPLING. I haven't read the telegram yet.

In response to the subpena served upon you summoning you to appear before the Committee on Un-American Activities, United States House of Representatives, in Washington, D. C., on October 23, you are hereby directed to appear on October 27 instead of October 23, at the hour of 10:30 a. m., room 226, Old House Office Building.

Signed: "J. Parnell Thomas, chairman."

Did you receive that telegram?

MR. LAWSON. I did.

MR. STRIPLING. You are here before the committee in response to this subpena and in response to this summons in the form of a telegram from the chairman?

MR. LAWSON. I am.

MR. STRIPLING. What is your occupation, Mr. Lawson?

MR. LAWSON. I am a writer.

MR. STRIPLING. How long have you been a writer?

MR. LAWSON. All my life—at least 35 years—my adult life.

MR. STRIPLING. Are you a member of the Screen Writers Guild?

MR. LAWSON. The raising of any question here in regard to membership, political beliefs, or affiliation—

MR. STRIPLING. Mr. Chairman—

MR. LAWSON. Is absolutely beyond the powers of this committee.

MR. STRIPLING. Mr. Chairman—

MR. LAWSON. But—

(The chairman pounding gavel.)

MR. LAWSON. It is a matter of public record that I am a member of the Screen Writers Guild.

MR. STRIPLING. I ask—

[Applause.]

THE CHAIRMAN. I want to caution the people in the audience: You are the guests of this committee and you will have to maintain order at all times. I do not care for any applause or any demonstrations of one kind or another.

MR. STRIPLING. Now, Mr. Chairman, I am also going to request that you instruct the witness to be responsive to the questions.

THE CHAIRMAN. I think the witness will be more responsive to the questions.

MR. LAWSON. Mr. Chairman, you permitted —

THE CHAIRMAN (pounding gavel). Never mind—

MR. LAWSON. (continuing). Witnesses in this room to make answers of three or four or five hundred words to questions here.

THE CHAIRMAN. Mr. Lawson, you will please be responsive to these questions and not continue to try to disrupt these hearings.

MR. LAWSON. I am not on trial here, Mr. Chairman. This commtitee is on trial here before the American people. Let us get that straight.

THE CHAIRMAN. We don't want you to be on trial.

MR. STRIPLING. Mr. Lawson, how long have you been a member of the Screen Writers Guild?

MR. LAWSON. Since it was founded in its present form, in 1933.

MR. STRIPLING. Have you ever held any office in the guild?

MR. LAWSON. The question of whether I have held office is also a question which is beyond the purview of this committee.

(The chairman pounding gavel.)

MR. LAWSON. It is an invasion of the right of association under the Bill of Rights of this country.

THE CHAIRMAN. Please be responsive to the question.

MR. LAWSON. It is also a matter—

(The chairman pounding gavel.)

MR. LAWSON. Of public record—

THE CHAIRMAN. You asked to be heard. Through your attorney, you asked to be heard, and we want you to be heard. And if you don't care to be heard, then we will excuse you and we will put the record in without your answers.

MR. LAWSON. I wish to frame my own answers to your questions, Mr. Chairman, and I intend to do so.

THE CHAIRMAN. And you will be responsive to the questions or you will be excused from the witness stand.

MR. LAWSON. I will frame my own answers, Mr. Chairman.

THE CHAIRMAN. Go ahead, Mr. Stripling.

MR. STRIPLING. I repeat the question, Mr. Lawson:

Have you ever held any position in the Screen Writers Guild?

MR. LAWSON. I stated that it is outside the purview of the rights of this committee to inquire into any form of association—

THE CHAIRMAN. The Chair will determine what is in the purview of this committee.

MR. LAWSON. My rights as an American citizen are no less than the responsibilities of this committee of Congress.

THE CHAIRMAN. Now, you are just making a big scene for yourself and getting all "het up". [Laughter.]

Be responsive to the questioning, just the same as all the witnesses have. You are no different from the rest.

Go ahead, Mr. Stripling.

MR. LAWSON. I am being treated differently from the rest.

THE CHAIRMAN. You are not being treated differently.

MR. LAWSON. Other witnesses have made statements, which included quotations from books, references to material which had no connection whatsoever with the interest of this committee.

THE CHAIRMAN. We will determine whether it has connection.

Now, you go ahead—

MR. LAWSON. It is absolutely beyond the power of this committee to inquire into my association in any organization.

THE CHAIRMAN. Mr. Lawson, you will have to stop or you will leave the witness stand. And you will leave the witness stand because you are in contempt. That is why you will leave the witness stand. And if you are just trying to force me to put you in contempt, you won't have to try much harder. You know what has happened to a lot of people that have been in contempt of this committee this year, don't you?

MR. LAWSON. I am glad you have made it perfectly clear that you are going to threaten and intimidate the witnesses, Mr. Chairman.

(The chairman pounding gavel.)

MR. LAWSON. I am an American and I am not at all easy to intimidate, and don't think I am.

(The chairman pounding gavel.)

MR. STRIPLING. Mr. Lawson, I repeat the question. Have you ever held any position in the Screen Writers Guild?

MR. LAWSON. I have stated that the question is illegal. But it is a matter of public record that I have held many offices in the Screen Writers Guild. I was its first president, in 1933, and I have held office on the board of directors of the Screen Writers Guild at other times.

MR. STRIPLING. You have been employed in the motion-picture industry; have you not?

MR. LAWSON. I have.

MR. STRIPLING. Would you state some of the studios where you have been employed?

MR. LAWSON. Practically all of the studios, all the major studios.

MR. STRIPLING. As a screen writer?

MR. LAWSON. That is correct.

MR. STRIPLING. Would you list some of the pictures which you have written the script for?

MR. LAWSON. I must state again that you are now inquiring into the freedom of press and communications, over which you have no control whatsoever. You don't have to bring me here 3,000 miles to find out what pictures I have written. The pictures that I have written are very well known. They are such pictures as Action in the North Atlantic, Sahara—

MR. STRIPLING. Mr. Lawson—

MR. LAWSON. Such pictures as Blockade, of which I am very proud and in which I introduced the danger that this democracy faced from the attempt to destroy democracy in Spain in 1937. These matters are all matters of public record.

MR. STRIPLING. Mr. Lawson, would you object if I read a list of the pictures, and then you can either state whether or not you did write the scripts?

MR. LAWSON. I have no objection at all.

MR. STRIPLING. Did you write Dynamite, by M-G-M?

MR. LAWSON. I preface my answer, again, by saying that it is outside the province of this committee, but it is well known that I did.

MR. STRIPLING. The Sea Bat, by M-G-M?

MR. LAWSON. It is well known that I did.

MR. STRIPLING. Succcss at Any Price, RKO?

MR. LAWSON. Yes; that is from a play of mine, Success Story.

MR. STRIPLING. Party Wire, Columbia?

MR. LAWSON. Yes; I did.

MR. STRIPLING. Blockade, United Artists, Wanger?

MR. LAWSON. That is correct.

MR. STRIPLING. Algiers, United Artists, Wanger?

MR. LAWSON. Correct.

MR. STRIPLING. Earth Bound, Twentieth Century Fox.

MR. LAWSON. Correct.

MR. STRIPLING. Counterattack, Columbia.

MR. LAWSON. Correct.

MR. STRIPLING. You have probably written others; have you not, Mr. Lawson?

MR. LAWSON. Many others. You have missed a lot of them.

MR. STRIPLING. You don't care to furnish them to the committee, do you?

MR. LAWSON. Not in the least interested.

MR. STRIPLING. Mr. Lawson, are you now, or have you ever been a member of the Communist Party of the United States?

MR. LAWSON. In framing my answer to that question I must emphasize the points that I have raised before. The question of communism is in no way related to this inquiry, which is an attempt to get control of the screen and to invade the basic rights of American citizens in all fields.

MR. MCDOWELL. Now, I must object—

MR. STRIPLING. Mr. Chairman—

(The chairman pounding gavel.)

MR. LAWSON. The question here relates not only to the question of my membership in any political organization, but this committee is attempting to establish the right—

(The chairman pounding gavel.)

MR. LAWSON (continuing). Which has been historically denied to any committee of this sort, to invade the rights and privileges and immunity of American citizens, whether they be Protestant, Methodist, Jewish, or Catholic, whether they be Republicans or Democrats or anything else.

THE CHAIRMAN (pounding gavel). Mr. Lawson, just quiet down again.

Mr. Lawson, the most pertinent question that we can ask is whether or not you have ever been a member of the Communist Party. Now, do you care to answer that question?

MR. LAWSON. You are using the old technique, which was used in Hitler Germany in order to create a scare here—

THE CHAIRMAN (pounding gavel). Oh—

MR. LAWSON. In order to create an entirely false atmosphere in which this hearing is conducted—

(The chairman pounding gavel.)

MR. LAWSON. In order that you can then smear the motion-picture industry, and you can proceed to the press, to any form of communication in this country.

THE CHAIRMAN. You have learned—

MR. LAWSON. The Bill of Rights was established precisely to prevent the operation of any committee which could invade the basic rights of Americans.

Now, if you want to know—

MR. STRIPLING. Mr. Chairman, the witness is not answering the question.

MR. LAWSON. If you want to know—

(The chairman pounding gavel.)

MR. LAWSON. About the perjury that has been committed here and the perjury that is planned.

THE CHAIRMAN. Mr. Lawson—

MR. LAWSON. You permit me and my attorneys to bring in here the witnesses that testified last week and you permit us to cross-examine these witnesses, and we will show up the whole tissue of lie—

THE CHAIRMAN (pounding gavel). We are going to get the answer to that question if we have to stay here for a week.

Are you a member of the Communist Party, or have you ever been a member of the Communist Party?

MR. LAWSON. It is unfortunate and tragic that I have to teach this committee the basic principles of American—

THE CHAIRMAN (pounding gavel). That is not the question. That is not the question. The question is: Have you ever been a member of the Communist Party?

MR. LAWSON. I am framing my answer in the only way in which any American citizen can frame his answer to a question which absolutely invades his rights.

THE CHAIRMAN. Then you refuse to answer that question; is that correct?

MR. LAWSON. I have told you that I will offer my beliefs, affiliations, and everything else to the American public, and they will know where I stand.

THE CHAIRMAN (pounding gavel). Excuse the witness—

MR. LAWSON. As they do from what I have written.

THE CHAIRMAN (pounding gavel). Stand away from the stand—

MR. LAWSON. I have written Americanism for many years, and I shall continue to fight for the Bill of Rights, which you are trying to destroy.

THE CHAIRMAN. Officers, take this man away from the stand—

[Applause and boos.]

THE CHAIRMAN (pounding gavel). There will be no demonstrations. No demonstrations, for or against. Everyone will please be seated.

All right, go ahead, Mr. Stripling. Proceed.

MR. STRIPLING. Mr. Chairman, the committee has made exhaustive investigation and research into the Communist affiliations of Mr. John Howard Lawson. Numerous witnesses under oath have identified Mr. Lawson as a member of the Communist Party.

I have here a nine-page memorandum which details at length his affiliations with the Communist Party and its various front organizations.

I now ask that Mr. Louis J. Russell, an investigator for the committee, take the stand.

THE CHAIRMAN. Mr. Russell, raise your right hand, please.

Do you solemnly swear that the testimony you are about to give is the truth, the whole truth, and nothing but the truth, so help you God?

MR. RUSSELL. I do.

THE CHAIRMAN. Sit down.

MR. STRIPLING. In order to give the committee the type of affiliations that Mr. Lawson has had with the Communist Party, I should like to refer, Mr. Chairman, to an article which appeared in the Daily Worker, the official organ of the Communist Party. This article is dated September 6, 1935, and appears on page 5 of the Daily Worker. Under the headline "Artists, writers," it says:

We cannot let the Daily go under—

referring to the Daily Worker. It says:

Need for Daily Worker has grown a thousand times since 1934.

By John Howard Lawson. The article bears a picture of Mr. Lawson, and it appears on the front page of the Daily Worker.

Under the Daily Worker heading, the following language appears:

The Daily Worker—central organ of the Communist Party of the United States, section of the Communist International.

I have here, Mr. Chairman, another article from the Daily Worker by John Howard Lawson, dated February 26, 1935, page 5:

The Story of William Z. Foster, a tribute on the occasion of his fifty-fourth birthday, by John Howard Lawson.

I have here, Mr. Chairman, over 100 exhibits showing Mr. Lawson's affiliations with the party.

I see no point in taking the committee's time in reading each exhibit. If the Chair desires, I will read the nine-page memorandum, after Mr. Russell has testified. I will submit copies of this—

THE CHAIRMAN. Without objection, they will be made a part of the record.

MR. STRIPLING. Mr. Russell, you have been sworn in this hearing; have you not?

MR. RUSSELL. I have.

Testimony of Louis J. Russell

MR. STRIPLING. Your name is Louis J. Russell?

MR. RUSSELL. That is right.

MR. STRIPLING. You are a member of the investigative staff of the Committee on Un-American Activities?

MR. RUSSELL. I am.

MR. STRIPLING. You were formerly with the FBI for 10 years?

MR. RUSSELL. I was.

MR. STRIPLING. Were you detailed to make an investigation as to the Communist Party affiliations of John Howard Lawson?

MR. RUSSELL. I was.

MR. STRIPLING. What did your investigation disclose?

MR. RUSSELL. During the course of my investigation and the investigation concluded by the committee, we were furnished—or I was—with copies of Communist Party registration cards pertaining to certain individuals for the year 1941.

THE CHAIRMAN. Speak louder, please.

MR. RUSSELL. One of those cards bears the number "47275" and is made out in the name of John Howard Lawson, 4542 Coldwater Canyon; city, Los Angeles; county, Los Angeles, State, California. There is a notation contained on this registration card: "New card issued on December 10, 1944." Other information contained on this card, which referred to the personal description of the John Howard Lawson mentioned, on Communist Party registration No. 47275—the description is as follows:

Male, white. Occupation, writer. Industry, motion pictures. Member of CIO–A. F. of L. "Independent union or no union," "Independent union" is checked. There is a question asked on this registration card: "Is member club subscriber for Daily Worker?" The answer, "Yes," is checked.

MR. STRIPLING. That is all, Mr. Russell.

Now, Mr. Chairman, what is the committee's pleasure with regard to the nine-page memorandum? Do you want it read into the record or do you want it made a part of the record?

THE CHAIRMAN. The committee wants you to read it.

MR. STRIPLING (reading):

INFORMATION FROM THE FILES OF THE COMMITTEE ON UN-AMERICAN
ACTIVITIES, UNITED STATES HOUSE OF REPRESENTATIVES, ON THE
COMMUNIST AFFILIATIONS OF JOHN HOWARD LAWSON

John Howard Lawson is a screen writer and one of the most active
Communists in the Hollywood movie industry. He has written the
following scripts: Dynamite (M-G-M); The Sea Bat (M-G-M); Blush-
ing Brides (M-G-M); Ship From Shanghai (M-G-M); Bachelor Apartment (Radio Films); Success at Any Price (RKO–Radio), 1934;
Goodbye Love (RKO–Radio), 1934; Treasure Island (M-G-M), 1934;
Party Wire (Columbia), 1935; Blockade (United Artists–Wanger),
1938; Algiers (United Artists–Wanger), 1938; They Shall Have Music
(United Artists–Goldwyn), 1939; Four Sons (20th Century–Fox),
1940; Earthbound (20th Century–Fox), 1940; Sahara (Columbia),
1943; Counterattack (Columbia), 1945.

The files of the House Committee on Un-American Activities show
that—

1. Rena M. Vale, a former member of the Communist Party and a
screen writer, testified before the Special Committee on Un-American
Activities on July 22, 1940, that Mr. Lawson had been identified to
her as a Communist Party member when she met him at a Communist
Party fraction meeting. She further testified that Mr. Lawson during
the meeting gave advice on inserting the Communist Party line into
drama. The State legislative committee investigating un-American activities in California cited Mr. Lawson as "one of the most important
Marxist strategists in southern California," in its 1945 report, page
118. The California report notes on the same page that Rena M. Vale
also testified before the State legislative committee and that the witness identified Lawson as a member of the Communist Party fraction
of the Screen Writers Guild who had given advice on the Communist
Party program in the writing of the play, Sun Rises in the West. The
State legislative committee states further, in its 1947 report, page 260,
that Mr. Lawson directed a Communist bloc of about 65 members in
local 47, the Hollywood local of the American Federation of Musicians, AFL, between the years 1937 and 1940. . . .[1]

TESTIMONY OF ERIC JOHNSTON

I'm not here to try to whitewash Hollywood, and I'm not here to help
sling a tar brush at it, either.

1. Ed. Note: At this point, Mr. Stripling proceeded to read nine single-spaced type-
written pages of documentation supporting the allegations of Lawson's Communist
activities and affiliations. This pattern repeated itself for all ten of the "unfriendly witnesses." After each was ejected from the committee room for refusing to answer the
questions put to him, Stripling or Russell read a lengthy list of citations into the
Congressional Record.

I want to stick to the facts as I see them.

There are several points I'd like to make to this committee.

The first one is this: A damaging impression of Hollywood has spread all over the country as a result of last week's hearings. You have a lot of sensational testimony about Hollywood. From some of it the public will get the idea that Hollywood is running over with Communists and communism.

I believe the impression which has gone out is the sort of scare-head stuff which is grossly unfair to a great American industry. It must be a great satisfaction to the Communist leadership in this country to have people believe that Hollywood Communists are astronomical in number and almost irresistible in power.

Now, what are the facts? Not everybody in Hollywood is a Communist. I have said before that undoubtedly there are Communists in Hollywood, but in my opinion the percentage is extremely small.

I have had a number of close looks at Hollywood in the last 2 years, and I have looked at it through the eyes of an average businessman. I recognize that as the world's capital of show business, there is bound to be a lot of show business in Hollywood. There is no business, Mr. Chairman, like show business. But underneath there is the solid foundation of patriotic, hard-working, decent citizens. Making motion pictures is hard work. You just don't dash off a motion picture between social engagements.

The great bulk of Hollywood people put their jobs first. But I can assure you you won't find a community in the country where hearts are any bigger or the purses more open when it comes to helping out worthy endeavors. Take any national campaign for the public good, and you'll find Hollywood people contributing their time and their money.

Every other country in the world is trying to build up its motion-picture industry, and I can verify that, having just traveled in 12 countries in Europe where they are all trying to build up their motion-picture industry. These governments are trying to do it through government subsidies and devices of all kinds. The American motion-picture industry grew by its own efforts. It has rejected subsidies and Government assistance. It wants no hand-out from Government. All it asks is a fair shake and a chance to live and to grow and to serve its country without being unfairly condemned and crucified.

I wind up my first point with a request of this committee. The damaging impression about Hollywood should be corrected. I urge your committee to do so in these public hearings.

There is another damaging impression which should be corrected. The report of the subcommittee said that some of the most flagrant Communist propaganda films were produced as the result of White House pressure. This charge has been completely refuted by the testimony before you.

My second point includes another request of the committee.

The report of your subcommittee stated that you had a list of all pictures produced in Hollywood in the last 8 years which contained Communist propaganda. Your committee has not made this list public. Until the list is made public the industry stands condemned by unsupported generalizations, and we are denied the opportunity to refute these charges publicly.

Again, I remind the committee that we have offered to put on a special showing of any or all of the pictures which stand accused so that you can see for yourselves what's in them. The contents of the pictures constitute the only proof.

Unless this evidence is presented and we are given the chance to refute it in these public hearings, it is the obligation of the committee to absolve the industry from the charges against it.

Now, I come to my third point—a vitally important one to every American and to the system under which we live.

It is free speech.

Now, I've been advised by some persons to lay off it. I've been told that if I mentioned it I'd be playing into the hands of Communists. But nobody has a monopoly on the issue of free speech in this country. I'm not afraid of being right, even if that puts me in with the wrong company. I've been for free speech ever since I first read the lives of great men of the past who fought and died for this principle—and that was in grade school.

There is nothing I can add to what every great American has said on the subject since the founding of the Republic. Our freedoms would become empty and meaningless without the keystone of our freedom arch—freedom of speech—freedom to speak, to hear, and to see.

When I talk about freedom of speech in connection with this hearing, I mean just this: You don't need to pass a law to choke off free speech or seriously curtail it. Intimidation or coercion will do it just as well. You can't make good and honest motion pictures in an atmosphere of fear.

I intend to use every influence at my command to keep the screen free. I don't propose that Government shall tell the motion-picture industry, directly or by coercion, what kind of pictures it ought to make. I am as whole-souledly against that as I would be against dictating to the press or the radio, to the book publishers or to the magazines.

One of the most amazing paradoxes has grown out of this hearing. At one point we were accused of making Communist propaganda by not making pictures which show the advantages of our system. In other words, we were accused of putting propaganda on the screen by keeping it out.

That sort of reasoning is a little staggering, especially when you know the story of American pictures in some foreign countries. We are accused of Communist propaganda at home, but in Communist-dominated countries in Europe our motion-picture films are banned because they contain propaganda for capitalism.

We can't be communistic and capitalistic at one and the same time. I've said it before, but I'd like to repeat it. There is nothing more feared or hated in Communist countries than the American motion picture.

To sum up this point: We insist on our rights to decide what will or will not go in our pictures. We are deeply conscious of the responsibility this freedom involves, but we have no intention to violate this trust by permitting subversive propaganda in our films.

Now, my next point is this:

When I was before this committee last March, I said that I wanted to see Communists exposed. I still do. I'm heart and soul for it. An exposed Communist is an unarmed Communist. Expose them, but expose them in the traditional American manner.

But I believe that when this committee or any other agency undertakes to expose communism it must be scrupulous to avoid tying a red tag on innocent people by indiscriminate labeling.

It seems to me it is getting dangerously easy to call a man a Communist without proof or even reasonable suspicion. When a distinguished leader of the Republican Party in the United States Senate is accused of following the Communist Party line for introducing a housing bill, it is time, gentlemen, to give a little serious thought to the dangers of thoughtless smearing by gossip and hearsay.

Senator Robert Taft isn't going to worry about being called a Communist. But not every American is a Senator Taft who can properly ignore such an accusation. Most of us in America are just little people, and loose charges can hurt little people. They take away everything a man has—his livelihood, his reputation, and his personal dignity.

When just one man is falsely damned as a Communist in an hour like this when the Red issue is at white heat, no one of us is safe.

Gentlemen, I maintain that preservation of the rights of the individual is a proper duty for this Committee on Un-American Activities. This country's entire tradition is based on the principle that the individual is a higher power than the state; that the state owes its authority to the individual, and must treat him accordingly.

Expose communism, but don't put any American who isn't a Communist in a concentration camp of suspicion. We are not willing to give up our freedoms to save our freedoms. . . .

TESTIMONY OF DALTON TRUMBO

MR. TRUMBO. Mr. Chairman, I have a statement I should like to read into the record, if you please—

MR. STRIPLING. Mr. Trumbo, just a moment, please. We want to conduct the hearing as orderly as possible, and I am sure you desire to cooperate.

MR. TRUMBO. I do, indeed.

MR. STRIPLING. You have counsel with you?

MR. TRUMBO. I have.

MR. STRIPLING. And would you identify your counsel?

MR. TRUMBO. Mr. Bartley Crum and Mr. Robert Kenny.

May I request of the Chair the opportunity to read a statement into the record?

THE CHAIRMAN. Yes. May we see your statement?

MR. TRUMBO. Yes.

THE CHAIRMAN. To determine whether it is pertinent to the inquiry.

(Statement handed to the chairman.)

MR. STRIPLING. Do you have a copy?

MR. CRUM (addressing Mr. Trumbo). Do you have an extra copy for Mr. Stripling?

MR. TRUMBO. Yes.

MR. STRIPLING. Mr. Chairman—

THE CHAIRMAN. The Chair is ready to rule.

MR. TRUMBO. I beg your pardon, sir?

THE CHAIRMAN. Mr. Trumbo, we have looked over this statement very carefully. It has been our practice to permit witnesses to read statements that are pertinent to the inquiry, that is, the alleged infiltration of communism in the moving-picture industry.

We have read your statement here. We have concluded, and unanimously so, that this statement is not pertinent to the inquiry. Therefore, the Chair will rule that the statement will not be read.

MR. TRUMBO. The Chair has considered a statement from Gerald L. K. Smith to be pertinent to its inquiries.[2]

THE CHAIRMAN. That statement is out of order.

MR. TRUMBO. And where is mine different from that, sir?

THE CHAIRMAN. As a witness, if you conduct yourself like the first witness yesterday, you won't be given the privilege of being a witness before a committee of Congress, before this committee of Congress.

Go ahead, Mr. Stripling.

MR. STRIPLING. Mr. Trumbo—

MR. TRUMBO. I would like to know what it is that is in my statement that this committee fears to be read to the American people?

2. Ed. Note: Gerald L. K. Smith was a violently anti-Communist agitator with a large following in Los Angeles. He was openly anti-Semitic and antiblack.

THE CHAIRMAN. Go ahead, Mr. Stripling, ask a question—

MR. TRUMBO. I have some evidence to introduce—

THE CHAIRMAN (pounding gavel). Ask one question, Mr. Stripling—

MR. TRUMBO. I should like to introduce evidence—

THE CHAIRMAN (pounding gavel). You are out of order.

MR. STRIPLING. State your name, please.

MR. TRUMBO. Dalton Trumbo.

MR. STRIPLING. What is your present address?

MR. TRUMBO. 329 South Rodeo Drive, Beverly Hills, Calif.

MR. STRIPLING. When and where were you born, sir?

MR. TRUMBO. I was born in Montrose, Colo., on December 9, 1905.

MR. STRIPLING. What is your occupation?

MR. TRUMBO. My occupation is that of a writer.

MR. STRIPLING. How long have you been in the motion-picture industry as a writer?

MR. TRUMBO. I believe since 1934 or '35.

MR. STRIPLING. Are you a member of the Screen Writers Guild?

MR. TRUMBO. At this point, sir, I should like to introduce certain evidence bearing upon this case—

MR. STRIPLING. Mr. Chairman—

MR. TRUMBO. I—

MR. STRIPLING. Just a moment, please—

MR. TRUMBO. I should like to introduce statements—

THE CHAIRMAN (pounding gavel). Just a minute—

MR. TRUMBO. About my work—

THE CHAIRMAN. What was the question—

MR. TRUMBO. From General Arnold of the Army Air Forces—

THE CHAIRMAN (pounding gavel). Now, just a minute—

MR. TRUMBO. From a municipal judge—

THE CHAIRMAN (pounding gavel). Just a moment. The Chair wants to find out what the question was and to see whether your answer is pertinent to the question. What was the question?

MR. STRIPLING. Mr. Trumbo, I shall ask various questions, all of which can be answered "Yes" or "No." If you want to give an explanation after you have made that answer, I feel sure that the committee will agree to that.

However, in order to conduct this hearing in an orderly fashion, it is necessary that you be responsive to the question, without making a speech in response to each question.

MR. TRUMBO. I understand, Mr. Stripling. However, your job is to ask questions and mine is to answer them. I shall answer "Yes" or "No," if I please to answer. I shall answer in my own words. Very many questions can be answered "Yes" or "No" only by a moron or a slave.

THE CHAIRMAN. The Chair agrees with your point, that you need not answer the questions "Yes" or "No"—

MR. TRUMBO. Thank you, sir.

THE CHAIRMAN. But you should answer the questions.

MR. TRUMBO. Thank you, sir.

THE CHAIRMAN. Go ahead, Mr. Stripling.

MR. TRUMBO. May I, if the Chair please, I am not going to make a speech. I simply have evidence from responsible people as to the nature of my work. I have 20 scripts which I propose and wish to introduce into the record so that it may be known what my work is, and what this committee may seek to prevent the American people from seeing in the future.

MR. STRIPLING. Mr. Chairman—

THE CHAIRMAN. Now, don't make a statement like that. That is not correct.

May I ask how long one of these scripts may be?

MR. TRUMBO. I am sorry to say that they average from 115 to 160 or 170 pages, with very few of them of the latter type.

THE CHAIRMAN. And how many do you want to put in the record?

MR. TRUMBO. I have 20. They are not quite all that I have written.

THE CHAIRMAN. I think the Chair will have to rule—

MR. TRUMBO. But, sir—

THE CHAIRMAN. They are too long—

MR. TRUMBO. My work has been under attack.

THE CHAIRMAN. Too many pages.

MR. TRUMBO. Then may I introduce into evidence statements of responsible people concerning my work?

THE CHAIRMAN. All right, you let the investigator ask his questions, and then you answer them the best you can.

MR. STRIPLING. I will be glad to cover all of your works. Mr. Trumbo.

MR. TRUMBO. I realize that, but yesterday a man's work was covered after he had left the stand. I should like to discuss my work now.

MR. STRIPLING. Well, Mr. Trumbo, I will repeat the question: Are you a member of the Screen Writers Guild?

MR. TRUMBO. I shall answer that question in just a moment. I want only to protest the fact that I have been denied the right to introduce evidence, to introduce statements of General Arnold, of juvenile court judges, of the head of the Motion Picture Division of the UNRRA, of the Naval Chaplain in charge of motion-picture projects for the United States Navy. These I consider pertinent. And with that protest, I shall go to your question.

MR. STRIPLING. Are you a member of the Screen Writers Guild?

MR. TRUMBO. Mr. Stripling, the rights of American labor to inviolably secret membership lists have been won in this country by a great cost of blood and a great cost in terms of hunger. These rights have become an American tradition. Over the Voice of America we have broadcast to the entire world the freedom of our labor.

THE CHAIRMAN. Are you answering the question or are you making another speech?

MR. TRUMBO. Sir, I am truly answering the question.

THE CHAIRMAN. Because if you want to make another speech we can find a corner right up here where you can make some of these speeches.

MR. TRUMBO. I would be willing to do that, too.

THE CHAIRMAN. All right, now, what was the question, Mr. Stripling?

MR. STRIPLING. The question, Mr. Chairman, is—I asked Mr. Trumbo if he is a member of the Screen Writers Guild.

MR. TRUMBO. You asked me a question which would permit you to haul every union member in the United States up here to identify himself as a union member, to subject him to future intimidation and coercion. This, I believe, is an unconstitutional question.

THE CHAIRMAN. Now, are you making another speech, or is that the answer?

MR. TRUMBO. This is my answer, sir.

THE CHAIRMAN. Well, can't you answer: Are you a member of the Screen Writers Guild, by saying "Yes" or "No," or I think so, or maybe, or something like that?

MR. TRUMBO. Mr. Chairman, I should like to accommodate you. May I try to answer the question again?

THE CHAIRMAN. Well, we would certainly like to have you accommodate us.

MR TRUMBO. If there were a committee of Congress, all the members of which had voted in favor of the Taft-Hartley bill—

MR. MCDOWELL. Oh, that isn't answering the question.

(The chairman pounding gavel.)

MR. TRUMBO. It might be considered that committee was hostile to labor.

THE CHAIRMAN (pounding gavel). Now, Mr. Trumbo—

MR MCDOWELL. It is no disgrace, you know, to identify yourself as a member of a labor union in the United States. Most of us belong to something.

THE CHAIRMAN. Now the question is, Mr. Trumbo: Are you a member of the Screen Writers Guild?

MR. TRUMBO. Mr. Chairman, I would not consider it a disgrace to be a member of a labor union.

MR. MCDOWELL. Of course he wouldn't.

MR. TRUMBO. But labor unions have the right to secrecy of their membership lists.

THE CHAIRMAN. I am getting back to the question: Are you a member of the Screen Writers Guild?

MR. TRUMBO. Mr. Chairman, this question is designed to a specific purpose. First—

THE CHAIRMAN (pounding gavel). Do you—

MR. TRUMBO. First, to identify me with the Screen Writers Guild; secondly, to seek to identify me with the Communist Party and thereby destroy that guild—

THE CHAIRMAN (pounding gavel). Are you refusing to answer the questions?

MR. TRUMBO. I will refuse to answer none of your questions, sir.

THE CHAIRMAN. Well, you are refusing to answer this question.

MR. TRUMBO. I am, indeed, not refusing to answer the question.

THE CHAIRMAN. I will ask you the question—

MR. TRUMBO. You ask me.

THE CHAIRMAN. Are you a member of the Screen Writers Guild?

MR. TRUMBO. I repeat—

THE CHAIRMAN (pounding gavel). Excuse the witness—

MR. STRIPLING. Just a moment, Mr. Chairman—

MR. TRUMBO. Am I excused?

MR. STRIPLING. I have more questions—

MR. TRUMBO. Am I excused, or not?

THE CHAIRMAN. No; just a minute. The chief investigator wants to ask some questions.

MR. STRIPLING. Just a moment. I have some other questions, Mr. Trumbo, that I would like to ask you.

Are you now, or have you ever been a member of the Communist Party?

MR. TRUMBO. Mr. Chairman, first I should like to know whether the quality of my last answer was acceptable, since I am still on the stand?

THE CHAIRMAN. This hasn't got anything to do with your answer to the last question.

MR. TRUMBO. I see.

THE CHAIRMAN. This is a new question, now.

MR. TRUMBO. I see.

Mr. Stripling, you must have some reason for asking this question—

MR. MCDOWELL. Yes, we do.

MR. TRUMBO. You do.

I understand that members of the press have been given an alleged Communist Party card belonging to me—is that true?

MR. STRIPLING. That is not true.

THE CHAIRMAN. You are not asking the question—

MR. TRUMBO. I was.

THE CHAIRMAN. The chief investigator is asking the questions.

MR. TRUMBO. I beg your pardon, sir.

THE CHAIRMAN. Are you or have you ever been a member of the Communist Party?

MR. TRUMBO. I believe I have the right to be confronted with any evidence which supports this question. I should like to see what you have.

THE CHAIRMAN. Oh. Well, you would!

MR. TRUMBO. Yes.

THE CHAIRMAN. Well, you will, pretty soon.

(Laughter and applause.)

THE CHAIRMAN (pounding gavel). The witness is excused. Impossible.

MR. TRUMBO. This is the beginning—

THE CHAIRMAN (pounding gavel). Just a minute—

MR. TRUMBO. Of an American concentration camp.

THE CHAIRMAN. This is typical Communist tactics. This is typical Communist tactics. [Pounding gavel.]

(Applause.)

THE CHAIRMAN. Now, there will be no demonstration from the persons in the audience. People in the audience are the guests of this committee. This is a congressional committee and we must maintain order. Those standing up or walking around will please sit down.

Mr. Stripling, put on the next witness.

MR. STRIPLING. Mr. Chairman, I would like to place into the record the affiliations of Mr. Trumbo with the Communist Party.

THE CHAIRMAN. Louder, please.

MR. STRIPLING. Which have been compiled by the investigative and research staff of the Committee on Un-American Activities.

I should also like to place a witness on the stand to introduce the Communist registration card of Mr. Trumbo.

Do I have permission to read this memorandum?

THE CHAIRMAN. How many pages are there?

MR. STRIPLING. Like in the case of Mr. Lawson, Mr. Chairman, it is nine pages long.

THE CHAIRMAN. Mr. Stripling, will you come up here, please for a minute.

(Mr. Stripling confers with the chairman.)

THE CHAIRMAN. All right, Mr. Stripling, you read it.

MR. STRIPLING. Mr. Chairman, before I read this memorandum, I would like to refer to an article which appeared in the Hollywood Reporter, which is one of the important trade papers of the motion-picture industry, under date of August 2, 1946, in which they state:

The reporter herein now asks Trumbo to answer these questions: Are you a Communist? Is your party name or alias Hal Conger? Are you a member of group 3, branch A, of the American Communist Party? Are you the holder of Communist Book No. 36802?

So far as we have been able to determine, Mr. Trumbo has never answered that challenge from the Hollywood Reporter.

According to the International Motion Picture Almanac and other sources available to this committee, Dalton Trumbo was the writer of the following films—there is a long list of films here, Mr. Chairman, and I won't read those unless it is desired.

THE CHAIRMAN. Without objection, it is so ordered.

MR. STRIPLING. I would like to point out, however, that Mr. Trumbo is the author of Tender Comrade, about which Mrs. Lela Rogers testified. (The films are as follows:)

Love Begins at 20, Everybody Cheer, Tugboat Princess (Columbia), The Devil's Playground (Columbia, 1937), Fugitives for a Night (RKO, 1938), A Man to Remember (RKO, 1938), Sorority House (RKO, 1939), The Flying Irishman (RKO, 1939), Five Came Back (RKO, 1939), Career (RKO, 1939), The Kid From Kokomo (First National, 1939), Heaven With a Barbed-Wire Fence (Twentieth Century–Fox 1939), A Bill of Divorcement (RKO, 1940), Curtain Call (RKO, 1940), Kitty Foyle (RKO, 1940), We Who Are Young (RKO, 1940), The Widow Wouldn't Weep (Paramount 1940), Accent on Love (Twentieth Century–Fox 1941), A Guy Named Joe (M-G-M, 1943), Thirty Seconds Over Tokyo, Tender Comrade (RKO, 1943), Jealousy (Republic, 1945), Our Vines Have Tender Grapes (M-G-M, 1945).

MR. STRIPLING. According to Variety of March 14, 1941, page 2, Dalton Trumbo was the author of Remarkable Andrew, which was so anti-British and anti-war that Paramount refused to continue with the picture after paying $27,000 for it. That was written during the period of the Soviet-Nazi pact.

The files, records, and publications of the Committee on Un-American Activities contain the following information concerning the Communist-front affiliations of Dalton Trumbo:

1. According to the Hollywood Reporter, August 22, 1946, well-known trade publication of the motion-picture industry, Dalton Trumbo was asked if he was the holder of Communist Party Book No. 36802. The committee knows of no denial by Mr. Trumbo of this fact. He has, however, openly endorsed Communist candidates, Communist legal defendants, and has openly cooperated with the

Communist Party and its instruments. According to the Los Angeles Times of November 2, 1942, Mr. Trumbo endorsed Mrs. La Rue McCormick, Communist candidate for State senator. In a speech quoted in the Worker of June 22, 1947, page 11 (magazine), Mr. Trumbo is quoted as follows:

And the defense of the rights of the Communist Party, and of all real or alleged Communists, is the duty not only of liberal and progressives, but all men and women who have love for their country and respect for its Constitution.

At an official meeting of the Communist Party featuring as its chief speaker, William Z. Foster, party chairman, the poem, Confessional, by Dalton Trumbo, was presented, according to the People's World of September 10, 1947, page 4. . . .

TESTIMONY OF ALBERT MALTZ (ACCOMPANIED BY ROBERT W. KENNY AND BARTLEY CRUM)

MR. STRIPLING. Mr. Maltz, will you state your full name and present address for the record, please?

MR. MALTZ. My name is Albert Maltz. I live at 6526 Linden Hurst Avenue, Los Angeles.

Mr. Chairman, I would like the privilege of making a statement, please.

THE CHAIRMAN. Do you have a prepared statement?

MR. MALTZ. I have a prepared statement.

THE CHAIRMAN. May we see it, please?

MR. MALTZ. May I ask whether you asked Mr. Gerald L. K. Smith to see his statement before you allowed him to read it?

THE CHAIRMAN. I wasn't chairman at that time.

MR. MALTZ. Nevertheless you were on the committee, Mr. Thomas, were you not?

THE CHAIRMAN. I asked him a great many questions and he had a hard time answering some of them, too.

MR. MALTZ. I am interested in that, but I still would like to know whether he had his statement read before he was permitted to read it.

THE CHAIRMAN Well, we will look at yours.

MR. MALTZ. I gather that you don't want to answer my question, Mr. Chairman.

(After a pause:)

THE CHAIRMAN. Mr. Maltz, the committee is unanimous in permitting you to read the statement.

MR. MALTZ. Thank you.

I am an American and I believe there is no more proud word in the vocabulary of man. I am a novelist and screen writer and I have produced a certain body of work in the past 15 years. As with any other writer, what I have written has come from the total fabric of my life—my birth in this land, our schools and games, our atmosphere of freedom, our tradition of inquiry, criticism, discussion, tolerance. Whatever I am, America has made me. And I, in turn, possess no loyalty as great as the one I have to this land, to the economic and social welfare of its people, to the perpetuation and development of its democratic way of life.

Now at the age of 39, I am commanded to appear before the House Committee on Un-American Activities. For a full week this committee has encouraged an assortment of well-rehearsed witnesses to testify that I and others are subversive and un-American. It has refused us the opportunity that any pickpocket receives in a magistrate's court—the right to cross-examine these witnesses, to refute their testimony, to reveal their motives, their history, and who, exactly, they are. Furthermore it grants these witnesses congressional immunity so that we may not sue them for libel for their slanders.

I maintain that this is an evil and vicious procedure; that it is legally unjust and morally indecent—and that it places in danger every other American, since if the right of any one citizen can be invaded, then the constitutional guaranties of every other American have been subverted and no one is any longer protected from official tyranny.

What is it about me that this committee wishes to destroy? My writings? Very well, let us refer to them.

My novel, The Cross and the Arrow, was issued in a special edition of 140,000 copies by a wartime Government agency, the armed services edition, for American servicemen abroad.

My short stories have been reprinted in over 30 anthologies, by as many American publishers—all subversive, no doubt.

My film, The Pride of the Marines, was premiered in 28 cities at Guadalcanal Day banquets under the auspices of the United States Marine Corps.

Another film, Destination Tokyo, was premiered aboard a United States submarine and was adopted by the Navy as an official training film.

My short film, The House I Live In, was given a special award by the Academy of Motion Picture Arts and Sciences for its contribution to racial tolerance.

My short story, The Happiest Man on Earth, won the 1938 O. Henry Memorial Award for the best American short story.

This, then, is the body of work for which this committee urges I be blacklisted in the film industry—and tomorrow, if it has its way in the publishing and magazine fields also.

By cold censorship, if not legislation, I must not be allowed to write. Will this censorship stop with me? Or with the others now singled out for attack? If it requires acceptance of the ideas of this committee to remain immune from the brand of un-Americanism, then who is ultimately safe from this committee except members of the Ku Klux Klan?

Why else does this committee now seek to destroy me and others? Because of our ideas, unquestionably. In 1801, when he was President of the United States, Thomas Jefferson wrote:

> Opinion, and the just maintenance of it, shall never be a crime in my view; nor bring injury to the individual.

But a few years ago, in the course of one of the hearings of this committee, Congressman J. Parnell Thomas said, and I quote from the official transcript:

> I just want to say this now, that it seems that the New Deal is working along hand in glove with the Communist Party. The New Deal is either for the Communist Party or it is playing into the hands of the Communist Party.

Very well, then, here is the other reason why I and others have been commanded to appear before this committee—our ideas. In common with many Americans, I supported the New Deal. In common with many Americans I supported, against Mr. Thomas and Mr. Rankin, the anti-lynching bill. I opposed them in my support of OPA controls and emergency veteran housing and a fair employment practices law. I signed petitions for these measures, joined organizations that advocated them, contributed money, sometimes spoke from public platforms, and I will continue to do so. I will take my philosophy from Thomas Payne, Thomas Jefferson, Abraham Lincoln, and I will not be dictated to or intimidated by men to whom the Ku Klux Klan, as a matter of committee record, is an acceptable American institution.

I state further that on many questions of public interest my opinions as a citizen have not always been in accord with the opinions of the majority. They are not now nor have my opinions ever been fixed and unchanging, nor are they now fixed and unchangeable; but, right or wrong, I claim and I insist upon my right to think freely and to speak freely; to join the Republican Party or the Communist Party, the Democratic or the Prohibition Party; to publish whatever I please; to fix my mind or change my mind, without dictation from anyone; to offer any criticism I think fitting of any public official or policy; to join whatever organizations I please, no matter what certain legislators may think of them. Above all, I challenge the right of this committee to inquire into my political or religious beliefs, in any manner or degree, and I assert that not the conduct of this committee but its very existence are a subversion of the Bill of Rights.

If I were a spokesman for General Franco, I would not be here today. I would rather be here. I would rather die than be a shabby American, groveling before men whose names are Thomas and Rankin, but who now carry out activities in America like those carried out in Germany by Goebbels and Himmler.

The American people are going to have to choose between the Bill of Rights and the Thomas committee. They cannot have both. One or the other must be abolished in the immediate future.

THE CHAIRMAN. Mr. Stripling (pounding gavel).

Mr. Stripling.

MR. STRIPLING. Mr. Maltz, what is your occupation?

MR. MALTZ. I am a writer.

MR. STRIPLING. Are you employed in the motion-picture industry?

MR. MALTZ. I work in various fields of writing and I have sometimes accepted employment in the motion-picture industry.

MR. STRIPLING. Have you written the scripts for a number of pictures?

MR. MALTZ. It is a matter of public record that I have written scripts for certain motion pictures.

MR. STRIPLING. Are you a member of the Screen Writers Guild?

THE CHAIRMAN. Louder, Mr. Stripling.

MR. STRIPLING. Are you a member of the Screen Writers Guild?

MR. MALTZ. Next you are going to ask me what religious group I belong to.

THE CHAIRMAN. No, no; we are not.

MR. MALTZ. And any such question as that—

THE CHAIRMAN. I know.

MR. MALTZ. Is an obvious attempt to invade my rights under the Constitution.

MR. STRIPLING. Do you object to answering whether or not you are a member of the Screen Writers Guild?

MR. MALTZ. I have not objected to answering that question. On the contrary, I point out that next you are going to ask me whether or not I am a member of a certain religious group and suggest that I be blacklisted from an industry because I am a member of a group you don't like.

(The chairman pounds gavel.)

MR. STRIPLING. Mr. Maltz, do you decline to answer the question?

MR. MALTZ. I certainly do not decline to answer the question. I have answered the question.

MR. STRIPLING. I repeat, Are you a member of the Screen Writers Guild?

MR. MALTZ. And I repeat my answer, sir, that any such question is an obvious attempt to invade my list of organizations as an American citizen and I would be a shabby American if I didn't answer as I have.

MR. STRIPLING. Mr. Maltz, are you a member of the Communist Party?

MR. MALTZ. Next you are going to ask what my religious beliefs are.

MR. MCDOWELL. That is not answering the question.

MR. MALTZ. And you are going to insist before various members of the industry that since you do not like my religious beliefs I should not work in such industry. Any such question is quite irrelevant.

MR. STRIPLING. I repeat the question. Are you now or have you ever been a member of the Communist Party?

MR. MALTZ. I have answered the question, Mr. Quisling. I am sorry. I want you to know—

MR. MCDOWELL. I object to that statement.

THE CHAIRMAN. Excuse the witness. No more questions. Typical Communist line. . . .

■ ■ ■ ■

HOLLYWOOD ON TRIAL (1948), Gordon Kahn

Hollywood on Trial was written specifically to defend the actions of the "Hollywood Ten" to the American people. The book reflected their opinions and presented their attitudes toward the committee, the film industry, and the constitutional principles of dissent and freedom of speech. These sections from the book describe the industry's initial support for the witnesses (the formation of the Committee for the First Amendment) and its later surrender to the forces of fear and public pressure.

COUNTER-ATTACK

A gigantic backfire of publicity was started by the Committee for the First Amendment in the third week of October 1947.

It was sparked by such creative leaders in the industry as Paul Henreid, Sterling Hayden, Evelyn Keyes, John Huston, Humphrey Bogart, Lauren Bacall, Philip Dunne, William Wyler, Gene Kelly, Danny Kaye, Marsha Hunt, Jane Wyatt, Ira Gershwin, and many, many more.

They chartered a transport plane for a flight to Washington.

They arranged for two national broadcasts over the coast-to-coast network of the American Broadcasting Company. They carried into millions of American homes the truth about what was going on in Washington, describing it as the story of "informers, spies, invasions of privacy and

Gordon Kahn, *Hollywood on Trial* (Boni & Gaer, 1948).

the other violations of rights after the manner of dictatorships and police states."

These undertakings were neither easy nor cheap. They were costly in terms of organizational effort and money. Throughout the United States the effort was forthcoming. The money was raised, with J. Parnell Thomas contributing greatly to the financial campaign each time he banged his gavel and yelled: "No, no, no, no, no!"

The Hollywood collaborationists with the Thomas Committee used every contractual trick and every personal pressure to keep the stars and directors and writers off the air and out of that Washington-bound plane.

But on October 26 and November 2, 1947, the Committee for the First Amendment was on the air with two broadcasts, directed by Norman Corwin, and including the most distinguished scientists, political leaders, writers, actors, directors, lawyers in the United States.

After the second broadcast, Frank Sinatra said: "If this (Un-American Activities) Committee gets a green light from the American people, will it be possible to make a broadcast like this a year from today?"

On October 28, the Committee for the First Amendment was en route to Washington by air, with John Huston, Humphrey Bogart, William Wyler, Paul Henreid, Danny Kaye, and many others heading to carry the counter-attack against the Thomas Committee to the American people.

This backfire proved enormously effective. Now the Thomas Committee had real competition for the headlines. On the air and in the press, in San Francisco, Chicago, New York, in every American city, town, and village as well as in Washington and Hollywood the warning reached them from such people as Thomas Mann, Thurman Arnold, Fredric March, Helen Gahagan Douglas, Charles Boyer, Senator Claude Pepper, Harlow Shapley, John Garfield, alerting them to danger.

These men and women about whose sincerity and right to speak there can be no question sounded the warning against a *coup d'état* aimed not only at the freedom of the screen but at the very heart of constitutional freedom in the United States.

The response was immediate. The tempo of newspaper and radio criticism of the Thomas Committee was at once intensified. The *New York Times*, the New York *Herald Tribune*, the *Washington Post*, the *Detroit Free Press* and hundreds of other newspapers reemphasized the dangerous implications of the Thomas Committee procedures. Radio commentators began to speak with clarity and courage about the real meaning of this attempted Congressional invasion of the guaranteed individual right to privacy of opinion and conscience.

Before the motion picture personalities representing the Committee for the First Amendment departed from Washington they called upon the clerk of the House of Representatives and presented to him, as citizens, a petition for redress of grievances, which read:

> We, the undersigned citizens of the United States residing in the State of California, do hereby respectfully petition the Honorable Joseph W. Martin, Jr., and our Representatives in Congress, for redress of our grievances as we are privileged to do by the First Amendment to the Constitution.
>
> As citizens of a free country, we repose our trust and faith in the first ten Amendments to the Constitution (The Bill of Rights). In our opinion, the procedures adopted by the House Committee on Un-American Activities here persistently violated the civil liberties of American citizens, to the end that today no citizen is secure from informers, spies, invasions of privacy and the other violations of rights common to dictatorships and police states.
>
> As citizens of a great nation facing outward to the world, we believe the most powerful and persuasive argument for our way of life against all others is that provided by the free media of expression, including the press, radio and motion picture films. In our opinion the procedures adopted by the House Committee on Un-American Activities, in inquiring into the content of motion pictures which will be exhibited overseas, are damaging one of the most important instruments of expression available to the American people in presenting the case for their way of life in the entire world.
>
> As citizens of the first and greatest democracy, we believe that every social problem can be solved by the democratic process, provided that the ballot remains secret and inviolable and provided that all the media of expression remain free of intimidation or coercion by any agency of the government. In our opinion procedures adopted by the House Committee on Un-American Activities evince a lack of faith in the democratic process and the implied belief that our way of life is too weak to resist criticism and inquiry. In so doing we believe that this Committee is making a mockery of a foreign policy which seeks to demonstrate to the world the strength and unity of our democracy.
>
> As Members of the Committee for the First Amendment representing a large group of actors, directors, writers, and producers in the motion picture industry, we have come to Washington to attend hearings of the House Committee on Un-American Activities. We have observed and have reported our findings to those who are unable to come. They have instructed us to speak for them and to express their sense of outrage over the abuses of civil liberties which we believe to have occurred at these hearings.
>
> In our opinion, the folowing abuses have occurred:
>
> I. The investigative function of the Committee on Un-American Activities has been perverted from fair impartial procedures to unfair, partial and prejudiced methods.

II. The reputations and characters of individuals have been smeared and besmirched in the following manner:

a. The Committee on Un-American Activities has been guilty of a violation of the long estabished Anglo-Saxon-American principles of individual accountability. They have accomplished this by adopting the "mass guilt" principle, i.e. guilt by association. Not only have the subpoenaed witnesses suffered by these methods, but mass lists have been publicized that contained many names of other people. These people were included in lists which have been designated by Committee members and counsel as "subversive," "pinko," "radical," "communistic," "disloyal," "un-American," etc. These people were neither subpoenaed nor given the opportunity to defend their characters.

b. The proceedings of the Committee have come to be regarded by the American people as a criminal trial. Nevertheless, American citizens have not been given the American privilege of ordinary self-defense statements and the right to cross examine their accusers. The accused witnesses have become defendants in fact, have not been allowed the right of obtaining witnesses to testify on their behalf. Neither have they been allowed the full right of professional counsel in the defense of their characters.

c. Moreover, while theoretically the Committee is not supposed to apply punitive measures, because of its procedural abuses, it has punished individuals in a far more damaging way than the assessment of fines or personal imprisonment. They have done this by besmirching and damaging man's most precious possession, his reputation.

In view of the above stated abuses of civil rights by the House Committee on Un-American Activities, we respectfully petition the Government for a redress of grievances.

Robert Ardrey	Anne Frank	Evelyn Keyes
Humphrey Bogart	Ira Gershwin	Danny Kaye
Larry Adler	Sheridan Gibney	Arthur Kober
Lauren Bacall	Sterling Hayden	Marsha Hunt
Geraldine Brooks	Mrs. Sterling Hayden	Robert Presnell, Jr.
Jules Block	June Havoc	Henry Rogers
Richard Conte	David Hopkins	Sheppard Strudwick
Philip Dunne	Paul Henreid	Joe Sistrom
Melvin Frank	John Huston	Jane Wyatt
	Gene Kelly	

For a little while, at least, even the League of Frightened Producers took heart as they saw the results of this public action against reaction. Their spokesmen, the smiling Eric Johnston and the eminent Paul V. McNutt, found the courage to defy the Thomas Committee and to assert that the motion picture industry would not bow to the censorship of fear.

This display of managerial valor . . . was destined to fizzle out ignominiously. . . .

RETREAT

The details of the actual capitulation of the motion picture companies to the Thomas Committee and the ideological forces for which it played first fiddle, took place behind a velvet curtain of apprehensive secrecy. The press was barred and there was apparently an explicit understanding that none of the conferees would later reveal the processes of logic or its antithesis by which the great reversal had been achieved.

It is true that the two-day meeting ended with the release of a formal statement that the studios would "forthwith discharge or suspend without compensation" the ten men accused of being in contempt. But the authors of this decree were not sensitive to the stern compulsions which moved Thomas Jefferson and his collaborators in an earlier historic Declaration. No "decent respect to the opinions of mankind" seemed to require "that they should declare the causes which impel them to the separation."

Seventeen unrevealing words were considered enough to justify the new policy of the Motion Picture Association of America, which was also subscribed to by the theoretically autonomous Society of Independent Motion Picture Producers. They were black-listing the recalcitrant ten, they announced, because "their actions have been a disservice to their employers and have impaired their usefulness to the industry." The nature of the disservice was not explained nor was there a hint of how anyone could impair his usefulness by challenging the powers of the very committee which Johnston and McNutt had accused a few weeks earlier of attempted censorship and intimidation.

Speculation as to what went on behind those closed doors can only be based on the few facts at our disposal and the subsequent efforts of the chosen spokesmen of the group to rationalize their new and, in some cases, startlingly unfamiliar position.

The setting of the conference was one of the most handsome and expensive public rooms in the Waldorf-Astoria Hotel. It was the same room which has been on occasion graced by the governors of the National Association of Manufacturers and where it was determined what you shall pay for a gallon of gasoline, a carload of manganese, washing machine, or a roll of linoleum.

The cast of the drama included, of course, Eric Johnston, present in his capacity as president of the Motion Picture Association of America; James F. Byrnes and Paul V. McNutt, counsel for that organization; Barney Balaban, Nicholas Schenck, Harry Cohn, Joseph Schenck,

J. Cheever Cowdin, Walter Wanger, Mendel Silberberg, Donald Nelson, Samuel Goldwyn, Y. Frank Freeman, Henry Ginsberg, Albert Warner, Louis B. Mayer, Dore Schary, Spyros Skouras, Nate Blumberg, William Goetz, Ned Depinet, and many more.

Some were star-characters and some supernumeraries. Some knew a great deal about what makes a motion picture and some knew nothing except that a film is something contained in flat tin cans which is supposed to yield a profit when exhibited to the public.

There were even one or two who were interested chiefly in how many tons of popcorn can be sold in the lobby while a particular picture is being unreeled.

But it is reasonable to assume that all of them, the devotees of prestige, profits, and popcorn alike, were aware that the gathering was a momentous one, for here, as the New York *Herald Tribune* detected, a precedent would be set: making political belief a test of employability. And among the conferees were some of the studio heads who had indignantly rejected the same plan when it had been urged upon them by the agents of the Thomas Committee in advance of the October hearings. Dore Schary of RKO–Radio had said categorically on the witness stand in Washington, when the Committee insisted he should fire any employee of whom they disapproved: "I would still maintain his right to think politically as he chooses."

It was here, in the words of the *Chicago Sun*, that the motion picture industry caved in and turned defeat into victory for J. Parnell Thomas, John Rankin, their colleagues, and supporters. But all we know is that the doors closed at eleven o'clock Monday morning and reopened early Tuesday afternoon to release a statement which should be examined in its entirety as part of our search for clues to the painful labor which precipitated its birth:

> Members of the Association of Motion Picture Producers deplore the action of the ten Hollywood men who have been cited for contempt by the House of Representatives. We do not desire to prejudge their legal rights, but their actions have been a disservice to their employers and have impaired their usefulness to the industry.
>
> We will forthwith discharge or suspend without compensation those in our employ, and we will not re-employ any of the ten until such time as he is acquitted, or has purged himself of contempt, and declared under oath that he is not a Communist.
>
> On the broader issue of alleged subversive and disloyal elements in Hollywood, our members are likewise prepared to take positive action.
>
> We will not knowingly employ a Communist or a member of any

party or group which advocates the overthrow of the Government of the United States by force, or by any illegal or unconstitutional method.

In pursuing this policy, we are not going to be swayed by any hysteria or intimidation from any source.

We are frank to recognize that such a policy involves dangers and risks. There is the danger of hurting innocent people, there is the risk of creating an atmosphere of fear. Creative work at its best cannot be carried on in an atmosphere of fear. We will guard against this danger, this risk, this fear. To this end we will invite the Hollywood talent Guilds to work with us to eliminate any subversives; to protect the innocent, and to safeguard free speech and a free screen wherever threatened.

The absence of a national policy, established by Congress, with respect to the employment of Communists in private industry makes our task difficult. Ours is a nation of laws. We request Congress to enact legislation to assist American industry to rid itself of subversive, disloyal elements.

Nothing subversive or un-American has appeared on the screen, nor can any number of Hollywood investigations obscure the patriotic service of the 30,000 Americans employed in Hollywood who have given our Government invaluable aid in war and peace.

Two days later, when the news of the blacklist had been heard in every civilized quarter of the globe, the Screen Writers' Guild, whose members were most affected, received the following cryptogram:

IN THE INTEREST OF ALL OF US WE EARNESTLY SUGGEST TO YOU THAT YOU JOIN WITH WALTER WANGER AND L. B. MAYER AT A MEETING AT MGM FRIDAY MORNING AT ELEVEN O'CLOCK STOP. WE SEEK TO ACQUAINT YOU WITH THE INTENT OF THE PRODUCERS' STATEMENT AND TO REASSURE YOU THAT OUR ACTION IS DESIGNED TO PROTECT THE INDUSTRY AND ALL THOSE ENGAGED IN IT AND TO DISAVOW ANY INTENTION OF A WITCH HUNT STOP. MAY WE URGE YOU AGAIN IN THE INTEREST OF ALL OF US TO WITHHOLD ANY ACTION STATEMENT OR COMMENT BY YOUR GUILD UNTIL WE HAVE MET AND EXCHANGED OUR VIEWS AND ATTITUDES STOP. THIS COMMITTEE ORGANIZED TO MEET WITH YOU INCLUDES L. B. MAYER, WALTER WANGER, DORE SCHARY, JOE SCHENCK AND HENRY GINSBERG AND WE ASK THAT YOU CONSIDER WHAT THESE MEN WANT TO SAY TO YOU BEFORE INDIVIDUAL GUILD ACTION IS DETERMINED OR BEFORE THE PRODUCERS ACTION IS MISUNDERSTOOD STOP. THANK YOU SINCERELY FOR YOUR COOPERATION. L. B. MAYER, CHAIRMAN, WALTER WANGER, JOE SCHENCK, HENRY GINSBERG, DORE SCHARY.

Representatives of the Screen Actors' and Screen Directors' Guilds were similarly summoned to the conclave. The studio heads had previously, in matters which couldn't be handled without the concurrence of the guilds, told them they were an essential part of The Industry and must participate in deciding policy. In this instance, the officers of the employee organizations suspected, their role was to be limited to accepting an accomplished fact, but they agreed nevertheless to withhold their judgment and listen.

It turned out they had quite a lot of listening to do. The first small meeting was followed by a larger one, to which the entire executive boards of the guilds were invited. Then, since no less an authority than the Thomas Committee had characterized the Screen Writers' Guild as the focal point of the infection its whole membership was assembled to hear the producers' committee.

It was generally agreed that Louis B. Mayer, at the second of these sessions, hit on the most graphic way of expressing the official point of view. The British people, he said, had their Royal Family, in the veneration of which a certain deep human impulse was satisfied. American democracy had to have a similar object of worship, and it had found it in the personalities of the motion picture business. That was why any word or act from Hollywood which shook the loyalty of even a fraction of the royal subjects was a matter for grave alarm and a potential contribution to national disintegration.

Mr. Mayer didn't have to labor the implications of his analogy. Hollywood glamor, for the purposes of his present definition, included the entire personnel of the studios, not just the stars whose images graced the household shrines of America. And it was an essential tradition of constitutional monarchy that the reigning sovereigns be above politics and refrain from any significant expression of opinion whatsoever.

The Guild representatives were affected by mixed emotions at this unexpected revelation. They were learning that there is no place of honor among mankind unaccompanied by sacrifice. They were being simultaneousy enthroned and disfranchised.

But it was the statement of Dore Schary before the Writers' Guild of which he had once been a member, that was awaited with the greatest interest. For it was Schary who had answered back to Thomas and Stripling with the words "Up until the time it is proved that a Communist is a man dedicated to the overthrow of the government by force or violence, or by any illegal methods, I cannot make a determination of his employment on any other basis except whether he is qualified best to do the job I want him to do."

He had repeated his stand in other terms: "I will hire only those people I believe best qualified for their jobs until it is proven, until it is a matter of record and if that record is shown to me, of course I would not hire anyone who is dedicated to overthrow of the government by force." And he had explained in advance why these standards for dismissal did not apply to Adrian Scott and Edward Dmytryk, the two men in his company subsequently dismissed: "I must say, not in defense but in honesty that at no time in discussions have I heard—or films—these men make any remark or attempt to get anything subversive into the films I have worked on with them. I must say that in honesty."

E. J. Mannix and Walter Wanger accompanied Schary to the writers' meeting—and left it without speaking a word. Schary was the spokesman and his colleagues were simply "present, as observers," apparently to see that the newly-minted executive talked like one instead of reverting to former type under the sinister influence of his erstwhile brethren.

Mr. Schary did not fail their expectations. The general impact of his extemporaneous speech was that the producers were opposed to the Thomas Committee, in fact despised it. They felt the freedom of the screen was in jeopardy. They were terribly sorry that they had to fire anybody for any reason whatsoever, especially honest, talented people.

It was true that his own personal opinion had not been in accord with the determination of the New York meeting. That went for quite a few other producers, too. But in spite of their disagreement a unanimous decision had been reached to do exactly what the Thomas Committee had asked them to do. This was because the motion picture industry was very sensitive to public opinion. And any public opinion, even when it was manufactured by people out to control the thoughts and speech of American citizens, was still public opinion.

The producers had a threefold program, Mr. Schary told the writers. The first plank was to fire and blacklist the ten witnesses. "We do not ask you to condone this," he assured an audience that included seven of the ten. Second was the policy of not hiring anyone *believed* to be a Communist. "We do not ask you to condone this," Mr. Schary repeated.

The third plank in the program was a big all-industry public relations campaign to restore the good name of Hollywood by convincing the American people that the first two planks were justified. This campaign, he was confident, the writers would not only condone but lend it their wholehearted support. Here the guilds and the producers could join in united action for the benefit of all.

As Mr. Schary descended the platform, Mr. Mannix and Mr. Wanger stood up to accompany him out. Sitting on the aisle in the front row was Dalton Trumbo. Many eyes watched this encounter between the would-be executioners and one of their principal victims. The three producers rose to the occasion. In turn they stopped, bent over, touched a friendly hand to Mr. Trumbo's slightly stiffened shoulder and spoke a word of greeting.

Then they proceeded to leave the meeting, their gesture having demonstrated that the bonds of personal friendship transcended the unpleasant necessities of blacklist, career-wrecking, and character assassination.

The membership of the Screen Writers' Guild was so impressed by the Schary explanation that, with only eight dissenting votes, over four hundred men and women reaffirmed their decision to demand an end to the blacklist.

■ ■ ■ ■

DOCUMENTATION OF THE RED STARS IN HOLLYWOOD (1951), Myron C. Fagan

Not all the pamphleteering and agitatory writing in the period came from the left and from supporters of the Ten. Myron C. Fagan was one of the most noisy and most tireless authors of privately published pamphlets that attacked the Red menace in Hollywood and elsewhere. A writer of minor plays and novels for thirty years, Fagan turned to specifically anti-Communist plays (*Red Rainbow*) and pamphlets (*Red Treason in Hollywood*) in the mid-1930s. This passage from one of his pamphlets that attempted to document his previous charges reveals the tone of Fagan's writing, his rather strange definition of "documentation," and a very different opinion of the Committee for the First Amendment than that in *Hollywood on Trial*.

FELLOW TRAVELERS

One of the most potent weapons of the Communist Party in America is what is commonly known as the "Red Front" organization. It is their Fifth Column "Transmission Belt." In every case, every such organization is created *on direct orders from Moscow*, by highly placed and trusted *Members of the Communist Party*. But no such Member ever appears as an Officer, or a Sponsor. The chief objective of such an organization is to extend Communist agitation and propaganda to non-Communist masses. Hence, its true character must be camouflaged under a high-sounding *patriotic* or *humanitarian* name—its Officers and Sponsors must be distinguished individuals whose very names aid the camouflage . . . *but these Officers and Sponsors are chosen from a list of tried and proven Fellow-*

Myron C. Fagan's *Documentation of the Red Stars in Hollywood* was published privately in 1951.

Travellers—or those whose *secret* memberships in the Party have been closely maintained.

Now, it must be borne in mind and emphasized that the Communist Party is *in all respects* a secret, conspiratorial branch of a foreign government. J. Edgar Hoover has stated that its membership totals between 50,000 and 60,000. But it is an accepted fact that many of these members —in fact, the majority of them—joined the Party under assumed and fictitious names. In nearly every case the applicant for membership gives first his real name and then sets forth the fictitious name under which he desires to be known in Communist circles. This is not conjecture, but a matter of *record* with the F.B.I. and the California State Senate Fact Finding Committee.

The California Committee is in possession of a mass of evidence concerning many individuals' relationship with the Communist Party. Where such an individual is of prominence, and therefore of great value to the Communist strategy, no record is made of his or her affiliation. Among the Commies themselves such an individual is referred to as "a member at large." Because of his or her importance, no formal application for membership is ever demanded and no party-book or other recording of membership is issued. For general purposes such individuals are listed as "Fellow-Travellers"—*and their affiliation zealously guarded.* The "Fellow-Traveller" follows the party line without deviation. If his activities tally with the changing and twisting policies of the Communist Party you may be sure of his close association with the Party. For example: a Red Front has become too notorious, disbands—and emerges under a new name; if you find that a Frederic March was a Sponsor of the old "Front" and is also a Sponsor of the new one, it is reasonable to assume that it is not just a happenstance.

At this point I wish to emphasize that an individual's allegiance or value to Communism is not to be judged by the number of Fronts with which he has been connected. A half-way Red, or a three-quarter one, may be affiliated with 20 or 30 Front organizations, whereas an all-out Red may be affiliated with only one or two or three such organizations. In other words, it is often the case that the more useful an individual is to the Commies, the less often his name is put forward in Front organizations. Therefore, he is not always to be judged on a numerical basis, but rather on the character of his affiliations, and particularly on the nature of the organization with which he is affiliated. For example, some of the Hollywood Reds I have listed may have been affiliated with only one or two Red Fronts, such as "American-Soviet Friendship" or "Committee for the First Amendment", but these Fronts were known to be all-out Communist organizations, working in a manner which made the Commie line ridiculously easy to discern, so there can be very little doubt that those individuals knew they were working for Red organizations—*they were not innocents, duped by pretentious objectives announced by the organizations.*

In confirmation of that statement I will quote from a Report to Congress made in 1939 by the Special Congressional Committee investigating Un-American Activities:

"In the Communist Movement, the Fellow Travellers are more numerous than the card-holding members of the Party. As a rule, the Fellow Travellers go along in the limited duties expected of them as faithfully as if they were actually party members. It is, however, important to recognize that there are many degrees in Fellow Travelling. Some are closer to the Party than others. Usually the Fellow Travellers are middle-class intellectuals—professors, writers, clergymen, and even important government officials. In some respects, the Fellow Traveller is a far more valuable instrument of the Communist Party's purpose than a party member would be. He may, therefore, exert a more insidious influence in Communist subversive activities than the person who openly acknowledges his Communist Party membership."

In those days the House Un-American Activities Committee did not even dream that the Hollywood Reds and Fellow Travellers were the backbone, financially and morally, of the Red movement in America!!!

Red Front Organizations

The Red Front is the Yardstick which measures the Communist, or Fellow travelling degrees of the various Hollywood Celebrities I named in "RED TREASON IN HOLLYWOOD", so I will precede the individual documentations with a presentation of the backgrounds of the Fronts, together with listings of their Sponsors.

The complete list of Red Fronts would run into the HUNDREDS, so I will include only those which are essentially Hollywood . . . *all of them* have been pronounced Communist Front organizations by the Attorneys General of the United States and various official Federal and State Investigation Committees. *All of them* were created for one objective: to promote and advance the cause of Communism . . . all of them had more or less interlocking Boards of Directors and Boards of Sponsors . . . all of them followed the Party Line and co-operated with each other.

COMMITTEE FOR THE FIRST AMENDMENT . . . I name this one first because, although its life was brief, it was all-Hollywood—and it was potentially the most vicious of all the Red Fronts in its planned and intended objectives. In my curtain speech on the opening night of "Thieves' Paradise", April 12, 1948, I named the organizers and active sponsors of this

Front . . . *which was the direct cause of its hurried demise* . . . but in "RED TREASON IN HOLLYWOOD" I revealed its entire background and objectives via an open letter to Lewis E. Milestone, as follows:

"Now, Mr. Milestone, on behalf of the AMERICAN people, I'd like to ask you a few very pertinent questions:

"I have been informed, by very excellent authority, that in September 1947 William Z. Foster, Stalin's appointed Boss of the entire Commie gang in America, was an honored guest in your home—and that you organized a gathering of the most important of the "Faithful" in Hollywood to meet with him. According to that same very excellent authority, the main objective of that "gathering" was to offset the effect of the Congressional investigation held in Los Angeles earlier that year of Red activities in Hollywood—also to bolster the courage of those terrified Reds who were to be further questioned in Washington a few weeks later. Also —still according to that same very excellent authority—it was on that night that "The Committee for the First Amendment" was born. Is that true, Mr. Milestone? If it is, you and all the others who were in that 'gathering' were guilty of treason such as would automatically mean death without even a trial in the Red land you so zealously glorify . . . because, you know as well as I do, that 'The Committee for the First Amendment' was to have been the springboard for a series of attacks against Congressional investigations of Red activities in Hollywood . . . in Labor . . . in Washington . . . in our Armed Forces . . . until it inflamed the people of this country to revolt against our entire form of Government . . . *and advocate its overthrow by violence!!!* That vicious Red Front Organization died a'borning . . . never mind who killed it . . . but that does NOT ABSOLVE you and all the others who created it and worked for its success!"

On October 25, 1947, another meeting was held in the home of Ira Gershwin, at which the "Committee" was launched and sent on its way! The following "eager-beavers" attended that meeting: Evelyn Keyes, John C. Lee, Bernard Feins, Hal Horne, Burt Lancaster, Vincente Minnelli, Arthur H. Singer, Dr. D. N. Poe, Robert Ardrey, Mervyn Le Roy, Sidney Buchman, Jan Strudwick, Marcia Panama, Kirk Douglas, Humphrey Bogart, John Beal, Mortimer Offner, Sy Bartlett, Mrs. Van Heflin, William Wyler, Margaret T. Wyler, Richard Brooks, Leon S. Becker, Chas. Einfeld, John Edward Paxton, Olive Abbott, Richard Conte, Harry Kurnitz, Marsha Hunt Presnell, John Houseman, Irving Yergin, Edward Smith, Joseph Than, Henry Brum, Jane Wyatt, Sheridan Gibney, Lloyd R. Perkins, Edward G. Robinson, Sterling Hayden, Charles Boyer, Melvin G. Frank, Alexander Knox, Evelyn Rideout Rooks, A. Litvak, and Peter Lorre.

A full page advertisement in the Hollywood Reporter . . . also in Variety . . . stated "We are arranging for Radio broadcasts and other steps to protest the conduct of the Washington Hearings." It also contained the names of the Sponsors of "The Committee For the First Amendment", as follows:

Larry Adler, Stephen Morehouse Avery, Geraldine Brooks, Roma Burton, Lauren Bacall, Barbara Bentley, Leonardo Bercovici, Leonard Bernstein, DeWitt Bodeen, Humphrey Bogart, Ann and Moe Braus, Richard Brooks, Jerome Chodorov, Cheryl Crawford, Louis Calhern, Frank Callender, Eddie Cantor, McClure Capps, Warren Cowan, Richard Conte, Norman Corwin, Tom Carlyle, Agnes DeMille, Delmar Daves, Donald Davies, Spencer Davies, Donald Davis, Armand Deutsch, Walter Doniger, I. A. L. Diamond, Muni Diamond, Kirk Douglas, Jay Dratler, Philip Dunne, Howard Duff, Paul Draper, Phoebe and Henry Ephron, Julius Epstein, Philip Epstein, Charles Einfeld, Sylvia Fine, Henry Fonda, Melvin Frank, Irwin Gelsey, Benny Goodman, Ava Gardner, Sheridan Gibney, Paulette Goddard, Michael Gordon, Jay Goldberg, Jesse J. Goldburg, Moss Hart, Rita Hayworth, David Hopkins, Katharine Hepburn, Paul Henreid, Van Heflin, John Huston, John Houseman, Marsha Hunt, Joseph Hoffman, Uta Hagen, Robert L. Joseph, George Kaufman, Norman Krasna, Herbert Kline, Michel Kraike, Isobel Katleman, Arthur Kober, Evelyn Keyes, Gene Kelly, Danny Kaye, J. Richard Kennedy, Harry Kurnitz, Fred Kohlmar, Canada Lee, Anatole Litvak, Burt Lancaster, Herbert Clyde Lewis, Arthur Lubin, Mary Loos, Myrna Loy, Burgess Meredith, Richard Maibaum, David Miller, Frank L. Moss, Margo, Dorothy McGuire, Ivan Moffatt, Joseph Mischel, Dorothy Matthews, Lorie Niblo, N. Richard Nash, Doris Nolan, George Oppenheimer, Ernest Pascal, Vincent Price, Norman Panama, Marion Parsonnet, Frank Partos, Jean Porter, John Paxton, Bob Presnell, Jr., Gregory Peck, Harold Rome, Gladys Robinson, Francis Rosenwald, Irving Rubine, Irving Reis, Stanley Hubin, Sylvia Richards, Henry C. Rogers, Lyle Rooks, Norman and Betsy Rose, Robert Ryan, Irwin Shaw, Richard Sale, George Seaton, John Stone, Allan Scott, Barry Sullivan, Shepperd Sturdwick, Mrs. Leo Spitz, Theodore Strauss, John and Marti Shelton, Robert Shapiro, Joseph Than, Leo Townsend, Don Victor, Bernard Vorhaus, Billy Wilder, Bill Watters, Jerry Wald, and Cornel Wilde.

Now, it is possible that some of those who supported and helped to finance this Front were dupes, but, with very few exceptions, they were all *willing* dupes who knew what it was all about. The complexion of this Front was an open secret from the outset . . . Wm. Z. Foster's presence at the meeting in Milestone's home was an open secret . . . all the organizers were known Reds . . . the general objectives were commonly known. Hence only an absolute moron could have joined this brazen Front under any delusion as to its character.

■ ■ ■ ■

Communist Infiltration of Hollywood Motion-Picture Industry (1951-52), U.S. House of Representatives, Committee on Un-American Activities

The second HUAC investigation began on 8 March 1951, and lasted some fifteen months, generating about 4,500 pages of testimony (the two weeks of 1947 hearings generated about 450). The personnel of the committee had been almost entirely changed, as had the comportment of the witnesses. The first two witnesses set the pattern that would continue for the duration of the hearings. The first witness, Larry Parks (famous for his impersonation of Al Jolson in two biographical films), admitted he was a former member of the Communist party, resisted naming other members for as long as possible, and eventually caved in (during an executive session). Neither Parks nor his wife, the MGM musical-comedy star Betty Garrett, would remain in America; despite his cooperation, Parks's career in Hollywood was finished. The second witness, Howard Da Silva, refused to answer any questions at all pertaining to his political beliefs and associations, standing on the Constitution's Fifth Amendment provision against self-incrimination. Although Da Silva had difficulties finding work for a long while in Hollywood, he has worked (especially in New York) steadily in the years since the hearings; ironically, one of his most frequent and familiar roles has been that of the American patriot Ben Franklin. Much of the testimony of the remaining witnesses seemed to be *déjà vu*. As opposed to the flamboyant 1951–52 sessions, an intentional strategy of the 1951–52 witnesses seemed to have been to bore the public and the press with the hearings, in effect to kill them with dullness.

Public Hearing

The committee met pursuant to call at 10:30 a. m., in room 226, Old House Office Building, Hon. John S. Wood (chairman) presiding.

Committee members present: Representatives John S. Wood (chairman), Francis E. Walter, Morgan M. Moulder, Clyde Doyle, James B. Frazier, Jr., Harold H. Velde, Bernard W. Kearney, and Charles E. Potter.

Staff members present: Frank S. Tavenner, Jr., counsel; Louis J. Russell, senior investigator; John W. Carrington, clerk; and A. S. Poore, editor....

The House Committee on Un-American Activities hearings on *Communist Infiltration of Hollywood Motion-Picture Industry* began 8 March 1951.

TESTIMONY OF LARRY PARKS,
ACCOMPANIED BY HIS COUNSEL, LOUIS MANDEL

MR. TAVENNER. Will you please state your full name, Mr. Parks?

MR. PARKS. Larry Parks.

MR. TAVENNER. Are you represented by counsel?

MR. PARKS. Yes, I am. My counsel is Mr. Mandel.

MR. TAVENNER. Will counsel identify himself?

MR. MANDEL. Louis Mandel, 1501 Broadway, New York City.

In light of the testimony that Mr. Parks will give here he has prepared a statement that he would like to read at this point. I think it is a proper background to the testimony he will give and be very enlightening to the committee as his testimony unfolds. May he read that statement?

MR. WOOD. Is it your purpose, Mr. Tavenner, to ask the witness questions?

MR. TAVENNER. Yes, sir.

MR. WOOD. At the conclusion of his testimony, if he desires to read the statement that has been presented to the members here, he will be given that privilege, or he can put it in the record, as he desires, after he has finished his testimony.

MR. MANDEL. The only reason I asked for it at this point is because I think in light of the testimony it won't have the same effect after as it will when you connect it with the testimony. And I think there is no harm. There is nothing in the statement that can't be connected with the testimony. There is nothing there except the simple statement of facts. And I would, in fairness to the witness, urge very strongly that he be permitted, because there is a connecting link to what he will testify here in this statement, because it is with that spirit that he will testify.

And I think, in proper consideration of the witness and what he will do, this opportunity ought to be given to him, and I urge it very strongly if the committee will consider it.

MR. WOOD. Proceed, Mr. Tavenner.

MR. TAVENNER. Mr. Parks, when and where were you born?

MR. PARKS. I was born on a farm in Kansas. I suppose the legal town would be Olathe. That was the closest town.

MR. TAVENNER. Will you relate briefly to the committee the details regarding your educational background?

MR. PARKS. Well, I was born in Kansas on a farm. I moved when I was quite small to Illinois. I attended the high school in Joliet, Ill., and I also attended and graduated from the University of Illinois, where I majored in chemistry and minored in physics. I sometimes wonder how I got in my present line of work.

MR. TAVENNER. What was the date of the completion of your work at the university?

MR. PARKS. 1936.

MR. TAVENNER. Now, what is your present occupation?

MR. PARKS. Actor.

MR. TAVENNER. What is your present address?

MR. PARKS. 1737 Nichols Canyon, Hollywood, Calif.

MR. TAVENNER. Mr. Parks, I believe you were present when I made a statement as to the purpose of this series of hearings.

MR. PARKS. Yes; I was present, and I heard you.

MR. TAVENNER. Then you understand that we desire to learn the true extent, past and present, of Communist infiltration into the theater field in Hollywood, and the committee asks your cooperation in developing such information. There has been considerable testimony taken before this committee regarding a number of organizations in Hollywood, such as the Actors' Laboratory; Actors' Laboratory Theater; Associated Film Audiences–Hollywood Branch; Citizens' Committee for Motion-Picture Strikers; Film Audiences for Democracy or Associated Film Audiences; Hollywood Anti-Nazi League or Hollywood League Against Nazism; Hollywood Independent Citizens' Committee of the Arts, Sciences, and Professions; Hollywood League for Democratic Action; Hollywood Motion-Picture Democratic Committee; Hollywood Peace Forum; Hollywood Theater Alliance; Hollywood Writers' Mobilization; Motion Picture Artists' Committee; People's Educational Center, Los Angeles; Mooney Defense Committee–Hollywood Unit; Progressive Citizens of America; Hollywood Committee of the Arts, Sciences, and Professions; Council of the PCA; Southern California Chapter of the PCA; Workers School of Los Angeles.

Have you been connected or affiliated in any way with any of those organizations?

MR. PARKS. I have. . . .

MR. TAVENNER. Will you tell the committee whether or not in your experience in Hollywood and as a member of these organizations to which you have testified there were to your knowledge Communists in these various organizations which I have referred to, particularly those that you were a member of?

MR. PARKS. I think I can say "Yes" to that.

MR. TAVENNER. Well, who were these Communists?

MR. PARKS. There were people in the Actors' Lab, for instance—this, in my opinion, was not a Communist organization in any sense of the word. As in any organization, it has all colors of political philosophy. And there were in these I suppose—I know nothing about who belonged other than myself to the Independent Citizens Committee of the Arts, Sciences, and

Professions. This I won't say because I don't know. There were Communists attached to the lab.

MR. TAVENNER. Well, were there Communists attached to these other organizations which you say you were a member of?

MR. PARKS. This I'm not familiar with. I don't know. I don't know who else was a member of them besides myself.

MR. TAVENNER. Your answer is because you do not recall who were members of these other organizations?

MR. PARKS. I think that is the gist of my answer; yes.

MR. TAVENNER. But you do recall that at the Actors' Laboratory there were members of the Communist Party?

MR. PARKS. That's true. . . .

MR. TAVENNER. Well, what was your opportunity to know and to observe the fact that there were Communists in that organization?

MR. PARKS. I knew them as Communists.

MR. TAVENNER. Well, what had been your opportunity to know them as Communists.

MR. PARKS. May I answer this fully and in my own way?

MR. TAVENNER. I would like for you to.

MR. PARKS. All right.

MR. TAVENNER. I hope you will.

MR. PARKS. I am not a Communist. I would like to point out that in my opinion there is a great difference between—and not a subtle difference—between being a Communist, a member of the Communist Party, say in 1941, 10 years ago, and being a Communist in 1951. To my mind this is a great difference and not a subtle one.

It is also, I feel, not a subtle difference to be a member of the Communist Party and being a Communist. I do not believe in my own mind that this is a subtle difference either.

I would furnish you with—I guess you would call it an allegory as to what I mean so that you will see why I say it is not a subtle difference.

The President of this country is a Democrat. He is the head of the Democratic Party. They have a platform, certain aims. There are many people who call themselves Democrats. There are certain southern Democrats, for instance, that do not follow the aims and platform of the Democratic Party as we call it, yet they are called Democrats. Well, in fact, they in my opinion are Republicans really; at least, this is the way they work.

MR. TAVENNER. Well, now, that could be said and a similar analysis could be given of the Progressive Party or any other party, but let us—

MR. PARKS. Yes.

MR. TAVENNER (continuing). Confine ourselves to the question of communism—

MR. PARKS. Yes. Well, I'm drawing an allegory.

MR. TAVENNER (continuing). Rather than speaking in terms of allegory.

MR. PARKS. Well, I felt that it was necessary so that you could see that this is not a subtle difference, you see.

MR. TAVENNER. No; I think the committee can understand by speaking plainly—

MR. PARKS. Yes.

MR. TAVENNER (continuing). And to the point—

MR. PARKS. I'm trying to.

MR. TAVENNER (continuing). On communism.

MR. PARKS. I'm trying to. As I say, I am not a Communist. I was a member of the Communist Party when I was a much younger man, 10 years ago. I was a member of the Communist Party.

MR. TAVENNER. I wish you would tell the committee the circumstances under which you became a member of the Communist Party; that is, when and where and, if you left the Communist Party as you have indicated, when you did it and why you did it.

MR. PARKS. Well, I will do this if I may. I missed one point that I mentioned—that there is also a difference I feel in being a member of the Communist Party in 1941 and being a Communist in 1951. In 1941—all right?

MR. TAVENNER. Go ahead.

MR. PARKS (continuing). Being a member of the Communist Party fulfilled certain needs of a young man that was liberal in thought, idealistic, who was for the underprivileged, the underdog. I felt that it fulfilled these particular needs. I think that being a Communist in 1951 in this particular situation is an entirely different kettle of fish when this is a great power that is trying to take over the world. This is the difference.

I became a Communist—

MR. TAVENNER. Now, just a moment. In other words, you didn't realize that the purpose and object of the Communist Party was to take over other segments of the world in 1941, but you do realize that that is true in 1951? Is that the point you are making?

MR. PARKS. Well, I would like to say this: That this is in no way an apology for anything that I have done, you see, because I feel I have done nothing wrong ever. Question of judgment? This is debatable. I feel that as far as I am concerned that in 1941, as far as I knew it, the purposes as I knew them fulfilled simply—at least I thought they would fulfill as I said before—certain idealism, certain being for the underdog, which I am today this very minute.

This did not work out particularly this way. I wasn't particularly interested in it after I did become a member. I attended very few meetings, and I drifted away from it the same way that—I petered out the same way I drifted into it. To the best of my recollection, as I recall—the dates are not exact because at that particular time it wasn't an important step one way or the other; I feel as I say that the dates are approximate—it was in 1941, and to the best of my recollection I petered out about the latter part of 1944 or 1945. . . .

MR. POTTER. Who would call the meetings together?

MR. PARKS. Well, I don't really know. I can't really answer this.

MR. POTTER. Did you have a set, scheduled meeting once every month or once every week, or was it upon the call of some individual?

MR. PARKS. Well, as I recall, various individuals would call. I don't believe that there was any set—

MR. POTTER. Certainly it wasn't run by mental telepathy.

MR. PARKS. No; I didn't say that. I say certain individuals would call, and to the best of my knowledge there was no set schedule of meetings.

MR. POTTER. Somebody had to issue a call?

MR. PARKS. That's correct.

MR. POTTER. Did you ever issue a call for your cell to get together?

MR. PARKS. Did I?

MR. POTTER. Yes.

MR. PARKS. No, I didn't.

MR. POTTER. Then, somebody would have to tell you when the meetings would take place and where they would take place; is that not true?

MR. PARKS. That's correct. I would get a call from a member of the group and they would say, "Well, let's have a meeting tonight, tomorrow night."

MR. KEARNEY. Were the meetings always held at the same place?

MR. PARKS. No; they were not.

MR. KEARNEY. Were they held in halls or in your own homes?

MR. PARKS. These were held at homes. As I say—

MR. KEARNEY. Did you ever have any meetings at your own home?

MR. PARKS. Never.

MR. KEARNEY. Where were some of the meetings held?

MR. PARKS. If I might add as a word of explanation, that these were people like myself, small type people, no different than myself in any respect at all, and no different than you or I.

MR. KEARNEY. Where were some of these meetings held?

MR. PARKS. As I say, these were held in various homes in Hollywood.

MR. KEARNEY. Can you name some of them?

MR. PARKS. Well, as I asked the counsel and as I asked the committee, if you will allow this. I would prefer not to mention names under these circumstances: That these were people like myself who—and I feel that I—have done nothing wrong ever. I mean along this line. I am sure none of us is perfect. Again, the question of judgment certainly is there, and even that is debatable. But these are people—

MR. WOOD. Just a moment. At that point, do you entertain the feeling that these other parties that you were associated with are likewise guilt-less of any wrong?

MR. PARKS. The people at that time as I knew them—this is my opinion of them. This is my honest opinion: That these are people who did nothing wrong, people like myself.

MR. WOOD. Mr. Parks, in what way do you feel it would be injurious, then, to them to divulge their identities, when you expressed the opinion that at no time did they do wrong?

MR. PARKS. This brings up many questions on a personal basis, Mr. Congressman, as an actor. If you think it's easy for a man who has—I think I have worked hard in my profession, climbed up the ladder a bit. If you think it's easy for me to appear before this committee and testify, you're mistaken, because it's not easy. This is a very difficult and arduous job for me for many reasons.

One of the reasons is that as an actor my activity is dependent a great deal on the public. To be called before this committee at your request has a certain inference, a certain innuendo that you are not loyal to this country. This is not true. I am speaking for myself. This is not true. But the inference and the innuendo is there as far as the public is concerned.

Also as a representative of a great industry—not as an official represen-tative; I don't mean it that way—but as an actor of the motion-picture in-dustry that is fairly well known, in that respect I am a representative of the industry. This is a great industry. At this particular time it is being investigated for Communist influence.

MR. WOOD. Don't you think the public is entitled to know about it?

MR. PARKS. Hmm?

MR. WOOD. Don't you feel the public is entitled to know about it?

MR. PARKS. I certainly do, and I am opening myself wide open to you to any question that you can ask me. I will answer as honestly as I know how. And at this particular time, as I say, the industry is—it's like taking a pot shot at a wounded animal, because the industry is not in as good a shape today as it has been, economically I'm speaking. It has been pretty tough on it. And, as I say, this is a great industry, and I don't say this only because it has been kind to me. It has a very important job to do to enter-tain people, in certain respects to call attention to certain evils, but mainly to entertain, and in this I feel that they have done a great job. Always when our country has needed certain help, the industry has been in the forefront of that help.

MR. TAVENNER. Mr. Chairman, may I make an observation?

MR. WOOD. Yes.

MR. TAVENNER. You are placing your reluctance to testify upon the great job that the moving-picture industry is doing or can do?

MR. PARKS. Excuse me, Mr. Counsel. I really hadn't finished, and that was just part of it. If you'd let me finish, then—Is that all right?

MR. TAVENNER. Very well.

MR. PARKS. That's one part of it. On the question of naming names, it is my honest opinion that the few people that I could name, these names would not be of service to the committee at all. I am sure that you know who they are. These people I feel honestly are like myself, and I feel that I have done nothing wrong. Question of judgment? Yes, perhaps. And I also feel that this is not—to be asked to name names like this is not—in the way of American justice as we know it, that we as Americans have all been brought up, that it is a bad thing to force a man to do this. I have been brought up that way. I am sure all of you have.

And it seems to me that this is not the American way of doing things— to force a man who is under oath and who has opened himself as wide as possible to this committee—and it hasn't been easy to do this—to force a man to do this is not American justice.

I perhaps later can think of more things to say when I leave, but this is in substance I guess what I want to say.

MR. WOOD. Well, I am glad, of course, to give considerable leeway to the range of your statement, because I for one am rather curious to understand just what the reasons are in your mind for declining to answer the question.

MR. PARKS. I'm not declining. I'm asking you if you would not press me on this. . . .

To be an actor, a good actor, you must really feel and experience, from the top of your head to the tip of your toes, what you are doing. As I told you, this is probably the most difficult morning and afternoon I have spent, and I wish that if it was at all possible—you see, it is a little different to sit there and to sit here, and for a moment if you could transfer places with me, mentally, and put yourself in my place.

My people have a long heritage in this country. They fought in the Revolutionary War to make this country, to create this Government, of which this committee is a part. I have two boys, one 13 months, one 2 weeks. Is this the kind of heritage that I must hand down to them? Is this the kind of heritage that you would like to hand down to your children? And for what purpose? Children as innocent as I am or you are; people you already know.

I don't think I would be here today if I weren't a star, because you know as well as I, even better, that I know nothing that I believe would be of great service to this country. I think my career has been ruined because of this, and I would appreciate not having to—don't present me with the choice of either being in contempt of this committee and going to jail or forcing me to really crawl through the mud to be an informer, for what purpose? I don't think this is a choice at all. I don't think this is really sportsmanlike. I don't think this is American. I don't think this is American justice. I think to do something like that is more akin to what happened under Hitler, and what is happening in Russia today.

I don't think this is American justice for an innocent mistake in judgment, if it was that, with the intention behind it only of making this country a better place in which to live. I think it is not befitting for this committee to force me to make this kind of a choice. I don't think it is befitting to the purpose of the committee to do.

As I told you, I think this is probably the most difficult thing I have done, and its seems to me it would impair the usefulness of this committee to do this, because God knows it is difficult enough to come before this committee, and tell the truth. There was another choice open to me. I did not choose to use it. I chose to come and tell the truth.

If you do this to me, I think it will impair the usefulness of this committee to a great extent, because it will make it almost impossible for a person to come to you, as I have done, and open himself to you and tell you the truth. So I beg of you not to force me to do this.

MR. WOOD. Proceed. . . .

Testimony Resumed in Executive Session

MR. TAVENNER. Who were the members of the cell of the Communist Party to which you were assigned during the period from 1941 on up to the time you disassociated yourself from the Party about 1945?

MR. PARKS. This is what I have been talking about. This is the thing that I am no longer fighting for myself, because I tell you frankly that I am probably the most completely ruined man that you have ever seen. I am fighting for a principle, I think, if Americanism is involved in this particular case. This is what I have been talking about. I do not believe that it befits this Committee to force me to do this. I do not believe it befits this Committee or its purposes to force me to do this. This is my honest feeling about it. I don't think that this is fair play. I don't think it is in the spirit of real Americanism. These are not people that are a danger to this country, gentlemen, the people that I knew. These are people like myself.

MR. TAVENNER. Mr. Chairman, if the witness refuses to answer the question, I see very little use in my asking him about other individuals.

MR. WOOD. The witness, of course, has got to make up his own mind as to whether he will or will not do it. It isn't sufficient, as far as this Committee is concerned, to say that in your opinion it is unfair or un-American. The question is: Do you refuse to answer or will you answer it?

MR. MANDEL. At this point I would like to ask the Chairman whether he is directing the witness to answer.

MR. WOOD. The witness has been asked. He must answer or decline to answer.

MR. MANDEL. I think a little more is needed. He must be directed to answer, and if he refuses to answer, just merely asking him and not going beyond I don't believe under law is sufficient. I think he has to be directed and told, "You have got to answer."

MR. WOOD. I don't understand any such rule, but, in order to avoid any controversy, I direct the witness to answer the question.

MR. PARKS. I do not refuse to answer the question, but I do feel that this Committee is doing a really dreadful thing that I don't believe the American people will look kindly on. This is my opinion. I don't think that they will consider this as honest, just, and in the spirit of fair play.

MR. JACKSON. Mr. Chairman, might I interpose at this point? Mr. Parks, we are, each one of us, individually responsible to the American people. I think that our concept of our responsibility is a thing which we ourselves are fully conscious of. That determination must rest with the individual members of the Committee and the Committee as a whole. I, for one, resent having my duties pointed out to me.

MR. PARKS. I am not pointing the duty out.

MR. JACKSON. The inference is that we are doing something which is un-American in nature. That is a personal opinion of yours, and I merely think that it should be in the record. We have accountability for which we must account and for which we must answer.

MR. WOOD. The witness has said he doesn't refuse to answer, so I assume he is ready to answer.

MR. MANDEL. I think the Committee and the individual members of the Committee are all seeking within themselves to do the right thing. There is no question about that. I think, in the same spirit, no one can, with the heritage that Mr. Parks has to uphold, think that he isn't as loyal as any member of this Committee, and that he has to do the right thing as we Americans in our elections do and choose. Of course, when the final gong goes down, he intends, as he indicated, to respect the will of this Committee, but, I think justly, he reserves the right to talk to you gentlemen and possibly persuade you to think differently.

MR. WOOD. The Committee took the view, sir, that perhaps there might be some merit in your contention if we were still in an open hearing, but we are not. It is an executive session.

MR. MANDEL. I realize that, and I want to thank the Committee for this consideration. I think it should have been done first before we started here, but this session is a very private session or executive session, which is very considerate of the Committee, and the record should so state. May I have a minute to talk to Mr. Parks?

MR. WOOD. Yes. You may retire if you like.

MR. MANDEL. I make this request of the Committee: I want no promise from you, but just as a matter of finding what is the sportsmanlike attitude, that what he gives you will not be used in that way if it can be helped, without embarrassing these people in the same position he finds himself in today.

MR. WOOD. Nobody on this Committee has any desire to smear the name of anybody. That isn't of benefit to this Committee in the discharge of its duties. I think all of the American people who have viewed the work of the Committee dispassionately and impartially will agree with that.

MR. MANDEL. The reason I asked is because, in the struggle that Mr. Parks is going through, I think the internal struggle would go a little lighter having that statement from you.

MR. TAVENNER. If you will just answer the question, please. The question was: Who were the members of the Communist Party cell to which you were assigned during the period from 1941 until 1945?

MR. PARKS. Well, Morris Carnovsky, Joe—

MR. TAVENNER. Will you spell that name?

MR. PARKS. I couldn't possibly spell it. Carnovsky, Joe Bromberg, Sam Rossen, Anne Revere, Lee Cobb.

MR. TAVENNER. What was the name?

MR. PARKS. Cobb. Gale Sondergaard, Dorothy Tree. Those are the principal names that I recall.

MR. TAVENNER. What was the name of Dorothy Tree's husband? Was it not Michael Uris?

MR. PARKS. Yes.

MR. TAVENNER. Was he a member?

MR. PARKS. Not to my knowledge.

MR. TAVENNER. Do you know whether Michael Uris was a member of any other cell of the Communist Party?

MR. PARKS. No, I don't know this at all. . . .

MR. TAVENNER. Can you recall the names of others who were at one time members of that cell?

MR. PARKS. That's about all I recall right now.

MR. TAVENNER. Was Howard Da Silva a member?

MR. PARKS. No, I don't believe that I ever attended a meeting with Howard Da Silva.

MR. TAVENNER. Was Howard Da Silva a member of the Communist Party, to your knowledge?

MR. PARKS. Not to my knowledge. . . .

MR. TAVENNER. Was James Cagney a member at any time?

MR. PARKS. Not to my knowledge. I don't recall ever attending a meeting with him.

MR. TAVENNER. Was he a member of the Communist Party, to your knowledge?

MR. PARKS. I don't recall ever hearing that he was.

MR. TAVENNER. Sam Jaffe?

MR. PARKS. I don't recall ever attending a meeting with Sam Jaffe.

MR. TAVENNER. Was he a member of the Communist Party, to your knowledge?

MR. PARKS. I don't recall any knowledge that Sam Jaffe was ever a member of the Communist Party.

MR. TAVENNER. John Garfield?

MR. PARKS. I don't recall ever being at a meeting with John Garfield.

MR. TAVENNER. Do you recall whether John Garfield ever addressed a Communist Party meeting when you were present?

MR. PARKS. I don't recall any such occasion. . . .

MR. MANDEL. May I suggest to counsel, in view of the general feeling of the witness—I don't mean to rush you, but this whole thing being so distasteful—I wonder if we can proceed a little faster so he doesn't suffer so much while this is going on.

MR. TAVENNER. I want him to be accurate on it. I purposely do not want to rush him into answering about matters as important as these.

MR. MANDEL. I didn't mean that. I am just trying to be considerate of the man's feeling, doing something that—

MR. TAVENNER. I asked you this morning about Karen Morley. Was she a member of the Communist Party?

MR. PARKS. Yes, she was.

MR. TAVENNER. Was she in this particular cell that you have described?

MR. PARKS. Yes, she was.

MR. TAVENNER. Richard Collins, were you acquainted with him?

MR. PARKS. I know Richard Collins. He was not to my knowledge a member of the Communist Party.

(At this point Representative Clyde Doyle left the hearing room.)

MR. TAVENNER. Did Communist Party organizers from the State of California appear before your committee from time to time?

MR. PARKS. Not to the best of my recollection. I don't believe I ever met any of them or ever saw any of them.

MR. TAVENNER. Were lectures given at any time or study courses given in your cell in which persons outside of your cell took part?

MR. PARKS. The only one that I recall at this time was a talk by John Howard Lawson.

MR. TAVENNER. What was John Howard Lawson's connection with the Communist Party?

MR. PARKS. I don't really know. . . .

MR. TAVENNER. Sterling Hayden?

MR. PARKS. No, I don't recall ever being at a meeting with Sterling Hayden.

MR. TAVENNER. Will Geer?

MR. PARKS. No, I don't recall ever being in a meeting with Will Geer.

MR. TAVENNER. Victor Killian, Sr.?

MR. PARKS. Yes, I recall that he attended at least one meeting.

MR. TAVENNER. Victor Killian, Jr.?

MR. PARKS. I don't believe I am acquainted with the gentleman at all.

MR. TAVENNER. Lionel Stander?

MR. PARKS. I have met him. I don't recall ever attending a meeting with him.

MR. TAVENNER. Andy Devine?

MR. PARKS. I don't recall ever attending a meeting with Andy Devine.

MR. TAVENNER. Edward G. Robinson?

MR. PARKS. No, I don't recall ever attending a meeting with Edward G. Robinson. . . .

MR. TAVENNER. Gregory Peck?

MR. PARKS. I have no remembrance of ever attending a meeting with Gregory Peck.

MR. TAVENNER. Humphrey Bogart?

MR. PARKS. I don't recall ever attending a meeting with Humphrey Bogart.

(*At this point Representative Donald L. Jackson left the hearing room.*)

MR. WALTER. I think you could get some comfort out of the fact that the people whose names have been mentioned have been subpoenaed, so that if they ever do appear here it won't be as a result of anything that you have testified to.

(*At this point Representative Bernard W. Kearney left the hearing room.*)

MR. PARKS. It is no comfort whatsoever.

MR. TAVENNER. Do you know of any other person now whose name comes to your recollection?

MR. PARKS. No, I don't recall anyone else.

MR. TAVENNER. I think that is all, Mr. Chairman.

MR. POTTER. I would like to say, Mr. Chairman, that Mr. Parks's testimony has certainly been refreshing in comparison with the other witnesses that we have had today.

MR. WOOD. I am sure you reflect the sentiments of the entire Committee. We appreciate your cooperation. You are excused.

TESTIMONY OF HOWARD DA SILVA,
ACCOMPANIED BY ROBERT W. KENNY AND BEN MARGOLIS, AS COUNSEL

MR. TAVENNER. Will you state your full name, please?

MR. DA SILVA. I would like to voice my objection now, if I may.

MR. TAVENNER. Will you state your full name, please?

MR. DA SILVA. May I not voice my objection?

MR. TAVENNER. You have not yet been identified in the record.

MR. DA SILVA. My name is Howard Da Silva. I was born Howard Silverblatt. I was born in Cleveland, Ohio, May 4, 1909.

MR. TAVENNER. Will you furnish the committee, please, with a brief résumé of your educational background.

MR. DA SILVA. Mr. Chairman, I have a statement which I would like very much to make. It has been announced in the press that this committee has as its purpose complete objectivity, and I think in the face of that it is quite important that I present my own statement here for clarity and for objectivity. Here is the statement I would like to present [handing statement to counsel].

MR. TAVENNER. Is this the same statement that counsel sent in to the committee a while ago?

MR. KENNY. No; I don't think we sent a statement in. It may be a statement of which you have seen a copy.

MR. TAVENNER. Is it a statement that was given to the press?

MR. DA SILVA. It was given to the press.

MR. WOOD. This is a statement that you released to the press?

MR. DA SILVA. What is that?

MR. WOOD. This statement you now desire to read is a statement that you released to the press?

MR. DA SILVA. Simultaneously with my appearance; yes.

MR. WOOD. Let's see if I understand you correctly. When did you release this statement which you now propose to read?

MR. DA SILVA. I was called here at 10 o'clock this morning.

MR. WOOD. When did you release the statement to the press?

MR. DA SILVA. Shortly after I arrived here.

MR. WOOD. Shortly after 10, and it is now after 3. In the light of the fact it has been given this wide publicity, I see no purpose in burdening the record with a repetition of it.

MR. DA SILVA. My purpose is not to burden the record. My purpose is to achieve the kind of objectivity which was originally stated to the press by this committee.

MR. WOOD. Proceed with the questions.

MR. DA SILVA. I don't follow you. Did you say my statement was not to be read?

MR. WOOD. Yes, sir.

MR. DA SILVA. It is not to be read.

MR. TAVENNER. My question was, Will you please furnish the committee a brief statement of your educational background?

MR. DA SILVA. At this point, may I object to being called to testify against myself in this hearing. I object because the first and fifth amendments and all of the Bill of Rights protect me from any inquisitorial procedure, and I may not be compelled to cooperate with this committee in producing evidence designed to incriminate me and to drive me from my profession as an actor. The historical—

MR. WOOD. Would an answer to that question incriminate you? You were asked to furnish a statement of your educational background. Would a true answer to that question incriminate you? If so, you have a right to protect yourself.

MR. DA SILVA. You want me to make this objection at a time when I think an answer to the question will incriminate me?

MR. WOOD. If a true answer to any question asked you by counsel or any member of this committee would tend to incriminate you and you so swear, you have a right to claim it, as I understand the law.

MR. MARGOLIS. It is our position that this witness is in the same position as a defendant, and I think he should be allowed to complete this objection.

MR. WOOD. He is not a defendant here. He is a witness.

MR. MARGOLIS. It is our contention that he is and will suffer the consequences and pains in many respects.

MR. WOOD. He will suffer the consequences of testifying falsely, if he does so. If he refuses to answer without valid ground, he is subjecting himself, as you well know, to a proceeding for contempt of Congress. It is a matter you can advise him about. You have that privilege any time you want.

MR. TAVENNER. Now, will you answer the question, please?

MR. DA SILVA. I attended the public schools of New York City; Bronx High School; and for a term, City College of New York.

MR. TAVENNER. When did you spend a term in City College of New York?

MR. DA SILVA. I was born in 1909. I was about 17. That would make it about 1926.

I also attended Carnegie Tech in Pittsburgh for a short semester, working through college by working in the Jones & Laughlin steel mill.

MR. TAVENNER. What is your present address?

MR. DA SILVA. My present address is 936 North Stanley Avenue, Hollywood 46, Calif.

MR. TAVENNER. And what is your present occupation?

MR. DA SILVA. My present occupation is acting.

MR. TAVENNER. Have you ever held the position of vice president of the Civil Rights Congress, that is, the New York chapter of the Civil Rights Congress?

MR. DA SILVA. Mr. Chairman, it is very clearly the object of this committee to tie me in with organizations which are in its disfavor, and therefore I object, and now I will tell you my objection.

MR. WOOD. We are not interested in your objection. We are interested in knowing whether you will answer the question.

MR. DA SILVA. I refuse to answer the question on the following basis: The first and fifth amendments and all of the Bill of Rights protect me from any inquisitorial procedure, and I may not be compelled to co-operate with this committee in producing evidence designed to incriminate me and to drive me from my profession as an actor. The historical origin of the fifth amendment is founded in the resistance of the people to attempts to prosecute and persecute individuals because of—

MR. WOOD. Will you please wait a moment? Please ascribe to the committee the intelligence to determine these questions for itself, and don't argue about it.

MR. DA SILVA. I don't care to argue about it, but I wish to clarify my position.

MR. WOOD. You need not teach this committee a class in law.

MR. DA SILVA. It is not my position. It is my position to uphold the law and to make sure the committee does.

MR. WOOD. If you say you decline to answer for the reasons given, it will be understood.

MR. TAVENNER. Do you refuse to answer the question?

MR. DA SILVA. I refuse to answer the question on the basis of my statement here, on the basis that my answer might, according to the standards of this committee, tend to incriminate me. . . .

TESTIMONY OF ABRAHAM POLONSKY

MR. TAVENNER. There have been several witnesses who have appeared before the committee during the course of these hearings who have described their own participation and membership in the Communist Party, and who have also made reference to your alleged membership in the Communist Party, and who have referred to meetings of the Communist Party which were held in your home. The committee is inquiring into these activities, and I would like to ask you this specific question: The witness, Mr. Sterling Hayden, as appears on page 34 of the transcript of his testimony, was asked this question:

> Question. Do you know an individual by the name of Abe Polonsky?
>
> MR. HAYDEN. Yes. The meetings were frequently held at Abe's house.
>
> Question. Was he a member of this group?
>
> MR. HAYDEN. He was later. About the time I terminated he began to show up at meetings. In the early stages of the proceedings he did not sit in on these meetings as I remember it.
>
> Question. Was he known to you as a member of the Communist Party, from your association with him?
>
> MR. HAYDEN. Yes.

Do you desire to affirm, deny, or explain in any manner the statement made by Mr. Hayden under oath?

MR. POLONSKY. I have indicated to counsel here that I am going to refuse to answer all such questions on the grounds previously stated.

MR. WOOD. Do you refuse to answer this question?

MR. POLONSKY. I refuse to answer this question on the grounds previously stated.

MR. TAVENNER. The witness Mrs. Meta Rosenberg testified before this committee on April 13—Mr. Sterling Hayden having testified on April 10—and at page 73 of the transcript Mrs. Rosenberg is shown to have been asked this question:

> Tell us who were in this second group, and in giving us the names of them, state also whether or not they were connected with the Hollywood Writers' Mobilization, and if you can recall, in what capacity.

By the "second group," previous to that question I had asked her what she meant by second group by this question: "Of the Communist Party?" to which she replied, "Yes."

Then, to the question I read, Mrs. Rosenberg made this answer:

> Well, the first one that comes to my mind, the most natural one, of course, is Robert Rossen, who was the second chairman of the Mobilization.
>
> There was Abe Polonsky. I don't know that he had any special job in the Mobilization. He did a good deal of work. He is a very brilliant writer.

MR. POLONSKY. What is the date of that, sir?

MR. TAVENNER. The date is April 13, the date of her testimony.

MR. POLONSKY. I refuse to answer that question on the grounds previously stated.

MR. TAVENNER. You were associated with and connected with the Hollywood Writers' Mobilization, were you not?

MR. POLONSKY. I refuse to answer that question on the grounds previously stated.

MR. TAVENNER. The witness Richard Collins testified before this committee on April 12, 1951, and on page 69 of the transcript it appears that this question was asked:

> QUESTION. Were you acquainted with a person by the name of Abe Polonsky?
> MR. COLLINS. Yes.
> QUESTION. Was he known to you to be a member of the Communist Party?
> MR. COLLINS. Yes.

Do you desire to offer any explanation by way of affirmation or denial of that statement?

MR. POLONSKY. I refuse to answer that question on the grounds previously stated?

MR. TAVENNER. Are you acquainted in California with a person by the name of Sidney Benson, or Sid Benson?

MR. POLONSKY. I refuse to answer that question on the grounds previously stated.

MR. TAVENNER. Were you acquainted with a person by the name of Naomi Willett, W-i-l-l-e-t-t, often referred to as Betty Willett?

MR. POLONSKY (after consulting his counsel). To the best of my knowledge I have no recollection of that name or any name like that.

MR. TAVENNER. Do you recall of such person ever coming to your home?

MR. POLONSKY. I have no recollection whatsoever of any such person, even the existence of any such person.

MR. TAVENNER. Do you recall a meeting in your home attended by Waldo Salt, Samuel Moore—

MR. WOOD. Spell it.

MR. TAVENNER. Waldo Salt, S-a-l-t-; Samuel Moore; John Stapp, S-t-a-p-p; Charles Glenn; and John Howard Lawson. And in asking you this question, it has no relationship to the individual about whom I asked you a moment ago.

MR. POLONSKY. I refuse to answer that question on the grounds previously stated.

MR. TAVENNER. Were you affiliated with the Council of the Arts, Sciences, and Professions as a member of its steering committee in 1950?

MR. POLONSKY. I refuse to answer that question on the grounds previously stated. Those are all organizations that have been characterized by this committee—

MR. TAVENNER. As Communist-front organizations. Were you affiliated with any such organizations?

MR. POLONSKY. I refuse to answer that question on the grounds previously stated.

MR. TAVENNER. Will you state to the committee what the purposes of any of these organizations were, such as the one I just mentioned, the Council of the Arts, Sciences, and Professions?

MR. POLONSKY (after consulting his counsel). I refuse to answer that question on the grounds previously stated.

MR. TAVENNER. Are you a member of the Communist Party at this time?

MR. POLONSKY. I refuse to answer that question on the grounds previously stated.

MR. TAVENNER. I have no further questions, Mr. Chairman. . . .

MR. WOOD. Mr. Velde.

MR. VELDE. Mr. Polonsky, is your wife's name Sylvia Morrow?

MR. POLONSKY. Sylvia Marrow, M-a-r-r-o-w.

MR. VELDE. Did you formerly live in New York City?

MR. POLONSKY. Yes, sir.

MR. VELDE. You and your wife?

MR, POLONSKY. Yes, sir.

MR. VELDE. Did you move to Los Angeles about 1944?

MR. POLONSKY. No, sir. Well, I am not sure about that. I took up residence in Los Angeles myself, that is, when I returned from the war, and my wife came at some other period, I think while I was overseas. There was a period of 2 weeks in the early part of 1944 when I went to Paramount to get a cover story for my departure abroad, and to explain why I could not continue under my motion-picture contract, and I also got my shots.

MR. VELDE. Is your wife a member of the Communist Party?

MR. POLONSKY. I refuse to answer that question on the grounds previously stated.

MR. VELDE. Do you have any knowledge that there is a Communist movement in Hollywood?

MR. POLONSKY. That seems to go to the general sense of the questions which I said that I must not answer in order not to incriminate myself, sir, and I refuse to answer that question.

MR. VELDE. Mr. Polonsky, in refusing to answer these questions, I presume you know that you leave us—or me, at least—with the impression that you have been and still are a member of the Communist Party.

Further than that, in refusing to answer whether or not you signed a loyalty oath when you went into OSS, you leave me with the impression that you are a very dangerous citizen. That is all.

MR. POLONSKY. Do you wish me to comment upon that, sir? When I cite the fifth amendment in order not to incriminate myself, I am not affirming or denying anything. I am doing that because of the context of things today.

MR. WOOD. I am unwilling to let that statement go unchallenged. When a man says, in answer to a question of whether or not he is a member of an organization that has been cited by an arm of this Government as subversive, that he refuses to answer on grounds of self-incrimination, he means one of two things to any reasonable person, either that if he tells the truth he is a member, or that if he denied membership he perjures himself.

I am not willing to let the statement go unchallenged that your answer might be "No." It would either, in your opinion, incriminate you to answer it truthfully, or your statement that you hide behind the fifth amendment is a false statement. So let's not have any misunderstanding about that.

MR. POLONSKY. But that is not the meaning of the fifth amendment as I understand it and as the courts have stated it. It is one of the most basic and fundamental rights under the Constitution.

MR. WOOD. Absolutely, and no member of this committee seeks to place any impediment in the way of anyone using it, but when he uses it and then says he leaves the inference he is not a member of the organization interrogated about, it doesn't make sense.

MR. POLONSKY. I am not trying to leave that implication. The Founding Fathers wrote the fifth amendment for this type of interrogation. Am I right about that?

MR. WALTER. No, no, no; you are not right at all. I suggest you read the debates. That was not the purpose of the fifth amendment at all.

MR. POLONSKY. As I remember, the special courts of inquiry at that time, the inquisitorial courts, the Founding Fathers, had the idea that such a thing might occur, that people might be brought up under subpena or some other way and forced to speak about things that might incriminate them about their political ideas, their conscience, their morality, their feelings, and it was felt at that time—and I feel it very deeply myself —that what the Constitution means, what the fifth and first amendments mean, is that this is a kind of country where there is thorough freedom for those things. And it doesn't seem to me the committee should attempt to characterize my answers, where I use the fifth amendment, as Mr. Velde does when he says he thinks I am a dangerous man.

MR. WALTER. You would with one breath use the fifth amendment, and with the second breath deprive us of our right to reach a conclusion.

MR. POLONSKY. I am not trying to deprive you of any right.

MR. WALTER. You do deprive us of our right to reach the conclusion stated by Mr. Velde, and I think he speaks for all of us.

MR. KEARNEY. Do you think the Founding Fathers had in mind the ultimate formation of the Committee on Un-American Activities?

MR. POLONSKY. I don't know, sir, but this committee has, in its actions —and I am not characterizing this committee—

MR. KEARNEY. Mr. Chairman, I see no reason to ask further questions of this witness. He is following a pattern that apparently has been rehearsed by witness after witness.

MR. POLONSKY. It is not rehearsed. When you ask questions and cut me off in the middle of my answer—I don't know. I am willing to talk about anything that—

MR. KEARNEY. You are willing to talk; there is no question about that.

MR. WOOD. Mr. Jackson.

MR. JACKSON. Have you ever been associated with an organization known as the Silver Shirts?

MR. POLONSKY. I have not.

MR. JACKSON. Were you ever associated with an organization called the Communist Party?

MR. POLONSKY. I refuse to answer that on the ground previously stated.

MR. JACKSON. You make a very fine distinction?

MR. POLONSKY. That is a very broad distinction.

MR. JACKSON. There is no distinction at all. You are perfectly willing to crawl under the umbrella of the fifth amendment so far as the Communist Party is concerned but, so long as your toes are not trod upon in the realm of the Communist Party, you have no hesitation in answering questions about the Silver Shirts or fascism or nazism.

MR. POLONSKY. You draw the implication. . . .

■ ■ ■ ■

REPORT ON BLACKLISTING (1956), John Cogley

John Cogley's *Report on Blacklisting* was published in 1956 when the blacklist was still in effect. The two-part work (the first part devoted to movies, the second to television, radio, and other entertainment fields)

John Cogley, *Report on Blacklisting* (Fund for the Republic, 1956).

was supported and published by the Fund for the Republic, an organization closely related in spirit and personnel to the Commission on Freedom of the Press that had sponsored *Freedom of the Movies* nine years earlier. Cogley's work generated such controversy that the HUAC began an investigation of blacklisting that focused more on how and why Cogley wrote his study than on the conditions and practices he described. Many of those whom Cogley cited as performing various functions in connection with the blacklist (such as George Sokolsky of this excerpt) emphatically denied Cogley's allegations; despite these denials, Cogley's citations and investigations have gained acceptance and credibility with the passing of time. These sections from Cogley's study summarize the 1951–52 hearings and describe the blacklist that resulted from it.

Hollywood reacted to news of the impending investigation in 1951 with something like panic. A *Life* reporter wired her editor at the time that the movie people put her in mind of "a group of marooned sailors on a flat desert island watching the approach of a tidal wave." The industry was not sure it could take another investigation, which would inevitably bring on more "revelations" and bad publicity and might mean picket lines around the nation's movies houses. To add to this anxiety, business was spectacularly bad. In 1946 domestic film rental stood at a dizzy $400 million; weekly movie attendance climbed to an all-time record of 80 million. But by 1951 television was a going thing and movie attendance was in the lower depths of a decline that finally, about February 1953, levelled off at 46 million.

In the lush days of World War II movie companies had expanded enormously, buying up vast studio facilities and adding to their rosters of high-priced talent. All the major studios had stockpiled costly films. Things looked black indeed. Although the slump lasted for seven years, its most severe effects were felt in the period between Congressional probes. These were years marked by big lay-offs and frequent theater closings. The movie companies were finding it difficult to get bank credit and dreaded the consequences of political controversy. What banker in his right mind would put up the money for a picture that might be picketed because one of its stars had the habit of signing petitions? Trouble had piled up on trouble for the moviemakers. When the government won an antitrust action and theater chains were separated from their distributor-producer owners, the industry—as *Fortune* magazine put it—"began to feel like a man with a loud humming sound in his head."

In March, 1951, just before the hearings began, *Variety* reported that in New York, Joyce O'Hara, acting president of the Motion Picture Association, had met with studio advertising and publicity heads and announced that movie people who did not firmly deny communistic ties would find it "difficult" to get work in the studios after the hearings closed. The Association had no intention of repeating the mistakes that had made Hollywood look foolish in 1947.

The House Committee on Un-American Activities was different too. In December, 1949, J. Parnell Thomas was convicted of payroll padding and was later reunited with members of the Hollywood Ten in prison. If the film industry managed to salvage any consolation from that, it was short-lived. For this time the Committee returned to the subject of Communism-in-Hollywood under new auspices (Georgia's John S. Wood had succeeded Thomas as chairman) and vastly changed circumstances.

In 1947 the wartime friendship between the U.S. and Russia was still a fresh memory. By 1951 U.S. soldiers were at war in Korea with the forces of two Communist powers and the Cold War with Russia was at its height. With the Hiss-Chambers, Klaus Fuchs and Judith Coplon cases behind it, the nation was becoming ever more security-conscious and, in the opinion of many, was afflicted with a bad case of political jitters. A Senator named McCarthy was becoming a front-page fixture. And, above all, the House Committee itself had a spanking new policy implemented by the Committee's new research director, an ex-FBI man named Raphael I. Nixon. Nixon, comparing the 1947 with the later hearings not long ago, commended Parnell Thomas' work but said it was unfortunate that in 1947 the Committee had focussed its attack on movie content, "the weakest argument."

Parnell Thomas' pursuit of Communist propaganda in films admittedly had led the Committee up a blind alley. In Nixon's opinion, the 1947 Committee could have centered a more pertinent and fruitful enquiry on the "prestige, position and money" the Communist Party picked up in Hollywood. And that is what the Committee went looking for in 1951.

Hollywood was chosen for a "broad base investigation," Nixon explained to a reporter, because of the volume of cooperation the Committee got there. But a critical Democratic Congressman whose district borders on the movie capital once suggested another reason. "The yearning for publicity on the part of some members of the Committee," he said, "could only be satisfied by the famous names a movie hearing would produce." Nixon recognizes that such charges were made against the Committee but argues that it was the newspapers rather than the Committee itself which put the emphasis on big names. "We couldn't overlook our responsibilities just because prominent people were involved."

By 1951, a number of prominent persons were begging the Committee for a chance to testify and the Committee had to disappoint some of them. There were, first of all, the ex-Communists, who by now looked upon the hearings as the only public forum open to them. If they wanted to prove to the world that they had broken with the Party, they had to testify. And until they did prove this, they were unemployable in the studios. The Committee welcomed them. But another class—persons who had never belonged to the Communist Party but suffered from unfavorable rumors—were also eager to go on record as anti-Communist. Many wanted to be heard but, according to Nixon, Edward G. Robinson, Jose Ferrer and the late John Garfield were the only three called where the Committee had no proof of Party membership, past or present. Robinson requested a hearing. Garfield and Ferrer were subpoenaed because they had been "the subject of considerable interest on the part of private organizations."

At first the Committee wanted Garfield and Ferrer to testify in private session. "But," Nixon said, "we were catching it all over—from George Sokolsky, Victor Riesel and even from Ed Sullivan. No one came right out in print and said so, but there were intimations of payoffs. Mr. Moulder [Congressman from Missouri] was subjected to criticism for stating that he thought Garfield was all right." Nixon also recalls that at the time some inexperienced anti-Communist groups were given to making loose, unsubstantiated charges, and the Committee drew fire for not acting on the "leads" these groups provided. From the other extremity, the Committee was attacked for "establishing blacklists."

Whether or not the Committee was interested in "establishing blacklists," it is now beyond question that many who testified (or who refused to testify) found themselves "unemployable" after they appeared as uncooperative witnesses before the Committee. During the scattered movie hearings of 1951, 90 Hollywood figures, almost all well-established in their careers, appeared on the witness stand. They took a variety of positions. Ferrer and Garfield swore that they had never been Party members; their names did not appear in the Committee's long lists of unfriendly witnesses published later. Thirty others, like novelist Budd Schulberg and Sterling Hayden, said they had been Party members and named people they knew as Communists. Their names appeared in the Committee's 1952 Annual Report as "Individuals who, through the knowledge gained through their own past membership in the Communist Party, have been of invaluable assistance to the Committee and the American people in supplying facts relating to Communist efforts and success in infiltrating the motion-picture industry."

One of these witnesses, screenwriter Martin Berkeley, named 162 persons he swore he knew as members of the Communist Party. His list included Dorothy Parker, who had spent some time in Hollywood as a screenwriter, Donald Ogden Stewart, Dashiell Hammett, Lillian Hellman, Edward Chodorov, writer-producer, and Michael Gordon, now a Broadway producer. Berkeley had originally been named before the Committee by Richard Collins. Berkeley later testified that after he learned Collins mentioned him, he sent a "very silly" telegram to the Committee. "I charged Mr. Collins with perjury and said I'd never been a member of the Communist Party, which was not true. I was not at that time a member and have not been for many years. [Berkeley left the Party in 1943.] Why I sent the telegram—I did it in a moment of panic and was a damn fool." But before Berkeley realized his "foolishness" and admitted there was truth to Collins' charge, several friends had begun to organize a defense fund for him. This campaign was under way when Berkeley shepishly admitted that Collins had told the truth.[1]

Berkeley joined the Motion Picture Alliance for the Preservation of American Ideals after his sensational testimony and became a leading figure in the organization. An MPA spokesman said not long ago that the group relied more on Martin Berkeley than on any of its other members to identify Communists and "Communist sympathizers" in the movie industry.

During the hearings that followed the 1951 sessions, other cooperative witnesses who provided names for the House Committee included actor Lee J. Cobb, director Elia Kazan and playwright Clifford Odets.

A list of 324 names was made available to the public by the House Committee in its 1952 and '53 Annual Reports. Names of those cited as Communists by cooperative witnesses were listed alphabetically. Everyone cited was blacklisted in the studios. But methods varied from studio to studio and from person to person, perhaps to avoid the "illegal conspiracy" which Paul V. McNutt warned against in 1947.

If the named people were under contract when they were identified or called to testify, their contracts were cancelled, bought up, or simply not renewed. If they were free-lance workers, usually tkeir agents told them they could no longer find work for them, and they stopped receiving "calls." Most were urged by their agents or studio executives to "clear" themselves of the charges made against them, either by testifying fully before the Committee or putting themselves in the hands of Roy Brewer or Martin Gang. . . .

To prepare witnesses and to keep them from answering questions that might cause them to lose their immunity privilege under the Fifth Amendment, teams of lawyers rehearsed their Hollywood clients by simulating

1. In later years Berkeley was cited by columnist George Sokolsky as a prime example of an anti-Communist who suffered unemployment for cooperating with the Committee. Many in Hollywood, however, believe that by his erratic behavior Berkeley had made himself unpopular and it was this rather than his anti-communism *per se* which caused his difficulties.

the examinations they would be put to on the witness stand. Variations of the Fifth Amendment position were developed. For instance, Carl Foreman, who was the writer and associate producer of "High Noon," invoked what later became known as the "diminished Fifth." He denied that he was a Party member at the time he was testifying but would not answer the question as to whether he had been a Party member at some previous date. Another variation was employed by producer Robert Rossen ("All the King's Men," "Body and Soul," "The Brave Bulls"). The first time he testified, Rossen invoked what came to be kown as the "augmented Fifth." He said that he was not a member of the Communist Party, that he was "not sympathetic with it or its aims," but declined to say whether he had ever been a Party member in the past. Eventually, though, those who invoked variations on the Fifth Amendment position found themselves as thoroughly unemployable in Hollywood as those who simply "took the Fifth," as the position came to be described.

Tension gradually increased in Hollywood. Once it was clear that the hearings were not to be stopped before the Committee had unearthed every available witness who could provide it with names, pressure to give cooperative testimony was exerted on all sides. Families were divided. Some of the "unfriendly" witnesses moved to new neighborhoods to avoid the ostracism they felt certain they would meet once their testimony was publicized.

Among the prominent Hollywood figures subpoenaed by the Committee was Sidney Buchman, a Columbia producer. Buchman had been an executive assistant to Harry Cohn, in charge of production at Columbia. He wrote the screen plays for "Mr. Smith Goes to Washington" and "Here Comes Mr. Jordan," produced "The Jolson Story" and wrote and produced "Jolson Sings Again." As a Columbia executive Buchman had worked on films featuring many of Hollywood's top stars. When he testified before the Committee on September 25, 1951, he took a position many unfriendly witnesses say they too might have taken had they believed the penalties would be as light as those later inflicted on Buchman.

Buchman testified that he had been a Communist but refused to name anyone he had known in the Party. He did exactly the thing which, according to precedent, should have meant a contempt citation. Observers were puzzled, until it was noted that Congressman Donald Jackson, California Republican, had left the hearing room in the course of Buchman's testimony but before the producer had refused to answer questions. This left the Committee without a quorum and, consequently, unable to issue a contempt citation against Buchman for his refusal to give full testimony. Buchman's lawyer noted the lack of a quorum at the conclusion of the testimony.

Public curiosity about Buchman's good fortune was expressed in various sections of the press. The Committee served Buchman with another subpoena, but this time he did not appear at the appointed time and was cited for contempt of Congress. On March 17, 1952, Buchman was indicted on two counts of contempt—for having failed to appear on January 25 and again on January 28. One count was later thrown out because Buchman had been cited twice on the basis of a single summons.

On March 25 District Judge T. Blake Kennedy in Washington, D.C. fixed the bond at $1,000 after the movie producer had been arraigned and pleaded not guilty. On May 9 a motion to dismiss the indictment was filed, argued and denied. Ten months later, jurors were sworn and the trial started March 9, 1953. On March 10 a judgment of acquittal was entered on the first account. On March 12 the jury delivered a verdict of guilty. The jury was polled and Buchman was permitted to remain on bond pending sentence. On March 16, 1953, Judge Kennedy sentenced Buchman to pay a fine of $150. The court suspended imposition of a prison sentence, and the defendant was placed on probation for a period of one year.

Edward Bennett Williams, Buchman's lawyer, says that Congressman Jackson left the hearing room at the fortuitous time because he had to drive Senator Potter of Michigan, a guest in his home, to the airport. Williams claims that the reason Buchman got off with such a light sentence was that the jury had been deadlocked, so the judge delivered what is known as an Allen charge: the judge was required to inform the minority in the jury to remember that the majority was acting according to its best lights and then to turn to the majority and repeat the same admonition in favor of the minority. However, says Williams, Judge Kennedy, for some accountable reason, became confused and delivered both charges to the minority members of the jury. After the judge realized this, he felt constrained to prevent any further complications in the case and decided to let Buchman off with a light sentence.

Buchman no longer works in the motion-picture industry and is engaged in other business in New York City. . . .

Witnesses who invoked the Fifth Amendment were banished from the studios in a variety of ways. Most studio executives, remembering Paul V. McNutt's warning about the illegality of an industry-wide "conspiracy," took pains to conceal the reasons for firings. Howard Hughes, then chief at RKO, furnished an exception. Paul Jarrico, a screenwriter, was working at the Hughes studio at the time he invoked the Fifth Amendment before the House Committee on April 13, 1951. Jarrico recently described his subsequent experiences in Hollywood this way:

"In my case the evidence that I was blacklisted was simple and unmistakable. On March 23, 1951, I was subpoenaed to appear before the

House Committee on Un-American Activities. The serving of the sub-poena was publicized by the Los Angeles press, most of the newspapers quoting me accurately as saying I was not certain yet what my position before the Committee would be, but 'if I have to choose between crawling in the mud with Larry Parks or going to jail like my courageous friends of the Hollywood Ten, I shall certainly choose the latter.'

"I was fired from my employment as a screenwriter at RKO that very day, forbidden to come onto the studio lot even to pick up my personal belongings. I appeared before the Committee on April 13, 1951, and was a most unfriendly witness. I not only exercised my privilege under the Fifth Amendment, I assailed the Committee for trying to subvert the American Constitution.

"I was subsequently informed by my agents, the Jaffe Agency, that there were no further possibilities of my employment in the motion-picture industry, and on June 20, 1951, at their request, I released them from the obligation of representing me. Though I had worked as a screen-writer more or less steadily for almost 14 years prior to the date on which I was subpoenaed, I have not been employed by any Hollywood studio since.

"In the Spring of 1952, I became involved in a highly publicized legal controversy with Howard Hughes. As head of RKO, he had arbitrarily removed my name from a film called 'The Las Vegas Story,' which had been my last writing assignment at RKO. I had been awarded a screen credit on this film by the Screen Writers Guild, which, under its collective-bargaining agreement, had exclusive authority to determine writing credits.

"Hughes sued me for declaratory relief, asserting that I had violated the morals clause by my stand before the Committee. I filed a cross com-plaint, asking for damages. The Screen Writers Guild sued Hughes inde-pendently for breaching the collective security agreement. Hughes won, both as against the Guild and me. Successive appeals of the Guild were defeated and the Guild finally accepted a compromise in which it gave up its hard-won authority to determine credits solely on the basis of literary contribution. My appeals were also denied.

"In the course of these suits and in the public statements surrounding them, Hughes made it very clear that he maintained and intended to maintain a political blacklist. The New York Times reported on April 7, 1952, that RKO 'will operate on a curtailed production basis for an in-definite period . . . in a drastic move for time to strengthen a political "screening" program to prevent employment of persons suspected of being Communists or having Communist sympathies.' The Times quoted Hughes further as asserting that 'every one' of eleven stories, selected as the best for filming out of 150 read by the studio over a period of six months, had to be discarded because 'information concerning one or more persons involved in the past writing of the script or original story showed that those writers were suspected of Communist ideas or sympathies.' Added Hughes: 'All studios have at their disposal information concerning the people who have been connected with one or more of the well-known Communist front organizations.' "

At a meeting of the Motion Picture Alliance on May 15, 1952, according to the Los Angeles *Daily News,* Roy Brewer declared that not one of the witnesses who "hid behind the Fifth Amendment" in the previous year and a half of hearings had subsequently been offered employment in the film industry. Later, it became apparent in Hollywood that workers who were named as Communists but had neither been called to testify nor come forth to answer the charges made against them, were also blacklisted. Brewer confirmed this, too, in another public statement. In answer to a charge in *Frontier* magazine that he was "strawboss of the purge," Brewer replied that the only blacklist he knew of was the list "established by the House Committee on Un-American Activities containing names of persons who have not repudiated that [Communist] association by comparable testimony." . . .

The blacklisting proceeded through 1951, '52, and '53. Those dropped by the studios were not limited to persons who could influence film content, or who would receive screen credit for their work. The industry had accepted the Committee's new emphasis on "prestige, position and money."

For example, there is the case of composer Sol Kaplan, who had scored more than 30 pictures in Hollywood between 1940 and 1953. Kaplan received a subpoena while he was working on a 20th Century–Fox sound stage. He had never been publicly identified as a Communist. John Garfield, who denied before the Committee that he had ever been a Communist, said in the course of his testimony that Kaplan was a friend of his. Though Kaplan had been under contract to 20th Century–Fox for one year, he was fired when this happened. Later he was reinstated on a week-to-week "probation" basis after he protested that many top studio executives (including the man who was firing him) were also friends of Garfield. Kaplan was subpoenaed in April, 1953. Shortly before he was scheduled to testify, a Fox business executive in charge of the music department told him that his job, despite economy firings, was safe. During his testimony, on April 8, 1953, Kaplan challenged the Committee to produce his accusers and invoked almost the entire Bill of Rights when he refused to cooperate.

After the hearing, he returned to work at 20th Century–Fox. The musician says that his colleagues looked surprised when they saw him in the studio. Nothing happened the first day, but on the second he was told to call one of Fox's top producers. The producer, who was a friend of Kaplan, told him that Darryl Zanuck, production chief of the studio, did not want to fire him. Congressman Clyde Doyle, Democratic member of the Committee, the producer said, did not believe that Kaplan was a Communist. If Kaplan would appear privately before Doyle—which could be "arranged"—he might be able to keep his job at Fox. The producer added that "no one would even know you spoke to Doyle." Kaplan said that he would not consider taking such a position because he did not believe in "deals" where important principles were concerned. Fifteen minutes later he received a telephone call from the same executive who had assured him that his job would be safe in case of economy firings. A new order had made Kaplan's dismissal necessary, the executive told him. When Kaplan pressed him, the studio executive finally admitted that the musician was being fired for political reasons.

If the unfriendly witnesses before the Committee suffered social ostracism and loss of employment, the cooperative witnesses also paid a price. Not only Communists but many non-Communists looked upon them as "informers" (or, as they were described in the official Communist press, as "stool pigeons"). Everyone in the movie colony had seen the British officer contemptuously push the money across the table with his swagger stick in John Ford's classic "The Informer." Everyone remembered how Victor McLaglen, as the Irish Judas, had picked it up. Also, many Hollywood liberals were bitter about the uses to which, in earlier days, the Communists had diverted their innocent good will to Party causes. Now, when they saw some of these same people playing the "informer" role, they found even more reason to turn on them. The remaining Communists did all they could to encourage the feeling. . . .

In the 1954–55 edition of *Who's Who in America*, George E. Sokolsky listed himself as columnist, author, lecturer and industrial consultant. No doubt his work in all these capacities contributed to the effectiveness of the role he played in making judgments as to who of the Hollywood penitents were worthy of immediate absolution and who should be referred to the "experts" on the West Coast for further consideration. But probably more pertinent, though unlisted in *Who's Who,* is the image of Sokolsky as a kind of gray eminence, a behind-the-scenes operator bestowing on individuals and causes at will the benefits of his accumulated wisdom, ingenuity and undoubted influence. These benefits appear to be bestowed sometimes to serve specific political purposes, sometimes for capricious or romantic reasons—but more often Sokolsky seems to combine both.

Sokolsky is generally recognized as one who transcends factional differences within the anti-Communist movement that directs its energies toward the entertainment media. He is a court of last appeals, an almost universally accepted father-figure. One public-relations man, widely experienced in the field of "clearance," said of him not long ago: "He's impartial, generous, extremely practical, as objective as anyone writing, kind, with no meanness in him." That represents a widely held view of the columnist. Other "clearance" experts have at different times felt that he was not being as shrewd as he might be in his judgments and was giving his blessing to people who did not deserve it. There have been schoolboy grumblings about "Sok" among the lesser "clearance" men. But his authority is rarely questioned.

He has been variously described as the Pope of the Right Wing presiding over a loyal College of Cardinals and as Chairman of the Blacklisting Board of Directors. Certainly, in the Supreme Court that has grown up since blacklisting in the entertainment world began, he has served as Chief Justice. Run-of-the-mill cases can be handled in the lower courts, and in the normal course of events Sokolsky is not called upon. But when leaders of the movie industry looked around for a man to sit in judgment on the American Legion "letters," the columnist was readily suggested.

Sokolsky met all the requirements. He was eminently acceptable to the American Legion and other groups whose views Hollywood was learning to respect. He qualified as a "sophisticated anti-Communist" in the circles where no greater encomium than that can be given to anyone. He was generally reputed to be a reasonable man. He writes a widely syndicated column that is read and admired by the kind of people who are likely to start picketing movies. He was aggressively "conservative" in his political opinions, yet his intellectual attainments were equal to those of the totally unacceptable "egg-head liberals": no critic of the program could convincingly charge Sokolsky with being a yahoo or a bigot. Best of all, Sokolsky had at his command the results of his friend J. B. Matthews' long research endeavors into the field of "Communist infiltration." Not long ago the columnist told a harassed radio-television sponsor that since the "file" at his disposal contained several million items it is only a matter of a telephone call and a 20-minute wait before anyone in show business can be thoroughly "checked."

Sokolsky once stated that he would have no objection to a Communist's being employed in the motion-picture industry if it were not for the fact that such a Communist would be likely to give significant financial support to the Party. (The producers would see to it that a movie Communist did not use the screen to propagandize.) His main political interest in the films, he said, is in getting Hollywood people out of the Communist orbit and back again into normal American life. He is opposed to making that transition so difficult it is practically impossible. On this score, Sokolsky grows impatient at times with the extremists in his own political camp. During one of his visits to Hollywood, for instance, he appeared at a Motion Picture Alliance meeting and publicly chastised anti-Communists who were so rigid and unforgiving that they were hurting the cause.

The columnist insists that he was not responsible for any individual's being blacklisted in the Hollywood studios. He *did* assist in putting people back to work who without his approval might have found themselves "unemployable." Of course those who did not pass the tests Sokolsky applied were in greater difficulty than before their "letter" reached his desk. But, according to the American Legion itself, less than 30 persons out of all those listed failed to provide "satisfactory" explanations.

Sokolsky, unlike some lesser "clearance" men, was not interested in dealing out punishment and thoroughly disapproves of anyone's accepting money for what he regards as essentially "rehabilitation" work.

When he was satisfied that there was no danger of a performer's or a director's falling under Communist influence, he was willing to pass an "explanation" for past indiscretions, even though he and the writer of the explanatory letter might take quite different sides on legitimate political issues.

Sokolsky, who is not at all the unfeeling man his column sometimes suggests, did not relish the thought of consigning any artist to the limbo of "unemployability." In a speech given in 1940 he expressed a cultural attitude that has influenced his decisions as Chief Justice. "We have to find sanctuary here for great performers," he wrote in that pre-war column. "We have to find sanctuary here for people who just think, and who dare to think independently and freely. . . . We have to be big and broad about that. . . . We have to be so big and broad that when this holocaust is over we can give back to each country that which is priceless because it cannot be replaced if lost. The human mind, and the human spirit, and the human appreciation of things that are fine and beautiful."

Another hint of that side of Sokolsky was expressed in a column he wrote on September 24, 1953. In what seemed like a remarkable recognition of the misery the "house-cleaning" program caused in Hollywood, he praised Roy Brewer's "rehabilitation" program: ". . . men and women, whose careers appear to have been wrecked, are now working. . . . Great talents have been redeemed from fears attending their errors for a clear road to useful work."

But whatever his reservations about "wrecking careers," Sokolsky, "in the absence of a national policy"—as the Waldorf statement put it—

agreed to take on the burdens of a private citizen judging the political trustworthiness of other private citizens.

After listees turned in their "explanations" to the Hollywood front offices, the letters were forwarded to American Legion headquarters. Some "explanations" were patently satisfactory; others were sent on to the columnist and it was his grim duty then to separate the liberal lambs from the Communist wolves. Where there were lingering doubts, cases were referred to Brewer and Ward Bond in Hollywood.

A "letter" written by Z.Z., a top-flight Hollywood star, was typical of many. Z.Z. directed his letter to James F. O'Neil at Legion headquarters in Washington and sent copies of it to all the studios distributing either his own pictures or those made by the company he owns.

Dear Mr. O'Neil:

My name is [deleted]. I am one of the owners of [name of company]. I am also an actor in the motion-picture industry. It has come to my attention that a list attached to a letter from an official of the American Legion includes my name. I am informed that my name was included in that list because of certain activities with which I concerned myself some years ago. I have examined the items in question and I am writing to you to explain the use of my name. I also give you my permission and authority to show this letter to any person to whom you may wish. First, let me tell you what you wish to know. I am not a Communist. I have never been a Communist. I have never been a member of the Communist Party or of the Communist Political Association. To the best of my knowledge and belief I have never knowingly belonged to any organization which was a Communist front.

1. In 1947 together with hundreds of the foremost citizens of Southern California, both in and out of the motion-picture industry, I permitted the use of my name in connection with what was known as the Committee for the First Amendment. Even with the benefit of hindsight I cannot believe any fair-minded person would consider the use of my name in connection with that committee as the use of my name for a Communist front. To my personal knowledge, this Committee for the First Amendment never was a Communist front, nor was it ever used for any Communist purposes even though certain of its opinions may at that time have paralleled the opinions of the Communist Party. As far as I am concerned, I permitted the use of my name in connection with the Committee for the First Amendment for the most patriotic of motives.

2. My name was used in connection with the brief *amicus curiae* filed on behalf of Lawson and Trumbo seeking a hearing by the Supreme Court. The list of people who permitted their names to be used

in this connection is almost as illustrious as the list of names used in the formation of the Committee for the First Amendment. I permitted the use of my name because I felt that the Constitutional issues presented were of such importance that a decision by the Supreme Court would be helpful. Permitting the use of my name had nothing whatever to do with the individual beliefs of Trumbo or Lawson. I am sure that if anybody reads the brief *amicus curiae* the reader will see that the signers merely requested that the Supreme Court grant a hearing. To my knowledge no signer of that petition in any way condoned the actions of Trumbo or Lawson or indicated any sympathy with the political beliefs of the men.

3. My name appears in an advertisement published by the *Hollywood Reporter* on October 28, 1947 headed "Hollywood Fights Back." I permitted the use of my name because this was an ad sponsored by the Committee for the First Amendment, of which I was a member. My recollection is that this advertisement clearly sets forth the honest beliefs of all people who permitted the use of their names by the Committee and in the ad. I call to your attention the manner in which the Committee on Un-American Activities has conducted its hearings since January of 1951 in order to point out the difference between properly conducted hearings and the way in which the hearings were conducted in 1947.

4. I am also informed that I was listed as a sponsor of a dinner benefit rally for the Hollywood Ten supposedly held March 5, 1948 at the Beverly-Wilshire Hotel in Beverly Hills. I was not a sponsor, nor did I attend that dinner or that rally. I did not give any money to the Hollywood Ten. I have read the item in the 1948 Report of the Committee on Un-American Activities in California issued by the Senate Fact Finding Committee of that state and find on page 241 my name listed with many others as a sponsor for that dinner. I have been unable to find any document upon which the Senate Fact Finding Committee based that statement. The record itself does not show the form in which my name was used and there is nothing in the Senate Report which causes me to change the statement which I have heretofore made with reference to the use of my name in this connection.

The actor's "explanation" was acceptable.

This performer was not alone. A number of top stars were named on the list the Legion sent to the studios. Of these a few were getting special attention from the *Firing Line, Facts for Fighting Communism*, a publication of the Legion's National American Commission. The newsletter brought their damning "associations" to the attention of Legion leaders all over the nation. The studio executives, with heavy investments at stake, were particularly anxious for these stars to "explain" themselves. In the vast number of cases, the studio chiefs were convinced, the "associations" were meaningless; at the worst they represented bad judgment. Clearing them up was simply a matter of recalling past circumstances and expressing regret. The letters designed to do this were carefully worked out. In some cases "explanations" teetered on the abject.

This is the way *Firing Line* reported on one Hollywood star who had a big-budget picture ready for release:

"The following material has been compiled by the research staff in response to numerous requests for information on motion-picture actor [his name]. [This actor] plays the part of . . . in a movie to be released shortly . . ." A list of "Communist associations" was cited.

The actor directed his "explanations" to the head of his studio. *Firing Line* had cited him as a speaker at a rally of 1500 teenagers under the auspices of American Youth for Democracy. The AYD, the newsletter pointed out, was cited as a subversive Communist front by Attorney General Clark. In his letter to the studio head the actor explained that in the spring of 1946 he was in Chicago and was asked to address some high-school students. He was told that there had been some race rioting in the city around that time. In making the speech, he said, he felt he was doing his duty as a citizen. If the AYD perverted this action of his for its own propaganda ends, he wrote, it was a typical Communist maneuver and was abhorrent to him. In answer to another Legion charge, he admitted he had been an officer of the Hollywood Independent Citizens Committee of the Arts, Sciences and Professions; but he joined the organization because he wanted to work for President Roosevelt's re-election. He stated he was alerted when the organization became unnecessarily involved in studio strike matters. After the war he joined others in the group who were resisting the Communist Party line; but by the end of 1946 it was clear that the Communists were dominating HICCASP policy and he resigned.

The actor "explained" his interest in the Committee for the First Amendment by saying it was now obvious to him he had been drawn into a Communist-front activity, based on an appeal that at the time seemed to involve a decent American principle.

Six months later an executive of the studio releasing this actor's picture wrote to James F. O'Neil at American Legion headquarters:

> As you know, it is our very firm opinion, based on our knowledge of [the actor] and his activities, that he is a fine and upstanding American. I have gathered from our talks that there was no reservation in your mind regarding the patriotism and Americanism of [the actor]. It is our belief and our hope that, similarly, there should be none as far as the American Legion as a whole is concerned. . . .

The Legion accepted the star's "explanations." His picture was released and shown without crippling incidents.

Not all studio workers got through the investigation as successfully as most of the big stars in trouble.

In a letter to a friend, H. W., a screenwriter, described an interview he had with a studio executive who tried to get him to disavow the activities cited against him. The letter read as follows:

> Mr. M. (the studio executive) tells me the studio pictures are being picketed. Cannot afford it. Trying to clear everyone. Will I write Mr. P. (studio president) a letter? M. tells me what they want in the letter. Particularly names, names, names. Why such and such happened, when I got out, who got me in, etc., etc. And he said, even if I did write this letter and was cleared, this is no guarantee, he realizes, that the next day they may not say they don't like my tie or my hat. I ask what Mr. P. will do with the letter. He tells me that when some of these organizations come in protesting against a picture, Mr. P. will show my letter. Or he may give it out for publication. I will have no control whatsoever over the letter. Then he begins to read my dossier. . . .
>
> I walked politely out, saying I was going to think. I told my agent that I would not write the letter. He said it was fine with him. But they will settle my contract immediately. Just can't keep me. Everyone else, I gather, has conformed. So we no longer have any problems here of who to invite with who and so forth. Just the problem of selling the house and breaking off our lives here.

After the first interview, the screenwriter wrote the following letter to the studio executive:

> Dear Mr. M.:
>
> First let me thank you for your tactful handling of a situation which must have been just as unpleasant for you as it was for me.
>
> For some time I had been expecting a request to write a letter such as you outlined to me in our meeting. Long ago I had made up my mind that I could not dignify the real source of this request by writing. But because of your courtesy and consideration, I gave the matter further thought. However, I cannot alter my decision.
>
> I feel that if I wrote such a letter I would be violating every principle of democracy and freedom in which I believe.
>
> My patriotism, my love and loyalty for my country and for the principles for which it stands and for the form of government which I cherish has never been questioned and cannot now be questioned. I will match my feelings and my actions in this respect against anyone, particularly my accusers.

I am not a Communist. I have never been a Communist and never could be. I have never wavered in my devotion and loyalty to the United States.

I hope you understand why I must refuse your request. Why I must adhere to my principles. After all, I must live with myself for many years to come.

A second conversation took place at which the studio executive demanded again that the screenwriter disavow his political past. The screenwriter's notes on this conversation follow:

Mr. *M.* asked if I had thought over the problem. I told him it was difficult at times to think of anything else. He then asked if I had changed my mind. He said, "I think you owe it to the studio to write the letter. . . .

Mr. *M.* said they were beginning to put pressure on him—asking "what about *me?*" He said these groups were getting very violent. I asked if he meant that the American Legion would picket our pictures. He said yes. *M.* then cited a case of an actor who was a day player—getting a salary of $150 a day. He was playing in a studio film. They gave him a few lines to say—next thing he knew the studio had a phone call telling them about this man. *M.* called the actor up to his office and showed him the list of political charges. The actor refused to answer—saying it was an invasion of his rights. The studio paid him off and he is out of the picture.

M. then spoke of what Mr. Brewer was doing about the writers who had gone to London and who were writing pictures there—he explained that these writers were Communists. The substance was that Brewer had written a letter to Mr. Sokolsky—that Mr. Sokolsky had commented on it and they hoped that there would be legislation to stop these films from playing in this country. He said that the IATSE operators could refuse to run those pictures. I then asked if they would picket a picture of mine which was about to go into production. Mr. *M.* said that he did not know, explaining that certain stories that they had bought before they knew of this trouble had been given an okay. He said that they now ask everyone who comes to work for them if they have been cleared for the Legion—that they would never have signed me now to the contract I have without that letter. He then asked about my contract, and I told him that I had one more picture to do after the present one I was working on.

He then said he was afraid the studio would have to ask me to give them a release. I said I would have to speak to my agent about any business things, and then asked what a release meant. He said, "Tear up the contract." He then said he wondered about the Un-American Activities Committee and what was my attitude about that. I reminded him that I had talked of that before and that naturally I would answer anything they wanted to know. He asked if I would go before the Committee voluntarily. I said that I did not think I could live through it.

He told me that writing a letter to Mr. *P.* was not a hard thing to do. "If you write saying 'I am not a Communist. I have never been and could never be,' and telling about the list of things that you were supposed to have been a member of and to have contributed to— that have been found to be Communistic fronts—that you did not know it and that if you had you would never have joined them."

An actor confronted with the American Legion's citations against him who refused to answer the question of Communist Party membership had a different experience.

R. had worked in theater and motion pictures since 1925, both as actor and director. After serving in the Army for three and a half years during World War II, he came to Hollywood to study at the Actors' Laboratory under the G.I. Bill. In a short time he started getting small parts in motion pictures.

In 1952, he was called for a part in the M-G-M production of "Julius Caesar" and had been working on the picture for three days when he was summoned from the set to the office of a studio executive.

The actor went to the office wearing toga and make-up and was questioned at length. First the executive said that R. should understand that the studio was owned by stockholders and it was the studio's job to protect the interest of stockholders by making certain that there would be no person in the studio's pictures who would cause the public to shun the box office He then asked R. if he read the *People's World,* and in the same sentence gave the actor the date when he subscribed to the *People's World.* Next he asked if R. had signed the 1947 *Variety* advertisement. R. replied that if his name was on the advertisement, he must have signed it, though he could not recall signing it. The executive asked next if R. had belonged to the Actors' Laboratory, a Hollywood theater group listed as a "Communist venture" by the California Committee on Un-American Activities. R. replied that he had studied at the Actors' Laboratory under the G.I. Bill and later had joined the Theater. The executive then asked who invited R. to join the Actors' Laboratory. R. replied that no one had, he joined because he thought it was a good place to study. When the executive asked how he heard about the Actors' Laboratory, R. replied that he had read about it in *Life* or *Time.* The executive then said, "You will write a letter to Mr. Schenck and explain your reason for these various activities and associations." When the actor replied that he had no intention of writing such a letter to Schenck or anybody else, the executive said, "Then I will ask you, are you a member of the Communist Party?" R. answered, "You have no right to ask that question or any other like it, and I will not answer it." The executive concluded the interview. "Then you are no longer employed by M-G-M." After that, R. was called but not hired for one brief part at another studio, but he has not appeared in films since. . . .

■ ■ ■ ■

Hollywood Meets Frankenstein (1952), "X"

The *Nation* devoted much of its issue of 28 June 1952 to the blacklist. This article by "X" describes the film industry's reaction to the rounds of HUAC hearings. The *Nation* described "X" as a pseudonym for "a group of top-flight writers who have important positions in major Hollywood studios."

On October 24, 1947, three of Hollywood's top directors sent a telegram to scores of key figures in the film industry. The wire said:

> THIS INDUSTRY IS NOW DIVIDED AGAINST ITSELF. UNITY MUST BE RECAPTURED, OR ALL OF US WILL SUFFER FOR YEARS TO COME. YOUR AID IS REQUIRED IN THIS CRITICAL MOMENT. THIS IS MORE IMPORTANT THAN ANY PICTURE YOU EVER MADE. SIGNED,
>
> JOHN HUSTON, WILLIAM WYLER, BILLY WILDER

"This critical moment" was an investigation of Hollywood by the House Committee on Un-American Activities, and the issue of "The Ten," then still this side of prison.

In those first days of the committee's onslaught, a broad group of film people stood up and fought back. More than fifty stars appeared on two nation-wide broadcasts. Others made a junket to Washington to watch the shabby circus in action. Several top studio executives, among them Dore Schary and L. B. Mayer, said brave words. Both insisted that what mattered in the case of talent was performance, not politics.

But in the hierarchy of the film corporations, men like Schary and Mayer are less than kings. The overlords of the industry are the New York executives who control financing, distribution, and the theater chains. The motion-picture business is primarily a real-estate operation, and the real estate is in the hands of men like Loew's Nick Schenck, Para-

"Hollywood Meets Frankenstein," by "X," appeared in the 28 June 1952 issue of *Nation*.

mount's Barney Balaban, and Fox's Spyros Skouras. It was these big boys who, at the close of the committee hearings, whistled the studio heads to a meeting at the Waldorf-Astoria. The high-priced hired help were given a brisk caning and a lecture on the facts of life. They emerged from the meeting to issue a statement announcing the firing of "The Ten." A portion of that document is worth quoting, for it has become a Pike's Peak of irony:

> In pursuing this policy, we are not going to be swayed by any hysteria or intimidation from any source. We are frank to recognize that such a policy involves dangers and risks. There is a danger of hurting innocent people, there is the risk of creating an atmosphere of fear. Creative work at its best cannot be carried on in an atmosphere of fear. We will guard against this danger, this risk, this fear.

Actually, with the firing of "The Ten," Hollywood created for itself a monster that was to grow as gruesome as any that ever frightened the wits out of children at a horror matinee. Since that day, the film industry has been in panicky retreat before every attack on civil liberties. It is now a hapless pushover for any witch-hunting outfit that seeks to collect blood or blackmail.

The spectacle of a giant monopoly gibbering with fright may seem curious until one recalls a bit of Hollywood history. The film executives (not unlike those in other industries) have always had an abiding faith in "the fix." They would rather buy off a racketeering union boss than sit down with an honest labor leader. It was this policy that led to the B-picture episode, a few years back, when the studio heads left a satchel of greenbacks in a hotel room to buy off Willie Bioff. It was this faith in the fix that (when a cog slipped somewhere) led to the landing of 20th Century's Joe Schenck in the federal pokey for income-tax evasion.

Hollywood is a company town, and beneath the fancy publicity it is not so different from a coal town in Kentucky or a cotton town in Alabama. When a strike broke out in 1946, the studios smashed it by using tear gas, fire hoses, and gun-toting deputies.

A few final details to fill in the background. Nineteen fifty-one was a rocky year for motion pictures. The Supreme Court had handed down an anti-trust decision ordering the divorcement of theater chains from production facilities. The public, hit by high prices, began to cut down on money spent for entertainment. Television antennae darkened the sky. In Los Angeles, movie attendance dropped 30 per cent. Hundreds of neighborhoor theaters shut their doors. 20th Century's Skouras asked his 130 highest-paid personnel to take salary cuts, some up to 50 per cent. Warner

Brothers (showing a comfortable profit for the fiscal year) fired five department heads, one of them with twenty-three years' service.

The film industry, following a national pattern, was searching for a way to slash employees' paychecks and intimidate their unions. Many movie executives looked upon the investigations of Hollywood as a faintly noxious blessing. True, they created nasty publicity. But they also made workers fearful and reluctant to press wage demands. They also kept the unions from becoming militant. Hadn't the conviction of "The Ten" knocked off half a dozen leaders of the Screen Writers Guild?

Meanwhile, the witch hunters were busy. After "The Ten" came the hearings of last year, which used Larry Parks for a burnt offering. Then the Hollywood subcommittee session at which Sidney Buchman turned out to be the main event. Each of these investigations was regarded by the employer element as the big crisis which, once past, would get everybody off the hook and permit a return from panic to Hollywood's normal condition of twittering nervousness. A spokesman for the Un-American Activities Committee actually told an interviewer on TV that last year's hearing would definitely wind up the investigations of "Red influence" in films.

Early in 1952 there seemed to be some easing of the pressure against studio personnel. Studio heads were no longer (or less often) making rousing speeches against The Menace. (One top executive, at a *compulsory* meeting of the entire staff, from producers and stars to grips and messenger boys, demanded that every one of the workers become an informer and report immediately anything of a suspicious character in the words or actions of fellow employees.) But this sort of thing decreased and a numbed weariness settled over Hollywood. The monster had been fed, it seemed, and for a while would be content to digest its victims.

This prediction turned out to be wishful thinking. A new quarry was marked for the hunt—liberals and "fellow travelers." This meant attacks on more than isolated writers, directors, actors, and a few producers. It meant the impugning of certain top executives themselves, no matter how fervid their protestations of anticommunism, no matter how many anti-Communist pictures they had produced.

Dore Schary (in charge at Metro, the biggest studio of them all) became a prime target. So did Paramount's chief of production, Don Hartman. So did Stanley Kramer. The Wage Earners Committee, a local nuisance group, picketed theaters throughout the Los Angeles area and paid its respects to Schary and Kramer with placards, on one of which their names dripped blood.

Neither Schary nor Kramer took it lying down. Both filed suits for more than a million dollars against the Wage Earners, and these actions are now pending in the courts. Schary took a big ad in the movie trade papers and the Los Angeles dailies, defining his suit as "a challenge to all those who recklessly and viciously peddle the tawdry wares of defamation and personal slander." Even the right-wing Producers Association came out in behalf of the libel suits.

The picketing did not stop. But for a moment, there seemed to be a stiffening of resistance. The worm turned, ever so slightly. People who had long ago resigned themselves to a relentless and inevitable McCarthyism crawled up from their cyclone cellars. There even seemed to be a ray of sunlight. When the Republican faction of the Un-American Activities Committee released a report denouncing Hollywood for having failed to purge itself of Communist influence, elements of the Producers Association blasted the report. So vigorous was this reaction that the Democratic members of the committee later dissented from the Republican stand.

Had Hollywood had enough? Had the loss of talent and revenue and the acres of damaging publicity finally exasperated the studios? Had they glimpsed, in the light of events, the shadowy reflection of a lost principle, the principle of civil liberties? It almost seemed as though the saturation point had been reached when, as in the Salem witch hunts, the fanatics started to go after the higher echelons.

Perhaps by coincidence, perhaps by design, but at this moment—at a time when Schary and Kramer found themselves on the barricades lately manned by people who are now for the most part jobless—Howard Hughes joined battle with the Screen Writers Guild over the issue of monies and credit due screen-writer Paul Jarrico. The latter, a Fifth Amendment casualty, demanded both credit on a finished picture and $5,000. Hughes galloped into the fray, Sir Galahad in tennis sneakers, doing the noble thing to defend free America. That is, it began to be noble after $3,500, for which sum Hughes was originally willing to settle with Jarrico. The Guild, whose contract with the entire industry stipulates that it alone shall arbitrate credits, tried to force Hughes to honor a contract which he publicly and blandly renounced. So far, two courts have upheld Hughes, or at least relieved him of the obligation to fulfill his contract with the Guild.

And since we've come to the courts: recently a jury in federal court awarded Adrian Scott (one of the "The Ten") $80,000 due him under an unfinished contract with RKO. Judge Ben Harrison, acting on the appeal of the studio, reversed the decision on the ground that the jury didn't know everything it should have known about the case. In announcing his decision, Judge Harrison also made a pejorative statement concerning what he thinks of a man who refuses to answer a question at a Congressional hearing. At the same time, it is only fair to say that in the case of another member of "The Ten" the judge allowed a verdict for a smaller amount to stand.

The Hughes controversy broke at just about the time that Elia Kazan (with a juicy new contract pending) confessed all to the Un-American Activities Committee and published an advertisement in which he urged "liberals" to "speak out" and inform on associates. The blasts from Hughes and Kazan sent a good many liberals scuttling back to their cyclone cellars to sit it out in what they hoped would be silence.

Then came the development that reached down into the cyclone cellars.

The American Legion for some time has had a proscribed list which feeds the hungry maw of the *American Legion Magazine* whenever that publication feels the need for more red meat in its diet. About three months ago, the Legion's Americanism experts found a brilliant new way of harassing the studios and getting them to lop off reddish pinks and pinkish whites. The method: picketing.

One or two pictures were picketed in one or two cities, and immediately Representatives of the Industry (run when you hear that phrase) rushed to the Legion experts with a view to arranging some kind of truce. The idea was to arrive at a formula whereby the studios would get a guarantee that pictures would not be picketed. What was dreamed up was a clearance mechanism that may well become Exhibit A in the evidence of this era's corruption of the American tradition. The mechanism works something like this:

Actor or writer finds himself on the list. He is called in by the chief in charge of such matters at the studio which employs him and is given a dossier of "charges" against him. These range from parlor gossip to hearsay quotes from the Tenney Committee reports, to scuttlebutt from the pages of "Red Channels," to data from state and county volunteer committees. Mention in the *Daily Worker,* other than outright attack, is considered a charge.

Out of the "appeasement" meeting between the Legion and industry representatives came a preliminary list of some 300 names, furnished by letter to each studio. The letter stated that if the studio employed any of the listees, picketing on a national scale would ensue when the picture involving the person's services was released.

To meet this, the studio now calls the listee, presents him with the charges, and asks him to write a letter "to the head of the studio" answering, by what is known as an Affidavit of Explanation, the following questions:

1. Is this so?
2. The reasons for joining organizations cited in the charges.
3. The people who invited you to join.
4. Did you invite others to join?
5. Did you resign? When?

The letter or affidavit (copies of which go to various agencies and organizations, and to certain individuals, including, so it is said, George Sokolsky, Howard Rushmore, and Freddy Woltman) is then submitted to a vague "central committee" for "clearance."

What makes this of particular interest, even among the exhibits of atrocities against civil liberties that are so plentiful these days, is the unblushingly investigative character of the questions, as revealed in the third and fourth items. This goes beyond the Un-American Activities Committee in asking liberals or "sympathizers" to name other liberals or "sympathizers."

In addition to Hollywood's troubles with the Legion, the Un-American Activities Committee has announced a new round of hearings for this coming autumn. Its process-servers are as busy as ever. Throughout the spring, deputy marshals sought out Los Angeles physicians, lawyers, radio, and television artists. Film folk were not ignored. One of the latest to be subpoenaed is a screen writer who received his summons on the floor of a Screen Writers Guild meeting—a meeting presumably open only to members in good standing. Considering the fact that the writer's address and phone number appear in the local directory and that no attempt was made to serve him at home, so far as he knows, the choice of time and place was clearly a calculated intimidation. Fear, suspicion, and wild rumor can be kept at fever pitch without the necessity of formal hearings. All the committee needs is an unlimited supply of pink subpoena forms.

As matters stand today, Hollywood is using half a dozen blacklists, as well as supplementary graylists based upon the vaguest sort of innuendo. The assumption that a person is guilty until proved innocent has become standard operating procedure. A weedy growth of professional witchhunting outfits has sprung up. Fingermen are doing a brisk business, hourly supplying additional names. In an effort to protect themselves from the cruder forms of blackmail, the studios are hiring their own investigators. Quite likely the talent scouts who once signed up young starlets are now combing the country for promising ex-FBI men.

All this has its effect on the kind of films that are being made. A fair cross-section of the pictures now in production includes the following: "Time Bomb," "Tribute to a Bad Man," "Apache Trail," "Flat Top," "Road to Bali," "Pleasure Island," "Something for the Birds," "Springfield Rifle," and "Bela Lugosi Meets the Gorilla Man"—plus two others whose titles seem uncomfortably autobiographical: "Panic Stricken" and "Tonight We Sing."

It is the opinion of the seasoned if not shell-shocked observers out here that if the industry goes all the way with appeasement of the Legion or any other pressure group on the setting of standards for employability, it will finally deliver itself to the Sokolskys, the McCarthys, and the Wage Earners Committee. After that there can only be darkness and television.

■ ■ ■ ■

THE PARAMOUNT CASE AND ITS LEGAL BACKGROUND (1961), Michael Conant

This section from Michael Conant's book, *Anti-trust in the Motion Picture Industry,* describes the complicated and lengthy history of litigation in the Paramount case. Although the government's original complaint was only against the one major company, the decision would apply to all of them since their corporate structures and practices were identical.

COMPLAINTS

The *Paramount* case was filed July 20, 1938, and the amended and supplemental complaint was filed November 14, 1940. In the supplemental complaint the five majors, Paramount, Loew's, RKO, Warner Bros., and Twentieth Century–Fox, were charged with combining and conspiring to restrain trade unreasonably and to monopolize the production, distribution, and exhibition of motion pictures. The three minor defendants —Columbia, Universal and United Artists—were charged with combining with the five majors to restrain trade unreasonably and to monopolize commerce in motion pictures.

Defendants were charged with conspiring to fix film license terms, runs, clearances, and minimum admission prices. They were charged with concertedly engaging in block booking, blind selling, and systematically dis-

"The Paramount Case and Its Legal Background" is from *Anti-trust in the Motion Picture Industry,* by Michael Conant (University of California Press, 1961).

crimating in license terms in favor of circuit theaters. They were further charged with (1) conditioning licenses to theaters of their coconspirators on receiving similar preferences for their own theaters, (2) excluding independently produced films from their theaters, (3) excluding independent exhibitors from first and other runs in which defendants operated theaters, (4) using first and early runs in affiliated theaters to control the supply of films, runs, clearances, and admission prices of competing unaffiliated theaters, (5) pooling profits in cities where two or more defendants operated theaters, and (6) effecting a division of territories in the entire United States. The prayer requested injunctive relief against the practices restraining trade, the establishment of a nation-wide system of arbitration tribunals, and that the five majors be ordered to divest themselves of all theaters used by them unreasonably to restrain trade.

CONSENT DECREE: 1940

On November 20, 1940, the government and the five majors were parties to a consent decree in the *Paramount* case that was to last for three years. During this period the government agreed not to press for divorcement of the majors' theaters. The decree set up a broad system of rules for bargaining and for settling disputes which was remarkably similar to the plan of industry self-government that had operated in motion pictures under the National Recovery Administration. Organized control of the industry by the five majors, effected in each exchange by the local Film Board of Trade, was allowed to continue within the constraints of the decree. Only minor changes in film marketing were instituted.

The decree prohibited blind selling by requiring trade showings of films in each exchange district before licensing. It curtailed block booking by limiting blocks to 5 pictures. It prohibited agreements to tie licenses for shorts or foreign films to those for domestic films. Theaters in each exchange district were to license films separately from those in other exchanges. Refusal to license films to a theater at all, the use of unreasonable clearances, and the withholding of available prints were also proscribed. All five majors consented not to enter upon a general program of expanding theater holdings for the three-year period. The three minor defendants did not consent to the decree and were not bound by it. . . .

Exhibitors generally were not satisfied with the consent decree. Affiliated circuits still dominated exhibition. Arbitration costs averaged $48 a case and attorneys' fees paid by the exhibitor. Since there were no definite standards for awards, the outcome of an action was filled with uncertainty, and the action could involve a prolonged appeal proceeding. As a result, arbitration lost its popularity. Exhibitors had filed 148 cases in 1941, the first year of arbitration, but only 32 cases in 1945.

Although, after the trial, the statutory court ruled that it did not have power to order the continuance of arbitration, it recommended that it be continued. It was not abandoned until 1949.

As to the requirement of trade showings, most small exhibitors did not have time to attend them. The 5-picture limit on block booking also was a source of complaint, for one or two B pictures tied to each top production could accomplish the same result as block booking a full year's pictures.

District Court Opinion and Decree

In August, 1944, the government reactivated the *Paramount* case by petitioning the District Court to modify the decree. Primarily the Justice Department asked that the remedies of the amended complaint be ordered. This meant divorcement of the exhibition branches of the five majors from the main production-distribution activities. The case went to trial in late 1945, and in June, 1946, the three-judge, statutory court issued its opinion holding the distribution system to violate the Sherman Act. The holdings can be summarized as follows:

1. The uniform admission prices for any given theater specified in the film licenses of all eight defendants were held sufficient evidence from which to infer a horizontal price-fixing conspiracy among them. In addition each distributor-defendant was found to have engaged in an illegal vertical price-fixing conspiracy with its licensees.

2. The uniform systems of runs and clearances adopted by the distributors were found to be the result of illegal conspiracy. Although it was shown that the amount of clearance set before any run indirectly determined the admission price of the theater or theaters concerned, the court refused to hold a single clearance agreement between a single distributor and its licensee to be illegal per se. The court analogized the license of a film to a theater for a week, not to the sale of a product but to the sale of an entire business and its good will. Hence it said the clearance agreement was ancillary to the license of film and was legal if reasonable. A reasonable clearance was one that was not unduly extended as to area or duration and that afforded a fair protection to the interests of the licensee without interfering unreasonably with the interests of the public.

3. Formula deals and master agreements were held illegal because inclusion of the theaters of a circuit into a single agreement gave no opportunity for other theater owners to bid for the feature for their respective areas. Franchises covering more than one season and embracing all pictures were also illegal interference with the opportunities of rival theaters to bid for pictures.

4. Block booking in the form of tying one copyrighted film to another by conditioning the licensing of one on the licensing of the other was held illegal. The extension of a public grant of monopoly, such as a patent or copyright, to items other than the single patented or copyrighted product had been held illegal in a long series of cases. The blind-selling prohibition of the earlier consent decree which required trade showings resulted in very poor attendance. Hence, blind selling was not held illegal where exhibitors could reject films bought without trade showings.

5. Pooling agreements whereby two or more of the five majors or a major and an independent theater owner operated their theaters jointly were held illegal. These were clear efforts to reduce competition in exhibition through systems of price fixing and clearances.

6. Certain license terms discriminating in favor of circuit buyers were held illegal. Among these were (a) suspension of contract terms if a circuit theater remained closed for more than eight weeks with reinstatement without liability on reopening, (b) allowing large privileges in the selection and elimination of films, (c) allowing deductions in film rentals if double features were played, (d) granting moveovers and extended runs, (e) granting road-show privileges, (f) allowing overage and underage, (g) excluding foreign pictures and those of independent producers, and (h) granting rights to question the classification of features for rental purposes.

In December, 1946, a decree was issued by the statutory court pursuant to its opinion of the prior June. The decree prohibited: (1) fixing admission prices in film licenses, (2) agreements to maintain systems of clearances, (3) clearances between theaters not in substantial competition, (4) clearance in excess of what was "reasonably necessary" to protect the licensee in the run granted, (5) franchises, (6) formula deals, master agreements, and (7) conditional block booking. Where an exhibitor chose to license films in groups, he was to be given the right to reject 20 per cent of such films. All pooling agreements and joint interests in theaters of two defendants or a defendant and independents were ordered to terminate. Further theater expansion was limited to buying out other joint owners only where it was shown that such acquisition would not unduly restrain competition.

The court held the harsh remedy of divorcement of exhibition from production-distribution in the five majors, which had been requested by the government, to be unnecessary. Instead, it ordered a system of competitive bidding for films in each run open to all theaters. Licenses were to be given theater by theater and picture by picture, solely on the basis of merit. Past status or affiliation was to have no effect on licenses. The distributor was allowed to reject all bids. If he accepted any, however, he was required to grant it to "the highest responsible bidder, having a theatre of a size, location and equipment adequate to yield a reasonable return to the licensors."

SUPREME COURT DECISION

On appeal to the Supreme Court of the United States, most of the lower court rulings relating to the illegality of trade practices were affirmed. As to the horizontal and vertical conspiracies to fix admission prices, the court reiterated the basic rule that price-fixing combinations are illegal per se. The court pointed out that the film copyrights did not give the holder the right to fix admission prices, but that it was an illegal use of copyrights to use them to carry out a price-fixing scheme. The rulings on clearances were also affirmed. The court restated the criteria for reasonable clearance which had appeared in the trial court decision but not in the decree. The court also approved shifting to the defendant-distributors the burden of proof to show clearances to be reasonable. . . .

The District Court injunction against formula deals and master agreements was also affirmed. Such practices eliminated the possibility of independent theaters bidding for earlier runs and put a premium on the size of the circuit. The District Court prohibition of franchises was reversed. Although the five major circuits may have used their power illegally to obtain long franchises, the court felt that franchises were not illegal per se. The lower court was directed to reëxamine franchises in light of the elimination from the decree of competitive bidding.

The District Court prohibition on block booking was affirmed. The Supreme Court adopted the reasoning of the District Court which applied the rule of a number of recent patent antitrust cases; that is, extension of a public grant of monopoly beyond the specific patented item to augment monopoly power is illegal. The tying of one copyrighted film to another was therefore held an illegal extension of the copyright grant. The prohibitions of the other discriminatory practices detailed in the District Court opinion were also upheld.

The District Court mandate for competitive bidding, picture by picture and theater by theater, was reversed. Four of the five majors favored competitive bidding; Paramount, the three minors, and independent theaters generally opposed it. On appeal, even the Justice Department opposed it. The freedom to compete in all runs, for which independent exhibitors had so long fought, also meant the bidding up of rentals in most runs. The Court based its reversal on the ground that competitive bidding would involve the courts too deeply in the daily operation of the industry. As set up by the District Court, the bidding system had two fatal weaknesses. The system allowed incomparable bids, since an exhibitor could specify flat rental, percentage of gross, or both, and could also specify how much clearance he was willing to accept and when he wished to exhibit the film. It also set up no measurable standard of rank, since the film was to be licensed to the "highest responsible bidder, having a theatre of size, location and equipment adequate to yield a reasonable return to the licensor." The Court felt the judiciary was unsuited to administer business affairs in this manner. It also speculated that since the circuits had the most money, they would still take the choice films first.

As an alternative to the nullified competitive bidding, the Supreme Court directed the lower court to reconsider divestiture of theaters as a remedy. . . .

■ ■ ■ ■

United States v. Paramount Pictures, Inc. (1947), United States Supreme Court

This section from the Supreme Court opinion on the Paramount case is significant for its impact on the industry, for its recounting of revealing commercial statistics, and for its implying that the Court would probably rule in favor of the right of motion pictures to First Amendment protection, should the question ever be tested. This implication links the Paramount case with the *Miracle* case of three years later.

Third. Monopoly, Expansion of Theatre Holdings, Divestiture.
There is a suggestion that the hold the defendants have on the industry is so great that a problem under the First Amendment is raised. Cf. *Associated Press* v. *United States*, 326 U. S. 1. We have no doubt that moving pictures, like newspapers and radio, are included in the press whose freedom is guaranteed by the First Amendment. That issue would be focused here if we had any question concerning monopoly in the production of moving pictures. But monopoly in production was eliminated as an issue in these cases, as we have noted. The chief argument at the bar is phrased in terms of monopoly of exhibition, restraints on exhibition, and the like. Actually, the issue is even narrower than that. The main contest is over the cream of the exhibition business—that of the first-run theatres. By defining the issue so narrowly we do not intend to belittle its importance. It shows, however, that the question here is not

United States v. Paramount Pictures, Inc. was argued before the United States Supreme Court in October 1947.

what the public will see or *if* the public will be permitted to see certain features. It is clear that under the existing system the public will be denied access to none. If the public cannot see the features on the first-run, it may do so on the second, third, fourth, or later run. The central problem presented by these cases is which exhibitors get the highly profitable first-run business. That problem has important aspects under the Sherman Act. But it bears only remotely, if at all, on any question of freedom of the press, save only as timeliness of release may be a factor of importance in specific situations.

The controversy over monopoly relates to monopoly in exhibition and more particularly monopoly in the first-run phase of the exhibition business.

The five majors in 1945 had interests in somewhat over 17 per cent of the theatres in the United States—3,137 out of 18,076.[1] Those theatres paid 45 per cent of the total domestic film rental received by all eight defendants.

In the 92 cities of the country with populations over 100,000 at least 70 per cent of all the first-run theatres are affiliated with one or more of the five majors. In 4 of those cities the five majors have no theatres. In 38 of those cities there are no independent first-run theatres. In none of the remaining 50 cities did less than three of the distributor-defendants license their product on first run to theatres of the five majors. In 19 of the 50 cities less than three of the distributor-defendants licensed their product on first run to independent theatres. In a majority of the 50 cities the greater share of all of the features of defendants were licensed for first-run exhibition in the theatres of the five majors.

In about 60 per cent of the 92 cities having populations of over 100,000, independent theatres compete with those of the five majors in first-run exhibition. In about 91 per cent of the 92 cities there is competition between independent theatres and the theatres of the five majors or between theatres of the five majors themselves for first-run exhibition. In all of the 92 cities there is always competition in some run even where there is no competition in first runs.

In cities between 25,000 and 100,000 populations the five majors have interests in 577 of a total of 978 first-run theatres or about 60 per cent.

---

1. The theatres which each of the five majors owned independently of the others were: Paramount 1,395 or 7.72 per cent; Warner 501 or 2.77 per cent; Loew's 135 or .74 per cent; Fox 636 or 3.52 per cent; RKO 109 or .60 per cent. There were in addition 361 theatres or about 2 per cent in which two or more of the five majors had joint interests. These figures exclude connections through film-buying or management contracts or through corporations in which a defendant owns an indirect minority stock interest. These theatres are located in 922 towns in 48 States and the District of Columbia.

In about 300 additional towns, mostly under 25,000, an operator affiliated with one of the five majors has all of the theatres in the town.

The District Court held that the five majors could not be treated collectively so as to establish claims of general monopolization in exhibition. It found that none of them was organized or had been maintained "for the purpose of achieving a national monopoly" in exhibition. It found that the five majors by their present theatre holdings "alone" (which aggregate a little more than one-sixth of all the theatres in the United States), "do not and cannot collectively or individually, have a monopoly of exhibition." The District Court also found that where a single defendant owns all of the first-run theatres in a town, there is no sufficient proof that the acquistion was for the purpose of creating a monopoly. It found rather that such consequence resulted from the inertness of competitors, their lack of financial ability to build theatres comparable to those of the five majors, or the preference of the public for the best-equipped theatres. And the percentage of features on the market which any of the five majors could play in its own theatres was found to be relatively small and in nowise to approximate a monopoly of film exhibition.[2]

Even in respect of the theatres jointly owned or jointly operated by the defendants with each other or with independents, the District Court found no monopoly or attempt to monopolize. Those joint agreements or ownership were found only to be unreasonable restraints of trade. The

2. The number of feature films released during the 1943–44 season by the eleven largest distributors is as follows:

| | | PERCENTAGES OF TOTAL | |
	NO. OF FILMS	With "Westerns" Included	With "Westerns" Excluded
Fox	33	8.31	9.85
Loew's	33	8.31	9.85
Paramount	31	7.81	9.25
RKO	38	9.57	11.34
Warner	19	4.79	5.67
Columbia	41	10.32	12.24
United Artists	16	4.04	4.78
Universal	49	12.34	14.63
Republic	—29 features —30 "Westerns"	14.86	8.66
Monogram	—26 features —16 "Westerns"	10.58	7.76
PRC	—20 features —16 "Westerns"	9.07	5.97
Totals	397 335 without "Westerns"	100.00	100.00

District Court, indeed, found no monopoly on any phase of the cases, although it did find an attempt to monopolize in the fixing of prices, the granting of unreasonable clearances, block-booking and the other unlawful restraints of trade we have already discussed. The "root of the difficulties," according to the District Court, lay not in theatre ownership but in those unlawful practices.

The District Court did, however, enjoin the five majors from expanding their present theatre holdings in any manner. It refused to grant the request of the Department of Justice for total divestiture by the five majors of their theatre holdings. It found that total divestiture would be injurious to the five majors and damaging to the public. Its thought on the latter score was that the new set of theatre owners who would take the place of the five majors would be unlikely for some years to give the public as good service as those they supplanted "in view of the latter's demonstrated experience and skill in operating what must be regarded as in general the largest and best equipped theatres." Divestiture was, it thought, too harsh a remedy where there was available the alternative of competitive bidding. It accordingly concluded that divestiture was unnecessary "at least until the efficiency of that system has been tried and found wanting."

It is clear, so far as the five majors are concerned, that the aim of the conspiracy was exclusionary, *i.e.* it was designed to strengthen their hold on the exhibition field. In other words, the conspiracy had monopoly in exhibition for one of its goals, as the District Court held. Price, clearance, and run are interdependent. The clearance and run provisions of the licenses fixed the relative playing positions of all theatres in a certain area; the minimum price provisions were based on playing position—the first-run theatres being required to charge the highest prices, the second-run theatres the next highest, and so on. As the District Court found, "In effect, the distributor, by the fixing of minimum admission prices, attempts to give the prior-run exhibitors as near a monopoly of the patronage as possible."

It is, therefore, not enough in determining the need for divestiture to conclude with the District Court that none of the defendants was organized or has been maintained for the purpose of achieving a "national monopoly," nor that the five majors through their present theatre holdings "alone" do not and cannot collectively or individually have a monopoly of exhibition. For when the starting point is a conspiracy to effect a monopoly through restraints of trade, it is relevant to determine what the results of the conspiracy were even if they fell short of monopoly.

An example will illustrate the problem. In the popular sense there is a monopoly if one person owns the only threatre in town. That usually does not, however, constitute a violation of the Sherman Act. But as we noted in *United States* v. *Griffith, ante,* p. 100, and see *Schine Chain Theatres, Inc.* v. *United States, ante,* p. 110, even such an ownership is vulnerable in a suit by the United States under the Sherman Act if the property was acquired, or its strategic position maintained, as a result of practices which constitute unreasonable restraints of trade. Otherwise, there would be reward from the conspiracy through retention of its fruits. Hence the problem of the District Court does not end with enjoining continuance of the unlawful restraints nor with dissolving the combination which launched the conspiracy. Its function includes undoing what the conspiracy achieved. As we have discussed in *Schine Chain Theatres, Inc.* v. *United States, ante,* p. 110, the requirement that the defendants restore what they unlawfully obtained is no more punishment than the familiar remedy of restitution. What findings would be warranted after such an inquiry in the present cases, we do not know. For the findings of the District Court do not cover this point beyond stating that monopoly was an objective of the several restraints of trade that stand condemned. . . .

The District Court in its findings speaks of the absence of a "purpose" on the part of any of the five majors to achieve a "national monopoly" in the exhibition of motion pictures. First, there is no finding as to the presence or absence of monopoly on the part of the five majors in the *first-run* field for the entire country, in the *first-run* field in the 92 largest cities of the country, or in the *first-run* field in separate localities. Yet the *first-run* field, which constitutes the cream of the exhibition business, is the core of the present cases. Section 1 of the Sherman Act outlaws unreasonable restraints irrespective of the amount of trade or commerce involved (*United States* v. *Socony-Vacuum Oil Co.,* 310 U. S. 150, 224, 225, n. 59), and § 2 condemns monopoly of "any part" of trade or commerce. "Any part" is construed to mean an appreciable part of interstate or foreign trade or commerce. *United States* v. *Yellow Cab Co.,* 332 U. S. 218, 225. Second, we pointed out in *United States* v. *Griffith, ante,* p. 100, that "specific intent" is not necessary to establish a "purpose or intent" to create a monopoly but that the requisite "purpose or intent" is present if monopoly results as a necessary consequence of what was done. The findings of the District Court on this phase of the cases are not clear, though we take them to mean by the absence of "purpose" the absence of a specific intent. So construed they are inconclusive. In any event they are ambiguous and must be recast on remand of the cases. Third, monopoly power, whether lawfully or unlawfully acquired, may violate § 2 of the Sherman Act though it remains unexercised (*United States* v. *Griffith, ante,* p. 100), for as we stated in *American Tobacco*

Co. v. *United States,* 328 U. S. 781, 809, 811, the existence of power "to exclude competition when it is desired to do so" is itself a violation of § 2, provided it is coupled with the purpose or intent to exercise that power. The District Court, being primarily concerned with the number and extent of the theatre holdings of defendants, did not address itself to this phase of the monopoly problem. Here also, parity of treatment as between independents and the five majors as theatre owners, who were tied into the same general conspiracy, necessitates consideration of this question. . . .

These matters were not considered by the District Court. For that reason, as well as the others we have mentioned, the findings on monopoly and divestiture which we have discussed in this part of the opinion will be set aside. There is an independent reason for doing that. As we have seen, the District Court considered competitive bidding as an alternative to divestiture in the sense that it concluded that further consideration of divestiture should not be had until competitive bidding had been tried and found wanting. Since we eliminate from the decree the provisions for competitive bidding, it is necessary to set aside the findings on divestiture so that a new start on this phase of the cases may be made on their remand. . . .

■ ■ ■ ■

THE MIRACLE CASE: THE SUPREME COURT AND THE MOVIES (1961), Alan F. Westin

Alan Westin's monograph *The Miracle Case* was a casebook for law students, explaining the background, events, and implications of the landmark Supreme Court decision. These sections from the book develop the initial reactions to the film, the actions of New York City commissioner of licenses Edward McCaffrey, and the boycott campaign initiated by Francis Cardinal Spellman.

ENTER THE MIRACLE

On December 12, 1950, a movie called *Ways of Love* opened at the Paris Theater, a small foreign film house on West 58th Street in New York City. *Ways of Love* was a grouping of three short films into one feature. Two of these were French-made: *A Day in the Country,* based

From Alan F. Westin, *The Miracle Case: The Supreme Court and the Movies,* ICP Case Study #64, Copyright 1961 by The Inter University Case Program, Box 229, Syracuse, N.Y. 13210.

upon a story by Guy de Maupassant and directed by Jean Renoir; and *Jofroi,* directed by Marcel Pagnol. The third was an Italian picture written and directed by Roberto Rossellini from a story by Federico Fellini and featuring the volatile and celebrated Italian actress, Anna Magnani. Each film was presented as illustrating a different aspect of love and was introduced by a frame showing alternative definitions of the word "love" from the dictionary. All three films had English subtitles. *A Day in the Country* and *Jofroi* were received warmly by the critics and by the public, and at no time did they create a controversy. It was only *The Miracle* that caused explosions.

The Miracle was in four scenes and ran for forty minutes. A demented peasant woman living in a primitive Italian village is tending her goats when a bearded stranger strolls by. She thinks he is St. Joseph, returning to earth to bring her "grace." She gives him food and wine, drinks wine herself, and the scene closes with the clear implication that he seduces her. Toward the end of this episode, a deep voice on the soundtrack recites from the Bible (Matthew 1:20): "Behold, the angel of the Lord appeared unto him in a dream, saying, Joseph, thou son of David, fear not to take unto thee Mary thy wife: for that which is conceived in her is of the Holy Ghost." In the second scene, months later, she talks with two priests about the "miracle" which has happened to her. Later, while dancing after a church service, she faints, and the village women learn she is pregnant. In scene three, she refuses to work because she must "honor" the coming child. She is taunted by the young people of the village, who put a basin on her head, sing a religious hymn to "Mary," and throw her out of town with a mocking religious procession. In the final scene, after living alone for months in a grotto, the demented woman goes to an outbuilding of an abandoned but locked church on a mountainside, and in a moment of combined pain and religious ecstasy, delivers her own child.

The Miracle played to mixed notices. Howard Barnes of the *New York Herald Tribune* wrote: "The less said about *The Miracle* the better, except that it would be wise to time a visit to the Paris in order to skip it. Rosselini has imagined that an idiot shepherdess meets a handsome stranger whom she mistakes for St. Joseph and bears him a child. The Italian director has dragged out the theme with a great deal of revolting attitudinizing. Anna Magnani has the bad luck to play the subject of the supposed miracle and Federico Fellini is guilty of having written the tasteless script as well as having acted in it. Altogether it leaves a very bad taste in one's mouth." Rose Pelswick in the *Journal-American* echoed the view that the film was "in questionable taste" but added that it offered "a striking performance by Rossellini's pre-Bergman star, the fiery

Anna Magnani." Alton Cook in the *World-Telegram and Sun* considered *The Miracle* as "charged with the same overwrought hysteria that ran through [Rossellini's] *Stromboli*. . . . In addition to the unrelieved tone of hysteria, the picture has an unpleasant preoccupation with filth and squalor. The verdict in this corner on *Ways of Love* is two excellent films and one exceedingly trying experience." Archer Winsten in the *New York Post* found Miss Magnani's performance "profoundly impressive" but remarked that "the parallels with Christ's conception, birth in a manger and hard times give this picture implications and overtones that could well prove offensive to the religious. . . ."

Praise came from Bosley Crowther in the *New York Times*. Calling *The Miracle* the "most overpowering and provocative" of the three films and "probably the most intense dramatic piece that we have had from the sensational Italian director," Crowther predicted this would "certainly cause a lot of stir."

> Played by Anna Magnani with a passion and fluid forcefulness as could only come from a Latin who is inspired yet fully disciplined, this bold and extravagant character is a creature of such tragedy— and it is so subtly framed by Rossellini—that she may be interpreted in two ways. She may be logically accepted as a symbol of deep and simple faith, horribly abused and tormented by a cold and insensitive world; or she may be entirely regarded as an open mockery of faith and religious fervor—depending upon your point of view. However, it must be acknowledged—Rossellini's caustic picture is the topper to a brilliant lot of film.

ENTER COMMISSIONER MCCAFFREY

What audiences' reactions to *Ways of Love* would have been if it had continued its run at the Paris Theater unmolested will never be known. On December 24, 1950, twelve days after the first performance, the New York press reported that showings of *The Miracle* had been stopped the previous afternoon on orders of the New York City Commissioner of Licenses, Edward T. McCaffrey.[1] McCaffrey had a letter delivered to the manager of the Paris, Mrs. Lillian Gerard, on Friday, December 22, declaring that he found the film "officially and personally blasphemous." In a telephone call earlier the same day, a representative of the Com-

---

1. The License Commissioner of New York City is appointed by the Mayor and serves at the Mayor's pleasure. The appointment is made after consultation with Party leaders and does not involve negotiations with professional or other interest groups, as would, for example, the appointment of a Health Commissioner. The License Commissioner has authority over 77 different occupations or activities and is empowered to license and supervise these to protect the public from unfair practices or improper conditions.

missioner's office warned Mrs. Gerard that the theater's license would be suspended if *The Miracle* were shown at that day's 1:00 p.m. opening performance or thereafter. Mrs. Gerard contacted the distributor of the film, Joseph Burstyn, for advice. She asked the Commissioner's representative for a short period of grace to consult her attorneys. This was not granted, and Commissioner McCaffrey could not be reached to discuss the legal implications of withdrawal. For the two afternoon showings that Friday *The Miracle* was withdrawn and another film screened in its place.

At the same time that he notified the theater, Commissioner McCaffrey had a letter delivered to Burstyn. This stated that "all theaters under the jurisdiction of this department" were being advised by the Commissioner that he intended "to take immediate steps against their licenses in the event they are found showing such a film, which I find to be a blasphemous affront to a great many of our fellow citizens." McCaffrey called on Burstyn to "co-operate" by eliminating all bookings of *The Miracle* in New York City.

McCaffrey's suggestion was a potential economic disaster for Burstyn. His company was not an importer of large numbers of foreign films but rather of a few which Burstyn took on because he thought they had unusual artistic merit. He had brought *Paisan, Open City,* and *Bicycle Thief* to American audiences, and it was his practice to work with "100% effort" on one film at a time. He had a heavy financial investment in *Ways of Love* already, in preparation and advertising costs, and it was his major film of the winter season, 1950–1951. The New York City market was the most important in the nation for foreign films, and a ban in New York based on Catholic protests threatened to set off censors in other key cities such as Chicago or to frighten away theater owners even in cities without government censorship. Burstyn decided that he had to fight for his film, for economic reasons as well as for civil liberty.

The first thing Burstyn did after receiving McCaffrey's letter was to phone Mrs. Gerard and to agree that they should keep the ban out of the news, in an attempt to straighten it out with the License Commissioner. However, a *New York Times* editor attending the theater became curious about the substitution and broke the story in his paper. When Burstyn learned that the theater had withdrawn *The Miracle,* he informed Mrs. Gerard that failure to show the film was a violation of the theater's contract with him, and he persuaded her to stand up to the Commissioner. At the two evening performances on Friday, *The Miracle* was restored to the trilogy.

Commissioner McCaffrey was apparently keeping close tabs on the Paris. A letter delivered by messenger the next morning (Saturday, December 23) notified Mrs. Gerard that the theater's license was under suspension because of the Friday evening showings. While not required to do so, the Commissioner said he would give the theater a hearing before any further step of revocation was taken. At a press conference Commissioner McCaffrey told reporters that he had acted after having seen the film personally, not because he had received any outside complaints. "Officially, as a representative of the city government," McCaffrey explained, "I felt there were hundreds of thousands of citizens whose religious beliefs were assaulted by the picture." . . .

Enter Cardinal Spellman

The head of the Catholic Archdiocese of New York, Francis Cardinal Spellman, took a personal hand in the affair. He issued a statement that was read at all Masses at St. Patrick's Cathedral on Sunday, January 7 and made the headlines on Monday. The Cardinal's statement began by reminding Catholics that they had recently taken the annual "pledge of the Legion of Decency," promising to "remain away from indecent and immoral films, to unite with those who protest against them, and to stay away altogether from places of amusement which show them as a matter of policy":

> Today, we call upon you to make that pledge effective against a motion picture entitled *The Miracle,* and against any theater that is showing it now or may show it henceforth. Not only do we address this admonition to the one and a quarter million of our fellow Catholics of the Archdiocese of New York but also to the 26 millions of our fellow Catholics in these United States of America.

Cardinal Spellman summarized the condemnation of the film by the National Legion of Decency and mentioned its condemnation in Rome by the Pontifical Film Commission. Noting the report in Saturday's press of Justice Steuer's ruling, the Cardinal said:

> It is indeed a blot upon the escutcheon of the Empire State that no means of redress is available to the people to correct a mistake made by the State Board of Censorship. And in licensing *The Miracle* our State Board certainly made a mistake offending and insulting millions of people for which it will be censured by every decent man and woman. . . . Since the civil law sustains the showing of such a vile and harmful picture, we, as the guardians of the moral law, must summon you and all people with a sense of decency to refrain from seeing it and supporting the venal purveyors of such pictures which are so harmful to morality and the public welfare. Moreover if the present law is so weak and inadequate to cope with this desperate situation then all right-thinking citizens should unite to change

and strengthen the federal and state statutes to curb those who would profit financially by blasphemy, immorality and sacrilege.

The Cardinal then explained to his audiences why *The Miracle* was offensive:

> The theme of *The Miracle* is the seduction of an idiotic Italian woman. What is there in this theme to be approved or licensed? The seduction of any idiot-woman, regardless of race, is revolting to any decent man or woman. It is art at its lowest. And to give to this story of the seduction of an idiot-woman the title, *The Miracle,* is diabolical deception at its depths. The picture should very properly be entitled, *Woman Further Defamed,* by Roberto Rossellini. . . .
>
> *The Miracle* is a despicable affront to every Christian. It is a mockery of our Faith. We believe in Miracles. This picture ridicules that belief. . . .
>
> In a secondary way, *The Miracle* is a vicious insult to Italian womanhood. It presents the Italian woman as moronic and neurotic and, in matters of religion, fanatical. Only a perverted mind could so represent so noble a race of women. . . .
>
> We are a religious nation. The perpetrators of *The Miracle* unjustly cast their blasphemous darts of ridicule at Christian Faith and at Italian womanhood, thereby dividing Religion against Religion and race against race. . . . Divide and conquer is the technique of the greatest enemy of civilization, atheistic Communism. God forbid that these producers of racial and religious mockeries should divide and demoralize Americans so that the minions of Moscow might enslave this land of liberty.

Reminding Catholics of their pledge, Cardinal Spellman closed by expressing confidence that "all good Americans will unite with us in this battle for decency and Americanism."

In the wake of the Cardinal's message, the Catholic War Veterans set up a picket line outside the Paris Theater from opening to closing time. The pickets carried signs reading, "This Picture is an Insult to Every Decent Woman and Her Mother," "This Picture is Blasphemous," "Please Stay Out of This Theater." Some placards read, "Write to the Board of Regents in Albany to Remove the License of this Picture." The Ancient Order of Hibernians and New York Assemblyman Samuel Roman of the Fifteenth District telegraphed Governor Thomas E. Dewey to stop the exhibition of the picture, and the New York Chapter of the Knights of Columbus called on the Governor to "correct this error." A protest demonstration by 3,000 men of the New York Archdiocesan Union of the Holy Name Society was set for the following Sunday to picket in the plaza across from the Paris Theater. . . .

■ ■ ■ ■

THE CATHOLIC AS PHILISTINE (1951), William P. Clancy

Not all Catholic opinion was united behind Cardinal Spellman's boycott tactics. This article, using the terms and assumptions of Mortimer Adler's *Art and Prudence,* was written by William Clancy and appeared in *Commonweal,* the liberal Catholic journal. Chief Justice Felix Frankfurter, in writing his separate opinion concurring with that of the whole Court, cited Clancy's arguments specifically in support of the position that a Catholic ban against the film was neither necessarily good Americanism nor good Catholicism. Ironically, Mr. Clancy, who was an instructor of English at Notre Dame University, lost his job, perhaps as a result of this article. He became editor of *Commonweal,* however, in which capacity he served for over a decade.

The now celebrated crusade to suppress Rossellini's film, *The Miracle,* has followed closely upon two similar campaigns: the efforts to censor and suppress the Rutgers undergraduate magazine, *Antho,* for publishing a short story which certain elements in the local Catholic community considered "immoral" and "blasphemous," and the successful attempt to remove certain Charlie Chaplin comedies from movie and television screens in New Jersey because the Catholic War Veterans "suspected Chaplin of having Leftist sympathies." These three efforts have been attended by wide publicity, and the latest one, the battle over *The Miracle,* has been marked by particular bitterness on both sides.

The pattern of these campaigns has shocked thousands of non-Catholic Americans, and this shock is shared by many loyal Catholics. Our shock, however, is a deeper one than any that can be felt by our non-Catholic neighbors, for we have more at stake; we are profoundly disturbed to see certain of our co-religionists embarked upon crusades which we feel can result only in great harm to the cause of religion, of art, and of intelligence. These appeals to mass hysteria, these highly arbitrary invocations of a police censorship must ultimately result, we feel, in great harm to the cause of religion as well as art. They are, we feel, a most deplorable violation of the human spirit, a violation which will justly expose us to the enmity of many men of goodwill, and furnish ammunition to the enemies of the Church.

"The Catholic as Philistine," by William P. Clancy, appeared in the 16 March 1951 issue of *Commonweal.*

These three cases of *Antho,* the Charlie Chaplin films, and *The Miracle* have much in common; they form a pattern. They involve a question of art, of the right of the artist to the free choice and treatment of his materials, and the extent to which his freedom of choice and treatment can or should be limited by prudence. They also involve the attempt to limit this freedom by appeals to mass emotion, and by consequent mass pressure. The end result, in each case, has been a semi-ecclesiastical McCarthyism, accompanied by some of the odious methods which this now implies: its "guilt by association," its appeal to prejudice and non-intelligence, its hysteria. This has made the matter of art and prudence a question for debate in the marketplace, and it has called into the debate thousands of well-meaning but misguided voices that appear to know little of the profound meaning of that which they so noisily argue about. It is a spectacle which many of us, as Catholics, can view only with shame and repulsion, for we know that neither art nor prudence, religion nor country, intelligence nor morality can be served by such means.

Such discussion has already been raised by the attempts to suppress *The Miracle.* The critics have been almost unanimous in judging the film to be superbly acted and honestly executed. Some have questioned its dramatic validity; others, like the critic who reviewed the film in THE COMMONWEAL, have questioned the taste of the director in his choice of theme. No serious or responsible critic, as far as I know, however, has questioned the sincerity or honesty of Rossellini's intention in making the film, an intention abundantly moral, as Rossellini made clear in a cable to Cardinal Spellman: "In *The Miracle,*" Rossellini said, "men are still without pity because they have not gone back to God. But God is already present in the faith, however confused, of the poor persecuted woman. . . . 'The Miracle' occurs when, with the birth of the child, the poor demented woman regains sanity in her maternal love." As in his previous film, Rossellini said, he had here endeavored to show how the absence of charity made way for immense sorrow. A group of Catholics, headed by Mr. Otto L. Spaeth, president of the American Federation of Arts, gave *The Miracle* unanimous approval as a deeply moving, profoundly religious film. The only "blasphemy" in the film, they agreed, was "the blasphemy of the villagers, who stopped at nothing, not even the mock singing of the hymn to the Virgin, in their brutal badgering of the tragic woman." It would seem, then, that the film is not *obviously* blasphemous or obscene, either in its intention or execution. The wisdom, then, of attempts at suppressing this or other serious films through the medium of mass pressure is, at best, highly doubtful, and it is made more questionable if we recall some specific principles.

First of all, there is clearly no such thing as a theme which is denied to the artist because it is immoral *in itself*. Its ultimate morality or immorality will depend upon its treatment at the hands of the artist. Admittedly some themes, of their very nature, require moral sensitivity and insight of the artist if he is to handle them without himself being contaminated. As Maritain has said: "To write Proust's work as it asked to be written would require the inner light of a St. Augustine." Such a theme, admittedly, is that of *The Miracle*. Perhaps, in our present society, the artist is ill-advised to attempt the treatment of such a theme under any circumstances, no matter how pure his intention. But categorically to deny him his right to treat a theme, on the ground that it is *per se* "immoral," "blasphemous," or "dangerous" is to impose an intolerable limitation upon the freedom so absolutely necessary if art is to exist at all. Worse still, such a confusion of a theme with its treatment is plainly "bad philosophy," and "bad philosophy" can never, in any mature view, add up to good morality.

Second: Many Catholics *would*, undoubtedly, find such a theme as that of *The Miracle* "offensive in itself." They would, admittedly, be incapable of any nice philosophical discrimination between the theme itself and its treatment by the artist. On the same principle, however, these are the very same people who would be shocked by the themes of *Anthony and Cleopatra* (sexual passion), *Oedipus Rex* (incest), and *Lysistrata* (denial of marital rights to their husbands by a whole nation of wives). Fortunately for art, prudence and intelligence these dramas have not been made the subject of mass morality campaigns for quite some time now, so there is as little chance of these people seeing such plays as there would be of their seeing *The Miracle*, had not this film been forcibly brought to their attention. The real danger to public morality would seem to lie, not in the cause, but in the proposed cure. Vulgarity, like bad philosophy, can never bear good fruit.

Third: Even should we accept the hypothesis that, despite Rossellini's intention (and charity surely demands that we accept his word as the artist) the film is finally blasphemous, who is competent to decide this? Surely no one has ever claimed that along with the sacramental powers conferred by Holy Orders every cleric received the intuitive insights of a competent literary and art critic. Still less can we look for such subtle judgments on the nature and intent of art to the sensitivities of veterans' organizations, or Police Commissioners, be they Catholic or not. The problem is not as simple as this. If art and the integrity of the artist mean anything at all they mean that final judgment on them must be reached quietly, prayerfully and intelligently by those who are morally, intellectually, and aesthetically qualified to speak on them. Without the combination of these sensitivities, we shall have the pure aestheticism of an Oscar Wilde, blind to the legitimate claims of prudence, on the one hand, or the arid moralism of a Puritan, blind to the equally pressing claims of art, on the other. Both extremes are intolerable. Surely the last place such judgments can be reached is in the partisan atmosphere of the picket line. It seems obvious that to fail to recognize this is to fail to recognize the reverence due the being, complexity, and integrity of truth.

Fourth: Even should a particular work of art be found morally or theologically unsound by competent judges (i.e. those who can view it as an artistic whole, who can see its intentions and form as well as its theme and method), it would still seem highly doubtful that the way to deal with this in a contemporary secular society is to attempt to suppress it by means of mass campaigns and the use of secular power. Prudence indicates that public morality may very possibly suffer more in this process, with all its attendant publicity and bitterness, than it would were the work quietly ignored. For the type of educated person, Catholic or non-Catholic, in this country who makes a habit of attending outstanding foreign films is usually quite capable of protecting his own intellectual, spiritual, and moral integrity, of forming his own judgments. He is apt bitterly to resent attempts by organized force to make these judgments for him. And he will probably find the majority of "morality campaigns," with their hysteria and their disregard for the complexity of truth, much more subtly shocking and morally revolting than any "dangerous theme." The overwhelming bulk of the population, on the other hand, is so very unlikely to see or desire to see a film like *The Miracle* (unless, as I have said, it is made a matter of public controversy) that the danger in this direction is very small.

It seems that the Church, above all other institutions, since she is the very incarnation of Truth, is the one from which, even in her temporal aspects, the spectre of McCarthyism should be most conspicuously absent. For here this spectre of irresponsible disregard for complexity, this use of "labels," this conscious appeal to surface virtue, this exploitation of non-intelligence, must appear much more deplorable than on any Senate floor —*corruptio optimi pessima*. It is to the Church, as to no human society, that we should be able to look for a deep respect for art as well as for prudence. This respect must result in a reverence for art and the artist which will make any interference with that freedom slow, very slow, to come. If it must come (and there are indeed times when it must) it will be only when a truly grave threat to faith or morals exists in the community. And when it comes it will come prayerfully and quietly. Above all it will avoid arbitrary and hasty judgments on the artist; it will scrupulously avoid making art a matter for partisan debate; it will be the last to uphold, tolerate, or advocate a police censorship of the artist, a censorship which knows practically nothing of the profound nature of that on which it passes judgment, a censorship which carries within it the most serious dangers to the dignity of the human spirit and intelligence, to freedom and art. To support an overeager censorship exhibits an unconcern for the hierarchy of values; a profoundly Philistine and un-Catholic brand of arbitrary moralism.

We have the Catholic War Veterans, organized, it would seem, to bear loud witness to those aspects of popular American Catholicism which are most shocking in any mature view of the function of the Church in modern society. Is it not well past the time when a national association of Catholics, especially those who write or teach, should be formed for the purpose of publicly representing and influencing a more reasoned and mature Catholic attitude toward matters on which they could speak with some competence, matters affecting questions of art, education, and the structure of society? Is it not time we cease leaving the field open to those who, however pure and sincere their intentions, seem bent on proving that, perhaps, the Paul Blanshards of America may have something to say after all?

Has history taught us nothing?

■ ■ ■ ■

JOSEPH BURSTYN, INC., V. WILSON, COMMISSIONER OF EDUCATION OF NEW YORK, ET AL. (1952), United States Supreme Court

The New York State Board of Regents, which functioned as a branch of the New York State Department of Education, supported license commissioner McCaffrey's ban of *The Miracle* on the grounds of the film's being "sacrilegious." Joseph Burstyn, distributor of the film, brought suit against Lewis A. Wilson, New York State's commissioner of education. Although Burstyn lost his suit in the New York courts, his appeal to the Supreme Court led to a significant reversal. Here is the opinion of the Court which led to the reversal.

Joseph Burstyn, Inc., v. Wilson, Commissioner of Education of New York, et al., was argued before the United States Supreme Court 24 April 1952 and decided 26 May 1952.

APPEAL FROM THE COURT OF APPEALS OF NEW YORK

MR. JUSTICE CLARK delivered the opinion of the Court.

The issue here is the constitutionality, under the First and Fourteenth Amendments, of a New York statute which permits the banning of motion picture films on the ground that they are "sacrilegious." That statute makes it unlawful "to exhibit, or to sell, leave or lend for exhibition at any place of amusement for pay or in connection with any business in the state of New York, any motion picture film or reel [with specified exceptions not relevant here], unless there is at the time in full force and effect a valid license or permit therefor of the education department . . . ." The statute further provides:

> "The director of the [motion picture] division [of the education department] or, when authorized by the regents, the officers of a local office or bureau shall cause to be promptly examined every motion picture film submitted to them as herein required, and unless such film or a part thereof is obscene, indecent, immoral, inhuman, sacrilegious, or is of such a character that its exhibition would tend to corrupt morals or incite to crime, shall issue a license therefor. If such director or, when so authorized, such officer shall not license any film submitted, he shall furnish to the applicant therefor a written report of the reasons for his refusal and a description of each rejected part of a film not rejected in toto."

Appellant is a corporation engaged in the business of distributing motion pictures. It owns the exclusive rights to distribute throughout the United States a film produced in Italy entitled "The Miracle." On November 30, 1950, after having examined the picture, the motion picture division of the New York education department, acting under the statute quoted above, issued to appellant a license authorizing exhibition of "The Miracle," with English subtitles, as one part of a trilogy called "Ways of Love." Thereafter, for a period of approximately eight weeks, "Ways of Love" was exhibited publicly in a motion picture theater in New York City under an agreement between appellant and the owner of the theater whereby appellant received a stated percentage of the admission price.

During this period, the New York State Board of Regents, which by statute is made the head of the education department, received "hundreds of letters, telegrams, post cards, affidavits and other communications" both protesting against and defending the public exhibition of "The Miracle." The Chancellor of the Board of Regents requested three members of the Board to view the picture and to make a report to the entire Board. After viewing the film, this committee reported to the Board that in its opinion there was basis for the claim that the picture was "sacrilegious." Thereafter, on January 19, 1951, the Regents directed appellant to show cause, at a hearing to be held on January 30, why its license to show "The Miracle" should not be rescinded on that ground. Appellant appeared at this hearing, which was conducted by the same three-member committee of the Regents which had previously viewed the picture, and challenged the jurisdiction of the committee and of the Regents to proceed with the case. With the consent of the committee, various interested persons and organizations submitted to it briefs and exhibits bearing upon the merits of the picture and upon the constitutional and statutory questions involved. On February 16, 1951, the Regents, after viewing "The Miracle," determined that it was "sacrilegious" and for that reason ordered the Commissioner of Education to rescind appellant's license to exhibit the picture. The Commissioner did so.

Appellant brought the present action in the New York courts to review the determination of the Regents. Among the claims advanced by appellant were (1) that the statute violates the Fourteenth Amendment as a prior restraint upon freedom of speech and of the press; (2) that it is invalid under the same Amendment as a violation of the guaranty of separate church and state and as a prohibition of the free exercise of religion; and, (3) that the term "sacrilegious" is so vague and indefinite as to offend due process. The Appellate Division rejected all of appellant's contentions and upheld the Regents' determination. 278 App. Div. 253, 104 N. Y. S. 2d 740. On appeal the New York Court of Appeals, two judges dissenting, affirmed the order of the Appellate Division. 303 N. Y. 242, 101 N. E. 2d 665. The case is here on appeal. 28 U. S. C. § 1257 (2).

As we view the case, we need consider only appellant's contention that the New York statute is an unconstitutional abridgment of free speech and a free press. In *Mutual Film Corp. v. Industrial Comm'n*, 236 U. S. 230 (1915), a distributor of motion pictures sought to enjoin the enforcement of an Ohio statute which required the prior approval of a board of censors before any motion picture could be publicly exhibited in the state, and which directed the board to approve only such films as it adjudged to be "of a moral, educational or amusing and harmless character." The statute was assailed in part as an unconstitutional abridgment of the freedom of the press guaranteed by the First and Fourteenth Amendments. The District Court rejected this contention, stating that the first eight Amendments were not a restriction on state action. 215 F. 138, 141 (D. C. N. D. Ohio 1914). On appeal to this Court, plaintiff in its brief abandoned this claim and contended merely that the statute in question violated the freedom of speech and publication guaranteed by the Constitution of Ohio. In affirming the decree of the District Court denying injunctive relief, this Court stated:

"It cannot be put out of view that the exhibition of moving pictures is a business pure and simple, originated and conducted for profit, like other spectacles, not to be regarded, nor intended to be regarded by the Ohio constitution, we think, as part of the press of the country or as organs of public opinion."

In a series of decisions beginning with *Gitlow* v. *New York*, 268 U. S. 652 (1925), this Court held that the liberty of speech and of the press which the First Amendment guarantees against abridgment by the federal government is within the liberty safeguarded by the Due Process Clause of the Fourteenth Amendment from invasion by state action. That principle has been followed and reaffirmed to the present day. Since this series of decisions came after the *Mutual* decision, the present case is the first to present squarely to us the question whether motion pictures are within the ambit of protection which the First Amendment, through the Fourteenth, secures to any form of "speech" or "the press."

It cannot be doubted that motion pictures are a significant medium for the communication of ideas. They may affect public attitudes and behavior in a variety of ways, ranging from direct espousal of a political or social doctrine to the subtle shaping of thought which characterizes all artistic expression. The importance of motion pictures as an organ of public opinion is not lessened by the fact that they are designed to entertain as well as to inform. As was said in *Winters* v. *New York*, 333 U. S. 507, 510 (1948):

"The line between the informing and the entertaining is too elusive for the protection of that basic right [a free press]. Everyone is familiar with instances of propaganda through fiction. What is one man's amusement, teaches another's doctrine."

It is urged that motion pictures do not fall within the First Amendment's aegis because their production, distribution, and exhibition is a large-scale business conducted for private profit. We cannot agree. That books, newspapers, and magazines are published and sold for profit does not prevent them from being a form of expression whose liberty is safeguarded by the First Amendment. We fail to see why operation for profit should have any different effect in the case of motion pictures.

It is further urged that motion pictures possess a greater capacity for evil, particularly among the youth of a community, than other modes of expression. Even if one were to accept this hypothesis, it does not follow that motion pictures should be disqualified from First Amendment protection. If there be capacity for evil it may be relevant in determining the permissible scope of community control, but it does not authorize substantially unbridled censorship such as we have here.

For the foregoing reasons, we conclude that expression by means of motion pictures is included within the free speech and free press guaranty of the First and Fourteenth Amendments. To the extent that language in the opinion in *Mutual Film Corp.* v. *Industrial Comm'n, supra,* is out of harmony with the views here set forth, we no longer adhere to it.[1]

To hold that liberty of expression by means of motion pictures is guaranteed by the First and Fourteenth Amendments, however, is not the end of our problem. It does not follow that the Constitution requires absolute freedom to exhibit every motion picture of every kind at all times and all places. That much is evident from the series of decisions of this Court with respect to other media of communication of ideas. Nor does it follow that motion pictures are necessarily subject to the precise rules governing any other particular method of expression. Each method tends to present its own peculiar problems. But the basic principles of freedom of speech and the press, like the First Amendment's command, do not vary. Those principles, as they have frequently been enunciated by this Court, make freedom of expression the rule. There is no justification in this case for making an exception to that rule.

The statute involved here does not seek to punish, as a past offense, speech or writing falling within the permissible scope of subsequent punishment. On the contrary, New York requires that permission to communicate ideas be obtained in advance from state officials who judge the content of the words and pictures sought to be communicated. This Court recognized many years ago that such a previous restraint is a form of infringement upon freedom of expression to be especially condemned. *Near* v. *Minnesota ex rel. Olson,* 283 U. S. 697 (1931). The Court there recounted the history which indicates that a major purpose of the First Amendment guaranty of a free press was to prevent prior restraints upon publication, although it was carefully pointed out that the liberty of the press is not limited to that protection. It was further stated that "the protection even as to previous restraint is not absolutely unlimited. But the limitation has been recognized only in exceptional cases." *Id.,* at 716. In the light of the First Amendment's history and of the *Near* decision, the State has a heavy burden to demonstrate that the limitation challenged here presents such an exceptional case.

New York's highest court says there is "nothing mysterious" about the statutory provision applied in this case: "It is simply this: that no religion, as that word is understood by the ordinary, reasonable person, shall be

1. See *United States* v. *Paramount Pictures, Inc.,* 334 U. S. 131, 166 (1948): "We have no doubt that moving pictures, like newspapers and radio, are included in the press whose freedom is guaranteed by the First Amendment." It is not without significance that talking pictures were first produced in 1926, eleven years after the *Mutual* decision. . . .

treated with contempt, mockery, scorn and ridicule . . . ."[2] This is far from the kind of narrow exception to freedom of expression which a state may carve out to satisfy the adverse demands of other interests of society. In seeking to apply the broad and all-inclusive definition of "sacrilegious" given by the New York courts, the censor is set adrift upon a boundless sea amid a myriad of conflicting currents of religious views, with no charts but those provided by the most vocal and powerful orthodoxies. New York cannot vest such unlimited restraining control over motion pictures in a censor. Cf. *Kunz* v. *New York,* 340 U. S. 290 (1951). Under such a standard the most careful and tolerant censor would find it virtually impossible to avoid favoring one religion over another, and he would be subject to an inevitable tendency to ban the expression of unpopular sentiments sacred to a religious minority. Application of the "sacrilegious" test, in these or other respects, might raise substantial questions under the First Amendment's guaranty of separate church and state with freedom of worship for all. However, from the standpoint of freedom of speech and the press, it is enough to point out that the state has no legitimate interest in protecting any or all religions from views distasteful to them which is sufficient to justify prior restraints upon the expression of those views. It is not the business of government in our nation to suppress real or imagined attacks upon a particular religious doctrine, whether they appear in publications, speeches, or motion pictures.

Since the term "sacrilegious" is the sole standard under attack here, it is not necessary for us to decide, for example, whether a state may censor motion pictures under a clearly drawn statute designed and applied to prevent the showing of obscene films. That is a very different question from the one now before us. We hold only that under the First and Fourteenth Amendments a state may not ban a film on the basis of a censor's conclusion that it is "sacrilegious."

Reversed.

2. At another point the Court of Appeals gave "sacrilegious" the following definition: "the act of violating or profaning anything sacred." . . . The Court of Appeals also approved the Appellate Division's interpretation: "As the court below said of the statute in question, 'All it purports to do is to bar a visual caricature of religious beliefs held sacred by one sect or another. . . .' " Judge Fuld, dissenting, concluded from all the statements in the majority opinion that "the basic criterion appears to be whether the film treats a religious theme in such a manner as to offend the religious beliefs of any group of persons. If the film does have that effect, and it is 'offered as a form of entertainment,' it apparently falls within the statutory ban regardless of the sincerity and good faith of the producer of the film, no matter how temperate the treatment of the theme, and no matter how unlikely a public disturbance or breach of the peace. The drastic nature of such a ban is highlighted by the fact that the film in question makes no direct attack on, or criticism of, any religious dogma or principle, and it is not claimed to be obscene, scurrilous, intemperate or abusive." . . .

■ ■ ■ ■

HOLLYWOOD AND THE U.S.A. (1950), Hortense Powdermaker

Hortense Powdermaker was an anthropologist who brought her tools and training to a study of Hollywood, as if it were one of the tiny primitive societies of Micronesia that had been studied by many of her colleagues. Her classic study, *Hollywood, the Dream Factory*, serves as a testament to the values of the "Old Hollywood," just as that particular "primitive" society was becoming extinct. This final chapter of the book examines the relationship of Hollywood's mores and practices to those of the United States as a whole.

The anthropologist sees any segment of society as part of a whole; he views Hollywood as a section of the United States of America, and both in the larger frame of Western civilization. The problems of the movie industry are not unique to it. But some characteristics of the modern world have been greatly exaggerated in Hollywood while others are underplayed. Hollywood is therefore not a reflection, but a caricature of selected contemporary tendencies, which, in turn, leave their imprint on the movies. It is a three-way circular interaction between Hollywood, U.S.A. and movies.

Many people would agree with the characterization of our society by the poet W. H. Auden as "The Age of Anxiety." The present generation has known two world wars and is worried about the possibility of a third, even more devastating. We won the last war and are probably the strongest nation, and yet we are insecure in our relations with former enemies and allies. Our country is prosperous and we have demonstrated an enormous capacity for production, but we are worried about a possible recession and unemployment. We live in a fast changing world but have lost faith in our belief that change is always for the better, and that progress is inevitable. We are not so sure of the happy ending.

Man has become increasingly lonely. Although people live in close physical contact, their relationships have become more and more depersonalized. We have a sense of being with people, and yet do not feel in any way related to them. In cities we are accustomed to having strange people beside us in street car, bus, or uncomfortably close in the subway. The technique of business and many other organizations, in trying to personalize their selling relationships, such as by announcing the name

"Hollywood and the U.S.A." is from *Hollywood, the Dream Factory*, by Hortense Powdermaker (Little, Brown, 1950).

of employees to customers, really fools no one. The fact that the name of the post office clerk, the bank teller or the person who handles complaints in the department store, is posted, does not really influence their relationship with customers. The market place is still basically impersonal. Over the radio, we listen to the voices of strangers relating intimate domestic stories or giving us their opinions about the latest national or world event. All these factors give an illusion of companionship which, however, only increases the feeling of being alone. This loneliness is particularly striking when we compare modern to primitive man with his web of personal relationships within his clan. From birth to death he was tied through reciprocal duties and responsibilities to his clan kindred. Clan membership could not be lost and was as fixed for the individual as was his sex. He belonged to his group through basic biological ties and isolation was rare.

Many other factors contribute to modern man's anxiety. The traditional American belief that anyone, by working hard and industriously, may rise in the social hierarchy and become rich and successful is being questioned. There is considerable evidence that the American worker realizes that social mobility is decreasing. Workers increasingly believe that hard work no longer counts for as much as it did and that opportunities for advancement are restricted. Many employees do not even understand the immediate aspects of their work situation. A study made at an electric company, which had an unusually good relationship with its employees, showed that there was much that the worker did not understand about his job, even including the method of payment. The author thought that this lack of understanding caused a feeling of exasperation and sense of personal futility on the part of the workers. Modern man lives in a world which is difficult to comprehend. He is prosperous or unemployed in recurring economic cycles about which economists talk in learned words of cause and effect. But the average man see only the effect, and is confused as to the causes.

In Hollywood there is far more confusion and anxiety than in the society which surrounds it. Even in its most prosperous periods when net profits were enormous, far surpassing those of other businesses, everyone was scared. Now, when diminishing foreign markets, increasing costs of production, competition with European pictures, and changing box-office tastes threaten the swollen profits of past prosperity, fear rises to panic. Anxiety grips everyone from executive to third assistant director. The happy endings of at least 100 per cent net profit for the studio and a relatively long period of employment at high salaries for employees, are becoming less common. Yet, although this is well known, many individuals still cherish the fantasy for themselves. In the movies the happy ending is still almost universal. Perhaps the people who make the movies cannot afford to admit that there can be another kind of ending, and many of those who sit in the audience prefer this fantasy, too. But an increasing number are becoming dissatisfied with the so obviously contrived nature of these endings. The neat and unrealistic movie solution to all problems is neither satisfying nor entertaining.

Attitudes stem from the past and change slowly. In a rapidly changing society such as ours, some attitudes born out of a past situation continue under new conditions, even when inappropriate. Today there are people who will still believe in the *laissez-faire* economy of the frontier days and are hostile to planning designed for a country which no longer has a frontier. But many who stubbornly cling to the old *laissez-faire* thinking are uneasy lest they fight a losing battle, while many of those who plan are afraid that the planning may go too far. Neither side is really very sure of itself. In Hollywood the lack of planning and extemporizing has been carried to extremes probably not known even on the frontier, and greater certainly than in any contemporary industry. Even more important, extemporizing without a plan has long been regarded by many as a necessary and inherent part of movie making. However, the proper accompaniment, the frontier self-confidence and courage in taking chances, is very rare in Hollywood. The distinguished director-producer William Wyler appeals for

> " '. . . men of courage' in Hollywood to reach out for a wealth of picture material which the industry has shunned so far." He continues, "We need men of courage in high places who will not be intimidated or coerced into making only 'safe' pictures—pictures devoid of any ideas whatsoever." Too often he has bunked up against a situation where the top men were forced to decide between two stories and asked the question, "Which is the safest?" Mediocrity in films is the direct result of playing it safe.[1]

The men who make these decisions do not trust the public to like a picture which has ideas in it, Mr. Wyler says, in the same interview. It might be added that the men who do not trust the public usually do not trust themselves.

From the frontier past comes also the tradition of individual aggressive behavior. This persists although industry has become increasingly regimented and co-operation more essential. In the movie industry which depends on the collaborative effort of many people, the aggression is more ruthless than any described on the frontier, although, due to the insecurities of most people, it is masked under "Darlings" and "Sweethearts"

1. *Variety,* October 12, 1949.

and costly presents and parties. In the movies, however, the hatred and aggression comes through with a bang. Here is undiluted violence. This may meet the needs of the makers of our daydreams, as well as of those who consume them. Many people in our society experience a high level of frustration but are unable, either because of social pressures or inner fear, to express their resentment. In the movies they may find comfort and encouragement for their fantasies.

We have also inherited a Puritan tradition, stressing the sinfulness of human nature and giving us taboos to curb it. Today the doctrine of the innate evilness of man has lost much of its force and is far less a part of the conscious beliefs of many people. There is a growing awareness that babies are born neither sinful nor virtuous, but with potentialities for many different kinds of behavior, and even the definitions of sin and virtue continue to change. Hollywood, however, even more than the rest of society, feels the weight of Puritan traditions. The industry has imposed on itself a set of taboos derived in part from seventeenth-century New England Protestantism, in order to appease the Catholic Legion of Decency and other would-be censors. No one in Hollywood, and very few outside of it, believe in the Code, nor are the censors appeased or pleased. For while the taboos are applied in the production of each movie, they fail completely to achieve the Puritan concepts on which they are based. They serve merely to make movies more dishonest, which is the natural result of any hypocrisy.

The activities of the various censoring groups spring not only from our past Puritanism, but also out of our social system in which pressure groups are accustomed to playing an important role. Labor, big business, farmers, and others try to influence legislation and get what they want through their organizations. Pressure groups are not restricted to modern society. In *primitive* ones, the whole tribe may bring pressure on recalcitrant individuals to follow the mores. But the pressure groups which try to influence Hollywood represent only a small part of the population and of movie audiences and are always negative in their intentions. They try to enforce a list of "Thou shalt nots." Most people interested in good entertainment usually know enough to realize that good movies cannot be created by such actions and so do not belong to these groups. This raises the whole question of the function of pressure groups in different areas of society. It is possible that legislators can pass adequate laws through balancing the claims of different pressure groups, and the pluralistic theory of government has long been an accepted democratic practice. But legislation is one thing, and making a movie is another.

An important focus for much of the anxiety in our modern world is in our changing values and goals. The anthropologist knows that the important differences between groups of men are not biological, but lie in their goals. Among the same people the goals may change from one historical period to another, such as from Elizabethan to Victorian England, and they obviously vary from one society to another. In the early Middle Ages religion provided the sanctions for most behavior. Since then the church, while still a functioning institution, has continued to lose much of its vitality. As Kluckhohn writes:

> The anthropologist must characterize our culture as profoundly irreligious. More than half of our people still occasionally go through the forms, and there are rural and ethnic islands in our population where religion is still a vital force. But very few of our leaders are still religious in the sense that they are convinced that prayer or the observance of church codes will affect the course of human events. . . . Belief in God's judgments and punishments as a motive for behavior is limited to a decreasing minority.[2]

Even more important relatively few people today, as compared to a couple hundred years ago, have the kind of relationship with God to bring them security or comfort. Our society stresses the search for a good time rather than the quest for salvation.

Traditions, however, have a habit of living on in the deeper levels of our consciousness, even when they are overtly denied. Comparatively few people give the impression of really enjoying their wealth or their good times. Many of them appear to be consumed with an obsession to merely fill up time with more and more activity, and space with more and more costly objects. The frenzied and compulsive activity in the studios and outside of them is one of Hollywood's most striking characteristics. Another is the evaluation of not only objects, but people too, in terms of how much they cost. In making movies, this is reflected in the idea that the more a picture costs the better it must be. The tendency towards lavish sets, costumes, and other extravagances is now being curtailed because of the need for economy and the trend to shooting on location. But, with a few exceptions, the correlation of the value of pictures with their budgets is still the prevalent type of thinking in Hollywood. The greater the cost the more sure the studio feels of success, and hence high costs become one way of reducing anxiety. Actually, money can no more guarantee dramatic values than it can insure accuracy or significance in research.

The U.S.A. has been labeled by many students as a business civilization as contrasted to a religious one. This is obviously true, but not the whole truth. Roger Butterfield has described the dominant themes of American life as "the desire to see all men free and equal, and the desire

2. Clyde Kluckhohn, *Mirror for Man*, pp. 247–248. New York: McGraw-Hill.

to be richer and stronger than anyone else." This conflict between human and property rights has, as this author points out, generated much of the drama of American life. The political idealism and humanitarianism of the eighteenth and nineteenth centuries, as well as the earlier Puritanism, still influence our business civilization. In our Declaration of Independence is the quintessence of idealism, expressing for the first time the idea that all men have a right to happiness. If the anthropologist interested in our contemporary society digs under the top layers of people's beliefs, he will find still surviving the archaic concepts that money is not the road to happiness, or, at least, not the main one. If he is historically minded, he will note that when private capitalism was developing, the man who accumulated wealth through his own hard work was respected and admired; but that later when private capitalism changed to a corporate form, the corporation was regarded as an enemy of the people. Theodore Roosevelt became famous as a "trust-buster." No man in the U.S.A. becomes a national hero just through making a lot of money. He must have made some contribution to the welfare of his fellow men; most of the nation's heroes have been humanitarians.

In Hollywood the concept of a business civilization has been carried to an extreme. Property is far more important than man and human values have to struggle hard to exist at all. But, while the heroes in Hollywood are those with the most money, in the movies we find the opposite extreme. The wealthy tycoon is almost always the villain and the hero is the man of good will. The hero or heroine may be rich, but wealth does not give them their status. Often we are asked to admire the poor little rich girl who breaks away from her luxurious environment to marry the poor hero whom she loves. Hollywood leans over backward to sentimentalize love, which in the movies is always more important than wealth. Earning a living is never shown with any sense of reality and making a fortune is rarely portrayed sympathetically. True, most of the characters in the movies are better dressed and live more luxuriously than do their counterparts in real life. The secretary dresses like a wealthy debutante and the female psychoanalyst like the popular concept of a Hollywood star. But neither they nor any other heroine or hero are shown as fundamentally interested in or concerned about the problem of making a living or becoming rich. It is only possible to speculate on the reasons for this almost complete negation of economic motives which are so prevalent in our society. The very extremes to which most movies go in the negation may mean that the executives who control the contents of the movies have themselves some hidden ambivalence about their goals. After all, the executives, as well as the actors, do belong to the human species and are not completely unaffected by the conflicting values of our society. Or, they may think that this underplaying of economic motives in the movies is desired by the audience. Neither reason precludes the other, and both could be true, as well as other unknown ones. Whatever the reasons, Hollywood represents a caricature and overelaboration of the business motives and goals of our society, while the movies consistently underplay the same characteristics.

Art and aesthetic goals have always been less important in our society than either business or humanitarian ones. The artist in all societies has traditionally been a kind of barometer, more sensitive to nuances and changes than others, because he is more deeply immersed in his culture and more interested in its meanings. Since he rarely completely accepts all the conventions, he has a certain degree of objectivity and freedom, which of course also makes him seem different from other men. While the artists's status declined in all Western societies after the Industrial Revolution, many of the European countries with their older traditions of painting, music and literature, accorded him a higher position than he enjoys in the United States. Here, he is still considered peculiar, abnormal, sometimes feminine, and unimportant unless he achieves a commercial success comparable to that of a businessman. A Hollywood caricature of this concept is portrayed in the movie, *A Kiss in the Dark*. The hero, a successful concert pianist played by David Niven, is scared, nervous, withdrawn, and obviously infantile. He is saved by noticing, with appreciation, a model's legs (those of Jane Wyman). She has no interest in his music and leads him to her world of jazz and trombones. He finally frees himself from being an artist and wins his girl by using his musician's hands to knock down the heroine's fiancé, a former athlete. The hero is now a he-man, throws his practice keyboard away, and embraces the heroine as the train carries them away on a honeymoon.

So in the actual production of movies in Hollywood, the American concept of the unimportance of the artist is magnified. Those who know most about storytelling, who are gifted with imagination, and who have a knowledge of human beings, all raw materials which the camera transforms into a movie, do not have sufficient status to use their abilities. As one director expressed it, "the environment is hostile to them." The environment favors the latest developments in sound and color, but discourages new ideas from its artists. These men, who traditionally have known considerable freedom in expressing themselves, work under the direction of businessmen.

The movies have to earn their living. Unlike some of the fine arts, they are not privately endowed nor are they an esoteric medium for the enjoyment of the few. The goals of business and art are each justifiable and not necessarily irreconcilable. When art meets the needs of a large number of people in our society, it inevitably makes a profit. Some of our most creative popular artists, such as Chaplin, Gershwin, Walt Disney and Irving Berlin, have made fortunes. The problem is not the simple one of art versus business. The artist can contribute to business. But his stock-in-trade is not only his technical know-how: it includes the ability to interpret man to himself. This is true in folk art, popular art and fine art. But it makes little difference to the businessman whether he assuages man's anxieties by interpretation, or whether he exploits them; but the latter is easier. Or, if phoniness brings in money easily, why bother about the details of honesty? The front-office executives are not completely blind to humanitarian issues, but they seem far more interested in profits than in man. Most of them are not conditioned to be otherwise. Artists have a different kind of conditioning. While they are concerned about money, they must also, in order to be reasonably contented, use their gifts to give their interpretations. It has already been indicated that while only relatively few of the Hollywood writers, directors and actors are artists in this sense, they are far more important than the host of mediocre people.

The social organization of Hollywood has, however, permitted the businessman to take over the functions of the artists and to substitute his values for theirs. The movies are the first art form of any kind, popular, folk or fine, to become a trust. Quite early the major companies combined in their efforts to restrain competition and to blacklist those who would not do their bidding. The struggle between the Independents and the organization of the major studios still continues. At the same time movies increasingly make use of a developing technology and of the heritage from theater and literature. Under any circumstances such a combination would create complex problems. In this particular situation, the men with power have known how to exploit the advantages of a trust better than they could utilize the assets of literature and drama. They have not seemed to realize that the efficiency of the factory is possible because it turns out identical products, whether automobiles or coffeepots, and that this principle cannot be applied to the making of movies. Since these businessmen have neither understanding nor respect for the artists' ability, they attempt to negate or destroy it, partly out of ignorance and partly from a desire to satisfy their urge to dominate men. It is only an exceptional executive who does not give the impression that he would have been equally satisfied as a tycoon in any other industry.

Outside of Hollywood there is a certain freedom in choice of goals. A man can decide to be an artist, a scientist or a college professor, which means that most likely he will never be rich. Or he can plan to be a big business executive and have the possibility of acquiring great wealth. In Hollywood the same freedom of choice does not exist, because whatever role the individual plays, the goals of business are paramount. In the country as a whole there is the combination of humanism and materialism. But in Hollywood, money is always more important than man. It is this difference in goals which accounts for much of the deep hostility between the front-office and the artists' group. People with the same goals may argue on how to achieve them, but they speak the same language. People with conflicting goals speak a different language. The real artist in Hollywood cannot be completely satisfied, even though he earns a fortune, if he is not functioning as an artist, and this the head of a trust cannot understand.

Another trait of our civilization is its high level of ingenuity and inventiveness in the mechanical skills. Our heroes include men like Thomas Edison, Alexander Graham Bell, Eli Whitney and Henry Ford as well as the humanitarian, political figures. We are justly famous for the enormous number of additions to material culture which make life more comfortable. Movies are themselves a remarkable invention in their integration of electricity, photography, color, sound and acting. The history of inventions from the first stone ax is a fascinating story and one peculiar to our species. For only man is a tool-making and tool-using animal. Each succeeding example of his ingenuity and cleverness has brought, however, its own problems. This has always been true, but only recently has atomic energy forced a public recognition of the serious social consequences of technological developments.

The control of machines and of all our inventions for the benefit of man is one of the most pressing problems of our time. Machines can enslave people or free them. The Industrial Revolution brought young children into sweatshops and kept them and their parents for long hours at machines. Gradually changes in the social and economic organization reduced the hours of work, set age limits for workers, and enabled them, as well as other people, to enjoy the higher standard of living which machines made possible. But even the most casual observer of our society today recognizes its machinelike character. Not only do machines increasingly replace human labor, but what is left of it grows more mechanical. The role of the individual worker on the assembly line tends to be more and more automatic and he has less and less understanding of its relationship or his own to the whole. The ironic climax is his attempt to escape into fantasies and daydreams, themselves manufactured on an assembly line, far more concerned with technology than with meaning.

The way in which Hollywood has mechanized creativity and taken away most of its human characteristics again exaggerates the prevailing culture pattern, which gives little prestige to creativity not technological. This, of course, does not apply to the genius: an Einstein, Picasso, or a Rachmaninoff is given due honor. But we do little to bring out the creativity which lies in all human beings. Most people—just the everyday garden variety, not the geniuses—have far more potentialities for being creative than they use. But very few of them have the courage or desire to carry through their own ideas, big or little, because they have been conditioned to think routinely and follow the crowd. Our society tends, particularly today, to prize uniformity in thinking more than originality. The concern with the "know-how" rather than the "why," with technology rather than meaning, permeates much of the thinking even in the social sciences when method becomes more important than problems. The use of the most exact scientific methods on a sterile and meaningless problem is not too different from the employment of the most technically advanced camera work to produce a banal movie. It is the same when our educational system stresses the accumulation of facts rather than the meaningful relationship between them, and the taking of so many courses that there is little time for thoughtful reflection. The radio with its "Information, Please" and other quiz programs continues the emphasis. It is not that factual knowledge or scientific methods are unimportant, but rather that they are of use only in the larger context of problems and meanings. Hollywood expands these two features of our society to such an extent that it discourages and sometimes even forbids creativity in the very people whom it presumably pays to be creative. . . .

Hollywood represents totalitarianism. Its basis is economic rather than political but its philosophy is similar to that of the totalitarian state. In Hollywood, the concept of man as a passive creature to be manipulated extends to those who work for the studios, to personal and social relationships, to the audiences in the theaters and to the characters in the movies. The basic freedom of being able to choose between alternatives is absent. The gifted people who have the capacity for choice cannot exercise it; the executives who technically have the freedom of choice do not actually have it, because they usually lack the knowledge and imagination necessary for making such a choice. Much behavior is compulsive, springing from fears, hidden and open. The careful planning and good judgment of the exceptional people have been already described and are in dramatic contrast to the hysterical behavior of the others.

The Hollywood atmosphere of crises and continuous anxiety is a kind of hysteria which prevents people from thinking, and is not too different from the way dictators use wars and continuous threats of war as an emotional basis for maintaining their power. As the late Dr. Harry Stack Sullivan pointed out, there is considerable difference between fear and anxiety. Fear, he said, is often provoked by a new or novel situation and wears off as one becomes accustomed to it. Anxiety, however, arises out of relationships with other people which are disturbed, and "from its mildest to its most extreme manifestations interferes with effective alertness to the factors in the current situation that are immediately relevant to its occurrence, and thus with the refinement and precision of action related to its relief or reduction." Put more colloquially and applied to Hollywood, this means that a stage director who directs a movie for the first time might have some fear which would disappear as he became more accustomed to the new situation. In the meantime, the fear would not inhibit his learning as much as possible about the new situation and applying his knowledge and talent to it. But the anxiety of the average producer who has been in movies all his adult life springs out of his character and interpersonal relations, and the Hollywood situation calls forth and increases what is already there. Nor is it possible to become accustomed to anxiety-provoking situations. The very anxiety prevents an awareness of the factors which call it forth and of realistically doing something about them. These anxiety-ridden producers and executives of Hollywood try to reduce anxiety by spending more money, buying a best seller whether or not it is appropriate for a movie, using ten writers instead of one, having three "big name" stars in a movie, and so on. But none of these formulas rids him of his anxiety. Even where a picture is a big success, he knows the same anxiety on the next one.

In *Mein Kampf*, Hitler wrote about Fate as sometimes cruel and other times loving. Whether it is called Fate, destiny, or breaks, the underlying concept is the same: man gives up the attempt to exercise some control over his life through his own intelligence, because he thinks forces beyond his domain completely direct it.

The totalitarian concept of man is not limited to human relationships in Hollywood, but is reflected in many movies. Life, success or misfortune is usually portrayed as caused by luck or an accident. Only rarely does a movie show the process of becoming successful or the process of disintegration. Either one is treated as a *fait accompli* in the beginning of the picture or as caused by accidents during the course of the movie. Most movie characters, whether hero or villain, heroine or jade, are passive beings to whom things happen accidentally. Rarely do they even try to think through the situation in which they find themselves. They are buffeted about and defeated; or Fate smiles on them and almost magically they are successful. A few pictures have freed themselves from this formula. In *Home of the Brave* the Negro hero is shown as suffering realistically from prejudice. His escape is not on a magic carpet into a never-never world but through a painful psychological process, which the movie plainly says is kaleidoscoped. The Negro problem is seen as part of a large human one. Nor is the problem over at the end of the picture. The hero merely understands it better and has a way of handling it.

The totalitarian concept likewise extends toward the audiences, often regarded as suckers whose emotional needs and anxieties can be exploited for profit. Hollywood producers are, of course, not the only people with undue anxieties and many of the movies cater to the same kind of anxieties in their audiences, strengthening rather than reducing them, and contributing nothing to understanding. Only men who are not completely ridden with anxieties and who have some understanding of their own, as well as mankind's problems, can make other kinds of pictures. "The people," however, are always used as a rationalization—by dictators who say they rule for the good of the people, and by Hollywood producers who say they give the people what they want.

Until recently Hollywood offered very little more choice to audiences than it did to its artist employees. Today, because of competition from both exceptional Hollywood movies and foreign films, there is more choice.

The ultimate in totalitarian power is power for its own sake, although dictators offer various rationalizations for propaganda purposes. Some of the men with power in Hollywood present the same picture. These men have made millions, and more money means very little to them; but they cannot get enough of power: power over human beings in the studio and power over the daydreams of men and women who sit in the darkened theater.

For men of this type there is often enjoyment also in the power to humiliate, which they exercise in their relationships with their employees. There is a story about a well-known director, Mr. John Mighty, who was sleeping with the star of the picture he was directing. One morning she came on the set about a half hour late, and he bawled her out in loud, scolding language before the other actors, a crowd of extras, and the workmen. She tried to tell him that the hairdresser and make-up had taken longer than usual, but he refused to listen. Instead, he made her repeat after him an abject apology to the crowd on the set: "I apologize because I am late, and because I have caused loss of money to the studio and loss of time to all of you, and more particularly, because I know I am an actress without ability." At this point, she broke down and crying, said, "But please, John!" She got no further. The director bellowed,

" 'John in bed, you bitch; 'Mr. Mighty' on the set!" Humiliation as a technique for maintaining authority and for enjoyment is not confined to big people: assistant directors often show the same pattern in their treatment of extras. Those who take pleasure in degrading other people, whether in Hollywood or in a totalitarian state, are themselves degraded and may be even subconsciously aware of it.

Of course Hollywood is no more completely totalitarian than it is completely primitive. The genesis of Hollywood is different from that of any totalitarian state. In the latter the dictators either seize power through revolution, or attain it by making promises to relieve the misery and anxieties from which people suffer, or they do both. In Hollywood most of the men who enjoy power have it simply because they got there first and were able to form the social structure of movie making as they desired, rather than in the interests of movie making. The Hollywood dictators have not been able to make converts, in the way of any successful political dictator. He gets his subjects when young, and conversion begins in the kindergarten. The subjects in Hollywood arrive there as adults with fairly well-formulated ideas about how they can best work and live. They accept the dictatorship only nominally, because of the high salaries. They rarely accept it emotionally and, instead, are filled with resentment and bitterness toward it.

The rebels, in this case the artists, do not struggle in underground movements to outmaneuver the studio executives. They fight openly to gain power, that is, to get into positions in which they can make important decisions and influence the movies. A sufficient number of gifted writers, directors and actors are succeeding to indicate at least a trend which offers a variation and may, eventually, modify or change the system.

These exceptional individuals receive little help in their struggles. The Federal Government tries to reduce the monopolistic power of the industry and to regulate its buying and selling practices. Censorship groups attempt to regulate the morality of the pictures and succeed only in making them dishonest. Guilds fight for more money for their members, but do nothing about a contract, which allows the employer almost literally to own his employees for its duration. The exceptional individuals, with great strength of character and drive, with high talent, and with a true morality, work on their own as they try to dent the power situation in Hollywood, alter the human relationships, and give meaning to their movies.

Totalitarianism, whether in a foreign nation or in Hollywood, represents one of the backward swings in history. But primitive societies seldom knew the degradation that modern man can suffer under a dictator. Although primitive cultures have a similar lack of emphasis on the individual, there are wide differences between them and modern totalitarian states. The two situations differ widely in origin and effect. In primitive societies man has not yet emerged sufficiently from his primary ties to his family and clan kindred to emphasize his own individuality. But totalitarianism attempts to negate the individuality of men who *have* broken these primary ties, who *have* known, and valued, freedom. The force of tradition offers very little choice to primitive man. The force of the modern police state also offers very little choice. Primitive cultures lack the knowledge and awareness of man's potentialities. Modern totalitarian societies fear and distrust them. Evolutionary thinking is not in style in the social sciences, but it is possible to view the history of man as a gradual freeing of himself from primary ties and becoming freer to utilize and develop his uniquely human characteristics.

In every society there are a multitude of patterns, some overelaborated and others underplayed. The anthropologist is well aware that either process may be carried to such unnecessary extremes as to threaten the well-being and, occasionally, even the survival of the society. Among the aborigines of Australia the marriage regulations are worked out to such a fine point that it is almost impossible for a native to find a socially approved mate. His way out of this impossible situation is to elope. Some Eskimo tribes are not permitted to hunt seals in summer, and they will not touch seals in this season even if the land game fails and they are starving.

Hollywood has the elaborated totalitarian elements we have described: the concept of people as property and as objects to be manipulated, highly concentrated and personalized power for power's sake, an amorality, and an atmosphere of breaks, continuous anxiety and crises. The result of this overelaboration is business inefficiency, deep frustration in human relations, and a high number of unentertaining second- and third-rate movies.

There are, of course, other patterns in the U.S.A. which Hollywood could elaborate. They are the democratic ones of the dignity of man, the concept of freedom, a belief in man's capacity to think, create, and to exercise some control over his life—a belief that man is more important than property—all part of our cultural heritage. How far will Hollywood utilize them? It is not a matter of more brains and talent or of money, but of generating new modes of behavior and a system in which collaboration is more important than domination. Any changes that will occur will not come out of magical thinking or waiting for breaks. Nor is it possible to be sure of a "happy ending." No anthropologist ever expects a complete break from the past. But he does know that societies assume different forms through contact with others, through technological inventions, and through changes in values and goals. He can predict that Hollywood will not go back to its isolated position and that there will be new technological developments. The really difficult question to answer is, Can Hollywood change its ways of thinking and its values, so that the democratic concept of man becomes more important than a totalitarian one?

■ ■ ■ ■

Hollywood in the Television Age (1949/50), Samuel Goldwyn

This article by Samuel Goldwyn looks forward to the future rather than back at the past. Given the articulateness of the piece, its grammatical smoothness, and the avoidance of any of the malapropisms for which Goldwyn was famous, one might suspect that the essay was "ghosted" by some member of the Goldwyn staff. (In his autobiography, *Hollywood*, Garson Kanin claims to have given Goldwyn the ideas for the piece.) Several of Goldwyn's predictions seem to have been amazingly accurate: the showing of movies on television, the development of especially "made-for-TV" movies, the disappearance of mediocre program pictures and the emphasis on special movies to draw audiences out of the home, the development of pay television (although at a much slower pace than Goldwyn predicted). Several other predictions seems more optimistic than accurate: for example, the ownership and operation of television studios by the movie studios. In general, Goldwyn seems to have underestimated the power and procedures of the communications networks, which descended from radio programming, not from motion pictures. This essay originally appeared in *Hollywood Quarterly*, which changed its name to the *Quarterly Review of Film, Radio, and Television* in 1951, then to *Film Quarterly* in 1958, and is now one of America's leading film journals.

Motion pictures are entering their third major era. First there was the silent period. Then the sound era. Now we are on the threshold of the television age.

The thoroughgoing change which sound brought to picture making will be fully matched by the revolutionary effects (if the House Un-

"Hollywood in the Television Age," by Samuel Goldwyn, appeared in the Winter, 1949/50, issue of *Hollywood Quarterly*.

American Activities Committee will excuse the expression) of television upon motion pictures. I predict that within just a few years a great many Hollywood producers, directors, writers, and actors who are still coasting on reputations built up in the past are going to wonder what hit them.

The future of motion pictures, conditioned as it will be by the competition of television, is going to have no room for the deadwood of the present or the faded glories of the past. Once again it will be true, as it was in the early days of motion picture history, that it will take brains instead of just money to make pictures. This will be hard on a great many people who have been enjoying a free ride on the Hollywood carrousel, but it will be a fine thing for motion pictures as a whole.

Within a few years the coaxial cable will have provided a complete television network linking the entire country. Whether the expense that is involved in producing full-length feature pictures for television can possibly be borne by advertisers or will be paid for by individual charges upon the set owners, no one can say today. But we do know that with America's tremendous technological capabilities and our ability to adjust to new situations, nothing will stand in the way of full-length feature pictures in the home produced expressly for that purpose.

Even the most backward-looking of the topmost tycoons of our industry cannot now help seeing just around the corner a titanic struggle to retain audiences. The competition we feared in the past—the automobile in early movie days, the radio in the 'twenties and 'thirties, and the developing of night sports quite recently—will fade into insignificance by comparison with the fight we are going to have to keep people patronizing our theaters in preference to sitting at home and watching a program of entertainment. It is a certainty that people will be unwilling to pay to see poor pictures when they can stay home and see something which is, at least, no worse.

We are about to enter what can be the most difficult competition imaginable with a form of entertainment in which all the best features of radio, the theater, and motion pictures may be combined. Today there are fifty-six television stations on the air, with sixty-six additional stations in process of construction. The chairman of the Federal Communications Commission points out that by 1951 there may be 400 stations in operation. There are now 950,000 receiving sets installed, sets are being produced at the rate of 161,000 per month and next year that rate will be doubled. Soon there will be a potential audience of fifty million people or more.

Here we have the development that will change the whole entertainment business. Fifty million Americans will be able to sit at home and take their choice of visiting the ball park, the prize-fight matches, the wrestling bouts, the legitimate theater, and the motion pictures without stirring from their own living rooms. It is going to require something truly superior to cause them not only to leave their homes to be entertained, but to pay for that entertainment.

How can the motion picture industry meet the competition of television? Most certainly the basic business tactics—if you can't lick 'em, join 'em—apply in this case. If the movies try to lick television, it's the movies that will catch the licking. But the two industries can quite naturally join forces for their own profit and the greater entertainment of the public. Instead of any talk about how to lick television, motion picture people now need to discuss how to fit movies into the new world made possible by television. Here are some of the ways in which that tailoring process can be effected:

First, the reality must be faced that if the motion picture industry is to remain a going concern—instead of turning into one that is gone—it will have to turn out pictures several times as good as pictures are, on the average, today. Such recent pictures as *Joan of Arc, The Snake Pit, Portrait of Jennie, Johnny Belinda, The Search,* and *Miss Tatlock's Millions* are proof that Hollywood has creative capacities which are utilized all too rarely. Pictures like these, far above the average today, will have to be the norm in the future.

A factor on our side is that people will always go out to be entertained because human beings are naturally gregarious. But before the moviegoer of the future arranges for a baby sitter, hurries through dinner, drives several miles, and has to find a place to park, just for the pleasure of stepping up to the box office to *buy* a pair of tickets, he will want to be certain that what he pays for is worth that much more than what he could be seeing at home without any inconvenience at all.

Assuming that better pictures will be made, there remains the problem of how the motion picture industry is going to receive financial returns for pictures made for television. The greatest potentialities lie in a device called phonevision.

This device is not yet known to the American public because it has not yet been placed upon the commercial market, but to motion picture producers it may well be the key to full participation in this new, exciting medium of entertainment. Reduced to its simplest terms, it is a system by which any television-set owner will be able to call his telephone operator, tell her that he wishes to see *The Best Years of Our Lives* (if I may be pardoned for thinking of my favorite picture), or any other picture, and then see the picture on his television set. The charge for the showing of the picture will be carried on the regular monthly telephone bill.

Phonevision is normal television with the additional feature that it can be seen on the phonevision-television combination set only when certain electric signals are fed into the set over telephone wires. No television set without the phonevision addition is capable of picking up phonevision programs, and no phonevision-television set can pick up such programs without those electrical signals supplied over the telephone wires on specific order.

The fee paid by the set owner will presumably be divided between the television transmitter, the picture producer, and the telephone company. The range of possibilities which this prospect opens to motion picture producers is almost limitless, for every television owner becomes just as much a box-office prospect inside his home as outside it.

It must be borne in mind that full-length pictures in the home are not necessarily something which will be realized in the immediate future. Despite the rapid pace at which we hurtle ahead, I am inclined to believe that the production of full-length pictures designed especially for home television will not become a practical reality for at least five to ten years more. Although phonevision seems to be ready for commercial adaptation today, it is obvious that no motion picture producer can risk the huge investment required for a full-length feature picture for television alone unless he has some reasonable assurance of recovering his costs.

In addition to producing for television, motion picture companies will undoubtedly make strenuous efforts to participate in the ownership and operation of television stations themselves. Already several of the larger companies have made extensive plans along these lines. An element which could blight the development of television would be the introduction into that field of monopolistic controls and practices similar to those which, in the motion picture industry, have hurt independent production. But this possibility should be reduced to a minimum by the fact that television-station ownership by theater companies and their affiliated interests, as well as others, will be limited by the Federal Communications Commission rule which provides, in effect, that no single interest can own more than five television licenses.

What effect will the exhibition of films over television have upon the type of films produced? First, one must hedge by saying that until we know whether the use of phonevision can supply sufficient revenue, or until advertisers can bear the cost of such full-length productions—a remote possibility,—we will all remain in the dark as to the direction to be taken by pictures produced essentially for that medium. One can venture a few predictions, however, as to the reasonable probabilities.

There is no doubt that in the future a large segment of the talents of the motion picture industry will be devoted to creating motion pictures designed explicitly for this new medium. As today's television novelty wears off, the public is not going to be satisfied to look at the flickering shadows of old films which have reposed in their producers' vaults for many years. Nor will the public be content to spend an evening looking at a series of fifteen-minute shorts such as are now being made for television. There will be a vast demand for new full-length motion picture entertainment brought directly into the home.

I believe that when feature pictures are being made especially for television, they will not differ basically from those made for showing in theaters. The differences will be chiefly variations in techniques. The craving which all of us have to lose ourselves, temporarily at least, in the adventures, romances, joys, trials, and tribulations of characters created by storytellers does not change much, whether those characters are portrayed in a novel, on the stage, or on the screen—or whether that screen is in a theater or in one's own living room.

But in this new medium there will undoubtedly be a greater emphasis on story values than exists today. A person rarely walks out of a theater before he has seen the picture he came to see, regardless of whether it lives up to his expectations. A variety of reasons are behind this—the admission price he paid, the fact that he has no control over the program, the fact that if he leaves it will probably be too late to go to another theater, etc. At most, only one of those factors—the equivalent of an admission price—will be present in the home. The knowledge that the spectator will be able to move from one picture to another by the mere turn of the dial is bound to make those who will produce pictures primarily for television concentrate on keeping the audience vitally interested.

I believe, too, that there will be a reversion, for a time at least, to a lustier, broader type of acting than we have seen since sound changed motion picture acting techniques. Because of the small viewing surface of present-day home television screens, the subtleties of underplaying which can be observed on the large motion picture theater screen are lost to the television viewer. Unless the home screen becomes measurably larger, actors will find that the emotions which they can portray today by nuances will have to be conveyed by much broader expression.

Along the same general line, I am inclined to believe that the pacing of feature pictures designed primarily for television will be found to be more rapid than the normal tempo of motion pictures in the theater. Feature television pictures will probably not run over an hour—a reduction of from thirty to fifty per cent of the running time of present-day features. The need for compressing the essential elements of the story will inevitably result in accelerated tempo.

All of this makes for an exciting and stimulating future even though it is impossible to forecast what the specific nature of the interests of motion picture companies or individual theater owners in television stations will be. Ultimately, a pattern will evolve out of the jumbled jigsaw puzzle of experimentation.

The certainty is that in the future, whether it be five or ten or even more years distant, one segment of our industry will be producing pictures for exhibition in the theaters while another equally large section will be producing them for showing in the homes. The stimulus of this kind of competition should have nothing but good results. The people best fitted to make pictures for television will be those who combine a thorough knowledge of picture-making techniques with a real sense of entertainment values and the imagination to adapt their abilities to a new medium.

The weak sisters in our ranks will fall by the wayside. But no one in our industry who has real talent need fear the effects of television. I welcome it as opening new vistas for the exercise of creative ability, spurred on by intense competition.

I have always been basically optimistic about Hollywood and its potenialities. I see no reason to change my views now. I am convinced that television will cause Hollywood to achieve new heights and that, as time goes on, above these heights new peaks will rise.

■ ■ ■ ■

STEREOPHONIC SOUND

Today to get the public to attend a picture show
It's not enough to advertise a famous star they know.
If you want to get the crowd to come around
You've got to have
Glorious Technicolor, Breathtaking CinemaScope, and Stereophonic
  sound.

If Zanuck's latest picture were the good old-fashioned kind
There'd be no one in front to look at Marilyn's behind.
If you want to hear applauding hands resound
You've got to have
Glorious Technicolor, Breathtaking CinemaScope, and Stereophonic
  sound.

The customers don't like to see the groom embrace the bride
Unless her lips are scarlet and her bosom's five feet wide.

You've got to have
Glorious Technicolor, Breathtaking CinemaScope,
Or Cinerama, or Vista Vision, or SuperScope, or Todd A-O
And Stereophonic sound,
And Stereophonic sound.

You all remember Lassie that beloved canine star
To see her wag her tail the crowds would come from near and far.
But at present she'd be just another hound
Unless she had
Glorious Technicolor, Breathtaking CinemaScope, and Stereophonic
  sound.

I lately did a picture at the bottom of the sea;
I rassled with an octopus and licked an anchovee.
But the public wouldn't care if I had drowned
Unless I had
Glorious Technicolor, Breathtaking CinemaScope, and Stereophonic
  sound.

If Ava Gardner played Godiva riding on a mare
The public wouldn't pay a cent to see her in the bare

Unless she had
Glorious Technicolor, Breathtaking CinemaScope,
Or Cinecolor, or Warnercolor, or Pathécolor, or Eastmancolor, or Koda-
*   color, or any color,*
And Stereophonic sound,
And Stereophonic—
As an extra tonic—
Stereophonic sound.

Words and music by Cole Porter;
from *Silk Stockings,* 1955 (stage) and 1957 (film).

7

Hollywood in the Television Age

(1953–1977)

It might seem strange to consider the last twenty-five years of film history as a single era. One could perhaps divide this long period into various "waves": the technological gimmicks of the mid-1950s to mid-1960s, culminating in the "wide-screen revolution"; the invasion of foreign films in the mid-1950s to mid-1960s, culminating in the conversion of many American films to the values of "art films"; the loosening of moral standards in the mid-1960s with the collapse of the Hollywood Code, the institution of the rating system, the greater sexual explicitness of feature films, and the boom in pornography; the absorption of the movie studios in the 1970s by the great conglomerate corporations. But to break this lengthy period into such smaller ones would seem arbitrary and artificial, a disruption of a continuous and unchanging social relationship of the movies to American life.

The basis of that continuity can be found in the title of Mr. Goldwyn's article, "Hollywood in the Television Age." The two great cultural shifts in motion picture patterns that television has effected are, first, in the cultural impact of the movies and, second, in their economic strength. No longer is the projected motion picture in the movie house America's favorite form of mass entertainment. It has become a minority entertainment, with an audience estimated at 20 million per week (about one-fourth the estimate of 1907). As a minority entertainment it has come to fill a place in the culture closely related to that filled by those other minority entertainments toward whose artistic seriousness it aspired in its youth—theater, dance, opera. The audience that continues to go to movies does so for very specific reasons—almost inevitably to experience some kind of aesthetic gratification that television does not or cannot provide. So the entire twenty-five-year period after 1953 can be seen as the motion picture industry's attempt to transcend the limits of television—by the employment of technological gimmicks; the importation of foreign films; or the introduction of controversial American topics, breathtaking sights and sounds, complex plots and ideas, or sexual explicitness.

To television have fled most of the major social issues that previously attached themselves to movies. What will television make of the younger generation of Americans? What will be the effects of violence on the youthful audience? What will be the effects of television on the family, on literacy, on social intercourse, on consumer patterns, on dietary patterns and physical health? As a cultural phenomenon, television is clearly the descendant of movies and should, perhaps, be considered as an extension of the same social history. An an aesthetic object, however, as a medium of entertainment, it is questionable whether television can be considered an extension of movies; indeed, because of the small screen size, the weaker powers of sight and sound, the commercial interruptions, and the social fact of seeing it in the home, television may well not provide the same kind of entertainment as movies even when it transmits a movie (either one made for the large screen or one made especially for television). These aesthetic differences between the two media—as well as the different gratifications each provides its audiences—seem a justification for keeping the social history of the motion picture separate from that of television.

Along with the loss of its audience and its corollary loss of cultural importance has come a necessary loss of commercial power. The motion picture industry (insofar as it can be considered an *industry* at all) survives via television—filming commercials, the regular series programs, and "made-for-TV" movies. Many of the major "studios" have been abandoned and sold for shopping centers and real-estate developments. The surviving film companies, whether bearing the names of familiar companies or not, are primarily distributors now—engaged in the business of financing and selling films, rather than making them. These film companies have become branches of the huge conglomerates—Gulf and Western, Transamerica—and are managed by shrewd businessmen, not by showmen. The schizophrenic split between West Coast and East

Coast, between show business and money business, which became apparent in the mid-1930s, is even more obvious now.

The present relationship of the motion picture with its audience has evolved slowly over the last twenty-five years, probably settling into a stable commercial and cultural relationship with American life in the mid-1960s. There is no sign that any of these present patterns will be significantly altered in the future.

REVOLUTION IN HOLLYWOOD

THE MOVIE INDUSTRY HAS PLUNGED INTO THE BIGGEST CONVERSION JOB IT HAS UNDERTAKEN SINCE THE ARRIVAL OF TALKING PICTURES; THE RESULT WILL BE A NEW KIND OF PICTURE IN THREE DIMENSIONS, BUT MOVIE-GOERS WILL DECIDE WHAT FORM IT WILL FINALLY TAKE

CINERAMA is one of the three basic ways of making a picture in which objects in the foreground seem to stand out from the background, giving the audience the illusion of looking at a scene having three dimensions— height, width and depth. Cinerama has pulled huge crowds into the few theaters where it has been shown. But because this three-dimensional system requires the use of a screen too large for installation in the average-sized neighborhood theater, Cinerama probably will be limited to big-city theaters.

NATURAL VISION is one of several trade names for a process of stereoscopic photography that requires the use of polarized glasses by the spectator. Every major studio is experimenting with this method, which is the only truly three-dimensional process so far developed. Several Natural Vision pictures already are in general circulation, but the use of glasses or "viewers" by the audience may be a drawback. Movie makers are reserving judgment on the system till audiences have seen many more of these films.

CINEMASCOPE is the trade name coined by 20th Century-Fox for its version of a system that uses a curved screen wider than normal. The wide screen produces an illusion of three dimensions because it allows the spectator to see the spread-out picture from the sides of his eyes as well as straight forward. The first pictures in this form probably will be released this fall.

The 3-D experiments now in the works probably will result in some combination of three basic systems of three-dimensional cinematography.

■ ■ ■ ■

3-D: HIGH, WIDE, AND HANDSOME (1953), Chester Morrison

Just as synchronized sound had pulled it out of a small slump twenty-five years earlier, the film industry hoped that another technological novelty would do the same for this much larger slump. Although these novelties had been available since the 1930s (many of the articles in this collection from that period mention them), the motion picture industry avoided them until it became clear that the problems they would cause exhibitors might be rewarded by necessary additional profits. This article from *Look* magazine explains the processes and their principles to the public.

In six years movie attendance has dropped from a top of 76,000,000 to 50,000,000 a week. The businessmen of Hollywood, who operate the world's biggest entertainment industry, have been blaming the loss on competition from television. What they are now doing to get back customers has caused the biggest upheaval Hollywood has experienced since the arrival of the talkies a generation ago.

Hollywood wants to make pictures that will reproduce, as closely as possible, what the normal eye can see—to provide the third dimension of depth missing in movies made before. Skilled as they are, the movie technicians have not yet developed a scheme as good as Nature's, but they are at work on two methods of imitating Nature's 180-degree field of vision in which foreground objects stand out from the background.

These two approaches are: 1. Use of a wide, curved screen as in Cinerama, Cinemascope, Warnerscope and other variations of the same principle, which attempt to create peripheral extension of vision. Peripheral vision is what is seen out of the sides of a normal pair of eyes looking straight ahead. 2. Stereoscopic photography, which seems to bring objects off the flat background of the screen. This requires the spectator in a movie audience to wear polarized glasses.

"3-D: High, Wide, and Handsome," by Chester Morrison (© 1953 by Cowles Broadcasting, Inc.), appeared in *Look* magazine on 30 June 1953.

THE PROCESSES ARE NOT NEW

There are many variations of both these principles. None of them re-produces normal vision, but when some combination of both principles is developed, the result may be a movie vastly more lifelike than any we have seen up to now.

The only thing new about the wide-screen process and the stereoscopic process is that they are now being used for feature-length commercial films in general distribution. Stereoscopic movies were shown at the Paris Exposition fifty years ago and at the New York World's Fair fourteen years ago. The wide-screen principle was tried, without commercial success, twenty years ago. Yet pictures made by both methods in the past few months have been smash box-office successes in the few cities where they have been shown. There is a strong suspicion that the success was mainly a result of the novelty of the new techniques.

Cinerama, first shown in New York last September (also running in Los Angeles and Detroit) uses a huge screen that fills the entire width of the stage. The screen is curved inward and consists of three sections. The curved surface and the width of the screen bring the spectator "into the picture" by providing a field of vision of about 142 degrees that seems to wrap around the audience. The picture is photographed by three cameras placed at different angles and is thrown onto the screen by three projectors. The use of these three visual angles makes Cinerama seem so lifelike that audiences watching a shot of a roller coaster going down-grade often behave as though they were taking the ride. But Cinerama does not provide a truly three-dimensional picture.

HIGHER COSTS PLUS MORE PROBLEMS

Cinerama also has practical disadvantages. It costs more to produce, be-cause it requires three cameras. It costs more to exhibit, because it re-quires a huge new screen and three separate projection booths, each with an operator. There is still trouble about synchronizing the three pictures thrown onto the screen and about synchronizing the sound that goes with the pictures. And, because the method is more useful for panoramic pic-tures than for intimate close-up shots, it may be best suited to spectacles.

Moreover, Cinerama, like Cinemascope and other wide-screen sys-tems, depends also upon "stereophonic" sound for producing upon the spectator the sensation of being "in the picture." There are several trade names for stereophonic sound, but it is simply a system that gives a sense of motion and direction to sound. Several loud speakers are added to the theater's normal sound equipment and plugged in at various spots around the theater walls. Thus, the sound is given a point of origin and a sense of movement.

Cinemascope, a wide-screen system which 20th Century–Fox now plans to use for all its pictures next year, involves the same peripheral-vision principle used by Cinerama. It employs a smaller curved screen that can be adopted to the stage of any theater. But it has a vision field of 62 degres, compared with the 142 degrees of Cinerama and the 180 degrees of the natural eye. The familiar two-dimensional screen has a field of about 30 degrees. Cinemascope avoids some of Cinerama's disadvantages: It is photographed with only one camera, instead of three, and in the theater only one projector is used. Fox hopes to develop a film that will carry the picture and three stereophonic sound tracks in one strip.

The cost of remodeling the Broadway Theater in New York for Cinerama was $85,000. Fox has a Cinemascope package, including screen, special lenses for the projectors and sound equipment that comes to about $8000 but may run to almost $10,000 for an exhibitor who wants a more complete installation. Comparatively few exhibitors have actually installed it so far.

Fox Is Hedging Its Bet

Fox has, however, something else up their sleeves. Although Cinemascope is their pride and hope, pictures now in production are made for exhibition on both the wide and standard screens. This probably is a sensible precaution, because the production of pictures in the Cinemascope form requires the use of special lenses on camera and projector. The lens on the camera compresses the scene it photographs; a compensating lens on the projector expands the scene it flashes to the proportions of the Cinemascope screen. These are called anamorphoscope lenses. The word means, roughly, that the camera distorts what it photographs and the projector restores the correct proportions. The difficulty here is that it may be a long time before the optical companies can grind enough anamorphoscope lenses to equip all the theaters that may want to show Cinemascope pictures.

There is still another variation of the wide-screen process. It is a development by Paramount, which uses a screen 1.66 times as wide as it is high.

Stereoscopic photography is the other important contribution to three-dimensional movies. It is an adaptation of the principle grandpa used to appreciate when he spent a quiet evening at home looking through a clumsy focusing device at slides of Niagara Falls. An important contributor to its development in its early stages was Oliver Wendell Holmes, the elder. In its recent movie form, called Natural Vision, it is primarily the work of Milton Gunzburg, whose process was used in the Natural Vision movies now in circulation. Natural Vision does give the stereoscopic effect—that is, of objects standing out from their background and, indeed, appearing to move off the screen and out into the audience. But it does not provide peripheral vision—that is, vision from the sides of the eyes. And Natural Vision in any of the modifications, or under any of the several trade names that have been developed since the first pictures in that form were made, requires the spectator to wear polarized glasses.

POLARIZED GLASSES UNSCRAMBLE IMAGE

Polarized glasses are two pieces of a plastic substance developed by the Polaroid Corp., of Cambridge, Mass., and fitted like the lenses of a pair of spectacles into a cardboard frame. They are not lenses, but light filters. By a chemical process, fine diagonal lines are etched into the plastic.

How do these glasses fit into stereoscopic photography?

When a pair of naked eyes looks at any object, each eye sees the object from a slightly different angle. In the stereoscopic processes, two cameras are mounted on a stand, their lenses separated by the average distance between a pair of eyes, which is about two and a half inches. One camera photographs what the right eye would see, the other camera performs the function of the left eye.

The picture is thrown onto a screen by two projectors, one projecting the film from the right camera and the other the film from the left camera. The images on the screen overlap slightly, as do the images seen by the normal eyes. The left lens of the polarized glasses worn by a spectator in a theater admits one of the screen images, the right lens admits the other. The brain co-ordinates the two into a single image.

Without the polarized filters, the spectator sees the two overlapping images as a fuzzy blur which the optical scientists call noncoincidental image reconstruction. You can get the same effect by holding a pencil a foot away from your eyes. Focus the eyes on a distant object directly behind the pencil and you'll see two pencils. Focus on the pencil itself, and the pencil stands out against the background in true third dimension.

Although there is nothing new about stereoscopic photography, Natural Vision lays claim to the development of a technique that makes the principles practicable for Hollywood's purposes. And Natural Vision says it can equip a theater for stereopticon films for about $750. Once a theater is equipped for projection of one stereoscopic picture, it can show any picture in that form, in any of the variations now being developed by Hollywood studios.

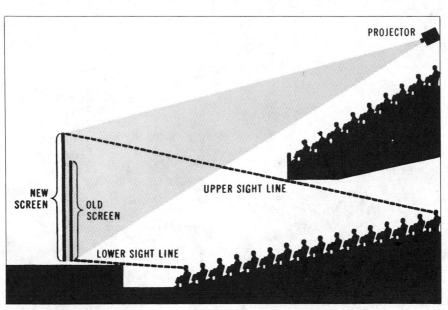

Paramount's wide, concave screen is higher and wider than the normal flat screen, provides a three-dimensional view from every seat in the theater

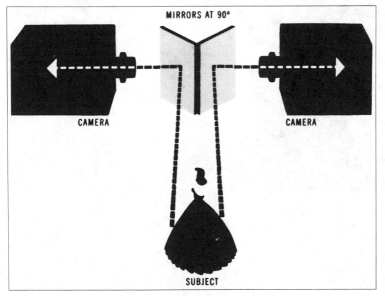

In the two-camera Natural Vision process, the cameras are focused on paired mirrors that reflect the scene that is to be shot, and not on the actual scene

In filming Cinemascope "The Robe,"
three microphones were used to record
stereophonic sound. Engineers later
learned to work with a single mike.

Twin cameras used for 3-D pictures
are mounted face-to-face in this huge
device and focused on mirrors that
reflect the scene to be shot

Audiences Go for 3-D

Audience reaction to all forms of 3-D films so far has been good. They liked Cinerama, which made its debut in New York last September and is still playing to packed houses. It opened recently in Los Angeles and preparations are underway to show it in several other large cities. So far Cinerama has released only one picture. The consesus in Hollywood is that, although Cinerama's production schedule may get moving in the near future, this form will remain a big-city show which always will be to the regular movie houses what extravaganzas are to the legitimate theater.

Natural Vision's first appearance was in a picture called *Bwana Devil*. Aside from its third dimension, it was a distinctly second rate motion picture. Newspaper critics panned it unanimously—but it broke box-office records everywhere.

After *Bwana Devil* came Warner Brothers' *House of Wax,* another esthetically inferior picture with three-dimensional Natural Vision. The critics panned that one, too—and people are packing the theaters wherever it is shown. Now everybody is in the act. All major studios in Hollywood are experimenting with three-dimensional processes. Some have developed their own variations of the basic principles, and the industry is well aware that it is involved in a revolution.

3-D Jokes and Slang

While the technicians worked, comedians produced 3-D jokes: About the man watching Cinerama who asked the lady in front of him to take off her hat and she said she couldn't, she was in the picture. And the switch about the man watching Cinerama who asked the lady *behind* him to take off her hat.

New 3-D slang began to develop in the studios: The frame of a stereoscopic picture is technically called the stereoscopic window; hence, when something appears to be thrown at the audience from a 3-D screen, it "goes out the window." When a 3-D picture is being filmed, the massive cameras are covered by a hood that masks the mechanical whir of the cameras. It is called a "blimp." The six men who remove and replace it while film is being reloaded are "pall bearers."

Just as the vocabulary expands, the technical know-how increases and the problems of 3-D multiply. Whatever form is ultimately developed as standard for all studios, the general changeover to any kind of 3-D production will involve heavy costs. Hollywood studios are carrying a $300,000,000 "inventory" of pictures already begun for flat production or already finished but not yet released, and of flat pictures that have made money in first-run theaters, but can make still more in neighborhood theaters on another go-round.

TV Is Experimenting with 3-D

Some studios—Fox is one of them—figure that if they decide to go all out for some 3-D form, they can unload the backlog of flat pictures on TV, which is not yet ready to show television in three dimensions (although TV, too, is experimenting and the results so far are promising). But some people in TV, who for a long time have wanted to buy big films from major studios, now are beginning to say that they don't want them; they're doing all right with films produced for TV or released to TV by independent film companies.

The prospect now seems to be that the Natural Vision method, or some variation of it, will continue to do well for a while at the box office, not only because of the novelty but also because theaters can equip for it quickly and at comparatively small expense. But there hasn't been a solid Grade-A stereopticon picture yet, and nobody in Hollywood will guess whether people are going to be willing to wear polarized glasses as a regular thing.

There are no better predictions forthcoming on the future of any of the wide-screen processes. None of them has yet been tested by a big enough audience to justify a judgment on public acceptance. But before long, most Americans will have seen 3-D in some form and Hollywood will have a basis for standardization. While the businessmen make up their minds, most of Hollywood's studios are shut down or operating at a much reduced pace.

Whether 3-D will lift the movies out of the doldrums is uncertain. Certainly it will not hurt TV. After all, TV is chiefly a way to bring movies into the home. The movie industry's big problem lies somewhere in the cumbersome method of distributing and exhibiting films.

Hollywood realizes that if 3-D is to last, the movie makers will have to give the customer something more than mere repetitive demonstrations of a novel technique. Smart producers acknowledge that it would be disastrous to leave the further development of the new system to the more pedestrian film-makers. They know that, from the professional point of view, the 3-D technique is a significant advance and that it will bring lasting rewards to those who are prepared to use it with skill, courage and imagination.

All such knowledgeable people will tell a visitor the same story: We don't know what the possibilities of 3-D are. We don't know yet how to get the best out of it, but everybody is learning something every day. We do know that in any kind of picture it's the story and the performances that count.

You can be sure, however, that inside the new technical wrapper you will be getting lots of the same old formulas: Alan Ladd will still be up there beside the supersonic airplane with George Sanders, the financier who owns the factory, wind whipping their trenchcoats. Then Stewart Granger, the designer, will dash out of the hangar and cry: "You're not going to send the boy up in that crate? My goodness, it's not even off the drawing board yet!" But Ladd will climb into the cockpit and say, "Roger!" (his only line in the film) and he will go and burst through the sound barrier, just as you knew he would.

Or here is Ladd in buckskins with Betty Grable bent over the stove in the simple log cabin, boiling up a mess of turnip greens. And she says: "You ain't a-goin' out in this blizzard to save them new-born calves, are you?" But out he goes and darned if he doesn't rescue them calves and save the ranch from foreclosure by George Sanders, the wicked financier who knows there's oil under that little old cabin.

Even if the old story formula turns out to be entertaining in the new form, there are other problems: How will the thousands of drive-in theaters like stereoscopic pictures that are distorted when customers watch them through windshields? How will the drive-in people like wide-screen movies that require greatly increased light power for projection? How will the proprietor of a little neighborhood movie like to pay the cost of installing equipment for every new kind of movie Hollywood may try to sell him? And above all, how are the customers going to like it?

Recently, Fox showed snatches of Cinemascope to audiences of theater owners in several key cities. The exhibitors who attended one such demonstration in New York watched with unmistakable interest and even applauded some especially spectacular shots on the wide screen. But a spectator moving among them afterwards, asking when they were going to remodel their own theaters, got a general, cautious answer: "Well, it's pretty good, but I don't know. Not right away, anyhow. Not right away. I'll wait and see what happens."

■ ■ ■ ■

M.G.M.: War Among the Lion Tamers (1957), Emmett John Hughes

As it did in the 1930s, *Fortune* magazine continued to take an interest in the commercial health of the film industry's giant, M.G.M. But if the strength of the giant company in the earlier decade was symptomatic of

"M.G.M.: War among the Lion Tamers," by Emmett John Hughes, appeared in the August 1957 issue of *Fortune*.

the entire industry's fiscal vitality, its chaotic near-collapse less than two decades later seemed equally symptomatic of industrial disease. This article, published in August 1957, exposes another skirmish in the continuing battle of East Coast finance and West Coast filmmaking.

The long fight for control of M.G.M. is rapidly approaching a decision. The thirty-three-year-old producing studio of Loew's Inc. is the biggest and, by appearances at least, the sickest giant of the motion-picture industry. And for possession of this somewhat flabby but immensely famed hulk there rages a struggle, as intricate as it is frenzied, that is now in its second year and nearing a climax.

In keeping with the times, the contest is being waged on a wide, wide screen that takes in not only Beverly Hills and Culver City, but Wall Street and lower Broadway. The formidable cast includes a former Secretary of Defense, a former Secretary of the Navy, a former Secretary of the Army, a former chairman of the board of a major auto maker, the president of a steamship line, and a New York newspaper publisher. Standing weightily in the background are two of Wall Street's most distinguished investment-banking houses, Lehman Bros. and Lazard Frères, which directly control some 400,000 of Loew's 5,300,000 outstanding shares. Ostentatiously in the foreground are a multimillionaire Canadian road builder, a man of elusive purpose and 180,000 shares; and a one-time TV producer with puny stock power (a mere 5,000 shares) but prodigious ambition—specifically, to be president of Loew's Inc.

The struggle swirls, incongruously, around a man of soft speech and mild temper. This central figure is Joseph R. Vogel, the president of Loew's since October, 1956. Surrounded by a board of directors both implacably divided and singularly inexperienced in the motion-picture business ("It's like Ava Gardner and Robert Taylor running U.S. Steel," says an openmouthed M.G.M. executive), Vogel today lives a life that is possibly more painful and precarious than that of any other chief executive of a major U.S. corporation. Or, as one of his anxious lieutenants picturesquely states the matter: "The poor guy is living in a Goddamn concentration camp. He's hanging by his thumbs."

An elongated shadow on the scene is the figure of seventy-six-year-old Nicholas Schenck, onetime carnival man, for twenty-eight years Loew's president, until misfortune and mismanagement precipitated his involuntary retirement in late 1955. And bellowing his cues from off stage to his favored principals in the drama is the irrepressible Louis B. Mayer, the seventy-two-year-old "Mr. Hollywood" who graduated from the junk business to preside over M.G.M. through most of its time of growth and glitter, until Schenck forced his retirement in 1951. Resentful of his rude fate, and contemptuous of M.G.M.'s misadventures since that date, Mayer, prowling the spacious rooms of his Beverly Hills mansion, hurls his grand challenge to all visitors: "*I could save this situation— turn it around right away—or I'll eat my shoes for breakfast.*"

Clearly, this is a unique collection of businessmen, bent upon discordant strategies, but as each has played his role, one touching harmony has emerged. As if some unseen director had instructed each and all in a single mannerism, there comes a moment when almost every individual draws himself upright, places his right hand over his heart, swallows hard with emotion, and intones: "I want nothing for myself—I only want to see this great company be really great once more. For the sake of M.G.M. For the sake of the industry. *I* don't want a thing. Not a *thing.*"

"LET 'EM SPEND THEIR OWN MONEY"

What is there to stir up such struggle? The answer is: a good deal more than Loew's slack earnings reports would ever suggest. At stake is a corporation with the greatest prestige in the industry and $220 million in assets; 187 acres of matchless studio property in Culver City, California; and—by 1956 fiscal reckoning—$172 million in gross revenues. There is, too, a reservoir of talent and technique great enough to make M.G.M. once again leader of the industry. And there is, in M.G.M.'s research laboratories, the capacity to revolutionize the business of movie making.

Yet only great and grave misfortune could have made M.G.M. the scene for such a power struggle. A good part of this misfortune was simply M.G.M.'s share of the whole movie industry's postwar troubles. Those included the competition of television, the shift of population away from metropolitan centers, the phenomenal soaring of production costs. A Supreme Court decision in 1948, in effect ordering separation of theatres and studios, cracked the traditional structure of the industry. On top of that came the rebellion of the industry's "independents"—stars, directors, and producers who incorporated, spurned the fixed salaries that they had to share so heavily with the government, and instead exacted fat percentage deals (50 per cent of profits or 10 per cent of gross).

The troubled industry might have hoped for vision and leadership from Loew's M.G.M.—glutted with stars as it was, and distinguished as the one great studio not to suffer bankruptcy during the depression of the 1930's. Instead, the management of Nicholas Schenck behaved with a sullen contempt for the forces that, in the decade from 1946 to 1956, drove corporate income down from $18,690,000 ($3.66 a share) to $4,840,000 ($0.91 a share). Action—or inaction—on three fronts contributed to this dismal decline:

• While Loew's stalled on the Supreme Court's 1948 decision, competitors went ahead and cut their theatres loose, and concentrated on making superior films worthy of booking by independent exhibitors.

• Loew's closed its eyes to the challenges of television, assuring itself that TV would need Hollywood in general and M.G.M. in particular. Louis B. Mayer recalls vividly (and wrathfully) the day in 1949 when R.C.A.'s David Sarnoff, urgently pounding the luncheon table, tried to persuade Schenck to put Loew's into fifty-fifty partnership with R.C.A. Schenck demurred, afterward nudged Mayer contentedly and mumbled: "Ya see how hungry they are for us? Let 'em spend a little more of their own money—we can come in any time."

• Loew's, under the stubborn Schenck, refused to come to terms with independent production at a time when all Hollywood talent was organizing itself in personal companies that would pay off in capital gains or corporate profits instead of straight income. Stars deserted the M.G.M. lot as fast as their contracts expired. Literary agents sold their best material (*The Caine Mutiny, Stalag 17,* etc.) to studios willing to make percentage deals. And the greatest studio extended its near-hitless streak: in fifteen years M.G.M. has produced but one Academy Award-winning film.

The final decline in M.G.M.'s prestige is linked by many in Hollywood to the regime of Dore Schary, who succeeded Louis B. Mayer as M.G.M. production boss in 1951. The triangular relationship of Mayer-Schary-Schenck was charged with such electric emotions as few businesses outside filmdom can generate. The aging Mayer himself, as studio head, had brought Schary to M.G.M.'s lot. But their personalities and prerogatives quickly clashed: they soon found themselves competing for the backing of Schenck and of Loew's New York business offices. Schenck, for some years, had grown increasingly resentful of Mayer's personal prestige, and Mayer's disdain for "the pencil pushers" who kept the company books. So Schenck thoroughly enjoyed Schary's appealing to him on production decisions, and was delighted to accept Mayer's angry resignation in 1951.

"A POT OF MESSAGE"

To the stocky, aggressive, and bombastic Mayer, Schary was quite a contrast: lean and scholarly-looking, self-cast for the role of Hollywood's leading liberal intellectual. Debate over Schary's performance and personality still goes on around Hollywood. No one doubts that he is a man of talent—and almost no one denies that he was notably unsuccessful as M.G.M.'s production chief. Collective decisions were rarely possible under his rule: he highhandedly bought stories and assigned production.

He seemed to M.G.M. veterans singularly uncritical of every M.G.M. product; he commonly scorned the warnings of adverse preview reaction. His contempt for the popular and his accent upon the "serious" led to the gibe, "We used to be in the entertainment business, but have sold our souls for a pot of message." The measurable failure came at the box office, where some of Schary's favorite projects scored striking losses: *Jupiter's Darling* lost $2,200,000, *Plymouth Adventure* $1,800,000.

The decade of M.G.M.'s misadventures thus encompassed both management and production failures. Beyond this, the Schenck regime carried a burden of inglorious memories that grew ever heavier with passing time and declining profits. There was the stain of the fabulous transaction in 1929, when Schenck and his treasurer literally tried to sell out their own company; they made $9 million by selling a block of 400,000 shares of Loew's stock at approximately twice the market value—to William Fox, Loew's chief competitor. There was the 1941 scandal of Schenck's payoff to labor racketeers Willie Bioff and George Browne of the stagehands' union—involving $50,000 raised (by Schenck's admission) by having his New York executives pad their expense accounts. There was the intricate web of nepotism that linked relatives of Schenck and Charles ("Carnation Charlie") Moskowitz, Schenck's intimate and Loew's treasurer, in many branches of Loew's—while four key suppliers of Loew's (carpets, posters, advertising, candy concessions) were at least partly owned by brothers or nephews or nieces of Schenck or Moskowitz. There were the bloated salaries paid to top executives regardless of M.G.M.'s revenues (in 1955, $171,786 to Schenck, $200,000 to Schary, $156, 429 to Moskowitz)—and a lush pension fund that, over a decade, sucked $3,500,000 a year from company profits. There was the arrogance of Schenck in disdaining to attend stockholders' meetings or to break down over-all profit-and-loss figures so that they would reveal the true picture about M.G.M. Thus it was possible while declaring dividends in excess of earnings to keep secret such statistics as these (never before made public):

• Over the ten-year period, 1947–56, the net result of all M.G.M. film production was a *loss* of more than $6 million. In 1956 alone losses on film production hit $4,600,000.

• Losses were offset (and hidden) only by profits from the re-issue of *old* films. These netted more than $16,800,000; the re-issue of *Gone With the Wind* netted over $11,500,000.

• All the while, M.G.M. facilities were maintained at a level capable of producing forty to fifty films a year, and these facilities cost the studio as much as $10 million in overhead in 1956. Actual production in 1956, however, was a mere twenty pictures.

THE NEW DISORDER

The end of the old disorder—and the beginning of the new disorder—came in the autumn of 1955. The fall-off in earnings (only $1.03 per share for the fiscal year ending August 31, 1955) stirred other ominous developments. Angry proxy fights threatened from several quarters, such as Dreyfus & Co., Hirsch & Co., and the Leon Lowenstein Foundation—whose holdings totaled perhaps 250,000 shares. The Wall Street "coroners" began to catch the scent of a lucrative liquidation operation. They knew that Loew's assets had been grossly understated—with the whole M.G.M. film library, salable to TV, not even listed on the books. Arthur Wiesenberger's investment reports had sharply raised the question whether Loew's Inc. was worth more dead or alive, and had concluded that "a $60 payout will make a far more appealing picture than any M.G.M. can produce for its shareholders today with the stock selling at 21⅜." Such critics noted that a company earning no more than 2 per cent on its investment was scarcely worth keeping alive.

To check these threats and tensions Loew's reshuffled the M.G.M. management, but the result was an uneasy interregnum that lasted less than a year. Schenck withdrew in December, 1955, from the presidency to become chairman of the board. It was impossible for him to press the candidacy of Charles Moskowitz for the president's job, for all dissidents would have assailed this as merely a move to perpetuate Schenck's rule. Instead, a man was picked from within the company who was sufficiently independent of Schenck to command confidence: fifty-six-year-old Arthur Loew, son of the company's founder. As head of Loew's International, he had done a notable job in overseas distribution—increasingly vital to M.G.M. as foreign revenues have come to make up almost 50 per cent of the company's gross. Arthur Loew, to support his position, turned to two Wall Street houses that had lately acquired substantial blocks of Loew's stock: Lehman Bros. and Lazard Frères. Both agreed to place representatives on Loew's board.

While these maneuvers sufficed to rout the "coroners" (Dreyfus shortly unloaded most of its Loew's stock), they were in fact only a weak kind of holding action. The two directors from Lehman Bros. and Lazard Frères found Loew slow to "clean house"—and slow to make the reforms they recommended. And one sharp issue soon arose: the Wall Street representatives on the board pressed urgently for outright sale of the pre-1949 film library to TV (there was one offer of $50 million), while Arthur Loew held out for a leasing arrangement, which in the long run will turn out to be more beneficial to M.G.M. The most serious weakness in the company's position, however, was the fact that Arthur Loew simply did not want to be president. He had taken the job reluctantly. He was impressed with the recollection that his father had died at the age (fifty-seven) that he was nearing. And he sensed new struggles for control of Loew's in the offing. So in October of last year he abruptly quit. The Lehman and Lazard representatives immediately resigned, retiring to the safety of the sidelines. And the open struggle for power was about to start.

It began eccentrically. Many people who were approached to take over the presidency (including Pat Weaver, recently departed from N.B.C., and Lew Wasserman, head of Music Corp. of America) spurned the job. Board Chairman Schenck (11,200 shares) made another vain effort to reaffirm his power through the candidacy of Moskowitz. And finally the task and title—after a remarkable fortnight when the greatest company in the movie industry was headless—went to Joseph R. Vogel. A man of calm and deliberation, Vogel had risen, over a period of more than forty years, from usher in a New York Loew's theatre to become head of the whole theatre chain in 1954. Along with this extended experience in distribution, his qualifications included: a knack of forecasting the gross of a picture within $100,000, a freedom from any intimate association with Schenck's fateful business decisions, the personal respect of the Wall Street banking houses—and an apparent unawareness of the conflicts that were about to afflict Loew's management. Indeed, at that date Vogel may not even have heard the name of Stanley Meyer.

WHAT MAKES STANLEY RUN

Stanley Meyer is a bold and voluble forty-four-year-old citizen of Hollywood, the son-in-law of Nate Blumberg, chairman of Universal; his title to film renown derives from once having been co-producer (with Jack Webb) of the serial *Dragnet*. In 1955, following the sale of his 25 per cent interest in *Dragnet,* Meyer found himself with a little more than a million dollars and nothing grand to do. His ambition was by no means so limited as his experience, the high point of which was his services to Webb. These entailed some contract negotiations, handling public relations, and negotiating Webb's divorce settlement with actress Julie London. As Meyer once summed it up, "I'm like the guy with the shovel that follows behind the elephant."

Early in 1956, as a change of pace, Meyer set out to stalk the lion: M.G.M., he strongly suspected, could be captured. He made a shopping trip to New York to explore the possibilities, found that his personal attorney also represented Lehman Bros., and conferred with Robert Lehman. Neither Lehman nor Lazard Frères seemed impressed with Stanley Meyer's managerial talents. But by chance Stanley Meyer heard from a Wall Street acquaintance of the existence of a Loew's stockholder named Joseph Tomlinson, formerly of Toronto, Canada, currently of Fort Lauderdale, Florida.

Seeking out Tomlinson, Meyer discovered him to be a gruff and blunt man of forty-seven, a Canadian citizen, and M.I.T. graduate who made his several millions building roads in Canada. Tomlinson had begun amassing shares of Loew's stock in 1954 until he and his family now had a pile of more than 200,000. Until 1956, the thought of control or even intervention in Loew's management had not apparently entered his head —which did, however, contain a lively appreciation of the company's real assets and potential earnings. But M.G.M. profits had kept getting smaller. Arthur Loew had not been able to achieve much. Could more be expected of another company veteran, Joseph Vogel? And here suddenly at Tomlinson's side stood Stanley Meyer—articulate, enormously earnest, seemingly steeped in knowledge of the mysteries of film making, uncompromising in his indictment of Schenck and his successors—a man of force and independence and talent, it seemed to Tomlinson.

And Stanley Meyer brought with him, it seemed, another quite special asset: the name of Louis B. Mayer. Mayer and Stanley Meyer had been acquainted for many years, and L. B. was godfather to one of Meyer's children. Meyer knew well L. B.'s bitter and abiding resentment over the way Schenck had treated him in 1951. He knew, too, that L. B. had a proud and simple formula for curing M.G.M.'s troubles: "If you want to save this company, you go to the man who made it great in the first place." And Stanley Meyer knew—or thought he knew—the impact the name of L. B. Mayer could have on baffled and irate Loew's stockholders.

Thus—just as Vogel assumed the presidency of Loew's—a hostile triumvirate was born. The sealing of the union took a little work. L. B. himself refused to travel to New York even to make the acquaintance of the Canadian road builder who might be the means of bringing him back from exile, so Tomlinson graciously traveled to Beverly Hills. Tomlinson was awed by the grand boast of the old producer: "Just let the word get around Hollywood that L. B. is back and the talent will come crowding back to M.G.M." In turn, L. B. hailed Tomlinson as "a real two-fisted guy." And Stanley Meyer for his part saluted two men perceptive enough to see the salvation of M.G.M. in the elevation of Stanley Meyer to the presidency.

DUEL WITH WOODEN SWORDS

The struggle for stockholder support—seemingly headed for a wide-open proxy fight—lasted from Vogel's assumption of the presidency last October until the annual stockholders' meeting last February. Sharp as it became, it was an odd struggle, essentially because neither Joseph Vogel nor Stanley Meyer was trained by any previous experience for this kind of contest. Meyer for some time nourished the illusion that Robert Lehman and André Meyer of Lazard Frères would respond enthusiastically to his cry that M.G.M. must "clean house"—economize, diversify, and bring in young talent to invigorate aging management. Vogel, for a while, was beguiled into thinking that Tomlinson was only a mildly restive stockholder, certainly not committed to Vogel's removal. . . . As the February stockholders' meeting approached, it was clear that Meyer and Tomlinson had made a serious miscalculation: they discovered that the name of L. B. Mayer, possibly an asset in terms of public relations, was a heavy liability on Wall Street. To both Lehman Bros. and Lazard Frères, L. B. was associated with the old regime and its prodigal spending habits. It became apparent, therefore, that the bankers would support Vogel if only to bar L. B.'s return.

Up to the very day of the stockholders' meeting on February 28, Meyer and Tomlinson tried to swing a seventh board member to their side. Among the men they had chosen as directors were onetime Chrysler Board Chairman K. T. Keller and former Defense Secretary Louis Johnson, who worked hard to swing possible waverers over to the Tomlinson-Meyer side. Stanley Meyer stormed the august offices of André Meyer at Lazard Frères, to hammer the desk in rage against bankers presuming to dictate the fate of M.G.M. All the while, Stanley Meyer cloaked his ambition to be elected president by various formulas: he would be content with direction of M.G.M. studios as a No. 2 man, or it might suffice if Tomlinson were just made chairman of the executive committee. To the last, the question of how the directors would vote stood in doubt. But at the meeting the stockholders approved the management slate, and the directors promptly confirmed Vogel in the presidency.

Thus the struggle shifted to the management level. And thus began Vogel's life in his "God-damn concentration camp."

GOODBYE MR. SCHENCK

Despite his unhappy position he achieved quite a bit.

In the area of general housecleaning, he dictated studio economies said to promise savings of $2,400,000 a year in overhead. The inherited nepotism of the Schenck era was almost totally swept out—Schenck is no longer even honorary chairman, and all M.G.M. purchasing has been opened to competitive bidding. The services of Charles Moskowitz are to terminate this year. And Vogel instituted a complete test-check audit of Loew's books.

Vogel promptly fired Dore Schary and paid off the balance of his contract. As administrative head of the studio, Vogel appointed Benjamin Thau, M.G.M.'s long-time casting director and one of Hollywood's shrewdest negotiators with talent. To provide Thau with artistic advice, Vogel named Sidney Franklin, the talented and respected creator of *Mrs. Miniver* and other M.G.M. hits of the past.

Meanwhile, in the television field, under Vice President Charles (Bud) Barry, M.G.M. made some headway. The leasing of old M.G.M. films to TV already has netted $45 million from some fifty stations. With title to the films remaining with M.G.M., allowing resale five years hence, Barry observes: "This library is like oil, it just keeps coming to the surface." At the same time, some of the huge M.G.M. facilities are being leased to outside companies producing for TV—which not only sops up some studio overhead but also gives M.G.M. technicians some valuable experience in TV production. For direct sale, M.G.M. is producing—in addition to TV commercials—its first dramatic serial, *The Thin Man,* whose outright sale is expected to bring close to $1 million. The TV budget was a modest one but Barry was inspired to declare: "There's nothing to keep this old colossus of M.G.M. from becoming the biggest producer of films for TV."

Vogel also made major contracts with independent producers and stars. Among those signed to long-term contracts, carrying percentage deals, were veteran producers Sol Siegel, Pandro Berman, Lawrence Weingarten, Aaron Rosenberg. Alfred Hitchcock's next film (*The Wreck of the Mary Deare*) will be released through M.G.M. William Wyler has been signed to direct a new *Ben Hur*—Loew's great hope for a smash success two years hence. And one of Hollywood's top box-office attractions, Yul Brynner, will play the lead in M.G.M.'s *The Brothers Karamazov,* currently being shot for early 1958 release.

Finally, Vogel brought to the office of chief executive of Loew's an integrity of person and of purpose widely recognized and respected. Even L. B. Mayer and Stanley Meyer acknowledged Vogel's personal honesty and worthy intentions. And on the M.G.M. lot he won regard for spending more time in Hollywood, studying production problems, than any other New York executive of Loew's has ever done. . . .

THE LION'S FUTURE

How dark or how bright is M.G.M.'s future under any constructive leadership?

The obituaries of late pronounced on the old lion—in trade journals and over cocktails at Romanoff's or the Brown Derby—seem premature. M.G.M. has always been a deliberate beast, almost always last in the industry to take every great forward step—sound, color, wide screen, independent production. Yet now, waking up to the new facts of film life, it is showing its latent vitality.

Committed as it is now to compete for independent production contracts, M.G.M. has more to offer the independents than almost any other studio. There is no finer distribution machinery in the business. There is no international organization so strong. There is no richer stock of literary properties to attract stars, directors, and producers hungry for material. And its technical resources are unmatched anywhere in the industry—from Douglas Shearer's sound department to M.G.M.'s ninety-seven acres of elaborate outdoor sets in Culver City.

At the same time the rise of the independent—only recently expected to render big studios obsolete—already is proving to be a trend with some severe limitations. "Freedom" from the big studio has its price: no art director, no make-up man, no prop man instantly ready at the producer's call. And once "freed," the independent creative talent has found itself more immersed in business details than ever before.

PRODUCERS CAN BE PRODUCERS

The wheel of change is thus slowly turning back half-circle, and it is likely to come to rest on the formula of "semi-independence," such as producers Pandro Berman and Sol Siegel now enjoy at M.G.M. As Berman says: "Under this setup I don't have to act like a promoter—running around town trying to make a package of a story and a male lead and a female lead, and peddle it to this bank and that bank. Here I can be what I am—a producer." Under such deals as Berman has, the independent producer makes contracts with M.G.M. for a specified number of pictures over a given number of years. The independent invests just enough money to qualify his company for capital-gains taxation; M.G.M. puts up the rest. The independent's contract calls for a specified percentage of the earnings of each picture under a scheme of "cross-collateralization." This device brackets pictures into groups of two to four for the computation of total earnings—so that the individual producer, for example, cannot make a handsome profit on one film and let M.G.M. take the loss on the others. The practical virtues of this system are many. For individual talent, it promises the best of both possible worlds: high potential earnings *and* the full facilities of a major studio. From the studio's viewpoint, it promises an advantage especially meaningful for M.G.M.: a built-in economy, since everyone working on a production has a personal interest in holding down costs. As Sol Siegel notes: "There's no easing up on the job now—every producer tries for a home run for his own sake." Berman, a veteran of seventeen years at

R.K.O. and seventeen more at M.G.M., says: "Right now I think this place is in healthier shape than at any time since 1940."

As Vogel is fond of pointing out, the potential earnings in the film industry—like its costs—are higher than ever. With the vast expansion in the overseas market, a successful picture today can make money unimagined in prewar years. Even a film so undistinguished as *Quo Vadis* has already grossed $22,500,000. So there is truth in Vogel's assertion: "M.G.M. suffers from nothing that two or three hits can't cure. Or let the next *Ben Hur* be a smash—and we'll record profits for five years on that alone."

On a more distant horizon looms the possibility that excites yet higher hopes—the prospect of toll television. There are many technical and legal matters unresolved here. But among toll TV's glittering attractions would be quick return on investment, and drastic cutting of present-day distribution costs.

MOVIES BY MAIL

And—on a yet more distant horizon—there exists in Douglas Shearer's research laboratory another possibility even more revolutionary. As the scholarly Shearer explains, with irrepressible excitement:

"Who knows more about distribution than anybody else? Publishers. What is indispensable to their system? Obviously, reproduction of their creation on cheap stock. Think along these lines. Suppose we could produce *films* on cellophane or a gelatin with no emulsion. And suppose we could ship them by mail just like a magazine. And suppose you have people subscribing to films just as they do to weeklies—you would have the most fabulous box office in the world—the home. Well, we *can* do it."

The scheme is no more advanced than Shearer's certainty of its technical practicality. The essential ingredient—a cheap stock—has been tested and proved. The possibilities certainly seem to justify Shearer's excitement. Films would be delivered by mail direct to customers, who could run them off in their homes on special projectors rented from local agencies. The film stock would sustain no more than three or four showings, but customers could buy new prints any time they wanted them. As a rough estimate of the economics involved: subscribers would pay $2.50 per film: production cost per film would be some 60 cents; and out of the $1.90 spread between cost and price, the producing company could probably take 60 cents—or 100 per cent profit.

This is the stuff that great corporations' dreams are made of. It's the stuff that could be part of a new life for old M.G.M. And it is the kind of stuff that makes a man like Joe Vogel hope very much that he will still be around M.G.M. for a while.

■ ■ ■ ■

HOLLYWOOD FACES THE WORLD (1962),
Richard Dyer MacCann

Although the audience for films in America was shrinking, the potential audience for Hollywood films abroad was expanding. But the American film industry's relationship to its global market became far more complex in the years following the war than it had previously been—when American films frequently occupied some 90% percent of the screen time in most foreign nations. This chapter from Richard Dyer MacCann's book, *Hollywood in Transition*, summarizes Hollywood's more delicate and dependent relationships with the film industries abroad. Professor MacCann, who was Hollywood correspondent for the *Christian Science Monitor*, now teaches cinema studies at the University of Iowa, is the former editor of *Cinema Journal*, and is the editor of the well-known anthology *Film: A Montage of Theories*.

"A tree is a tree, a rock is a rock: shoot it in Griffith Park!"
Old Hollywood proverb

Mid-century movie making has gone global. Hollywood is no longer even a geographical expression. It is a state of mind, operating world-wide. It is a starlet at Cannes and a producer on location in Rome. It is Ava Gardner, who lives in Spain, and Bill Holden, who has moved to Switzerland. It is a novelist at work on a screenplay in London and a screenwriter at work on a novel in Hawaii.

Hollywood has always been seen through many eyes—by a moviegoer in Bombay, a banker-stockholder in England, a theater owner in Peru. Its worldwide impact was great even in the silent days.

Now the impact is being felt in reverse. Hollywood still influences the world, but the world is also becoming a factor to reckon with in Hollywood. Foreign markets are no longer merely dumping grounds for films that have already made their profits. Foreign receipts are no longer merely "gravy." They are more than 50 percent of the gross.

This has direct effects on plans for film making in Hollywood. The democracy of the box office—not the anxious advice of diplomats and editorial writers—has begun to convince America's film companies that many of their decisions must be considered from an international point of view.

"Hollywood Faces the World" is from Richard Dyer MacCann's book, *Hollywood in Transition* (Houghton Mifflin, 1962).

This also means that the film producer is no longer restricted to satisfying American audiences. He is free to find his money anywhere in the world. The standards of Boston or Chicago need not deter him very much. American problems of urbanism or education or segregation or traffic are not of much interest to him if he doesn't think they will interest the foreign audience. He is a worldwide communicator and he reports to nobody but the national censors and the banks.

THE COMPETITIVE FOREIGN MARKET

The facts are not well known, and they are illuminating. At last count, according to the U.S. Department of Commerce, there were 154,852 motion picture theaters in the world. Of this number, only 16,991 are in the United States (4700 of them drive-ins). Here are some comparative figures for other regions and nations (the Soviet figure, here and below, includes mobile 16-millimeter theaters and is therefore greatly inflated):

Europe: 103,990

USSR	45,600	West Germany	6,884
United Kingdom	3,457	East Germany	1,550
France	5,778	Sweden	2,403
Spain	6,080	Italy	10,508

Other European countries 21,730

Mexico and Central America	2,927	Far East	15,697
		Middle East	694
South America	6,973	Africa	2,168
Caribbean	857	Atlantic Islands	216
Canada	1,727	South Pacific	2,311

Audience statistics tell more about the actual impact of films, since theaters vary greatly in size. But even the estimates of audience potential must be viewed with caution, since theater men are fond of rounding off numbers upward. The number of theater seats in four-wall theaters in the United States is only 11,300,000 of the 73,826,349 in the world.

Europe: 42,863,551

USSR	17,000,000	West Germany	2,843,963
United Kingdom	3,450,000	East Germany	550,000
France	2,785,655	Sweden	600,000
Spain	3,663,000	Italy	4,700,000

Other European countries 7,270,933

Mexico and Central America	2,025,723	Far East	7,918,969
		Middle East	451,000
South America	4,518,187	Africa	1,459,760
Carribbean	592,226	Atlantic Islands	97,173
Canada	810,000	South Pacific	1,463,710

Since 1955, the number of theater seats has increased by 35 per cent in Africa and in Europe, by 43 per cent in the Far East, and by 63 per cent in the Middle East.

Competition among nations has always been a factor in international film distribution, but the extent of it has ebbed and flowed with technological change. In the silent days, of course, motion pictures moved freely across boundaries. Only the occasional printed titles had to be changed from one language to another—and some of the best German films of the early 1920's had few titles to change.

The coming of sound raised language barriers too steep for any but the most outstanding films to surmount. Printed titles had to be burned right into the face of the photography. This was all right for the enthusiasts in the slowly growing number of "art theaters." But not until the skill of "dubbing in" voices reached a level slightly above embarrassment could translated films reach a mass audience in other countries. The development of dubbing skills made it easier for American films to reach foreign audiences, at least in those countries which would accept this technique. The process has been used by the major companies for many years. On the other hand, dubbing can also make it easier for a small country with a small film industry to seek wider distribution. Because of the growing popularity of foreign films, dubbed sound tracks have recently become much more common in this country.

With wider distribution, foreign films can have bigger budgets. With bigger budgets, a small country can turn out product more like Hollywood's. This means the loss of individuality, artistry, and even identity—and eventually a falling-off in world interest in the small country's films, once they lose their unique background and atmosphere. But the immediate chance for more profits and bigger budgets is hard to resist.

Italian producers have been especially active in seeking world markets during the decade since early low-budget film makers like Rossellini and DeSica made a name for Italian films. Competing in their own country with TV sets in the cafés, competing both at home and overseas with the big-screen products of Hollywood, the Italians have put less emphasis on competition and more on "co-production." This new financial invention means the sharing of costs and stars with American or French or British companies, and after that, a mutual sharing of markets. Paramount found it useful for *War and Peace* and many lesser subjects since. Co-production is a good way for American companies, too, to enlarge film budgets, expand audiences, and generally soften the blows of competition in the world arena.

Motion picture production is being seriously undertaken in an increasing number of countries. In Sweden, when Ingmar Bergman began making films, his budgets were strictly limited to the national audience he could expect to reach. His astonishing international success proves once more that a unique contribution to film can find a world audience despite language barriers and the supposed illiteracy of audiences. The popularity of Japanese films, based mainly on early directing achievements by Akira Kurosawa (especially *Rashomon*) has been paralleled by the same expanding of production costs and cheapening of content that has occurred in Italy. Japan is now the largest producer of films in the world. Some of the statistics for 1959 feature production are instructive:

Japan	502	U.S.	187	West Germany	100
India	310	Italy	167	Mexico	86
Hong Kong	273	France	136	Spain	68

Since motion pictures are probably the most expensive form of national self-expression, it is noteworthy that we are beginning to see film production come from such countries as Greece, Yugoslavia, Brazil, Argentina, and even Holland. Iron Curtain countries, of course, obeying Lenin's dictum about the importance of films, are busy: Hungary, Bulgaria, Poland, Czechoslovakia, Cuba. Russia has expanded production prodigiously in the years since Stalin's death.

The weekly world audience for American films is estimated by the Film Daily Yearbook to be 200,000,000 people. Of these, only 44,000,000 are in the United States. But foreign audiences pay much less for their tickets. In order to bring in from overseas that other half of every dollar earned, movie distributors must attract *more than three times* as many patrons as they do in this country.

Such figures reveal the box the American box office is in. While the audience abroad is growing larger in proportion to the declining domestic audience, selling pictures in foreign markets is getting harder all the time.

From a combination of factors, it seems clear that America's competitive position in film distribution abroad has declined. Fewer films are being produced by Hollywood companies. More are being made in other countries. In many instances co-production arrangements have blurred American contributions to the final result on the screen. The impact of TV is beginning to be felt, notably in Japan, Great Britain, and western Europe.

Foreign screen time for American films has been proportionately falling, year by year. American films are still more popular than those from any other single country, but if there ever was a danger of a Hollywood monopoly, it no longer exists. Ten years ago, American motion pictures occupied from 80 to 90 per cent of the screen time in foreign theaters. Five years ago this figure was 68 per cent. Today it averages 60 per cent—60 per cent in England, 50 in Italy, 35 in France, 30 in Germany, 50 in Argentina, 30 in Japan. Recently a handful of current films have been seen for the first time in Russia.

Official restrictions by foreign governments are continually changing and are the subject of endless international conferences. Eric Johnston, president of the Motion Picture Association, is seldom seen in Hollywood. He and his chief lieutenants are overseas much of the time, trying to wring concessions little by little, country by country, from boards of trade, economic commissions, tariff experts, and censors.

The restrictions occur on several levels. In certain countries, like India and Indonesia, the censors are particularly hard on the kind of "action" films Americans like to make. In most countries, there are general limitations like taxes, import duties, and license procedures. In between are the elaborate problems of quotas and "frozen funds."

Quotas are primarily intended to encourage national film production by keeping out more than a certain number of American movies each year. Some countries have no specific import quotas but specify that theaters must include a certain number of nationally produced films or show them during a certain percentage of their screen time.

French authorities, for example, decided that no more than 10 films by major American companies could come in during 1960. These are divided up by the MPA among its members. Independent film-makers have to fight for their own quotas. After all that, of course, each company must still seek out specific theater men and sell the product to them.

The quota system not only encourages national film-making. It tends to discourage American production. If only about 15 pictures from the studio can get into the major markets this year, then there isn't much point in making more than 15. Thus the foreign market, so important to the success of a release schedule, often reduces the American market to strictly secondary consideration. When the decision is between two pictures, one for the American market and one that can be expected to go well everywhere, the decision is likely to go against the picture for the U.S.

PRESSURES FOR OVERSEAS PRODUCTION

The ingenious notion of blocking or "freezing" American dollars has had a different kind of effect. It has served to force more American producers to make their films abroad.

Although the accounting problems for the film maker may be baffling, the basic concept of frozen funds is simple. The producer makes a picture, distributes it in Japan, and receives only one fourth of his box office in dollars. The rest is in yen, unconverted to dollars, held by the government in a blocked account in Tokyo. It's the producer's money, but all those millions of yen won't buy a single star or story or crew in the United States of America. The answer is to find a project like *Sayonara* that can be done in Japan. The only trouble is that the film made in Japan may then be very popular at the Japanese box office and eventually the frozen funds are bigger than ever.

Motion picture companies found themselves becoming diversified in a hurry as they struggled to get their dollars out of foreign lands. All sorts of schemes have been worked out. American film companies have bought beef in Argentina and polo ponies in Chile. M-G-M used some of its blocked lire to buy Italian marble and sold it to the Vermont Marble Company. In 1955, the MPA went so far as to advance a $7,500,000 loan to the Japanese government (out of frozen yen), repayable in dollars in three to seven years.

Recently film companies willing to produce in foreign countries have been confronted with a carrot as well as a stick. Special subsidies for national film production in England, France, and elsewhere have been interpreted to apply also to co-production arrangements with American companies, if certain requirements are met. The money comes from an entertainment tax levied on the customer at the box office, but it is untaxed income when the film companies get it. Naturally it is a strong temptation to "make a British film" (with a basically British crew and some British financing) when this means sharing in the box-office rebates provided by the Eady plan. Some of this money, too, is frozen, which of course means further involvement in foreign production.

There are many reasons for using foreign locations. The decision to shoot most of the picture abroad is not necessarily based entirely on blocked balances, subsidies, and the blandishments of Italian or British co-financiers.

The determining reason may often be an artistic one. The producer-director sometimes options a script on the assumption that it can only be shot in Israel or in Africa. The story demands it. The action could not be effectively developed against familiar American backgrounds, even if they "look like" the foreign locale.

Furthermore, the distant place may be just as important as the expensive star in building the "production value" that makes the picture sell. In fact, the star may already be overseas (seeking income tax advantages) or may want to take a trip overseas, and the two factors will reinforce each other.

Thus the artistic reason is inextricably mingled with the search for elements of audience appeal. The basic story may call for geographical splendor, but the publicity office may call for it even more strongly.

Ever since *Three Coins in the Fountain* gave moviegoers their first Cinema-Scope tour of Rome, the foreign locale has been judged an "exploitable" factor. A producer-director, by the very tension of his hyphenation, has to think about commerce and aesthetics at the same time. When he thinks about the "values" of overseas location, he doesn't try too hard to distinguish between the demands of the story itself and the expectations of the big audience he hopes it will appeal to.

Furthermore, the American audience—so much more familiar with faraway places since World War II, so much more exposed to them by the wide screen—is now joined by an equally potent worldwide audience. Authenticity of background is a most important appeal in foreign lands. A story about Israel, filmed in Israel, may be of outstanding interest in Japan, and vice versa. Certainly it is hard to get away with a studio-produced picture about the Orient in the Oriental market.

None of these pressures can be altered much by the conscious resolve of individual producers to stay and work in Hollywood. Nor are they likely to be much affected by union resolutions, pickets, or boycotts. Hollywood labor-management meetings, however, have justifiably called attention to those "runaway" producers who try to save a few dollars by incorporating under a foreign flag—pretending to be foreign for tax purposes but claiming to be American for distribution advantages.

There will always be a Hollywood, technically speaking. The tradition is there, the laboratories are there, the skills are there. A great center of trained technicians draws business to itself, as the enormous volume of TV-film production attests. But there are also changing currents of comparative wage scales, import quotas, and national currency restrictions. There are broad shifts in audience interest, story sources, and directorial desires. There are some stars and directors who don't want to work in Hollywood any more, for reasons of their own. Sometimes they just don't want to have studio executives peering over their shoulders. If they can't have all the financial independence they want, at least they can have distance.

As for the labor costs of shooting in foreign countries, apparently the advantages and disadvantages tend to cancel out. Producers who have tried it say: "Yes, sometimes foreign crews can be smaller and cheaper than in Hollywood. But they may also work less efficiently, and sometimes they make costly mistakes."

The biggest labor advantage in foreign production is the availability and cheapness of extra players—onlookers, armies, and mobs. The cost of a first-rate revolution or massive battle is prohibitive in present-day Hollywood. The rise in the American standard of living has made spectacular films into foreign affairs.

■ ■ ■ ■

FANTASIES OF THE ART-HOUSE AUDIENCE (1954), Pauline Kael

Films came to America from abroad in greater numbers in the 1950s and 1960s than they had in any period since the 1920s. The fact that the *Miracle* case was triggered by a foreign film playing a small "art house" dedicated exclusively to the showing of such films is itself indicative of the growing importance of these films in the period. The film critic in America who was one of the most responsive to these films and may have been one of the most influential in their acceptance and understanding was Dwight Macdonald, who became film critic for *Esquire* in 1960 and continued in that position during the entire decade. Another influential writer on film whose opinions began to be heard at about the same time as Macdonald's was Pauline Kael. As opposed to Macdonald, whose judgments tended to concentrate exclusively on the formal and thematic issues of the films themselves, Ms. Kael's criticism combined an interest in such qualities with a greater tolerance for and understanding of the problems of the American film industry and a greater awareness of the relationship between a film on the screen and the audience that chose to watch it. The material reprinted below, excerpted from an article which appeared in *Sight and Sound* in 1954, takes issue initially with a single aesthetic judgment of Macdonald's about a single "art film." Ms. Kael's real goal in the piece is to examine the assumptions behind the new film audience's acceptance of these new, foreign "art films."

For several decades now educated people have been condescending toward the children, the shopgirls, all those with "humdrum" or "impoverished" lives—the mass audience—who turned to movies for "ready-made" dreams. The educated might admit that they sometimes went to the movies designed for the infantile mass audience—the number of famous people who relax with detective fiction makes this admission easy —but presumably they were not "taken in"; they went to get away from the tensions of their complex lives and work. But of course when they really want to enjoy movies as an art, they go to foreign films, or "adult" or unusual or experimental American films.

I would like to suggest that the educated audience often uses "art" films in much the same self-indulgent way as the mass audience uses the Hollywood "product," finding wish fulfillment in the form of cheap and easy congratulation on their sensitivities and their liberalism. (Obviously

"Fantasies of the Art-House Audience," which originally appeared in 1954 in *Sight and Sound,* was reprinted in *I Lost It at the Movies,* by Pauline Kael (Atlantic–Little, Brown, 1965).

any of my generalizations are subject to numerous exceptions and infinite qualifications; let's assume that I know this, and that I use large generalizations in order to be suggestive rather than definitive.)

By the time Alain Resnais's *Hiroshima Mon Amour* reached American art houses, expectations were extraordinarily high. Dwight Macdonald in *Esquire* had said: "It is the most original, moving, exciting and important movie I've seen in years, somehow managing to combine a love story with propaganda against war and the atomic bomb without either losing its full force." The rest of the press seemed to concur. The *Saturday Review* considered it "a masterpiece." The New York *Herald Tribune* decided that "it establishes beyond any man's cavilling the potentialities of the film as an art"—something one might have thought already established. *Time* decided that the theme was that "Hiroshima, like God, is love. It is the Calvary of the atomic age. It died for man's sins . . ." I met a couple who had seen the film five nights in a row; a University of California professor informed me that if I didn't like *this* one, he would never speak to me again. Dwight Macdonald wrote more and went further:

> It is as stylised as *Potemkin* or *Ten Days that Shook the World*, as pure and powerful as cinema . . . It is also a novelistic exploration of memory, a *recherche du temps perdu* comparable to Proust. . . . For the first time since Eisenstein—we have a cinematic intelligence so quick, so subtle, so original, so at once passionate and sophisticated that it can be compared with Joyce, with Picasso, with Berg and Bartok and Stravinsky. The audience was extraordinarily quiet—no coughing, whispering, rustling of paper; a hypnotic trance. . . . It was oddly like a religious service, and if someone had made a wisecrack, it would have seemed not an irritation but a blasphemy.

Surely movies—even the greatest movies—are rarely received in such an atmosphere of incense burning. *Breathless* and *L'Avventura* were to be either admired or disliked or ignored, but *Hiroshima Mon Amour* was described in hushed tones; it was some sort of ineffable deep experience. Why?

The picture opened with those intertwined nude bodies—this could be symbolic of a true intermingling, but it irresistibly set off some lewd speculations about just *what* was going on. And what was that stuff they were covered with? Beach sand? Gold dust? Ashes? Finally, I accepted it as symbolic bomb ash, but I wasn't happy with it. (Later I discovered that it was supposed to be "sweat, ashes and dew.") Then the French girl said she had seen everything in Hiroshima, and the Japanese man told her she had seen nothing in Hiroshima. Then they said the same things over again, and again, and perhaps again. And I lost patience. I have never understood why writers assume that repetition creates a lyric mood or underlines meaning with profundity. My reaction is simply, "OK, I got it the first time, let's get on with it." Now, this is obviously not how we are supposed to react to Marguerite Duras's dialogue, which is clearly intended to be musical and contrapuntal, and I was going to try to get in the right, passive, receptive mood for a ritual experience, when some outright fraud made me sit up and pay attention. The action— or inaction—in bed was intercut with what purported to be documentary shots of the effect of the bomb on Hiroshima. Only I had seen some of the footage before in a Japanese atrocity movie that was about as documentary as *Peyton Place*. This clumsily staged imposture made me suspect that the Japanese man didn't know Hiroshima either, and I began to look askance at the truth he was supposed to represent. Where did he get this metaphysical identity with Hiroshima? As the film went on, and the heroine recounted her first love for a German soldier, how he had been killed on the last day of fighting, how she had been dragged away and her head shaved, how she had gone mad and been hidden away in the cellar by her shamed parents, I began to think less and less of the movie and more about why so many people were bowled over by it.

Was it possibly an elaborate, masochistic fantasy for intellectuals? Surely both sexes could identify with the girl's sexual desperation, her sensitivity and confusion—and had anyone dreamed up worse punishments for sexuality? Only a few years ago it had looked as if James Dean in *East of Eden* and *Rebel Without a Cause* had gone just about as far as anybody could in being misunderstood. But this heroine not only had her head shaved by people who didn't understand her love and need of the German, but she went *crazy* and was locked in a cellar. You can't go much further in being misunderstood. And, at the risk of giving offense, is this not what sends so many people to analysts—the fear that they'll go crazy if they don't get love?

The Japanese, it may be noted, is rather dull and uninteresting: he says no more than an analyst might; he is simply a sounding board. And if, being Japanese, he is supposed to represent the world's conscience, he brings an unsuitably bland, professionally sympathetic and upper-class manner to the function. But everybody who has suffered sexual deprivation—and who hasn't?—can identify with her and perhaps fantasize brutal parents and cellars. Even her insanity can be equated with those rough nights when a love affair fell apart or that nervous exhaustion at the end of the academic year that sends so many to the hospital or the psychiatric clinic.

It seemed to be a woman's picture—in the most derogatory sense of the term. And still she went on talking: her feelings, her doubts, her memories, kept pouring out. It began to seem like True Confession at the higher levels of spiritual and sexual communion; and I decided the great lesson for us all was to shut up. This woman (beautifully as Emmanuelle Riva interpreted her) was exposing one of the worst faults of intelligent modern women: she was talking all her emotions out—as if bed were the place to demonstrate sensibility. It's unfortunate that what people believe to be the most important things about themselves, their innermost truths and secrets—the real you or me—that we wish up when somebody looks sympathetic, is very likely to be the driveling nonsense that we generally have enough brains to forget about. The real you or me that we conceal because we think people won't accept it is slop—and why *should* anybody want it?

But here was the audience soaking it up—audiences of social workers, scientists, doctors, architects, professors—living and loving and suffering just like the stenographer watching Susan Hayward. Are the experiences involved really so different? Few of us have seen our lovers killed by partisan bullets, but something kills love anyway—something always does—and it's probably highly gratifying for many people to identify with a heroine who isn't responsible: it is the insane world that has punished her for her sexual expression. Emmanuelle Riva's sexual expression is far more forthright than a Hollywood heroine's, which makes it more appealing to an educated audience, and, of course, her character and her manner of indicating her emotional problems have a higher "tone." (It may be relevant to note that the educated audience, which generally ignores Miss Hayward, did turn out for *I Want to Live,* in which the character of Barbara Graham was turned into a sort of modern Tess of the d'Urbervilles—not only innocent of crime but horribly sinned against and *nobler* than anybody else.)

But what does her sad story have to do with Hiroshima and the bomb? Would not some other psychosexual story of deprivation (say, *Camille* or *Stella Dallas*) be just as relevant to the horrors of war if it were set in Hiroshima? It would seem so. However, the setting itself explains another aspect of the film's strong appeal, particularly to liberal intellectuals. There is a crucial bit of dialogue: "They make movies to sell soap, why not a movie to sell peace?" I don't know how many movies you have gone to lately that were made to sell soap, but American movies *are* like advertisements, and we can certainly assume that indirectly they sell a way of life that includes soap as well as an infinity of other products. But what makes the dialogue crucial is that the audience for *Hiroshima Mon Amour* feels virtuous because they want to buy peace. And the question I want to ask is: who's selling it?

Recently, at a cocktail party of artists and professors, I noticed displayed on a table right next to the pickled Jerusalem artichokes, two French publications—Lo Duca's new volume on *Eroticism in the Cinema* and Kenneth Anger's *Hollywood Babylon*. Both books are like more elegantly laidout issues of *Confidential* and all those semi-nameless magazines which feature hideously outsized mammary glands, only these books are supposed to be chic—the latest intellectual camp. The Lo Duca book features stills from a Kenneth Anger movie in which nude ladies are wrapped in chains. Anger, you may recall, made his reputation with a film called *Fireworks,* in which a roman candle explodes inside a sailor's fly. His own book has a dust jacket photograph of Jayne Mansfield— an aerial view down her dress that makes her breasts look like long strips of cooked tripe. The book itself is a recounting of the legends (that is to say the dirty stories, scandals, and gossip) that Anger heard while growing up in southern California.

What struck me about these books, which function as entertainment to what might be called highbrows, was that their chic seemed to consist largely in a degradation of the female image. The stars and starlets are displayed at their most grotesque, just as they are in the cheapest American publications (in fact the photos are probably derived from those sources). This female image is a parody of woman—lascivious face, wet open mouth, gigantic drooping breasts. She has no character, no individuality: she's blonde or brunette or redhead, as one might consume a martini, an old-fashioned, or a gin and tonic.

Now I am told that even the junior-high-school boys of America use photographs like these as pinups, and that this is their idea of the desirable female. I don't believe it. I would guess that they pretend to this ideal because they're afraid they won't be considered manly and sexy if they admit they find this image disgusting. I don't believe that these photographs are erotic in any ordinary sense. I think that the grotesqueness of this female image is what people enjoy. Here are some possible reasons. First, these spongy, subhuman sex images reduce women to the lowest animal level. And in the modern world, where women are competent, independent, and free and equal, the men have a solid, competitive hostility —they want to see women degraded even lower than they were in the Victorian era. Here is woman reduced to nothing but a blob that will gratify any male impulse. And, of course, a woman who has no interest in life but love presents no challenge to the male ego. Second, there's the old split between sacred and profane love—and many men feel that the more degraded the female, the more potent they would become. Third, there's the vast homosexual audience which enjoys derision of the female. I would guess, and here's a big generalization, that more homosexuals than heterosexuals love to chortle over the nude photos of Anita Ekberg. She's so preposterous—a living satire of the female. It's my guess that the audience for nudie-cutie magazines uses them in much the same way the wealthy and educated use expensive French publications on the same theme: they want to laugh at the subjects and/or feel superior to them.

When the parodied female becomes known, becomes a "personality," derision gives way to admiration and sympathy and "understanding." In publications like the British *Sunday Times* you will find discussions with passages like "Marilyn Monroe grew up without affection and at times she was near suicide. When she talks about herself the awareness of her bitter past is never quite absent." *Time* and *Life* present her psychoanalytical comments on herself. And Dwight Macdonald in *Esquire* explains that "the expensive difficulties she makes for her employers are not so much prima donna assertiveness as symptoms of resentment and boredom." Sociologists read Zolotow's book on her character changes, and Cecil Beaton rhapsodizes that "she was born the postwar day we had need of her. Certainly she has no knowledge of the past. Like Giraudoux's Ondine, she is only fifteen years old; and she will never die." He's right at least, about her not having knowledge of the past: she seems to have swallowed all the psychoanalytical clichés about maltreated children, and when she talks about her past she simply spews them up. And the educated public loves these burbling bits of Freudian "insight" when they come out of the mouths of "babes." In *The Misfits,* our heroine, with the sure instincts of the faithful dog, and the uncorrupted clarity of the good clean peasant, looks at each character in the film and knows him for what he is. The innocent eye can see the inner man—she's the female of the species of the strong, silent hero, but she's also the traditional whore with the heart of gold. Her performance in *The Misfits* appears uncontrollably nervous, but it's almost as if her confused state were the final proof of her sincerity. The public loves her the more because life seems too much for her. . . .

The educated American is a social worker at heart: he feels especially sympathetic toward these slovenly ladies because their slovenliness marks them as misfits who couldn't function in his orderly world. The same man who is enchanted with Monroe in the seduction scene of *Some Like It Hot*—crawling all over Tony Curtis while hanging out of her dress both fore and aft—expects his girl friends or wife to be trim, slender and well-groomed. The decor in the homes and offices of the American professional classes is clean and functional—Scandinavian with a guilty dash of Japanese (as reparation for the bomb, we sit close to the earth). Upon occasion, the American will desert the art house for an American picture, particularly if it is advertised with the intellectually fashionable decor. For this decor is an article of faith: it is progressive and important; it calls businessmen and artists to conferences at Aspen, where it is linked with discussions of such topics as "Man the Problem Solver." And so American movies now often come, packaged as it were, with several minutes of ingenious, abstract, eye-catching titles. This send-off—the graphics look provided by Saul Bass and other designers—has virtually nothing to do with the style or mood of the picture, but it makes the movie look more *modern*. (How can the picture be dismissed as trash when it looks like your own expensive living room?) This type of design, using basic colors and almost no soft lines, was, of course, devised so that advertising would be clear and effective with a minimum of cost. In movies, a photographic medium, complexity and variety and shadings of beauty are no more expensive than simplification. But modern graphic design, which has built an aesthetic on advertising economics, has triumphed: new big productions (like *The Misfits*) open with such a proud array of flashy designs that the movie itself comes on rather apologetically.

The advertising campaign for new films often uses a motif that appears again at the opening of the film: presumably, if the ad was good enough to get you there, you'll appreciate having it amplified. Perhaps the next Hollywood "genius" will be the man who can design the whole movie to look like a high-powered ad. At present, the movie that begins when the packaging is out of the way is in a different, and older, style of advertising art. This style was summed up by a member of the audience a few weeks ago when I was looking at a frightfully expensive, elaborately staged movie. The beautiful heroine, in pale blue, was descending an elegant beige staircase, when a voice from the dark piped up—"Modess, because . . ." When the beautiful heroine in pale blue finally got into her creamy white lace and the properly nondenominational clergyman intoned, "Wilt thou, Robert, take this woman . . . ," another voice in the theater groaned, "I wilt."

The social worker-at-heart finds true reassurance when the modern-designed movie also has modern design built into the theme: a movie like *Twelve Angry Men*. Ask an educated American what he thought of *Twelve Angry Men* and more likely than not he will reply, "That movie made some good points" or "It got some important ideas across." His assumption is that it carried these ideas, which also happen to be his ideas, to the masses. Actually, it didn't: this tense, ingenious juryroom melodrama was a flop with the mass audience, a success only at revivals in art houses.

The social psychology of *Twelve Angry Men* is perfectly attuned to the educated audience. The hero, Henry Fonda—the one against the eleven—is lean, intelligent, gentle but strong; this liberal, fair-minded architect is *their* hero. And the boy on trial is their dream of a victim: he is of some unspecified minority, he is a slum product who never had a chance, and, to clinch the case, his father didn't love him. It isn't often that professional people can see themselves on the screen as the hero— in this case the Lincolnesque architect of the future—and how they love it! They are so delighted to see a movie that demonstrates a proposition they have already accepted that they cite *Twelve Angry Men* and *The Defiant Ones* as evidence that American movies are really growing up.

It is a depressing fact that Americans tend to confuse morality and art (to the detriment of both), and that, among the educated, morality tends to mean social consciousness. Not implicit social awareness (Antonioni isn't "saying anything," they complain of *L'Avventura*) but explicit, machine-tooled, commercialized social consciousness. "The old payola won't work any more," announces the hero of *The Apartment*, and even people who should know better are happy to receive the message. How reassuring *The Apartment* is, with its cute, soft-hearted Jewish doctor and his cute, soft-hearted, fat, mama-comic Jewish wife—so unworldly and lovable that they take the poor frustrated sap for a satyr (almost as deadly in its "humor" as Rock Hudson being mistaken for a homosexual in *Pillow Talk*). In *The Apartment*, the little people are little dolls; the guys at the top are vicious and corrupt and unfaithful to their wives as well. The moral is, stick at the bottom and you don't have to do the dirty. This is the pre-bomb universe; and its concept of the "dirty" is so old-fashioned and irrelevant, its notions of virtue and of vice so smugly limited, that it's positively cozy to see people for whom deciding to quit a plushy job is a big moral decision. The "social consciousness" of the educated is so unwieldy, so overstuffed, that the mass audience may well catch up before the intellectuals have found any grounds to move on to—though surely many should be happy to vacate the premises of Freud and Marx.

The art-house audience is at its dreamiest for Russian films like *Ballad of a Soldier* and *The Cranes Are Flying*. How eager they are to believe the best about the Soviet Union, to believe that love is back, propaganda is out, and it's all right to like Russian movies because the Russians are really nice people, very much like us, only better. These sentiments have been encouraged by the theaters and by the cultural exchange agreement, and at showings of *The Cranes Are Flying* there was a queasy little prefatory note: "At the same time you are watching this Soviet film, Soviet audiences are watching an American motion picture." I was happy for the voice in the theater which piped up, "But it's six A.M. in the Soviet Union."

The Cranes Are Flying and *Ballad of a Soldier* are both good examples of nineteenth-century patriotism and nineteenth-century family values; neither seems to belong to the Communist period at all—they're reminiscent of American war epics of the silent era. And sophisticated Americans love the simple, dutiful characters that they would laugh at in American movies. It's a long time since audiences at art houses accepted the poor, ravished unhappy heroine who has to marry the cad who rapes her. They go even farther toward primitivism at *Ballad of a Soldier:* they love the "touching" and "charming" hero and heroine who express such priggish repugnance at a soldier's unfaithful wife (how would these two react if they caught the wife sleeping with a German, like the heroine of *Hiroshima Mon Amour?*). *Ballad of a Soldier* takes us back to the days when love was sweet and innocent, authority was good, only people without principles thought about sex, and it was the highest honor to fight and die for your country. These homely values, set in handsome, well-photographed landscapes, apparently are novel and refreshing—perhaps they're even exotic—to art-house audiences. It's a world that never was, but hopeful people would love to associate it with life in the Soviet Union.

Are these recruiting posters so morally superior to American lingerie ads like *Butterfield 8?* Are they as effective in the U.S.S.R. as in the outside world? We can see the results of *Butterfield 8:* half the junior-high-school girls in America are made up to look like Elizabeth Taylor, and at the Academy Award Show it was hard to tell the stars apart—there were so many little tin Lizzies. It's more difficult to gauge the effects of Russia's antique middle-class morality. Perhaps educated Americans love the Russians more than the Russians do. All over America people are suddenly studying Russian; and they sometimes give the impression that the first word they want to learn is "Welcome."

A congressional subcommittee headed by Kathryn Granahan, a Democrat from Pennsylvania who is known as America's leading lady smut-hunter, is exploring the possibility that the influx of foreign films, most especially the French film *Les Liaisons Dangereuses,* may be a Communist plot to undermine American moral structure—that is to say that Americans are being offered a preoccupation with sex so that they will become degenerate, corrupt, too weak to combat the Communist threat. Mrs. Granahan has stated that the social, cultural and moral standards of France are among the greatest impediments to a strong NATO stand against international Communism.

In other words, she takes the position that a strong state, a state capable of defending itself, must be a Puritan state, and that individual freedom and the loosening of sexual standards threaten the state. This is, of course, the present Communist position: even American jazz is regarded as a threat. Nothing could be *cleaner*—in nineteenth-century terms—than Russian movies. Observers at the Moscow Film Festival reported that the Russians were quite upset after the showing of *The Trials of Oscar*

Wilde: they had been under the impression that Wilde was imprisoned for his revolutionary politics—for socialism, not for sodomy. Russians have been protected from just such information, discussion and art as Mrs. Granahan would protect us from. Apart from what appears to be a wholly unfounded notion that the Russians are trying to poison us via French sexual standards, there is an interesting issue here. For absurd as the Granahan position seems to be, I have heard a variant of it from many people who would scoff at the way she puts it.

Everywhere in the United States enthusiasts for *La Dolce Vita* explain that it's a great lesson to us—that Rome fell because of sexual promiscuity and high living, and we will too—that the Communists are going to win because of our moral laxity, our decay. It's as if poor old Gibbon had labored in vain, and the churches' attitudes have triumphed. Even those who no longer believe in God seem to accept the idea that European and American habits and values are loose and sinful and will bring destruction down upon us.

May I suggest that this is just as nonsensical as the Granahan line? If all Europeans and all Americans suddenly became heterosexual and monogamous—if everyone took the pledge and there were no more drinking, if all nightclubs were closed, and if the rich turned their wealth over to the poor—I cannot see that our *power* position in this nuclear age would in any way be affected. And it's astonishing that sensible people can get so sentimental about Russian movies with their Puritan standards, the bourgeois morality that developed out of the rising salaried classes and the Stalinist drive to stamp out individual freedom. Queen Victoria squats on the Kremlin; and Americans who fought to rid themselves of all that repressive Victorianism now beat their breasts and cry, look how *good* they are, look how *terrible* we are—why, we don't *deserve* to win. Has Puritanism so infected our thinking that we believe a nuclear war would be won by the pure in heart?

■ ■ ■ ■

THE NEW HOLLYWOOD: MYTH AND ANTI-MYTH (1959), Robert Brustein

In addition to importing films from Europe, the American film industry sought to make its own products more "adult," more complex, more sensitive to serious social and psychological issues. This rare article on film by

"The New Hollywood: Myth and Anti-Myth," by Robert Brustein, appeared in *Film Quarterly* in 1959.

Robert Brustein (former head of the Yale Drama School and the author of such books on drama as *The Theater of Revolt*) questions the maturity, the complexity, and the seriousness of the "New Hollywood" and its offerings. The article originally appeared in *Film Quarterly*.

It must now be apparent even to the most indifferent movie-goer that something unusual has recently been happening on the screen. Although for years he has been accustomed to suspending his cares in the soft black impersonal lap of his neighborhood auditorium, the spectator is now more frequently jolted than caressed by many of the films he sees—they seem especially designed to disturb his tranquillity. The celluloid is losing its sharpness of focus and assuming the murkier tones hitherto associated with European realism. The settings are changing from plushy modern apartments atop imposing skyscrapers to shanty-town slums in rotting southern or northern towns. The costumes, apparently acquired no longer from Mainbocher but from the surplus stores of the Salvation Army, hang on the actors as dashingly as skivvies on a scarecrow.

At the same time, the glamor queen is unpinning her hair, exposing her faulty skin and puffy eyes, and reverting to the untutored accents of her original speech; the matinee idol is yielding before a tousled, scratching, stammering, frequently unhandsome average Joe as distinguished as you or I; and the extras are being recruited not from Central Casting but from taverns and corner drugstores. The heyday of Hollywood glamor is drawing to a close, hastened by catcalls from the wings. Behind the scenes one can almost hear the fading tread of the cosmeticians, the speech teachers, and the beauty consultants—that vast army of unfamiliar names inscribed on a film's opening credits—who have hitherto played so large a part in creating "screen magic."

It would seem, then, that Hollywood is making room among its old formulas for radical new developments; it would seem also that the film-makers are beginning to assume attitudes toward their products which, twenty years ago, they would have considered visionary and impractical. Certainly, pictures like *On the Waterfront, A Hatful of Rain, Wild Is the Wind, The Goddess, Come Back, Little Sheba, Baby Doll, The Rose Tattoo, The Long Hot Summer, Hot Spell* (and countless others) embody, whatever their actual merits, a conscious artiness at which producers would formerly have shivered.

Is it possible that our celebrated dream factory has abandoned its artificial merchandise for the complex stuff of life? Is the industry undertaking to agitate the populace with harsh truths rather than lull them asleep with comforting fantasies? Is Hollywood, in short, now prepared to subsidize works of art? In order to answer these questions, it is necessary to recall the conditions that brought these new films into being.

After the war, of course, television absconded with a large portion of the audience the movies once held captive. Since millions of Americans, sitting in a drugged stupor before their sets, became deaf to the call of the box office, the movie moguls began to conclude that the old formulas were no longer sufficient. Only two classes of movie-goers remained faithful, and even these were beginning to desert: the teen-agers, who used the balconies of movie theaters as trysting places, and the inveterate celluloid-eaters, who preferred foreign films and the occasional art movie. The first attempt to woo back the deserters was the technique of the giant screen. CinemaScope, VistaVision, Todd-AO, Cinerama, and stereophonic sound were originally designed to awaken the spectator to the limitations of TV's constricted universe. The giant screen tried to demonstrate that the price the spectator paid for entertainment in his own home was to be eternally trapped in his own domestic troubles. This was a discerning judgment. At the time that the new movie techniques were introduced, the predominant video form was the domestic drama, only a cut above soap opera. The prophet of the new drama was Paddy Chayefsky, and its new heroes were middle-aged men in quest of romance, loveless butchers, nervous white-collar workers, and dissatisfied wives. Even the "adult western" soon developed into a family drama where a hero in a cowboy suit set about solving a minor domestic crisis not too far removed from the problems of the viewer.

The giant screen, on the other hand, emphasized the boundless dimensions available to Hollywood. Besides exulting in their leisurely tempo, the movies could stretch themselves in limitless space. While the TV viewer sweated and gasped for air in sympathy with a quiz contestant in a coffin-like isolation booth (the authentic symbol of TV's world), Todd-AO took the movie-goer for a three-hour trip around the world.

But rather than offer anything new in the way of material, the giant screen attempted primarily to preserve and enhance the old formulas. The movie-makers were trying to feed a traditional public appetite that to a large extent no longer existed: the craving for colossal screen glamor. The old matinee idols, despite their graying hair and sagging jowls, were still expected to attract admiration from the spectator through the time-worn methods: their extraordinary good looks, their superhuman deeds, and their freedom from petty human complaints. On the assumption that few would dispute the heroic proportions of a man over thirty feet tall, these qualities were now exaggerated by the hero's enormous size. On the giant screen, Gary Cooper grew lankier, Jayne Mansfield bosomier, and Richard Widmark meaner, while the cleft in Kirk Douglas chin enlarged into a minor Grand Canyon. It was Hollywood's last attempt to exploit America's old hunger for giantism: Paul Bunyan was breaking the plains on a horse as big as a mountain, its hoofbeats magnified a thousandfold by the magic stereophonic sound.

Although the giant screen had a few big successes and recaptured a few of the deserters, it could not hold them past the initial novelty. The public, preferring claustrophobia to agorophobia, remained largely apathetic, still immobilized before their sets. What is worse, even the faithful began to desert. The teen-age girls might identify with Audrey Hepburn as Gary Cooper made love to her under a table, but the teen-age boys were finding it hard to identify with a hero who looked old enough to be their grandfather. Similarly, the more discerning film-goers were generally cold, in some cases positively antagonistic, to the lure of the giant screen. The movie-makers decided to surrender their claim to the confirmed TV addicts and try to consolidate their position with the audience that still remained. They cast around for a new form which might be acceptable to all their patrons, and discovered—"realism."

It was, of course, an extremely belated discovery; realism, in various guises, had been flourishing on European and American stages for over a hundred years. But, considering Hollywood's traditional reluctance to agitate anybody, it was inevitable that the movie-makers would turn to the most inoffensive type. Rather than the Ibsenite form which rigorously exposed the cant, hypocrisy, fraud, and humbug beneath the respectable appearance, Hollywood's realism was to become more akin to Zola naturalism—dedicated to a purely surface authenticity.

The postwar Italian movies of deSica and Rossellini, concerned with poverty-stricken characters of the lower class and focusing on the unpleasant physical conditions of Italian city life, had caught the eye of the critics and collected a vigorous following among intelligent film-goers. When Paddy Chayefsky turned an inexpensive film like *Marty* into a surprising commercial success by reproducing the atmosphere (and junking the moral concerns) of Italian movies, Hollywood had to conclude that television had conditioned the American public to commonplace reality. It was becoming clear that the aimless and boring lives of people like Bronx drugstore cowboys could—if seasoned generously enough with sentimentality—attract box-office gold. Hollywood, in consequence, ever alert to changes in mass taste, began to retool in preparation for the new form.

The first move was a radical change in personnel: Hollywood went on an exhaustive quest for new experts. Zola realism, for a number of years, has been the artistic domain of the New York theater, so it was inevitably to the New York theater artist that the industry turned. Directors especially were in great demand. Elia Kazan was provided by

Warner Brothers with his own production unit and absolute freedom in chosing his subjects, casts, and associates; Sidney Lumet and Delbert Mann were kidnaped from TV; Joshua Logan was periodically imported to energize such films as *Bus Stop* and *Sayonara;* even fledging directors like Martin Ritt (*Edge of the City, The Long Hot Summer*) and Daniel Mann (*Come Back Little Sheba, Hot Spell*), with only a few Broadway shows to their credit, were whisked to Hollywood, where they are now afforded a respect they never enjoyed in New York.

Along with the directors came their collaborators—Broadway dramatists, television writers, and novelists. The plays of Tennessee Williams, William Inge, Robert Anderson, and Michael Gazzo, for example, are finding their way to the screen, sometimes transferred by the author, sometimes by an able adapter, frequently with surprising fidelity. In mounting competition over literary material, studios are purchasing off-Broadway plays, TV scripts, and even as yet unpublished novels. If, in the 'thirties and 'forties, William Faulkner and Aldous Huxley could write films in complete anonymity, today Tennessee Williams and Paddy Chayefsky draw almost as large an audience as the star.

Inevitably, a whole new crop of young stars was introduced as well, many of them trained in New York naturalistic theater schools like the Actors Studio and already familiar to Broadway and television audiences. Marlon Brando, Anthony Perkins, Paul Newman, Ernest Borgnine, Anthony Quinn, Anthony Franciosa, Don Murray, Steven Hill, and Ben Gazzara have become the matinee idols of the 'fifties, with actresses like Eva Marie Saint, Julie Harris, Barbara Bel Geddes, Anna Magnani, Shirley Booth, Kim Stanley, and Carroll Baker as their romantic counterparts. Few of these people are notable for their outstanding good looks, for there is an increasing tendency to deglamorize the Hollywood star. The new actors attract attention by their intensity of feeling, rather than by physical attractiveness, and have developed a style of acting which even some of the older stars are beginning to adopt.

In other words, New Yorkers have begun to infiltrate the film industry and to influence it with many of the convictions of the Broadway stage, including a traditional distaste for the old Hollywood products. In the past, Broadway's antagonism toward Hollywood took the form of moralistic condemnations and satiric attacks. The Group Theatre, that dynamic production unit which flourished in the 'thirties and which reluctantly fed so many of its associates into the films, always regarded Hollywood as Inferno and the Hollywood producer as a vulgar Mephistopheles who purchased the soul of the serious artist and degraded his talent with attractive offers of money, fame, swimming pools, and the love of beautiful women. Elia Kazan attacked, in an article, the "manufactured entertainment" of the movies, while Clifford Odets took his revenge on the film colony for enticing him from the stage with a venomous play (*The Big Knife*) exposing Hollywood's corruption, artificiality, and acquisitiveness. To Broadway, Hollywood has traditionally been a land of phony dreams created of tinsel and cotton candy where the real questions of existence are generally ignored.

Today, however, instead of overtly attacking the industry, the Broadway people are covertly attempting to reform it from the inside. They now constitute a highly influential unit within the larger circle of Hollywood movie-making. Such is Hollywood's desperation over declining receipts that the studios (and banks) are willing to subsidize the new artists, provide them with independent companies, and distribute their pictures. The result is that Hollywood has been underwriting the destruction of its old forms. Most of the conventions of the realistic film seem to have been created almost in purposeful contrast to the conventions of the traditional Hollywood romance. Consistent with their own tradition ("real," in the Broadway lexicon, has generally been a synonym for "seamy"), the realistic film-makers are dedicating themselves to the exposure of the unsavory truth behind the manufactured dream.

With suggestions of incest in *Desire Under the Elms,* sadism in *Baby Doll,* adultery in *God's Little Acre,* and homosexuality in *The Strange One,* the realistic movie works manifold variations on conventional sexual themes. Similarly, violence becomes more open and frequent. A brawny hero in a Hollywood epic by John Ford might batter another for hours with chairs, sticks, stones, and broken bottles and emerge from the melee with no more than an attractive little bruise on the cheek. When Marlon Brando is beaten up by labor racketeers in *On the Waterfront,* he streams cascades of blood from open wounds, loses a few of his teeth, and suffers visibly from broken bones.

Not only does the realistic film stand in purposeful contrast to romantic films, but it sometimes even derives its effects by playing on the spectator's memory of the old Hollywood myths. Marilyn Monroe's performance in *Bus Stop,* for example, in which she played a dissipated, anemic, peroxide-blonde "chantoosy," has significance primarily if one remembers her in more well-groomed roles—say, as the glamorous idiot of *Gentlemen Prefer Blondes.* Similarly, the dilapidated, weather-stained Mississippi mansion used in *Baby Doll* calls to mind, and even comments on, the movie magnificence of Tara's enormous halls and curving staircases in *Gone With the Wind.* The dirt and the cobwebs, and the sex and the violence, of the realistic film serve a partial debunking function. They expose the glittering and hyperbolic lies of Hollywood glamor.

This is further emphasized by the techniques of the genre. In contrast to the technical virtuosity of the CinemaScope epic, the realistic film is singular for the modesty of its presentational devices. It is frequently shot in black and white and designed for projection on the smaller, conventional screen. The director furthermore prefers to work in actual locales rather than on the more artificial studio lots—many movie actors today spend more time in Arkansas, Mississippi, and New York than they do in Hollywood. Similarly, like the realistic play the realistic film employs interiors more often than exteriors. Despite the hypothetical advantage of the movies over the stage in its flexibility of locale, the new film is generally content to keep its hero fixed in and around the four walls of his house.

The character of the hero undergoes a corresponding change. The old matinee idols were groomed as romantic leading men, at pains to exhibit their charms in the most attractive possible manner; the new idols are less concerned with their persons than with their agonized spirits. If Clark Gable and Cary Grant could set a million female hearts aflutter merely by exposing their teeth, Anthony Quinn and Ben Gazzara struggle —lest they violate some secret agreement—never to smile. Glowering, slumping, and scowling, the new actors exert their appeal not through graceful dash but through sullen bad humor. Furthermore, if the hero of the romantic film is accustomed to performing mighty deeds, usually in an open-air setting, the realistic hero is more often victimized by the confining world in which he lives. And he is trapped not only in the interior of his world but in the interior of his soul. Rather than holding an enemy at bay with a couple of loaded pistols, he is himself held at bay by the power of his neurosis. . . .

Now the anti-hero is the central character of the anti-myth in which the "real" is juxtaposed with the "illusion," the tawdry with the grand. Considering that realism feeds to such a large extent off the extant Hollywood myths and illusions, it is inevitable that at least one realistic film should be an explicit anti-myth—in other words, that it should take for its very theme the debunking of Hollywood glamor.

The Goddess, written by Paddy Chayefsky, is the life history, from childhood to her late thirties, of a movie queen. When this film was first announced it caused a little stir because, in taking a movie queen for his heroine, Chayefsky was reported for the first time to have created a figure out of the ordinary. The reports were wrong. Chayefsky's is possibly the most commonplace "goddess" in the history of drama or mythology. . . . As played by Kim Stanley, she is unimaginably seedy: puffy-faced, tending to fat, and endowed—even in her adolescence—with the heaviest bags two young eyes have never sustained.

The film is exclusively concerned with the heroine's psychological history. Growing up in a Maryland slum (the camera hovers affectionately above the dirty dishes), she is traumatized by a loveless childhood with an indifferent mother. The heroine, in consequence, begins to seek love wherever she can find it, first in the arms of the local swains and later in two unsuccessful marriages and innumerable affairs. Her first husband is an alcoholic—she finds him lying drunk and begrimed in a gutter—who later turns out to be the unwanted son of a movie actor. He is "damaged"—passive and suicidal—and the marriage ends when he storms off to war, followed by her curses. Her second marriage—to an inarticulate athlete (from time to time, the parallel with a living movie queen asserts itself)—is dissolved because of their inability to communicate and her voracious ambition to get into the movies.

It is difficult to understand how, considering her plainness, but the heroine eventually becomes a famous movie star. Although as Rita Shawn she is now loved by multitudes, she is still isolated and unhappy. She grows alcoholic and emotionally unbalanced, throwing frequent fits of hysteria. She quarrels violently with her mother, now a religious fanatic, who disapproves of her daughter's immoral life in Beverly Hills, where she lives between sanitariums. Later she becomes addicted to barbiturates and is last seen in a deranged stupor being cared for by an imposing female presence who represents the tender mother she never had in her childhood. The suggestion of Lesbianism in this relationship completes the deviant circle of the heroine's sexual history.

Instead of an examination of Hollywood life, we are here given a clinical study of a heroine indistinguishable from Pavlov's dogs: a victim of internal and external forces, completely incapable of exercising her will, imprisoned in the structure of her heredity and environment. Her aspirations, we are told, are specious and unsatisfying, she is unable to love, and she can find no faith to sustain her; without redeeming features of any kind, she leads a life of noisy desperation.

Now, this picture may attract patrons to the theater by its promise of glamor—which is, after all, the only interesting thing about a movie star—but glamor is the one biographical quality which Chayefsky neglects to include. Instead of someone distinctive and unique, Chayefsky has purposely created a quite commonplace figure, similar in temperament to his butchers and white-collar workers. Rita Shawn's nymphomania, her Lesbianism, her alcoholism, and her drug addiction may tally with underground reports of Hollywood behavior but these qualities are, nevertheless, the standard ingredients of Zola realism, common to most films of this type. In contrast to the heroine of another anti-Hollywood film of some years back (*Sunset Boulevard*) who though gaudy and vulgar at least had a fascinating Hollywood style, this goddess has nothing unusual about her at all. Rita Shawn is an expressionless shell barraged by traumas, more ordinary than anyone in the theater. One is encouraged to ask the reason.

One answer gives us some clue to the kind of spectator response the realistic film tries to evoke, for Rita Shawn's stunning lack of physical and mental equipment is obviously designed so that the average female spectator will identify with her. A new kind of identification is being urged, quite distinct from the way Hollywood tried to manipulate us in the past. If movie-goers were once allowed to daydream that they were Clark Gable kissing Grace Kelly, or Ingrid Bergman being pursued by Gregory Peck, they are today supposed to identify with Don Murray and Kim Stanley in the grip of damnable neurotic torments amidst dirty linen.

And yet, one must ask just how close to the average spectator's situation the material of these films really is. Undoubtedly, a drug addict and a nymphomaniac seem more "real" to us than a cowboy, a big game hunter, or a ballroom dancer; but why, when America has the largest middle-class population in the world (when, in one sense, it sees itself as entirely middle class), are its predominant movie heroes dock workers, motor-cyclists, juvenile delinquents, prostitutes, butchers, Southern farmers, seamen, and drifters, the economically and the emotionally dispossessed?

For the adult audience, I think, these heroes are interesting precisely because of their *distance* from everyday life. Americans can now afford to be indulgent toward grubbiness and poverty because they have been enjoying over the past ten years a prosperity unparalleled in their history. Having achieved what Hollywood once presented as the comfortable illusion—the well-stocked refrigerator, the well-furnished apartment, and the gleaming new car—the great middle of the American population can now regard the torn T-shirt, the dirty fingernails, and the cluttered sink as the "truth about existence." What once was immediate and painful can now be viewed with cheerful equanimity because, although it *seems* close and real, it is becoming remote from our experience. For the adult audience, in other words, the anti-myth is in the process of becoming the myth, its images almost as exotic as Hollywood's old close-ups of spotless clothes and faultless features.

For the adolescent audience, on the other hand, the appeal of the realistic film is immediate and direct. It is no accident that, although movie heroes like Humphrey Bogart and Jimmy Stewart never seemed to have any families and were remote even from their women, the heroes of the realistic film are invariably involved in conflicts with their parents and hang on to their girls for dear life. (Even films like *A Hatful of Rain* and *The Goddess,* with supposedly "adult" content, derive their action and motivation from parent-child conflicts.) For his relations with his parents provide the crucial dilemma of the adolescent's life. It is hardly a coincidence that actors like Marlon Brando, Jimmy Dean, and Anthony Perkins—the mainstays of the realistic film—have become the central heroes of adolescent culture, or that teen-age images like Natalie Wood, Julie Harris, and Susan Strasberg (rather than mature women of the type represented by, say, Norma Shearer and Greta Garbo) are generally the new heroines. The huge blow-up of Carroll Baker in *Baby Doll* lying in a crib and sucking her thumb is a more articulate symbol of the new genre than its creators know.

What has happened is that Hollywood, resigned to the fact that the majority of its audience is now composed of people between the ages of fifteen and twenty, has yielded to the teen-ager's demand to see himself and his problems depicted. Sometimes this results in an amalgamation of realism and adolescent drama—Andy Hardy is provided with a switchblade. Films like *Rebel Without a Cause, East of Eden, The Blackboard Jungle, The Wild One,* and *High School Confidential* employ realistic techniques to depict the delinquent adolescent's troubled relations with his parents, his girl, or his gang. But Zola realism, whether directly aimed at adolescents or not, is admirably suited to mirror the problems of the young because it offers a youthful, rather than a mature, picture of the world. Like the hero of the realistic film, the adolescent feels himself a victim of forces beyond his control. Like this hero, he feels manipulated against his will into situations he does not desire and traumatized by a world he never made. In limiting its world to the domestic scene, the realistic movie provides the adolescent with scenes that he can recognize. In centering on delinquents, addicts, and escapists, it gives him a perfect expression for his own feelings of rebellion and isolation.

Needless to say, such a form has no more claim to art than a comic book—realism has become another peg on which Hollywood hangs its commercial hat. Although its traditions are auspicious enough, the realistic film has now settled into rigid formulas, no more true to life than the formulas of the Western and a good deal more restricting to the imagination. The Broadway people who come to Hollywood are simply swapping their own conventions for the conventions of the romantic film. And though these conventions are more sophisticated and in some cases (the films of Elia Kazan) more expertly controlled, they are really as ingratiating, as false, and as far removed from the moral concerns of art as the old. Films of high quality do occasionally emerge from Hollywood: John Huston's early films were first-rate and Stanley Kubrick promises to be an authentic movie talent if his anger holds out. But such films are infrequent, seldom box-office successes, and never written to formulas. For films of quality proceed not from the demands of a mass audience but from the painful prodding of an artists's conscience. They do not creep along the surface of the skin, but journey deep into the recesses of the soul.

■ ■ ■ ■

SEE NO EVIL (1970), Jack Vizzard

As Robert Brustein's article implied in its discussion of the new anti-myths, Hollywood's evolving artistic values were linked to a shift in moral values. The old Production Code of 1930 was no longer consistent with the "New Hollywood," nor with the values of its new audiences, nor, for that matter, with the values of the new America as a whole. The result was a transition from a code which eliminated certain kinds of material altogether to a rating system that indicated the kind of material audiences could expect to find in the films. Jack Vizzard was a close observer of this transitional process, for in 1942 he became a member of the Production Code Administration under Joseph Breen, and he continued to serve as a member of the board for over two decades under Breen's more lenient and liberal successor, Geoffrey Shurlock. These sections from his book, *See No Evil*, record his experiences as a member of the PCA during the most difficult transitional years between the two systems.

At this point arose the case that has become a minor household word in the lore of modern censorship. I refer to *The Moon Is Blue*.

This was a picture made by Otto Preminger from a popular stage play by F. Hugh Herbert. It was refused a certificate by the Code, and condemned by the Legion of Decency. On appeal, it was turned down by the Board of Directors of the Motion Picture Association. To release the film, United Artists had to resign from the Association. This they did, and, despite a storm of controversy and a mass of pressures, they succeeded in achieving a smash hit. It was a bellwether of things to come.

Most people thought that the issue with *The Moon* was one of "blue" language. Even the usually careful New York *Times* stated that one of the reasons this film fell into disfavor with the custodians of the Code "obviously" was the absolute lack of inhibition with which sex was discussed. It cited such "taboo" words as "virgin," "seduce," and "pregnant," which, said the paper, were used "with bland insouciance and cool forthrightness."

Jack Vizzard, *See No Evil* (Simon & Schuster, 1970).

Such was not the problem. Even while the picture was still in the early stages of preparation, Joe Breen wrote to Martin Quigley, who was negotiating behind the scenes with Arthur Krim, the President of United Artists. Joe declared that Krim was definitely misled if he believed that "if questionable language was properly treated in production, the picture would probably prove acceptable."

Within the hard little knot of the film makers themselves, there was a consciousness of being daring in taking this enterprise in hand. The star, William Holden, was quoted in an interview as saying that Preminger, Herbert, and himself entered into an agreement before the picture went into production that the screenplay would not be submitted to the Breen office for approval. "I didn't see anything unmoral about the picture," the actor said. But the pact, by such sophisticated people, made later protestations of surprised innocence at the reaction to the picture sound suspiciously hollow indeed. At any rate, somebody must have slipped up, for the script was, in fact, sent in to the Code office in the waning days of 1952, and, after much soul-searching, a letter was returned to the studio by way of a New Year's present.

True, the letter contained such minuscule prohibitions as "The broken expression 'son of a . . .' is unacceptable"; and "The reference to marijuana should be omitted." But other lines got closer to the heart of the matter. There was dialogue like "Men are usually bored with virgins," and ". . . godliness does not appeal to me," followed by "steaks—liquor—and sex. In that order." Elsewhere there was the line "I always feel uncomfortable on a high moral plane." It was the flavor of talk such as this that created the question.

More specifically, the problem arose from the plot. The premise of the story was this. Maggie McNamara, a talkative aspiring television actress has allowed herself to be picked up by a successful architect, William Holden. He has just had a spat with the girl upstairs, Dawn Addams, daughter of the charming scamp David Niven. It seems that Dawn had come home the night before, only to find her father under the influence of alcohol and preparing to bed down with his current lady friend. Coming downstairs, she had appealed to Holden for a place to sleep. He surrendered his bed in a chivalrous manner and slept on a couch in the living room. In the great spate of misunderstandings that followed this arrangement, Holden categorically denied that nobility or moral principle had anything to do with his decency. He had drawn back because the girl had forced the issue on his malehood, taking away from him the right to choose the time, the place, and the circumstances. To prove his point, he had gone out and found Maggie McNamara.

Right here lay the first root problem. Inferentially, the story was saying that "free love" was something outside the scope of morality altogether, was a matter of moral indifference. Had the architect chosen to pursue the opportunity on his own terms, that was his business. Later, a lady viewer of the film wrote in without solicitation to splutter that this premise was so alien to our moral concepts that she intended to call the picture to the attention of the "UnAmerican Activities Committee of the United States."

What came into contention was the Code clause that stated, "Pictures shall not infer that low forms of sex relationship are the accepted or common thing." Philosophically this was one of the most important provisions in the entire Code document. If "free love" were a commonplace, and were something widely accept*ed*, it was only a small elision over into the conclusion that it was accept*able*. This then became a matter of condoning evil in principle, which in turn became a question of embracing corrupt standards.

The plot went on to take another twist. David Niven, our swinger, came storming downstairs in the role of outraged father to horsewhip Holden when he heard that his daughter had slept in an alien bed. However, as he discovers that nothing happened, he is at first nonplussed and then chagrined that the girl's vanity has been so sorely wounded. He decides that he ought to horsewhip the architect for compromising the girl by *not* making a pass at her.

Naturally, this element in the plot did nothing but bruise an already sore point. But the main item was yet to come. Circulating like a vestal virgin in the midst of all these complications was the aggressively chaste figure of Maggie McNamara. So emphatic does she become about her virtue that William Holden eventually accuses her of being a "professional virgin." When she asks him what that means, he tells her that she is always advertising her virginity. She wants to know, indignantly, what is wrong with that. He says that those who advertise usually have something to sell. This, incidentally, is probably the most remembered dialogue in the piece. It is a big laugh on Maggie McNamara, putting her in her place.

The only trouble was that, to the devotees of sexual continence, the figure of Maggie McNamara is the main rooting interest. The architect is someone to be looked at with envy, but not cheered on. He has to be overcome. But (and this was the key to the entire controversy) when he so patently tops Maggie, he is made to seem to win. She, on the other hand, is made to seem eccentric for being "clean," an oddball for clinging to her virtue in the midst of this "characteristically" loose way of life.

It was the recognition of this factor that made the hackles rise on the back of Joe Breen's neck and prompted him to make of this picture his last great orchestral flourish. To Joe, this was an issue involving the original set of values on which the Code was founded. To support his point of view, he called in the friendly opinion of the man who was, at that time, his favorite spokesman of the old-fashioned verities, the Hearst newspaper columnist, George Sokolsky. "Sound as a nut," Joe used to dub him, and he repeated the accolade so often that we never referred to the man except as "sound-as-a-nut-Sokolsky." To back Joe, Sokolsky wrote a column blasting the film.

The one individual close to the scene who was not in accord with this assessment of the play was Geoff Shurlock. From the very outset, he could not see what all the fuss was about. But inasmuch as he was, like the Centurion, "a man subject to orders," he did what he was told, and wrote letters on terms dictated by the man who was still Boss. But in conferring with Preminger, Geoff did not discuss any of the details of the letter which he had dumbly written, but simply encouraged the entrepreneur to make the picture according to the dictates of his "integrity" and "taste." There are those who will argue that Geoff was drawing a long bow by putting it on this basis, but Preminger loved it, and ultimately made Geoff his pet.

Actually, those who could not understand the objections raised against this film were looking at the story from the opposite end of the telescope. They believed the character portrayed by Maggie McNamara. They were not overpowered by the character of William Holden. They realized that the girl was being a bit extravagant and a bit too aggressive about her virtue, but on the whole they knew she was right, and Holden wrong. Such was the way Preminger argued. He pointed out, in an impassioned argument with Breen, that it was Maggie, the virtuous girl, who wins, in the sense that she gets her man because she is decent, and without giving the precious commodity in her loins away. Thus, virtue triumphs. Furthermore, she was a person who worked for a living, who neither drank nor smoked, and who was completely honest and outspoken.

Even the Legion of Decency was tempted to look on the picture in this manner. After the furor had died down and the picture had gone into limbo, an influential party in this organization confessed that they had acted to condemn the film, not out of intrinsic reasons, but for extrinsic considerations—namely to support the Code and prevent the seamless garment from being rent.

It is not, however, as though Joe Breen were naïve by the standards of that particular moment in history, or that people did not agree with him in formidable array. Even the secular press, which was clearly more sensitive in the early fifties than it is in the late sixties, was aghast at the brassiness of the film. A trade magazine like the *Showmen's Trade Review* (nothing prim here) said that to hear for the first time from the motion picture screen such words as "virgin" and "seduce" "is a shock even for the most sophisticated." We have come a long way since then. Amusingly, *Variety's* London correspondent indicated that it all got veddy, veddy boring to the English, because "British audiences don't take to unrelieved sex with the same enthusiasm as their counterparts in America." On the local scene, the *Motion Picture Daily* warned exhibitors: "If your audiences are prepared to take . . . outspokenness [they] will be amused. If your audiences are of a different stripe, you'd better see this before your house falls in on you."

The Catholic Hierarchy did not see the situation as good-naturedly as some of the journeymen in the Legion of Decency. The Cardinal's Residence in New York issued a proclamation against the picture, saying that it openly spurned the Code and was an attempt to ignore and override the moral law and to challenge the ideals of morally wholesome standards in public entertainment. It was labeled as "an occasion of sin," and Catholics were not only reminded of their obligation to avoid it, but of their pledge to refrain from attendance at theaters that flout decency by exhibiting such a picture. The Archbishop of Philadelphia, John F. O'Hara, issued a similar edict and strove strongly to keep the film out of that city. And the President of the Archdiocesan Council of San Francisco wrote to say that "Whoever was brazen enough and had the temerity to proceed lacking approval of the established standards of the Code reviewers is a direct challenge to the public."

Finally, the picture was refused acceptance by the Maryland Board of Censors, and the case was brought into the courts. On December 7, 1953, the answer was returned by Judge Herman Moser, upsetting the Board of Censors, and ordering them to license the film. In his memorandum opinion, Judge Moser said, among other things, that the film "is a light comedy telling a tale of wide-eyed, brash, puppy-like innocence routing or converting to its side the forces of evil it encounters." Preminger was vindicated.

So, incidentally, was Geoff Shurlock. All during the heated discussions involving the rejection of the picture, he kept echoing like a stuck needle that *The Moon Is Blue* was a story of the triumph of goodness. Several times he was verbally overrun by Joe Breen for clinging stubbornly to this point of view. But Geoff did not waver. He kept his secret locked in his heart and, when he finally got the chance, took it on himself personally to issue the Certificate of Approval on *The Moon* as a private accommodation to Otto Preminger. On June 28, 1961, a full eight years later, Geoff sent Certificate No. 20017 to United Artists, who came back into the fold.

The support afforded the film by the public made Joe realize that the jig was truly up.

In recognition of his feats, the Academy of Motion Picture Arts and Sciences bestowed on him one of its special Golden Oscars, largely through the good offices of Walter Wanger, a member of the Board of Governors.

Joe threw a party, and the Oscar cost him plenty. An Oscar for the Censor was surely never dreamed of when the Code was signed in 1930....

No sooner had [Jack] Valenti taken his place in the chair of honor than he was struck his first blow.[1]

WHO'S AFRAID OF VIRGINIA WOOLF?

It was more than three years earlier, in 1963, that we had written our first Code letter on the famous Albee play. In that pace-setting report, a hundred cautions, objections, and admonitions were listed on words, phrases, sentences, and situations. The letter was replete with "god-dams," "bastards," and "for Christ's sakes," but also contained more juicy morsels such as the phrases "monkey nipples" and "angel tits." To traffic in these details too much is to run the risk of harpyism, that is, a proclivity to feast on waste products at the expense of larger issues. Nevertheless, there is no way of telling this whole story, in fact or in truth, without coming out bluntly with a sampling of the blue stuff.

Neither is this to imply that the sordities are in themselves vulgar. It is intention that makes vulgarity, and anyone with one eye in the back of his head would see that the dimensions of this important play are not coextensive with the crudities. The story, basically, is more in the order of a Greek tragedy, and has to do with a New England history professor, George, and his wife, Martha, the daughter of the college's president. Returning home late at night from a faculty party, they have brought along a young couple for a nightcap.

The four proceed to drink heavily, and the intoxication brings on a convulsion of truth-telling that almost tears both couples to shreds. This savage honesty leads to confessions regarding a fantasy the professor and his wife have nurtured, that they have a nonexistent son. The burden

---

1. Ed. Note: Valenti, one of Lyndon Johnson's closest advisers, became president of the Motion Picture Association of America (formerly the MPPDA) in 1966, succeeding Will Hays and Eric Johnston. As of 1982 he was still its president.

of the story seems to be that if we disgorge our falsehoods, no matter how painfully, we can face the dawn of a new reality with at least the hope of love beginning.

When Jack Valenti and Lou Nizer (who, as an alternative, had been hired as legal counsel for the association) saw this picture they were caught almost completely off guard. What they beheld was a scene of Elizabeth Taylor looking straight into the camera and yelling, "Screw you!" Add to this scene a dance in a local juke joint that was so extreme as to be an expression of agony rather than of lust; and such occasional expressions as, "Let's play hump-the-hostess," and one begins to get a measure of the disconcertment of these two men. Undoubtedly they had not seen as many films of current vintage as they might have, and so their surprise was compounded.

Valenti subsequently admitted that his first reaction had been to confront Jack Warner, and to have it out with him then and there. Nizer, whose traditional sense of decency seems to have been particularly irritated, afterward hinted that he had prodded Valenti to throw down the gauntlet and threaten to quit, and that he would stand behind him. Perhaps he knew the axiom that those issues which you do not make in the first ninety days are next-to-impossible to make later.

However, the movie industry is more stubborn and more shrewd than it sometimes allows the public to believe. It knew very well that there was no backing out of the situation now. Warner Brothers had, reportedly, $7½ million in this project. What could it do with the film, eat it? The fact that the studio had put itself in that position with full consciousness, and had taken the risk, was justified by the fact that the play had won the Drama Critics' Award in 1963 and had been seen by countless thousands on the legitimate stage without any undue uproar.

And so, the voices of the statesmen went to work and began arguing sweet reason. Valenti was in no easy spot. He did not want to seem to be used; to be lending the prestige that trailed him from the White House as a cloak for this film. But at the same time some dim, dark instinct was at work in the man, assuring him that beyond the initial impact of the film, its basic validity would prevail, and it would ultimately—in the theatrical sense—play.

The company presidents used some style. In executive session, they ruled on Warners' Appeal from the Production Code's (mandatory) rejection of this film, and permitted it to have their blessing, with certain saving graces. First of all, some concessions were made by way of editing. The "Screw you!" was deleted, and replaced by a protection shot in which Liz yells "Goddam you!" ("Some improvement," growled certain critics.) Other cuts were made, too. But most importantly, Warners' introduced a new "first" into the system. It advertised the film as S.M.A. (Suggested for Mature Audiences),[2] but even more, it agreed to insert a clause into all contracts with exhibitors making it incumbent on the retail end of the business to police the box office. The stipulation was that no one under eighteen could see this film unless accompanied by a parent. The word was that this promise was kept, at least initially, by the theater owners, and created an illusion of seriousness and of high tone about the picture. This muted, to use a favorite word of Valenti, the feeling of scurrility about the language.

In an elegantly worded statement accompanying the approval of the picture by the Board of Directors, the Movie Industry took the burden to its own breast. It said:

> This exemption means exactly that—approval of material in a specific, important film, which would not be approved for a film of lesser quality, or a film determined to exploit language for language's sake. This exemption does not mean that the floodgates are open for language or other material. Indeed Exemption means precisely the opposite. We desire to allow excellence to be displayed and we insist that films, under whatever guise, which go beyond rational measures of community standards will *not* bear a Seal of Approval.

Somewhere along in here the Legion of Decency had wisely decided to take the flavor of militancy out of its name, and had changed over to the title of National Catholic Office for Motion Pictures. This awkwardly abbreviated into N.C.O.M.P.

The N.C.O.M.P., expected to be *Virginia's* severest critic, screened the film for a special review group of over eighty people, experts and everyday viewers alike, and in sum, took out its finest feather pen, and rated it "A-IV" (morally unobjectionable for adults, with reservations). One of the consequences of this liberal action by the N.C.O.M.P. was a flareup of indignation on the part of conservative Catholics. In La Jolla, California, a group of twenty-one "outraged Catholic laymen" petitioned bishops, newspapers, and Catholic organizations to help them get rid of the "N.C.O.M. Petants" and "to clean house."

Mike Nichols, the director, was accused of not caring ahead of time whether he got a Code Certificate or not, but he denied this politely, saying that he did not want to bite the hand that freed him.

In sum, the industry got what it wanted, and Valenti's sense of honor

---

2. Although not numerically the first. This distinction belongs to British made, Columbia distributed *Georgy Girl*.

was preserved. He was liberated now to spit on his hands, as it were, and begin to take a hard look at that baroque old document, the Code itself.

What he saw was not altogether pretty. There was a holdover provision from the dear dead days beyond recall that read, "Brothels in any clear identification as such may not be shown." Any intelligent meaning had been squashed out of this clause by *The World of Suzie Wong,* but it had been the root of such hypocrisies as calling the fun house in *Mamie Stover* a social club, in which the sailor boys in Hawaii had to buy tickets to "talk" with the hostesses. There were also comic provisions, such as the one "Children's sex organs are never to be exposed. This provision shall not apply to infants." (The secret information around the P.C.A. quarters was that this stricture was traceable back to a fix on the part of Y. Frank Freeman, when he was head of production at Paramount.)

More troublesome were those clauses which represented blanket prohibitions, such as ". . . a story must not indicate that an abortion has been performed." This clause reflected a certain amount of Catholic theology, and was dangerous to tinker with; but the days of blanket taboos were past. This was the sort of thing that could easily come back to haunt you.

In the midst of considerations like these, hardly before he had time to absorb the shock waves from *Virginia Woolf,* Valenti was struck his second major blow.

ALFIE

What *Alfie* was all about, to borrow the catch phrase from the popular title song, was that nettlesome clause concerning abortion.

Fundamentally, *Alfie* was a morality play. That is, it carried a strong and eloquent message against the bad life. The bad life, in this case, is a life of sex without love. Alfie was a cockney Don Juan who collected women like ornithologists gathered their specimens. He used them, and threw them aside. He referred to them as his "birds," and tabbed them "it"—"It does a marvelous egg custard." Alfie took, and gave nothing back.

This led to a life of emptiness that, in the eyes of the producer-director Lewis Gilbert, was little better than the life of a dog. To emphasize this point, he framed the film with this symbol. In the very closing shot, he had Alfie straying off down the street, without "me piece o' mind," with a little cur, his counterpart, trotting after him. And in the very earliest frames, he forecasts what's coming by showing a scene of two mongrels perilously close to the suggestion that they were mounting each other. This bit, of course, was in proximity to a sequence of Alfie having a go with a married woman in a parked car. Lest there be any doubt as to what he is doing, he finishes the scene by throwing her her panties.

A picture with so strong a moral point is excused for much grittiness that might be intolerable in a lesser work.

Alfie was one of those increasing cases in which the Code office did not have a script. Therefore, it took the staff by surprise. It dropped, quite literally, out of the blue, having been flown in from England by Paramount. Attending the showing in the projection room were both Valenti and Nizer. In the semi-darkness, one could almost sense their indignation. At the same time, some of us on the staff irritated what was already a sore provocation by openly enjoying the funnier lines. It was clear that there were two sets of opinion here that were at odds.

The next morning, in "huddle," we addressed ourselves formally to the contents of the film. There had been a chance to weigh the issues overnight, and everybody had his dialogue ready.

Chairing the conversation, Valenti asked how many men in the room had children. Several of the staff members raised their hands.

"What age?" he wanted to know, pistoling a finger at me.

"In their teens."

"A daughter?"

"Yes."

"How old?"

"Fifteen."

"Very well, then. Let me put it this way. If you had a choice, which would you rather that she see—*Alfie* or *Virginia Woolf?*"

"In the company of her mother? In controversial films like this—"

"No, no, I don't mean in the company of her mother. I mean if she were to walk in off the street with her boyfriend."

I thought hard. "In that case, then—I'd say *Alfie.*"

Startled, he asked, "Why?"

Groping, I tried to explain. "In the case of *Virginia Woolf,* what would she see? A sick and repellent view of marriage. As if a relationship with a woman were something out of hell, leading to two people tearing each other to shreds. In the case of *Alfie* she'd see something that was fundamentally sound, what I mean is—basically moral."

He interrupted with an impatient gesture. "I'm not asking about morality," he said. "I don't think any man has the right to pass judgment on the rightness or wrongness of another man's actions. What a person does in his private life is his own business. What I'm talking about is taste. What about that abortion scene?"

The abortion scene had been protracted and extremely graphic. But it had ended with Alfie peering down in stark horror at the pitiful remains of the embryo, his child, that had just been taken from his friend's wife. The shock led him to a scene in which, for the first time in his life perhaps, he exhibited feelings toward another human entity. It was a powerful therapeutic encounter, and showed the fact of abortion in all its shabby, cruel reality.

Perhaps, due to overexposure to seamy material, those of us on the staff had become too case-hardened to scenes like these. We tended to feel that the very offensiveness of the sequence was its antidote, and its moral quotient. But Valenti was reflecting the reactions of a more normal audience, and did not care for highly specialized reactions on the part of technicians. Therefore he was nonplussed. He did not want to contradict his staff. But neither did he want to get trapped by a second outrage.

In a reversal of roles, it was we, who had been looking for some relief from permissiveness, who were now defending a notorious piece of material. But we were the old order. Before our eyes, a new set of criteria for judging pictures was being created.

In the end, Valenti felt he had no choice but to insist that an Appeal be taken in the case of *Alfie*. If nothing else, there was a clear-cut violation of the Code in the *fact* of abortion. Nobody had given the Code office the right to say it didn't count because the picture contained an eloquent lesson.

To keep the central question uncomplicated, the Studio compromised on a few of the more glaring details. It agreed to remove the hint of the dogs in the act of sex and left only a preliminary shot of them sniffing intimately at each other. It agreed to take out the shot of Alfie throwing the woman's panties at her, as being too specific. Thirdly, there was a line, tossed by Alfie at Shelley Winters, while he is setting her up for a candid camera shot. Seemingly referring to the camera, but actually being on the make for her, he says, "Well, I've got two positions [for taking pictures]—straight up or sideways, depending on your nationality." This, they thought, was too pointed. And finally, there was a line delivered about a bathtub with a mirror in the ceiling, which would not make sense unless told in conjunction with the whole scene; and which, therefore, we pass over.

Paramount, of course, while conceding the technical violation, wanted another exemption just like Warner Bros. In accepting this petition, Valenti must have felt that he had been blindsided by his household professionals; the quarter from which he had least expected trouble. He rather clearly wanted to make the issue of which he felt he had been deprived in *Virginia Woolf*.

The Board of Directors saw it for Paramount. On August 2, 1966, they granted an exception, labeling the film S.M.A.

The manifesto issued to cover the single case of *Virginia* was breached in about six weeks. Talking about making only one exemption is like talking about eating only one potato chip.

Many will remember that *Alfie* competed strongly for next spring's Oscar, and, for what it is worth, it was called a "highly moral film" by the Protestant publication *The Christian Century*. The N.C.O.M.P. rated it "A-IV," with the comment that "in spite of the light treatment of immoral situations, the film develops the theme that an individual must accept responsibility of his actions." . . .

■ ■ ■ ■

OFFICIAL CODE OBJECTIVES (1968), Motion Picture Association of America

The "S.M.A." exceptions which Jack Vizzard described were already, in effect, a rating system rather than a code that prohibited certain kinds of films and filmed activities altogether. In 1968 the Motion Picture Association of America instituted a formal rating system, abandoning the old Production Code Administration in favor of the new Code and Rating Administration. This statement of the principles and purposes of the new Code is from a brochure intended to provide information about the new system—primarily to producers and the press. The rhetoric of this 1968 Code, which stresses freedom of expression and creativity, is radically different from that of the one written in 1930, mirroring both the shift in movie attitudes and in American mores.

This Code is designed to keep in close harmony with the mores, culture, the moral sense and change in our society.

The objectives of the Code are:

1. To encourage artistic expression by expanding creative freedom.

2. To assure that the freedom which encourages the artist remains responsible and sensitive to the standards of the larger society.

Censorship is an odious enterprise. We oppose censorship and classification by governments because they are alien to the American tradition of freedom.

Much of this nation's strength and purpose is drawn from the premise that the humblest of citizens has the freedom of his own choice. Censorship destroys this freedom of choice.

"Official Code Objectives" is from a brochure published by the Motion Picture Association of America in 1968.

It is within this framework that the Motion Picture Association continues to recognize its obligation to the society of which it is an integral part.

In our society parents are the arbiters of family conduct. Parents have the primary responsibility to guide their children in the kind of lives they lead, the character they build, the books they read, and the movies and other entertainment to which they are exposed.

The creators of motion pictures undertake a responsibility to make available pertinent information about their pictures which will assist parents to fulfill their responsibilities.

But this alone is not enough. In further recognition of our obligation to the public, and most especially to parents, we have extended the Code operation to include a nationwide voluntary film rating program which has as its prime objective a sensitive concern for children. Motion pictures will be reviewed by a Code and Rating Administration which, when it reviews a motion picture as to its conformity with the standards of the Code, will issue ratings. It is our intent that all motion pictures exhibited in the United States will carry a rating. These ratings are:

(G) SUGGESTED FOR GENERAL AUDIENCES

This category includes motion pictures that in the opinion of the Code and Rating Administration would be acceptable for all audiences, without consideration of age.

(M) SUGGESTED FOR MATURE AUDIENCES
—ADULTS & MATURE YOUNG PEOPLE[1]

This category includes motion pictures that in the opinion of the Code and Rating Administration, because of their theme, content and treatment, might require more mature judgment by viewers, and about which parents should exercise their discretion.

(R) RESTRICTED—Persons under 16 not admitted
unless accompanied by parents or adult guardian.

This category includes motion pictures that in the opinion of the Code and Rating Administration, because of their theme, content or treatment, should not be presented to persons under 16 unless accompanied by a parent or adult guardian.

(X) PERSONS UNDER 16 NOT ADMITTED

1. Ed. Note: Early in 1970 the M rating was changed to GP. In 1972 it was changed again, this time to PG ("Parental Guidance Suggested; some material may not be suitable for pre-teenagers"). The R and X categories have raised their age limit to 17.

This category includes motion pictures submitted to the Code and Rating Administration which in the opinion of the Code and Rating Administration are rated (X) because of the treatment of sex, violence, crime or profanity. Pictures rated (X) do not qualify for a Code Seal. Pictures rated (X) should not be presented to persons under 16.

The program contemplates that any distributors outside the membership of the Association who choose not to submit their motion pictures to the Code and Rating Administration will self-apply the (X) rating.

The ratings and their meanings will be conveyed by advertising; by displays at the theaters; and in other ways. Thus, audiences, especially parents, will be alerted to the theme, content, and treatment of movies. Therefore, parents can determine whether a particular picture is one which children should see at the discretion of the parent; or only when accompanied by a parent; or should not see.

We believe self-restraint, self-regulation, to be in the American tradition. The results of self-discipline are always imperfect because that is the nature of all things mortal. But this Code, and its administration, will make clear that freedom of expression does not mean toleration of license.

The test of self-restraint—the rule of reason . . . lies in the treatment of a subject for the screen.

All members of the Motion Picture Association, as well as the National Association of Theatre Owners, the International Film Importers and Distributors of America, and other independent producer-distributors are cooperating in this endeavor. Most motion pictures exhibited in the United States will be submitted for Code approval and rating, or for rating only, to the Code and Rating Administration. The presence of the Seal indicates to the public that a picture has received Code approval.

We believe in and pledge our support to these deep and fundamental values in a democratic society:

Freedom of choice . . .

The right of creative man to achieve artistic excellence . . .

The importance of the role of the parent as the guide of the family's comfort . . .

STANDARDS FOR PRODUCTION

In furtherance of the objectives of the Code to accord with the mores, the culture, and the moral sense of our society, the principles stated above and the following standards shall govern the Administrator in his consideration of motion pictures submitted for Code approval:

• The basic dignity and value of human life shall be respected and upheld. Restraint shall be exercised in portraying the taking of life.

• Evil, sin, crime and wrong-doing shall not be justified.

• Special restraint shall be exercised in portraying criminal or anti-social activities in which minors participate or are involved.
• Detailed and protracted acts of brutality, cruelty, physical violence, torture and abuse shall not be presented.
• Indecent or undue exposure of the human body shall not be presented.
• Illicit sex relationships shall not be justified. Intimate sex scenes violating common standards of decency shall not be portrayed.
• Restraint and care shall be exercised in presentations dealing with sex aberrations.
• Obscene speech, gestures or movements shall not be presented. Undue profanity shall not be permitted.
• Religion shall not be demeaned.
• Words or symbols contemptuous of racial, religious or national groups, shall not be used so as to incite bigotry or hatred.
• Excessive cruelty to animals shall not be portrayed and animals shall not be treated inhumanely.

■ ■ ■ ■

THE MOVIE RATING GAME (1972), Stephen Farber

Although the new rating system "opened up" film content in both fact and theory, it did not cure all the abuses of the old Code. The system created one new problem: the definition of precise standards for determining which sorts of films belonged in each category. (The rating a film received translated into the number of people who could pay to see it.) The system therefore perpetuated an old problem: the give-and-take bargaining between a producer and the board about what would need to be cut from a film in order to obtain a commercially more favorable rating. For six months Stephen Farber, now a leading American film critic, served as one of two voting student interns on the Code and Rating Administration board. The purpose of these internships was both to provide a lesson in practical problems for the two film students as well as to get the attitudes and opinions of younger people (the bulk of the movie audience) into the decisions of the board. These sections from the book which Mr. Farber wrote to record his experiences in movie rating, *The Movie Rating Game*, also reveal his dissatisfactions with both the practice and principle of movie rating.

Stephen Farber, *The Movie Rating Game* (Public Affairs Press, 1972).

How are ratings actually determined? Official brochures on the rating system provide only very brief general definitions of the four categories, and I do not believe the categories can or should be defined much more specifically. It is impossible to set hard-and-fast rules; every film is different from every other film, and no precise definition could possibly cover all films made. Valenti has frequently toyed with the idea of more detailed definitions, though any rigid demarcations between the categories inevitably seem hopelessly arbitrary.

In most of his public appearances, Valenti has stressed that the board does not rate for adults, but for children; it aims to give parents the information that will enable them to make decisions about their children's moviegoing. But how does one decide what is suitable or unsuitable for children? I never found a satisfactory answer to that question, and over the six-month period that I was rating films, the decisions came to seem more and more difficult. The other board members rarely seemed troubled by doubts, and they showed an amazing ability to come up with a rating on a film the very instant the lights went on in the screening room. Their ballots were terse and unqualified. They were impatient with the lengthy discussions that Estelle Changas and I tried to initiate;[1] to them the job seemed simple and the issues elementary.

In devising my own criteria for rating, I tried to see beyond the visual and verbal details that so often paralyzed the other board members, and to consider the impact and maturity of the film as a whole. I tried to distinguish between movies with themes of general interest but a few isolated strong elements—nudity or sex or profanity or violence—and movies with genuinely disturbing adult themes and treatment. But there was no way of making absolutely clear distinctions.

The very first day I was on the board we screened *Catch 22*, and although it contained female pubic hair, a brief suggestion of fellatio, the word "prick" (and one moment of ghastly violence—a wounded man's intestines spilling out—that concerned me quite a bit more), I rated it GP. When the other members saw those elements, they *knew* the film was R; just a few months before, those same elements would have automatically consigned the film to the X category, and they felt they were quite liberal in rating it R. It was admittedly a borderline case, a demanding film for young audiences, but I thought an R rating was more of a distortion than a GP. The central theme—the insanity of war, and the difficulty of surviving within an authoritarian military bureaucracy —had universal appeal, and it was dramatized with a minimum of brutality and, considering the army milieu, with relatively minor emphasis on

1. Ed. Note: Ms. Changas was the other student intern on the board.

sex or vulgarity. Anyone twelve or thirteen could respond to the anti-war passion of the film, and to the humanity in the characterization and performance of the central role of Yossarian. Excluding all unaccompanied children and teenagers under seventeen seemed to me too severe a restriction.

I may be able to give more sense of the difficulty of rating films by discussing in detail a more perplexing decision that we faced about a month later. *They Call Me* Mister *Tibbs,* a detective film in which Sidney Poitier played the same character he had originally created in *In the Heat of the Night,* was finally rated GP after two screenings. The film opens with a very shocking scene in which a nude prostitute pulls away from a man with whom she has apparently just had intercourse (he is off-screen) and taunts him for being a bad lover, whereupon he strangles and bludgeons her to death. The rest of the film follows Virgil Tibbs in his detection of the crime. There is a bit of clinical police dialogue (including a reference to semen stains in the prostitute's room), a rather sordid feeling to scenes surrounding several minor characters—a vaguely homosexual, reptilian landlord who runs a narcotics ring, a prostitute who works for him and more than once tries to seduce Tibbs—and a couple of scenes of strong violence toward the end. I felt that each of these items taken alone could probably be handled in a GP film. (Even the opening scene was very brief, no longer than necessary to establish the crime.) But cumulatively these elements probably did give the film a more adult atmosphere.

I was also troubled by some thematic distortions. The man who turns out to be the murderer is a crusading minister (Martin Landau), a friend of Tibbs, presented throughout as a sympathetic character who is working with blacks in the ghetto to win votes for a controversial community control program. I felt that children unable to comprehend the psychological motive for the crime would be quite confused and upset to learn that a man who seemed to them decent, liberal and humane was involved in a lurid sexual murder. Estelle Changas suggested that children, searching for some explanation, might even draw a connection between the minister's controversial social activities and his crime. It seemed a good deal to ask children to handle, and I felt the film was basically adult in theme and should probably be restricted. Yet I was extremely reluctant to restrict it because of my own political sympathies. In addition, in spite of the murky adult theme and the sordid atmosphere of much of the film, there were other elements in it that seemed deliberately aimed at a family audience—particularly the charming, intelligent scenes portraying Tibbs' home life and his rather strained relationship with his young son. I also believed that Tibbs' central problem in the film—a

conflict between his responsibility to his job and his loyalty to his friend
—was a moral problem that children might find comprehensible and
meaningful.

Not all of our decisions were as troublesome as this one, but this film
exemplifies the difficulty of trying to fit complex, irregular motion pictures—which have not been designed to meet a rating—into one of four
simple categories. On first viewing I rated *They Call Me* Mister *Tibbs* R,
but after seeing it again, I felt the subplot regarding the minister, his
social consciousness and his sexual inadequacy might be as confusing
to adults as to children—it was very superficially treated—and perhaps
just indirect and insignificant enough in the film as a whole to permit a
rating of GP. When uncertain, I generally inclined toward the less restrictive rating, as most of the time I preferred to err on the side of len-
iency. (The GP rating on *Tibbs* was, incidentally, criticized as too lenient
by a number of parents.) . . .

While I was on the board, pubic hair was [a] taboo for the GP
category. During an unusually liberal period in early 1970, the board
had allowed a flash of full female nudity in the GP-rated *Halls of Anger,*
and got some complaints (one trade reviewer even called it a "beaver
film")—which goes to show that the board members are not the *only*
literal-minded people seeing films. (Along these lines I might mention
an amusing meeting the board had with Russ Meyer, who was very upset
with the X rating given his film *Beyond the Valley of the Dolls;* although
the film was filled with sex and violence, Meyer felt he had used very
good taste in refusing to show any pubic hair.)

The word "fuck" was also strictly verboten in the GP category (along
with words like "cunt" and "cocksucker"), and *The Landlord* was
rated R because it had one "fucking" and one silently-mouthed "motherfucker"—even though it was unusually restrained in the love scenes,
and quite a humane morality play that might have been meaningful to
audiences of all ages.

There were some revealing distinctions in the area of language. When
General Patton or Brian Keith in *The McKenzie Break* used the word
"shit," that was no problem for GP; when Ali MacGraw, the heroine of
Love Story, said "bullshit," the board grew more nervous. They finally
did rate *Love Story* GP, with trepidation, but the fact that a *girl* used
strong profanity made some difference. Similarly when Raquel Welch,
early in *Myra Breckinridge,* turned to the camera and taunted the audience, "All right, you motherfuckers," the board was not amused. One
board member said, "Now when we have a picture about Negroes in the
ghetto, and some of the characters use the word 'motherfucker,' that is
valid. But to hear Raquel Welch say it—there's no excuse for *that!*" A

little later I mentioned ironically that Raquel Welch seemed to have her own code of good taste because she never appears nude in her films; and another board member replied, without irony, "I'd rather see her take her clothes off than hear her use language like 'motherfuckers'."

These were the elements that a few months earlier had been taboo even in R films; now the same prohibitions were operating in GP. Explicit scenes of lesbianism or homosexuality or masturbation or "group sex"—no matter how brief—remained "X elements," almost invariably. Orgasm was forbidden in GP and, except for unusual cases, even in R. The group grew nervous as soon as someone started to breathe heavily or moan during a scene of lovemaking, even if the camera remained on the actors' faces. The board preferred sex without satisfaction. Thus, the desert orgy sequence in *Zabriskie Point* was probably approved for R because it was all so "abstract" and so completely passionless.

In addition to anticipating parents' objections to "nudity, nude lovemaking, and language"—the gruesome threesome—the board paid a great deal of attention to drugs, and often overreacted to films on the subject. Almost any film dealing with drugs was automatically restricted. Yet drug addiction is presented very frankly on television now, and many people feel that unglamorous films about addiction (like *The Panic in Needle Park, Believe in Me, Cisco Pike, Dusty and Sweet McGee*) should be rated GP instead of R so that teenagers could have easy access to these movies. Several exhibitors showing *The Panic in Needle Park* announced that they were disregarding the R rating and allowing anyone over ten or twelve to see the film unaccompanied.

At times I could understand the board's concern about very strong films on drug addiction. What amazed me was the board's sensitivity to marijuana, which I discovered when we re-reviewed *Alice's Restaurant* in March 1970. It had originally been rated R in the summer of 1969, but the producer, Hillard Elkins, resubmitted it to see if the rating could be changed to GP. I could not imagine why the film had ever been restricted, and a couple of the other board members admitted that the sex scenes now looked awfully mild; Geoffrey Shurlock even felt that this film *should* be seen by young people because of its clear condemnation of hard drugs. But Dougherty mentioned the pot-smoking in the film as a reason for the R rating, and I was bewildered.

It turned out that there had been some kind of "gentleman's agreement" with the Los Angeles police to the effect that films condoning the use of marijuana would not be placed in unrestricted categories. (Apparently the matter had come up in reference to *I Love You, Alice B. Toklas,* the first big-studio film to treat pot sympathetically.) In *Alice's Restaurant* there was hardly any pot-smoking anyway, and it was mainly confined to minor characters in the background of two scenes, the Thanks-giving dinner scene and the wedding of Alice and Ray at the very end. But Dougherty insisted that the shots of these unidentified people passing joints around would have to be eliminated before the film could be con-sidered for a GP rating. Several board members honestly felt that a film like *Alice's Restaurant*—which presented pot-smoking as a casual, ac-cepted part of people's lives—was insidious; apparently they were over-whelmed by that fear of children "imitating" what they see presented sympathetically on the screen. Interestingly, John Cassavettes' *Husbands,* about three sympathetic alcoholics, was rated GP. . . .

With the R category broadened, few major films have been released with an X during the last two years, and most of the big-studio films that *have* been rated X—*Myra Breckinridge, Beyond the Valley of the Dolls, Performance, The Devils*—have been savagely attacked by a number of short-sighted critics as proof of the decline of Western civilization.

By now the X has lost whatever chance it might have had to achieve respectability. Several studios have made it a policy to produce *no* X films, and most studio contracts with directors stipulate that the director must win an R or less restrictive rating on the finished film. The X may even keep some films from being made at all. An independent pro-ducer submitted to the board a realistic, non-exploitative script about sailors, and an X rating was threatened simply on the basis of the pro-fanity that was necessarily a part of the dialogue. As a result of the projected X, the producer lost financing for the film.

Film-makers know that sexually frank material will be "punished" with an X, so even while they are writing their scripts and shooting, they are very conscious of the need to temper themselves to escape the brand of shame. Writer-director Ernest Lehman was under great pressure at Fox to make *Portnoy's Complaint* into an R film—a virtual impossibility if he wanted to be true to the obsessively clinical, scatological humor of Philip Roth's novel; finally Fox gave up and turned the project over to Warners. Abby Mann reported at a film conference in 1971 that his script for *The Todd Killings,* a serious attempt to explore a Manson-like cult and the phenomenon of teenage violence, was emasculated because of the studio's desperation to avoid an X rating; he eventually asked that his name be removed from the credits of the finished film.

Some of this censorship pressure is simply an unspoken threat that hovers over the film-maker as he works. Some of it is expressed more directly in the "script letters" from the rating office, which relentlessly detail all the items to be eliminated in order to avoid an X. But the most obvious result of the confusion and increasingly foul smell sur-rounding the X rating is that producers and distributors of X-rated films have been re-editing their films to achieve an R rating. The X has always been somewhat undesirable from a commercial viewpoint since it bars a large segment of the potential audience for a film. Now, with theaters refusing X films, newspapers refusing to advertise them, and the public reading X as a synonym for smut—a misreading never vigorously challenged by the MPAA—the obstacles to commercial success are even greater. One irony is that sexploitation films can still get quick release in specialty theaters; they are shown uncut and uncensored. The films that suffer are the more serious and unconventional—though explicit—X movies, the movies that are not intended for a grind house but that may well be kept out of more respectable theaters by their X rating.

The distributors of *Joe*, for example, were very upset when their film was rated X by the New York branch of the Code and Rating Administration. They insisted on getting the film into the R category, so the New York representative of CARA, Jim Bouras, itemized some deletions—mainly from the orgy scene, with a couple of other minor cuts—and eventually rated the film R. More recently, Sam Peckinpah's *Straw Dogs* was rated X by the board, but because the distributing company, ABC, has committed itself to making no X films, *Straw Dogs* was edited for an R. At the direction of the Code and Rating Administration, part of a brutal rape scene necessary to understanding the plot, themes, and characterizations was deleted, and some of the other violence was trimmed, softening the film. The board refuses to accept responsibility for this re-editing, blaming the distributing companies and the exhibitors, insisting that the censorship is "voluntary." But these film-makers do not *want* to cut their films; because of the stigma attached to the X rating, they *have* to cut their films if they are to achieve nationwide release and reach an intelligent diversified audience.

At this point it is probably too late to redefine the X category or to re-educate the public about the meaning of the X rating. But it is naive to assume that the problem will go away. I am convinced, as I often told the board, that more and more of our most serious and committed film-makers will want to deal boldly with mature sexual themes (and, for that matter, with extremes of violence). Sex is one of the few film subjects that has not yet been dramatized with passion and insight. We are only now seeing the first film equivalents of D. H. Lawrence's experiments in literature some fifty years ago—films that explore radical new conceptions of sexual identity, the connection between the sexual revolution and other forms of cultural and social revolution. The MPAA rating system was designed to free the film-maker for this exploration, but the pressures to avoid an X may in fact constrain him as much as the old Production Code. . . .

During my six months on the board, there was some effort—short-lived—to reduce the amount of censorship, though a good deal of it still went on. About 35 of the 170 films I saw were re-edited while I was on the board. (Several more were resubmitted months after their initial release, and edited for a new rating.) Few of these, I must admit, were major films. But I am not sure this should make any difference. Many of the films I fought to save from the censors' scissors were very cheap, badly-made films. There is an interesting moral issue involved here: Do film-makers deserve to be treated more harshly, their work more cavalierly sheared, simply because they are untalented, or because they work on a low budget?

The public is astonishingly ignorant about this whole business. Most people assume that a film is magically assigned a rating which it never loses. But the widespread editing does a disservice to everyone—to the film-makers who see their work hacked against their wishes, and to the moviegoers who do not realize the sort of compromises made before a film is rated.

I have touched on some of the main reasons that the board continues to regard re-editing as one of its most important responsibilities. The primary problem is the legacy of the Breen office. Several of the people on the rating staff worked for years under a system that required them to be vigilant and petty; they were explicitly charged with the responsibility of expurgating films—removing those elements that were direct violations of a stringent Code. Through editing almost any film could be "cleaned up" sufficiently to qualify for a seal. As Geoffrey Shurlock explained recently, the Code office did not want to reject films outright: "We never refused seals. We were in the business of granting seals. The whole purpose of our existence was to arrange pictures so that we could give seals. You had to give a seal." The editing was, in many cases, the price exacted by the board for doing the studios' bidding and approving their films. . . .

When he learned of the negotiations under way to recut *Alice's Restaurant,* Vincent Canby wrote a cogent attack on the rating board in the *New York Times,* pointing up the most basic reason for re-editing of films: "Thus, it seems, the sort of carving up of films—an activity that often makes censors feel they are equal partners with the artist in a creative endeavor—has continued into this enlightened age of G, GP, R, and X." The board deeply resented that article, as might be imagined, but Canby was right; the board members do take satisfaction in "improving" a film through editing. (Certain prejudices were revealed in their casual conversation: They often accidentally referred to a less restrictive rating as a "better" rating; and when I once questioned Dougherty about why a film was to be cut, since the majority had voted for the less restrictive rating anyway, another board member told me, "We may vote a film R, but that doesn't mean we are opposed to editing to make it a *better* R." They used an ugly euphemism for re-editing—they called it "correcting" a film.)

One of my most appalling experiences on the board was the first editing session I witnessed, a conference held to "correct" a routine George Peppard film, a melodrama about the Mexican Revolution called *Cannon for Cordoba*. Most of us had initially rated it R because of a great deal of violence and slaughter all through the film, a particularly gruesome torture scene at the beginning (a man is hung upside down over a fire, his face horribly burned, and finally he is shot to death), and one moderately explicit sex scene, featuring bare breasts and heavy breathing, which a couple of the board members had found too strong even for R. The Mirisch Company, obviously realizing it had a loser on its hands, wanted to bring the film into the GP category in order to get wider distribution. According to the usual practice, the board saw certain "trouble spots" out of context, thus losing all sense of the impact of the film as a whole. They were most concerned, of course, by the sex scene; someone suggested that if the nude lovemaking were excised, the scene could open with the girl lighting Peppard's cigar and handing it to him as he is getting dressed. The board members were all delighted with this suggestion, and when they saw the scene again after it had been recut, they congratulated themselves and the producers on how much better the scene now played. . . .

■ ■ ■ ■

Art in Court: City of Angels vs. "Scorpio Rising" (1964), Fred Haines

Although in its *Miracle* decision the Supreme Court prohibited the banning of films on ideological grounds (such as sacrilege), it specifically affirmed the right to prohibit the showing of obscene films. Most of the legal actions against films in recent decades have been on the grounds of obscenity. This report of the Los Angeles trial of Kenneth Anger's *Scorpio Rising* appeared in the *Nation* on 14 September 1964. The article reveals the difficulties of defining obscenity (from the 1960s on, one of the

"Art in Court: City of Angels vs. 'Scorpio Rising,' " by Fred Haines, appeared in the 14 September 1964 *Nation*.

persistent problems for both the American public and the courts), the residue of morally conservative opinion in America (despite the implications of the new rating system for films), and the emerging importance of a new kind of film which was outside the aims and control of the motion picture industry altogether.

Last spring half a dozen vice-squad officers barged into a Hollywood art film house and sat down to watch *Scorpio Rising*, an experimental work by Kenneth Anger. When they left they took *Scorpio* with them; in their opinion it was a pretty dirty movie. Several days later they returned to arrest theatre manager Mike Getz.

Gaiety prevailed when the trial opened in April in the Los Angeles Municipal Court. Jurors were eager to be empaneled: this case promised to be far more exciting than the customary trials of junkies, drunks and hustlers. With censorship rapidly vanishing under ten years of progressive court rulings, those defending the film weren't too worried. *Tropic of Cancer, Naked Lunch*, even *Fanny Hill* (which may be a truly pornographic novel, depending on what you think "pornographic" means), are freely sold all over the city. And *Scorpio* would be tried under the California State Penal Code's definition of obscenity, which combines the sense of recent court rulings with the American Law Institute's 1957 "model" definition.

Obscenity, in California, is that which, to "the average person applying current standards . . . the predominant appeal of the material taken as a whole is to the prurient interest, i.e., a shameful or morbid interest in nudity, sex or excretion." Obscenity "goes substantially beyond customary limits of candor in description of such matter and is . . . utterly without redeeming social importance."

Not a bad definition—in spite of the vagueness of terms like "appeal," "customary limits" and "prurient." In order to be legally obscene, a work must meet all of the criteria at once, and the clause on social importance seems to guarantee immunity to serious art. It does not mean that social importance must outweigh obscenity; the courts have held that *any* social importance redeems an otherwise obscene work. If one concedes that serious art necessarily has social importance, the radical's axiom that art is never obscene seems enshrined in California law.

The prosecutor presaged the drift of his case against *Scorpio* in the selection of jurors. Deputy City Attorney Warren Wolf dismissed all those who customarily enjoyed books or movies—an easy task, since only a few were guilty of such conduct. Defense counsel Stanley Fleishman was satisfied with the all-woman jury eventually empaneled; he feared that a male juror with anxieties about his masculinity might respond hysterically to the homoerotic undertones of Anger's film.

Scorpio Rising investigates the American motorcycle cult in purely visual terms. There is no narration. Anger's camera explores the sensual nature of the cyclist's relationships to his machine-sex object, to his buddies and to his heavily symbolic leather clothing, chain belts and jewelry. He portrays the cyclist as an alienated, death-oriented hipster, whose masculinity is expressed as violence and whose femininity emerges in his clothing, in his masochistic devotion to cults and in the kind of homoerotic horseplay common to authoritarian, all-male groups like fraternities or veterans' clubs. Anger's motorcyclist is not unlike Fromm's Fascist in *Escape from Freedom* or Lindner's psychopath in *Rebel Without a Cause*.

Mr. Wolf opened by warning the jury ladies that they would actually see a "male penis" (throughout the trial he seemed to think there might be another kind). His expert witness would testify to the utter lack of "redeeming social importance." In fact, Mr. Wolf told them, *Scorpio Rising* is a cancerous film about a bunch of sick people that ought to be stamped out. It was not clear whether he was talking about the film or the sick people.

Scorpio was shown to the jury, and then the prosecution introduced eleven stills made from frames of the film. They were admitted into evidence over the defense objection that they hardly constituted "best evidence," since the film itself was an exhibit. These represented shots picturing a penis or other nudity. All were from a single scene.

Anger shot his film in Brooklyn, using a real motorcycle club. In order to film a party he threw one himself, hanging dime-store Halloween decorations around to provide some of the death symbols he wanted. He asked the cyclists' wives to stay behind the camera. Once the party, complete with improvised costumes, got under way, Anger asked his cast to make an entrance he could film. The first guy through the door came in wearing one of the decorations, a cardboard skeleton, which he had adorned—as a joke on the film-maker—with a rubber dildoe from a Times Square novelty shop. This artificial penis figured in much of the night's revelry, which included a lot of that childish pseudosexual play so aptly characterized by the slang term "grab-ass." In cutting his final footage, Anger emphasized this sexual clowning to create the impression that an ugly sort of orgy was taking place.

The jury ladies couldn't make much of the stills, but Mr. Wolf helpfully explained that they depicted "attempted" oral intercourse, "attempted" anal intercourse, and so forth. He next brought his expert to the stand. Vagueness, which ordinarily invalidates an indictment, is the essence of an obscenity trial, since there is no objective test for obscenity. (Ladies donning silk stockings are obscene to some people; motorcyclists donning leather jackets are obscene to others.) Consequently, if there is no question as to whether the material was actually exhibited, the only relevant evidence is the opinion of experts. Even more confusing, this "evidence" is not binding on the jury, which is instructed to make up its own mind no matter what the experts say.

The prosecution's expert was J. Warren Day, a 26-year-old Boy Scout leader from La Crescenta. A graduate of Scarritt College, Tennessee, Mr. Day serves as education director for a Methodist Church. Mr. Day sees two movies a month and calls himself something of a movie fan. He knew the film was homosexual right from the first scenes, which were portrait shots of jazzed-up motorcycles.

Oddly enough, Mr. Day remembered all the scenes that showed penises, but could not recall the spectacular motorcycle wreck that climaxed the film. Nor did he notice another key scene, a man taking a drug. Shown a reproduction of a Courbet painting, Day judged it obscene. The fact that motorcyclists admire Nazis was of no social importance. *Scorpio* might have social importance for some people, he admitted, but not for the average person. The film was largely unintelligible to the average person. Moreover it was trite. How could that be? Well, it was trite to Mr. Day, but "above" the average person.

Shown photos of Indian temple sculpture, Mr. Day opined that it would be obscene if "on public view" (which it is). On the other hand, a Greek vase depicting fellatio and buggery would not be obscene if it illustrated an ancient Greek play (which it did), but would be otherwise.

Then came defense experts: James Powers, film critic for the Hollywood *Reporter,* felt that Anger was a gifted film-maker meriting serious attention. Showing the penis does not go "beyond customary limits"—travelogues occasionally show the male organ. Paul Sawyer, a Unitarian minister, said that *Scorpio,* like the Bible, dealt with morality by depicting immorality. Sex organs are often shown in art, even great religious art.

Cinematographer Archer Goodwin testified that he had timed the objectionable shots. Their total duration was eighteen and two-thirds seconds. Of this, two shots—the cardboard skeleton shot and another revealing the bare buttocks of a man on a cycle—lasted more than six seconds each. The remaining nine shots occupied the screen less than six seconds all together—none lasted long enough for the viewer to assimilate their content. In other words, nine of the eleven shots were essentially "subliminal."

Goodwin found no sexual contact in any of the shots, and even microscopic analysis did not reveal whether any of the penislike objects were in fact penises. One of the stills—showing a man's head on another's lap—had been cropped. The full frame clearly showed several people who were merely scuffling. In any case, excepting the skeleton shot, a penis-like object appeared in only nine frames out of a total 44,500.

Judge Bernard Selber asked Goodwin why a film-maker would use shots a viewer could not, in any ordinary sense, "see." Goodwin thought Anger wanted to suggest homosexuality without showing it. In any case, Goodwin said, a true pornographer would hardly hide his best shots that way.

More defense experts followed: Mel Sloan, a professional film-maker and USC teacher; film critic and teacher Colin Young; *Saturday Review* critic Arthur Knight, one of the judges who selected Anger for a $10,000 Ford Foundation grant; Ted Carpenter, chairman of Valley State College's anthropology department; art critic Jules Langsar; film editor Verna Fields, who testified that she would let her children see *Scorpio;* Rabbi Leonard Bierman; Ruth Hirschman of KPFK-FM; and the producer-director of *Hud,* Martin Ritt.

Twelve witnesses in all. None thought the film obscene according to the law. Several thought *Scorpio* went well beyond customary limits of candor —at least for a film—but all conceived it to be of redeeming social importance.

At last the defendant took the stand. (Actually, the defendant serves mostly as a sort of "body bail"—if the film is guilty, he goes to jail.) Technically, at least, it was necessary to prove that Getz knew the film to be obscene in order to convict him, but no one seemed to care very much about that. The 26-year-old Cornell graduate did not, and still does not, believe the film to be obscene.

On rebuttal the prosecution brought in two more witnesses. The first was the 26-year-old student who had filed the complaint. He thought *Scorpio* was a stag film. We all know about motorcyclists and prostitutes, he said, but we don't have to see films about them. He admitted he had seen other films about prostitutes, even on TV, and Fleishman dropped his cross-examination.

The last witness, Dr. Fred Goldstein, was a clinical psychologist who treats many homosexuals. Dr. Goldstein obviously had good claim to expert status, but he almost seemed not to have seen the same film the others saw. He objected that *Scorpio* did not portray all homosexuals fairly; it dealt with a vicious minority, and its only apparent purpose was to arouse the prurient interest of that minority. Asked whether he believed the film would arouse the average person, Dr. Goldstein said it would be as confusing to the average person as an Ingmar Bergman film.

Fleishman, in summing up, pointed out that Mr. Day's definition of obscenity was more restrictive than the law's, since he condemned works previously exonerated by various courts. Dr. Goldstein, on the other hand, had admitted that the film would not arouse the prurient interest of the *average* person as required by the law.

Mr. Wolf told the jurors they need not heed the experts, that the problem was one of moral standards. He read a passage from *Tropic of Cancer* and asked them how they would like to see that on a wide screen, in color—even Panavision! He predicted that *Scorpio Rising* would be shown on television, a possibility that could only have astonished its maker.

Judge Selber instructed the jury to find for acquittal if they agreed the film had any social importance whatever, which, apparently, they did not. After less than five hours of deliberation, the twelve ladies reached their verdict: guilty. Mike Getz received a sentence of $500 or fifty days, which is now being appealed.[1]

Anyone who sat through the trial heard twelve people—artists, critics, educators, a minister and a rabbi—recommend *Scorpio Rising* as a worthwhile aesthetic experience, a film of insight and social importance which one might want to see. At the trial's end, another twelve people delivered a contrary opinion. But the second group's decision was far more than a recommendation not to see *Scorpio;* they told the spectator, in effect, they he *may not* see the film. They made it clear that no matter how "progressive" the obscenity statute, a court of law is a poor device for making artistic judgments. The legal process is directed toward securing a verdict; that is the way we deal with facts. In debate about values, though, we insist that the verdict is never in, that no one has the right to close off debate.

■ ■ ■ ■

Linda Lovelace: The Blue-ing of America (1973)
Richard Smith

The successful legal appeals of serious, experimental films like Anger's *Scorpio Rising* also opened the legal door for the making, distributing, and screening of many hard-core sexual exploitation films in the 1970s, some of which achieved mass distribution. This chapter from Richard Smith's *Getting into Deep Throat,* a book which examines the back-

1. Ed. Note: The appeal reversed the conviction. The same film was also seized and tried in the State of New York. The eventual result was the elimination of New York's Board of Censors.

"Linda Lovelace: The Blue-ing of America" is from *Getting into Deep Throat,* by Richard Smith (Playboy Press, 1973).

ground, the economics, and the legal battles which attended the most famous of these films, treats the press's reactions to the film and its star. One can only imagine the reaction of those early members of the National Board of Censorship (who found even the gleam in a pirate's eye too energetic) to this sort of film.

Faster than Raquel Welch, more powerful than Gloria Steinem, able to swallow tall men in a single gulp. Look! Up on the screen! It's a sword-swallower! It's a vacuum cleaner! It's Linda Lovelace! Yes, Linda Lovelace, strange visitor from Bryan, Texas, who came to the World Theatre with powers and abilities far beyond those of mortal women. Linda Lovelace, who can change the course of film history, bend flesh in her bare throat, and who, disguised as a mild-mannered nymphomaniac for a small metropolitan film company, fights a never-ending battle for free speech, free love, and the French way!

It may have been the Year of the Cock in China, but in America, 1972 will undoubtedly be remembered as the Year of the Throat.

During that summer, a film intriguingly titled "Deep Throat" opened quietly at the New Mature World Theatre in the loins of Manhattan's Times Square area. The movie featured a fluffy-headed, freckle-faced young actress named Linda Lovelace who did for fellatio what Nureyev had done for the leap—taken a standard part of the repertory of the art and refined and developed it to the point where it seemed to defy the laws of nature. Her unprecedented esophagal acrobatics so deeply impressed SCREW magazine editor Al Goldstein, New York's ultimate arbiter of taste in sexual entertainment, that he hailed the film as "the very best porno ever made," setting off an orgy of obscenity controversy that made the "I Am Curious, Yellow" furor of a few years before look like harmless foreplay.

By the end of the summer, the theater had been hit with two arrests for promoting obscenity, with a trial date set for Mid-December. Deep Throat had become the test case in the mayoral election year campaign to clean up Times Square, and business started booming at the World.

Until it played Deep Throat, the New Mature World Theatre, like the Eros, the Love, the Doll, and about twenty other grind houses in the neighborhood, catered almost exclusively to the raincoat-on-the-lap set, a small but dedicated cadre of footage fetishists made up mostly of middle-class, middle-aged men carrying out a joyless, furtive campaign of guerilla raids on respectability. Whether they thought of what they were seeing as blue movies, skin flicks, sexploitation films, fuckfilms, stag films, adult movies, erotic films, pornography, porno, or porn, as a group they were more interested in fucking and sucking than in lighting and writing. Many, according to a study by sociologist Charles Winick, also had an academic interest.

"It really is educational," one patron reported. "I saw one film about fifteen minutes long, where you actually could see a vagina covering the whole screen and throbbing, with fluid running. You know for sure that she is coming, the same way you know a man is coming when you see the sperm moving out. Where else could you see a vagina 20 feet high, and learn how it works and looks?"

Another gynecologist-manqué confided, "I look carefully at the vagina. The longer it is on the screen, the better. You have enough time to study it and it is very real." Then, stepping away from the clinical viewpoint momentarily, he added, "The younger they are the more I like it."

"You learn a lot by seeing the girls walk around with their breasts bouncing," said another, "the different shapes the breasts have, the space between them, how they are connected—that's all good to know."

One fan observed that "the asses of the girls I know have blotches and are pimply and hairy. In the movies, the girls' asses are clear-looking. It may be the photography, but I like it. I like to see an ass that looks clear; that's the way I prefer to think of them."

For the raincoat brigade, the Sixties were a long striptease of greater and greater explicitness, starting with the virginal breast-and-buttock displays of the "nudie-cuties" like Russ Meyer's "The Immoral Mr. Teas" and ending with the tentative thrusting of "I Am Curious, Yellow." Along the way there were the nudist colony epics, equating volley ball with virtue; the sex-and-violence sagas, equating sex with violence; and the striptease shorts, equating eroticism with pubic hair. By 1972, the tease was over, and the only thing left to the imagination was the salaries of the actors and actresses. What had previously been available only in the grainy black-and-white of under-the-counter stag films was appearing in living color in the theatres of Times Square.

What was remarkable, then, about Deep Throat was not what it showed, but who saw it. Before it was ordered closed in March of 1973, the film played to almost a quarter of a million people, grossing over a million dollars. For the first time in its history, the World theatre was playing to packed houses, audiences of men and women who laughed and cheered. Those who came included not only the regular hard-core corps, but a group that ranged from celebrities to secretaries to suburban matrons to U.N. delegates. Many of them were seeing real sex on the screen for the first time, prompting reactions that varied from delighted incredulity ("I can't believe she ate the whole thing") to outright revulsion ("I vomited").

When the trial started in December, business at the theatre doubled as fashionable New York dinner party chatter moved enthusiastically from Nixon politics to blowjobs and hard-ons. "Not to have seen it," wrote Nora Ephron in Esquire, "seemed somehow . . . derelict."

The threadbare plot of Deep Throat revolves around the trials and tribulations of a young woman, Linda Lovelace, who try as she might is unable to experience orgasm. Her roommate Helen, extravagantly gifted in that department, suggests that Linda may simply not have hit on the right technique—"different strokes for different folks." To remedy the situation, Helen arranges a party consisting of herself, Linda, and a dozen men who line up delicatessen style, each with a number, each hoping to come up with the magic combination of oomph and orifice that will set bells ringing, dams bursting, and rockets exploding for the hapless heroine. All to no avail.

Convinced that Linda's problem may be psychological, Helen recommends a Dr. Young. After one of the briefest history-takings in the annals of psychiatry, the light-headed, heavy-hung young doctor dismisses the possibility of emotional disorder. His thorough physical examination, however, conducted in part with a child's toy telescope, reveals the patient to be the victim of a rare physiological anomaly—her clitoris is located at the base of her throat.

Linda is despondent, but the good doctor assures her that orgasmic ecctasy is still within her reach thanks to his revolutionary "deep throat" treatment. Volunteering his own penis in the interest of therapy, he teaches her a variation of fellatio that could make a circus sword-swallower choke. Linda's problems soon dissolve in a climactic montage of the proverbial bells, bombs, and rockets, leaving her so overwhelmed with gratitude that she offers to marry her benefactor on the spot. The doctor, who seems to have his hands full servicing his magnificently-endowed blonde nurse, begs off and offers her instead a position working for him as a "physiotherapist."

The remainder of the film is devoted to a series of "case histories" in which Linda applies liberal doses of her therapeutic thorax to a variety of sexual unfortunates, including one poor fellow who insists on sipping Coca-Cola from a hollow glass dildo in her vagina to work out his obsession to find out if things really *do* go better with Coke, a horny widower who pays for his "treatments" with Blue Cross, and a young man with a small ego and a large penis who can only be potent in the role of a bandit/rapist. Everything turns out happily, with Linda engaged to marry the last patient and Dr. Young looking forward to a rest from his exertions.

Most of Deep Throat's hour and two minutes is devoted to sexual activity of one form or another. In fact, the diligent statisticians at the New York Times counted fifteen overt sexual acts, including seven of fellatio and four of cunnilingus. What dialogue there was time for under the circumstances often had the tone of an X-rated Laugh-in. Some examples:

> HELEN: (to her partner in cunnilingus) Do you mind if I smoke while you're eating?

and,

> SWISHY NEWCOMER: (to boyfriend at orgy) What's a nice joint like you doing in a girl like this?

and,

> DOCTOR: It's not so bad. You should be thankful you have a clitoris at all.
> LINDA: (sobbing) That's easy for you to say. How would you feel if your balls were in your ears?
> DOCTOR: (ponders deeply, sudden inspiration) Why then I could hear myself coming!

The part of the soundtrack not dedicated to jokes and moans features a score that includes a parody version of the Fifties rock 'n' roll classic "Love is Strange" (for anal penetration), a raunched-up rendition of the Coke jingle ("I'd like to teach the world to screw in perfect harmony . . ."), and a title tune that provides a vivid description of Linda's stupendous swallow, and a chorus so cryptic it could have been written by the acid-phase Bob Dylan. To wit:

> Deep Throat
> Don't row a boat
> Don't get your goat
> That's all she wrote
> Deep Throat

Not surprisingly, serious critics approached the job of reviewing Deep Throat with all the enthusiasm that Henry Kissinger might be expected to show at the prospect of negotiating a barroom brawl. The problem, for many, was to express distaste for the film without giving ammunition to the forces of censorship, and much of the verbiage that resulted displayed the tortured introspection of a law-and-order liberal who has just been mugged. Vincent Canby of the New York Times, who thought the movie was "junk," juggled the hot potato this way:

"Trying to write honestly about pornographic films is like trying to tie one's shoe while walking: it's practically impossible without sacrificing stride and balance and a certain amount of ordinary dignity, the sort one uses with bank tellers who question a signature. Almost any attitude the writer adopts will whirl around and hit him from the other side. The haughty approach ("it's boring") has long-since been suspected as evidence of a mixture of embarrassment and arousal. The golly-gee-whiz style ("They've gone as far as they can go!") is patently untrue, while to make fun of pornography is to avoid facing the subject at all. To call it a healthy development is another vast oversimplification that refuses to acknowledge that it may be fine for some people, and quite upsetting for others. Then, too, to suggest that pornography degrades the audience as well as the performers assumes a familiarity with all of the members of all audiences that I, for one, do not have."

Mort Sheinman of Women's Wear Daily responded to clitoris-in-throat with tongue-in-cheek. He called Deep Throat a "remarkable film" that "provides a bold thrust forward in the history of contemporary cinema, plunging deeply into areas seldom, if ever, explored on screen. . . . The poignancy of [Linda's] plight and the exultation of her eventual triumph rank with the most moving bits of film in this reviewer's memory. . . . A delightful surprise for cineastes is director Gerard's tribute to Alfred Hitchcock in the fireworks sequence, calling to mind those wonderful scenes between Cary Grant and Grace Kelly in "To Catch a Thief." . . . Len Camp's set designs provide the proper ambiance and the clothes, by Royal Fashions, are as much a part of the script as anything else. All in all, a rare treat."

Others were not amused. Judith Crist of New York magazine characterized the film as an example of "idiot moviemaking" and the actors as "awful"; while at the Village Voice, Andrew Sarris found it to be a "joyless, repetitious documentary on the latest oral-genital techniques in the Kingdom of Pornalia." Noting the film's "whimsical self-hatred and mechanical slobbering," he asked rhetorically, "Where is the charm? Where is the humor? Where is the eroticism? Where is the liberation? And, finally, where is the exit?" In a piece in Esquire magazine that featured an Alice-in-Wonderland interview with Linda Lovelace, Nora Ephron described Deep Throat as "one of the most unpleasant, disturbing films I have ever seen—it is not just anti-female but anti-sexual as well." Ellen Willis of the New York Review of Books called it "witless, exploitive, and about as erotic as a tonsillectomy."

If the critics were less than enthusiastic, the news editors went for Deep Throat with a voraciousness equal to Linda's own. In addition to extensive local and national coverage of the New York trial, scarcely a week went by after it without a report of some new Throat incident to titillate the readership.

There was the story of Deep Throat replacing a children's matinee on the Upper East Side, featuring a picket line of four adults and eight children demanding that the film be sent back to Forty-second Street "where it belonged." The issue was resolved a few days later with the capitulation of the theatre management and the moving of the movie a few blocks east to a less community-minded neighborhood.

There was the Milwaukee incident in which local residents picketed the Parkway Theatre where the film was attracting audiences from Chicago. The picketers claimed that they were not so much protesting the film as the unprecedented volume of traffic it brought into the area, threatening the safety of their children and making it impossible for them to find parking spaces. When the picketing failed to get results, the citizens lined up for the show themselves, purchasing their $3.00 tickets with bags of pennies, causing such a serious delay that the manager decided to let 500 people in free. This well-intentioned tactic backfired when patrons already inside the theatre took it as a cue to demand their money back. The next night the protesters returned, this time approaching the box office with hundred-dollar bills. After ten had been admitted, the theatre was out of change.

Then there was the story of a Lansing, Michigan garbage collector who refused to service the Cinema X theatre where Deep Throat was playing. "We may be in the trash business," the president of the company explained, "but we want nothing to do with *that* kind of trash."

In Syracuse, New York, Deep Throat turned up on the university's cable television station one night, shocking the dean, but delighting the news media.

The most thorough piece of journalism on the subject was Ralph Blumenthal's article "Porno Chic," which appeared in the magazine section of the Sunday New York Times two weeks after the trial. Describing the Times Square area as "an unmistakable vista of sexploitation gone berserk," he reported that the audience for Deep Throat had recently included such notables as Johnny Carson, Mike Nichols, Sandy Dennis, Ben Gazzara, Jack Nicholson, and Truman Capote ("you see it at your own peril").

Blumenthal also took his readers behind the scenes and revealed that the film had been made on a budget of $25,000 in six days the previous winter in Florida. The director was a veteran porno producer named Gerard Damiano (he called himself "Jerry Gerard" in the credits), who had made the film on a bankroll supplied by his partners Lou Perry and Phil Parisi. Damiano had written, directed, and edited the movie. It was ready for distribution by the summer.

"There are different versions of what happened next," Blumenthal wrote. "According to Lou Perry, Damiano, the third partner in Film Productions, Inc., asked to sell his share when the film faced legal problems and had not yet begun to make money. 'He was compensated what he asked for—$25,000,' Perry said. 'He was even asked to stay. This was his decision.' "

An unidentified source told Blumenthal a different story, however. In this version, Perry and Parisi simply informed Damiano that the three-way split was over as soon as the film started to do well at the box office, giving the director a parting $25,000 as his share of the future profits. When Blumenthal confronted Damiano with this story, Damiano reportedly said that he couldn't talk about it, and when asked why not replied, "Look, you want me to get both my legs broken?" Further questioning produced only a roll of the eyes and total silence.

After the Blumenthal article, Perry and Parisi, along with the film's distributor, Terry Levene of Aquarius, adopted a public profile so low it made President Nixon's look like Everest on the Sahara. But Linda Lovelace was everywhere.

The girl who had done for the throat what Grable had done for legs was staking out her claim in American popculture somewhere between Raquel Welch and Tiny Tim.

Her first appearance in print took place in the September 1 issue of Women's Wear Daily, where she described herself to columnist Rosemary Kent as "just a simple girl who likes to go to swinging parties and nudist colonies." . . .

Time magazine good-naturedly described Linda as a "MAD magazine cloning of Little Annie Fanny and Mary Marvel" in an article about the trial entitled "Wonder Woman."

Playboy described her as "The all-American girl without the all-American hang-ups. Bright as a button, sweet as honey, carnal as hell." In a full-length pictorial feature called "Say 'Ah!,' " she revealed a "warm, friendly personality that falls short of being gregarious" and a "free and easy sensuality that seems healthy, natural, spontaneous."

"Linda came to *Deep Throat,* or vice versa," the Playboy article explained, "because of her boyfriend. She was living in Texas when she met J. R. Traynor, a New York free-lance photographer working on an agricultural assignment. After returning with him to Manhattan, she went to work as a clerk in a head shop until Traynor met a local film maker and told him about Linda's unique erotic gifts." The piece went on to quote her on the subject she knows best:

> It makes me so mad that sex films are called obscene when movies full of slaughter are rated PG. Kids learn that killing is accepted; what they should learn is that sex is good. Then there wouldn't be so many neurotics in the world.

> You're only here once, to enjoy life. I don't have any hangups at all.
> I do what I do because it feels good.
>
> I really do dig getting it in the throat. Everything turns me on,
> actually; my preferences depend on my mood, but I'd say right now
> I like throat, ass, cunt, one, two, three, in that order.

The article ended by describing Linda as a girl who is "sexually fear-less, knows who she is and what she wants, and has a deep respect for other people as individuals, as long as they reciprocate. . . . Linda would rather spend a quiet evening at home puttering around with a new recipe than dine out in an elegant restaurant. And she says she likes keeping house as much as she does cooking." . . .

Whatever else remains to be revealed or concealed about the woman who has done the most for the human throat since Caruso, her impact on American culture can be measured as much by the jokes she has spawned as by the profits. Here are some samples:

> There's a sucker born every minute, but a Linda Lovelace comes along once in a blue movie.
>
> After Deep Throat, Linda Lovelace is going to go legit and star in one of those Hollywood biblical spectaculars. She's reading for the part of the whale in the Jonah episode.
>
> Linda had to cancel her plan to address the French Film Academy on the subject of "Sex in the Cinema"—She had a Frog in her throat.
>
> Don Imus, an early morning disk jockey in New York, singled Linda Lovelace out as one woman who would not be observing the April meat boycott.
>
> And, of course, the Linda Lovelace doll: Wind it up and it swallows the key.

■ ■ ■ ■

Synaesthetic Cinema and Polymorphous Eroticism (1970), Gene Youngblood

Nowhere has the relationship between radically new cinema and radically new American mores been made more clear than in Gene Youngblood's book *Expanded Cinema*. This chapter from the book relates the bizzarre sexuality of the "underground" films to the new sexual values and consciousness which Youngblood saw emerging in America in the late 1960s.

"Synaesthetic Cinema and Polymorphous Eroticism" is from Gene Youngblood's *Expanded Cinema* (E. P. Dutton, 1970).

Mr. Youngblood's discussion indicates (as did the trial of *Scorpio Rising*) that the sexuality of "underground" films is merely one more chapter in the perpetual saga of sex in the cinema. The very terms and tone of Youngblood's "flower-child" prose affix its date as precisely as does the Victorian rhetoric of John Collier's discussion of the National Board of Censorship (see pp. 144–53).

> The Western consciousness has always asked for freedom: the human mind was born free, or at any rate born to be free, but everywhere it is in chains; and now at the end of its tether.
>
> *Norman O. Brown*

For the majority of the mass public, "underground" movies are synonymous with sex. Although this conclusion was reached for all the wrong reasons, it is nevertheless accurate. If personal cinema is indeed personal, and if we place any credence at all in Freud, personal cinema is by definition sexual cinema. A genuine social underground no longer is possible. The intermedia network quickly unearths and popularizes any new subculture in its relentless drive to satisfy the collective information hunger. Jean-Luc Godard once remarked that the only true twentieth-century underground was in Hanoi. But I would suggest that in the history of civilization there never has been a phenomenon more underground than human sexuality.

The vast political and social revolution that is now irreversible in its accelerating accelerations around the planet is merely a side effect of the more profound revolution in human self-awareness that is producing a new sexual consciousness.

We hold the radical primacy of the passions to be self-evident. Norman O. Brown: "All Freud's work demonstrates that the allegiance of the human psyche to the pleasure-principle is indestructible and that the path of instinctual renunciation is the path of sickness and self-destruction." If there is a general debasement of the sexual act among the bourgeoisie, it is precisely because that sexuality has been repressed. Charles Fourier: "Every passion that is suffocated produces its counter-passion, which is as malignant as the natural passion would have been benign."

Nowhere is this more evident than in commercial cinema. Hollywood movies are teasers whose eroticism is a result of psychological conditioning that is not, fundamentally, the enjoyment of sex itself. Girlie and Hollywood films "for mature adults" are founded on puritanical concepts of "sin" and other repressive measures, no matter how "honest" or "artistic" or "redeeming" the presentation may seem. The absurd notion that sex must somehow be "redeemed" is exploited by Hollywood as much as by the makers of girlie or stag films. Hollywood presents "re-deemed" sex, suggesting there's an unredeemed way of doing it and therefore we're getting away with something. Girlie and stag films take the opposite approach: they represent sex in various stages of "unredemption" until the point of watching them becomes more an act of rebellion, of something "dirty," clandestine, without redeeming qualities, than the enjoyment of sex. That is to say, the present socioeconomic system actually contributes to the corruption of the institution it claims to uphold.

However, it is now only a matter of a few years until the final restrictions on sexuality will disintegrate. The revolution that seeks the restructuring of social arrangements—a utopia of material plenty and economic freedom—is secondary by far to that other revolution that demands the total release of psychic impulses. This imminent utopia of the senses has been described by the neo-Freudian psychoanalyst A. H. Maslow as *Eupsychia*, a view oriented to the liberation and satisfaction of inner drives as prerequisite to any effective reorganization of the exterior social order. It implies the necessary transformation of a bourgeois society that perpetrates the three cardinal crimes against human sexuality: delayed sexual gratification, restricted to "adults only"; heterosexual monogamy; specialization of sexual activity limiting pleasure to the genitals.

Eupsychia and utopia are both quite inevitable and both quite out of our hands, for they are the irreversible result of technology, the only thing that keeps man human. The most comprehensive, reliable, and respected future-forecasts attempted by scientific man indicate that individual sensorial freedom is virtually synonymous with technological progress.

Buckminster Fuller is among many who have noted the effects of industrialization and cybernetics on sexual activity: "We may glimpse in such patterning certain total behaviors in Universe that we know little about. We noted, for instance, that as survival rate and life-sustaining capability increase, fewer birth starts are required. This may be related to our developing capacities in interchanging our physical parts, or producing mechanical organs, of having progressively fewer organisms to replenish. The drive in humanity to reproduce as prodigally as possible decreases considerably. This may be reflected in social behavior—when all the girls begin to look like boys and boys and girls wear the same clothes. This may be part of a discouraging process in the idea of producing more babies. We shall have to look askance on sex merely as a reproductive capability, i.e., that it is normal to make babies. Society will have to change in its assessment of what the proclivities of humanity may be. Our viewpoints on homosexuality, for example, may have to be reconsidered and more wisely adjusted."

Repression and censorship become impossible on an individual level when technology outstrips enforcement. The new image-exchange and duplication technologies are a formidable obstacle to effective sexual censorship. Home videotape recorders, Polaroid cameras, and 8mm. film cartridges render censorship nearly powerless. One prominent scientist working in laser holography has suggested the possibility of "porno-grams"—pornographic, three-dimensional holograms mass-produced from a master and mass-distributed through the mail since their visual information is invisible until activated by plain white light.

When sexual material is readily available in the home, it changes the public attitude toward sex in commercial cinema. We aren't likely to be dazzled by discreet nudity on the Silver Screen when our home videotape library contains graphic interpretations of last week's neighborhood bi-sexual orgy. This is precisely what is happening in thousands of sub-urban homes, which otherwise are far from avant-garde. Within the last three years intermarital group sex has become an industry of cor-porate business, particularly in the Southern California area where a new world man is evolving. Computer firms compete with one another, match-ing couples with couples and compiling guest lists for orgies at homes and private country clubs. Home videotape systems are rented by the month and tapes of flagrant sexual activity are exchanged among the participants, many of whom regularly attend two orgies a week, some-times as frequently as four or five, as the will to sexual power overtakes their outlaw consciousness. They discover the truth in Dylan's remark that you must live outside the law to be honest.

Thus man moves inevitably toward the discovery of what Norman O. Brown describes as his polymorphous-perverse self. A society that re-stricts physical contact in public to handshakes and discreet heterosexual kisses distorts man's image of his own sexual nature. However, anyone who has ever participated in even the most chaste encounter groups or sensory awareness seminars such as those conducted at the Esalen In-stitute in Big Sur, is impressed with the new sensual identity he discovers within himself, often accompanied by surprise and embarrassment.

The effects of habitual group sex, even when exclusively heterosexual, becomes obvious: man inevitably realizes that there is no such thing as "perversion" apart from the idea itself. We begin to recognize that our sexual potential is practically limitless once psychological barriers are erased. We see that "heterosexual," "homosexual," and "bisexual" are social observations, not inherent aspects of the organism. Freud, and re-cently Brown, Marcuse, and R. D. Laing have noted that the qualities of "maleness" and "femaleness" are restricted to genital differences and do not even approach an adequate description of the human libido. And so, "Genital man is to become polymorphously perverse man, the man of love's body, able to experience the world with a fully erotic body in an activity that is the equivalent of the play of childhood."

Personal synaesthetic cinema has been directly responsible for the recent transformation in sexual content of commercial movies. After all, *I Am Curious* begins to seem a bit impotent when Carolee Schneemann's *Fuses* is playing at the Cinémathèque around the corner. Synaesthetic cinema, more than any other social phenomenon, has demonstrated the trend toward polymorphous eroticism. Because it is personal it's a manifestation of consciousness; because it's a manifestation of consciousness it is sexual; the more probing and relentlessly personal it becomes, the more polymorphously perverse it is. (Dylan: *"If my thought/dreams could be seen, they'd put my head in a guillotine."*) Because eroticism is the mind's manifestation of body ego, it is the one offensive quality that we cannot be rid of by slicing off a particular appendage. We are forced to accept it: synaesthetic cinema is the first collective expression of that acceptance.

The art and technology of expanded cinema will provide a framework within which contemporary man, who does not trust his own senses, may learn to study his values empirically and thus arrive at a better understanding of himself. The only understanding mind is the creative mind. Those of the old consciousness warn that although the videotape cartridge can be used to unite and elevate humanity, it also can "degrade" us by allowing unchecked manufacture and exchange of pornography. But the new consciousness regards this attitude itself as a degraded product of a culture without integrity, a culture perverse enough to imagine that love's body could somehow be degrading.

John Dewey reminds us that when art is removed from daily experience the collective aesthetic hunger turns toward the cheap and the vulgar. It's the same with the aesthetics of sex: when the art (i.e., beauty) of sex is denied and repressed we find a "counter-passion" for the obscene ". . . as malignant as the natural passion would have been benign." There is no basis for the assumption that synaesthetic cinema will contribute to the debasement of sex. We know that precisely the opposite is true: for the first time in Western culture the aesthetics of integrity are about to liberate man from centuries of sexual ignorance so that he may at last understand the infinite sensorium that is himself.

THE PANSEXUAL UNIVERSE OF ANDY WARHOL

It might be said of Warhol that what he did for Campbell's Soup, he did for sex. That is, he removed sex from its usual context and revealed it both as experience and cultural product. From the verbal jousting of *My Hustler* and *Bike Boy* to the casual intercourse of *Blue Movie,* Warhol has expressed an image of man's sexuality unique in all of cinema. Although partial to homosexuality, his work nevertheless manages to generate an overwhelming sense of the polymorphous-perverse. This is particularly evident in his most recent work.

For example, a romantic heterosexual relationship of warm authenticity develops between Viva and Louis Waldron in the notorious *Blue Movie*. In *Lonesome Cowboy* and Paul Morrissey's *Flesh*, however, Waldron is equally convincing as a brusque homosexual. Ironically, it is Morrissey's beautiful film that epitomizes the unisex world of The Factory. The Brandoesque Joe Dallasandro is virtually the embodiment of polymorphous-perverse man as Morrissey interprets him: the archetypal erotic body, responding to the pleasures of the flesh without ideals or violence in a pansexual universe.

Because of their objective revelatory purpose, Warhol's and Morrissey's films are not synaesthetic. Yet, because of their nondramatic structure, neither are they spectacles. It is spectacle (". . . *something exhibited to view as unusual or entertaining; an eye-catching or dramatic public display*.") that defeats whatever erotic purpose may exist in conventional narrative cinema. Eroticism is the most subjective of experiences; it cannot be portrayed or photographed; it's an intangible that arises out of the aesthetic, the manner of experiencing it. The difference between sex in synaesthetic cinema and sex in narrative cinema is that it's no longer a spectacle. By definition synaesthetic cinema is an art of evocative emotion rather than concrete facts. The true subject of a synaesthetic film that includes fucking is not the act itself but the metaphysical "place between desire and experience" that is eroticism. It ceases to be spectacle because its real subject cannot be displayed.

Virtually the entire range of erotic experience has been engaged by the new cinema. Carl Linder is concerned with the surreal/psychological aspects of sexuality in films like *Womancock* or *The Devil Is Dead*. Jack Smith's *Flaming Creatures* and *Normal Love*, Ron Rice's *Chumlum*, Bill Vehr's *Brothel* and *Waiting for Sugar*, and *The Liberation of Mannique Mechanique* by Steven Arnold and Michael Wiese all explore the polymorphous subterranean world of unisexual transvestism. Stephen Dwoskin's exquisite studies, such as *Alone* or *Take Me*, reveal a Minimalist's sensibilities for latent sexuality and nuances in subtle autoeroticism. Warhol's *Couch*, Barbara Rubin's *Christmas on Earth*, and Andrew Noren's *A Change of Heart* confront, in various ways, the immortal subject of "hard core" pornography. . . .

■ ■ ■ ■

ON THE FUTURE OF MOVIES (1974), Pauline Kael

As she has done for more than three decades, Pauline Kael continues to speculate perceptively on the relationships between film art, the film business, and the tastes of the film audience. This pessimistic article, excerpted from the *New Yorker,* wonders if the movies have any future at all—if the corporation presidents who run the film companies and the sensation-hungry audiences who consume them have left any room for the gifted, serious film artists at all.

Sometime during the last year, a number of the most devoted moviegoers stopped going to the movies. I say "a number" because I have no idea how many are actually involved, but I keep meeting people—typically, men in their late twenties and early thirties—who say, "You know, I just don't have the impulse to go to a movie anymore," or "There aren't any movies anymore, are there?" The interest in pictures has left these people almost overnight; they turned off as suddenly as they'd turned on, and, since they no longer care to go, they feel that there's nothing to see. It was no accident that the Americans walked off with most of the top awards at Cannes this year. Right now, American movies —not the big hits but many of the movies that Hollywood considers failures—are probably the best in the world. No country rivals us in the diversity of skilled, talented filmmakers, but there are few lines for the sorts of films that young audiences were queuing up for a couple of years ago. They talked fervently then about how they loved movies; now they feel there can't be anything good going on, even at the movies.

Whatever their individual qualities, such films as "Bonnie and Clyde," "The Graduate," "Easy Rider," "Five Easy Pieces," "Joe," "M*A*S*H," "Little Big Man," "Midnight Cowboy," and "They Shoot Horses, Don't They?" all helped to form the counterculture. The young, anti-draft, anti-Vietnam audiences that were "the film generation" might go to some of the same pictures that the older audience did, but not to those only. They were willing to give something fresh a chance, and they went to movies that weren't certified hits. They made modest—sometimes large —successes of pictures that had new, different perceptions. A movie like the tentative, fumbling "Alice's Restaurant" would probably be a flop now, because student audiences are no longer willing to look for feelings,

"On the Future of Movies," which originally appeared in the 5 August 1974 issue of the *New Yorker,* was reprinted in *Reeling,* by Pauline Kael (Atlantic–Little, Brown, 1976).

to accept something suggestive and elliptical and go with the mood. Students accept the elliptical on records—the Joni Mitchell "Court and Spark," say, and some of the more offbeat Carly Simon cuts—but not in movies. The subdued, fine-drawn "McCabe & Mrs. Miller," which came out in 1971, managed to break even, but the soft-colored "Thieves Like Us," the latest film by the same director, Robert Altman, has been seen by almost nobody. Those who might be expected to identify with Jeff Bridges in "The Last American Hero" are going to see Clint Eastwood in "Magnum Force" instead. They're going to the kind of slam-bang pictures that succeed with illiterate audiences in "under-developed" countries who are starved for entertainment. The almost voluptuously obsessive "Mean Streets"—a film that one might have thought would be talked about endlessly—passed through college towns without causing a stir. The new generations of high-school and college students are going to movies that you can't talk about afterward—movies that are completely consumed in the theatre.

There is no way to estimate the full effect of Vietnam and Watergate on popular culture, but earlier films were predicated on an implied system of values which is gone now, except in the corrupt, vigilante form of a "Dirty Harry" or a "Walking Tall." Almost all the current hits are jokes on the past, and especially on old films—a mixture of nostalgia and parody, laid on with a trowel. The pictures reach back in time, spoofing the past, jabbing at it. Nobody understands what contemporary heroes or heroines should be, or how they should relate to each other, and it's safer not to risk the box-office embarrassment of seriousness.

For many years, some of us alarmists have been saying things like "Suppose people get used to constant visceral excitement—will they still respond to the work of artists?" Maybe, owing partly to the national self-devaluation and partly to the stepped-up power of advertising, what we feared has come about. It's hardly surprising: how can people who have just been pummelled and deafened by "The French Connection" be expected to respond to a quiet picture? If, still groggy, they should stumble in to see George Segal in Irvin Kershner's "Loving" the next night, they'd think there was nothing going on in it, because it didn't tighten the screws on them. "The Rules of the Game" might seem like a hole in the screen. When "The Getaway" is double-billed with "Mean Streets," it's no wonder that some people walk out on "Mean Streets." Audiences like movies that do all the work for them—just as in the old days, and with an arm-twisting rubdown besides. College students don't appear to feel insulted (what's left to insult us?); they don't mind being banged over the head—the louder the better. They seem to enjoy seeing the performers whacked around, too; sloppy knockabout farce is the newest smash, and knockabout horror isn't far behind. People go for the obvious, the broad, the movies that don't ask them to feel anything. If a movie is a hit, that means practically guaranteed sensations—and sensations without feeling.

I often come out of a movie now feeling wiped out, desolate—and often it's a movie that the audience around me has reacted to noisily, as if it were having a high, great time—and I think I feel that way because of the nihilism in the atmosphere. It isn't intentional or philosophical nihilism; it's the kind one sometimes feels at a porn show—the way everything is turned to dung, oneself included. A couple of years ago, I went with another film critic, a young man, to see a hard-core movie in the Broadway area, and there was a live stage show with it. A young black girl—she looked about seventeen but must have been older—did a strip and then danced naked. The theatre was small, and the girl's eyes, full of hatred, kept raking the customers' faces. I was the only other woman there, and each time her eyes came toward me, I had to look down; finally, I couldn't look up at all. The young critic and I sat in misery, unable to leave, since that would look like a put-down of her performance. We had to take the contempt with which she hid her sense of being degraded, and we shared in her degradation, too. Hits like "The Exorcist" give most of the audience just what it wants and expects, the way hardcore porn does. The hits have something in common: blatancy. They are films that *deliver*. They're debauches—their subject might almost be mindlessness and futurelessness. People in the audience want to laugh, and at pictures like "Enter the Dragon" and "Andy Warhol's Frankenstein" and "The Three Musketeers" and "Blazing Saddles" they're laughing at pandemonium and accepting it as the comic truth.

The counterculture films made corruption seem inevitable and hence something you learn to live with; the next step was seeing it as slapstick comedy and learning to enjoy it. For the fatalistic, case-hardened audience, absurdism has become the only acceptable point of view—a new complacency. In "The Three Musketeers," Richard Lester keeps his actors at a distance and scales the characters down to subnormal size; they're letching, carousing buffoons who don't care about anything but blood sport. The film isn't politically or socially abrasive; it's just "for fun." At showings of "Chinatown," the audience squeals with pleasure when Faye Dunaway reveals her incest. The success of "Chinatown"—with its beautifully structured script and draggy, overdeliberate direction—represents something dialectically new: nostalgia (for the thirties) openly turned to rot, and the *celebration* of rot. Robert Towne's script had ended with the detective (Jack Nicholson) realizing what horrors the Dunaway character had been through, and, after she killed her incestuous

father, helping her daughter get to Mexico. But Roman Polanski seals
the picture with his gargoyle grin; now evil runs rampant. The picture
is compelling, but coldly, suffocatingly compelling. Polanski keeps so
much of it in closeup that there's no air, no freedom to breathe; you don't
care who is hurt, since everything is blighted. Life is a blood-red maze.
Polanski may leave the story muddy and opaque, but he shoves the rot at
you, and large numbers of people seem to find it juicy. Audiences now
appear to accept as a view of themselves what in the movies of the past
six or seven years counterculture audiences jeered at Americans for being
—cynical materialists who cared for nothing but their own greed and lust.
The nihilistic, coarse-grained movies are telling us that nothing matters
to us, that we're all a bad joke.

It's becoming tough for a movie that isn't a big media-created event to
find an audience, no matter how good it is. And if a movie has been turned
into an event, it doesn't have to be good; an event—such as "Papillon"—
draws an audience simply because it's an event. You don't expect Mount
Rushmore to be a work of art, but if you're anywhere near it you have
to go; "Papillon" is a movie Mount Rushmore, though it features only
two heads. People no longer go to a picture just for itself, and ticket-
buyers certainly aren't looking for the movie equivalent of "a good read."
They want to be battered, to be knocked out—they want to get wrecked.
They want what "everybody's talking about," and even if they don't like
the picture—and some people didn't really care for "A Touch of Class,"
and some detested "The Three Musketeers," and many don't like "Blazing Saddles," either—they don't feel out of it. Increasingly, though, I've
noticed that those who don't enjoy a big event-film feel out of it in another way. They wonder if there's something they're not getting—if the
fault is theirs.

    The public can't really be said to have rejected a film like "Payday,"
since the public never heard of it. If you don't know what a movie is and
it plays at a theatre near you, you barely register it. "Payday" may not
come at all; when the event strategy really works, as it has of late, the
hits and the routine action films and horror films are all that get to most
towns. And if a film turns up that hasn't had a big campaign, people assume it's a dog; you risk associating yourself with failure if you go to
see Jon Voight in "Conrack" or Blythe Danner in the messed-up but
still affecting "Lovin' Molly." When other values are rickety, the fact
that something is selling gives it a primacy, and its detractors seem like
spoilsports. The person who holds out against an event looks a loser:
the minority is a fool. People are cynical about advertising, of course,
but their cynicism is so all-inclusive now that they're indifferent, and so
they're more susceptible to advertising than ever. If nothing matters any-

way, why not just go where the crowd goes? That's a high in itself.

There are a few exceptions, but in general it can be said that the public no longer discovers movies, the public no longer makes a picture a hit. If the advertising for a movie doesn't build up an overwhelming desire to be part of the event, people just don't go. They don't listen to their own instincts, they don't listen to the critics—they listen to the advertising. Or, to put it more precisely, they do listen to their instincts, but their instincts are now controlled by advertising. It seeps through everything—talk shows, game shows, magazine and newspaper stories. Museums organize retrospectives of a movie director's work to coördinate with the opening of his latest film, and publish monographs paid for by the movie companies. College editors travel at a movie company's expense to see its big new film and to meet the director, and directors preview their new pictures at colleges. The public-relations event becomes part of the national consciousness. You don't hear anybody say, "I saw the most wonderful movie you never heard of;" when you hear people talking, it's about the same blasted movie that everybody's going to—the one that's flooding the media. Yet even the worst cynics still like to think that "word of mouth" makes hits. And the executives who set up the machinery of manipulation love to believe that the public—the public that's sitting stone-dead in front of its TV sets—spontaneously discovered their wonderful movie. If it's a winner, they say it's the people's choice. But, in the TV age, when people say they're going to see "Walking Tall" because they've "heard" it's terrific, that rarely means a friend has told them; it means they've picked up signals from the atmosphere. It means "Walking Tall" has been plugged so much that every cell in a person's body tells him he's got to see it. Nobody ever says that it was the advertising that made him vote for a particular candidate, yet there is considerable evidence that in recent decades the Presidential candidates who spent the most money always won. They were the people's choice. Advertising is a form of psychological warfare that in popular culture, as in politics, is becoming harder to fight with aboveboard weapons. It's becoming damned near invincible.

The ludicrous "Mame" or the limp, benumbed "The Great Gatsby" may not make as much money as the producing companies hoped for, but these pictures don't fail abjectly, either. They're hits. If Hollywood executives still believe in word of mouth, it's because the words come out of their own mouths.

The businessmen have always been in control of film production; now advertising puts them, finally, on top of public reaction as well. They can transcend the content and the quality of a film by advertising. The new blatancy represents the triumph—for the moment, at least—of the businessmen's taste and the businessmen's ethic. Traditionally, movies were thought linked to dreams and illusions, and to pleasures that went way beyond satisfaction. Now the big ones are stridently illusionless, for a public determined not to be taken in. Audiences have become "realists" in the manner of businessmen who congratulate themselves for being realists: they believe only in what gives immediate gratification. It's got to be right there—tangible, direct, basic, in their laps. The movie executives were shaken for a few years; they didn't understand what made a film a counterculture hit. They're happy to be back on firm ground with "The Sting." Harmless, inoffensive. Plenty of plot but no meanings. Not even any sex to worry about.

Much—perhaps most—of the students' and educated moviegoers' unresponsiveness to recent fine work can be traced to the decisions of the movie companies about what will sell and what won't. With their overweening campaign budgets for "The Great Gatsby" and "Chinatown," the Paramount executives didn't even take a full-page ad in the *Times* to announce that "The Conversation" had won the Grand Prize at Cannes. They didn't *plan* on "The Conversation" being a success, and nothing now is going to make them help it become one. "Gatsby" and "Chinatown" were their pictures, but "The Conversation" was Francis Ford Coppola's, and they're incensed at his being in a position (after directing "The Godfather") to do what he wanted to do; they're *hurt* that he flouts their authority, working out of San Francisco instead of Los Angeles. And they don't really have any respect for "The Conversation," because it's an idea film. It's the story of a compulsive loner (Gene Hackman), a wizard at electronic surveillance who is so afraid others will spy on him that he empties his life; he's a cipher—a cipher in torment. There's nothing to discover about him, and *still* he's in terror of being bugged. (Hackman is a superlative actor, but his peculiarity, his limitation, like Ralph Richardson's when he was younger, is his quality of anonymity: just what is right for this role.) "The Conversation" is driven by an inner logic. It's a little thin, because the logic is the working out of one character's obsession, but it's a buggy movie that can get to you so that when it's over you really feel you're being bugged. Maybe the reason the promotion people didn't try to exploit the Watergate tie-in was that they suspected the picture might also be saying something about movie companies. If a film isn't promoted, it's often because something about it—the idea itself, or the director's obstinate determination to make it—needles the bosses. . . .

An actor or a director can become an "artist with discipline" when he has a huge box-office, and his reputation for discipline will soar if, like Paul Newman or Robert Redford, he has a string of hits. Actually, to the moneymen discipline means success plus a belief in success. Coppola isn't called disciplined, despite the success of "The Godfather," because he wants to work on his own projects (such as "The Conversation"), but George Roy Hill ("Butch Cassidy and the Sundance Kid," "Slaughter-house Five," "The Sting") is disciplined, because he believes in big-name, big-star projects. Peter Yates ("Bullitt," "John and Mary") is considered a man you can do business with, despite a flop like "Murphy's War" and the far from successful "The Hot Rock" and "The Friends of Eddie Coyle;" his flops aren't held against him, because he believes in the same kind of projects that the moneymen do and he doesn't try to do anything *special* with those projects. His latest, "For Pete's Sake," probably won't bring in much of a bundle, but it's a model of Hollywood "discipline."

Peter Yates's lack of distinction, like the veteran Richard Fleischer's, is a proof of trustworthiness. The moneymen want a director who won't surprise them. They're scared of a man like Altman, because they just don't know what he'll do on a picture; they can't trust him to make it resemble the latest big hit. They want solid imitations, pictures that reek of money spent and money to come, pictures that look safe—like those Biblical epics that came rumbling off the assembly lines in the fifties. Twentieth Century–Fox and Warner Brothers are jointly producing a burning-skyscraper picture, "The Towering Inferno," with Steve McQueen, Paul Newman, William Holden, Jennifer Jones, Robert Wagner, Fred Astaire, Richard Chamberlain, and other assorted big names. It's Grand Hotel in flames at last. Universal, for starters, has signed up Anne Bancroft and George C. Scott for "The Hindenburg," described as "a multilayered drama with a gallery of international characters." In other words, Grand Hotel in flames in the sky. Every couple of years, the American movie public is said to crave something. Now it's calamity, and already the wave of apocalyptic movies—which aren't even here yet—is being analyzed in terms of our necrophilia. The studio heads are setting up disaster epics like kids reaching hand over hand up a baseball bat—all because of the success of "The Poseidon Adventure," which probably had about as much to do with a public interest in apocalypse as Agatha Christie's old "Ten Little Indians" had. I doubt whether there's a single one of the directors mounting these disaster specials—becoming commanders-in-chief in an idiot war—who wouldn't infinitely rather be working on something else. By the time the public is gorged with disasters and the epics begin to flop, the studio heads will have fastened on another get-rich-quick gimmick (pirate capers are said to be on the agenda), and the people who work for them will lose a few more years of what might have been their creative lives. The producers gamble on the public's wanting more of whatever is a hit, and since they *all* gamble on that, the public is always quickly surfeited, but the failures of the flaccid would-be hits never anger the producers the way the failures of the films that someone really fought for do. The producers want those films to fail; they often make them fail. A Sam Peckinpah film, an Altman film, a Kershner film—the executives get pleasure out of seeing those films fail. It's a *punishment* of the artist.

Since all the businessmen's energy goes into strategy and manipulation, they can outfox the artists damn near every time; that's really the business they're in. Their right of "final cut"—one of the great symbolic terms in moviemaking—gives them the chance to chop up the film of a director who has angered them by doing it his own way; they'll mutilate the picture trying to remove the complexities he battled to put in. They love to play God with other people's creations. Movie after movie is mangled, usually by executives' last-minute guesses about what the public wants. When they've finished, they frequently can't do anything with the pictures but throw them away. That's their final godlike act—an act easy for them to live with, because they always have the director to blame. To them, the artist is the outsider; he's not a member of the family, to be protected. A few years ago, when word was out in the industry that Brando didn't mean anything at the box office, the producer David Merrick fired him from a picture; I asked an executive connected with the production what Brando had done. "Nothing," he said. "Brando was working hard, and he was coöperative with everyone. But he suggested some ways to improve the script; they were good suggestions—the script was a mess. But legally that was interference, and Merrick could fire Brando and collect on the insurance." "But why?" I persisted. He shrugged at my ignorance. "What could make David Merrick bigger than firing Marlon Brando?" he said. . . .

There's no way for movies to be saved from premature senility unless the artists finally abandon the whole crooked system of Hollywood bookkeeping, with its kited budgets and trick percentages. Most directors are signed up for only one picture now, but after the deal is made the director gets the full de-luxe ritual: fancy hotels, first-class travel, expense money to maintain cool, silky blond groupies for travelling companions. Directors are like calves being fattened—all on the budget of the picture. The executives and their entourage of whores and underlings are also travelling and living it up on the same budget; that's how a picture that cost $1,200,000 comes in on the books at $3,000,000, and why the director who has a percentage of the profits doesn't get any.

It isn't impossible to raise money outside the industry to make a movie—the studios themselves finance some of their biggest pictures with tax-shelter money ("Gatsby," in part)—but even those who raise independent financing and make a picture cheaply ("Mean Streets" was brought in for $380,000, plus $200,000 in deferred costs, "Payday" for $767,000) are stuck for a way to distribute it and fall victim to the dream of a big Hollywood win. So they sell their pictures to "the majors" to exhibit, and watch helplessly as the films die or the swindled profits disappear. And they are beggars again. Brian De Palma's "Greetings" was made for $20,000, plus $23,000 in deferred costs in 1968; back in the fifties, Irvin Kershner made "Stakeout on Dope Street" for $30,000, plus $8,000 in deferred costs. If there had been an artists' co-op to distribute the films, the directors might have been able to use the profits to continue working, instead of pouring energy into planning films that they could never finance, and seeing the films they did make get sliced to ribbons.

If the directors started one distribution company, or even several (they could certainly get backing), they might have to spend time on business problems, but, with any luck, much less time on dealmaking sessions: those traumatic meetings at which the businessmen air their grievances while the artists anxiously vulgarize the projects they're submitting, hoping to make them sound commercial enough. If they have a book they want to film or if they try to get development money for a story idea, the lack of enthusiasm is deadly. One director says, "You look at them and you give up. And if, after a year or two years, they finally give you the go-ahead, then they cut you down to a twenty-five-day shooting schedule and *dare* you to make a picture." Right now, all but a handful of Hollywood directors spend most of their time preparing projects that they never get to shoot. They work on scripts with writers, piling up successions of drafts, and if they still can't please the producers and get a deal, the properties are finally abandoned or turned over to other directors, who start the process all over again, with new writers. One could outline a history of modern Hollywood by following the passage of one such project—the French novel "Choice Cuts," say, which more than a dozen of the best writers and close to a dozen of the best directors have worked on: script after script in insane succession, and the waltz still goes on, each person in turn thinking that he's got a deal and his version will be made. The directors spend their lives not in learning their craft and not in doing anything useful to them as human beings but in fighting a battle they keep losing. The business problems of controlling their own distribution should be minor compared to what they go through now—the abuse from the self-pitying bosses, the indignity, the paralysis. And if the directors had to think out how their movies should be presented to the public—what the basis for the advertising campaign should be—this mightn't be so bad for them. If they had to worry about what a movie was going to mean to people and why anybody should come to see it, they might be saved from too much folly. A fatal difference between the "high" arts and the popular, or mass-culture, arts has been that in one the artist's mistakes are his own, while in the other the mistakes are largely the businessmen's. The artist can grow making his own mistakes; he decays carrying out the businessmen's decisions—working on large, custom-made versions of the souless entertainment on TV.

Privately, almost every one of the directors whose work I admire tells the same ugly, bitter story, yet they live in such fear of those spiteful, spying bosses that they don't dare even talk to each other. Hollywood is a small, ingrown community where people live in terror that "word will get back." They inhabit a paranoia-inducing company town, and within it they imagine the bosses to have more power in the outside world than they actually do. If such talents as Sam Peckinpah, Paul Mazursky, Martin Scorsese, Coppola, Kershner, Altman, De Palma, Woody Allen, Frederick Wiseman, Lamont Johnson, John Korty, Steven Spielberg, Michael Crichton, and even some of the older directors, such as Kazan and Fred Zinnemann, joined together to distribute their own films, they'd be able to work on the projects they really want to work on, and they'd get most of the writers and performers and craftsmen they want, too. The main obstacles are not in the actual world. It's not impossible to buck the majors and to book movies into theatres, and it's not really hard to publicize movies; the media are almost obscenely eager for movie news, and the businessmen, who know only one way to advertise a film— by heavy bombardment—often kill interest in an unusual picture by half-heartedly trying to sell it as if it were the kind of routine action show they wanted it to be.

There's no way of knowing whether a new audience can be found; it's a matter of picking up the pieces, and it may be too late. But if the directors started talking to each other, they'd realize that they're all in the same rapidly sinking boat, and there'd be a chance for them to reach out and try to connect with a new audience. If they don't, they'll never test themselves as artists and they'll never know whether an audience could have been found for the work they want to do.

The artists have to break out of their own fearful, star-struck heads; the system that's destroying them is able to destroy them only as long as they believe in it and want to win within it—only as long as they're psychologically dependent on it. But the one kind of winning that is still possible in those terms is to be a winner like William Friedkin or George Roy Hill. The system works for those who don't have needs or aspirations that are in conflict with it; but for the others—and they're the ones who are making *movies*—the system doesn't work anymore, and it's not going to.

■ ■ ■ ■

THE RAISE OF THE YEAR FROM A "BOARD OF ROBOTS" (1977), Dan Dorfman

This article by *New York* magazine's business editor seems to support many of Ms. Kael's contentions about the movie business and movie executives of the 1970s. The Warner Bros. of 1977 bears little resemblance to the family company of fifty years ago that was indeed run by four brothers who "staked all" (or, at least, staked something) on making synchronized sound motion pictures. Note that the Warner Bros. company has been swallowed by Warner Communications, a conglomerate with an interest in many entertainment and communications industries (paperback books, video games, and, most recently, cable television) rather than just movies. The reduction of Warners' commitment to movies seems metaphoric for the entire culture's attraction to other leisure pleasures. The salaries of movie executives continue to fascinate the American public—as they did in the 1930s when Louis B. Mayer earned the highest salary in America. And the Steven J. Ross of this study, when he observes that making a dozen pictures is much safer than making only one, seems to have recognized a principle that the 1930s movie mogul knew well. The Warner Bros. of 1977 and after makes much closer to one movie a year than a dozen.

SALARY UNLIMITED

Box-office smash *Star Wars* has not only been a bonanza for its producer, Twentieth Century–Fox, but it has created an avalanche of investor excitement in the movie business. With that thought in mind, I decided to visit another one of the film biggies, Warner Communications, Inc., the fast-stepping leisure-time conglomerate that owns Warner Bros. Surprisingly, though, Steven J. Ross, Warner's stock-conscious chief executive, was less than ecstatic about the big rise in Fox shares (from about

"The Raise of the Year from a 'Board of Robots,'" by Dan Dorfman, appeared in the 4 July 1977 issue of *New York* magazine.

10½ to a recent high of 24⅝). "It scares the hell out of me," Ross said, "because it could be the hit syndrome all over again."

The "hit syndrome" Ross is so fearful of is the erratic price fluctuations of movie securities following the critics' reaction to each new film. "People will think it's a crap-shoot business when it's really not," he complained repeatedly throughout a three-hour interview last week at his posh executive offices in the Warner building at 75 Rockefeller Plaza. "Look at the shares of Columbia Pictures," he said, grumbling that they were off a point during the day in reaction to the negative reviews of Columbia's new film, *The Deep*. "It's crazy time again [with movie stocks]," he said.

Manny Gerard, a top Warner executive and one of the brightest minds I've ever come across in the entertainment business, echoed his boss's thinking. "Those assholes on Wall Street expect every film to be another *Star Wars*. And there's no way to tell those idiots that it can't be . . . because those clowns won't know what the f--k you're talking about. *The Deep* looks like a hit, but Columbia's selling off because of unrealistic expectations. Go figure those jerks."

I could readily understand Ross's concern about the gyrations in Warner's stock. The handsome, silver-haired 49-year-old executive personally owns about 130,000 shares of the company's approximately 14.3 million shares (on a fully diluted basis). Obviously, his net worth, on paper at least, is affected by the slightest movement either way in Warner's shares. But there'll be no need, I assure you, ever to pass the collection plate around for Ross—certainly not as long as there are boards like Warner's in existence. Its obviously smitten directors, including consumer advocate Bess Myerson, voted him a new 1977 contract that must surely be the envy of almost every American businessman.

In the past year, Ross earned a base salary of $260,000, a livable wage by most standards. Apparently, though, some people thought it wasn't enough even though Ross also received a bonus of nearly $255,000, raising his 1976 take-home pay to around $515,000. And so a highly charitable four-man compensation committee, which included a consultant to Warner's, set out to do right by Ross. And they surely did that. We should all have such worker-oriented people negotiating over our salaries. The group eventually put together a marvelous contract calling for a base salary of $350,000, plus a bonus equal to ⅝ of 1 percent of the after-tax consolidated income for every year of full-time employment as long as the most recent five-year average of the earnings is not less than $45 million. Warner's most recent five-year earnings average was $49.5 million, meaning that Ross's 1976 bonus under the new plan would have yielded him an extra $383,000 for a total year's compensation of $733,000.

Based on some analysts' estimates of roughly $65 million in earnings this year for Warner's, Ross's total 1977 pay should easily exceed $750,-000 and probably top $800,000.

Some Wall Streeters were privately up in arms. "It's an excessive, grabbing plan . . . a flagrant act that gives big business a bad name and demeans what a corporate board is supposed to stand for," said one top entertainment analyst. He was also critical of the fact that Ross would still get a huge bonus even if earnings were to decline sharply. And from another entertainment analyst: "It's a wonder that Ross's board of robots didn't give him all the earnings."

"The board of robots," as it's called, didn't stop at just salary and bonus boosts. It also granted Ross $150,000 bonus units. Each unit represents the right to receive in cash, at the time of exercise, the amount by which the stock exceeds $27 a share. With a current Warner's price of about $30, that's another $450,000 gift.

But wait, there's more. The board also tossed in 50,000 incentive units, based on the performances of three-year earnings cycles starting in 1977 and ending in 1983. Assuming a 15 percent earnings growth rate over the seven-year period, these incentive units—which Ross doesn't pay for —are worth $25 each (or $1,250,000). But let's say Warner's is unable to maintain that growth rate as it gets bigger. The units are still worth $14 each at a 10 percent growth rate ($700,000 all told) or $7 each for 6 percent growth rate ($300,000). Ross also received options on 50,000 shares.

If you figure roughly $800,000 in potential salary and bonus, another $450,000 for the bonus units, and a maximum of $1,250,000 on the incentive units, that's a combined package of $2.5 million.

Too much, you say? That's not what I hear from a source inside Warner's who told me that Ross wasn't overjoyed with the package. "He thought he was worth more," the source said.

Ross, smoking one cigarette after another and occasionaly taking a break to nibble on one of his fingers, had a ready retort. "The board initiated the contract, not me," he said. "I had been asked about a contract, but put it on the back shelf. It had led to some irritation [among the directors]." But then the cocky Brooklyn-born Ross, a onetime bathing-suit salesman and funeral-parlor operator, hastened to add: "I was worth it because I was giving up my freedom." (This is a reference to the fact that Ross has never had a contract at Warner's, a firm he has headed since its founding in 1961.)

But if you weren't planning to leave, I asked Ross, what kind of freedom were you giving up? I never did get a satisfactory answer to that one.

In fairness to Ross, though, it should be pointed out that he gets high

marks from Wall Street for his leadership qualities. As one money manager with a fair-sized stock position in Warner's put it: "I don't trust
wheeler-dealers like Ross, because they are too damn unpredictable. But
then you go through the company and it's impressive as hell." Ross wins
praise for developing topflight management at both the corporate and
operating levels, also for his savvy in moving into fields with seemingly
above-average growth prospects—namely such leisure-time activities and
products as records, movies, publishing, and cable television.

Ross, hardly the inhibited type, was quick to tick off another one of
his achievements—a snappy 15.2 percent rate of annual earnings growth
over the last ten years.

In reaction to these pluses, an enthusiastic Wall Street has bid up the
price of Warner's shares nearly 50 percent from their 1976 low of 17½
(the stock was as low as 8¾ in 1975) to a shade below their 1977 high
of 32¾. It's a far cry from the early 1970s, when some analysts ridiculed
the company for its hodgepodge of unrelated business, its debt-heavy
leveraged balance sheet, and the lack of management depth.

Ross clearly believes that Wall Street's renewed interest in Warner's
is not without justification. "I feel very comfortable that we can continue to grow [in earnings] at 15 percent a year over the next five years,"
he said. His reasoning: "We're a cash-flow machine [a reference to the
fact that most of Warner's businesses, such as records, need no capital
expenditures to regenerate earnings]. We can use the cash flow [now
running at about $60 million net annually] to retire stock, make acquisi-
tions, or just earn money on it. How can we miss?"

A good question. It's interesting to note, though, that Warner's did
miss in 1975, when write-offs of discontinued operations cost the company $41 million and net earnings that year plunged to 53 cents a share
from $2.40 the year before. And who's to say—with Warner's hunger
for acquisitions—that it can't happen again?

Ross indicated that 1977's earnings growth rate would be considerably
higher than 15 percent. Noting that the company is doing "very good"
in all divisions, Ross told me he wouldn't quarrel with Wall Street's 1977
estimates of $4.50 a share (fully diluted), and indicated 22 percent gain
over 1976's $3.68.

Despite Ross's ebullience, a number of things bother Wall Street. One
is the trading patterns in Warner's $135-million portfolio. The firm takes
sizable stock positions in corporations, in turn leading to widespread
speculation that Warner's may follow with a bid for the company. Recent examples are Coca-Cola Bottling Company of New York, Bausch &
Lomb, and Franklin Mint.

Are you studying to become a portfolio manager? I asked Ross.

He quickly said no, and emphasized Warner's shouldn't be compared with Gulf & Western Industries. "We're like night and day. They buy stock to acquire—we're buying to invest."

Rumors recurred last week that Warner's bid for Coca-Cola Bottling was imminent and the bottler's stock touched a 1977 high of 9⅜. Ross emphasized that Warner's, which owns nearly 2 million of the bottler's shares (equivalent to 12 percent of the stock), has no plans to seek control of the company. The Bausch & Lomb shares were unloaded for a modest profit, but Warner's, unfortunately, is still sitting with a 395,000-share position in Franklin Mint. The Franklin Mint shares were purchased at 29, and they were trading last week at about 11½, representing a paper loss of about $7 million. Here again, Ross said there was no plan to acquire Franklin Mint.

Another criticism from Wall Street concerns Warner's recent purchase of Atari, a West Coast electronics-game manufacturer, for $28 million in cash and notes. The company has fine management and a topflght product line—but there's strong concern that the field will get intensely competitive (like the semiconducter industry), leading to shrinking profits. Ross strongly disagrees. "It's a fantastic business with great management," he says. "The company did $75 million in sales in 1976, and it should do over $100 million this year." Atari (acquired last October) should turn in a cash flow of about $20 million in its first fifteen months under Warner's. Ross said, "Tell me, do you really think I can get hurt starting in?"

What about the ups and downs of the movie business? Isn't it risky as hell? "It's the worst business," Ross responded, "if you make one film a year, but the best business if you make say, ten, twelve, sixteen, or eighteen films . . . because there's an enormous appetite out there. You can lose maybe $1 million or $2 million on one film, but you can make $20 million, $30 million, or $40 million on another. It's a fantastic risk-reward business."

The leverage factor also bothers some analysts—namely, its $235-million long-term debt. Manny Gerard argues, though, that this concern should be mitigated by the company's ability to offset much of the debt through the potential sale of the securities portfolio.

Ross has a reputation in some quarters of being a big-time spender on the expense account. In fact, I was told by one company source that Ross, on a recent business trip to Europe, took his barber along in the corporate jet to cut his hair each day. Ross denied it, explaining that the "barber wanted to go to Italy for a week and so we took him [and his lady friend] along."

I had heard that Ross and his steady companion, Amanda Burden, recently flew to a Cosmos soccer game (Warner's owns the team) in New Jersey, in the company helicopter. And I wondered if Warner's shareholders footed the bill for Ms. Burden. Ross quickly assured me that while he hadn't yet filed an expense report on it, he intended to pay for Ms. Burden's flight.

With $827 million in sales last year and on the way to becoming a billion-dollar company, Warner has clearly established itself as a business force to be reckoned with. But with its plan to buy Knickerbocker Toy (the parent of Raggedy Ann), its purchase of Atari, and its entry into men's and women's cosmetics—and who knows what else—there's a big question of whether Warner really has a strong view of what it wants to be. As one source intimately familiar with Warner's top management puts it:

"When I talk to these guys I'm never quite sure that what I'm really looking at is not a bunch of kids trying to build castles in the sand. . . ."

Bibliography

Despite the length of this collection, the anthologized pieces represent only a small fraction of the relevant and valuable material for each period and issue. The selections were culled from the following books and articles, organized according to the chronological structure of the anthology, except for the first section, which lists those books that treat or refer to more than one of the book's chronological sections.

GENERAL

Anger, Kenneth. *Hollywood Babylon*. Phoenix: Associated Professional Services, 1965.

Barsam, Richard. *Nonfiction Film*. New York: Dutton, 1973.

Bogle, Donald. *Toms, Coons, Mulattoes, Mammies, and Bucks: An Interpretive History of Blacks in American Films*. New York: Viking, 1973.

Brownlow, Kevin. *The Parade's Gone By*. New York: Knopf, 1968.

Conant, Michael. *Anti-trust in the Motion Picture Industry*. Berkeley and Los Angeles: University of California Press, 1960.

Cripps, Thomas. *Black Film as Genre*. Bloomington, Ind.: Indiana University Press, 1977.

———. *Slow Fade to Black: The Negro in American Film, 1900–1942*. New York: Oxford University Press, 1977.

Everson, William K. *American Silent Film*. New York: Oxford University Press, 1978.

French, Philip. *The Movie Moguls*. Baltimore: Penguin, 1971.

Green, Abel, and Joe Laurie, Jr. *Show Biz: From Vaudeville to Video*. New York: Holt, 1951.

Hampton, Benjamin. *A History of the Movies*. New York: Covici-Friede, 1931.

Haskell, Molly. *From Reverence to Rape*. New York: Holt, Rinehart, 1974.

Jacobs, Lewis. *The Rise of the American Film*. New York: Columbia Teachers' College Press, 1969.

Jarvie, Ian C. *Movies and Society*. New York: Basic Books, 1970.

Jowett, Garth. *Film: The Democratic Art.* Boston: Little, Brown, 1976.

Kennedy, Joseph P., ed. *The Story of the Films.* Chicago: A. W. Shaw, 1927.

Knight, Arthur. *The Liveliest Art.* New York: Macmillan, 1957.

Leab, Daniel J. *From "Sambo" to "Superspade": The Black Experience in Motion Pictures.* Boston: Houghton Mifflin, 1975.

Lewis, Howard T. *The Motion Picture Industry.* New York: Van Nostrand, 1933.

MacGowan, Kenneth. *Behind the Screen.* New York: Delacorte, 1965.

Mast, Gerald. *A Short History of the Movies.* 3d ed. Chicago: University of Chicago Press, 1981.

Mellen, Joan. *Big Bad Wolves: Masculinity in the American Film.* New York: Pantheon, 1977.

———. *Women and Their Sexuality in the New Film.* New York: Horizon Press, 1973.

Pratt, George C. *Spellbound in Darkness.* Greenwich, Conn.: New York Graphic Society, 1973.

Ramsaye, Terry. *A Million and One Nights.* New York: Simon & Schuster, 1964.

Randall, Richard S. *Censorship of the Movies.* Madison: University of Wisconsin Press, 1968.

Robinson, W. R., ed. *Man and the Movies.* Baltimore: Penguin, 1969.

Rosen, Marjorie. *Popcorn Venus.* New York: Coward, McCann, 1973.

Ross, Murray. *Stars and Strikes.* New York: Columbia University Press, 1941.

Rotha, Paul. *The Film till Now.* London: J. Cape, 1929. Rev. ed. with Richard Griffith. New York: Funk & Wagnalls, 1949.

Seldes, Gilbert. *The Great Audience.* New York: Viking, 1950.

Sklar, Robert. *Movie-Made America.* New York: Random House, 1975.

Slide, Anthony, with Paul O'Dell. *Early American Cinema.* New York: A. S. Barnes, 1970.

Zierold, Norman. *The Moguls.* New York: Avon, 1972.

Beginnings (1882–1900)

Armat, Thomas. "My Part in the Development of the Motion Picture Projector." *Journal of the Society of Motion Picture Engineers* 24, no. 3 (Mar. 1935): 241–50.

Balshofer, Fred J., and Arthur C. Miller. *One Reel a Week.* Berkeley and Los Angeles: University of California Press, 1967.

Barnet, Philips. "The Record of a Sneeze." *Harper's Weekly* 38 (4 Mar. 1894): 280.

Barr, J. Miller. "Animated Pictures." *Popular Science Monthly* 52 (Dec. 1897): 177–88.

Bellamy, Edward. "With the Eyes Shut." *Harper's* 79 (Oct. 1889): 736–45.

Blackton, J. Stuart. "An Interview with Thomas Alva Edison." *School Arts* 31 (Dec. 1931): ix–xii.

Cassady, Ralph, Jr. "Monopoly in Motion Picture Production and Distribution, 1908–1915." *Southern California Law Review* 32 (Summer 1959): 325–90.

Circuit Court of Appeals, Second Circuit. *Edison v. American Mutoscope Company.* 10 Mar. 1902. 114 Fed Rep 926 (1902) at 934–35.

Crawford, Merritt. "Some Accomplishments of Eugene Lauste." *Journal of the Society of Motion Picture Engineers* 16, no. 1 (Jan. 1931): 105–9.

Dickson, W. K. L. and Antonia Dickson. "Edison's Invention of the Kineto-phonograph." *Century* 48 (June 1894): 206–14.

———. *History of the Kinetograph, Kinetoscope, and Kinetophonograph.* New York, 1895.

"Edison Kinetoscope." *Scientific American* 71 (10 Nov. 1894): 298.

"First Days of the Movies." *Literary Digest* 108 (10 Jan. 1931): 18.

"Frozen Movies." *Independent* 77 (2 Mar. 1914): 311.

Grau, Robert. *The Businessman in the Amusement World.* New York: Broad-way Publishing, 1910.

———. *The Theater of Science.* New York: Broadway Publishing, 1914.

Hamilton, Harlan. "*Les Allures du Cheval:* Eadweard James Muybridge's Con-tribution to Motion Pictures." *Film Comment* 5, no. 1 (Fall 1969): 16–35.

Hendricks, Gordon. *Beginnings of the Biograph.* New York: Beginnings of the American Film, 1964.

———. *The Edison Motion Picture Myth.* Berkeley and Los Angeles: University of California Press, 1961.

———. *The Kinetoscope.* New York: Beginnings of the American Film, 1966.

Hepworth, Cecil M. *Animated Photography.* 2d ed. London: Hazell, Watson, & Viney, 1900.

Hill, Roland. "Louis and August Lumiere." *Camera* 45 (Dec. 1966): 74–77.

Hopwood, Henry V. *Living Pictures.* London: Optician & Photographic Trades, 1899.

Jenkins, C. Francis. *Animated Pictures.* Washington, D.C.: H. L. McQueen, 1898.

Lathrop, George Parsons. "Edison's Kinetograph." *Harper's Weekly* 35 (13 June 1891): 446–47.

McBride, Joseph, ed. *Persistence of Vision.* Madison: University of Wisconsin Press, 1968.

Marey, E. J. *Animal Mechanism.* New York: D. Appleton, 1874.

Muybridge, Eadweard. "The Attitudes of Animals in Motion." *Scientific Ameri-can Supplement* 343 (29 July 1882): 5469–70.

Newhall, Beaumont. "Muybridge and the First Set of Motion Photographs." *Image* 5 (Jan. 1956): 4–11.

Quigley, Martin, Jr. *Magic Shadows: The Story of the Origin of Motion Pictures.* Washington, D.C.: Georgetown University Press, 1948.

Smith, Albert E., with Phil A. Koury. *Two Reels and a Crank.* Garden City, N.Y: Doubleday, 1952.

Stainton, Walter. "Movie Pre-history." *Films in Review* 16 (June/July 1965): 333–42.

NICKELODEON (1900–1913)

Addams, Jane. *The Spirit of Youth and the City Streets.* New York: Macmillan, 1909.

"The Birth of a New Art." *Independent* 77 (6 April 1914): 9–10.

Bourne, Randolph S. "The Heart of the People." *New Republic* (3 July 1915): 233.

Bowen, Louise de Koven. *Five and Ten Cent Theatres*. Chicago, 1911.

Chandler, Edward H. "The Moving Picture Show." *Religious Education*, Oct. 1911, pp. 344–49.

Chicago Vice Commission. *The Social Evil in Chicago*. Chicago: Gunthorp-Warren, 1911.

Collier, John. "Censorship and the National Board." *Survey* 35 (2 Oct. 1915): 9–14.

———. "Cheap Amusements." *Charities and the Commons* 20 (11 Apr. 1908): 73–76.

Currie, Barton W. "The Nickel Madness." *Harper's Weekly* 51 (24 Aug. 1907): 1246.

"The Drama of the People." *Independent* 69 (29 Sept. 1910): 713–15.

Dunbar, Olivia Howard. "The Lure of the Films." *Harper's Weekly* 57 (18 Jan. 1913): 20–22.

Dyer, John. "Sex, Sin—and Revolution." *Films and Filming* 4 (May 1958): 13–15.

"The Early Years." *Arts in Society* 4 (Winter 1967): 105–16.

Eaton, Walter P. "The Menace of the Movies." *American Magazine* 76 (Sept. 1913): 55.

Fulk, Joseph R. "The Effect on Morals and Education of the Moving Picture Shows." *National Education Association Annual Meeting*, 1912, pp. 456–61.

Graham, Charles. "Acting for the Films in 1912." *Sight and Sound* 4 (Autumn 1935): 118–19.

Griffith, Linda Arvidson. *When the Movies Were Young*. New York: Dutton, 1925.

Holliday, Carl. "The Motion Picture and the Church." *Independent* 74 (13 Feb. 1913): 353–56.

Howe, Frederic C. "Leisure for the Millions." *Survey* 31 (1914): 415–16.

Howells, William Dean. "Editor's Easy Chair." *Harper's* 125 (Sept. 1912): 634–37.

"In the Interpreter's House." *American Magazine* 76 (July 1913): 102–5.

Lanier, Henry W. "The Educational Future of the Moving Picture." *American Review of Reviews* 50 (Dec. 1914): 725–29.

Lawrence, Florence. "Growing Up with the Movies." *Photoplay*, Jan., Feb., Mar. 1915.

Levien, Sonya. "New York's Motion Picture Law." *American City* 9 (Oct. 1913): 319–21.

McDonald, Gerald D. "Origin of the Star System." *Films in Review* 4 (Nov. 1953): 449–58.

Merritt, Russell. "Nickelodeon Theatres: Building an Audience for the Movies." *AFI Report*, May 1973, pp. 4–8.

"The Moving Picture and the National Character." *American Review of Reviews* 42 (Sept. 1910): 315–20.

"The Nickelodeon." *Moving Picture World and View* 1 (4 May 1907): 149.

North, Joseph H. *The Early Development of the Motion Picture, 1887–1909*. New York: Arno, 1973.

O'Dell, Paul. "Biograph, Griffith, and Fate." *Silent Picture* 1 (Winter 1968): 2–6.

Parsons, Louella O. "Essanay Days." *Theatre Arts* 35 (July 1951): 33.

Pierce, Lucy F. "The Nickelodeon." *World Today* 19 (Oct. 1910): 1052–57.

Sennett, Mack. *King of Comedy*. Garden City, N.Y.: Doubleday, 1954.

Slide, Anthony. *The Big V: A History of the Vitagraph Company*. Metuchen, N.J.: Scarecrow, 1976.

Stern, Seymour. "11 East 14th." *Films in Review* 3 (Oct. 1952): 399–406.

Tevis, Charles V. "Censoring the Five-Cent Drama." *World Today* 15 (Oct. 1908): 1132–39.

Vardac, A. Nicholas. *Stage to Screen*. Cambridge, Mass.: Harvard University Press, 1949.

Wagenknecht, Edward. *The Movies in the Age of Innocence*. Norman: University of Oklahoma Press, 1962.

Walsh, George E. "Moving Picture Drama for the Multitude." *Independent* 64 (6 Feb. 1908): 306–10.

Waters, Theodore. "Out with a Motion Picture Machine." *Cosmopolitan* 40 (Jan. 1906): 251–59.

Feature Films and Hollywood (1914–1927)

Amid, John (Myron Morris Stearns). *With the Movie Makers*. Boston: Lothrop, Lee, & Shepard, 1923.

Bakshy, Alexander. "The Language of Images." *Nation* 127 (26 Dec. 1928): 720–21.

———. "The Russian Contribution." *Nation* 127 (25 July 1928): 360–64.

"The Birth of a Nation." *New York Times*, 4 Mar. 1915, p. 9.

Bitzer, Billy. *Billy Bitzer: His Story*. New York: Farrar, Straus, 1974.

Brooks, Louise. "Gish and Garbo." *Sight and Sound* 28 (Winter 1958–59): 13ff.

Brown, Karl. *Adventures with D. W. Griffith*. New York: Farrar, Straus, 1973.

Carter, Huntly. *The New Theatre and Cinema of Soviet Russia*. New York: International Publishers, 1925.

Chase, William Sheafe. *Catechism on Motion Pictures in Interstate Commerce*. 3rd ed. Albany, N.Y.: New York Civic League, 1922.

Conners, Marilynn. *What Chance Have I in Hollywood?* New York, 1924.

Croy, Homer W. *How Motion Pictures Are Made*. New York: Harper, 1918.

De Mille, William C. "A Message of Hope." *Photoplay*, May 1921, p. 54.

Deutsch, Babette. "The Russian Theatre Today." *Theatre Arts* 9 (Aug. 1925): 537–47.

Eaton, Walter P. "A New Epoch in the Movies." *American Magazine* 78 (Oct. 1914): 44ff.

Eisenstein, Sergei M. "Mass Movies." *Nation* 125 (9 Nov. 1927): 507–8.

Evans, Ernestin. "The Soviet Idea in the Kino." *Asia* 26 (Aug. 1926): 698ff.

Franklin, Harold B. *Motion Picture Theatre Management*. New York: Doran, 1927.

Gish, Lillian, and Ann Pinchot. *The Movies, Mr. Griffith, and Me*. Englewood Cliffs, N.J.: Prentice-Hall, 1969.

Grierson, John. "The Product of Hollywood," "Putting Punch in a Picture," and four other articles in *Motion Picture News*, vol. 34 (1926).

Griffith, D. W. *D. W. Griffith and the Wolf.* Unpublished autobiography. New York, Museum of Modern Art.

———. *D. W. Griffith: The Man Who Invented Hollywood.* Edited by James Hart. Louisville, Ky.: Touchstone, 1972.

———. *The Rise and Fall of Free Speech in America.* Los Angeles: the author, 1916.

Hall, Ben S. *The Best Remaining Seats.* New York: Bramwell House, 1961.

Hamilton, Clayton. "Movies, Censor, and Public." *New York Evening Post,* 30 Dec. 1922.

Hays, Will H. "The Motion Picture Industry." *American Review of Reviews* 67 (Jan. 1920): 65ff.

———. "Motion Pictures and their Censors." *American Review of Reviews* 75 (Apr. 1927): 393–98.

Hecht, Ben. *A Child of the Century.* New York: Simon & Schuster, 1954.

Hibben, Paxton. "The Movies in Russia." *Nation* 121 (11 Nov. 1925): 539–40.

Irwin, Will. *The House that Shadows Built.* Garden City, N.Y.: Doubleday, 1928.

Jones, Charles Reed, ed. *Breaking into the Movies.* New York:. Unicorn, 1927.

Kennedy, Minnie E. *The Home and Moving Pictures.* New York and Cincinnati: Abingdon, 1921.

Kinsila, Edward Bernard. *Modern Theatre Construction.* New York: Chalmers, 1917.

Lane, Tamar. *What's Wrong with the Movies?* Los Angeles: Waverly, 1923.

Lawson, W. P. "The Miracle of the Movie." *Harper's Weekly* 60 (2 Jan. 1915): 7–9.

Lindsay, Vachel. *The Art of the Moving Picture.* New York: Macmillan, 1915.

Love, Bessie. "Jokers Wild." *Films and Filming* 12 (Aug. 1966): 21–22.

Lyons, Timothy J. "Hollywood and World War I." *Journal of Popular Film* 1, no. 1 (Winter 1972): 15–29.

Marsh, Mae. *Screen Acting.* Los Angeles: Photostar Publishing, 1922.

Meloy, Arthur S. *Theatres and Motion Picture Houses.* New York: Architects Supply & Publishing, 1916.

Mencken, H. L. *Prejudices.* 6th series. New York: Knopf, 1927.

Merritt, Russell. "Dixon, Griffith, and the Southern Legend." *Cinema Journal* 12, no. 1 (Fall, 1972):26–45.

Moore, Colleen. *Silent Star.* Garden City, N.Y.: Doubleday, 1968.

Morris, L. "Merchants of Dreams." *Theatre Arts* 35 (Aug. 1951): 12–13.

Motion Picture Association. *National Conference on Motion Pictures.* New York: Motion Picture Producers and Distributors of America, 1923.

"Movie Manners and Morals." *Outlook* 113 (26 July 1916): 694–95.

Münsterberg, Hugo. *The Photoplay: A Psychological Study.* New York: D. Appleton, 1916.

Murnau, F. W. "The Ideal Picture Needs No Titles." *Theatre Magazine* 47 (Jan. 1928): 41–2.

National Board of Review of Motion Pictures. *Motion Pictures Not Guilty.* New York: National Board of Review, 1920.

————. *The Question of Motion Picture Censorship*. New York: National Board of Review, 1914.

Oberholtzer, Ellis Paxson. *The Morals of the Movie*. Philadelphia: Penn Publishing, 1922.

Page, William A. "The Movie-Struck Girl." *Woman's Home Companion* 45 (June 1918): 18ff.

Peet, Creighton. "Hollywood at War, 1915–1918." *Esquire*, Sept. 1936, pp. 60ff.

Pettijohn, Charles C. *The Motion Picture*. New York: 1923.

Poffenberger, A. T. "Motion Pictures and Crime." *Scientific Monthly* 12 (Apr. 1921): 336–39.

Potamkin, Henry Alan. "The New Kino." *Close Up* 8, no. 1 (Mar. 1931): 64–70.

Rice, Elmer. *A Voyage to Purilia*. New York: Cosmopolitan, 1930.

Richmond, Jack. *Hollywood*. Los Angeles, 1928.

Rutland, J. R., ed. *State Censorship of Motion Pictures*. The Reference Shelf series. New York: Wilson, 1923.

Saroyan, William. "Year of Heaven." *New Republic* 97 (4 Jan. 1939): 255–56.

Seabury, William Marston. *The Public and the Motion Picture Industry*. New York: Macmillan, 1926.

Schulberg, Budd. "It Was Great to Be a Boy in Hollywood." *Holiday* 17 (Jan. 1955): 70–72.

"The Screen in Politics." *Independent* 110 (6 Jan. 1923): 6.

Seldes, Gilbert. "A Letter to the International Art Guild." *New Republic* 44 (18 Nov. 1925): 332–35.

————. "Russian and American Movies." *New Republic* 59 (7 Aug. 1929): 317.

————. "Some Russian Films." *New Republic* 59 (3 July 1929): 179–80.

Sheehan, Perley Poore. *Hollywood as a World Center*. Hollywood: Hollywood Citizen Press, 1924.

The Sins of Hollywood. New York and Los Angeles: Hollywood Publishing, 1922.

Stearns, Harold. "Art in Moving Pictures." *New Republic* 4 (25 Sept. 1915): 207–8.

Stelze, Charles. "Movies instead of Saloons." *Independent* 85 (28 Feb. 1916): 311.

Stern, Seymour. "The Birth of a Nation." *American Mercury* 68 (Mar. 1949): 308–19.

————. "Griffith I: The Birth of a Nation." *Film Culture*, vol. 36 (Spring/Summer 1965), special issue.

————. "Russian and American Movies." *New Republic* 59 (7 Aug. 1929): 317.

Tully, Jim. "Erich von Stroheim," "A Napoleon of Shadows," "Ernst Lubitsch," plus nine other articles on the movie colony in *Vanity Fair*, 1926.

Waterbury, Ruth. "Don't Go to Hollywood." *Photoplay*, Mar. 1924.

Wilson, Harry Leon. *Merton of the Movies*. Garden City, N.Y.: Doubleday, 1922.

Wright, W. H. "The Romance of the Third Dimension." *Photoplay*, Sept. 1921, pp. 41ff.

Young, Donald R. *Motion Pictures: A Study in Social Legislation*. Philadelphia: Westbrook, 1922.

Woolf, Virginia. "The Movies and Reality." *New Republic* 47 (4 Aug. 1926): 308–10.

THE TALKIES (1924–1930)

Ahern, Maurice L. "Hollywood Horizons." *Commonweal* 12 (21 May 1930): 71–73.
Allighan, Garry. *Romance of the Talkies*. London: Stacey, 1929.
Bakshy, Alexander. "Notes on Sound and Silence." *Theatre Arts* 13 (Feb. 1929): 99–103.
Brown, Bernard. *Talking Pictures*. London: Pitman, 1931.
"Color and Sound on Film." *Fortune* 2 (Oct. 1930): 33ff.
DeForrest, Dr. Lee. "Pictures That Talk." *Photoplay*, July 1924, pp. 78–79.
Franklin, Harold B. *Sound Motion Pictures*. Garden City, N.Y.: Doubleday, 1930.
Geduld, Harry. *The Birth of the Talkies*. Bloomington: Indiana University Press, 1975.
Glassgold, C. A. "Canned for Eternity." *Arts* 14 (Oct. 1928): 219–20.
———. "More Talk." *Arts* 15 (Oct. 1929): 278–80.
Green, Fitzhugh. *The Film Finds Its Tongue*. New York: Putnam, 1929.
Hall, Mordaunt. "The Vitaphone." *New York Times,* 7 Aug. 1926, p. 6.
Henry, Ralph L. "The Cultural Influence of the Talkies." *School and Society* 29 (2 Feb. 1929): 140–50.
Howard, Clifford. "The Menace around the Corner." *Close Up* 6, no. 1 (1930): 59–66.
Huxley, Aldous. "Do You Like the Talkies? No." *Golden Book* 11 (Apr. 1930): 51–54.
Kent, George. "A New Crisis in the Motion Picture Industry." *Current History* 33 (Mar. 1931): 887–91.
Lenauer, Jean. "In Praise of Simplicity." *Close Up* 6, no. 2 (1930): 134–40.
Nathan, George Jean. *Art of the Night*. New York: Knopf, 1928.
Potamkin, Henry Alan. "In the Land Where Images Mutter." *Close Up* 5, no. 6 (1930): 11–19.
Scotland, John (pseud.) *The Talkies*. London: Lockwood, 1930.
Seldes, Gilbert. "The Movies Commit Suicide." *Harper's* 157 (Nov. 1928): 706–12.
———. "Some Current Talkies." *New Republic* 59 (12 June 1929): 97–99.
———. "Talkies' Progress." *Harper's* 159 (Aug. 1929): 454–61.
Sherwood, Robert E. "With All Due Respect to Mr. Huxley." *Golden Book* 11 (Apr. 1930): 54–55.
———. "*Don Juan* and the Vitaphone." *Life* 88 (26 Aug. 1926): 26.
———. "*The Jazz Singer*." *Life* 90 (27 Oct. 1927): 24.
Trumbo, Dalton. "Frankenstein in Hollywood." *Forum* 87 (Mar. 1932): 142–46.
"Wanted—A New Name for the Talkies." *Photoplay*, Mar. 1929.

THE THIRTIES (1931–1940)

Adler, Mortimer J. *Art and Prudence*. New York: Longman's, 1937.
Ames, R. S. "The Screen Enters Politics." *Harper's* 171 (May 1935): 473–82.

"Anti-Block-Booking Bill Reported to Senate." *Christian Century* 56 (17 May 1939): 630–31.

Behlmer, Rudi, ed. *Memo From: David O. Selznick.* New York: Avon, 1972.

Bergman, Andrew. *We're in the Money.* New York: New York University Press, 1971.

Berman, Sam. "The Hays Office." *Fortune* 18 (Dec. 1938): 68ff.

Blumer, Herbert. *Movies and Conduct.* New York: Macmillan, 1933.

Blumer, Herbert, and Philip Hauser. *Movies, Delinquency, and Crime.* New York: Macmillan, 1933.

Capra, Frank. *The Name above the Title.* New York: Macmillan, 1971.

"Censorship of Motion Pictures." *Yale Law Review Journal* 48 (Nov. 1939): 87–113.

Charters, W. W. *Motion Pictures and Youth.* New York: Macmillan, 1933.

Corliss, Richard. "The Legion of Decency." *Film Comment* 4, no. 4 (Summer 1969): 24–61.

———. *Talking Pictures.* Woodstock, N.Y.: Overlook, 1974.

Dale, Edgar. *Children's Attendance at Motion Pictures.* New York: Macmillan, 1935.

———. *The Content of Motion Pictures.* New York: Macmillan, 1933.

———. *How to Appreciate Motion Pictures.* New York: Macmillan, 1937.

Dysinger, Wendell S., and Christian A. Ruckmick. *The Emotional Responses of Children to the Motion Picture Situation.* New York: Macmillan, 1935.

Facey, Paul W. *The Legion of Decency: A Sociological Analysis of the Emergence and Development of a Pressure Group.* New York: Arno, 1974.

"First Three-Color Feature Awaits Public Verdict." *Motion Picture Herald,* 25 May 1935, pp. 11–13.

Forman, Henry James. *Our Movie-Made Children.* New York: Macmillan, 1933.

Gussow, Mel. *Don't Say Yes until I Finish Talking.* Garden City, N.Y.: Doubleday, 1971.

Harley, John Eugene. *World-Wide Influence of the Cinema.* Los Angeles: University of Southern California Press, 1940.

Hays, Will H. *The Memoirs of Will H. Hays.* Garden City, N.Y.: Doubleday, 1955.

———. *See and Hear.* New York: Motion Picture Producers and Distributors of America, 1929.

Holaday, Perry W., and George D. Stoddard. *Getting Ideas from the Movies.* New York: Macmillan, 1933.

Huettig, Mae D. *Economic Control of the Motion Picture Industry.* Philadelphia: University of Pennsylvania Press, 1944.

Kanin, Garson. *Hollywood.* New York: Viking, 1974.

Karpf, Stephen. *The Gangster Film: Emergence, Variation, and Decay of a Genre, 1930–40.* New York: Arno, 1973.

Kellogg, Arthur. "Minds Made by the Movies." *Survey Graphic* 22 (May 1933): 245–50.

Klingender, F. D., and Stuart Legg. *Money behind the Screen.* London: Lawrence & Wishart, 1937.

"Loew's Inc." *Fortune* 20 (Aug. 1939): 25ff.

Loos, Anita. *Kiss Hollywood Goodbye*. New York: Viking, 1974.

MacDonald, Dwight. "Notes on Hollywood Directors." *Symposium* 4 (Apr. and July 1933): 159–77 and 280–300.

Martin, Olga. *Hollywood's Movie Commandments*. New York: Wilson, 1937.

"M. G. M." *Fortune* 6 (Dec. 1932): 50ff.

Mitchell, Alice Miller. *Children and the Movies*. Chicago: University of Chicago Press, 1929.

Moley, Raymond. *Are We Movie-Made?* New York: Macy-Masius, 1938.

———. *The Hays Office*. Indianapolis: Bobbs-Merrill, 1945.

Motion Picture Association. *The Community and the Movies*. New York: Motion Picture Producers and Distributors of America, 1929.

Naumberg, Nancy, ed. *We Make the Movies*. New York: Norton, 1937.

Nizer, Louis. *New Courts of Industry*. New York: Longacre, 1935.

"Paramount." *Fortune* 15 (Mar. 1937): 87ff.

Patterson, Francis Taylor. "Bread and Cinemas." *North American Review* 246, no. 2 (Dec. 1938): 259–66.

Perlman, William J., ed. *The Movies on Trial*. New York: Macmillan, 1936.

Peters, Charles C. *Motion Pictures and Standards of Morality*. New York: Macmillan, 1933.

Peterson, Ruth, and L. I. Thurstone. *Motion Pictures and the Social Attitudes of Children*. New York: Macmillan, 1933.

Pitken, Walter B. "Screen Crime vs. Press Crime." *Outlook and Independent* 158 (29 July 1931): pp. 398–99.

Priestley, J. B. *Midnight on the Desert*. New York: Harper, 1937.

Quigley, Martin. *Decency in Motion Pictures*. New York: Macmillan, 1937.

Renshaw, Samuel, Vernon A. Miller, and Dorothy P. Marquis. *Children's Sleep*. New York: Macmillan, 1933.

Rorty, James. "Dream Factory." *Forum* 94 (Sept. 1935): 162–65.

Rosten, Leo C. *Hollywood: The Movie Colony, the Movie Makers*. New York: Harcourt, Brace, 1941.

Sarris, Andrew. "Films of the 30s." *Arts Magazine* 42 (Sept./Oct. 1967): pp. 17–18.

Schlesinger, Arthur, Jr. "When the Movies Really Counted." *Show* 1, no. 1 (Apr. 1963): 77–78.

Seldes, Gilbert. *The Movies Come from America*. New York: Scribner's, 1937.

———. "The Movies in Peril." *Scribner's* 97 (Feb. 1935): 81–86.

Shaw, Albert. "Will Hays: A Ten Year Record," *American Review of Reviews* 85 (Mar. 1932): 30–31.

Shenton, Herbert. *The Public Relations of the Motion Picture Industry*. New York: Federal Council of the Churches of Christ in America, 1931.

Shuttleworth, Frank K., and Mark A. May. *The Social Conduct and Attitudes of Movie Fans*. New York: Macmillan, 1933.

Sinclair, Upton. *Upton Sinclair Presents William Fox*. Los Angeles: the author, 1933.

Stott, William. *Documentary Expression and Thirties America*. New York: Oxford University Press, 1973.

Taylor, Winchell. "Secret Movie Censors." *Nation* 147 (9 July 1938): 38–40.

Thomas, Bob. *King Cohn.* New York: Putnam, 1967.

———. *Selznick.* Garden City, N.Y.: Doubleday, 1970.

———. *Thalberg.* Garden City, N.Y.: Doubleday, 1969.

Thorp, Margaret. *America at the Movies.* New Haven: Yale University Press, 1939.

"Twentieth-Century Fox." *Fortune* 12 (Dec. 1935): 85ff.

"Warner Bros." *Fortune* 16 (Dec. 1937): 110ff.

White, E. B. "One Man's Meat." *Harper's* 179 (July 1939): 217–19.

Young, Kimball. "Review of the Payne Fund Studies." *American Journal of Sociology* 41 (Sept. 1935): 249–55.

Zukor, Adolf. *The Public Is Never Wrong.* New York: Putnam, 1953.

THE WAR ABROAD, A WAR AT HOME (1941–1952)

Agee, James. "So Proudly We Fail." *Nation* 157 (30 Oct. 1943): 509–10.

"Anti-Trust Scenario." *Business Week* 627 (6 Sept. 1941): 32–33.

Alpert, Hollis. "Strictly for the Art Houses." *Saturday Review* 34 (28 Apr. 1951): 27–28.

Bentley, Eric, ed. *Thirty Years of Treason.* New York: Viking, 1971.

Bessie, Alvah. *Inquisition in Eden.* Berlin: Seven Seas, 1967.

Carlson, Oliver. "The Communist Record in Hollywood." *American Mercury* 66 (Feb. 1941): 135–43.

Clancy, William P. "The Catholic as Philistine." *Commonweal* 53 (16 Mar. 1951): 567–69.

Cogley, John. *Report on Blacklisting. I: Movies.* New York: Fund for the Republic, 1956.

Crichton, Kyle. "Hollywood Gets Its Teeth Kicked In." *Collier's* 111 (9 Jan. 1943): 34–35.

Davidman, Joy. "The War Film: An Examination." *New Masses* 45 (24 Nov. 1942): 29–30.

———. "The Will and the Way." *New Masses* 45 (27 Oct. 1942): 28–31.

Dawson, Anthony H. "Motion Picture Economics." *Hollywood Quarterly* 3 (Spring 1948): 217–40.

Delahanty, Thornton. "Disney Studio at War." *Theatre Arts* 27 (Jan. 1943): 31–39.

Deming, Barbara. *Running Away from Myself.* New York: Grossman, 1969.

"Drive-Ins." *Time* 38 (14 July 1941): 66.

Fagan, Myron C. *Documentation of the Red Stars in Hollywood.* The author, 1951.

———. *Red Treason in Hollywood.* The author, 1949.

Film Culture, vols. 50–51 (Fall and Winter 1970–71). Issue on blacklisting.

"Films to Entertain Soldiers." *Theatre Arts* 27 (Mar. 1943): 169–76.

Fox, M. S. "The Art of the Movies in American Life." *Journal of Aesthetics and Art Education* 3, nos. 9–10 (1944): 39–52.

Frakes, Margaret. "Why the Movie Investigation?" *Christian Century* 58 (24 Sept. 1941): 1172–74.

Goldwyn, Samuel. "Hollywood in the Television Era." *Hollywood Quarterly* 4 (Winter 1949): 145–51.

Goodman, Jack, ed. *While You Were Gone.* New York: Simon & Schuster, 1946.

Goodman, Walter. *The Committee.* New York: Farrar, Straus, 1968.

Griffith, Richard. "The Audience over 35." *Films in Review* 1 (Sept. 1950): 19–23.

Handel, Leo A. *Hollywood Looks at Its Audience.* Urbana: University of Illinois Press, 1950.

Harmon, Francis S. *The Command Is Forward.* New York: R. R. Smith, 1944.

"Hollywood Learns How to Live with TV." *Business Week* 1197 (9 Aug. 1952): 46–48.

"Hollywood in Uniform." *Fortune* 25 (Apr. 1942): 92ff.

"Hollywood Wows Wall Street." *Business Week,* 11 May 1946, p. 58.

Houseman, John. "Hollywood Faces the Fifties." *Harper's* 200 (Apr. 1950): 50–59.

Houston, Penelope. "Mr. Deeds and Willie Stark." *Sight and Sound* 19 (Nov. 1950): pp. 276–79.

Inglis, Ruth A. *Freedom of the Movies.* Chicago: University of Chicago Press, 1947.

Isaacs, H. "Whistling in the Dark." *Theatre Arts* 27 (Dec. 1943): 727–33.

Jacobs, Lewis. "World War II and the American Film." *Cinema Journal* 7 (1967–68): 1–21.

Jarrico, Paul. "They Are Not So Innocent Abroad." *New Republic* 120 (31 Jan. 1949): 17–19.

Jones, Dorothy B. "Hollywood Goes to War." *Nation* 160 (27 Jan. 1945): pp. 93–95.

———. "The Hollywood War Film, 1942–44." *Hollywood Quarterly* 1 (Oct. 1945): 1–19.

———. "Is Hollywood Growing Up?" *Nation* 160 (3 Feb. 1945): 123–25.

Kahn, Gordon. *Hollywood on Trial.* New York: Boni & Gaer, 1948.

Kanfer, Stefan. *A Journal of the Plague Years.* New York: Atheneum, 1973.

Kempton, Murray. *Part of Our Time.* New York: Simon & Schuster, 1955.

Kracauer, Siegfried. "National Types as Hollywood Presents Them." *Public Opinion* 13, no. 1 (1949): 53–72.

Look magazine editors. *Movie Lot to Beachhead.* New York: Doubleday, Doran, 1945.

Luther, Rodney. "Television and the Future of Motion Picture Exhibition." *Hollywood Quarterly* 5 (Winter 1950): 164–77.

Marlowe, Fredric. "The Rise of the Independents in Hollywood." *Penguin Film Review* 3 (Aug. 1947), pp. 72–75.

Martin, Pete. "Tonight at Beachhead Bijou." *Saturday Evening Post* 217 (12 Aug. 1944): 20ff.

Miller, Merle. *The Judges and the Judged.* Garden City, N.Y.: Doubleday, 1952.

"The Motion Picture Industry." *Annals of the American Academy of Political and Social Science,* vol. 254 (Nov. 1947), special issue.

Othman, Frederick C. "War in the World of Make Believe." *Saturday Evening Post* 215 (17 Oct. 1942): 28ff.

Powdermaker, Hortense. *Hollywood: The Dream Factory*. Boston: Little, Brown, 1950.

"Propaganda or History?" *Nation* 153 (20 Sept. 1941): 241–42.

Putnam, Harold. "The War against War Movies." *Educational Screen* 22 (May 1943): 162ff.

Seldes, Gilbert. "Law, Pressure, and Public Opinion." *Hollywood Quarterly* 1 (1946): 422–26.

———. "A Short Angry View of Film Censorship." *Theatre Arts* 35 (Aug. 1951): 56–57.

Shaw, Irwin. "Hollywood People." *Holiday* 5 (Jan. 1949): 53–59.

Sodergergh, Peter A. "The Grand Illusion: Hollywood and World War II, 1930–1945." *University of Dayton Review* 5 (1968): 13–22.

———. "The War Films," *Discourse*, 11 (Winter, 1968), pp. 87–91.

Solovay, Jacob. "Reply." *Saturday Review* 26 (6 Feb. 1943): 13.

Taylor, John Russell. "The High Forties." *Sight and Sound* 30 (Autumn 1961): 188–91.

Trumbo, Dalton. *Additional Dialogue: The Letters of Dalton Trumbo, 1942–1962*. Edited by Helen Manfull. New York: M. Evans, 1970.

———. *The Time of the Toad*. The author, 1949.

Tyler, Parker. *The Hollywood Hallucination*. New York: Simon & Schuster, 1944.

———. *Magic and Myth of the Movies*. New York: Simon & Schuster, 1947.

U. S. Congress, House, Committee on Un-American Activities. *Hearings*. 1947.

———. *Hearings. Communist Infiltration of the Motion Picture Industry*. 1952.

U. S. Congress, Senate, Committee on Interstate Commerce. *Propaganda in Motion Pictures. Hearings*. 1941.

United States Supreme Court. *Joseph Burstyn, Inc. v. Wilson, Commissioner of New York, et al*. 343 US 495 (1951) at 1098.

———. *United States v. Paramount Pictures, Inc*. 334 US 131 (1949) at 166.

Vaughn, Robert. *Only Victims*. New York: Putnam, 1972.

Wanger, Walter. "Hollywood and the Intellectuals." *Saturday Review* 25 (5 Dec. 1942): 6–8.

———. "Motion Pictures in the Fight for Freedom." *Free World* 6 (Nov. 1943): 443–47.

———. "Movies with a Message." *Saturday Review* 25 (7 Mar. 1942): 12.

———. "The Role of Movies in Morale." *American Journal of Sociology* 47 (Nov. 1941): 378–83.

Westin, Alan F. *The Miracle Case*. University: University of Alabama Press, 1961.

Wolfenstein, Martha, and Nathan Leites. *Movies: A Psychological Study*. Glencoe, Ill.: Free Press, 1950.

"X." "Hollywood Meets Frankenstein." *Nation* 174 (8 June 1952): 628–31.

HOLLYWOOD IN THE TELEVISION AGE (1953–1977)

Alpert, Hollis. "American Motion Picture: 1966." *Saturday Review* 49 (24 Dec. 1966): 17–19.

———. "The Lion Meows." *Saturday Review/World* 1 (26 Jan. 1974): 56–57.

"Art House Boom." *Newsweek* 59 (28 May 1962): 101.

Atkins, Thomas R., ed. *Sexuality in the Movies.* Bloomington: Indiana University Press, 1975.

"Baby Doll." *Commonweal* 65 (11 Jan. 1957): 371–72.

Balio, Tino, ed. *The American Film Industry.* Madison: University of Wisconsin Press, 1976.

Battcock, Gregory, ed. *The New American Cinema.* New York: Dutton, 1967.

Benedict, John. "Movies Are Redder than Ever." *American Mercury* 91 (Aug. 1960): 3–23.

Brown, Stanley H. "Hollywood Rides Again." *Fortune* 74 (Nov. 1966): 181ff.

Brustein, Robert. "The New Hollywood: Myth and Anti-Myth." *Film Quarterly* 12 (Spring 1959): 23–31.

Carmen, Ira H. *Movies, Censorship, and the Law.* Ann Arbor: University of Michigan Press, 1966.

Cassady, Ralph, Jr. "Impact of the Paramount Decision on Motion Picture Distribution and Price Making." *Southern California Law Review* 31 (1958): 150–80.

Chayefsky, Paddy. "Big Changes in Hollywood." *Saturday Review* 40 (21 Dec. 1957): 9–17.

Clancy, William P. "Censorship and the Court: Freedom of the Screen." *Commonweal* 59 (19 Feb. 1954): 501–2.

Clayton, George. "Classification—and the Right to Be 'Obscene' but Not Absurd." *Cinema* 5, no. 2 (1969): pp. 22–23.

Dunne, John Gregory. *The Studio.* New York: Farrar, Straus, 1969.

"Fade Out for Blockbuster Films." *Business Week* 1729 (20 Oct. 1962): 172–74.

Fadiman, William. *Hollywood Now.* New York: Liveright, 1972.

———. "Hollywood: Shivering in the Sun." *New Republic* 162 (27 June 1970): 17–19.

Farber, Stephen. *The Movie Rating Game.* Washington, D.C.: Public Affairs Press, 1972.

"Film-Rating Fiasco." *America* 124 (29 May 1971): 557.

Fleishman, Stanley. "Movies, Politics, and the Supreme Court." *Journal of the Screen Producers Guild* 10 (Sept. 1968): 35–38.

"Getting Them Back to the Movies." *Business Week* 1364 (22 Oct. 1955): 58.

Goodman, Ezra. *The Fifty Year Decline and Fall of Hollywood.* New York: Simon & Schuster, 1961.

"Growth of Drive-Ins." *Commonweal* 65 (16 Nov. 1956): 166.

Guback, Thomas H. *The International Film Industry.* Bloomington: Indiana University Press, 1969.

Guber, Peter. *Inside "The Deep."* New York: Bantam, 1977.

Haines, Fred. "Art in Court: City of Angels vs. *Scorpio Rising.*" *Nation* 199 (14 Sept. 1964): 123–25.

Higham, Charles. *Hollywood at Sunset.* New York: Saturday Review Press, 1972.

"Hollywood Unions Say Too Many Films Shot Abroad." *Business Week* 1433 (16 Feb. 1957): 169.

Houston, Penelope. *The Contemporary Cinema.* Baltimore: Penguin, 1963.

———. "Hollywood in the Age of Television." *Sight and Sound* 26 (Spring 1957): 175–79.

———. "Lion Rampant." *Sight and Sound* 24 (Summer 1954): 21–30.

Hughes, Emmett John. "M.G.M.: War among the Lion Tamers." *Fortune* 56 (Aug. 1957): 99ff.

"Hullabaloo over *The Moon Is Blue*." *Life* 35 (13 July 1953): 71–74.

Kael, Pauline. "On the Future of the Movies." *New Yorker* 51 (5 Aug. 1974): 43ff.

———. *I Lost It at the Movies*. Boston: Little, Brown, 1965.

MacCann, Richard Dyer. *Hollywood in Transition*. New York: Houghton Mifflin, 1962.

Macdonald, Dwight. *Dwight Macdonald on Movies*. Englewood Cliffs, N.J.: Prentice-Hall, 1969.

MacKaye, Milton. "The Big Brawl: Hollywood vs. Television." *Saturday Evening Post* 224 (19 Jan., 26 Jan., and 2 Feb. 1962): 17–19, 30ff, 30ff.

Madsen, Axel. *The New Hollywood*. New York: Crowell, 1975.

Mast, Gerald. "In Memoriam: Central Casting." *New Republic* 173 (27 Dec. 1975): 25–27.

Mekas, Jonas. "A Call for a New Generation of Film Makers." *Film Culture* 19 (1959): 1–3.

Monaco, James. *American Film Now*. New York: Oxford University Press, 1979.

Morrison, Chester. "3-D: High, Wide, and Handsome." *Look* 17 (30 June, 1953): 27–33.

Rosten, Leo C. "Hollywood Revisited." *Look* 20 (10 Jan. 1956): 17–28.

Rotsler, William. *Contemporary Erotic Cinema*. New York: Random House, 1973.

Sarris, Andrew. "After *The Graduate*." *American Film* 3 (July/Aug. 1978).

Schary, Dore. "Hollywood: Fade Out, Fade In." *Reporter* 16 (18 Apr. 1957): pp. 20–25.

Schechner, Richard. "Pornography and the New Expression." *Atlantic* 219 (1 Jan. 1967): 74–78.

Schecter, Rosalyn. *An Open Letter to the Supreme Court*. Baltimore: Four Star, 1970.

Schulberg, Budd. "How Are Things in Panicsville?" *Life* 55 (20 Dec. 1963): pp. 79ff.

Schumach, Murray. *The Face on the Cutting-Room Floor*. New York: Morrow, 1964.

Sklar, Robert. "Hollywood's New Wave." *Ramparts* 10 (Nov. 1971).

Steiner, Gary A. *The People Look at Television*. New York: Knopf, 1963.

Stuart, Fredric. *The Effects of Television on the Motion Picture and Radio Industries*. New York: Arno, 1975.

Turan, Kenneth, and Stephen F. Zito. *Sinema*. New York: Praeger, 1974.

"TV and Hollywood Sing a Duet." *Business Week* 1911 (16 Apr. 1966): 106–8.

Tyler, Parker. *Screening the Sexes: Homosexuality in the Movies*. New York: Holt, Rinehart, 1972.

———. *Underground Film*. New York: Grove, 1970.

Valenti, Jack. "A Message to Film-Makers." *Action!* 3 (Mar./Apr. 1968): 19–21.
———. "Motion Picture Code and the New American Culture." *PTA Magazine* 61 (Dec. 1966): 16–19.
Vizzard, Jack. *See No Evil.* New York: Simon & Schuster, 1970.
Young, Colin. "Hollywood's War of Independence." *Film Quarterly* 12 (Spring 1959): 4–15.
Young, Colin, and Gideon Bachman. "New Wave—or Gesture?" *Film Quarterly* 14 (Spring 1961): 6–14.
Youngblood, Gene. *Expanded Cinema.* New York: Dutton, 1970.